Less managing. More teaching. Greater learning.

 STUDENTS...

Want to get **better grades**? *(Who doesn't?)*

Prefer to do your **homework online**? *(After all, you are online anyway...)*

Need **a better way** to **study** before the big test?

(A little peace of mind is a good thing...)

 With **McGraw-Hill's *Connect® Plus Economics*,**

STUDENTS GET:

- **Easy online access** to homework, tests, and quizzes assigned by your instructor.

- **Immediate feedback** on how you're doing. (No more wishing you could call your instructor at 1 a.m.)

- **Quick access** to lectures, practice materials, eBook, and more. (All the material you need to be successful is right at your fingertips.)

- A Self-Quiz and Study tool that **assesses your knowledge** and **recommends** specific readings, supplemental study materials, and additional practice work.*

*Available with select McGraw-Hill titles.

Want an online, **searchable version** of your textbook?

Wish your textbook could be **available online** while you're doing your assignments?

 ### *Connect® Plus Economics* eBook

If you choose to use *Connect® Plus Economics*, you have an affordable and searchable online version of your book integrated with your other online tools.

Connect® Plus Economics eBook offers features like:

- Topic search
- Direct links from assignments
- Adjustable text size
- Jump to page number
- Print by section

 Want to get more **value** from your textbook purchase?

Think learning economics should be a bit more **interesting**?

 ### Check out the STUDENT RESOURCES section under the *Connect®* Library tab.

Here you'll find a wealth of resources designed to help you achieve your goals in the course. Every student has different needs, so explore the STUDENT RESOURCES to find the materials best suited to you.

ECONOMICS
THE BASICS

McGraw-Hill/Irwin Series in Economics

ESSENTIALS OF ECONOMICS

Brue, McConnell, and Flynn
Essentials of Economics
Second Edition

Mandel
Economics: The Basics
Second Edition

Schiller
Essentials of Economics
Eighth Edition

PRINCIPLES OF ECONOMICS

Colander
*Economics, Microeconomics,
and Macroeconomics*
Eighth Edition

Frank and Bernanke
*Principles of Economics,
Principles of Microeconomics,
Principles of Macroeconomics*
Fourth Edition

Frank and Bernanke
*Brief Editions: Principles of
Economics, Principles of
Microeconomics, Principles of
Macroeconomics*
Second Edition

McConnell, Brue, and Flynn
*Economics, Microeconomics,
and Macroeconomics*
Nineteenth Edition

McConnell, Brue, and Flynn
*Brief Editions: Economics,
Microeconomics,
Macroeconomics*
First Edition

Miller
Principles of Microeconomics
First Edition

Samuelson and Nordhaus
*Economics, Microeconomics,
and Macroeconomics*
Nineteenth Edition

Schiller
*The Economy Today, The Micro
Economy Today, and The Macro
Economy Today*
Twelfth Edition

Slavin
*Economics, Microeconomics,
and Macroeconomics*
Tenth Edition

ECONOMICS OF SOCIAL ISSUES

Guell
Issues in Economics Today
Sixth Edition

Sharp, Register, and Grimes
Economics of Social Issues
Nineteenth Edition

ECONOMETRICS

Gujarati and Porter
Basic Econometrics
Fifth Edition

Gujarati and Porter
Essentials of Econometrics
Fourth Edition

MANAGERIAL ECONOMICS

Baye
*Managerial Economics and
Business Strategy*
Seventh Edition

Brickley, Smith, and Zimmerman
*Managerial Economics and
Organizational Architecture*
Fifth Edition

Thomas and Maurice
Managerial Economics
Tenth Edition

INTERMEDIATE ECONOMICS

Bernheim and Whinston
Microeconomics
First Edition

Dornbusch, Fischer, and Startz
Macroeconomics
Twelfth Edition

Frank
Microeconomics and Behavior
Eighth Edition

ADVANCED ECONOMICS

Romer
Advanced Macroeconomics
Fourth Edition

MONEY AND BANKING

Cecchetti and Schoenholtz
*Money, Banking, and Financial
Markets*
Third Edition

URBAN ECONOMICS

O'Sullivan
Urban Economics
Eighth Edition

LABOR ECONOMICS

Borjas
Labor Economics
Fifth Edition

**McConnell, Brue, and
Macpherson**
*Contemporary Labor
Economics*
Ninth Edition

PUBLIC FINANCE

Rosen and Gayer
Public Finance
Ninth Edition

Seidman
Public Finance
First Edition

ENVIRONMENTAL ECONOMICS

Field and Field
*Environmental Economics:
An Introduction*
Fifth Edition

INTERNATIONAL ECONOMICS

Appleyard, Field, and Cobb
International Economics
Seventh Edition

King and King
*International Economics,
Globalization, and Policy: A
Reader*
Fifth Edition

Pugel
International Economics
Fifteenth Edition

ECONOMICS

THE BASICS, 2/e

Michael Mandel

Chief Economist, Visible Economy LLC

Former Chief Economist, *BusinessWeek*

Senior Fellow, Mack Center for Technological Innovation

at The Wharton School of the University of Pennsylvania

ECONOMICS: THE BASICS

Published by McGraw-Hill/Irwin, a business unit of The McGraw-Hill Companies, Inc., 1221 Avenue of the Americas, New York, NY, 10020. Copyright © 2012, 2009 by The McGraw-Hill Companies, Inc. All rights reserved. Printed in the United States of America. No part of this publication may be reproduced or distributed in any form or by any means, or stored in a database or retrieval system, without the prior written consent of The McGraw-Hill Companies, Inc., including, but not limited to, in any network or other electronic storage or transmission, or broadcast for distance learning.

Some ancillaries, including electronic and print components, may not be available to customers outside the United States.

This book is printed on acid-free paper.

1 2 3 4 5 6 7 8 9 0 RJE/RJE 1 0 9 8 7 6 5 4 3 2 1

ISBN   978-0-07-352318-7
MHID   0-07-352318-6

Vice president and editor-in-chief: *Brent Gordon*
Publisher: *Douglas Reiner*
Executive director of development: *Ann Torbert*
Sponsoring editor: *Scott Smith*
Managing development editor: *Christina Kouvelis*
Editorial coordinator: *Emily Kline*
Vice president and director of marketing: *Robin J. Zwettler*
Marketing director: *Brad Parkins*
Marketing manager: *Katie White*
Marketing specialist: *Jennifer M. Jelinski*
Vice president of editing, design, and production: *Sesha Bolisetty*
Senior project manager: *Dana M. Pauley*
Buyer II: *Debra R. Sylvester*
Senior designer: *Mary Kazak Sander*
Senior photo research coordinator: *Keri Johnson*
Photo researcher: *Allison Grimes*
Senior media project manager: *Bruce Gin*
Media project manager: *Cathy L. Tepper*
Interior design: *Cara Hawthorne, cara david DESIGN*
Typeface: *10.5/12 Times New Roman MT Std*
Compositor: *Aptara®, Inc.*
Printer: *R. R. Donnelley*

Library of Congress Cataloging-in-Publication Data

Mandel, Michael J.
   Economics : the basics / Michael Mandel.—2nd ed.
      p. cm.—(McGraw-Hill/Irwin series in economics)
   Includes index.
   ISBN–13: 978–0–07–352318–7 (alk. paper)
   ISBN–10: 0-07–352318–6 (alk. paper)
   1. Economics. I. Title.
HB171.5.M262 2012
330—dc23

                                      2011028977

www.mhhe.com

DEDICATION

To Judy, Elliot, and Laura

ABOUT THE AUTHOR

Michael Mandel

Michael Mandel holds a PhD in economics from Harvard University. After teaching at New York University's Stern School of Business, he moved to *BusinessWeek* in 1989, where he wrote about a wide range of topics, ranging from the economics of crime, to immigration, to healthcare, to technology, to the global economy. Mandel helped supervise *BusinessWeek*'s domestic and global economic coverage while writing many of the magazine's economic cover stories.

Mandel specializes in making complex economic concepts understandable, relevant, and exciting for a broad audience while emphasizing economic accuracy. He has won numerous awards, including the Economic Journalism Award from the Institute on Political Journalism, given to the writer "who has done the most to shape public opinion by giving the public a better understanding of economic theory and reality"; the Gerald Loeb Award, the most prestigious prize for economic and financial journalism; and the Economic Journalist of the Year Award from the World Leadership Forum. He was also named one of the top 100 business journalists of the 20th century.

Mandel is the author of several books, including *Rational Exuberance: Silencing the Enemies of Growth and Why the Future is Better Than You Think*. He also helped revise the 1995 edition of Paul Samuelson's classic economics textbook.

Currently, Mandel is Chief Economic Strategist at the Progressive Policy Institute in Washington, DC. He is also a Senior Fellow at Wharton's Mack Center for Technological Innovation, and runs the news and education company, Visible Economy LLC, which produces news videos on economic topics to accompany college textbooks. His blog, Mandel on Innovation and Growth, can be found at innovationandgrowth.wordpress.com. Mandel lives in Millburn, NJ, with his wife Judy and his two children, Elliot and Laura.

PREFACE

When I started writing this textbook, I had two goals. First, I wanted to clearly explain basic economic principles, using the tools that I learned during my years as an economist and as an economic journalist. Second, I wanted to provide an introduction to the vibrant, but increasingly perplexing economy that we all live in.

What you see here is the result of my effort to achieve these two goals. The first half of the textbook, which includes the introduction and 11 core chapters, presents the essential economic concepts. I designed this section to be accessible to people with a wide range of economic and mathematical backgrounds. The second half of the textbook covers topics such as financial markets, globalization, technological change, healthcare, and environmental economics.

Throughout the textbook, I have consistently used fresh examples from today's global economy. My goal is to make the textbook, in part, a window into what is happening in the economy right now, including globalization and the aftermath of the financial crisis.

Fundamental Objectives

This textbook will accomplish three goals for you:

- You will get the basic tools of economics to learn a new way of thinking about today's world, so you can think more like an economist.
- By using these tools of economics, you will begin to understand markets and the global market economy.
- You will see the ways in which the possibilities of today's economy are expanding.

Distinguishing Features and Organization

This textbook emphasizes the main forces shaping today's economy: technological change, globalization, and the evolution of financial markets. The basic tools of economics are presented in the first 12 chapters to lay a foundation for understanding how the economy evolves and changes.

Current and Real Examples Economic concepts and ideas are illustrated in recent newsworthy events to help you see that economics is in action everywhere around you. Each chapter starts with a brief vignette that applies the concept to be learned to real-world events so you can see how the chapter concept relates back to everyday life.

Clear and Simple Graphs This book's simple, easy-to-follow graphs translate complex economic concepts into effective visual tools for the beginning student.

Historical Context Economic Milestone boxes sprinkled throughout each chapter provide interesting historical facts and references that relate to the material at hand.

Assurance of Learning Ready Many educational institutions today are focused on the notion of assurance of learning, an important element of many accreditation standards. *Economics: The Basics, 2/e* is designed specifically to support your assurance of learning initiatives with a simple yet powerful solution.

Each chapter in the book begins with a list of numbered learning objectives, which appear throughout the chapter as well as in the end-of-chapter assignments. Every Test Bank question for *Economics: The Basics, 2/e* maps to a specific chapter learning objective in the textbook as well as topic area, Bloom's Taxonomy level, and AACSB skill area. You can use our Test Bank software, *EZ Test,* or *Connect Economics* to easily search for learning objectives that directly relate to the learning objectives for your course. You can then use the reporting features of *EZ Test* to aggregate student results in similar fashion, making the collection and presentation of assurance of learning data simple and easy.

AACSB Statement McGraw-Hill/Irwin is a proud corporate member of AACSB International. Understanding the importance and value of AACSB accreditation, *Economics: The Basics, 2/e* recognizes the curricula guidelines detailed in the AACSB standards for business accreditation by connecting selected questions in the Test Bank and end-of-chapter material to the general knowledge and skill guidelines in the AACSB standards.

The statements contained in *Economics: The Basics, 2/e* are provided only as a guide for the users of this textbook. The AACSB leaves content coverage and assessment within the purview of individual schools, the mission of the school, and the faculty. While *Economics: The Basics, 2/e* and the teaching package make no claim of any specific AACSB qualification or evaluation, we have, within *Economics: The Basics, 2/e,* labeled selected questions according to the six general knowledge and skills areas.

Changes in the Second Edition

The narrative in all chapters has been evaluated and streamlined where necessary. Content and data updates to the figures, tables, and chapter narrative have been made throughout the book to reflect currency. In addition, select "Spotlight" and "How It Works" boxes have been updated or replaced to provide scenarios from today's economic landscape. All end-of-chapter problems have been reworked and are now aligned with the learning objectives presented at the beginning of each chapter. Additionally, all of the end-of-chapter problems of are assignable through McGraw-Hill *Connect Economics,* and select problems are available as algorithmic variations (for more information on *Connect Economics* please refer to p. xvi and xvii). Chapter-by-chapter changes are as follows:

Chapter 1 Introduction features an updated chapter opening vignette discussing the Great Recession of 2007–2009. The learning objectives have been reevaluated, resulting in the deletion of one learning objective and the addition of another about key disagreements in economics. The "Economic Policy Debate" section has been revised and renamed: "The Role of Government" and current examples of recent government interventions have been added. Also, an appendix covering the basics of graphs has been included.

Chapter 2 Demand and Supply: The Basics of the Market Economy starts with a revised listing of learning objectives. Additional coverage is devoted to how prices affect the quantity supplied in relation to the financial crisis.

Chapter 3 Market Equilibrium and Shifts contains an updated chapter opening vignette that details events of April 2010, like the release of the iPad and the Gulf of Mexico oil spill. A brief mention of the changes in loan standards in relation to the housing boom was added to the "Changes in Financial Markets" section.

Chapter 4 How Businesses Work starts with a revised listing of learning objectives. Figure 4.2 has been deleted, and the remaining features have been renumbered accordingly. The "Spotlight" box on Boeing has been updated and streamlined.

Chapter 5 Competition and Market Power features data updates to the "Spotlight" boxes on the furniture and auto industries. Additionally, the "How It Works" box on well-known brand names has been updated.

Chapter 6 Government and the Economy begins with a new chapter opening vignette about President Obama's healthcare reform. Coverage of government intervention in response to the Great Recession is now scattered throughout the chapter. Chapter 18 of the previous edition has been transformed into an appendix called *Delving Deeper into Microeconomics* and is featured at the end of this chapter.

Chapter 7 The First Step into Macroeconomics contains four learning objectives; the previous edition's learning objective number four was deleted. Figures 7.4 and 7.5 and Table 7.2 were deleted, and the remaining figures have been renumbered accordingly.

Chapter 8 Inflation has substantially revised data throughout. Additionally, updates have been made to the "How it Works" boxes to accurately reflect changes in the economy to housing, air travel, and oil.

Chapter 9 Growth features revised learning objectives. Additions to Figure 9.5 show the clear signs of the Great Recession, and a brief discussion has been added to further illustrate this event. Substantial revisions to data are featured throughout. Material on the information revolution and globalization has been added to the "History of U.S. Productivity Growth" section.

Chapter 10 Business Cycles, Unemployment, and Inflation features a new section on the Great Recession and its impact on the U.S. economy. The subsection on problems in financial markets has been heavily revised and moved to another location within the chapter. Again, substantial revisions to data are featured throughout. The "How It Works" box on local unemployment has been revised to reflect currency. Figures 10.4 and 10.5 were deleted, and the remaining figures have been renumbered accordingly.

Chapter 11 Fiscal Policy begins with a new chapter opening vignette that details a few strategies the government took to combat the Great Recession. The learning objectives have been streamlined. Material on the American Recovery and Reinvestment Act (ARRA) and a new table on major fiscal stimulus legislation from 2008 to 2010 has been added. The "Spotlight" box on the economic impact of military bases has been deleted and replaced with material on the impact of the ARRA. The "Spotlight" box on outsourcing and government spending has been replaced with material on the fiscal stimulus and the buy-American provision.

Chapter 12 Monetary Policy starts with an updated chapter opening vignette that discusses the government's response to the financial crisis of 2007–2009. The section on "Ensuring Financial Stability" now details the Fed's role in the financial crisis. A new section describing the three types of monetary policy tools available to the Federal Reserve has been included. Details have been added about the aftermath of the financial crisis and how the crisis changed the way the Fed reacted. Chapter 19 of the previous edition has been transformed into an appendix, *Delving Deeper into Macroeconomics,* and is featured at the end of this chapter.

Chapter 13 The Financial Markets features added information on the financial crisis in a new section "The Causes of the Financial Crisis." In addition, data detailing the effect of the crisis on the auto industry has been included. The "Spotlight" box on microfinance has been deleted.

Chapter 14 International Trade has substantially revised data throughout, including a number of revised figures. The "Trade Balance" section from Chapter 19 of the previous edition has been folded into this chapter.

Chapter 15 Technological Change now incorporates the affects of the Japanese Fukushima incident and how it impacted the United States The "How It Works" box on e-commerce has been updated.

Chapter 16 Economics of the Labor Market features updated data to reflect the unemployment statistics of early 2011. Figures 16.3 and 16.11 have been deleted, and the remaining figures have been renumbered accordingly. Updated information has been included in the "Spotlight" box on global movie stars.

Chapter 17 The Distribution of Income has substantially revised data throughout, including a number of revised figures and new data in the chapter opening vignette. The "How It Works" box on the distribution of wealth has been deleted and replaced with a new box titled "Global Catch-Up," which discusses how the rest of the world compares to America's living standard.

Chapter 18 Economics of Retirement and Healthcare was Chapter 20 in the previous edition. This chapter now features an updated discussion of Obama's healthcare plan throughout, including an extended discussion in a new subsection titled "Health Insurance Coverage." A new "Spotlight" box on why Americans don't save more has been added.

Chapter 19 Economics of Energy, The Environment, and Global Climate Change was Chapter 21 in the previous edition. This chapter features substantially revised figures and updated information about nuclear power and the effects of the Fukushima disaster. In addition, "Spotlight" boxes on gasoline tax and windmill pollution have been updated, and a new box on energy-related disasters has been added.

DYNAMIC FEATURES

Learning Objectives appear at the beginning of each chapter and are referenced again in the summary and among the end-of-chapter problems to which they relate. The Learning Objectives (LO) serve as a quick introduction to the material and concepts to be mastered before moving to the next chapter.

LEARNING OBJECTIVES

After reading this chapter, you should be able to:

LO1-1 Understand the importance of markets.

LO1-2 Identify three of the main forces shaping today's economy.

LO1-3 Explain the debate over the role of government in the economy.

LO1-4 Define economics and discuss how prosperity is measured.

LO1-5 Name some key disagreements in economics.

Toward the end of 2007 the United States plunged in economic downturn now known as the **Great Reces** The number of unemployed Americans doubled between and 2010. The financial system nearly collapsed in fall forcing the federal government to intervene. Home fo sures became depressingly common as families strugg pay their mortgages. State and local governments were to lay off teachers, firefighters, and other workers as tax nues dropped.

The economic picture was equally dismal in much rest of the world. Countries such as the United King Italy, Ireland, Spain, and Greece experienced sharp, lasting economic contractions that threw millions of p out of work. By contrast, some developing countries, as China and India, continued to grow through the crisis.

The question now is what the future will bring. He tory may be a guide. Back in 1929 the United States by the Great Depression, an economic crisis that w worse than the current one and lasted for most of the 1

Economic Milestone features help students place themselves in the historical continuum of economics while reinforcing important concepts.

Economic Milestone

1994 THE GREAT COFFEE CRUNCH

Coffee drinkers were hit by a very large relative price shift in 1994 because of a spate of natural disasters in coffee-growing countries that made coffee beans scarce: insects in Colombia, frost in Brazil, civil war in Rwanda. A pound of ground roast coffee rose from $2.50 in January of that year to $4.50 by August—a much bigger rise than the overall price level.

Spotlight and **How It Works** boxes highlight examples from current events to help students identify how economics works in the real world.

SPOTLIGHT: THE GREAT ETHANOL BOOM

For an example of the law of supply in action, look no further than the great corn ethanol boom of 2007. As the name suggests, corn ethanol, an alte native to gasoline, is made from corn. In 2007 the growing demand for ethanol sent the price of corn soaring from roughly $2.00 a bushel in 2005 to $4.20 a bushel in 2007.

Farmers, the main suppliers of corn, responded the rising price by increasing the quantity supplied. They planted more corn—a lot more corn. The result was the largest corn crop in history at the time: 13.0 billion bushels.

Not all farmers were happy about the higher price of corn, however. In particular, farmers raising pigs and cattle were used to feeding corn to their animals. As it grew more expensive, they had to fi alternative sources of feed or reduce the number pigs and cattle they were raising.

Source: U.S. Department of Agriculture.

HOW IT WORKS: FINDING MORE REVENUE

One of the most important tasks of a business is finding new ways to make money from the same products. That requires figuring out what people are willing to pay for.

For example, electronics retailers get revenue from selling you an LCD television or computer. But in addition, they get quite a bit of money from selling you an extended warranty—that is, a promise to fix the TV or computer if something goes wrong over the next few years.

Consider movie theaters. They get money from ticket sales, obviously, but the concession stands also bring in a tremendous amount of money selling giant candy bars, bags of popcorn, and cups of soda so large they could swallow a small dog.

And sports teams have had great success broadening their sources of revenue. Originally they made money from ticket sales and concession sales. Then came television rights, with the National Football League selling its first major television contract in 1962. Looking for more revenue, sports teams turned to selling the naming rights for their stadiums and arenas. For example, the Washington Redskins football team is being paid about $200 million by FedEx. In exchange, FedEx gets to put its name on the team's stadium.

SUPPLEMENTS

Economics: The Basics, 2e comes with a complete array of instructor and student tools that make both teaching and learning easier.

Test Bank
Available in both Microsoft Word and EZ Test computerized formats, the test bank includes a full complement of multiple-choice and short answer/essay questions to choose from. Created by Paul Fisher of Henry Ford Community College, the test bank is composed of over a thousand unique questions that serve as a barometer of student mastery.

PowerPoint Presentations
Learn as graphs come alive! Developed by Paul Kutasovic of the New York Institute of Technology, the PowerPoint presentations that accompany Mandel's text incorporate both the fundamental concepts of each chapter and the graphs essential to each topic. Where appropriate, the graphs themselves are animated to demonstrate movement within a coordinate axis—something printed figures simply cannot do. The PowerPoint presentations successfully enhance the lessons in the text *without* providing a substitute for chapter reading or class attendance.

Instructor's Manual
Authored by Paul Fisher of Henry Ford Community College, the Instructor's Manual includes pop quiz resources, common student stumbling blocks, and lecture notes. The manual is an invaluable resource for professors new to the course, as well as for TAs or other graduate instructors.

Solutions Manual
Suggested answers to the end-of-chapter questions are provided in this manual authored by Peggy Dalton of Frostburg State University.

Student Study Guide
The Student Study Guide offers students a wealth of additional resources to master the course. Authored by Derek Yonai of Campbell University, the Student Study Guide includes chapter overviews, discussion of issues relevant to the topics in the chapters, practice quizzes, and a common myths section to help students get past points of confusion.

Online Learning Center: www.mhhe.com/mandel2e
The website accompanying this book is a central resource for students and instructors alike. Students can review PowerPoint presentations and test their knowledge of chapter concepts with auto-gradable practice quizzes. In addition, students will have access to the Student Study Guide just described. The password-protected Instructor Center houses the Test Bank, PowerPoint presentations, Instructor's Manual, and the tables and figures used in the text.

DIGITAL SOLUTIONS

 Less Managing. More Teaching. Greater Learning.

McGraw-Hill *Connect® Economics* is a web-based assignment and assessment platform that connects students with the tools and resources they'll need to achieve success.

McGraw-Hill *Connect® Economics* helps prepare students for their future by enabling faster learning, more efficient studying, and higher retention of knowledge.

Connect® Economics offers a number of powerful tools and features to make managing assignments easier so faculty can spend more time teaching. With *Connect® Economics*, students can engage with their coursework anytime and anywhere, making the learning process more accessible and efficient. *Connect® Economics* offers the features described here.

Simple Assignment Management

With *Connect® Economics*, creating assignments is easier than ever so you can spend more time teaching and less time managing. The assignment management function enables you to

- Create and deliver assignments easily with selectable end-of-chapter questions and test bank items.
- Streamline lesson planning, student progress reporting, and assignment grading to make classroom management more efficient than ever.
- Go paperless with the eBook and online submission and grading of student assignments.

Smart Grading
When it comes to studying, time is precious. *Connect® Economics* helps students learn more efficiently by providing feedback and practice material when they need it, where they need it. When it comes to teaching, your time also is precious. The grading function enables you to

- Have assignments scored automatically, giving students immediate feedback on their work and side-by-side comparisons with correct answers.
- Access and review each response; manually change grades or leave comments for students to review.
- Reinforce classroom concepts with practice tests and instant quizzes.

Instructor Library
The *Connect® Economics* Instructor Library is your repository for additional resources to improve student engagement in and out of class. You can select and use any asset that enhances your lecture.

Student Study Center
The *Connect® Economics* Student Study Center is the place for students to access additional resources. The Student Study Center

- Offers students quick access to lectures, practice materials, eBooks, and more.
- Provides instant practice material and study questions, easily accessible on the go.
- Gives students access to the Self-Quiz and Study described below.

Self-Quiz and Study
The Self-Quiz and Study (SQS) connects each student to the learning resources needed for success in the course. For each chapter, students

- Take a practice test to initiate the Self-Quiz and Study.
- Immediately upon completing the practice test, see how their performance compares to the chapter learning objectives to be achieved within each section of the chapters.
- Receive a Study Plan that recommends specific readings from the text, supplemental study material, and practice work that will improve their understanding and mastery of each learning objective.

Student Progress Tracking *Connect*® *Economics* keeps instructors informed about how each student, section, and class is performing, allowing for more productive use of lecture and office hours. The progress-tracking function enables you to

- View scored work immediately and track individual or group performance with assignment and grade reports.
- Access an instant view of student or class performance relative to learning objectives.
- Collect data and generate reports required by many accreditation organizations, such as the AACSB.

Lecture Capture Increase the attention paid to lecture discussion by decreasing the attention paid to note taking. For an additional charge Lecture Capture offers new ways for students to focus on the in-class discussion, knowing they can revisit important topics later. Lecture Capture enables you to

- Record and distribute your lecture with a click of button.
- Record and index PowerPoint presentations and anything shown on your computer so it is easily searchable, frame by frame.
- Offer access to lectures anytime and anywhere by computer, iPod, or mobile device.
- Increase intent listening and class participation by easing students' concerns about note taking. Lecture Capture will make it more likely you will see students' faces, not the tops of their heads.
- To learn more about Tegrity, watch a two-minute Flash demo at http://tegritycampus.mhhe.com.

McGraw-Hill *Connect Plus Economics*

McGraw-Hill reinvents the textbook learning experience for the modern student with *Connect*® *Plus Economics*. A seamless integration of an eBook and *Connect*® *Economics*, *Connect*® *Plus Economics* provides all of the features mentioned above plus the following:

- An integrated eBook, allowing for anytime, anywhere access to the textbook.

- Dynamic links between the problems or questions you assign to your students and the location in the eBook where that problem or question is covered.
- A powerful search function to pinpoint and connect key concepts in a snap.

In short, *Connect*® *Economics* offers you and your students powerful tools and features that optimize your time and energies, enabling you to focus on course content, teaching, and student learning.

For more information about Connect, please visit www.mcgrawhillconnect.com, or contact your local McGraw-Hill sales representative.

McGraw-Hill Customer Care Contact Information

At McGraw-Hill, we understand that getting the most from new technology can be challenging. That's why our services don't stop after you purchase our products. You can e-mail our product specialists 24 hours a day to get product training online. Or you can search our knowledge bank of frequently asked questions on our support website. For customer support, call **800-331-5094,** e-mail hmsupport@mcgraw-hill.com, or visit www.mhhe.com/support. One of our technical support analysts will be able to assist you in a timely fashion.

CourseSmart

CourseSmart is a new way for faculty to find and review eTextbooks. It's also a great option for students who are interested in accessing their course materials digitally. CourseSmart offers thousands of the most commonly adopted textbooks across hundreds of courses from a wide variety of higher education publishers. It is the only place for faculty to review and compare the full text of a textbook online. At CourseSmart, students can save up to 50% off the cost of a print book, reduce their impact on the environment, and gain access to powerful web tools for learning including full text search, notes and highlighting, and e-mail tools for sharing notes between classmates. Your eBook also includes tech support in case you ever need help.

Finding your eBook is easy. Visit www.CourseSmart.com and search by title, author, or ISBN.

ACKNOWLEDGMENTS

I want to thank the people who were good enough to read and comment on chapters from this text, including Chris Farrell, Sue Helper, Elliot Mandel, Judy Scherer, and Robert Stavins. I'd like to express my appreciation to my former colleagues at *BusinessWeek,* including Editor-in-Chief Steve Adler and Economics Editor Peter Coy. I couldn't have done this textbook without my editors at McGraw-Hill/Irwin, who helped steer me though this long process. Finally, my deepest thanks to my family, Judy, Elliot, and Laura, who had to put up with the many hours that I spent working on the textbook.

Michael Mandel

Ryan Amacher
University
of Texas–Arlington

Lee Ash
Skagit Valley College

Tami Bertelsen
Arapahoe Community
College

Laura Jen Bhadra
Northern Virginia Community College–Manassas
Campus

Richard Bilas
The Citadel

Grant Black
Indiana University–
South Bend

R. Morris Coats
Nicholls State University

Bruce Domazlicky
Southeast Missouri State
University

Susan Doty
University of Southern
Mississippi

Eugene Elander
Brenau University

William Farr
Georgia College and State
University

Cynthia Foreman
Maui Community College

David Garraty
Virginia Wesleyan College

Armagan Gezici
Keene State College

David Hoover
Cambridge College

Zhining Hu
Gettysburg College

Jim Klein
Savannah Technical
College

Khawaja Mamun
Sacred Heart University

Kelly Manley
Gainesville State
College

Michael Marlow
California Polytechnic
State University

Louis Martinette
University of Mary
Washington

Roger Meiners
University of Texas–
Arlington

Mark Nadler
Ashland University

Charles Newton
Houston Community
College–Southwest

Suzanne Palmer
Albright College

Steve Price
Butte College

Charles Rambeck
Saint John's University

Terry Riddle
Central Virginia Community
College

Nancy Rumore
University of Louisiana–
Lafayette

Mike Ryan
Gainesville State College

Sara Saderion
Houston Community
College–Southwest

Ayuba Sarki
Hampton University

Dawn Saunders
Castleton State
College

Deborah Savage
Southern Connecticut
State University

Dennis Shannon
Southwestern Illinois
University

Stephan Silver
The Citadel

Harindar Singh
Grand Valley State
University

Martha Stuffler
Irvine Valley College

John Swinton
Georgia College and State
University

Susanne Toney
Hampton University

Janice Wirtjes
Piedmont Technical
College

Ben Young
University of Missouri–
Kansas City

BRIEF CONTENTS

CONTENTS

ECONOMICS
THE BASICS

01 INTRODUCTION

LEARNING OBJECTIVES

After reading this chapter, you should be able to:

LO1-1 Understand the importance of markets.

LO1-2 Identify three of the main forces shaping today's economy.

LO1-3 Explain the debate over the role of government in the economy.

LO1-4 Define economics and discuss how prosperity is measured.

LO1-5 Name some key disagreements in economics.

Toward the end of 2007 the United States plunged into the economic downturn now known as the **Great Recession.** The number of unemployed Americans doubled between 2007 and 2010. The financial system nearly collapsed in fall 2008, forcing the federal government to intervene. Home foreclosures became depressingly common as families struggled to pay their mortgages. State and local governments were forced to lay off teachers, firefighters, and other workers as tax revenues dropped.

The economic picture was equally dismal in much of the rest of the world. Countries such as the United Kingdom, Italy, Ireland, Spain, and Greece experienced sharp, long-lasting economic contractions that threw millions of people out of work. By contrast, some developing countries, such as China and India, continued to grow through the global crisis.

The question now is what the future will bring. Here history may be a guide. Back in 1929 the United States was hit by the Great Depression, an economic crisis that was far worse than the current one and lasted for most of the 1930s.

At the low point of the Great Depression, roughly one-quarter of the American workforce was unemployed. Construction came to a halt, farmers were desperate, and banks were closing. The rough economic stretch lasted a full decade.

But surprise! That terrible period was followed by 75 years of strong economic growth and rising living standards. Someone who graduated from school during the Great Depression may have had a miserable time finding a first job but probably ended up enjoying a lifetime of rising wages, improved health, bigger homes, better education, and far more options for travel and entertainment. One example: In 1929 air travel was a rarity, available only to a few people. Today traveling by air across the United States or to other countries is common. Or consider health: People are far more likely to live 65 years or more today than they were in 1929, when illnesses such as diptheria and tuberculosis were major causes of death.

What will the next 75 years bring? Change happens so quickly now that even 5 or 10 years can dramatically alter our lives. By some forecasts, China could pass the United States as the world's largest economy sometime in the next 20 years, with India not far behind. The Internet brings us more entertainment and information every day, as well as increasing amounts of misinformation and opportunities for fraud. Advances in health technology may significantly advance our life spans, bringing all the societal implications of a large elderly population. And the threat of global climate change has increased pressure to move away from fossil fuels such as coal and oil to other energy sources such as solar, wind, and nuclear power.

As the global economy speeds into the future, the big question is, Who is steering? Or to put it another way, how much should the

MARKET
A way for buyers and sellers to voluntarily exchange goods and services for money.

government intervene in the economy? This issue came up in fall 2008 when Treasury Secretary Henry Paulson and Federal Reserve Chairman Ben Bernanke led a successful government response that stopped the financial system from collapsing. Then in spring 2009 President Barack Obama and his economic team pushed through a massive stimulus plan to help prop up the economy and the labor market. Politicians and economists are still debating whether these efforts were too small or too large or could have been done better. Consider, for example, the question of who pays for health care—one of the biggest and fastest-growing sectors of the economy. Few are satisfied with the current system in the United States, which is expensive and leaves many Americans without any health care coverage. President Obama signed a major health care reform bill in spring 2010 that improved access to health insurance for many Americans. Yet there is still disagreement about whether the right solution is to get the government more involved or to rely more on private businesses. This question will continue to come up in the future—not just in the United States but in the rest of the world as well.

THE BIG PICTURE

This textbook will accomplish three goals for you. *First,* you'll get the basic tools of economics, starting in Chapter 2 with supply and demand. When you're finished, you won't be an economist, but you will have learned a new way of thinking about today's world.

Second, using these tools of economics, you can begin to understand **markets** and the 21st-century **global market economy.** In a market, buyers and sellers come together—not necessarily in the same place—to voluntarily exchange goods and services for money. It may be the smallest of transactions, such as downloading an iPhone app for 99 cents, or the

$200 million purchase of a passenger jet from Boeing by an airline or a wealthy individual. The market economy consists of all the different markets going on simultaneously.

Today the vast majority of economic activity worldwide is organized by **market transactions:** activities that produce and exchange goods and services that other people are willing to pay for. From poor rice farmers in Cambodia to multi-millionaire investment bankers on Wall Street, the market rules, and this book will show you how it works.

Third, you'll see the ways in which the possibilities of today's economy are expanding. More precisely, at any moment households are limited in what they can purchase by their income and by the range of products and services available (you can't yet buy your own spaceship). Businesses are limited in what they can produce by technology and by their past investments in factories, processes, and materials. Whole countries remain poor and thus limited in their economic capabilities.

But these constraints change every day. Some things that were impossible or very expensive a few years ago have now become commonplace. New technologies let us communicate globally far more cheaply than ever before. Countries that were once poor, such as China and India, have become productive dynamos. The stock market and other financial markets are now far more accessible to ordinary people and small businesses.

For all these reasons, we'll pay special attention to the main forces driving change in today's economy.

TECHNOLOGICAL CHANGE
An improvement in knowledge that increases the quantity and range of goods and services that the economy can deliver.

KEY FORCES SHAPING TODAY'S ECONOMY

Let's look individually at three of the main forces shaping today's economy: technological change, globalization, and the evolution of financial markets.

Technological Change

The forward progress of technology and science is the primary force for economic growth—not just in the United States but everywhere. From the development of the steam engine, the automobile, and electricity through the creation of computers and the Internet, technological change has been the critical factor in raising living standards.

Technological change, broadly speaking, is an improvement in knowledge that increases the quantity and range of goods and services the economy can deliver. It can include the introduction of a sophisticated electronic product, such as the first microprocessor or the first mobile telephone, that lets people do things they couldn't do before (see the accompanying "Economic Milestone" box). Technological change includes the invention of Google's "page rank" search algorithm, which makes it much easier to find exactly what you want on the Internet (and which made its inventors billionaires). And it includes the invention of decaffeinated coffee or sugar substitutes that provide sweetness without calories.

Technological change also includes new ways of doing things. One of the best examples of technological change is McDonald's, which applied assembly-line methods to the restaurant industry.

Economic Milestone

1971 THE FIRST MICROPROCESSOR

The first microprocessor—a "computer on a chip"—was created in 1971 by Intel. At the time, Intel was a small start-up company, and the tiny chip, called the 4004, was designed to run a Japanese calculator. What was new, though, was that the 4004 could be programmed to do a wide variety of tasks. This was the true beginning of the Information Age. Today Intel is one of the best-known companies in the world, and microprocessors are found in everything from computers and cell phones to televisions and cars.

AT&T Picturephone

Technological change is uneven, moving much faster in some industries than others. Although information technology has evolved rapidly in recent decades, the pace of change in energy technologies has been much slower. Virtually all cars are still powered by internal combustion engines—a technology first invented in Germany in the 1880s. Nuclear power has turned out to be far more expensive and troublesome than expected, and the 2011 disaster at Japan's Fukushima nuclear power plant has raised more questions about safety. Meanwhile renewable energy sources, such as solar, wind, and hydropower, still provide only 8 percent of U.S. energy needs as of 2009.

The result was "fast food" mass-produced at low prices. Technological change includes creativity in entertainment as well. Walt Disney, who died in 1966, created the animated feature film. Originally hand-drawn by teams of animators, those early films evolved into the computer animation we know today.

However, with global climate change on everybody's minds these days, and the price of oil so high, companies and governments have more incentive to invest in developing new energy technologies that either are cheaper or emit fewer greenhouse gases. As a result, the pace of energy-related technological change may accelerate.

Successful technological change or innovation is much more difficult than it looks. Plenty of ideas look promising at first, but they take years or decades to get turned into successful products or businesses. For example, the first video telephone, which allowed you to see the person on the other end of the call, was demonstrated at the 1964 World's Fair in New York City. This was the AT&T Picturephone, and it was a commercial failure. It wasn't until many years later that videoconferencing became available for most businesses.

Globalization

Globalization is the increasing exchange of goods, services, ideas, and people among countries. To a greater extent than ever before, we live in a global economy. The United States imports cheese from New Zealand, television sets from Taiwan, fish from Ecuador, tires from Romania, clothing from Turkey . . . the list is almost endless.

GLOBALIZATION
The increasing exchange of goods, services, ideas, and people among countries.

Most products take multiple attempts to become practical. For example, before the Apple iPod came a whole generation of music players that were either too expensive or too hard to use—or that simply didn't give users what they wanted.

But trade in manufactured goods and foodstuffs is only one aspect of globalization. More and more international trade—both exports and imports—consists of intangible services. For example, when you call customer support for your new computer, you may get routed to a call center in India. The services of those Indian customer representatives are being

Economic Milestone

1983 THE FIRST TOYOTA CAMRY

In 1983 Japan-based carmaker Toyota introduced the Camry in the United States. The success of the Camry, the top-selling car in the United States over the past decade, helped make Japan-based Toyota the top global automaker. Today most Camrys sold in the United States are assembled in Toyota's factory in Georgetown, Kentucky.

imported into the United States or wherever you might be located.

Global flows of information—ideas, research, entertainment, and other forms of communication—have vastly increased as well. Many more people are also crossing international borders for business, for tourism, or to immigrate permanently. The number of international travelers—not including immigrants—rose by 50 percent from 1998 to 2008, before dropping a bit in 2009 because of the global recession.

Why are countries so much more interconnected these days? Technological change is one reason. It is now possible to communicate from virtually any spot on the globe to virtually any other spot at almost no cost. If a retailer like Walmart in the United States is running low on, say, size 12 jeans, it can immediately flash a new order to a clothing factory in China, Thailand, or wherever the production is done.

Technology by itself, however, is not enough to explain the pull of globalization. Most people accept that being open to the global economy brings enormous advantages. Poorer countries such as Korea, China, and India started growing only when they focused on becoming exporters—that is, when they focused on figuring out what the rest of the world wanted and responding.

For a rich country like the United States, a big benefit of foreign trade is access to cheaper goods and services. The price of clothing has fallen by 10 percent since 1995, mainly because of soaring imports from low-cost producers overseas. In addition, a global economy greatly expands the size of the potential market for exporters. Companies such as Boeing and Intel, the giant U.S. semiconductor manufacturer, get much of their revenue from outside the United States.

Globalization also acts as a reality check. In an economy walled off from the global economy, it's easy for companies and workers to grow complacent and sluggish. Foreign competition shakes things up, forcing everyone to try harder and to look for better ways of doing things.

Of course, the impact of the global economy is not all positive. Foreign competition can wipe out jobs at home, force down wages and profits, and cause deep-seated insecurity. The flood of cheap imports in recent years has ravaged manufacturing industries in the United States, eliminating millions of domestic jobs.

In response to such effects, it's tempting to pull up the drawbridge, close the gates, and pretend the outside world doesn't exist. The United States is a big country; in theory, U.S. factories could produce almost everything we import today, from toys to clothing to computers. The single big exception might be oil, but even there a determined effort to use alternative fuels could substantially cut oil imports.

Yet today every successful national economy is tied into the broader global economy. Closed economies—that is, ones that are cut off from the rest of the world—may do better in the short run, but history shows they quickly lose their vitality and fall behind. Over time it has become clear that countries that are open to international trade do better than those that are isolated (see "Spotlight: The Chinese Economy").

SPOTLIGHT: THE CHINESE ECONOMY

If you check the label on your clothing, there's a good chance it will say "Made in China." Your iPod, if you own one, says "Made in China" as well. The same is true for many laptop computers, toys, motorcycles, appliances, and all sorts of other goods.

Thirty years ago, it would have been almost impossible for you to find anything in the United States that was made in China. In 1978 China was the most populous country in the world, with a billion people. But it was also one of the poorest countries, barely able to feed itself, and certainly possessing no ability to compete economically with the United States.

Since then China has undergone one of the great economic transformations in history. Starting in the late 1970s, the government relaxed some aspects of its control over the economy, encouraged markets, and took steps to foster trade with the rest of the world.

The result: China is now the largest global exporter of goods. Perhaps more important, many Chinese are far better off than their parents were 30 years ago. The country still has poor regions and political unrest, and some of the growth has caused problems like pollution. But at least up to this point, China has become an economic success story.

The Evolution of Financial Markets

The third force driving today's economy forward is the evolution of the financial markets. The **financial markets** (sometimes also called the **financial system**) encompass all parts of the economy that have to do with borrowing, investing, or transferring money. That includes the stock market, where investors can buy and sell shares of companies; the residential mortgage market, where people can borrow money to buy homes; and the venture capital market, where start-up companies can raise funds to finance their early years. The financial markets also include banks, brokerage firms, mutual funds, credit card providers, and financiers. Government regulators, which in the United States include such agencies as the Securities and Exchange Commission and the Federal Reserve Board, are part of the financial markets as well.

Over the long run, the spread of financial markets has helped fuel economic growth. Companies, individuals, and governments can use financial markets to raise money for useful activities. As just one example, Facebook, the social networking company, was able to expand faster because it received venture capital funding.

Most people justifiably have mixed feelings about financial markets, which can experience violent swings. For Americans who have a lot of their retirement money in the stock market, these downturns can seem devastating. Over the long run—say, 20 years—the stock market has historically almost always gone up. But in the short run it is subject to wide swings that can create large fortunes or steal hard-earned investments. Pick the right stock, and you can turn a small stack of money into a much larger pile. But make a bad investment or get caught in a stock market crash, and you can see your life savings disappear.

Over the past few years, the financial markets went through some particularly nasty gyrations that damaged the rest of the economy. We will read more about this financial crisis later in the textbook. Basically, what happened is that between 2000 and 2007, Americans took on an enormous amount of mortgage debt, including so-called subprime loans given to people who did not have enough income to qualify for ordinary mortgages. When housing prices started to turn down, suddenly many Americans found that they owed more money on mortgages than their homes were worth. The problems hit many financial institutions as well, who had lent large sums of money under the assumption that home prices would keep going up. The result: billions of dollars of losses at big financial institutions. Moreover, there was a danger of a chain reaction, where the losses at one big bank or other financial institution would cause it to fail, and pull down other companies with it. That's why the government had to intervene to keep the financial markets from collapsing in fall 2008.

> **FINANCIAL MARKETS**
> The parts of the economy connected with borrowing, investing, or transferring money.

THE ROLE OF GOVERNMENT

In response to the Great Recession and the financial crisis, the U.S. government took aggressive steps to fight unemployment and the economic slowdown. Yet Washington policymakers were criticized both for not doing enough and for interfering too much in the economy.

This debate is an example of a more general concern: Should the economy be guided by politicians and government regulators, or should individuals and private businesses be allowed to make business decisions as they please? This question comes up in all sorts of situations. At one extreme is a **centrally planned economy,** in which most economic activities are controlled by the government. In the past, the Soviet Union—which collapsed in 1991—approached this mode. The government owned all the factories and decided what they would produce, how much, and at what selling price. At the other extreme would be an imaginary economy with few or no government regulations or laws at all—what economists call a **laissez-faire economy.**

Obviously neither of these two extremes is workable. But virtually every debate over economic policy boils down to finding the right balance between government intervention and free competition. Let's get a better idea of what these terms mean.

Economic Competition

The common definition of competition is "a rivalry between contestants to achieve a goal or reward." Workers compete for jobs and promotions. Universities compete to attract good students. Companies compete for customers or for market dominance. States compete to attract new businesses.

Economic competition is the effort by people and businesses to achieve a desirable outcome, given what everyone else is doing. The most important economic competition happens within the context of a market. Buyers compete to get the best deals at the lowest prices; sellers compete to sell the most products for the highest prices. McDonald's competes with Wendy's, while Google competes with Facebook and Apple.

History suggests that economic competition—conducted within a fair set of rules—is the most consistent force for growth and progress. A company has a much stronger incentive to innovate and to produce a better and cheaper product if it knows that its rival down the block or across the ocean is trying to take its customers. The influx of inexpensive, reliable cars from Japan in the 1980s forced General Motors, Ford, and Chrysler to improve the reliability of their own cars and to come up with a whole new type of vehicle—the minivan. More recently the success of the hybrid gas–electric cars from Toyota and Honda compelled U.S. auto manufacturers to move more quickly to introduce their own hybrid models.

The most competitive large economy in the world, by most reckonings, is the United States. Developing countries such as China and India have prospered by introducing more elements of a U.S.-style economy, including more competition, start-ups of new companies, and much less top-down management by government.

What is the attraction of the U.S. economic model? The simplest answer is that it has a long track record of success. Despite recent problems, the United States has enjoyed consistently strong economic growth over time. Most people living in the United States enjoy a high living standard, meaning they have ample access to necessities such as food, clothing, and shelter and luxuries such as entertainment and travel. U.S. companies and workers have also shown a remarkable ability to adapt to new technologies

ECONOMIC COMPETITION
The effort by people and businesses to achieve a desirable outcome, given what everyone else is doing.

and a changing global economy, in part because they have always been used to competing.

Still, the idea of unbridled economic competition with no government intervention troubles many people because it seems to lead to insecurity, waste, and unnecessary hostility. After all, if there is a winner, there must be losers. If companies are competing for the same customers, the one who comes in second may be forced to lay off workers. And economic competition seems to leave behind large pockets of poverty—people who are jobless and homeless.

Government Intervention

Government intervention represents the actions taken by government to affect the economy. Indeed, it would be impossible to do business without basic laws governing fraud and contracts. The government issues money, insures bank deposits so people can trust banks, and regulates the banks and the financial system. Regulations govern the details of daily life. They dictate how our homes are wired and whether our cars have seat belts or airbags, and they ensure that you can use your computer in the same room as your television without the signals creating interference on the screen. The Food and Drug Administration must approve new drugs for safety and usefulness before they can be sold, and the Federal Aviation Administration certifies new aircraft before they can be flown.

Moreover, the government generally takes responsibility for making sure the economy doesn't fall into deep slumps in which a lot of people lose their jobs. This role has been highlighted during the Great Recession. In 2008 the Federal Reserve lent financial institutions billions of dollars to ensure that they would not fail and drag down the economy when the overheated housing market crashed. Also in 2008, President George W. Bush signed into law the Troubled Asset Relief Program (TARP), which made $700 billion available to help prop up the troubled financial sector. After President Obama took office in 2009, he signed the American Recovery and Reinvestment Act (ARRA), which spent almost $800 billion in an effort to create jobs across the whole economy.

Even during normal times, every country draws a different line between the appropriate role of the government and the appropriate role of private businesses and individuals. In Canada and the United Kingdom, health care is provided by the government. And the Chinese government regularly exercises control over where its citizens live and how many children they can have. The "one-child" policy is no longer enforced in China as strictly as it once was, but families may still be penalized financially if they have too many children.

In practice, centrally planned economies seem to do poorly over the long run. Top-down management reduces insecurity, but at the cost of reducing incentives to innovate and make improvements. In a competitive economy, businesses react quickly to changing conditions; they don't have any choice if they want to stay in business. And unlike businesses in planned economies, they can use new technology without waiting for permission from a central authority.

Over the past 30 years, most countries have moved in the direction of less intervention by government, a process known as **deregulation.** For example, in the United States, President Jimmy Carter started reducing government control over the airline and trucking industries in the late 1970s. That process was greatly accelerated by President Ronald Reagan when he took office in January 1981.

About the same time on the other side of the globe, Chinese leader Deng Xiaoping began the process of shifting China away from a centrally planned economy. Today China still has many people working in state-owned factories, but it also has a vibrant private business sector that has made China the largest exporter in the world.

Finding a Balance

In practice, both competition and government are present in every part of the economy. The housing market is a good example. Most homes are built by private developers, not by the government. But developers and builders must work within a framework of zoning rules and construction codes set by the government.

When people want to borrow money to buy a home, they usually go to a private lender (a bank) or a mortgage broker. But the government has arranged the tax code to benefit home buyers who take out mortgages: Mortgage interest payments are typically tax-deductible, which helps save households billions in taxes. And during the recent troubles in the housing market, the government intervened to ensure that mortgage money would keep flowing.

THE DEFINITION OF ECONOMICS

Economics is a very broad subject that covers everything from global growth to the price of apples at a local supermarket. That's why we need a broad definition. From a wide perspective, economics is about how we make decisions, given that we can't have everything. To put it more precisely, **economics** is the study of how individuals, businesses, and governments make decisions and trade-offs in the face of scarce resources.

You could be a home owner trying to decide whether to allocate your money to buying a new car or to fixing the roof. Or you could be a business manager trying to decide whether to open a new store or put money into fixing up an existing one. Or you could be a government official choosing whether to create educational scholarships or fund health care for the elderly. In each of these cases, it's necessary to make a trade-off because only a limited amount of money is available.

This way of thinking about economics will be very important in this textbook, especially when we consider the behavior of consumers, workers, and businesses in the early chapters. It reflects the reality of the world.

Indicators of Prosperity

Economics is always concerned with what can be done to improve people's lives, keeping in mind the need to make trade-offs. Ultimately we judge

---

DEREGULATION
The process of reducing government control over markets.

ECONOMICS
The study of how individuals, businesses, and governments make decisions and trade-offs in the face of scarce resources.

HOW IT WORKS: GROSS DOMESTIC PRODUCT

Suppose you had to fill out a government form that asked, "How big are you?" You could give your height, your weight, your waist size, your shoe size, your hat size, or any other possible physical measurement.

Similarly, there are plenty of ways to measure an economy. But one key indicator is known as **gross domestic product** (GDP), which is the dollar value of the total output of a national economy over a year.[1] GDP includes the value of all the food produced in the country, the value of its cars and trucks, and the amount of money spent on health care plus more. GDP also includes the value of tickets for sporting events, the money paid by consumers for phone service, and the cost of all the goods and services provided by federal, state, and local governments, such as defense, education, and road repair.

In the United States, the value of GDP is calculated by the Bureau of Economic Analysis, one of the major statistical agencies of the federal government. For 2009 the GDP of the United States was $14.1 trillion, an almost unimaginably large number. This comes to roughly $46,000 for every woman, man, and child in the country. (We'll look at GDP in more detail in Chapter 7.)

Other countries calculate GDP as well, using roughly the same set of rules as the United States. Figure 1.1 shows the 10 largest economies in the world in 2009, measured by GDP.

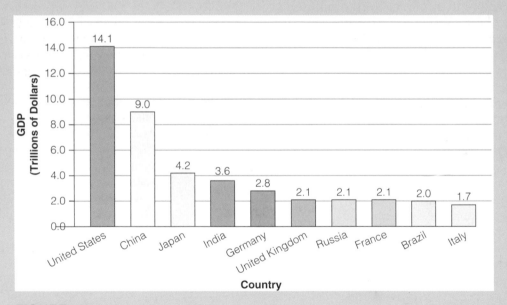

FIGURE 1.1
The 10 Largest Economies in the World in 2009: This chart shows the gross domestic product (GDP), measured in dollars, of the 10 largest economies in the world. The United States leads with a GDP of $14.1 trillion. China is number 2 with a GDP of $9 trillion.
Source: International Monetary Fund as of October 2010
[1] Taking care not to double count.

the success or failure of an economy by the prosperity of its inhabitants. Of course this leaves open the question of precisely how to measure prosperity. As you will see in this textbook, economists like to quantify (or put numbers on) the things they study, and there are lots of different ways to measure how well an economy and its members are doing.

For example, we can look at the total output of an economy, also called its **gross domestic product** (see "How It Works" on page 10). In an important sense, the more goods and services an economy can produce, the better it is doing. That's why economists want to make sure the total output of the economy keeps growing.

But economists look at other measures as well to gauge economic success. For example, government statisticians produce reams of data on wages and benefits. That's certainly one indicator of how well people are doing. Another important statistic is annual household income, which includes pay for workers plus other sources of money such as Social Security and income from investments. Economists also keep an eye on household consumption, which is the amount of goods and services a typical household consumes in a year.

Depending on which indicator you look at, there can be a big difference in a person's prosperity. For example, a student in college may have no income but may still have a good standard of living, including travel and entertainment. A rich person who is not working won't receive any wage payments but may still have plenty of money from investments.

Then there are nonmonetary measures of prosperity. We can survey people and ask them how happy they are. We can look at whether life expectancy—the number of years that people are expected to live—is rising. And we can ask whether the quality of the environment is getting better or worse. Although these indicators are not purely economic, they are still important to an overall feeling of prosperity.

The Safety Net

Any successful modern economy must allow all its members to share in its prosperity. It's not politically or morally acceptable for most of the population to live good lifestyles while a smaller number are much worse off.

That's why the United States and other industrialized countries have a **safety net,** the government programs that provide a measure of security for the poor, the sick, and the vulnerable.

SAFETY NET
The government programs which provide a measure of security for the poor, sick, and vulnerable.

In the United States, the safety net consists of a wide array of programs with familiar names: Social Security, Medicare, Medicaid, unemployment insurance, food stamps, housing subsidies, and tax credits for low-income wage earners.

The safety net makes an enormous difference in the well-being of low-income households. The food stamp program, for example, provided low-cost food to roughly 40 million Americans in 2010, with the average person getting $1,600 in benefits. The Medicaid program helped about 50 million low-income people with medical costs. And the earned income tax credit—a tax program designed to help low-income wage earners—gave an average benefit of over $2,000 to 25 million U.S. tax filers.

Still, there is widespread disagreement about whether the United States is doing enough to help the poor. The income and wealth gap between rich and poor has increased in recent years, so that the top 20 percent of U.S. households get about half the country's income. In 2009, the Census Bureau reported that there were 44 million Americans who were officially designated as living below the poverty line.

By comparison, European countries such as France and Germany pride themselves on the strength of their social safety nets, which offer comprehensive medical care, better retirement benefits, and more job security than in the United States. Yet until very recently these countries have also consistently suffered from a worse unemployment problem than the United States has. For all its shortcomings, no one has yet come up with an economic model clearly superior to that of the United States.

DISAGREEMENTS IN ECONOMICS

In some areas of economics there is little disagreement. However, plenty of important policy questions divide economists when it comes to the right amount of government intervention in the economy. For example, reputable economists disagree about whether the government's response to the Great Recession was too big, too small, or just right.

Then there is the debate over how big the government's role should be in health, education, and retirement. How can we pay for Social Security and Medicare as the baby boom generation retires? Some critics of President Obama's health care reform argued that it called for too much government interference in the private sector. Meanwhile, other economists thought that health care should be completely paid for by the government.

Likewise, although everyone agrees that education is crucial, there is no consensus among economists—or anyone else, for that matter—about how best to improve the educational system. Many economists argue that "money talks," so spending more resources on education, especially for the younger grades, is the right thing to do. But an influential group of economists believes, based on empirical studies, that spending money to reduce class size has little impact on educational achievement.

And then there's higher education. Some economists want the federal government to provide more scholarship funds, enabling more poor children to go to college. Others argue that if the government provides more scholarship funds, colleges will simply cut their financial aid packages or raise tuition by the same amount, leaving poor students in the same spot.

What about the government's role in determining the course of technology? Right now cable companies and phone companies are vying to provide broadband connections to homes. Will market forces produce the best solution, or could government intervention improve the outcome? Should Congress pass legislation to force auto manufacturers to sell more fuel-efficient vehicles, or would that deprive us of our right to drive gas-guzzling sport utility vehicles?

Perhaps most important is the ongoing controversy about the right level of federal taxes. Should federal taxes be higher, lower, or completely revamped to make them simpler? President Bill Clinton raised federal income taxes in 1993 to reduce the federal budget deficit, and his actions were applauded by many well-known economists. But when President George W. Bush sharply cut taxes in 2001 and 2003, he received applause from equally well-known economists. There is simply no consensus in the economics profession about this question (and don't let anyone tell you there is).

Why do economists disagree about so many vital policy questions? In many cases we don't have enough data to be sure of the right answer. In other cases the controversy is aggravated by the political agendas of those who stand to gain or lose from policy changes. In this textbook, we will present both sides of controversial issues, and help you understand the reasoning behind each of them.

Economics is a dynamic subject, always evolving to keep up with changes in the economy. With any luck, this textbook will help you better understand both the subject of economics and the economy we live in.

01   SUMMARY

1. The basic tools of economics developed in this textbook, such as supply and demand, are essential for understanding markets and the global market economy that we all live in. (LO1-1)

2. Three key forces shaping today's economy are *technological change*, *globalization*, and the evolution of *financial markets*. Technological change is an improvement in knowledge that increases the range of products and services the economy can deliver. Globalization is the increasing exchange of goods, services, ideas, and people among countries. And financial market changes affect any person or business who borrows, invests or, spends money. (LO1-2)

3. An important economic policy debate is the appropriate role of government in the economy—

that is, the degree to which individuals and private businesses can make decisions as they please without interference from politicians and government regulators. Most economists believe that economic competition–conducted within a fair set of rules–is the most consistent force for growth and progress. *(LO1-3)*

4. Economics is defined as the study of making decisions in the face of scarce resources.

The goal of economic policy, broadly defined, is to raise the prosperity of the inhabitants of a country. *(LO1-4)*

5. Economists often disagree about the right way to raise prosperity. Important economic policy debates include the level of taxes, and the nature of the government's role in such areas as health care and education. *(LO1-5)*

KEY TERMS AND CONCEPTS

Great Recession

markets

global market economy

market transactions

technological change

globalization

financial markets (financial system)

centrally planned economy

laissez-faire economy

economic competition

government intervention

deregulation

economics

gross domestic product

safety net

PROBLEMS

1. Economic activity around the world is mainly organized by _____ *(LO1-1)*

   a) Internet connections.
   b) family connections.
   c) informal arrangements.
   d) market transactions.

2. Technological change _____ *(LO1-2)*

   a) moves faster in some industries than others.
   b) is found equally in all parts of the economy.
   c) moves fastest in the energy sector.
   d) never benefits the economy.

3. One benefit of globalization is _____ *(LO1-2)*

   a) higher prices.
   b) lower prices.
   c) less international communication.
   d) a lower standard of living.

4. Many people have mixed feelings about financial markets because financial markets _____ *(LO1-2)*

   a) can experience violent swings.
   b) can work only in a centrally planned economy.
   c) only hurt the economy.
   d) always go down.

5. For each of the following, indicate whether it is more likely to be the result of economic competition or government intervention. *(LO1-3)*

   a) Protection against unsafe drugs.
   b) Rapid innovation.
   c) Help for poor families.
   d) Strong economic growth.

6. At its extreme, a laissez-faire approach to the economy means no government regulation at all. Let's suppose we got rid of the rule that you need a medical degree to practice medicine. One disadvantage of such a change would be _____ *(LO1-3)*

   a) more time spent in waiting rooms.
   b) fewer doctors.
   c) a higher price for medical care.
   d) a lower quality of medical care.

7. One indicator of prosperity is gross domestic product. Gross domestic product measures the economy by _____ *(LO1-4)*

   a) adding up annual household income.
   b) looking only at household consumption.
   c) counting the dollar value of the total output of a national economy over a year.
   d) measuring annual wages and benefits.

8. If the government safety net were to disappear, which of the following outcomes would be likely to occur? *(LO1-4)*

   a) Elderly Americans would live longer.
   b) Poor families would be able to buy less food.
   c) The income and wealth gap between rich and poor would narrow.
   d) The United States would spend less on health care.

9. Disagreements among economists are _____ *(LO1-5)*

    a) unusual.

    b) limited to health care and education.

    c) frequent when considering the appropriate degree of government intervention.

    d) rare when considering new technologies.

10. Is the following statement true or false? Reputable economists agree that the response to the Great Recession was too small. *(LO1-5)*

APPENDIX
THE BASICS OF GRAPHS

LEARNING OBJECTIVES

After you read this appendix you should be able to:

LO1A-1 Read data from a line graph or a bar graph.

LO1A-2 Plot points on a graph using data from a table.

In this textbook we use several different kinds of graphs. But don't be scared: The purpose of graphs is to help you by giving a visual representation of economic concepts or numerical relationships. For example, we can compare the sizes of two economies with numbers, or we can use the visual representation of a bar graph, like Figure 1. 1. We also use graphs to plot the behavior of individuals or firms in markets, or to help understand the behavior of the whole economy.

READING DATA FROM GRAPHS

Graphs can be used to convey economic information visually. Figure 1.1, reproduced here as Figure 1A.1, is a **bar graph** that compares the size of different economies, measured in dollars. This graph has a **horizontal axis** (sometimes called the *x*-axis) and a **vertical axis** (sometimes called the *y*-axis). In this graph, the horizontal axis contains a list of countries, and the vertical axis reports on the size of each country's economy. The

---

FIGURE 1A.1 | **An Example of a Bar Graph**

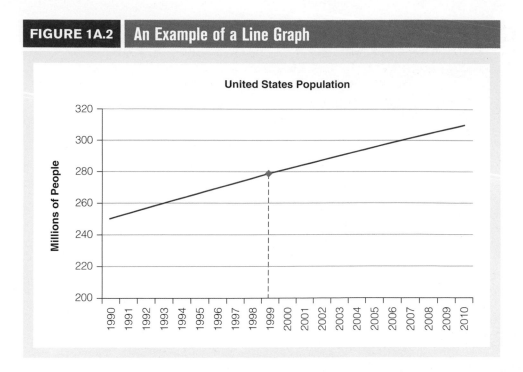

FIGURE 1A.2 | **An Example of a Line Graph**

height of the bars represents the size of each economy. So the United States has a bigger economy than France, measured in dollars.

We can read the size of each economy off the graph. For example, the bar labeled "Brazil" comes right up to the line labeled '2.0'. That means Brazil's economy is $2.0 trillion.

Another type of data graph is a **line graph.** A line graph, as the name shows, conveys information using a line. For example, Figure 1A.2 shows the population of the United States since 1990. To determine, for example, the population of the United States in 1999, we start from 1999 on the horizontal axis and trace straight up until we reach the line. Then we look to the vertical axis and see that there were 280 million Americans in 1999.

PLOTTING GRAPHS FROM DATA

With the data graphs just described, you can read the data from the graph. But often in economics you will be asked to go the other direction: Given a table of numbers, you have to be able to graph it. That is, you plot the data points on the graph, one by one. Then if necessary you connect the points.

Consider Table 1A.1, which reports on entertainment spending per person for households headed by people of different ages. For example, a household headed by a person 45–54 years old

TABLE 1A.1 | **Age and Entertainment Spending**

Household Headed by Person	Amount Spent on Entertainment per Person*
Under 25 years old	$ 800
25–34 years old	1,000
35–44 years old	1,100
45–54 years old	1,200
55–64 years old	1,400
65 and older	1,100

*Rounded to nearest $100.

Data: Bureau of Labor Statistics Consumer Expenditure Survey, 2008.

FIGURE 1A.3 | **Age and Entertainment Spending**

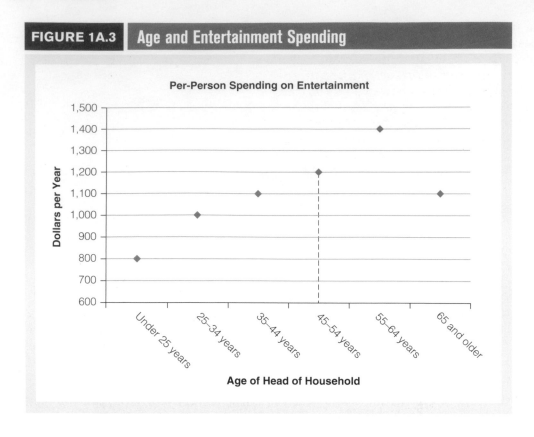

FIGURE 1A.4 | **Age and Entertainment Spending (with Connected Lines)**

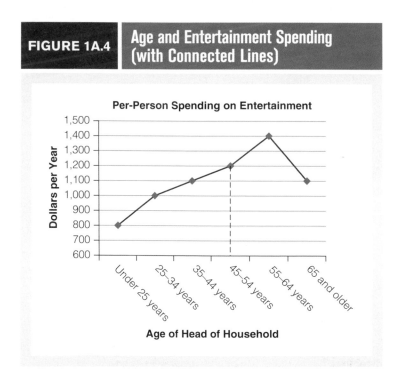

will spend $1,200 on average per person in the household on entertainment. (This includes teenage children, of course!) Entertainment spending includes tickets for sporting events, movies, and concerts; purchases of consumer electronics, sports equipment, and toys; and spending on pets.

How do we turn this into a graph? The first column of categories—in this case, the different age groups—goes along the horizontal axis. Then for each number, we go to the corresponding level of the vertical axis. So for a household headed by a 45–54-year-old, we run our finger up until we get to the $1,200 level, and that's where we put our point. We do that for each category on the horizontal axis.

We can leave those points like that, or we can connect them with lines, as in Figure 1A.4.

One thing to notice about Figure 1A.4 is that the line is **upward-sloping** from the category "under 25 years" to the category "55–64 years." That means the line goes from the bottom left to the top right. An upward-sloping line means, in this case, that entertainment spending per person increases as the age of the head of household increases.

Now let's look at a downward-sloping line. Since 1950 the population of the city of Cleveland, Ohio, has been steadily falling, as shown in Table 1A.2.

We will graph these data in Figure 1A.5. The first column, which is the years, goes on the horizontal axis. The vertical axis is the population. As before, we begin by plotting each data point, starting from the horizontal axis and moving up. For example, the population of Cleveland in 1990 was roughly 500,000, so we go up from 1990 to the line labeled 500 and put a point there. Then we connect the points in sequence.

This graph is **downward-sloping.** That means the population of Cleveland decreases as we move to the right along the graph.

TABLE 1A.2	Population of Cleveland
	(Thousands)
1950	915
1960	876
1970	751
1980	574
1990	506
2000	478
2009	432

Data: U.S. Census Bureau

CONCLUSION

This appendix has described the basics of graphs. As we move on in the textbook, we will see more ways that graphs can be used to understand the economy.

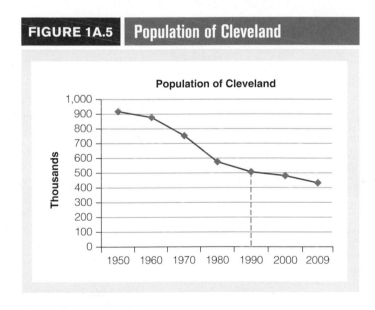

FIGURE 1A.5   Population of Cleveland

KEY TERMS AND CONCEPTS

bar graph	line graph	downward-sloping
horizontal axis	vertical axis	upward-sloping

PROBLEMS

1. The following graph plots the number of unemployed workers in the United States from 2000 to 2010. What is the number of unemployed workers in 2007? *(LO1A-1)*

a) 4 million

b) 7 million

c) 9 million

d) 14 million

Number of Unemployed Workers

Data: Bureau of Labor Statistics

2. The following table reports on the average price of a gallon of unleaded gasoline in the United States, rounded to the nearest 10 cents. *(LO1A-2)*

a) Plot the points to make a line graph.

b) From 2004 to 2008, is the line upward-sloping or downward-sloping?

Average Price of a Gallon of Unleaded Gasoline*

2002	1.40
2003	1.60
2004	1.90
2005	2.30
2006	2.60
2007	2.80
2008	3.30
2009	2.40
2010	2.80

*To nearest ten cents.

Data: Bureau of Labor Statistics.

3. At a (hypothetical) minor league baseball stadium, the team owner has tried three different prices for tickets and has found that his attendance per game varies according to the following table. Label the points on a graph, with attendance on the horizontal axis and ticket price on the vertical axis. Is this graph upward- or downward-sloping? *(LO1A-2)*

Attendance per Game (in Thousands)	Ticket Price
5	$15
10	10
15	5
20	3

02 DEMAND AND SUPPLY: THE BASICS OF THE MARKET ECONOMY

LEARNING OBJECTIVES

LO2-1 Describe the key elements of a market.

LO2-2 Explain how the price in a market affects the quantity demanded.

LO2-3 Explain how the price in a market affects the quantity supplied.

LO2-4 Discuss why the number of markets can increase.

Remember Legos, those little plastic building blocks? In April 2009 the world's then-tallest Lego tower was built in Nasu, Japan. Constructed from more than 400,000 Lego bricks, the tower stretched an impressive 97 feet high.

A **market economy,** such as that of the United States or Japan, is a bit like a Lego tower. It's an economic system made up of smaller "building blocks" of individual markets for trading all the different goods and services used in a country.

The variety of different markets is almost too big to grasp. It ranges from the market for homes in Chicago, to the online market for video games, to the market for airline tickets between London and Shanghai, to the market for pizza in Missoula, Montana (which in early 2011 included 29 pizza stores, according to the Yahoo! yellow pages).

This chapter introduces the basics of the market economy. First we'll explore the differences among local, national, and global markets. Next we'll look separately at demand and supply in markets—that is, the behavior of buyers and sellers. Then we'll briefly discuss the creation of new markets.

PRICES, BUYERS, AND SELLERS

Any market has one or more **buyers** and one or more **sellers.** In the market the buyer pays money in exchange for a **product**—a good or service. The sellers receive money in exchange for supplying the product. The rate at which the buyer and seller exchange money for the good or service is known as the **price.**

A simple example is the market for apples, say, in your town. There may be several sellers—the local supermarkets, the organic food store, and the corner deli. There are generally many buyers, such as people who enjoy eating apples and restaurants that make apple pie. The price is the amount a buyer pays per pound of apples (in 2010 the average price of a pound of Red Delicious apples was $1.22).

It's usually easy to figure out who are the buyers and sellers in a market. The individuals or businesses with the cash or credit cards in their hands, or writing the checks, are the buyers. The people or businesses collecting the money are the sellers.

PRICE
The rate at which the buyer and seller exchange money for a good or service.

But keep in mind that each individual or business is typically a buyer in some markets and a seller in others. For example, the typical worker is a seller in the **labor market.** That is, workers sell their time on the job for money. Meanwhile, they are buyers in most other areas of their lives, purchasing food, coffee, video games, and other necessities and luxuries. A business such as Starbucks is a seller in the market for premium cups of coffee—but it's also a buyer of coffee beans, coffee cups, espresso machines, office computers, and the labor of its workers.

Local, National, and Global Markets

Buyers and sellers who are geographically close to each other are part of a **local market.** For example, certain perishable food products like milk are generally sold in local markets (see "Spotlight: The Milk Market" on page 24). Dental services are typically local because you are unlikely to travel to a different part of the country to have your teeth cleaned. Similarly, many personal services such as haircuts, dry cleaning, and shoe repairs are handled in local markets. Even in today's global economy, no one is going to ship their dresses or shirts to China to be dry-cleaned!

In contrast, a **national market** lets buyers and sellers conduct transactions across the country. Thanks to the Internet and fast transportation, an increasing number of goods and services are traded in national markets. Do you want to open a stock account? No matter where in the United States you live, you can buy those stock-trading services from a broker anywhere else in the country. You can go house-hunting on the Internet and buy books, clothes, electronics, and music online. You can hire professionals in other parts of the country to improve your résumé or do your taxes.

Similarly, **global markets** allow buyers and sellers to be anywhere in the world. Crude oil has been sold on global markets for decades, as have steel, fish, natural gas, and memory chips. Global markets are often the province of globe-spanning companies called **multinationals,** which have operations in multiple countries. The

SPOTLIGHT: THE MILK MARKET

When you drink a glass of milk, there is a good chance it hasn't traveled more than a few hundred miles from the cow. Virtually every state has its own dairy industry, with distinctively named brands of milk from Shamrock Farms in Arizona to Golden Fleece Dairy in Florida. As a result, the market for fluid milk is mainly local.

In theory, refrigerated milk could be safely shipped much farther than current distribution patterns. But a complicated set of government regulations—in place since the 1930s—discourages but does not prohibit long-distance shipments of fluid milk.

In contrast, the market for dairy products such as cheese and butter is clearly global. The butter you put on a piece of bread may have come from as far away as New Zealand, and the cheese you eat may have come from France or even from Bulgaria, Lithuania, and Poland.

giant oil company ExxonMobil, for example, does energy exploration and production in 39 countries and sells oil, natural gas, gasoline, and lubricants almost everywhere around the globe.

One of the most remarkable changes in recent years is the seemingly overnight transformation of some local markets into vibrant national or global markets. The creation of the online auction site eBay in 1995

in the living room of founder Pierre Omidyar enabled the traditional yard sale to reach a national audience. Rather than simply advertising in a local paper, individuals can now sell their antique lamps or comic book collections to buyers around the country. And to an increasing degree, services that used to be done locally in the United States can now be outsourced to other countries. Preparing tax returns, for example, used to be the classic local service: You brought your box of receipts to your local accountant, who put your tax return together. Now the information can be transmitted to India, where the return is prepared at a much lower cost and transmitted back to the United States.

The Market Price

In economics we balance the wonderful complexity of the real world with the useful simplicity and clarity of economic models. In the previous section, for example, we talked about the *price* of a good or service as if there were only one price. In the real world, however, even identical cars may sell at different prices depending on which dealerships they are bought from and how well the buyers negotiate.

That's why we define the **market price** as the *typical* price at which a good or service sells in a market. In many cases the price for a good or service may be obvious and easy to identify. For example, the covers of most newspapers and magazines list their newsstand prices.

But sometimes identifying the price of a good or service is not as easy as reading it off a printed list. Sellers are always adjusting their prices to pull in more customers. A **sale price**, for example, is intentionally set below the market price to stimulate purchases.

Then there are **negotiated prices**, which are determined by individual buyer and seller on a case-by-case basis. Go to an auto dealer's showroom, and you will see the sticker price of a car or SUV listed on its window. But that sticker price is just the starting point for negotiation, after which different buyers may pay hundreds of dollars more or less for the same model car. Negotiated prices are more common in markets for big-ticket items like cars or homes.

MARKET PRICE
The typical price at which a good or service sells.

In some markets, buyers may be offered a **volume discount,** or a lower price for making a large purchase. For example, a hospital may charge an individual patient one price for an operation such as an appendectomy. But insurance companies may be able to negotiate a much lower price for the identical procedure, based on the large volume of operations they pay for on behalf of their customers—firms and individuals who buy medical insurance.

In other markets, an **advance purchase discount** means that prices differ according to when purchases are made (see "Economic Milestone," below). In air travel, two identical seats on the same plane may sell for different prices depending on how far ahead of time the travelers purchased them.

HOW PRICE AFFECTS THE QUANTITY DEMANDED

Some words in economics have meanings different from ordinary usage. Usually a *demand* refers to a forceful request, with the threat of consequences if the request is not met. Bank robbers demand money; babies demand their bottles.

Demand in a market, though, is a gentler concept. The **quantity demanded** by a particular buyer is the amount that a buyer is willing to purchase at a given price. For example, the weekly quantity demanded for gasoline at $3.00 per gallon is the amount a consumer is willing to buy at that price over a week.

To really understand a market, though, it's not enough to know what consumers are buying today. We also need to know what would happen to demand if the price of a good or service went up or down.

QUANTITY DEMANDED

The amount a buyer is willing to purchase at a given price.

In the market for gasoline, for example, it's extremely important for government agencies and oil companies to know how much the demand for gasoline will drop if the price rises from $3.00 a gallon to $4.00 a gallon or even more.

The link between a buyer's quantity demanded and the price is called the **demand schedule.** For example, consider how many songs a person—call him Sam—might download from an online music site in a month. If the price is $0.50 per song, Sam might download 20 songs and try out some unusual ones. If the price is $2.00 per song, Sam might download only the three songs he really likes. At $4.00 a song, Sam might decide not to download any songs.

Table 2.1 shows what Sam's demand schedule might look like. The first column is the price per song, and the second column is the number of songs Sam would be willing to buy at that price.

In theory we can build a demand schedule for every possible good or service that someone could buy. For example, your demand schedule for basketball tickets would reveal how many basketball games you might attend over the next year, depending on the price. Even if you are a vegetarian, we could construct your demand schedule for hamburgers. It would show zero quantity demanded at every price because no matter how low the price of hamburgers, you wouldn't buy any.

The **market demand schedule** sums the demand schedules for all the individual buyers in a market. So the market demand schedule in a town for hamburgers, for example, tells us how many hamburgers will be bought by the people in that town at any given price. That includes vegetarians who never buy hamburgers and people who eat a cheeseburger every day for lunch.

Economic Milestone

1986 THE FIRST PREPAID TUITION PLAN

In 1986 Michigan enacted the nation's first prepaid tuition plan. The plan enabled the parents of young children to pay for future tuition costs at state public higher education institutions at the current prices, thus avoiding all future tuition increases. About 13, or so, states now have similar plans—an example of an advance purchase discount.

TABLE 2.1	Sam's Demand Schedule for Music Downloads

The demand schedule tells us how many songs Sam will want to download, given the price per song.

Price per Song (Dollars)	Quantity Demanded (Number of Songs to be Downloaded in a Month)
$0.50	20
$1.00	10
$2.00	3
$3.00	1
$4.00	0

One final note: When we think about a demand schedule for a market, we are implicitly assuming that everything else about the buying situation stays the same when the price changes. For example, the market demand schedule for basketball tickets assumes that key factors like the quality of the team, the cost of the concessions, and the ease of traveling to the arena don't change when the price goes up or down. This assumption is called *ceteris paribus*—Latin for "all other things equal." Economists often use this simplifying strategy to determine the effect of a single change on a complex system.

The Law of Demand

When a local supermarket wants to bring in more shoppers, it advertises a sale—lower prices for detergent, say, or for lamb chops. And when Ford wants to attract more buyers for its cars or SUVs, it lowers its prices or offers rebates. The sellers expect that a lower price will increase the quantity demanded.

Alternatively, as the price of a good or service goes up, some people will simply stop buying the item, especially if it is a luxury and not a necessity. For example, if the price of a basketball ticket goes up enough, some people will simply cut basketball games out of their budgets and stop going.

Generally speaking, the lower the price, the greater the quantity demanded. This relationship between price and quantity demanded is known as the **law of demand.** Here's a good way to think about it: If the price of a good goes up, you look at your spending and ask yourself, "Is this the best use of my money?" If it's not, you spend a little bit less on the item that has gone up in price, and a little bit more on something else.

Suppose you drink three cups of coffee a day at $1 a cup. The local coffee vendor raises the price of a cup of coffee to $1.50 a cup. Now you have to ask yourself whether that third cup of coffee is still worth it, or whether you want to spend that $1.50 on a pack of gum or a piece of fruit. The principle works on a bigger scale as well. If tuition per class goes up, you may cut back on the number of college courses you take at a time.

Keep in mind that the law of demand is a general tendency, not an ironclad rule. In some cases, rising prices will *increase* demand. For example, when the prices of homes in a city are rising rapidly, buyers sometimes feel that they have to jump in quickly before the prices go even higher. Conversely, when the prices of homes start to fall in a market, buyers sometimes hold back from purchases hoping that home prices will decline further. However, despite such exceptions, you can usually expect that demand will fall as prices rise, and vice versa.

LAW OF DEMAND
A lower price tends to increase the quantity demanded, all other things equal.

The Special Case of Zero Price

Economists will be the first people to tell you that there's no such thing as a free lunch. And in fact almost everything in life seems to come with a price tag attached. But there actually *are* a few products that come with a **zero price,** so that you can get an additional unit of a good or service at no extra charge.

HOW IT WORKS: THE iPHONE AND THE LAW OF DEMAND

Not even Steve Jobs, the billionaire head of Apple who recently stepped down as CEO, can break the law of demand. When Apple first released its iPhone in June 2007, it got great reviews, but it sold for a stunning $599—a bit steep for most people. Two months later Apple reduced the price to $399. The result? Demand jumped. At the higher price, Apple sold just under a million iPhones, or about 14,000 per day. But after the price cut, average sales over the next four months were 20,000–25,000 per day. The price cut may not have been the only reason for the increase in sales, but it certainly helped.

When Jobs announced the price cut, many people who had rushed to buy iPhones at the earlier higher price felt cheated. As a result, Jobs was forced to write a letter on Apple's website apologizing and offering a $100 credit to those who had bought the phone at the higher price

Source: www.apple.com/hotnews/openiphoneletter.

There is no trick. In today's technology-based economy, we consume plenty of goods and services in unlimited quantities without paying anything beyond an initial fee. For example, most cable television plans allow you to watch as many shows as you want without paying extra, and many cell phone plans offer unlimited calling to other cell phones on the same network. Similarly, at least for now most broadband Internet plans allow you to connect for as long as you want for a fixed monthly charge.

Zero prices sometimes occur outside the technology sector as well. Some restaurants offer unlimited refills on coffee, and all-you-can-eat buffets are not uncommon. So if the price is zero, why don't you consume an infinite amount?

First, you generally reach **satiation** at some point, meaning that eventually the value to you of consuming any more of the good disappears. You can drink only so much free coffee at one sitting before you get full or you start to shake from too much caffeine.

There's another consideration as well. Many products and services require some time to consume. For example, if you are sitting in front of the television, you are not doing something else like taking a walk, going to the mall, or spending time with friends. And no matter how adept you are at multitasking, you cannot talk on the cell phone while you are sleeping.

In other words, even at a zero price there's an *opportunity cost* to consuming more of a good or service if it requires some of your time. In doing one thing, you are giving up the opportunity to do something else. In a world in which there are only 24 hours to the day, that's a real cost. So the

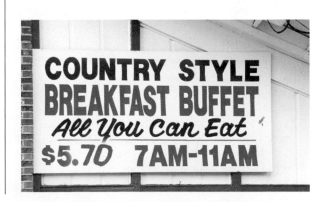

opportunity cost of watching television is not zero; it's the value to you of the other activities you could be doing instead. Your long-distance calls on your cell phone may be free, but if you spend all your time on the phone, you are not studying for exams, earning money at work, or taking a walk in the park. Such trade-offs will limit how much you consume, even at a zero price.

Opportunity cost is an important concept in economics. In general, the **opportunity cost** of a choice or action is defined as the value or benefit of the next best alternative. This embodies the basic principle that individuals have to choose between different uses of their time and money. We'll meet this idea again.

Graphing the Demand Curve

Now let's look at the demand schedule for coffee consumption in a week for an individual—call her Sally. For many people, drinking a cup of coffee is an essential part of their day. However, one principle of economics is that even the demand for necessities responds to price.

In Table 2.2, the first column is the price per cup, and the second column is the number of cups demanded during the week. For example, if the price is $1.00 per cup, Sally may consume 18 cups per week. But if she must pay $5 a cup, she will restrict herself to only six cups a week.

This demand schedule for coffee can be represented visually on a graph (shown as Figure 2.1).

HOW IT WORKS: UNCOVERING THE DEMAND SCHEDULE

Suppose you were running a record company. You want to sell music online, but how much should you charge for each song? $0.99? $0.75? $1.50?

Obviously the answer to this question depends on how many songs will be purchased at each price—the market demand schedule. For example, if the quantity demanded drops little when the price goes from $0.99 to $1.50, then it makes sense to charge the higher price.

But knowing the demand schedule for a market is often not easy, especially with a new product. One way to uncover a demand schedule is to survey consumers and ask them how much they would pay for a new product. Companies regularly show new products to groups of selected people and ask their opinions. The problem, though, is that consumers may say they highly value a product and then spend their money on something else.

For established products, one way to see a demand schedule is to actually look at how much consumers buy at various prices. This is most useful for widely used products, like gasoline, where economists can review how buyers have reacted to past price increases in order to predict the response to future price increases or decreases.

TABLE 2.2	Sally's Demand Schedule for Coffee

This demand schedule represents how many cups of coffee Sally will want to buy in a week, depending on the price.

Price per Cup (Dollars)	Quantity Demanded (Cups per Week)
$1.00	18
$2.00	15
$3.00	12
$4.00	9
$5.00	6
$6.00	3

Going up the vertical axis of the graph are the different prices Sally could pay. Going across the horizontal axis of the graph are the different quantities she could demand. To plot the demand schedule on the graph, we start from a price on the vertical axis and move right until we get to the corresponding quantity.

For example, when the price is $2 per cup, the quantity demanded is

FIGURE 2.1 | **Sally's Demand Curve for Coffee**

Each point on the demand curve says how many cups of coffee Sally will demand, given the price. Point *A*, says that at $2 per cup, Sally will demand 15 cups of coffee in a week. Point *B* corresponds to a price of $3 and a quantity demanded of 12 cups.

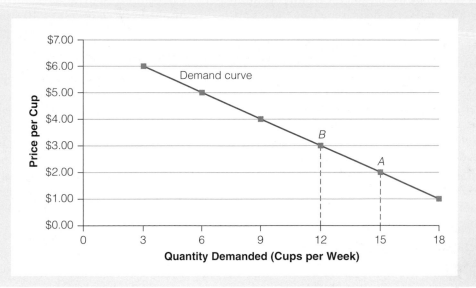

15 cups. So we find that price on the vertical axis, and go from left to right until we reach 15 cups per week (point *A* on graph). That becomes a point on the demand curve. Next, when the price is $3 per cup, the quantity demanded is 12 cups. We find the price $3 on the vertical axis and move right until we reach 12 cups (point *B*).

We do this for every price, and then we connect the points in a line, called a **demand curve.** The demand curve shows the link between price and quantity demanded. It is the graphical counterpart to the demand schedule.

The result is known as a **downward-sloping demand curve** because the curve we plotted from our data starts at the top left side of the graph and slopes downward to the right. The law of demand suggests that most demand curves will slope downward because price increases reduce the quantities demanded, all other things being equal.

HOW PRICE AFFECTS THE QUANTITY SUPPLIED

Now we turn our attention to the supply side of markets. Let's start by looking at the market for new homes. In 2000 the average sale price of a new single-family house in the United States was $207,000. By 2005 the average sale price of a new single-family home had risen to $297,000, a big jump in only five years.

How did home builders react to this enormous increase in the price of their product? They began constructing a lot more houses in every part of the country. The pace was frenetic: In 2005 home builders started almost 1.7 million new homes, up from 1.2 million in 2000. With prices so high, they built homes wherever they could find the space—even in the middle of deserts.

The process worked in reverse as well. When housing prices began to plummet in 2007, it became a lot less worthwhile for home builders to put up new homes. By 2009 new home construction had almost completely dried up.

In any market, the **quantity supplied** by a particular seller is the amount of goods and services that the seller is willing to provide at a given price. As the price changes, the quantity supplied changes as well. The **supply schedule** for a good or service reports the quantity supplied at different selling prices.

Let's think about the supply schedule for women's haircuts. A hair salon hires hairstylists, who are available to shape, trim, and dry the hair of anyone who walks through the door. For simplicity, assume it takes an hour to give a good haircut. So the quantity supplied of haircuts at any price in this market is determined by the number of hairstylists employed.

Notice that the quantity supplied of haircuts can exceed the quantity demanded. What does this mean? The stylists may spend part of the day not giving haircuts but reading the newspaper next to an empty chair or sweeping the floor while waiting for customers. But as long as they are available if and when someone comes in wanting a haircut, their time at work is part of the supply of haircuts.

Let's take a look at a hypothetical supply schedule for Helen's Haircutting Salon, as shown in Table 2.3. At a price of $5, there are only 40 haircuts available per week, with perhaps one hairstylist working full-time. As the price per haircut rises, however, running a hair salon becomes much more lucrative. At $10 per haircut, the number of haircuts available is 60 (perhaps because the existing stylist works extra hours during the week). As the price rises further, more people are put to work. At $35 per haircut, 160 haircuts are available, which reflects employment of perhaps four stylists, each working a 40-hour week and taking one hour for each haircut.

The **market supply schedule** adds up the quantity supplied by all the sellers in a market. For example, suppose there are 10 haircutting salons in a town, all with the same supply schedule as Table 2.3. Then if the price per haircut is $20, there will be a total of 1,000 haircuts supplied (100 haircuts × 10 stores).

The Law of Supply

The **law of supply** says that higher prices tend to increase the quantity supplied of a good or service, assuming nothing else changes. If the price a business can get for its goods and services rises, it has an incentive to increase production. There are plenty of ways to do that. It can hire more workers; it can have existing workers put in longer hours; it can open up a new store or a new factory; it can buy new computers or new machinery to beef up its productive capabilities.

Suppose the market price of a haircut goes up. That will make it more attractive for a hair salon to hire more stylists. It will also increase the willingness of would-be entrepreneurs to open up their own businesses. But if the price goes down, haircutting will be less profitable; some hairstylists will be let go or be given reduced hours; and some existing salons may close. The quantity supplied will drop along with the price. This is part of the natural ebb and flow of markets.

The law of supply operates in global markets as well. Suppose a department store chain is selling blue shirts imported from China. If the price of that kind of shirt goes up—perhaps because men are dressing better—the department store chain will order more shirts from its supplier in China. The Chinese factory will need a little time to respond because it must first hire more workers and train them. But higher prices increase the quantity supplied, even though it may take a while.

A key market where the law of supply generally holds is the labor market. The price of labor is the wage rate—that is, the price per hour a worker gets paid. Generally

TABLE 2.3	**The Supply Schedule for Helen's Haircutting Salon**

For any price of a haircut, this table reports how many haircuts are supplied.

Price per Haircut (Dollars)	Quantity Supplied (Haircuts Available in a Week)
$ 5.00	40
$ 10.00	60
$ 15.00	80
$ 20.00	100
$ 25.00	120
$ 30.00	140
$ 35.00	160

SPOTLIGHT: THE GREAT ETHANOL BOOM

For an example of the law of supply in action, look no further than the great corn ethanol boom of 2007. As the name suggests, corn ethanol, an alternative to gasoline, is made from corn. In 2007 the growing demand for ethanol sent the price of corn soaring from roughly $2.00 a bushel in 2005 to $4.20 a bushel in 2007.

Farmers, the main suppliers of corn, responded to the rising price by increasing the quantity supplied. They planted more corn—a lot more corn. The result was the largest corn crop in history at the time: 13.0 billion bushels.

Not all farmers were happy about the higher price of corn, however. In particular, farmers raising pigs and cattle were used to feeding corn to their animals. As it grew more expensive, they had to find alternative sources of feed or reduce the number of pigs and cattle they were raising.

Source: U.S. Department of Agriculture.

speaking, a higher wage rate will not have much effect on the labor supplied by people who are already working full-time. However, economic research generally shows that higher wages do increase the labor supply of people who are less committed to working, such as teenagers.

Like the law of demand, the law of supply does not hold true in every circumstance. In some cases, an increased

LAW OF SUPPLY
A higher price tends to increase the quantity supplied, all other things equal.

price can lower supply. For example, suppose your goal is to work enough hours during a semester to pay your expenses—let's say $2,000. If you earn $10 an hour, you will have to work 200 hours to achieve your goal. But if you earn $20 an hour, it will take only 100 hours to earn enough to pay your expenses—so a higher price for your labor will decrease, not increase, the amount of labor you supply. However, in most situations the law of supply does hold.

Graphing the Supply Schedule

Just as we did with the demand schedule on page 29, we can plot the supply schedule for a market on a graph. Let's think about a suburban town where home owners hire other people to mow their lawns. They might be paying neighborhood teenagers or a landscape service.

The market price per lawn determines the quantity of lawn-mowing services supplied. If the price is high, then teenagers tear themselves away from their video games and offer to mow their neighbors' lawns, and landscape services hire more workers.

Table 2.4 shows a hypothetical market supply schedule for the lawn-mowing market in a town. As the market price per lawn increases, so does the quantity supplied.

Now let's plot this supply schedule on a graph (Figure 2.2). Going up the vertical axis are the various prices that could be charged per lawn. Going across the horizonal axis is the quantity supplied—the number of lawns mowed. To plot the supply schedule, we start with a price on the vertical axis and move right horizontally until we come to the number of lawns mowed.

For example, if the market price is $10 per lawn, the supply schedule tells us that the quantity supplied is 15 mowed lawns. That's point *A* in Figure 2.2. Plotting all the combinations of price and quantity supplied and connecting the points gives us the **supply curve.** The supply curve shows the link between the price and the quantity supplied.

The result is an **upward-sloping supply curve** that starts at the lower left corner and goes to the upper right corner of the graph. We have drawn it as a straight line, but real-world supply curves are generally not straight.

TABLE 2.4	The Market Supply Schedule for Lawn Mowing

As the price to mow a lawn rises, so does the quantity supplied. For example, if the going market price for mowing a lawn in a town is $15, then suppliers make themselves available to mow 25 lawns.

Market Price per Lawn Mowed (Dollars)	Quantity Supplied (Lawns Mowed per Week)
$ 5.00	5
$ 10.00	15
$ 15.00	25
$ 20.00	35

NEW MARKETS

Here's one final note for this chapter. Demand and supply schedules describe how buyers and suppliers behave in existing markets, but the number of markets is not fixed. **New markets** are created every day to meet the changing needs of consumers and to take advantage of the changing capabilities of producers. New markets can provide new products or services, or bring in new buyers and sellers.

Some goods and services we buy today were not available 10, 20, or 30 years ago or were not available in the same form. We're surrounded by new technologies and new products—everything from the iPad to the latest product for hair straightening.

New types of services, too, have proliferated, such as web design—a new market that didn't exist before the mid-1990s.

New markets also arise as incomes rise in developing countries like China. For example, as recently as the early 1990s, few families owned cars in China. But as the country grew richer and incomes soared, the market for automobiles in China went from minuscule to enormous almost overnight.

We will return to the notion of new markets in Chapters 13, 14, and 15 when we look at financial markets, globalization, and technological change in more detail. For now, keep in mind that one of the biggest positives of a market economy is its ability to adapt quickly to changing circumstances.

FIGURE 2.2	The Market Supply Curve for Lawn Mowing

Each point on the market supply curve says how many lawns suppliers are willing to mow, given the price. Point A says that at $10 per lawn, the quantity supplied is 15 mowed lawns. Point B corresponds to a price of $15 and a quantity supplied of 25 lawns.

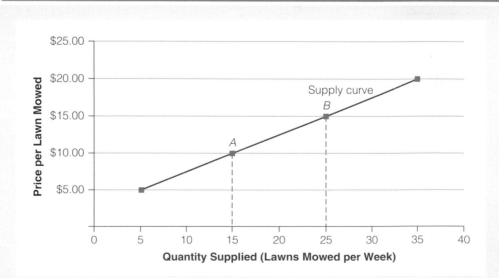

SUMMARY

1. Markets are composed of buyers and sellers who exchange goods and services for money at a rate called the price. Markets can be local, national, or global. *(LO2-1)*

2. A demand schedule describes the behavior of buyers in a market. For each price, the demand schedule reports the quantity demanded at that price. A demand curve is usually downward-sloping, which means that the quantity demanded drops as the price increases. *(LO2-2)*

3. A supply schedule describes the behavior of sellers in a market. For each price, the supply schedule reports the quantity supplied at that price. A supply curve is usually upward-sloping, which means that the quantity supplied increases as the price increases. *(LO2-3)*

4. The number of markets is not fixed. New markets can provide new goods or services or bring in new buyers and sellers. *(LO2-4)*

KEY TERMS AND CONCEPTS

market economy

buyers

sellers

product

price

labor market

local market

national market

global market

multinational

market price

sale price

negotiated price

volume discount

advance purchase discount

quantity demanded

demand schedule

market demand schedule

ceteris paribus

law of demand

zero price

satiation

opportunity cost

demand curve

downward-sloping demand curve

quantity supplied

supply schedule

market supply schedule

law of supply

supply curve

upward-sloping supply curve

new markets

PROBLEMS

1. Which of the following is an example of a buyer in a market? *(LO2-1)*

   a) An airline offering low fares for seats on a flight.

   b) A student paying for a haircut.

   c) A restaurant selling a meal.

   d) An amusement park selling admissions to a ride.

2. Which of the following is an example of a global market? *(LO2-1)*

   a) The market for haircuts in New York City.
   b) The market for dry cleaning in a town.
   c) The market for homes in Dallas.
   d) The market for crude oil.

3. The typical price at which a good or service sells in a market is the _____ *(LO2-1)*

   a) sale price.
   b) market price.
   c) negotiated price.
   d) volume discount.

4. When a person becomes unwilling to consume more of a good even at a zero price, he or she has reached _____ *(LO2-2)*

   a) the market price.
   b) ceteris paribus.
   c) satiation.
   d) the sale price.

5. The demand curve is the graphical representation of the _____ *(LO2-2)*

   a) opportunity cost.
   b) sale price.
   c) supply schedule.
   d) demand schedule.

6. Sam lives in a small town with only one restaurant. The restaurant, run by an eccentric old gentleman, offers a dinner menu on which every dish is the same price. Each month he posts the price of the meal in the window. The following table lists the number of times Sam goes out to dinner at the restaurant during the month, according to the posted price of the dinner. *(LO2-2)*

Price per Meal (Dollars)	Quantity Demanded (Number of Times Sam Eats at the Restaurant in the Month)
$ 3.00	24
$ 6.00	12
$ 9.00	8
$12.00	6
$15.00	4
$18.00	2

   a) Plot the demand curve for meals.
   b) How many times per month does Sam eat at the restaurant if the price per meal is $12?

7. All other things being equal, when the price of a good increases, the quantity supplied typically _____ *(LO2-3)*

   a) stays the same.

   b) decreases.

   c) increases.

8. In a small town there's only one construction company that builds new homes. The following table lists the number of new homes built in a year at different selling prices. *(LO2-3)*

Sale Price of a New Home (Dollars)	Quantity Supplied (Number of New Homes Built in a Year)
$150,000	1
$200,000	4
$250,000	7
$300,000	10
$350,000	13

   a) Plot the supply curve for new homes.

   b) How many homes are built if the price is $250,000 per home?

9. Over the past few years, smartphones, such as the iPhone, have become much more common. Which of the following statements is true? Explain your answer. *(LO2-4)*

   a) The rise of the smartphone did not lead to any new markets.

   b) The rise of the smartphone created many new markets, including the market for iPhone applications (apps).

   c) The only new market created is the market for smart phones.

   d) The price of smartphones is lower than the price of the phones they replace.

03 MARKET EQUILIBRIUM AND SHIFTS

LEARNING OBJECTIVES

After reading this chapter, you should be able to:

LO3-1 Define excess supply and excess demand.

LO3-2 Explain market equilibrium, and identify the equilibrium point on a supply–demand diagram.

LO3-3 Describe the impact of supply and demand shifts.

LO3-4 Discuss some causes of markets shifts.

LO3-5 Illustrate how changes in income affect the demand curve.

LO3-6 Review the basics of elasticity.

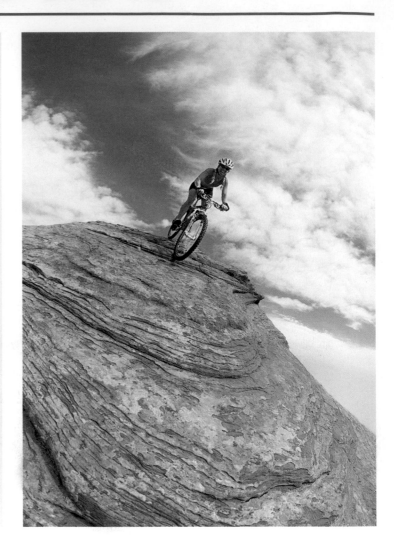

The economy is always changing in ways large and small. Consider one month: April 2010. In that month Apple Computer introduced the first iPad. The Deepwater Horizon drilling rig exploded in the Gulf of Mexico, leading to an enormous oil spill. And the population of China grew by about 545,000 people (in one month).

Each of these events affected at least one market. People had a new electronic gadget to purchase. As the oil spill spread, fishing was banned in much of the Gulf of Mexico, hurting the commercial fishery industry there. And the number of future consumers and workers in China rose, potentially affecting the whole world.

In this chapter we will look at how markets react to change. First we'll examine what might happen when buyers want more than sellers are prepared to produce, or when sellers produce more than buyers are prepared to consume. Then we'll outline the key concept of *market equilibrium*—that special point where both buyers and sellers are satisfied and supply equals demand. We'll see how buyers and sellers react to events, or *shifts,* that can push markets away from equilibrium. Finally, we'll discuss the basics of elasticity of demand and supply, which tell us how much buyers and sellers react to changes in their economic environment.

MATCHING SUPPLY AND DEMAND

Recall from the previous chapter that markets have two sides: buyers and sellers. Each side makes decisions independently, so in theory the amount buyers wish to purchase may be very different than the amount sellers wish to provide. But as we will see in this section, one of the great strengths of a market economy is that quantity demanded tends to roughly equal quantity supplied.

The Case of Excess Demand

A market has **excess demand** if buyers want more than sellers are prepared to supply at the current market price. In other words, quantity demanded exceeds quantity supplied at the current market price. During the housing boom of 2003–2006, home buyers in hot cities like Boston, New York, San Francisco, and San Diego lined up to make competing bids whenever a desirable property came on the market. Often the final selling price of a home was higher than the original price it was listed for—a clear sign of excess demand.

EXCESS DEMAND
When quantity demanded exceeds quantity supplied at the current market price.

EXCESS SUPPLY
When quantity supplied exceeds quantity demanded at the current market price.

The employment market for nurses also occasionally shows signs of excess demand in some regions. The combination of an aging population's need for more medical care and healthcare providers' unwillingness to raise nursing wages means hospitals sometimes have a hard time finding all the nurses they need.

The Case of Excess Supply

Other markets may suffer from **excess supply** when suppliers are willing to sell more at the market price than buyers are prepared to pay for. Quantity supplied then exceeds quantity demanded at the current market price. After the housing market collapsed in 2007, there were far more homes for sale than there were buyers in most parts of the country.

But it's not just housing. If the restaurant around the corner from you has few customers at dinnertime—perhaps because it serves overpriced bad food—that's a situation of excess supply. This is why thousands of restaurants go out of business each year. Similarly, a roadside motel with empty rooms faces a situation of excess supply (as we see in "Spotlight: Excess Supply on the Highways").

The Invisible Hand

Situations of excess demand and excess supply frustrate sellers and disappoint consumers. Every day some business owners and managers look unhappily at the poor sales in their stores. On the other side, consumers see empty shelves and vow to get to the store earlier next time.

How do markets react to a gap between quantity supplied and quantity demanded? The difference between the two is usually closed by what economists call the **market mechanism**—or, more poetically, the **invisible hand.**

The reason the mechanism is "invisible" is that no central planning agency has to issue explicit orders to close the supply–demand gap; buyers and sellers act on their own. Excess supply usually puts downward pressure on prices. For example, when retailers have too many shirts or DVD players on

SPOTLIGHT: EXCESS SUPPLY ON THE HIGHWAYS

Before the construction of the interstate highway system in the 1950s and 1960s, long-distance car and truck traffic flowed along relatively slow two-lane highways. The fabled Route 66, for example, stretched from Chicago to Los Angeles, going through places like Groom, Texas, and Hackberry, Arizona, along the way. These were not big towns, but because the road brought truckers who needed dinner and a bed, the towns had a reason for existence.

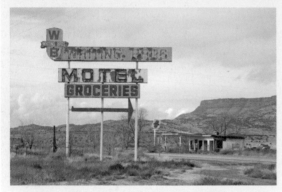

A deserted motel on Route 66 in Groom, Texas.

After the interstate highway system was built, however, the trucks and cars that used to stop in Groom and Hackberry instead hurtled down broad highways at 65 miles per hour, making many fewer stops. As a result, there was suddenly an excess supply of diners and motel rooms in small towns across the United States. In the end, this situation of excess supply was resolved by widespread closures.

Source: Guy Randall, www.cart66pf.org/66caravan.

A lower price simultaneously increases the quantity demanded and reduces the quantity supplied. A reduced price for hotel rooms, say, increases quantity demanded by encouraging tourists to stay longer and enticing local parents to take a quick weekend break from their kids rather than just going out to eat. The lower price also eventually decreases the quantity supplied of hotel rooms. Fewer new hotels get built, and some existing ones may go out of business or get turned into apartments.

Similarly, excess demand usually puts upward pressure on prices. Just like a price decline, a price increase affects both buyers and sellers. It decreases the quantity demanded by buyers, who buy less or substitute cheaper goods. At the same time, a higher price is a lure for sellers to increase production and add capacity by building a new store or a new factory. When there is excess demand in the real estate market, several people bid for the same house, and the price rises. The high selling prices of homes in 2004, 2005, and 2006 led to the construction and sale of a record number of new single-family houses because builders could sell new homes at a high price just as fast as they could put them up.

MARKET EQUILIBRIUM

Left to themselves, most markets will eventually reach a **market equilibrium,** where the quantity supplied and the quantity demanded are equal. Prices move up or down, buyers change the amount they demand, and sellers adjust the quantity they supply. True, the process of adjustment may be stop-and-go (prices may go up and down and then up again), and it may take a long time, perhaps years. Consumers and businesses get accustomed to their routines and the way they've done things in the past, and change is difficult. Yet one of the truly distinguishing features of a market economy is that eventually the forces of supply and demand are enough to overcome such inertia and restore the balance.

The price at which the quantity supplied equals the quantity demanded is the **equilibrium price.** At the equilibrium price, there's a match between how much buyers want

hand, or too many new cars in the lot, they run a sale. Motels with spare rooms offer them at cut-rate prices to tour operators or online resellers. Hair salons may trim their prices by offering newspaper coupons or specials on coloring.

EQUILIBRIUM PRICE
The price at which quantity supplied equals quantity demanded.

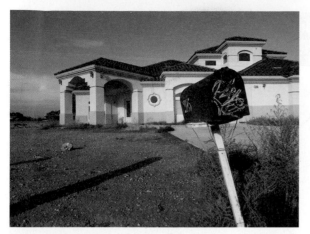

Builders could sell homes just as fast as they could put them up during the housing boom.

markets, left to their own devices, will tend toward the equilibrium price that balances supply and demand. As a result, most markets either are near equilibrium or are trying to get there.

The Basic Supply–Demand Diagram

We can depict the market equilibrium by drawing the market supply and demand curves on the same graph. The price at which the two lines intersect is the equilibrium price. At that price, quantity supplied is equal to quantity demanded: the equilibrium quantity.

Figure 3.1 is perhaps the most famous—and useful—diagram in economics. In this figure, the equilibrium price is P, and the equilibrium quantity is Q. Think about it this way: buyers and sellers make decisions independently from each other. However, at the equilibrium price, it happens that the quantity picked by suppliers is equal to the quantity chosen by sellers.

To make the idea of market equilibrium a bit more concrete, let's look at the market for new motor vehicles. We know that the demand curve for motor vehicles is downward-sloping because consumers will buy more cars, sport utility vehicles (SUVs), and other vehicles if they are

and how much sellers are willing to supply: the **equilibrium quantity,** which is the quantity supplied and demanded at the market price. For example, the market for hotel rooms would be at equilibrium if all hotel rooms were filled, but there were no potential guests standing outside in the cold with no place to sleep.

In the real world, few markets are exactly at the equilibrium price. There might be some excess demand or some excess supply. However, most

> **EQUILIBRIUM QUANTITY**
>
> The quantity supplied and demanded at the equilibrium price.

FIGURE 3.1   A Market Equilibrium

We find the equilibrium price P and the equilibrium quantity Q at the point A, where the supply and demand curves intersect. At that price the quantity supplied is equal to the quantity demanded.

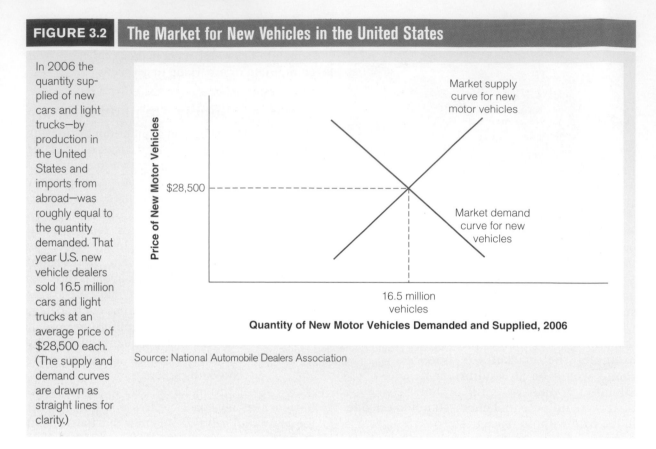

FIGURE 3.2 | **The Market for New Vehicles in the United States**

In 2006 the quantity supplied of new cars and light trucks—by production in the United States and imports from abroad—was roughly equal to the quantity demanded. That year U.S. new vehicle dealers sold 16.5 million cars and light trucks at an average price of $28,500 each. (The supply and demand curves are drawn as straight lines for clarity.)

Market supply curve for new motor vehicles

Price of New Motor Vehicles

$28,500

Market demand curve for new vehicles

16.5 million vehicles

Quantity of New Motor Vehicles Demanded and Supplied, 2006

Source: National Automobile Dealers Association

less expensive. And the supply curve for vehicles is upward-sloping: if dealers can get more money for each car or SUV, manufacturers hire more workers, run the assembly lines longer, or bring in more vehicles from overseas.

Figure 3.2 illustrates the 2006 market equilibrium in the new car and light truck market. At an average price of $28,500, vehicle manufacturers were willing to supply 16.5 million vehicles to the market. At the same price level, buyers were willing to shell out enough money to take home 16.5 million vehicles. Quantity supplied and quantity demanded are equal, making this an equilibrium. (Inventories—the number of vehicles held in stock by manufacturers and dealers—changed very little that year.)

Equilibrium in Numbers

Sticking to the theme of vehicles, let's look at a numerical example of market equilibrium. Think about the market for go-karts—small, gasoline-powered vehicles that look like the

one pictured on this page. Made today mostly by Asian companies, they range in price from roughly $600 to well over $2,000, with a maximum speed of 35–40 miles per hour. Some are made for kids; some are driven by adults in go-kart races (including "endurance karting," where the races can last up to eight hours).

A go-kart in action.

TABLE 3.1	Supply and Demand in the Go-Kart Market

This table lays out hypothetical supply and demand schedules for go-karts. For example, if the price were $800 per go-kart, the quantity demanded would be 5,500 go-karts, and the quantity supplied would be 3,500 go-karts.

Price (Dollars)	Quantity Demanded	Quantity Supplied
$ 600	6,000	3,000
$ 800	5,500	3,500
$ 1,000	5,000	4,000
$ 1,200	4,500	4,500
$ 1,400	4,000	5,000
$ 1,600	3,500	5,500
$ 1,800	3,000	6,000

Both the quantity supplied and the quantity demanded of go-karts are sensitive to price. On the demand side, go-karts are strictly a discretionary purchase; if the price rises too much, buyers will put off the purchase. On the supply side, the same Asian factories that make go-karts can also make a wide range of other products, including small scooters and golf carts. That makes it easy to switch workers to making more go-karts if their price should rise—or to making other products if the price of go-karts should suddenly drop.

Table 3.1 shows hypothetical market supply and demand schedules for the go-kart market; the left column of the table lists the price per go-kart. For any price, if you read across the table, the second column reports the quantity demanded at that price, and the third column reports the quantity supplied. For example, if the price per go-kart is $800, the market quantity demanded is 5,500 go-karts and the market quantity supplied is 3,500. In other words, we have a situation of excess demand: more people want go-karts than are able to get them at the going price. But if the price is $1,800 per go-kart, the quantity demanded is 3,000 go-karts and the amount supplied is 6,000 go-karts: a situation of excess supply. Producers are willing to make more go-karts at this price than buyers are willing to purchase.

The equilibrium for this market, as for every market, occurs at the price where quantity demanded equals quantity supplied. For this example, the equilibrium price is $1,200, where both quantity supplied and quantity demanded equal 4,500 go-karts.

We can also draw the corresponding supply and demand curves on a graph, just as we did in Chapter 2. Look at Figure 3.3. The upward-sloping

FIGURE 3.3	Equilibrium in the Go-Kart Market

The supply and demand curves for go-karts cross at the point labeled A. That's where the price is $1,200 per go-kart, and 4,500 go-karts are demanded and supplied.

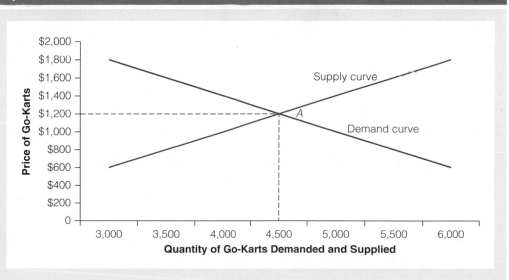

line is the market supply curve, and the downward-sloping line is the market demand curve. For example, start at a price of $1,600 per go-kart and move right. The first line we run into is the demand curve, which shows a demand of 3,500 go-karts at this price. If we keep going right, we run into the supply curve at 5,500 go-karts.

On the diagram we can immediately identify the point *A* where the two lines intersect. This is the market equilibrium because it's where quantity supplied equals quantity demanded.

MARKET SHIFTS

Markets are continually being bombarded by outside forces, large and small, that affect buyers or sellers or both. As one example, the market for music compact disks (CDs) was dramatically affected by the expansion of the Internet. When songs became widely available online, potential music purchasers could download desired songs for free. As a result, they became less likely to buy a music CD, even if the price of the CD didn't change.

DEMAND SHIFT
A change in the amount buyers want to purchase at a given price.

SUPPLY SHIFT
A change in the amount sellers supply at a given price.

Economists call the changes caused by such forces **market shifts.** A **demand shift** is a market shift that affects buyers, changing the amount buyers want to purchase at any given price. For example, when music became widely available online, the demand curve for music CDs shifted to the left, as Figure 3.4 shows.

Similarly, a **supply shift** affects sellers, either raising or lowering the amount they supply at any given price. For example, a loosening of restrictions on clothing imports, combined with improved manufacturing capabilities, has allowed countries like China, Vietnam, and Indonesia to ship a lot more clothing to the United States. The increase in imports means the supply curve for clothing shifted to the right, as Figure 3.5 shows. For any given price, more clothing is supplied.

Demand Shifts and Market Equilibrium

A market shift will change the market equilibrium. After a market experiences a demand or

---

FIGURE 3.4   A Shift in the Demand for Music CDs

The ease of downloading music from the Internet means the demand curve for music compact disks has shifted to the left. At the price *P*, the quantity demanded drops from *Q* to *Q'*.

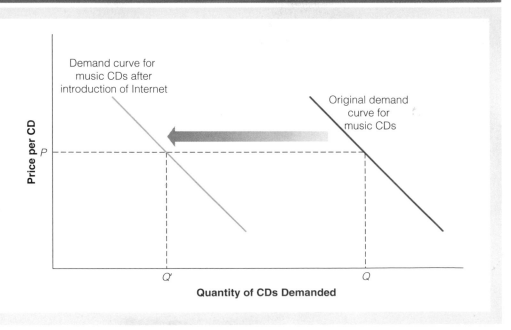

Demand curve for music CDs after introduction of Internet

Original demand curve for music CDs

Price per CD

P

Q'   *Q*

Quantity of CDs Demanded

FIGURE 3.5 | **A Shift in the Supply of Clothing**

Looser restrictions on clothing imports and increased manufacturing capabilities abroad mean that the supply curve for clothing in the United States has shifted to the right. At the price *P*, quantity supplied rises from *Q* to *Q'*.

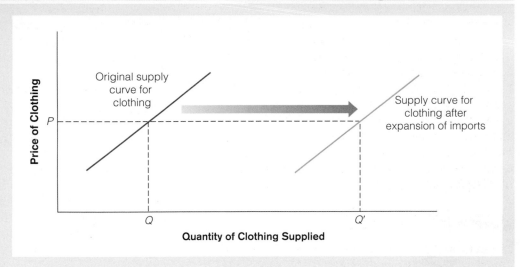

supply shift, it eventually finds a new equilibrium. For example, if the demand curve shifts to the left—as in the case of the market for music CDs—that will temporarily create a situation of excess supply, which tends to drive down the price until a new equilibrium is reached.

Looking at Figure 3.6, we see that the original equilibrium in the music CD market was at point *A*, where the pre-Internet demand curve and the supply curve cross. When music downloads reduced demand for CDs, the demand curve shifted to the left and the equilibrium shifted to point *B*,

FIGURE 3.6 | **Changing Equilibrium in the Music CD Market**

The decrease in demand for compact disks means that the market equilibrium shifts from *A* to *B*. The result is a lower price and a lower quantity supplied and demanded.

FIGURE 3.7 Changing Equilibrium in the Clothing Market

The increase in supply of clothing means that the market equilibrium shifts from *A* to *B*. The result is a lower price and a higher quantity supplied and demanded.

Quantity of Clothing Demanded and Supplied

with a lower price and a lower quantity supplied and demanded.

Supply Shifts and Market Equilibrium

Let's look now at the impact of a supply shift on market equilibrium. Suppose the supply curve shifts to the right, as in the case of the clothing market. That will temporarily create a situation of excess supply, which tends to drive down the price until a new equilibrium is reached.

Looking at Figure 3.7, we see that the original equilibrium in the clothing market was at point *A*, where the original supply and demand curves cross. The combination of fewer restrictions on clothing imports and improved manufacturing capabilities overseas caused the supply curve to shift to the right. The new equilibrium is at point *B*, with a lower price of clothing and a higher quantity supplied and demanded.

Even though these supply and demand curves are hypothetical, they accurately convey what happened. Between 2000 and 2010 the price of clothing fell by 8 percent, even while the prices of all sorts of other goods and services were rising. Meanwhile American consumers dramatically increased their purchases of clothing over this stretch.

An Example of an Increase in Demand

Let's look at a demand shift in a market that few people think much about: the market for cement. Cement is used for construction everywhere around the world. Starting around 2004 or so, there was a dramatic construction boom in China—factories, office buildings, apartment buildings, and highways. This surge in Chinese construction moved the global demand curve for cement to the right (see the arrow in Figure 3.8) because Chinese builders suddenly bought up a big chunk of the worldwide cement production. At any price for cement, the quantity demanded was higher.

Before China came into the worldwide cement market, the global market equilibrium was at the point labeled *A*. The price of cement was *P*, and the amount supplied and demanded was *Q*. Everyone was getting their needs met: The buyers of cement—construction companies—were getting enough to fulfill their needs, and the sellers of cement were keeping their plants running. (As an aside, the largest producer of cement in North America is Cemex, a company headquartered in Mexico.)

After China started exerting its cement-buying muscles, the demand curve shifted to the right.

FIGURE 3.8 | Demand Shifts in the Cement Market

When the global demand for cement increased, the market equilibrium shifted from *A* to *B*. The result was that the price surged higher and the quantity of cement supplied and demanded rose as well.

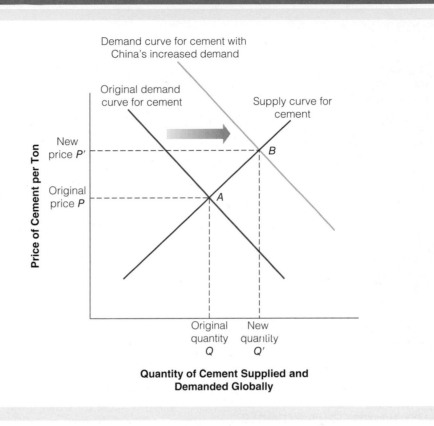

The new equilibrium point *B*—where the old supply curve crosses the new demand curve—has a higher price and a higher quantity Q'. A demand shift to the right generally leads to higher prices and eventually higher output. And in fact that's what happened.

Remember that excess demand in a market creates pressure to raise prices. So with prices leaping, making cement became a more attractive business, and cement producers sped up the construction of new plants in the United States and around the world.

In an amazing turnabout, China greatly expanded its production and exports of cement in 2005 and 2006. In fact, China became the biggest exporter of cement, helping to rebuild New Orleans after Hurricane Katrina. Nevertheless, the price of cement in the United States continued to rise through 2007, responding to the residential construction boom. After 2007, construction slowed, and the price of cement dropped again.

An Example of a Decrease in Supply

When Hurricane Katrina struck New Orleans in August 2005, it closed down refineries and oil rigs both onshore and in the Gulf of Mexico. As a result, the price of gasoline jumped almost instantaneously around the country. Newspapers wrote about service stations boosting prices by $1 or more per gallon within a short period. In New Jersey the state attorney general charged 20 gas stations with violating a 1938 law prohibiting them from raising prices more than once in a 24-hour period.

Figure 3.9 shows the impact of Hurricane Katrina on the gasoline market. Before Katrina hit, the market was at the equilibrium labeled *A*. The average national price of gasoline was $2.36 in July 2005. After the hurricane, the supply curve for gasoline shifted to the left. That is, at the same price, the quantity of gasoline supplied fell. As a result,

FIGURE 3.9	Hurricane Katrina's Impact on the Gasoline Market

When Katrina damaged refineries and drilling rigs on the Gulf Coast and in the Gulf of Mexico, the effect was to shift the supply curve for gasoline to the left. The market equilibrium shifted from *A* to *B*, prices rose, and the quantity of gasoline produced and bought fell.

the new equilibrium price was much higher. In September 2005 the average price of gasoline was $2.97. (That number seems low compared to more recent gas prices, but it was horrifying back then.)

Shifts versus Movements

Let's end this section by making an important distinction. In each of two examples we have just examined—the market for clothing and the market for cement—the equilibrium quantity increased. Yet the reason was different in each case.

In the clothing example, the equilibrium quantity increased because the supply curve shifted and the demand curve stayed the same. This is

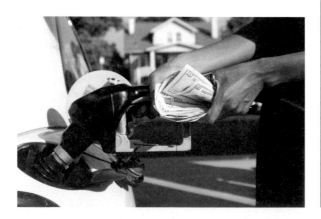

an example of a **movement along a demand curve**. You can see in Figure 3.7, on page 44, that the equilibrium just slides along the demand curve from *A* to *B* as the supply shifts.

On the other hand, in the cement example, the equilibrium quantity increased because the demand curve shifted and the supply curve stayed the same. This is an example of a **movement along a supply curve**. You can see in Figure 3.8, on page 45, from that the equilibrium just slides along the supply curve *A* to *B* as the demand shifts.

The music CD market is also an example of a movement along a supply curve, as the demand curve shifts to the left (Figure 3.6). And the gasoline market after Katrina is an example of a movement along a demand curve, as the supply curve shifts to the left (Figure 3.9).

SOME CAUSES OF MARKET SHIFTS

We've now seen several examples of how supply and demand shifts can affect market equilibrium. Table 3.2 summarizes the impacts, which depend on whether the demand or supply curve is shifting, and in which direction it shifts.

TABLE 3.2	Summarizing the Effect of Supply and Demand Shifts

All other things being equal, an increase in demand boosts both equilibrium price and quantity. An increase in supply reduces equilibrium price and increases equilibrium quantity.

Shift and Direction	How We Say It	Effect on Equilibrium Price	Effect on Equilibrium Quantity
Demand curve shifts left.	"Demand decreases."	−	−
Demand curve shifts right.	"Demand increases."	+	+
Supply curve shifts left.	"Supply decreases."	+	−
Supply curve shifts right.	"Supply increases."	−	+

In fact, many economic changes can be described in terms of shifts in supply and demand, including the key forces driving today's economy, described in Chapter 1: technological change, globalization, and the evolution of financial markets. Other major causes of market shifts include changes in the prices of raw materials and changes in tastes. Let's look at these.

Technological Change

We already mentioned the impact of the Internet on the demand for music CDs. Historically some of the biggest market shifts have been created by technological breakthroughs. Looking back a century, Henry Ford introduced the first mass-produced automobile, the Model T, in 1913. That caused the supply curve for automobiles to shift dramatically to the right, driving down prices and boosting quantities sold. Because his factories were so productive, Ford could sell cars for under $300 each—far less than the $1,000 his competitors were charging. (In Chapter 8 we will learn how to adjust historical prices for inflation. A car sold for $300 in 1913 would cost the equivalent of about $6,000 today—still not expensive.) The dramatically lower prices for cars enabled many more families to afford them, so the shift in the supply curve led to a movement along the demand curve.

Of course we don't have to look back a hundred years to see technology-driven shifts. In recent years, the supply of telephone services has been shifting to the right rapidly because of advances in communications technology. As a result, phone service—especially long-distance service—has dropped steeply in price, and people spend far more time on the phone than ever before.

Globalization

By introducing new buyers and sellers into a market, globalization can create shifts on either the demand or supply side of a market, or both. We already mentioned the impact of China on cement demand and the impact of China and other countries on the supply of clothing. Now let's consider the impact of globalization on the supply of furniture. Between 2000 and 2007, U.S. furniture companies started making more furniture in China because it was considerably less expensive to produce there. As a result, the supply curve for furniture shifted to the right. A sharp fall ensued in the price of dining room and living room furniture, along with a big increase in the amount of furniture purchased by American households, as we will see in Chapter 5.

Changes in Financial Markets

One important cause of market shifts is a change in the cost of borrowing money. Most of us don't have enough cash on hand to pay for the car or home we want or to pay for our education. So we take out loans—auto loans, home mortgages, education loans. The price of a loan is its **interest rate,** which says how much we have to pay the lender in exchange for the use of the money. For example, a 5 percent annual interest rate means we owe the lender an extra 5 percent of the original loan value (the

FIGURE 3.10   The Impact of Rising Interest Rates on the Car Market

Higher interest rates cause the demand curve for cars to shift to the left. All other things being equal, that means the equilibrium shifts from *A* to *B*, leading to a lower equilibrium price and equilibrium quantity.

amount we borrowed) in return for using the money for a year. (Interest rates and loans are discussed further in Chapter 13.)

If interest rates rise, then cars, homes, and education become harder to pay for. So higher interest rates mean we perhaps stick with our old houses or cars for a while, or we go to school only part-time. In other words, a rise in interest rates causes demand to decline: the demand curve for autos, homes, or education shifts to the left.

Figure 3.10 shows the result of an increase in interest rates on auto loans. At any price for cars, the quantity demanded falls because potential customers are paying more for their loans. The result is that the equilibrium quantity falls, and so does the price. We'd see the same basic pattern in other markets in which many consumers use loans to buy a product or service (like education and housing).

Finally, market shifts can also be caused by changes in loan standards. During the housing boom, it became very easy for Americans to get mortgages and home equity loans, even if they didn't have much income. This "easy credit" helped shift the demand curve for many goods and services to the right. Then, when the economy fell into the Great Recession, financial institutions tightened up on standards for credit cards, mortgages, and other borrowing, so demand curves shifted to the left.

Government Action

Any type of government action—such as the creation of new rules or requirements—can cause a significant market shift, changing supply and demand in a market almost overnight. For example, if a state legislature passes a law requiring that drivers use child safety seats or booster seats for passengers through age 7 (as New Jersey did in 2001), the demand curve for child car seats and booster seats immediately shifts to the right. Similarly, if a state requires that hands-free headsets be used for cell phones while people drive, that shifts the demand curve for headsets to the right.

Government action can also affect the supply side of markets. Suppose a town decides to change its land use regulations—say, by requiring builders to leave 100 feet between new homes rather than only 10 feet. That causes the supply curve for new homes in that town to shift left because now fewer homes than before can be built on the same amount of land.

Changes in Raw Material Prices

Shifts in the price of raw materials can be a major cause of supply shifts across a wide range of markets. Frost can wipe out an orange crop, shifting the supply curve to the left and driving orange prices up. Discovery of a major new oil field in Africa would cause the oil supply curve to shift to the right.

One important future cause of supply shifts may be global climate change, which will affect temperature and rainfall patterns in different parts of the world. By some estimates, global warming may reduce food production in countries near the tropics, which are already hot. Areas that start off cooler—such as the northern United States, Canada, and Russia—may see a shift to the right in the supply of grain and other agricultural products. (The economic implications of environmental change and global warming are explored more deeply in Chapter 19.)

Shifts in Tastes

Often markets are rocked by nothing more or less than a **shift in tastes**—that is, an unexplained shift in the consumer demand curves for various products and services. One day reality shows are all the rage; the next day television viewers don't care for them. If every family needs a minivan today, next year minivans may be completely out of fashion. One month skirts are short; the next month they're long.

Businesses learn to live with these essentially unpredictable changes. In some industries, like fashion and entertainment, the whole game is to catch these shifts in taste as they occur. But changes in consumer tastes also regularly affect more mundane industries such as food. (See "How It Works: The Fall of the Red Delicious Apple.")

THE EFFECT OF INCOME ON DEMAND

One important influence on demand deserves special attention: income. A family earning $50,000 a year will have a very different demand curve than one earning $500,000 a year. For most goods and services, an increase in income will shift a family's demand curve to the right. For example, at price P a low-income household might consume Q of a

HOW IT WORKS: THE FALL OF THE RED DELICIOUS APPLE

Go to your local grocery store, and you might see 20 different varieties of apples, from Granny Smith and Gala to Jazz, Cameo, and Pacific Rose. It wasn't that way a few years ago. Red Delicious apples—bright, firm, and easy to store—used to be the clear favorites. As recently as 1998, Red Delicious apples accounted for 40 percent of all the apples produced in the United States.

The problem was that consumers found them tasteless. Growers had spent years breeding Red Delicious apples that looked good and stood up well to shipping—but lost flavor in the process. "They eventually went too far and ended up with apples the public didn't want to eat," Lee Calhoun, an apple historian, told the *Washington Post* in 2005. The Red Delicious "is an apple that has done its duty and is on its way out."

With consumers tiring of the Red Delicious, the demand curve for that variety of apple shifted left. As a response, production and sales have been dropping, even though the apple's price remained more or less flat. By 2009 Red Delicious apples made up less than 25 percent of all U.S. apple production.

Source: "Why the Red Delicious No Longer Is," by Adrian Higgins, *Washington Post,* August 5, 2005

good. But the demand curve for a high-income household is shifted to the right, so their quantity demanded is higher at Q', as Figure 3.11 shows.

The Bureau of Labor Statistics tracks consumer spending by households with different income levels. For every major category of consumption—food, clothing, housing, transportation, healthcare, and entertainment—higher-income households spend more.

But if we look more closely within the spending categories, it's not simply that high-income families buy more; their whole pattern of consumption is different. For example, a family earning $50,000 a year might own a modest used car and a small house and eat out at the local pizzeria. Does a family earning 10 times as much own 10 modest used cars and 10 small houses

| **FIGURE 3.11** | **Higher Income Usually Means Higher Demand** |

All other things being equal, consumers with higher incomes usually spend more on food, clothing, housing, and other broad categories of consumption. So for a given price P, the quantity demanded will rise from Q to Q′.

and order 10 pizzas a week? Of course not—that would be absurd.

As their incomes rise, then, people don't just consume more of the same goods. They shift their consumption patterns to other goods. Instead of a small used car, they buy a luxury automobile. They live in a bigger home, with more bedrooms and more land, and eat at expensive restaurants. They take long vacations overseas and send their kids to expensive colleges.

This shift in spending patterns holds true for countries as well. Take China, for example. As the incomes of its citizens have risen, they have bought a lot more cars and taken a lot more vacations to places like Australia and the United States. Energy use has shifted from woodstoves to electricity, and food consumption has shifted from staples such as rice to more expensive items such as meat.

It's helpful to classify goods and services into three different groups according to how their consumption changes with income. A **normal good** is one whose demand rises more or less in step with income,

NORMAL GOOD

A good or service whose demand rises more or less in step with income.

LUXURY GOOD

A good or service whose demand rises very sharply as income increases.

which includes a wide variety of goods and services such as housing, medical care, and motor vehicles. As you earn more, you buy more of these goods, though perhaps of different types. (By *goods,* of course, we mean goods *and* services.)

A **luxury good** is one whose demand rises very sharply as income increases. Some examples of luxury goods include restaurant meals, travel abroad, and air travel in general, to which higher-income households devote a much larger percentage of their income. Another luxury good, of a sort, is education. High-income families are more likely to send their kids to expensive private schools and colleges rather than free public elementary and secondary schools and low-cost public universities and community colleges. As a result, high-income families put a much bigger share of their budgets toward education.

How much? Take a look at Figure 3.12, which reports education spending as a share of overall budgets. A family in the $40,000–$50,000 income range spends 1.1 percent of

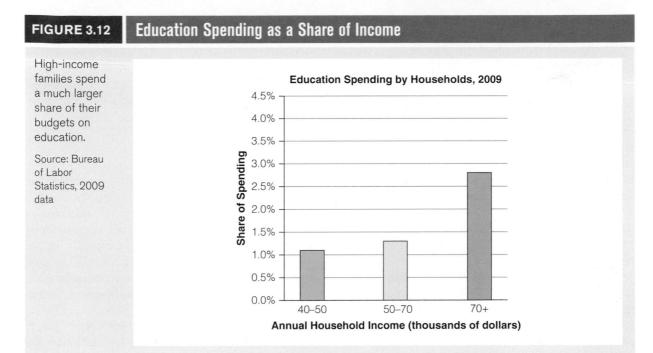

FIGURE 3.12 | **Education Spending as a Share of Income**

High-income families spend a much larger share of their budgets on education.

Source: Bureau of Labor Statistics, 2009 data

Education Spending by Households, 2009

Share of Spending (y-axis: 0.0% to 4.5%)

Annual Household Income (thousands of dollars) (x-axis: 40–50, 50–70, 70+)

its budget on education. In contrast, a family with an income over $70,000 devotes 2.8 percent of its budget to education—quite a difference!

There's one more category of goods whose demand changes with income, called **inferior goods.** Inferior goods are those whose demand might actually *fall* as incomes increase. In most cities, for example, public transportation—bus and rail—is an inferior good used mainly by people who cannot afford cars. In Los Angeles, a city that revolves around its cars and freeways, the great majority of the people who use public transportation to get to work—mainly buses—earn $25,000 or less a year. Once people can afford a car, they stop riding public transportation. Other U.S. cities—with a few exceptions like New York—have much the same pattern.

Other inferior goods include cheap beer, shoddily made clothing, and rental housing. Corporations often target different products toward low-income and high-income consumer sectors. The automakers, for example, have a range of models that run from relatively inexpensive to very pricey as a way to appeal to the widest possible array of purchasers.

INFERIOR GOOD
A good or service whose demand falls as income increases.

A BRIEF LOOK AT ELASTICITY

We've seen that equilibrium price and quantity change in response to supply and demand shifts. Let's finish up by asking which will change *more*—price or quantity? If frost suddenly destroys a big portion of the orange crop—a supply shift—does that create a small increase in orange juice prices or an enormous one? A small change in the quantity of orange juice demanded or a big one? If Chinese consumers suddenly develop a desire to vacation in Hawaii—a demand shift—do hotel prices there jump a lot or a little? Does the quantity supplied of hotel rooms change a little or a lot?

The answers depend on the supply and demand curves. In some markets, shifts show up mainly in price rather than quantity. For example, in the case of the Chinese tourists in Hawaii, the number of hotel rooms in Hawaii won't change much, at least until new hotels can be built, so a sudden increase in Chinese tourists will cause hotel prices to rise.

In the language of economics, hotel rooms in Hawaii have an **inelastic supply**—that is, the quantity supplied doesn't change much even if the price changes a lot. Other examples of inelastic supply include the number of golf courses in California and the amount of land in New York City. Of course, eventually new golf courses can be built and new land might be added by landfill—but it's a long process.

Similarly, **inelastic demand** means that the quantity demanded doesn't change much even if the price changes a lot. For example, let's suppose a lot of visitors are coming to a town for a big event—the Olympics, say, or a political convention. Now suppose a hotel burns down (of course no one is hurt), which is equivalent to a decrease in supply. The price of hotel rooms is likely to skyrocket, but the quantity of rooms demanded is not likely to change much.

On the other hand, **elastic demand** means that a small change in price has a big impact on quantity demanded. For example, the demand for orange juice is elastic because many people are willing to switch to other kinds of juice or to other beverages when orange juice is too expensive. Looking at the other side of the market, **elastic supply** implies that a small price change has a big impact on quantity supplied. (The appendix to Chapter 6 defines the concept of **elasticity** more precisely.)

The use of the word *elastic* for this economic idea makes sense when you think of a rubber band that's elastic: you can stretch it a long way without much effort—like demand or supply that changes readily with only a small change in price. A steel bar, by contrast, is inelastic and can't be bent without a great deal of effort or special machinery.

CONCLUSION

We've covered a lot of ground in this chapter. We started with the basics of market equilibrium, examined the different kinds of supply and demand shifts, and finished up with a short discussion of elasticity. Along the way, we gained better insight into how we can think about the impact of some of the most important changes in the economy, including the expansion of the Internet, the rise of China, and the large fluctuations in raw material prices.

In the next chapter we will look more closely at the supply side of markets. In particular we will consider how businesses make their production decisions. How do they decide how much to produce, how many people to hire, how many machines to buy, or how many stores to open? These are the key questions we will address next.

03   SUMMARY

1. Excess supply in a market means that quantity supplied is greater than quantity demanded. Excess demand means that quantity demanded is greater than quantity supplied. The gap between quantity supplied and quantity demanded is usually closed over time by the market mechanism, also known as the invisible hand. *(LO3-1)*

2. Left to themselves, most markets eventually reach an equilibrium, which means that the quantity supplied and quantity demanded are reasonably in balance. At the equilibrium price, quantity supplied equals quantity demanded. On a graph, the market equilibrium is the point where the supply and demand curves cross. *(LO3-2)*

3. The market equilibrium changes when either the supply or demand curve shifts. If supply increases, equilbrium price falls and equilibrium quantity rises. If supply decreases, equilibrium price rises and equilibrium quantity falls. If demand increases, equilibrium price and quantity both rise. If demand decreases, equilibrium price and quantity both fall. *(LO3-3)*

4. Important causes of market shifts include technological change, globalization, changes in financial markets, government action, changes in raw material prices, and shifts in tastes. *(LO3-4)*

5. Increases or decreases in income can exert a major influence on demand. Consumption patterns differ for low-income and high-income households. *(LO3-5)*

6. If supply is inelastic, then the quantity supplied doesn't change much even if the price changes a lot. If demand is inelastic, then the quantity demanded doesn't change much even if the price changes a lot. *(LO3-6)*

KEY TERMS AND CONCEPTS

excess demand

excess supply

maarket mechanism

invisible hand

market equilibrium

equilibrium price

equilibrium quantity

market shift

demand shift

supply shift

movement along a demand
 curve

movement along a supply curve

interest rate

shifts in tastes

normal good

luxury good

inferior good

inelastic supply

inelastic demand

elastic demand

elastic supply

elasticity

PROBLEMS

1. The market for new automobiles has excess supply if _____ (LO3-1)
   a) potential buyers have to wait several months for the car they want.
   b) car dealers have more autos than they can sell at the market price.
   c) car dealers temporarily run out of autos to sell at the market price.

2. The following table reports the (hypothetical) market supply and demand schedules for the iPod and other portable music players. (LO3-2)

Price per Player (Dollars)	Quantity Demanded (Millions)	Quantity Supplied (Millions)
$ 50	7	0
$ 100	5	1
$ 150	4	2
$ 200	3	3
$ 250	2	4
$ 300	1	5

   a) When the price per music player is $100, what is the quantity demanded? What is the quantity supplied? Is the market in excess supply, excess demand, or equilibrium?
   b) When the price per music player is $300, what is the quantity demanded? What is the quantity supplied? Is the market in excess supply, excess demand, or equilibrium?
   c) What is the equilibrium price for the music player market? What is the equilibrium quantity?

3. In 2007 the Nintendo Wii video game console was in short supply. Many retailers ran out of stock, and especially around the holiday season, parents ran from store to store hoping to find a Wii for their kids. (LO3-1, LO3-2)
   a) At the time, was the Wii market facing a situation of excess demand, excess supply, or equilibrium?

b) If the list price for the Wii unit was $250. Was the equilibrium price higher than, lower than, or equal to $250?

c) The company sold 7.4 million Wii consoles in the United States in 2007. Was the equilibrium quantity higher than, lower than, or equal to 7.4 million?

4. The following graph represents the market for yachts. *(LO3-2, LO3-3)*

a) Label the supply and demand curves.

b) Label the market equilibrium.

c) Suppose there is a sudden increase in the demand for yachts because there are more billionaires in emerging markets. Show how the demand curve shifts, and label the new market equilibrium.

5. A sudden discovery of an enormous gold mine in Florida would mean a _____ *(LO3-3)*

a) rightward shift in the supply curve for gold.

b) rightward shift in the demand curve for gold.

c) leftward shift in the supply curve for gold.

d) leftward shift in the demand curve for gold.

6. In a shorefront tourist town, a hurricane washes away the beach. All of the town's hotels, however, are still intact. *(LO3-4)*

a) Does the supply curve for hotel rooms shift to the left, shift to the right, or stay in the same place? Explain your answer.

b) Does the demand curve for hotel rooms shift to the left, shift to the right, or stay in the same place? Explain your answer.

c) After the hurricane, what happens to the equilibrium price and quantity of hotel rooms?

d) Suppose the neighboring town still has its beach. After the hurricane, what happens to the market for hotel rooms in that town?

7. Here are some examples of new technologies and the markets they affect. Identify whether each of these is a supply or demand shift, and describe its impact on equilibrium price and quantity. *(LO3-4)*

Technological Change	Affected Market	Supply or Demand Shift?	Impact on Equilibrium Price and Quantity
A new way to cheaply generate electricity from sunlight	Market for electricity	?	?
A new car engine that gets much better gas mileage	Market for gasoline	?	?
A new additive for milk that improves its taste	Market for milk	?	?

8. The following table reports spending on food in 2009 by households with incomes of less than $70,000 and by households with incomes greater than $150,000. "Food eaten at home" refers mainly to food that is purchased at supermarkets and brought home. "Food eaten away from home" refers mainly to food eaten at restaurants, though it also includes college dining rooms and similar situations. *(LO3-5)*

	Households with Incomes Less Than $70,000	Households with Incomes Greater Than $150,000
Average Spending on Food Eaten at Home	$3,064	$6,529
Average Spending on Food Eaten Away from Home	$1,734	$6,704

Source: Bureau of Labor Statistics.

a) How much do households with incomes of less than $70,000 spend on food eaten at home? Do they spend more on food at home or food away from home?

b) How much do households with incomes greater than $150,000 spend on food eaten away from home? Do they spend more on food at home or food away from home?

c) From this table, would you conclude that food eaten away from home is a normal good, a luxury good, or an inferior good? Is food eaten at home a normal good, a luxury good, or an inferior good? Explain your answers.

9. In the early days of the Internet, relatively few Americans had access. Now more than three-quarters of Americans have access to the Internet. That suggests, Internet access turned from _____ *(LO3-5)*

a) a normal good into a luxury good.

b) a luxury good into an inferior good.

c) a luxury good into a normal good.

10. The store down the street increases the price of bananas by $2 per pound. As a result, most customers switch to buying candy instead. This is an example of what? *(LO3-6)*

a) Inelastic supply.

b) Inelastic demand.

c) Elastic demand.

d) Elastic supply.

11. If the quantity supplied doesn't change much, even if the price changes a lot _____ *(LO3-6)*

a) supply is inelastic.

b) supply is elastic.

c) demand is inelastic.

d) demand is elastic.

04 HOW BUSINESSES WORK

LEARNING OBJECTIVES

After reading this chapter, you should be able to:

LO4-1 Explain and apply the economic perspective on business operations.

LO4-2 Define and apply the production function, average product, and marginal product.

LO4-3 Discuss the implications of the cost function, average cost, and marginal cost. Explain the difference between variable costs and fixed costs.

LO4-4 Define and apply the revenue function and marginal revenue.

LO4-5 Determine the profit-maximizing level of output.

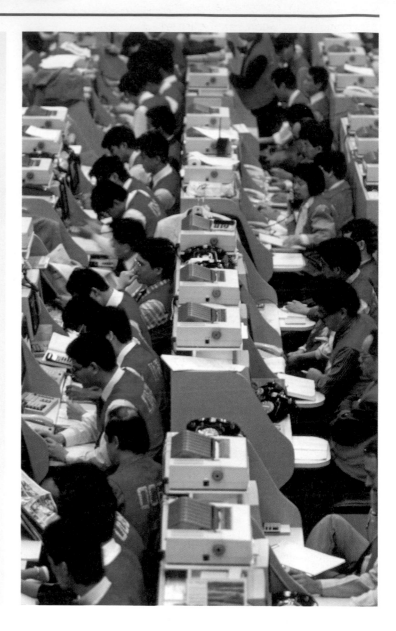

Most U.S. employees work in a business that has profit maximization as its main goal. Some work in megacorporations like the giant retailer Walmart, the largest private employer in the world with 2.1 million workers (called "associates") in the United States and around the globe. That's as many people as live in Philadelphia plus Las Vegas.

At the other extreme are more than 3 million U.S. businesses with fewer than five employees. Almost every town has its local hairdresser, a small law office with a receptionist and an assistant, and a two- or three-person web design firm run from home. Such small businesses are the heart and soul of any modern economy.

Obviously Walmart and the neighborhood hair salon are different. Yet every business, large or small, runs on the same economic principle: turning inputs into goods and services and selling them for money, with the goal of making the biggest possible profit.

In this chapter we study the basics of business, including production, cost, revenue, and profit maximization. Since businesses are the key source of production and supply in the economy, this will help us understand how supply works in markets.

THE NATURE OF BUSINESS

Let's start with the big picture of how businesses operate, from an economic perspective. The **outputs** of a business are the goods and services it sells to customers. The **inputs** are the goods and services the business uses to produce the outputs. **Production** is the process of turning inputs into outputs.

PRODUCTION
The process of turning inputs into outputs.

PROFIT
The difference between revenues and costs.

For example, think about your favorite restaurant. The outputs of the restaurant are the meals it feeds its customers. The inputs required to produce the meals include workers: chefs in the kitchen and staff to bring you the food and clean the restaurant. Other inputs include the food ingredients and the physical objects that make up the restaurant: the oven and refrigerators in the kitchen, the chairs and tables, and the roof over the whole thing. A final but important input is the book of recipes for the dishes on the menu; the recipes are essential because without them the dishes would come out different each time.

Let's consider a much bigger business: Caterpillar, the world's largest maker of construction and mining equipment. Caterpillar's output in 2010 included bulldozers, excavators, paving equipment, and all sorts of other heavy machinery, sold in virtually every country. The company is based in Peoria, Illinois, but its products were made in manufacturing facilities around the world, using labor and other inputs such as buildings, steel, rubber, electronics, and energy. At the end of 2010, Caterpillar employed 104,490 full-time workers around the world.

The Flow of Money

In a market economy, a business does not simply produce outputs using inputs—it also collects and spends money. **Revenue** is the money a business receives from the sales of its outputs to customers. **Cost** is what the business pays for its inputs.

For example, in 2010 Caterpillar received roughly $43 billion in revenues for all the bulldozers and other products it sold. Caterpillar's costs were $39 billion to pay its workers, to build and maintain its factories, and to pay for the raw materials it used, like steel and electricity.

Profit is the difference between revenues and costs. In 2010 Caterpillar reported a profit of about $4 billion, which was the difference between its revenues ($43 billion) and its costs ($39 billion).

On a smaller scale, your favorite restaurant collects revenues from customers paying for meals, and it uses that money to pay its workers and suppliers. With any luck, revenues will exceed costs, so the restaurant will make a profit and be able to stay in business. Figure 4.1 shows the basics of how a business operates.

Profit Maximization

For better or worse, the main objective of any business in a market economy is **profit maximization.** That is, the people running a business want to operate it in a way that yields the largest difference between revenues and costs. True, a business might have all sorts of goals, including providing jobs for the local population, giving the lazy son of the founder something to do, or being a

FIGURE 4.1 | **How a Business Operates**

A business uses inputs from its suppliers to produce outputs to sell to its buyers. In return, it receives revenue from the buyers, and it pays its suppliers. Any money that remains is profit.

Flow of goods and services

Business

Suppliers of labor and other inputs

Inputs → Production → Output

Profit maxmization

Cost of inputs ← → Revenue from selling outputs

Buyers

Flow of money

---

socially responsible corporate citizen. But any business must try to make a good profit—defined as the difference between the revenue of the business and its total cost of production—or it will have trouble surviving in a competitive world.

Profit maximization is shorthand for "trying to produce something with the biggest difference between the costs and what someone is willing to pay." In the real world, maximizing the profit of a business is difficult. Running even a small business requires a multitude of large and small decisions. Managers have to deal with a constantly changing world, tough competitors, tougher employees, machines that break down, products consumers don't want to buy, corporate scandals, and natural disasters.

Businesses in the United States make a very wide range of profits. For example, oil giant Exxon Mobil reported $30 billion in profits in 2010. That same year many businesses large and small reported losses—that is, their costs exceeded their revenues. The car company Chrysler had a loss of $652 million in 2010.

The difficulty of consistently producing a good profit is the reason successful chief executives of large corporations get paid so handsomely—and it is also why most of them have such a short tenure on the job.

Of course profit-maximizing businesses are not the only source of production, since there are productive enterprises with other goals. Nonprofit organizations such as private

LABOR
The inputs supplied by various kinds of workers.

universities and hospitals also supply goods and services. Governments provide services, such as police forces and education. And most child care activities are still done by parents or other household members; most families are not run as profit-making enterprises.

PRODUCTION

At the core of any business is production—turning inputs into outputs that customers will buy. In this section we take a deeper look at these inputs and production.

Types of Inputs

The inputs used by a business in the production process can be divided into five big categories—*labor, capital, land, intermediate inputs,* and *business know-how.* Let's take a closer look at each one.

LABOR **Labor,** of course, refers to the inputs supplied by the various types of workers that enable a business to function. At an airline, for example, labor might include the hours of work put in by pilots, flight attendants, ticket agents, mechanics, crew schedulers, gate agents, menu planners, accountants, and so forth. At a television station, the labor inputs include the work time of the camera crews, the makeup staff, the public relations people, the newswriters, and of course the high-priced on-air talent.

We can measure labor inputs either by the number of workers a business employs or by the total number of hours worked. Measuring labor input by number of workers is especially common when the labor comes from executives and professionals because most businesses do not track the hours of their more educated workers.

CAPITAL **Capital,** the second input, is another name for all the long-lived physical equipment, software, and structures a businesses uses in its production process. For example, an airline needs at least one airplane (usually many more) to accomplish its most important function, which is to fly passengers from one point to another. But most airlines generally also need hangars to keep the planes in, tools for the mechanics who service the planes, computers and phones for the reservation agents, and office buildings for the airline managers. A television station may have its own studios, complete with cameras, props, and equipment for transmitting its signal. And of course an amusement park needs its roller coasters and haunted houses. All these physical goods are part of the capital used in production.

A business need not own all the capital it uses, however. For example, a law firm can either own its office building or rent it. Similarly, an airline can either own the commercial aircraft it operates, like a Boeing 747, or lease it from some other company that actually owns the plane. For example, the International Lease Finance Corporation—a company you likely have never heard of—owned over 900 commercial aircraft as of 2010, leasing them out to big carriers like Continental Airlines

CAPITAL
The long-lived equipment, software, and structures used in the production process.

LAND
The actual ground used by a business.

INTERMEDIATE INPUTS
Goods and services purchased from other businesses and used up in production.

and Southwest Airlines and small ones like Air Malta and Vietnam Airlines.

LAND Another input to most productive activities is **land,** the actual ground used by a business. Factories need land, as do office buildings. Shopping malls, of course, require large amounts of land. Even Internet retailers such as Amazon.com require land for their warehouses, offices, and computer facilities.

Agriculture and mining are especially land-intensive. It's not possible to grow wheat or extract oil from the ground without plenty of land. In fact, in these industries land can be the major input.

INTERMEDIATE INPUTS **Intermediate inputs** is really a catch-all category that refers to any goods and services purchased from other businesses and used up in production. For example, almost every business needs to buy electricity and telephone services; these are intermediate inputs. A pizzeria must buy flour, cheese, tomato sauce, pepperoni, anchovies, and all the other ingredients for its pizzas. A steel mill buys either iron ore or scrap metal as an input to its production process. A construction company buys cement, steel beams, rivets, and hard hats for its workers.

In fact, much economic activity in the United States consists of business-to-business (B-to-B) transactions like these, in which businesses buy and sell intermediate inputs. When you, as a consumer, go into a store to buy an article of clothing, that simple sale is just the visible strand of a broad web of B-to-B transactions. The store has to pay the local electric utility for power, an accounting

Economic Milestone

1962 THE FIRST WALMART OPENS

From its humble beginnings in tiny Bentonville, Arkansas, Walmart has grown into the world's largest retailer. How did that happen? Walmart's executives have made better use of business know-how than have their competitors. For one thing, Walmart was a pioneer in harnessing computers to track and order goods. The company was also one of the earliest retailers to extensively import cheap goods from China.

firm for managing its books, and a wholesaler for the clothing it sells. It pays a trucking company to bring the clothing to the store. The trucking company, in turn, pays for gasoline, truck repairs, the drivers' salaries, accident insurance, and so forth.

BUSINESS KNOW-HOW One underappreciated input is **business know-how,** which includes all the knowledge and technology necessary for the production process. An automaker, for example, must know how to design, build, and market cars. That includes knowledge of everything from how internal combustion engines work to the wind resistance that a car encounters on the highway.

In many cases, the necessary knowledge or technology is built into or embodied in the equipment a company buys. For example, a company that buys a computer can use its capabilities without knowing the details of how the hard disk works. Similarly, the computer may come with accounting and word processing programs already installed.

Sometimes necessary know-how is less tangible and much more specific to a particular business. A restaurant, for example, has recipes for each dish on its menu. It likely also has rules, either explicit or implicit, for how and when to clean the tables, how to manage the cash register, and what to do with unruly customers. These contribute to the business's success by ensuring that customers are satisfied enough to come back or recommend the restaurant to their friends.

Business know-how can be why a company succeeds or fails. For example, the success of Google rests on two crucial pieces of business know-how. The first is its search algorithm, invented by founders Sergey Brin and Larry Page, which typically gives users better results than any of its competitors. The second piece of business know-how is a proprietary method for pricing and selling search-based advertisements (those little ads that pop up next to Google searches). That's how the company makes most of its money. Other companies, such as Yahoo!, have tried to duplicate the success of Google's search ads, but this hasn't been easy.

> **BUSINESS KNOW-HOW**
> All the knowledge and technology necessary for the production process.

The Production Function

Economists sometimes like to think of a business as a sort of machine—a giant black box. At one end of the machine we put in the inputs—the labor, the capital, the intermediate inputs, the land, and the business know-how. From the other end come the outputs—the goods and services the business produces, whatever they may be.

Economists give this machine a catchy name: the **production function.** A production function tells you, given the inputs, what the output is going to be. In practice this is difficult to do for a large company. A major corporation may have hundreds of thousands or even millions of different inputs and outputs, making it nearly impossible to write down its production function. For example, General Electric makes everything from jet engines to train headlights to nuclear power plants to television shows.

It's much easier to think about the production function for a small business that has only one or two inputs and one output. Let's think about a lawn-mowing business, which for a small fee will take care of that green expanse in front of your house (as mentioned in Chapter 2). The simplest such business is one consisting of your next-door neighbor's son or daughter, who for a fee will cut your lawn. This business has two inputs: cheap labor and the old push mower from the garage. The output is the number of lawns cut in a day. If you know how many hours the teenager works, you can calculate the output of the business.

Table 4.1 shows a simple production function that relates the amount of labor to the amount of output. For a given number of hours worked, it tells you how many lawns will be mowed. Figure 4.2 graphs the same production function. For example, if the workers put in 2 hours of labor, move along the horizontal axis until you get to 12. Then move vertically until you get to the output—4 lawns mowed, in this case. As the number of hours worked rises, so does the output.

The Marginal Product of Labor

The production function gives an important piece of information: how much output the business

TABLE 4.1   A Simple Production Function

This table gives the production function for a small lawn-mowing business. The first column is the number of hours worked; the second column is the number of lawns mowed. For example, 2 hours of work will result in 4 lawns mowed.

Hours of Labor	Number of Lawns Mowed Using a Hand Mower
0	0
1	2
2	4
3	5
4	6

can produce given its inputs. But the production function also answers another question: If the business expands by adding more workers or by having them work more hours, how much does its output increase? The **marginal product of labor** (or simply *marginal product* for short) is the

MARGINAL PRODUCT OF LABOR

The extra amount of output a business can generate by adding one more hour of labor or one more worker.

extra amount of output the firm can generate by adding one more hour of labor or one more worker.

This is the first time in this textbook that we have encounted the idea of a *marginal* change, but it won't be the last. Economists often think about decision making in terms of small incremental steps.

We can apply this idea to the small lawn-mowing business of the previous section. The first hour of labor yields two lawns mowed. That means the marginal product of the first hour is 2, as shown in the third column of Table 4.2. The second hour of work yields another two lawns mowed, so the marginal product is still 2.

But what happens when the teenager works a third hour? By that time, he or she is tiring, so the marginal product of the third hour is only 1. To put it a different way, going from two hours worked to three hours worked yields only one additional lawn mowed, so the marginal product is 1.

Let's consider a business trying to hire a worker. When a potential employee is interviewed for a job, the manager may ask, "Why should I

FIGURE 4.2   Graphing a Simple Production Function

This graph corresponds to the production function in Table 4.1. The horizontal axis measures the input (the number of hours of labor), and the vertical axis measures the output (the number of lawns mowed). For example, 2 hours of work will result in 4 lawns mowed.

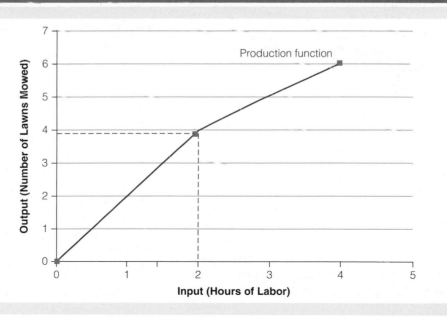

TABLE 4.2 — The Marginal Product of Yard Workers

In this table, the first two columns are the same as in Table 4.1, reporting the hours of labor and the number of lawns mowed. The third column reports the marginal product of each additional hour of work.

Hours of Labor	Number of Lawns Mowed	Marginal Product of Labor: Additional Lawns per Hour
0	0	
1	2	2
2	4	2
3	5	1
4	6	1

hire you? What will you add to my company?" In effect, what the worker will add to the company is his or her marginal product—the additional output from one more worker.

Think about an accounting firm that does tax returns. The marginal product of an additional accountant is the number of tax returns he or she can complete. Table 4.3 shows the production function for this accounting firm. The first column is the number of accountants, the second column is the output of those accountants, and the third column is the marginal product.

TABLE 4.3 — The Marginal Product of Accountants

In this table, the third column shows the marginal product of each additional accountant.

Input: Number of Accountants	Output: Number of Tax Returns Done in a Week	Marginal Product of Labor: Additional Tax Returns per Worker
1	10	10
2	20	10
3	29	9
4	37	8
5	44	7

For example, the marginal product of the third accountant is nine tax returns. That's because the first two accountants can produce 20 returns without him and 29 returns with him. The difference, 9, is the marginal product of the third accountant.

In general, as a business adds workers without changing the amount of capital or other inputs, each additional worker will have **diminishing marginal product.** That is, the marginal product will fall as the number of workers rises, holding other inputs constant. To see this, consider a restaurant. The inputs are cooks, kitchen equipment, and ingredients, and the output is the number of meals cooked. If there's only one cook, he or she has to do everything—cut the onions, fry the potatoes, watch the pasta—which obviously limits the output of meals. Adding a second cook will likely double the output of meals just by dividing the labor. But eventually, if we add enough cooks, they will get in each other's way because the kitchen offers only limited space. As the old saying goes, too many cooks spoil the broth.

Table 4.3 shows diminishing marginal product for the accounting firm. Perhaps there isn't enough room in a small office for all the workers, or perhaps they have to wait for the single copy machine. In some cases, output can even decline with an additional worker.

The Production Function with Capital

Now let's look at what happens when we add another input: capital. In this case, capital comes in the form of a gasoline-powered mower, which cuts grass a lot faster. Table 4.4 shows the production function of the lawn-mowing business both with and without the gasoline-powered mower. With more capital, the same number of labor hours will result in more lawns mowed. Figure 4.3 graphs the production function with and without the power mower.

What is the marginal product of an additional hour of work, with the power mower? Suppose the teenager goes from working for one hour to working for two hours. Then his or her output goes from three lawns to six lawns, so the marginal product is 3.

	The Production Function
TABLE 4.4	**with Capital**

This table gives the production function for a lawn-mowing business. The first column is the number of hours worked. The second column is the number of lawns mowed with a push mower, and the third column is the number of lawns mowed if the business uses a gasoline-powered mower.

Hours of Labor	Number of Lawns Mowed with a Push Mower	Number of Lawns Mowed with a Power Mower
0	0	0
1	2	3
2	4	6
3	5	9
4	6	11

Similarly, Table 4.4 shows that the marginal product is 3 for three hours of work as well. Eventually, though, the teenager starts to get bored and a bit tired, even using the power mower. That's why the marginal product of the fourth hour of work is only 2.

Average Product

The production function also gives us a third piece of information: **average product,** which is the output divided by the number of labor hours or by the number of workers—in other words, output per hour or output per worker. For a lawn-mowing service this would be lawns mowed per worker. For an automaker the average product is vehicles manufactured per worker, perhaps with some adjustment so that big sport utility vehicles count more than compact cars. For an electric utility, the average product is megawatts of energy delivered per worker.

How can we interpret average product? In the past we could say that a business with a higher average product was better off than a competitor with a lower average product, all other things being equal. So if one automaker could produce more vehicles than another automaker using the same number of workers, the first company would have an advantage. In fact, automakers would spend a lot of time comparing their average products with those of their competitors.

These days, however, average product is a less reliable indicator of the strength of a business. Businesses now have the option of **outsourcing**

FIGURE 4.3	**Graphing the Production Function with Capital**

This graph shows that using a power mower produces more output than using a hand mower. For example, two hours of labor with a power mower will yield 4 lawns mowed rather than 2. This figure corresponds to Table 4.4

part of their operations, either within the United States or overseas. That is, they hire outside sellers to handle tasks their own employees once did. In the 1970s and 1980s, for instance, many businesses decided they didn't want to run their own cafeterias or vacuum the office floors in the evening. Instead they contracted out housekeeping and food services to specialized firms.

In the past few years, outsourcing has become a way of life. Businesses have systematically sent their manufacturing and customer service processes overseas. Call centers and customer support operations have moved to India, the Philippines, and other low-wage, English-speaking countries.

SPOTLIGHT: "CUT YOUR TREE, MISTER?"

Utility companies are supposed to be good at running power-generating plants cheaply and safely and delivering an uninterrupted supply of electricity. But over time it has become apparent that an important part of maintaining overhead power lines is trimming the trees and vegetation that grow alongside them—and that's something in which utilities have little expertise.

That's why they tend to outsource their tree work. The result is an entire industry of companies that specialize in utility tree trimming. One of the biggest, Asplundh Tree Expert Company, reported in 2010 that it had over 26,000 workers around the world.

Source: Asplundh Tree Expert Company, www.asplundh.com.

Computer companies have outsourced production of many laptop and desktop computers to Asian manufacturers. That means businesses have been able to lower their employee counts without cutting their output. This boosts the average product.

COST

So far our discussion of business has mostly omitted any mention of money. We've focused on the process of production, turning inputs into outputs. But every input has a *cost*—that's the nature of a market economy. If a business wants to make the best profit-maximizing decisions, it has to know how its costs vary with its production decisions. We'll start by looking at the cost of each input, and then at how they are put together.

Types of Cost

COST OF LABOR The **cost of labor** of a business is its monetary outlays for workers. In the simplest case, it is the price of labor per unit times the amount of labor used, where the price of labor is the workers' wages—either hourly wages or monthly salaries, depending on the jobs. On top of that, many businesses provide additional benefits at their own cost, such as vacation days, retirement benefits, and medical and dental insurance. Top managers at large companies often get a wide variety of other types of compensation, including use of corporate jets, health club memberships paid for by the company, and sometimes even paid housing.

COST OF CAPITAL AND LAND The **cost of capital and land** is the outlay for buying or renting equipment, structures, and land. Businesses can generally either buy or rent physical capital—like a building, a truck, or a computer. The same is true for land: A copper mining company will either buy land with copper ore or rent the right to mine from the owner of the land.

If a business rents a truck, the truck's cost per period is (not surprisingly) the price of the rental for that period. Similarly, if your business occupies space in somebody else's building, you generally pay rent monthly. But what happens if you buy a truck or a building yourself? There will be a big up-front cost—thousands for the truck, hundreds of thousands or even millions for the building—but you expect to use that truck or building over several years. As the business owner, you want to figure out the annual cost of your purchase and spread the initial cost over the projected life of the physical capital. If you buy a $40,000 truck and you expect it to last 10 years, you can look at your $40,000 cost as being spread over 10 years, or $4,000 a year. If you take out a loan to make your purchase, you'll also have to figure the interest on the loan as part of your costs. We'll go into this in more detail in Chapter 13.

COST OF INTERMEDIATE INPUTS The **cost of intermediate inputs** is the money a business pays for goods and services purchased from other companies. For example, a restaurant buys ingredients for making meals—vegetables, meats, spices, and the like—from its suppliers. For many businesses, the cost of intermediate inputs can be quite large.

COST OF ACCUMULATING BUSINESS KNOW-HOW Finally, let's look at the **cost of accumulating business know-how.** Any outlays that increase a company's knowledge and capabilities are part of the cost of accumulating business know-how. This includes the cost of setting up scientific laboratories to research new technologies, hiring engineers and designers to develop new products, conducting marketing studies to see what customers want, bringing in management consulting firms to tell you how to run your business better, sending your workers to conferences to learn the latest techniques, paying other companies for the right to use their technologies, and so on.

Most companies do not officially report all their business know-how costs. However, they usually report their spending on research and development (R&D) on their annual financial statements. In 2010, for example, chip giant Intel spent more than $6 billion on research and development, with the goal of producing faster, cheaper, and more energy-efficient semiconductor chips.

In some cases the cost of getting smarter is simply making mistakes and figuring out how to do things better. This is known politely as learning by doing. For now, however, we will focus on the monetary costs of accumulating business know-how.

COST FUNCTION
Reports the total cost of producing each level of output.

Total Cost of Production

The **total cost** of production is the sum of costs for each of the inputs:

Total cost = (Cost of labor) + (Cost of capital and land) + (Cost of intermediate inputs) + (Cost of accumulating business know-how)

Here's one way to think about total cost. If you own and operate a McDonald's restaurant, your labor cost is wages and benefit payments to your hamburger flippers and cashiers. Your cost of capital and land is the rent on your store plus the cost of the food preparation equipment. The cost of intermediate inputs includes the money you pay for the all-beef patties, the buns, and the employees' uniforms. And the cost of accumulating business know-how is the time and money you need to go through McDonald's extensive training program for prospective owner–operators, including a stint at "Hamburger University." All of these added together make up your total cost.

The Cost Function

Imagine for a moment that you work for a company that makes candy. The members of the National Confectioners Association include candy manufacturers such as the American Licorice Company and Tootsie Roll Industries. The top company managers are going to decide how many thousands of pieces of candy to make in their factory, and they want to know how much each production level will cost.

So you spend a week doing the calculations for each potential level of output: how many workers and candy machines are needed, the cost of the sugar and the wrapping paper, whether the company will need extra security guards if the factory has to run an extra shift at night. When you're done, you know the total cost of producing 1,000 pieces of candy, 2,000 pieces, and so on. (The appendix following Chapter 6 goes deeper into the economics of the cost function and profit maximization.)

Your bosses don't need to know all the details of the calculation, though. All they need is the summary. The **cost function** summarizes the results of your calculations.

TABLE 4.5	The Candy Cost Function

The left column reports the output of the factory, and the right column reports the total cost for that level of output.

Candy Produced (Pieces)	Total Cost (Dollars)
0	$ 500
1,000	$ 1,500
2,000	$ 2,500
3,000	$ 3,600
4,000	$ 4,850
5,000	$ 6,350
6,000	$ 8,100
7,000	$ 10,100

That is, the cost function is like a calculator that tells you the total cost of producing each level of output, using the cheapest and best methods known to the company at the time.

The cost function for your candy company might look something like Table 4.5. The left column of this table gives the possible levels of output for the company, while the right column reports the total cost for that level of output. The right column says, for example, that producing 3,000 pieces of candy will cost $3,600, producing 7,000 pieces of candy will cost $10,100, and producing no candy will cost $500 (the wages for the security guard, perhaps, to watch the empty factory).

We can also graph the cost function, as shown in Figure 4.4. If you want to know the cost of producing 5,000 pieces of candy, move across the horizontal axis until you come to 5,000. Then the graph tells you the total cost is $6,350. The cost function is upward-sloping because it costs more to produce more candy.

Marginal Cost

Knowing the cost function for different levels of output is useful. But for profit maximization, what's more important is **marginal cost.** The marginal cost, or MC, is the added expense of producing one more unit of output. To put it a slightly different way, if a company decides to

FIGURE 4.4	Graphing the Candy Cost Function

The horizontal axis reports the number of candy pieces produced by the factory, and the vertical axis gives the total cost. This graph corresponds to the numbers in Table 4.5.

TABLE 4.6   Calculating Marginal Cost

As the business increases production from 1,000 to 2,000 pieces of candy, the cost rises from $1,500 to $2,500. The marginal cost is $1 per piece (the additional cost divided by the additional number of pieces of candy).

Candy Produced (Pieces)	Total Cost (Dollars)	Marginal Cost (Dollars)
0	$ 500	
1,000	$ 1,500	$ 1.00
2,000	$ 2,500	$ 1.00
3,000	$ 3,600	$ 1.10
4,000	$ 4,850	$ 1.25
5,000	$ 6,350	$ 1.50
6,000	$ 8,100	$ 1.75
7,000	$ 10,100	$ 2.00

Table 4.6, shows how we can calculate the marginal cost for the candy factory. Notice that the first two columns repeat Table 4.5. For example, the cost of producing 1,000 pieces of candy is $1,500, and the cost of producing 2,000 pieces of candy is $2,500. The added cost to produce an extra 1,000 pieces (2,000 − 1,000) is $1,000 ($2,500 − $1,500), so the marginal cost in the third column is $1.00 per piece ($1,000 ÷ 1,000).

Figure 4.5 graphs the marginal cost curve. We can see from both the fig-

expand output by one unit, the marginal cost is the additional total cost. More precisely,

Marginal cost = (Added cost of producing additional units of output) ÷ (Number of additional units of output)

ure and the table that the marginal cost rises as the plant's production increases. Why should each additional piece become more expensive? Workers have to be paid overtime, machines break down more often if they run all the time, and the factory has to hire inexperienced workers who make more mistakes and require training.

FIGURE 4.5   Graphing Marginal Cost

The horizontal axis measures output, and the vertical axis measures marginal cost. This graph corresponds to the third column of Table 4.6. In general, marginal cost rises as the output increases.

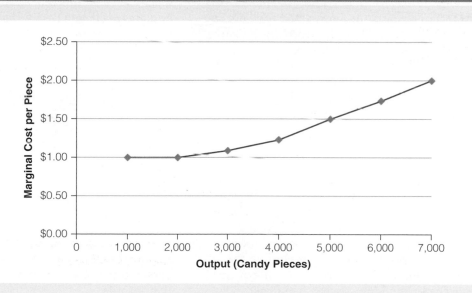

assume
oduced.

as if we
In real-
e inputs
mple, if
ses, it's
prepare
her din-

Production send a note to Paulos

We can think of businesses as having two types of costs: **variable costs** and **fixed costs.** Variable costs, also known as **short-term costs,** are those that managers can quickly raise or lower by decisions they make today. For example, it's easy for a retailer to adjust the number of hours its salespeople work. Similarly, advertising is a variable cost for a retailer, who can decide week to week how much advertising to buy in the local newspaper or on the Internet.

By contrast, fixed costs, also known as **long-term costs,** are harder to change; more precisely, a decision by a business to change its fixed costs will take longer to have an effect. For example, the rent a retailer pays for its building is a fixed cost. The business can certainly change that cost—but it takes a lot longer to open a new location somewhere else than it does to hire a new worker.

There's one quirk you should remember about this terminology of *fixed* and *variable.* Fixed costs, of course, are not really fixed forever. The retailer could close down the store, for example. But in the short run, it's much easier to change variable costs than fixed costs.

For that reason, variable costs are more relevant for short-term, everyday decision making, whereas fixed costs are properly the domain of long-term strategic planning. An example of variable costs can be found in your local newspaper. Each day the publisher of the newspaper has to decide how many pages the paper should include. A thick paper with more pages has more room for news, for advertisements, and for humorous feature stories. But a thick paper costs more money—for printing, for ink, and for workers to run the printing presses. Including the additional pages is a variable cost. In contrast, buying the printing presses is a fixed cost.

Or consider retailers such as Starbucks, Walmart, and Home Depot. Each day or week their managers decide how to staff their stores—how many workers to have on each shift. That's a short-term decision. A key long-term decision for these companies is how many new stores to open and where. In 2010, for example, Starbucks added new company-operated stores in China and Canada while reducing the number of stores in the United States and the United Kingdom. Such long-term decisions alter the fixed costs of doing business.

In some parts of the economy, hiring decisions may actually be tougher to reverse than brick-and-mortar investments. In the government sector many workers are protected by unions and civil service rules, which make it tough to fire them except in cases of severe misconduct. On many college campuses it is easier and faster to put up a new building than it is to fire a tenured professor.

On the other hand, outsourcing turns some decisions that used to be about fixed costs into decisions about variable costs. Suppose a U.S. company designs a new laptop computer and hires a Taiwanese company to make it. The cost of building and operating the computer factory—which is owned by the Taiwanese company—is now a variable cost for the U.S. company instead of a fixed cost.

We can distinguish between the *short-term cost function* and the *long-term cost function.* The **short-term cost function** assumes fixed costs can't be changed. If you own a building or a factory or have a long-term contract with your workers, you can't easily alter these inputs in the short term.

The **long-term cost function,** in contrast, puts everything up for grabs, including all the fixed costs (which are not so fixed in the long run). For example, the short-term cost function for Starbucks assumes all its retail locations are fixed. The long-term cost function, though, assumes the coffee chain can open new stores and close those that are not making a profit.

REVENUE

Now we come to the final piece of the business: revenue. Once we understand revenue, we can understand the basics of how companies maximize their profits.

A Simple Example

Revenue is the amount of money companies get from selling their products or services. In the simplest case, a business sells only one product at a fixed price. Then the revenue is equal to the number of units sold times the price per unit.

For example, a hot dog stand cooks hot dogs and then sells them. If the price is $1.50 each, the revenue equals the number of hot dogs sold times $1.50. Table 4.7 shows the revenue, given the number of hot dogs sold (assuming that all the hot dogs can be sold). If the price per hot dog were higher, the revenue would be higher too.

More generally, a business may have several different ways to bring in money, beyond just selling a single product. Banks, for example, take in money by charging interest on the loans they make. But they also may charge people fees for withdrawing money from their automated teller machines. (For other examples, see "How It Works: Finding More Revenue.")

Marginal Revenue

What happens to revenue when a business expands production and sales? Typically revenue will go up, but by how much?

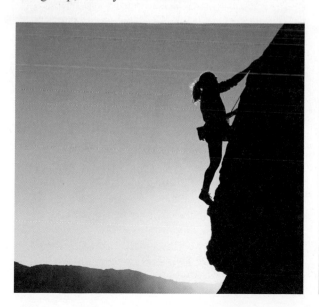

TABLE 4.7	A Revenue Example

The first column gives the output of the hot dog stand, and the second column gives the revenue amounts, assuming the price per hot dog is $1.50. Assuming all hot dogs that are made can be sold, the revenue is simply the number of hot dogs times $1.50.

Output: Number of Hot Dogs Cooked and Sold in a Day	Revenue (Assuming All Hot Dogs Can Be Sold at $1.50 Each)
10	$15
20	$30
30	$45
40	$60
50	$75

HOW IT WORKS: FINDING MORE REVENUE

One of the most important tasks of a business is finding new ways to make money from the same products. That requires figuring out what people are willing to pay for.

For example, electronics retailers get revenue from selling you an LCD television or computer. But in addition, they get quite a bit of money from selling you an extended warranty—that is, a promise to fix the TV or computer if something goes wrong over the next few years.

Consider movie theaters. They get money from ticket sales, obviously, but the concession stands also bring in a tremendous amount of money selling giant candy bars, bags of popcorn, and cups of soda so large they could swallow a small dog.

And sports teams have had great success broadening their sources of revenue. Originally they made money from ticket sales and concession sales. Then came television rights, with the National Football League selling its first major television contract in 1962. Looking for more revenue, sports teams turned to selling the naming rights for their stadiums and arenas. For example, the Washington Redskins football team is being paid about $200 million by FedEx. In exchange, FedEx gets to put its name on the team's stadium.

The **marginal revenue** is the additional money a business gets from producing and selling one more unit of output (we're assuming at this point that the business sells everything it makes). In the simplest case, the business can sell as much as it wants at the going market price. This usually reflects the business being small relative to the total market. (We will see in Chapter 5 that this kind of market is known as *perfect competition*.)

In this case, the marginal revenue from selling one more unit—that is, the extra revenue from the additional unit—is equal to the price. The more the business produces, the more it can sell at the same price. For our hot dog vendor, the marginal revenue is $1.50 per additional hot dog cooked and sold.

PROFIT MAXIMIZATION

Now we get to the bottom line of this chapter: if profit depends on the difference between revenue and cost, both of which are affected by production, how does a business owner or manager decide *how much* to produce? The answer is that once we have both the cost and revenue functions, we can slowly increase the output of the business until we find the level that maximizes profit.

The **profit-maximizing rule** is a simple one:

A profit-maximizing business will increase production as long as marginal revenue exceeds marginal cost.

That is, as long as the added revenue from an additional unit of output is greater than the additional cost of producing that unit, expansion will earn more profit for the business. For example, suppose the cost of hiring an additional landscape worker is $300 for a 40-hour week. Now suppose the extra worker can mow enough lawns to produce an additional $500 of revenue. Adding this extra worker makes sense because she can produce an additional $200 in profits over the $300 cost of hiring her.

For most businesses, marginal cost increases as output rises. Such a business will keep expanding up to the point that marginal cost is equal to marginal revenue (think about walking up to a line but no further). So the profit-maximizing rule is sometimes written this way: At the profit-maximizing output, marginal cost is equal to marginal revenue.

An Example

Let's look at an example in detail. Let's revisit the candy factory discussed earlier in this chapter.

Table 4.8, on page 71, is probably the most complicated table you'll see in this textbook, so let's take it step by step. We've seen the first three columns before in Tables 4.5 and 4.6—the output of the factory, the cost of production, and the marginal cost. The fourth column is total revenue, assuming each piece of candy sells for $1.50 (perhaps a chocolate bar or a whole pack of gum). For example, 4,000 pieces of candy bring in $6,000 in revenue. The fifth

HOW IT WORKS: WHO GETS THE PROFIT?

Suppose a business makes a million dollars in profit. Who gets it? The short answer is that the profit belongs to the owners of the business, but they may not always be able to take it home with them.

A small business may be owned by one person or a small number of partners. They can choose to take the profit out of the business and use it to send their kids to college, or they can reinvest the earnings to expand the business. Their hope in doing so is that their investment will make the company worth even more in the future.

The situation is similar for a large company. As we will see in Chapter 13, a large public company may have millions of shareholders who are all part owners of the company. The company will typically distribute some profit to them in the form of dividends, which are quarterly payments of cash per share of stock. The rest of the profit the firm either reinvests in the company or keeps in the bank.

TABLE 4.8 The Profit-Maximizing Candy Company

Marginal Revenue from Marginal Cost

The candy company will increase output as long as marginal revenue exceeds [...] pieces, the marginal revenue of $1.50 per piece is greater than the marginal c[...] of 6,000 pieces, the marginal revenue of $1.50 per piece is less than the marg[...] profit-maximizing level of output is 5,000 pieces, where marginal revenue equals [...]

Candy (Pieces)	Total Cost (Dollars)	Marginal Cost (Dollars)	Revenue, Assuming Each Piece of Candy Sells for $1.50 (Dollars)	Revenue (Dollars)	Profit (Dollars)
0	$ 500	–	0	–	–$500
1,000	$1,500	$1.00	$1,500	$1.50	$0
2,000	$2,500	$1.00	$3,000	$1.50	$500
3,000	$3,600	$1.10	$4,500	$1.50	$900
4,000	$4,850	$1.25	$6,000	$1.50	$1,150
5,000	**$6,350**	**$1.50**	**$7,500**	**$1.50**	**$1,150**
6,000	$8,100	$1.75	$9,000	$1.50	$900
7,000	$ 10,100	$2.00	$10,500	$1.50	$400

column, marginal revenue, is the extra money the company earns by selling one more piece of candy. The final column, profit, is revenue minus costs.

Following our profit-maximizing rule, we expand production as long as marginal revenue exceeds marginal costs. For example, at the 2,000-piece level of production, marginal revenue is $1.50 and marginal cost is $1.00, so it makes sense to produce and sell more because the extra revenue exceeds the extra cost.

The expansion continues up to the 5,000-piece level of production (highlighted in the table). This is the profit-maximizing level of production because up to that point we can still earn extra revenue. At higher levels of output, marginal cost rises to $1.75, which is more than marginal revenue. Thus profit falls if output goes above 5,000 pieces.

One final note: It is sometimes true that there is more than one level of output that maximizes profit. In this example, an output of 4,000 pieces gives the same profit as 5,000 pieces. In such a situation, choose the output where marginal revenue equals marginal cost.

The Law of Supply Revisited

Suppose that in Table 4.8 the price was $2.00 per piece rather than $1.50. What would happen to production? According to the profit-maximizing rule, the company will increase production as long as marginal revenue exceeds marginal cost. If the price is $2.00 per piece, the company will want to increase production up to 7,000 pieces of candy. In other words, a higher price leads to increased production because the company wants to maximize profit.

Now we can better understand the law of supply described in Chapter 2, which said that the quantity supplied in a market generally rises as the price increases. Because businesses are profit-maximizing, they can generally make more money by expanding production when the market price increases, assuming they are able to sell all they make.

SPOTLIGHT: BOEING'S LONG-TERM DECISION

The long-running competition between Boeing and Airbus, two giant commercial airplane manufacturers, offers a classic example of long-term decision-making. Designing and testing a new commercial airplane is an expensive proposition requiring billions of dollars. Airplane manufacturers make investments like this in the expectation that the payoff will come over decades. For example, Boeing started developing the 747 in 1963; its first flight was in 1969; and the model is still being sold as of 2010.

In the mid-1990s, both plane makers had to place bets for the future. The executives leading Airbus chose to build the giant A380, capable of carrying up to 800 people (and requiring landing strips to be strengthened at airports around the world).

On the other hand, Boeing designed a smaller, more fuel-efficient plane called the Dreamliner or the 787. It turned out that most airlines preferred the 787. Boeing had almost 900 orders for its new plane as of mid-2008 with the expectation that the first 787s would soon be carrying passengers. That proved overly

optimistic—a series of production problems meant that the new planes were still in testing as of early 2011. A three-year delay in introducing a new product would probably be disastrous for many companies. However, because the 787 will likely be sold for many years into the future, Boeing still expects to make good profits on the new model.

Short-Term Profit Maximization and Long-Term Decisions

We can distinguish between short-term and long-term profit maximization. In **short-term profit maximization** we focus on achieving the highest profit, assuming that fixed costs cannot be changed. The managers of the candy company make their production decisions taking the current size of the factory as a given.

In contrast, when we consider **long-term profit maximization** we assume a business can vary all its inputs, even going as far as shutting down. The candy company can expand its factory, close part of it down, or move its operations to Canada or China (the United States imported $160 million in confectionery products from China in 2010, up from almost nothing in 2000).

Long-term profit maximization also includes the results of a company's big strategic decisions, like coming up with new products or entering new markets. Some companies like Apple maximize their profits by innovating. Others do it by offering low prices and trying to get maximum efficiency from their workforce.

For an automaker like Ford or Toyota, long-term decisions are connected with the design and development of new models—what they will look like, what performance characteristics they will have, and what market segments they will address. Take Toyota's development of the Prius, the first widely selling hybrid car, able to run on both gasoline and electricity. A team of Japanese engineers started designing the hybrid car in 1993. The biggest decision—what kind of engine to use—wasn't made until 1995. The Prius was first offered for sale in December 1997.

For executives at big drug companies, two key decisions are how much to invest in developing new drugs and where the most profitable opportunities might be. It can take up to 10 years to develop a new drug in the laboratory, test it on animals, make sure it is safe for humans, run some large-scale studies to see whether it actually is beneficial, and then wait for the Federal Drug Administration (FDA) to approve the drug for sale. At each step along the way the drug company has to decide, based on its analysis of costs and revenues, whether it makes sense to keep funding the new drug.

Long-term decisions are inherently uncertain ones. Especially when companies are committing themselves to new technologies and new markets, it's tough to know what is going to happen. (For an example of long-term decision making in the airplane industry, see "Spotlight: Boeing's Long-Term Decision.")

CONCLUSION

We started this chapter with Walmart and ended it with Boeing. In between we looked at hair salons, lawn-mowing enterprises, giant oil producers, and fast-growing Internet search firms, all examples of profit-maximizing businesses with production, revenues, and costs. The basic logic of profit maximization that we saw here is essential for understanding how today's economy works.

In the next chapter we will show how competition—or the lack of competition—affects the production and pricing behavior of businesses, and what that means for the broader economy.

04   SUMMARY

1. A business buys inputs from its suppliers. It uses those inputs to produce output—the goods and services it sells to its customers. The money the business pays for the inputs is its cost, and the money it receives from its customers is its revenue. Profit is the difference between revenue and cost. *(LO4-1)*

2. The inputs to production include labor, capital, land, intermediate inputs, and business know-how. The production function summarizes the output of a business, given the levels of its inputs. The marginal product of labor is the extra amount of output a business can generate by adding one more hour of labor or one more worker. *(LO4-2)*

3. The total cost of production is the sum of the costs for all of the inputs.The cost function for

a business reports how much it will cost to produce a given level of output. Marginal cost is the added cost to produce one more unit of output. Variable costs can be quickly changed by the decisions of managers. Fixed costs take longer to change. *(LO4-3)*

4. Revenue is the amount of money companies get from selling their products or services. Marginal revenue is the added revenue from producing and selling one more unit of output. In perfect competition, the marginal revenue will be equal to the price. *(LO4-4)*

5. A profit-maximizing business will increase production as long as marginal revenue exceeds marginal cost. Short-term profit maximization holds fixed costs constant. Long-term profit maximization allows all inputs to vary. *(LO4-5)*

KEY TERMS AND CONCEPTS

outputs	cost	capital
inputs	profit	land
production	profit maximization	intermediate inputs
revenue	labor	business know-how

production function	cost of accumulating business know-how	long-term costs
marginal product of labor		short-term cost function
diminishing marginal product	total cost	long-term cost function
average product	cost function	revenue
outsourcing	marginal cost	marginal revenue
cost of labor	variable costs	profit-maximizing rule
cost of capital and land	fixed costs	short-term profit maximization
cost of intermediate inputs	short-term costs	long-term profit maximization

PROBLEMS

1. A business has revenues of $4 million per month and costs of $3 million per month. Its annual profits are _____ *(LO4-1)*

   a) $1 million.

   b) $7 million.

   c) $12 million.

   d) $36 million.

2. Many hospitals and private universities are nonprofit institutions. This means _____ *(LO4-1)*

   a) their costs exceed their revenues.

   b) they do not seek to maximize their profits.

   c) they try to maximize revenues.

   d) they do not try to minimize costs.

3. In 2010 American Electric Power (AEP), an electric utility with operations from Texas to Michigan, produced 206 million megawatt-hours of electricity (a megawatt-hour measures the output of an electricity-generating plant). The company also had 19,000 U.S. employees. What is the average product of AEP? *(LO4-2)*

4. A medical office does MRI (magnetic resonance imaging) scans on patients. It has two MRI machines. Each scan requires a technician to run the MRI machine. Here is the production function for the office, which shows how many patients the technicians can scan. *(LO4-2)*

Number of Technicians	Number of Scans Completed per Day	Marginal Product	Average Product
1	5	?	?
2	10	?	5
3	14	?	?
4	17	3	?
5	20	?	?

a) Fill in the table with the appropriate marginal product and average product for each level of hiring.

b) Graph the production function.

c) Suppose the office buys a new type of MRI machine that that can do one extra scan per day. Show graphically what will happen to the production function.

5. In the previous problem, suppose that the price of the labor input (the MRI technician) is $200 per day in wages and benefits. Suppose also that the capital input (the MRI machines) has a price of $150 per day for each machine, on a long-term lease. *(LO4-3)*

a) To do 10 scans in a day, how many technicians are needed?

b) What is the labor cost of doing 10 scans in a day?

c) What is the total cost of doing 10 scans per day (assuming there are two MRI machines in the office)?

d) What is the variable cost of doing 17 scans in a day?

e) What is the fixed cost of doing 17 scans in a day?

6. Think about a Starbucks coffee shop. Identify whether each of the following inputs is a fixed cost or a variable cost. *(LO4-3)*

a) An espresso machine.

b) Electricity to run the machine.

c) The lease on the store.

d) Workers.

7. A local handyman offers to install new windows in your home. Here is his cost function. *(LO4-3)*

Number of Windows	Cost (Dollars)	Marginal Cost (Dollars)
0	100	—
1	150	?
2	200	?
3	250	?
4	325	?
5	425	?
6	550	?

a) Fill in the marginal cost column in the table.

b) Graph the cost curve.

c) What is the fixed cost of window installation?

8. All other things being equal, a business making shirts would choose not to expand when _____ *(LO4-4)*

a) Marginal revenue per shirt equals $10 and marginal cost per shirt equals $10.

b) Marginal revenue per shirt equals $7 and marginal cost per shirt equals $10.

c) Marginal revenue per shirt equals $20 and marginal cost per shirt equals $10.

d) Marginal revenue per shirt equals $20 and marginal cost per shirt equals $10.

9. Here is the cost function for a bicycle repair shop, including the labor cost for the repair technicians. *(LO4-4)*

Bicycles Repaired per Day (Number)	Cost (Dollars)	Marginal Cost (Dollars)	Revenue (Dollars)	Marginal Revenue (Dollars)
0	100	–	?	–
1	150	?	?	?
2	200	?	?	?
3	260	?	?	?
4	330	?	?	?
5	410	?	?	?
6	500	?	?	?
7	600	?	?	?
8	710	?	?	?

   a) Fill in the blanks for marginal cost. Is the marginal cost increasing or decreasing?

   b) Suppose the market price for repairing a bicycle is $80. Fill in the blanks for the revenue and marginal revenue.

10. Using the table in question 9, answer the following questions. *(LO4-5)*

   a) How many bicycles must the store repair per day to maximize profits? (Remember the profit-maximizing rule.)

   b) Now suppose the market price for repairing a bicycle goes up to $100. How many bicycles will the shop repair?

11. In 2008 the cost of oil soared, and so did the cost of jet fuel. In response, American Airlines announced in May of that year that it was cutting some routes and reducing the frequency of flights on other routes. *(LO4-5)*

   a) Is jet fuel a variable cost or a fixed cost?

   b) What did American Airlines gain from reducing the number of flights?

   c) Was the airline more likely to cancel flights that tended to be filled to capacity, or ones that typically flew partly empty? Explain.

   d) The next generation of airplanes from Boeing, the 787, uses less fuel than many of the aircraft currently being flown (see "Spotlight: Boeing's Long-Term Decision"). If American Airlines could replace its aircraft with more fuel-efficient models, would it want to increase or decrease the number of flights?

05 COMPETITION AND MARKET POWER

LEARNING OBJECTIVES

After reading this chapter, you should be able to:

LO5-1 Define perfect competition, and identify its key characteristics.

LO5-2 Describe how businesses maximize profits in perfectly competitive markets.

LO5-3 Discuss the long-term outcome of perfect competition.

LO5-4 Compare and contrast the four types of market structure.

LO5-5 Explain how market power affects price and quantity supplied.

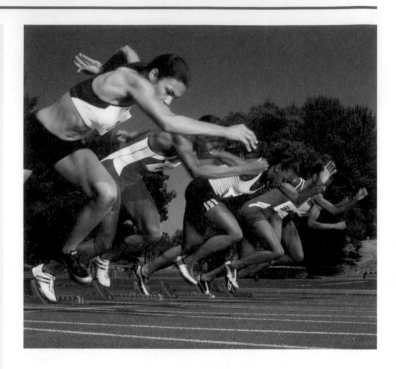

We've all been brought up on the idea of competition in sports and in life. I win, you lose; you win, I lose.

Yet competition plays a very different role in a market economy. What economic theory says—and experience confirms—is that under the right circumstances competition is a win–win proposition. Companies compete against each other to deliver to consumers what they want at the lowest cost. In the short run and the long run, competition in the market leads to more production, more innovation, and higher standards of living.

These benefits of competition are the key reasons the market economy remains popular. If competition did not deliver a higher standard of living, there would be much more political opposition to all the insecurity and turmoil that inevitably come along with a market economy.

India offers a good illustration of the impact of competition on the standard of living. Until 1991 the Indian government exerted direct control over its economy. For example, government bureaucrats determined which factories were allowed to operate, what they could produce, what raw materials they could use, and so on. Competition was discouraged. The problem was that this system of direct control did not result in a rising living standard. After an economic crisis in 1991, India's political leaders changed course, embracing competition and a market economy, leading to faster economic growth and a rising living standard.

In this chapter we begin by examining how perfect competition works in a single market. Then we'll examine alternatives to perfect competition and where they fall short. Finally, we'll explain the benefits of perfect competition, which are a key justification for the market economy.

PERFECT COMPETITION

Let's start by looking at **perfect competition**, which is sometimes also called a **competitive market.** Perfect competition is in some sense an extreme type of market that is rarely found in the real world. Nevertheless, it is a useful benchmark for understanding how real market economies behave.

What makes perfect competition special is that all buyers and sellers are **price takers.** Being a price taker means just what it sounds like—buyers and sellers take the market price as given and make their buying and production decisions accordingly. Imagine that as the manager of a grocery store you are trying to decide what price to put on your Red Delicious apples. Your competitors are selling apples for $1.00 per pound. If you are a price taker, you charge the going rate in the market—$1.00 per pound, the same as your competitors. If you are a price taker, you'd be foolish to charge more than $1.00 because all your customers would buy their apples elsewhere. And you'd be foolish to charge less because you can sell all your apples at the (higher) going rate.

If you are a buyer of the apples, being a price taker means that you accept the posted price as given without trying to bargain it down. In perfect competition, buyers and sellers bow to the will of the market. No seller can boost its price above the market without losing its customers to competitors. No buyer can push the price below the market because there are plenty of other buyers willing to pay the going rate.

Under what circumstances will we expect to see price-taking behavior? First, products have to be standardized so buyers can readily compare them. **Standardized products** differ in a small number of easily identifiable features. In the United States, corn comes in five grades, depending on factors such as the percentage of broken kernels.

Likewise, it's now easier to compare the price of different desktop computers because computer capabilities are becoming increasingly standardized. Two computers with the same microprocessors, random access memory, and hard disk space are pretty much equivalent, so a purchaser can choose the cheaper one. (Laptop computers, by contrast, are not so easily standardized.) Similarly, memory chips are standardized according to size and response time.

PERFECT COMPETITION
A situation in which all buyers and sellers are price takers.

Economic Milestone

1980 FIRST STANDARDIZED ENERGY USE LABELS

To help consumers make comparisons, the government requires air conditioners, dishwashers, and other major appliances to be labeled with estimated energy consumption or efficiency. Such standardized information brings the market closer to perfect competition by making it easier for consumers to decide whether they are getting a good deal.

Second, for price-taking behavior to occur, sellers and buyers must be well informed about what all the sellers are charging. That means if any seller lowers its prices, buyers immediately know and flock there. Similarly, if a seller raises its price, buyers immediately know they have better alternatives, and they quickly leave.

Third, and perhaps most important, a market with perfect competition will typically have many sellers and many buyers. They don't all have to be in the same place, however. In national or global markets (defined in Chapter 2), buyers and sellers may be in different parts of the country or different parts of the world.

A market with perfect competition will typically have many sellers and many buyers.

In perfect competition, a profit-maximizing business will expand until its marginal cost equals the market price.

for Number 2 yellow corn (a particular grade of corn) was $7.21 per bushel.

Some manufactured products also trade in markets that are close to perfect competition, with many suppliers and many buyers, and standardized products. For example, memory chips for personal computers are made by many companies, the chips are standardized, and it's possible to find the current market price for memory chips of different sizes.

Examples of Perfect Competition

Most markets do not meet all three conditions of perfect competition. Products may not be standardized; one dress, for example, is not exactly like another. It may not be easy to compare prices charged by different suppliers. And there may be relatively few buyers or sellers; in any area there are usually few providers of cell phone service, for example.

However, in some ways today's economy is moving closer to perfect competition. As markets become global, individual businesses, no matter how large, are less able to affect prices. Buyers have access to many more potential suppliers—not just in their town or their state, but around the world. And many businesses in the United States have to worry about matching prices charged by Asian or European competitors.

Some markets that are close to perfect competition include basic foods such as wheat and corn. There are many suppliers and buyers in the United States and around the world, the products are standardized, and the current market price can be seen by anyone with access to a computer. For example, on March 28, 2011, the price

PROFIT MAXIMIZATION IN PERFECT COMPETITION

Remember from Chapter 4 that a profit-maximizing business increases production as long as its marginal revenue (MR) is greater than its marginal cost (MC). In perfect competition, the business can sell as much as it wants at the market price (P), so the marginal revenue from selling an extra unit of output is just equal to P.

In general, marginal cost rises as production increases. Thus in perfect competition, a profit-maximizing business will expand until its marginal cost equals the price (P = MC). Once we know the market price, we also know the level of production for the firm in perfect competition.

For example, a company producing low-end desktop computers today is in a market that's close to perfect competition because the machines' capabilities are so similar. Suppose the company can sell its computers for $500 each. Then it will produce up to the point where its marginal cost of producing the next computer is equal to $500 (see Table 5.1).

For an individual business in a competitive market, the supply curve is the same as the marginal cost curve. Look at Figure 5.1. To see how much the business will produce at a market price of $500, we find the point A where marginal cost is equal to $500. That gives us the profit-maximizing output of 4,000 units.

<table>
<tr><td>**TABLE 5.1**</td><td>**Marginal Cost and Marginal Revenue Schedule for a Computer Maker**</td></tr>
</table>

This table gives the marginal cost schedule for a computer maker. For example, the marginal cost of the 4,000th computer is $500.

Output (Number of Computers)	Marginal Cost (Dollars)	Marginal Revenue (Assuming the Market Price Is $500 per Computer) (Dollars)
1,000	$ 200	$ 500
2,000	$ 300	$ 500
3,000	$ 400	$ 500
4,000	$ 500	$ 500
5,000	$ 600	$ 500

As we saw in Chapter 2, the market supply curve is the sum of the individual supply curves. For example, if there are 10 identical businesses with the same marginal cost schedule shown in Table 5.1, then at each price the quantity supplied to the market will be 10 times the individual quantity supplied. Figure 5.2 shows the market supply curve. Note that at a market price of $500, the quantity supplied is 40,000 computers (10 × 4,000).

Market Equilibrium in Perfect Competition

As in any other market, equilibrium for a perfectly competitive market occurs where market quantity supplied equals market quantity demanded. At the market equilibrium, price equals the marginal cost of production for each business. If price were greater than the marginal cost, the business would have an incentive to expand production. If price were less than the marginal cost, the business would reduce production. As a result, all businesses end up producing at the same marginal cost, which is equal to the market price.

<table>
<tr><td>**FIGURE 5.1**</td><td>**Profit Maximization by a Single Business in a Competitive Market**</td></tr>
</table>

If the market price is $500 per computer, the profit-maximizing business expands to the point where marginal cost is equal to $500 (labeled *A*). This figure corresponds to the numbers in Table 5.1.

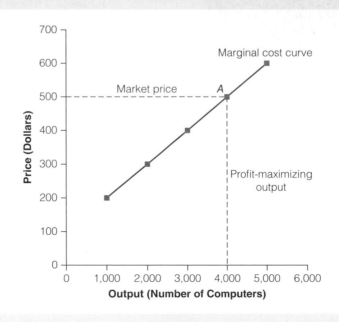

FIGURE 5.2 | Market Supply with 10 Identical Businesses

In perfect competition, all businesses in the market produce at the point where the market price equals marginal cost. In this case, with 10 businesses, each produces 4,000 computers.

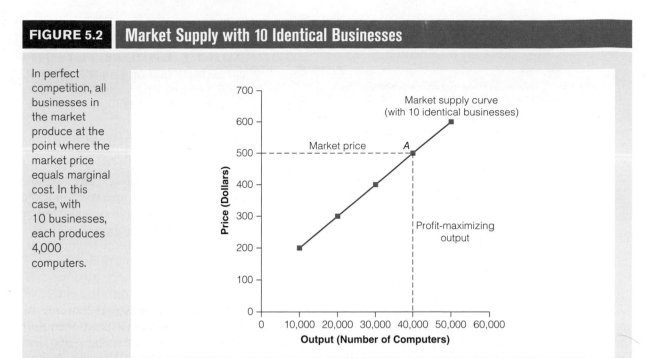

Let's stick with the example of the market for computers. Take a look at Figure 5.3, which shows the market supply curve that we have already seen in Figure 5.2. In addition, Figure 5.3 includes a possible market demand curve. The market equilibrium is the point *A* where quantity supplied equals quantity demanded—that is, the point where the two curves cross.

FIGURE 5.3 | Graphing Market Equilibrium

This graph corresponds to the supply and demand schedules shown in Table 5.2. Point *A* identifies the market equilibrium.

TABLE 5.2	An Example of a Market with Perfect Competition

In this market there are 10 suppliers, all of them price takers, with the marginal cost curve shown in Figure 5.1. The equilibrium for this market comes where the price is $500 per computer, and the quantities supplied and demanded are both 40,000.

Price (Dollars)	Quantity Demanded by All Buyers (Number of Computers)	Quantity Supplied by All Sellers (Number of Computers)
200	70,000	10,000
300	60,000	20,000
400	50,000	30,000
500	40,000	40,000
600	30,000	50,000

Table 5.2 shows the numbers corresponding to the supply and demand curves. At a market price of $500, the quantity demanded is 40,000 computers and so is the quantity supplied. But we know even more than that. Each of the 10 computer manufacturers produces 4,000 computers—and at that level of production, their marginal cost is $500, according to Table 5.1. In perfect competition, marginal cost is equal to the market price.

PERFECT COMPETITION IN THE LONG RUN

What happens in a competitive market in the long run? If businesses in a market are making a profit, those profits attract new entrants to the market, just as sugar attracts ants. **New entrants** are just what they sound like—new businesses competing in the same market, or existing businesses in other markets that are expanding into a new market. In fact, if there is nothing to stop them—such as government regulations or high start-up costs—a market will have new entrants as long as it looks profitable. Figure 5.4 shows how the market equilibrium changes with new entrants.

What happens when a new electronics store opens in a small town? Let's assume all the stores sell the same brand-name computers, big-screen digital televisions, video game machines, and iPods. Each new store increases the supply of electronics and causes the supply schedule to shift to the right. That drives down the price for everyone. Eventually profits fall low enough that no one else is willing to take the plunge and enter the market.

Let's call this the Big Squeeze. As more and more competitors move into a market, any business with a higher-than-average cost function gets forced out. For example, in the computer industry, companies that couldn't match a low-cost producer like Dell have been squeezed out. In retailing, Walmart's ability to consistently offer low prices has put the squeeze on higher-priced competitors. Eventually those that cannot make a profit are forced out of business.

Stores that cannot make a profit are forced out of business.

FIGURE 5.4   **New Entrants Drive Down the Market Price**

As new businesses enter a competitive market, the market supply curve shifts to the right, and the market price falls.

In a market with perfect competition, as long as there is enough time and there are no barriers to entry, profits will tend toward zero. A **barrier to entry** is anything that might make it difficult for a competitor to enter a market. For example, if Best Buy or Walmart wanted to open a new store in a town, it might need approval from the town government, especially if it needed a change in zoning laws. In this case government regulation is a barrier to entry. Another barrier to entry is the lack of a key resource. Perhaps not enough land is available in town to put up another big store, or it might take a long time for a large enough parcel of land to become available.

BARRIER TO ENTRY
Anything that makes it difficult for a new competitor to enter a market.

If there are no barriers to entry, only the lowest-cost businesses survive over the long run in a market with perfect competition.

Long-Term Survival

The Big Squeeze leads us to another implication of perfect competition. If there are no barriers to entry, only the lowest-cost producers survive over the long run. Let's suppose you'd like to buy a tuna sandwich from a local restaurant or some other store that sells food. You are therefore a buyer in the market for tuna sandwiches. Now suppose there are two types of restaurants. One type—the high-cost producers—can make a tuna sandwich at a marginal cost of $3 per sandwich (ingredients and labor). The second type of restaurant—the low-cost producers—can make the sandwich at a marginal cost of $2 (using the same ingredients but a much faster, more efficient sandwich-making technique).

Over the long run, the low-cost providers will consistently be able to drive down the price below $3, and at that price the high-cost providers won't be able to make a profit. After they lose enough money, they will have to close or adopt the same sandwich-making techniques as their rivals. Indeed, in the long run a market with perfect competition is driven by survival of the fittest.

This process by which the low-cost producers drive out the high-cost producers over the long run occurs in any industry in which there are no barriers to entry. Consider department stores. Remember Marshall Field's? How about Stern's? Or Bradlees? Probably not—but all these were department store chains that either closed or were sold between 2001 and 2006. That period saw massive consolidation in the department store industry—the result of intense competition from online retailers and discount chains such as Walmart and Target. Many existing retailers simply could not cut costs low enough to compete. As a result, employment at nondiscount department stores dropped by a stunning 23 percent over this period.

The long-run shift to low-cost producers is a central trend in manufacturing as well, especially for such products as basic clothing. As mentioned in Chapter 3, most apparel manufacturing has moved to low-cost countries like China and Vietnam because United States–based factories simply can't match the prices of the imports. More recently, furniture manufacturing has been moving to lower-cost producers overseas (see "Spotlight: The Furniture Industry").

SPOTLIGHT: THE FURNITURE INDUSTRY

Few parts of the U.S. economy have been affected so quickly or so completely by Chinese competition as the furniture industry. In 1998 the United States imported only $2 billion worth of furniture from China. By 2000 that number had risen to $5 billion, and by 2010 it was $17 billion.

U.S. furniture makers found themselves suddenly competing with literally thousands of Chinese furniture factories, all vying to offer anything furniture retailers wanted at the lowest possible cost. In 2006 the big furniture fair in Shanghai attracted 1,500 exhibitors and 10,000 international buyers, spread over two enormous buildings.

In effect, the market moved much closer to perfect competition. That benefited consumers because the price of furniture in the United States fell almost every year from 2000 to 2010. In particular, living room, dining room, and kitchen furniture became 13 percent cheaper.

The downside? The furniture manufacturing industry in the United States lost about 48 percent of its jobs over the same period. North Carolina has seen more than half of its furniture-making jobs disappear. Competition, foreign or domestic, is a tough taskmaster.

Source: Census Bureau, Bureau of Labor Statistics.

The Shutdown Decision

Not only do new businesses enter markets, but existing businesses also close down. Let's take a closer look at the **shutdown decision**—the decision of whether a business will keep operating. A shutdown decision involves closing a store, factory, or office and letting workers go. Usually the decision to shut down is irreversible, and it can seriously harm employees and the local community, depending on the size of the business.

Businesses shut down because their costs exceed their revenues. However, they don't make shutdown decisions simply because they lose money for one or two years. New businesses almost invariably lose money at first, and even many established companies record losses during economic downturns. For example, American Airlines reported big losses in 2008, 2009, and 2010, yet its planes continued to fly and carry passengers. Businesses shut down because it becomes clear that they are going to keep losing money—or they simply run out of cash to pay their bills.

Escaping Perfect Competition

Perfect competition is good for consumers because it drives down prices. But before finishing this section, let's note there's a force pushing against perfect competition over the long run. When businesses find themselves stuck in anything that looks like a perfectly competitive market, they try to escape it. They want to show potential customers that they are different and better than the competition in order to charge higher prices.

How can a business escape perfect competition? The best way is to build a better product—or at least do something that differentiates your product from those of your rivals. Consider, for example, the market for music players. When Apple introduced the first iPod in October 2001, there were already plenty of portable music players on the market. But Apple was able to differentiate itself through better design, a hard disk that stored a lot more songs, and an online music store that worked better than anyone else's. As a result, the iPod quickly became the market leader and the standard to beat.

Apple was able to differentiate its iPod from other portable media players on the market.

HOW IT WORKS: WELL-KNOWN BRAND NAMES

A well-known and respected brand name helps differentiate a product and allows a company to charge higher prices and earn higher profits than it could in perfect competition. In 2009 *BusinessWeek* published a list of the "most valuable" brands—that is, products whose brand names helped boost sales and profits. The list was led by Coca-Cola, IBM, Microsoft, GE, and Nokia. In all these cases the companies' names convey positive messages about their products and services.

Source: "100 Best Global Brands," *Businessweek,* September 28, 2009, www.businessweek.com/interactive_reports/best_global_brands_2009.html.

Another way to differentiate a product is through **advertising.** Advertising, of course, is paid communication with potential customers through a public medium, such as television, the Internet, a magazine, or a billboard. One role of advertising is to provide information about what a product does and how much it costs, but good advertising also has an emotional impact. It gives potential buyers a sense of comfort or excitement, along with a reason to buy. Advertising is especially valuable for brand names such as Crest, Tide, and Coke, to which consumers can become intensely loyal (see "How It Works: Well-Known Brand Names").

For example, if you go into a drugstore, you will find perhaps 40 different kinds of shampoo for men and women. They all accomplish the same thing—cleaning hair. However, they have different ingredients and perhaps different levels of effectiveness. They all have different brand names and brand images, aided by copious amounts of advertising. And unlike goods in a perfectly competitive market, they can sell for very different amounts, ranging from $2 to $20 for 16 ounces.

Some economists argue that consumer devotion to a well-advertised brand name is justified because all that advertising creates a reputation effect. This means a company that spends millions of dollars advertising a product—especially one that is used repeatedly like

shampoo or razors—will want to make sure its financial investment in the ad campaign will pay off and not be eroded by consumer complaints or well-publicized problems with the product. So economists argue that heavy advertising often means a product does indeed deliver what its producer promises. (By contrast, heavy advertising of a single-use product like a new movie may just be a way of getting people into the theater before they hear how bad the film is.)

MARKET STRUCTURE

If a market does not operate under perfect competition, how do we describe it? Economists have classified markets into several different types, or **market structures,** according to the number of buyers and sellers and the intensity of competition. Other than perfect competition, the main types of market structure are *monopolistic competition, oligopoly,* and *monopoly.*

MARKET STRUCTURE
A way of classifying markets according to the number of buyers and sellers and the intensity of compitition.

Monopolistic Competition

Perhaps the most common market structure in today's economy is **monopolistic competition.** This type of market is characterized by a large number of sellers with similar but not standardized products.

A good example of monopolistic competition consists of restaurants in a neighborhood. There may be 5 or 10 restaurants within a short distance of each other, all offering the basics—a meal and a clean place to sit. But some may be quiet, others noisy. Some may offer pizza, others Thai food. And some may be expensive while others serve meals for a few dollars.

> **MONOPOLISTIC COMPETITION**
> A situation where a large number of sellers offer similar but not standardized products.

These restaurants are competitors in the sense that they are all trying to attract the same pool of potential diners. However, it is not perfect competition—no market price applies to all the restaurants. Each offers a different meal or dining experience from the others, so each can charge a different price.

What's more, the restaurants are not price takers. If a restaurant lowers its prices, it knows it will take business away from the other restaurants and boost its number of diners. If it raises its prices, its quantity demanded will fall, but it will still keep the customers who really like its food. In other words, monopolistic competitors each face a downward-sloping demand curve.

PROFIT MAXIMIZATION WITH MONOPOLISTIC COMPETITION

The rule for profit maximization from Chapter 4 was that a business boosts output as long as marginal revenue exceeds marginal cost. For perfect competition, marginal revenue is equal to price because a business can sell as much as it wants at the market price.

But for a monopolistic competitor, marginal revenue is actually less than the price. The reason is that if the business wants to sell another unit of output, it will have to cut the price it is charging everyone. That means it will lose some revenue from the goods and services it was originally selling, even as it gets additional revenue from the added sales.

Think about a restaurant serving 100 meals a night at $20 each. To increase sales to 101 meals a night, it will have to lower the menu price of the meals below $20. It gets additional revenue from the extra meal, but it loses some from the lower price for the first hundred meals it was already selling.

Auto dealers face the same problem. Typically auto dealers are monopolistic competitors. They compete with other dealers in the same area selling other models of cars. The Ford dealer competes with the GM dealer and the Toyota

HOW IT WORKS: PERFORMERS AS MONOPOLISTIC COMPETITORS

Musicians and actors—or indeed any kind of performers—are great examples of monopolistic competition. Performers who play the same type of music—whether classic rock, hip-hop, or country—obviously compete for the same audience. Listeners have only a limited amount of money and time, and the more they spend on concerts and music downloads for one performer, the less money and time they have for others. If too many performers are giving concerts in the same city at the same time, it becomes harder for any of them to sell out their shows.

If the market for music were perfectly competitive, all performers would have to charge the same price for their concerts. (Or perhaps they would charge by the hour so that longer concerts would cost more!) And it wouldn't matter to you which performer you went to see.

In reality, performers do not produce a standardized product. No one would ever mistake Jason Mraz for Ke$ha (or substitute any two performers of your choice). So some performers can charge much higher prices than others without losing all their ticket sales.

TABLE 5.3	Marginal Revenue and Marginal Cost at a Car Dealer

A car dealer who is a monopolistic competitor knows that selling more cars requires lowering the price. The profit-maximizing output comes where marginal revenue equals marginal cost—in this example, at three cars sold per day.

Cars Sold per Day	Price per Car (Dollars)	Total Revenue (Dollars)	Marginal Revenue (Dollars)	Marginal Cost (Dollars)
1	30,000	30,000	30,000	24,000
2	29,000	58,000	28,000	25,000
3	28,000	84,000	26,000	26,000
4	27,000	108,000	24,000	27,000
5	26,000	130,000	22,000	28,000

dealer, who may be on the same block or even across the street.

To make things simple, imagine that the dealers post prices for the cars on their lots, and they have to offer these prices to everyone (there's no individual negotiation). The price each dealer picks depends on how many cars he or she wants to sell—that is, on the output of the dealership. To attract more customers, the dealer has to set a lower price, which lures customers away from the dealers across the street.

However, two things happen when a dealer sells one more car. The dealer gets the revenue from the additional car, but the lower price means he or she also has to give up a bit of revenue from the other cars that were already selling. As a result, the marginal revenue will be less than the price.

Table 5.3 gives an example of a revenue function, a marginal revenue function, and a marginal cost function for a car dealer. If the dealer sets the price at $30,000 per car, he or she can sell one car per day. But to sell two cars, the dealer must lower the price to $29,000 for both cars. How much extra revenue comes in? The original revenue from selling one car was $30,000. The revenue for the two cars is $29,000 per car, or $58,000 in total. Hence the marginal revenue is $28,000 ($58,000 minus $30,000).

So the marginal revenue from selling the second car ($28,000) is lower than the price ($29,000). You can see from the table that's true at every level of sales—the marginal revenue is less than the price.

How many cars will the dealer sell? The dealer will expand output until marginal revenue equals marginal cost. In this example, the profit-maximizing output is three cars sold per day.

MONOPOLISTIC COMPETITION IN THE LONG RUN

Generally monopolistic competitors compete not only on price but also on other attributes of their products. For example, restaurants may try to distinguish themselves by quality of food or by friendliness of service. The more successful they are in differentiating themselves positively from their rivals, the more they can escape perfect competition, and the more they can raise their prices without fear of losing customers.

But here's a big problem for a business in monopolistic competition: if you successfully differentiate yourself from your competitor, what's to stop your competitor, or a new entrant, from imitating you? Suppose you run a restaurant, and you have been successful with your "Hawaiian Pizza." For a while that draws big crowds, but soon the other restaurants in town are offering their own versions, and your competitive edge disappears.

In the long run, monopolistic competition starts looking more and more like perfect competition as more businesses enter the market. The big challenge for successful businesses is to continually come up with new ways of defending their competitive advantage or creating new points of difference.

In fact, this is one of the great advantages of a market economy. The pressure to escape perfect competition forces successful companies to devote considerable resources to creating new products and services or to refining and upgrading their existing ones. In a market economy, standing still is a sure way to lose ground.

Oligopoly

Oligopoly occurs when a small number of sellers in a market produce similar products. (*Small* is usually defined in this context as four or fewer.) In most cities, for example, there are only two or three wireless telephone service companies. And except for the most heavily traveled routes, most cities are served by only a few air carriers. These suppliers are oligopolists.

In some situations, oligopolists can compete intensely. They can wage price wars to lure each other's customers away. Such intense rivalry can make an oligopoly look much like perfect competition, at least for a time.

Alternatively, two or more oligopolists can engage in illegal **collusion,** working together to keep the prices of their products artificially high and to split the market. For instance, two local drugstores could agree that they'll both sell shampoos or tissues at a higher price and neither will try to undercut the other.

Sometimes oligopolists engage in **implicit collusion.** That means they do not communicate directly about price; however, they let one company—the market leader—set prices in the market. Whatever price the leader sets, the others follow. For example, two or three airlines may fly between the same two cities. When one airline raises ticket prices by $10, the other two follow immediately. This is not officially collusion, but it has the same

OLIGOPOLY
A market containing a small number of sellers producing similar products.

MONOPOLY
A market in which there is only one seller, and buyers have no good alternatives.

effect of keeping prices higher than they would otherwise be.

In practice, however, it's difficult for oligopolists to collude effectively without talking to each other. There will always be temptation for one party to cheat, which means undercutting the oligopoly price by a bit to sell a lot more. Supplier cheating in an oligopoly actually benefits consumers by lowering prices.

Monopoly

At the opposite extreme from perfect competition is a **monopoly.** A monopoly is a market in which there is only one seller, and buyers have no good alternatives. As you might expect, a profit-maximizing monopolist will push up its price to take advantage of its control over the market. If you own the only gas station for miles around, you can charge more than if you face a lot of competition.

But to charge a higher price, a monopolist has to restrict its output. That's because buyers generally obey the law of demand—higher prices mean lower quantity demanded. Because quantity supplied equals quantity demanded in equilibrium, higher prices mean supply has to be reduced.

How high can a monopolist raise prices? It depends in part on the elasticity of market demand, as defined in Chapter 3. If demand is inelastic—that is, if buyers don't react much to price changes—then the monopolist can raise the price high above the competitive level. Suppose on an island only one store sells food. This store can push prices up a lot because there are no alternatives for food buyers.

But in a monopolistic market in which demand is elastic, consumers will significantly reduce

Economic Milestone

1960 BIGGEST OLIGOPOLY FOUNDED

The title of the biggest oligopoly goes to OPEC, the Organization of Petroleum Exporting Countries. OPEC started with 5 members and now has 13, led by Saudi Arabia, which has one-fourth of the world's proven oil reserves. OPEC members meet regularly to set the price of oil and to allocate quotas for how much each country will produce. However, several large oil-exporting countries, including Russia, Norway, and Mexico, are not part of OPEC.

their purchases when prices go up even a little. Then the monopolist won't be able to boost prices much above the competitive level. For example, suppose you have exclusive rights to sell something few people want, such as land in the middle of the desert. Your monopoly on the land won't do you much good; if you try to raise prices much above the competitive level, your potential buyers will look elsewhere.

True monopolies are even harder to find than markets with perfect competition. For example, the National Basketball Association is the only professional men's basketball league in the United States, so it has a monopoly on providing professional men's basketball games. But there are plenty of close substitutes for your sports entertainment dollar, including women's professional basketball, other major league men's sports, and college games. For that reason, there's a limit to how far NBA teams can raise their ticket prices despite their monopoly power in men's basketball.

Most monopolies have been undermined, to a large extent, by globalization and technology. The local department store in a small town, which once was the main source of clothing and hardware, now faces competition from online sellers such as Amazon.com that ship anywhere in the world. People have access to nearly infinite sources of news, classified ads, and other information, rather than just the local newspaper. And even when only one company manufactures a product in a country (Boeing is the only manufacturer of commercial airliners in the United States), it is not a monopoly because it must contend with competition from overseas companies, like Airbus.

Even so-called natural monopolies have been eaten away by technological change. A **natural monopoly** is an industry in which it may make economic sense to have only one supplier. The classic example is the old AT&T (known originally as American Telephone & Telegraph), which for most of the 20th century was the sole provider of telephone service to most of the United States. At that time, all telephones had to be physically connected to each other by wires that ran from people's homes to central switching offices. That was an expensive investment; once the wires were installed, it didn't cost the phone company much to provide the service.

Moreover, everyone had to be tied into the same network. As a result, it didn't make economic sense to have more than one provider of telephone service.

Today, of course, there are multiple sources of telephone service in your home. You can use a cell phone, get your phone service from your cable company, or make calls over the Internet. As a result, the conditions for a natural monopoly no longer exist.

Other natural monopolies used to include the local electric power company, cable company, and water company. These all shared two characteristics with the old telephone company. First, they had large *fixed costs* for infrastructure (wires, pipes, power stations, water filtration equipment) and low *variable costs* for providing service. Second, customers had to be tied into physical networks, so they could not easily switch.

Technological advances have made it possible to choose which company generates the electricity you use, even though there is still generally only one supply conduit to your home. And you can get your television shows from the local cable company, the local phone company, or a satellite TV company.

The 1990s witnessed wide debate about whether technology was creating new natural monopolies. Microsoft, in particular, seemed to control two large markets. Microsoft Windows had a very large share of the operating system market for personal computers, and Microsoft Office dominated the market for word processing, spreadsheets, and other business productivity programs. What's more, these markets seemed to have the two characteristics essential for a natural monopoly: there were high fixed costs to develop the software, making it difficult for a new company to enter into the market, and customers were generally locked into their software (people within the same company all had to use Microsoft Office so their documents would be compatible).

Yet technological change is gradually eroding Microsoft's commanding position. The focus of digital innovation has gradually shifted from the computer to the Internet. Google, in particular, has a huge share of the market for online search, which in the future may turn out to be as important as the desktop operating system.

Still, probably the easiest way to keep a monopoly these days is to have the government protect it for you. For example, the post office still has a monopoly on home delivery of first-class mail. The fact that many areas are served by only one cable company is the result of a government licensing procedure that acts like monopoly protection.

PERFECT COMPETITION VERSUS MARKET POWER

Why have we made such a big deal about the difference between perfect competition and other types of market structure? Why does it matter how many competitors are in a market and whether they are price takers?

The Benefits of Perfect Competition

The essence of a market economy is that all economic activities in a market are voluntary. Businesses choose to produce and sell because they benefit by earning the highest profit possible. Buyers make purchases because the value of the goods or services to them is greater than the prices they pay. In a market, all trades of money for goods and services are mutually beneficial—both buyers and sellers win.

But perfect competition goes further. In a market with perfect competition, businesses are price takers. As long as the market price exceeds the marginal cost, businesses automatically choose to increase output. To put this another way, as long as buyers are willing to pay enough to cover the extra costs of production, suppliers will oblige them.

To better understand the benefits of perfect competition, think again about that tuna sandwich you might buy at a local restaurant. Suppose you are willing to pay $3 or less for it. Now suppose its marginal cost—the cost of the ingredients and of the cook's time to make it—is only $2.50. As long as the price of the sandwich is between $2.50 and $3.00, the restaurant can profitably sell the sandwich, and you will be willing to buy it.

In perfect competition, that tuna sandwich will always be made and eaten. If a restaurant is not willing to make it for you, the one next door will. In essence, that's what perfect competition means—there are plenty of potential suppliers.

This idea holds not just for sandwiches but for any other type of good or service sold in perfect competition. Perhaps you want to buy an office chair. As long as the marginal cost of producing that chair is less than the price you are willing to pay, in perfect competition you will be able to find a business willing to make and sell the chair to you.

The Downsides of Market Power

A profit-maximizing monopolist will always charge a higher price than a perfect competitor would. More generally, monopoly, monopolistic competition, and oligopoly all feature sellers with some degree of **market power**. Market power is the ability to raise prices above the level that perfect competition would produce—by restricting the quantity supplied.

Higher prices and lower quantities supplied lead to higher profits for a business with market power. These higher prices hurt customers, of course. What's more, businesses with market power have to artificially hold down production and sales to keep up their prices.

Let's examine the general problem of market power using Figure 5.5. In perfect competition, suppliers and buyers reach the market equilibrium *A* where price equals marginal cost. Now let's suppose suppliers have some degree of market power. They band together and raise the price a bit to boost their profits. Buyers cut back on purchases because of the higher price (the result of a downward-sloping demand curve). The new market equilibrium is point *B* on the graph, and the new quantity supplied is less than the original quantity supplied.

Suppose a town has lots of restaurants engaged in cutthroat competition. As a result, the restaurants price their meals low at their marginal cost (which is the cost of the ingredients in the meals plus the labor required to prepare and serve them). Everyone in this town, even relatively poor people, can afford to eat out once a

FIGURE 5.5 | Comparing Market Power and Perfect Competition

In perfect competition, market equilibrium occurs at point A. When businesses have market power, they can charge a price higher than the price with perfect competition, pushing the market to point B and reducing the amount produced and sold.

week. The restaurants are not making much money—just enough to stay in business. This is point A in the diagram.

Now imagine that the restaurant owners get together and agree to raise the prices they charge for their meals. So instead of charging $10 for dinner, they charge $15. What happens? In the diagram, the new market equilibrium corresponds to point B. The poorer people in this town stop eating out. The middle class eats out less often. The number of meals served drops a lot.

The restaurant owners are making more money—or they wouldn't have raised their prices. The people of the town are worse off—paying more and eating out less. But perhaps most important, dinners that could have been served aren't. This decrease in production and consumption represents a real loss to society.

There are other downsides to market power. Because it can make higher profits, a business with market power has little incentive to make the best possible cost-minimizing decisions. In other words, it can use some of its market power to pay higher wages. Alternately, the business can let its employees work less hard or take longer vacations. Market power can make work easier

SPOTLIGHT: THE AUTO INDUSTRY

For many years after World War II, the Big Three automakers—GM, Ford, and Chrysler—controlled the U.S. auto market. They were able to keep prices high enough to earn good profits and often made local car dealers wealthy. Autoworkers did well too. They were among the best-paid factory workers, with generous benefit packages that included free healthcare even after retirement.

The market power of U.S. automakers began disappearing in the 1970s, when competition arrived in the form of Toyota and other foreign automakers selling small, fuel-efficient cars that the Big Three didn't have. Detroit's market power gradually ebbed, and the Big Three could no longer boost prices as fast as overall inflation. In fact, from 1994 to 2007, the average price of new vehicles sold in the United States didn't rise at all, which benefited car buyers. Finally, the Great Recession sent both Chrysler and General Motors into bankruptcy. The market power of U.S. automakers had vanished.

Source: Bureau of Labor Statistics.

for managers and workers—but it may not be the best thing for society.

True, businesses with market power have sometimes used their high profits to research new products and technologies with long-term payoffs. The classic example is the old AT&T, which had a near-monopoly on telephone service in the United States until 1982. It used its powerful position to do some of the most important research in the country such as the invention of the transistor and the laser. Businesses with market power have also been big contributors to charity and cultural institutions—once again drawing on their higher profits.

Nevertheless, most economists believe that an economy with more competition performs better in the sense that it has higher production levels and lower costs. As we proceed through this textbook, we will return to this theme.

CONCLUSION

This chapter could be summarized with the phrase "why competition among sellers is (usually) a good thing for buyers." Competition yields lower prices and more production. Lack of competition leads to higher prices and, sometimes, a lack of incentives for businesses to try as hard as they might.

Yet there are economic situations for which competition and markets are not the right solution. That's why the next chapter is devoted to the role of government in the economy.

05   SUMMARY

1. In perfect competition, buyers and sellers are price takers. Perfect competition is more likely if products are standardized, if buyers and sellers are well informed about what other sellers charge, and if there are many buyers and sellers. *(LO5-1)*

2. In perfect competition, a profit-maximizing business will set its output level so that price (P) is equal to marginal cost (MC). *(LO5-2)*

3. In a market with perfect competition and no barriers to entry, profits will tend toward zero in the long run. New entrants will come in and drive down prices. Only the lowest-cost businesses will survive over the long run. Businesses with higher costs will shut down if they keep losing money. Businesses try to escape perfect competition by differentiating their products from those of their rivals. *(LO5-3)*

4. Perfect competition is just one type of market structure. The other types are monopolistic competition, oligopoly, and monopoly. Monopolistic competition is characterized by many sellers with similar but not standardized products. Oligopoly features a few sellers with similar products. Monopoly has one seller with no good alternatives for buyers. *(LO5-4)*

5. In monopolistic competition, profit-maximizing businesses choose an output level so that marginal revenue (MR) equals marginal cost (MC). Prices in markets with monopolistic competition are often driven down in the long run by the entry of other competitors. *(LO5-4)*

6. A business with a monopoly will also choose an output level so that marginal revenue equals marginal cost. That means a higher price and a lower quantity supplied and demanded than in a comparable market with perfect competition. This is true whenever businesses have market power. *(LO5-4)*

7. In general, markets that are closer to perfect competition perform better than markets where suppliers have more market power. As markets have more competition, production rises and costs fall over the long run. *(LO5-5)*

KEY TERMS AND CONCEPTS

perfect competition	shutdown decision	implicit collusion
competitive market	advertising	monopoly
price takers	market structure	natural monopoly
standardized product	monopolistic competition	market power
new entrants	oligopoly	
barrier to entry	collusion	

PROBLEMS

1. Answer the following questions. *(LO5-1)*

    a) Are standardized products easy to compare, hard to compare, or high-priced?

    b) Are markets with one or two sellers more likely to be perfectly competitive, less likely to be perfectly competitive, or more likely to be innovative?

    c) In a perfectly competitive market, do buyers and sellers need information about prices so they can identify cheaters, gain market power, or find the best deal?

2. Consider the following products. For each one, identify whether the market has one, few, or many sellers. *(LO5-1)*

    a) Apples in the grocery store.

    b) Plane tickets from New York to Seattle.

    c) Tickets to a professional football game in your town.

    d) Passenger train service.

3. The following table shows the cost function for a business producing beach chairs. *(LO5-2)*

Quantity of Beach Chairs Produced (Number)	Total Cost (Dollars)	Marginal Cost (Dollars)
0	3	–
1	13	?
2	24	?
3	36	?
4	49	?
5	63	?

a) Fill in the column for marginal cost.

b) Assume the business is operating under conditions of perfect competition. If the market price is $14 per chair, how many chairs does the business produce? What is the total profit of the business?

c) If the market price is $13 per chair, how many chairs does the business produce? What is the total profit of the business?

4. The following table shows the maximum amount five potential buyers are willing to pay for a car. *(LO5-2)*

	Maximum Amount He or She Would Pay for the Car
Buyer 1	$40,000
Buyer 2	$35,000
Buyer 3	$30,000
Buyer 4	$25,000
Buyer 5	$20,000

a) What is the quantity demanded if cars sell for $30,000 each?

b) Under conditions of perfect competition, how many cars are bought if the marginal cost of producing a car is $25,000?

c) How many cars are bought if the marginal cost of producing a car falls to $20,000?

5. There are 15 hair salons in town, and the local haircut market is operating under conditions of perfect competition. *(LO5-3)*

a) What happens to the market supply curve in the short run if one of the hair salons goes out of business?

b) What happens to the price of haircuts sold?

c) What happens to the number of haircuts sold?

6. Someone wants to open a new restaurant in town. Identify which of the following would be a barrier to entry. Explain. *(LO5-3)*

a) None of the available property in town is zoned for business use.

b) The price of tablecloths has risen.

c) Consumers buy only from businesses they know.

d) The town requires all businesses to pay a hefty annual permit fee.

e) The town requires new businesses to pay a hefty permit fee.

7. You are running a restaurant under conditions of monopolistic competition. For each of the following situations, explain whether the demand schedule you face shifts right, shifts left, or stays the same. *(LO5-4)*

a) Another restaurant opens across the street.

b) You advertise in the local newspaper.

c) You develop a tasty new dish that appeals to the local population.

8. A small business makes 1970s-style lava lamps. There aren't many competitors. The business can sell the first few lamps for $30 each, but the business owners have found that they need to reduce the price if they want to sell more. *(LO5-4)*

Number of Lava Lamps Sold	Price	Revenue	Marginal Revenue
10	$30	?	
20	$25	?	?
30	$23	?	?
40	$21	?	?
50	$19	?	?

a) Fill in the table with the revenue and marginal revenue for each level of output. (Marginal revenue is calculated here as the change in revenue divided by the change in quantity sold.)

b) Suppose the marginal cost of making each lamp is $14. How many lamps should the business make to get the highest profit?

9. The following table shows the maximum amount five potential car buyers are willing to pay for each level of sales. Suppose that the cars are being sold by a car dealer operating as a monopoly (perhaps because there are no other car dealers in the market). *(LO5-4)*

	Maximum Amount He or She Would Pay for the Car
Buyer 1	$40,000
Buyer 2	$35,000
Buyer 3	$30,000
Buyer 4	$25,000
Buyer 5	$20,000

a) What is the revenue if the price of the car is $30,000?

b) If the marginal cost of each car is $20,000, how many cars will the monopolistic car dealer want to sell? What will the price be?

c) How many cars will be sold in perfect competition?

10. In November 2010, Google had almost 64 percent of all online searches, according to comScore, an Internet tracking company. By comparison, Yahoo! and Microsoft had only 19 percent and 11 percent respectively. *(LO5-5)*

   a) Clearly Google is the choice of many people for searching. If Google started charging for searches, would demand for its services go down a lot or a little?

   b) Does Google have market power in the market for searches, as defined in this chapter?

   c) Google does charge advertisers for placing their ads next to related searches. For example, if you search for "Toyota," you will see car-related ads. Do you think Google has market power in the market for advertising?

   d) Suppose Google had 100 percent of the online search market (perhaps by buying up Microsoft and Yahoo!). Would Google be able to raise the price it charges advertisers? Explain.

11. In general, as markets have _____ *(LO5-5)*

   a) more competition, production rises, and costs fall over the long run.

   b) less competition, production falls, and costs fall over the long run.

   c) more competition, production falls, and costs fall over the long run.

   d) less competition, production rises, and costs rise over the long run.

06 GOVERNMENT AND THE ECONOMY

LEARNING OBJECTIVES

After reading this chapter, you should be able to:

LO6-1 Discuss the changes in the economic role of the government over time, including the New Deal and deregulation.

LO6-2 Explain the benefits of government action.

LO6-3 Describe the limits and downsides of government action.

LO6-4 List and illustrate circumstances in which government intervention in the economy may be useful.

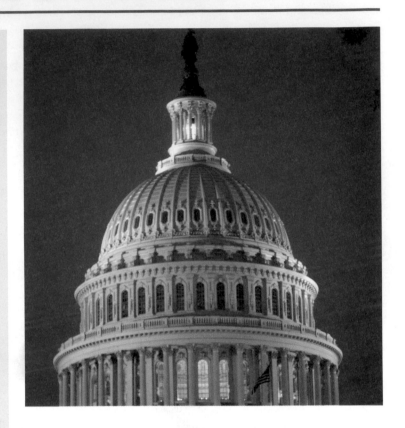

In March 2010 President Barack Obama signed legislation to reform the entire United States healthcare system. The goals were admirable: to provide health care coverage for many uninsured Americans and to hold down medical costs.

But to accomplish these goals, the government had to take a much more active role in guiding and controlling the healthcare system, including requiring most people to purchase some sort of insurance. The legislation was intensely controversial as soon as Obama proposed it, in large part because many opponents objected to the increased role of government. Indeed, voter opposition to the healthcare legislation helped the Republican Party win back control of the House of Representatives in the November 2010 election.

The fight over healthcare reform is just one example of a long-running debate: how big a role should the government play in the economy?

Generally economists start from the belief that markets are innocent until proven guilty. That is, providing goods and services through the **private sector**—which includes privately owned businesses—is preferable to taking government action unless there's a good reason to think otherwise. Big Macs should be sold by McDonald's, not by the U.S. government. Similarly, it would be absurd to expect that consumer electronics—iPods, big-screen TVs, and the like—should be sold or subsidized by the government.

But it's also true that markets alone are not enough: every successful country has a large **public sector.** In the United States the public sector includes the federal, state, and local levels of government, which collect taxes, employ workers, allocate money, regulate industries, and participate actively in the economy. The public sector provides goods and services such as national defense and police. After all, no one would seriously contemplate the idea of a nuclear weapon being privately owned.

However, the right place to draw the line between the public and private sectors is often the subject of vehement debate. Should passenger trains be partly funded by the government, as they are in the United States and in most European countries, or should train transportation be left to the private sector? Should state governments run liquor stores, as they do in Pennsylvania and Utah? And should the federal government be able to regulate the gas mileage of sport utility vehicles?

Then there's the government response to the Great Recession. After the financial crisis hit, the federal government took a very active role in propping up the economy and the financial system. As one example, the government bailed out General Motors and Chrysler, propping up the ailing automakers with loans and direct aid until they could get back on their feet again. (In Chapter 11 we'll examine fiscal policy during the Great Recession, and in Chapter 18 we'll take a closer look at healthcare reform.)

In this chapter we'll explore the history of government intervention in the economy. We'll consider the advantages and disadvantages of the public sector. Then we'll explore the different justifications for a public sector role in the economy, including public goods, externalities, regulation, and redistribution,

HISTORICAL BACKGROUND

When you go to bed tonight, take a close look at your mattress. Your bedding has been regulated by the federal government for nearly 30 years under the Flammable Fabrics Act. The U.S. Consumer Product Safety Commission (CPSC) administers this standard, giving detailed directions for manufacturers to test each mattress for resistance to burning when exposed to cigarettes. For example, the standard specifies how many cigarettes will be used to test for flammability, exactly how they should be placed, and how badly a mattress can be charred and still pass the test. The standard even explains what testers should do if a test mattress ignites (see "Spotlight: The Cigarette Test for Mattresses"). An additional regulation, approved by the CPSC commissioners in 2006, ensures that new mattresses will be less likely to burst into flames when exposed to candles or matches.

Or consider your car, which has to meet a long list of federal and state regulations. The gas mileage it gets, the pollution that comes out of its tailpipe, the composition of the gasoline in its tank, the seatbelt that fits securely around you—all are influenced or controlled by government action. The National Highway Traffic Safety Administration, for example, has a 76-page manual describing how rearview mirrors are to be placed and tested. Measuring "roof crush resistance" rates a 35-page manual. And let's not forget that the highways and streets

SPOTLIGHT: THE CIGARETTE TEST FOR MATTRESSES

Through the Consumer Product Safety Commission, the government gives precise instructions for how the potential flammability of mattresses should be tested. Here's one example:

> In the interest of safety, the test operator should discontinue the test and record a failure before reaching the 2 inch (5.1 cm) char length if an obvious ignition has occurred. If an ignition has occurred, immediately wet the exposed area with water, cut around the burning material with a knife or scissors and pull the material out of the mattress prototype with tongs. Make sure that all charred or burned material is removed. Ventilate the room.

Source: Consumer Product Safety Commission, www.cpsc.gov/businfo/testmatt.pdf, downloaded 12/19/2010.

you ride on are almost all built and maintained by local or state governments, using tax dollars or the proceeds from tolls.

You can't avoid government regulation when you go to the bank or use your credit card. Your deposits are insured by the Federal Deposit Insurance Corporation up to $250,000, so your money is safe even if your bank goes under. The Federal Reserve regulates how the bank processes your canceled checks, including whether it is obliged to provide you with paper copies. The new Consumer Financial Protection Bureau and the Federal Trade Commission help protect you against abusive practices by lenders. And of course the $10 and $20 bills you use are printed by the Bureau of Engraving and Printing, which is part of the Treasury Department.

Finally, higher education is a mixture of private and public, with the public predominating. About 75 percent of college students attend public institutions: four-year or two-year colleges that are funded and run primarily by state and local governments. Even at many private institutions, a significant chunk of funding comes from public sources.

The Great Depression and the New Deal

Today the hand of the government is apparent in every corner of the economy. But if we look back about 80 years or so, we see a much different world in which the government played a considerably smaller role. The dividing line was 1929—the year the Great Depression began. We'll discuss this period in more detail in Chapter 10, which covers the ups and downs of the business cycle. However, the key point is that economic conditions were so bad during the Depression that everyone was hoping the government could help. At the low point, one of every four workers was out of a job. There were widespread bank failures, the collapse of crop prices sent many farmers into bankruptcy, and it looked like the entire economy was about to come to a shuddering halt.

As a result, after President Franklin Roosevelt was elected in 1932, businesses and voters demanded that the federal government do something—anything—to get the economy moving again. In an amazingly short span of time the Roosevelt administration passed a flurry of legislation to help U.S. families and businesses. This collection of public programs to alleviate economic suffering was called the **New Deal.**

Before 1929 the government played a much smaller role in the economy.

The New Deal included almost any program the Roosevelt administration thought might work. For example, the Works Progress Administration, approved in 1935, was designed to put the unemployed to work building bridges, highways, and airport landing fields, as well as painting murals on public buildings. At its peak the WPA employed 3.4 million people, or more than 5 percent of the total labor force.

The WPA and similar New Deal work programs faded away as the economy gradually recovered at the end of the 1930s. However, many New Deal programs became a permanent part of the economic landscape and are still

TABLE 6.1	**Legacies of the New Deal**

Many government programs begun under the New Deal are still with us today, including Social Security.

Program Created during New Deal	What It Does Today
Social Security	Financial support for the elderly
Unemployment insurance	Financial support for the unemployed
Securities and Exchange Commission	Protection for stock market investors
Federal Deposit Insurance Corporation	Protection for bank depositors from bank failures
Federal minimum wage	Minimum wage for workers
Ban on child labor	Tight restrictions on children being forced to work
Welfare for dependent mothers and children	Financial support for poor families

with us today. Social Security, for example, was a New Deal program. So were unemployment insurance, the federal minimum wage, and the Federal Deposit Insurance Corporation (see Table 6.1).

The Era of Government Growth

The Depression and its subsequent economic recovery were followed by World War II, which pushed government spending and employment even higher as the United States geared up for war against Japan and Germany. After the war ended in 1945, government spending and employment dropped, but they did not return to their low pre-1929 levels (see Figure 6.1). In fact, after a short pause in the late 1940s, the government's role in the economy gradually expanded through the 1950s, 1960s, and 1970s.

It is interesting that during these three decades, the expansion of government's economic roles took place during the terms of both Republican and Democratic presidents. For example, the interstate highway program was started by President Dwight Eisenhower, a Republican who took office in 1953. Under this program, the federal government poured huge sums of money into one of the largest public works projects in history, eventually leading to the construction of almost 50,000 miles of high-speed, limited-access highways.

Eisenhower's successor, President John F. Kennedy, a Democrat who took office in 1961, did not stint on spending either. This is what Kennedy said in a May 1961 speech:

> I believe that this nation should commit itself to achieving the goal, before this decade is out, of landing a man on the moon and returning him safely to the earth....This decision demands a major national commitment of scientific and technical manpower, materiel and facilities, and the possibility of their diversion from other important activities where they are already thinly spread.

The manned space program Kennedy started *was* expensive and required an enormous commitment of people and resources. In fact, between 1961 and 1972 the federal government spent as much on space exploration as it did on building highways.

President Lyndon B. Johnson, a Democrat who became president when Kennedy was assassinated in 1963, made his mark with the Great Society programs, which were designed to help poor Americans. These included Head Start, which funds early childhood education for low-income children; Medicare, which provides medical care for senior citizens; and Medicaid, which does the same for poor Americans.

Under Johnson, the federal government also increased its involvement in other ways. This period saw the creation of the National Endowment

FIGURE 6.1 | **Government's Share of Employment**

The federal, state, and local governments employed about 10 percent of all workers in 1929. The government share of employment skyrocketed during World War II, going as high as 31 percent in 1944 and 1945, including military. In 2009 government employed roughly 18 percent of all workers.

Source: Bureau of Economic Analysis.

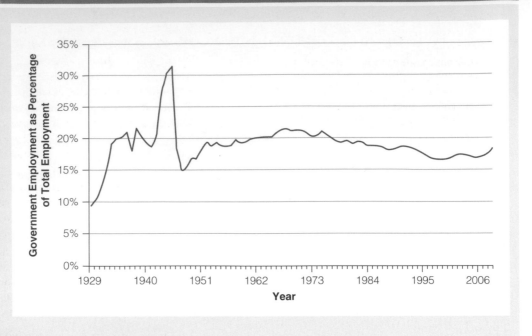

for the Arts and the National Endowment for the Humanities, two government agencies that fund artistic and cultural projects. Johnson also signed legislation authorizing the nonprofit, government-funded television and radio networks, Public Broadcasting Service (PBS) and National Public Radio (NPR). (Today PBS still receives a substantial portion of its revenue from the government, whereas NPR receives little government funding.) When Richard Nixon, a Republican, took over as president in 1969, government involvement in the economy continued to grow. Nixon signed legislation approving the creation of the Environmental Protection Agency (EPA), which focuses on preserving the environment; the Occupational Safety and Health Administration, which monitors and improves worker safety; and the Equal Employment Opportunity Commission, which tries to reduce labor market discrimination. (Labor market discrimination will be discussed in Chapter 17. The economics of the environment will be discussed in Chapter 19.)

Perhaps most notably, Nixon aggressively used the power of government to control rapid price

Landing a person on the moon required large government expenditures.

and wage increases. In an August 1971 speech he said the following:

> I am today ordering a freeze on all prices and wages throughout the United States for a period of 90 days. In addition, I call upon corporations to extend the wage–price freeze to all dividends.
>
> I have today appointed a Cost of Living Council within the government. I have directed this council to work with leaders of labor and business to set up the proper mechanism for achieving continued price and wage stability after the 90-day freeze is over.

This was an amazing exercise of government control over the economy. The federal government actually told businesses what prices they could charge, and it told unions what wages they could ask for. These directives would be almost inconceivable today.

The mid-1970s saw the beginning of the era of deregulation, when the role of government in the economy was reduced.

The Era of Deregulation

Starting in the mid-1970s, the public began to feel that government interference in the economy had gone far enough. The defining moment was the **oil price shock** of 1973. In October of that year, the Organization of Petroleum Exporting Countries (OPEC) put an embargo on oil shipments to the United States and several European countries that supported Israel. The result of the cutback in oil supplies was, not surprisingly, a sharp run-up in the price of gasoline and other petroleum products, which is exactly what you'd expect from a competitive market.

Americans, long used to low gasoline prices, had a strong negative reaction. President Nixon and Congress, then run by the Democratic party, responded quickly, but everything the government tried to do seemed to make things worse. For example, the government implemented odd–even gasoline rationing. If your license plate ended in an odd digit, you could buy gasoline only on odd-numbered days.

This rationing plan seemed to make sense, but in practice it worked badly. Because drivers wanted to make sure they didn't run out of gas, they started trying to keep more gasoline in their tanks than usual. Thus the demand for gasoline actually grew. And because people were scared of running out of gas on the "wrong" days, motorists made sure to stop at a service station on their "right" days. As a result, gasoline stations were likely to have long lines of customers and sometimes to run out of fuel.

At the same time, the economy turned sluggish, and consumer prices rose a lot. Americans began to feel the United States had taken the wrong path—not just in response to the oil embargo, but more generally. President Jimmy Carter, a Democrat, made the first attempts at **deregulation**—the reduction of government control over markets. In particular, he rolled back government oversight of the airline and trucking industries. The Airline Deregulation Act of 1978 allowed existing airlines to change fares, abandon old routes, and start new ones without asking for government permission. New airlines could enter the industry as well, subject only to safety regulations.

However, the antigovernment movement did not get into full swing until the 1980 election of Republican President Ronald Reagan. In his first term Reagan dramatically cut personal taxes, reduced government spending on job training programs, and generally tried to restrict the government's role in the economy. Philosophically, the idea at the time was that less government was better.

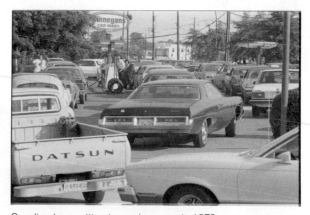

Cars lined up waiting to purchase gas in 1973.

Here's one example of deregulation. From 1933 to 1980 a government rule—called "Regulation Q"—had put a ceiling on the interest rates banks could pay on savings and checking accounts. That artificially limited the interest rates small depositors could get: if a bank wanted to offer a high interest rate on its savings accounts, it wasn't allowed to do so.

In 1980 Congress—then controlled by Democrats—passed legislation that called for the elimination of interest rate ceilings, but it did not give a timetable for doing so. The Reagan administration aggressively took up this mandate, and by 1986 virtually all interest rate ceilings were a thing of the past.

Still, for all the deregulation, the antigovernment movement was a slow and moderate one rather than a revolution. Take another look at Figure 6.1. In the mid-1970s the government employed about 19 percent of the total workforce, the high-water market for public sector hiring in the past half century. In 2009 government employed 18 percent of the U.S. workforce; this is a drop, but is still way above the pre-Depression level.

Over the past 20 years we've seen what's essentially a stand-off between supporters of an increased role for the public sector and those who think the public sector should shrink. Indeed, this public debate looks much like a territorial battle between two neighboring countries, in which the border shifts back and forth without much real change.

International Comparisons

Among industrialized countries, the United States has one of the smallest public sectors when we measure the ratio of government spending to the size of the economy. In 2009 during the Great Recession U.S. government spending at all levels was 43 percent of gross domestic product according to the International Monetary Fund. (Remember from Chapter 1 that gross domestic product, or GDP, measures how much an entire economy produces.) In contrast, the three biggest European economies—Germany, France, and the United Kingdom—have government spending that exceeds 45 percent of GDP, as shown in Figure 6.2. In part that's because these governments handle most of the healthcare spending for the countries. They also tend to offer more generous government benefits for citizens, such as better unemployment insurance.

Still, all the industrialized countries, without exception, qualify as **mixed economies;** that is, they are mainly market-based but also include a significant role for government. Moreover, the most successful developing economy, China, offers support for both private sector and public sector advocates. The country encourages business owners to be entrepreneurial and make money exporting. But on the other hand, China's economy looks nothing like the hands-off, perfect competition ideal. Businesses owned by the government—also called *state-owned enterprises*—still make up a big chunk of the Chinese economy.

THE BENEFITS OF GOVERNMENT ACTION

What's the biggest strength of the public sector? In the public sector, it's possible to identify a social or economic goal and take action to achieve it directly.

Economic Milestone

1981   FIRST DISCOUNT AIRLINE

Deregulation of the airline industry allowed the entry of new carriers that could offer cheap tickets. The first of these was People Express, which started flying in 1981. Operating from a dingy terminal at Newark Airport just outside New York City, People Express offered fares as low as $19 off-peak to Washington, DC, and $29 to Boston. Unfortunately this "bus in the sky" lasted only six years because such low fares did not allow enough profits.

| FIGURE 6.2 | Comparing Government Spending in Different Countries |

This chart shows government spending as a percentage of gross domestic product for nine major countries in 2009. A higher number means that the government has a greater role in that economy.

Source: IMF.

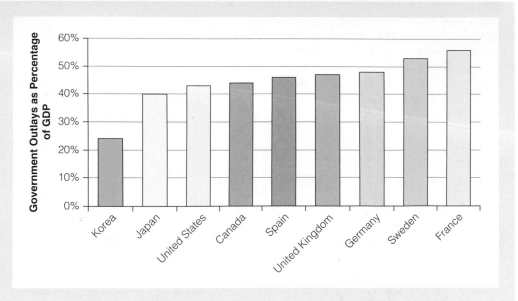

If you want more money spent on education, for example, you allocate more funds for teachers, schools, and college scholarships. You need a stronger defense against external threats? Spend more on spy satellites, jet fighters, and tanks. You don't want people driving too fast and wasting gasoline? Pass a law that sets the national speed limit at 55 miles per hour, as Congress did in March 1974 after OPEC cut off oil supplies in December 1973. Other public sector initiatives include bans on smoking in restaurants, bars, and office buildings, and aid to the poor in the form of welfare payments, food stamps, and housing vouchers.

The Benefits of the Command-and-Control Approach

Such a **command-and-control approach** to social and economic goals directly specifies certain market outcomes and activities to achieve desirable goals. This approach can seem appealing. For example, most people agree that it's desirable for everyone to be able to receive at least a high school education. In the United States, this goal was mostly achieved by the middle of the

20th century because local governments built and staffed elementary and high schools using public money.

In other words, the goal of giving everyone at least a high school education was achieved by government action rather than by relying on markets. These public schools were open to everyone, without regard to income, family background, or gender. Such mass education caused the percentage of high school graduates to rise dramatically, with beneficial effects for the economy. This shift could not have happened so quickly or so completely if schooling had been left primarily in the hands of the private sector. What's more, every state passed a compulsory attendance law requiring children to attend school up to some level. Such laws were especially important in agricultural regions, where families could be tempted to rely on older children to work on farms instead of sending them to school.

Figure 6.3 shows the spending that resulted from these government education policies. First, government spending on public elementary and secondary schools soared, going from roughly

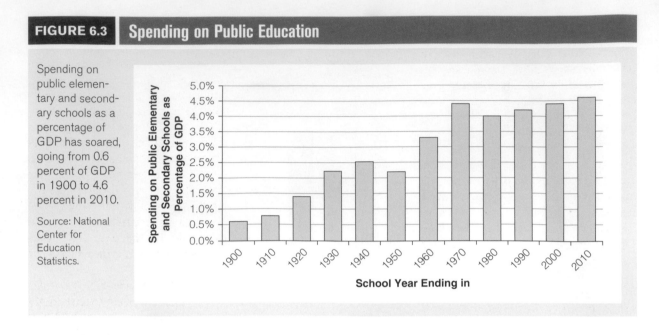

FIGURE 6.3   Spending on Public Education

Spending on public elementary and secondary schools as a percentage of GDP has soared, going from 0.6 percent of GDP in 1900 to 4.6 percent in 2010.

Source: National Center for Education Statistics.

0.6 percent of GDP in 1900 to 4.4 percent in 1970—roughly where it is today.

Government also plays an essential role in managing globalization, encouraging technological change, and shaping financial markets—the forces that guide today's economy. For example, the U.S. Trade Representative negotiates the treaties that control trade with other countries, which then have to be approved by the Senate. As we will see in Chapter 14, these agreements set trading rules that the private sector has to follow.

Similarly, government funds the basic research that underlies many technological advances. For example, the Defense Department sponsored much of the original research that led to the development of the Internet. And long experience has shown that financial markets work best when they are tightly supervised and regulated.

Finally, government action is also a remedy for deficiencies in private markets. The Environmental Protection Agency sets pollution exhaust standards for passenger vehicles. Without government regulation, it's unlikely that new car buyers would spend several hundred dollars for pollution control equipment despite its benefits for overall air quality. We'll discuss the different types of government action later in this chapter.

THE DOWNSIDES OF GOVERNMENT ACTION

So why don't we just let the government control everything? One reason is that for every clear example of the need for the public sector, there's an equally convincing case of government waste and foolishness. Most of us have had the experience of dealing with an unresponsive or obstructive government bureaucracy (such as the Department of Motor Vehicles).

There are several disadvantages to government intervention in the economy. First, public sector managers face an **incentive problem.** Because governments don't need to make a profit, and because they can always raise more money through taxes, there's little pressure on them to be efficient. That means a government agency can overspend unless closely watched. In contrast, private sector managers are judged on the profits they produce, which means they have an incentive to hold down costs.

Second, the bigger the role played by government in the economy, the more businesses and individuals lobby public officials. This lobbying is what economists call **rent-seeking behavior.** If you need a license to open a supermarket, and there are only a limited number available, you will probably hire lobbyists, give campaign contributions, initiate lawsuits, take the appropriate politicians and bureaucrats to lunch, offer their relatives jobs, start malicious rumors about their opponents, and otherwise try to influence government decisions. In fact, there's an entire industry of lobbying firms in Washington, DC, devoted to persuading legislators and government officials to do special favors for their clients.

The problem with rent-seeking behavior is that an enormous amount of talent, time, and resources goes into beating or influencing the system rather than improving the production of existing businesses or inventing new products or services. In 2010, lobbyists in Washington spent roughly $3.5 billion trying to influence government decisions.

Rent-seeking behavior can also cross the line into **corruption**: illegal activities intended to influence government action. Bribery and other forms of political corruption are pervasive features of many economies around the world. Economists generally agree that government corruption slows economic growth because special favors go to businesses that are willing to cheat rather than to those offering the best products and services. (See "Spotlight: Corruption.")

Third, government often suffers from a **lack of flexibility and innovation.** The government can make investments in far-sighted research and development, including such breakthroughs as the Internet. The problem, though, is that the public sector has little incentive to put breakthroughs into widespread use because the government can't make a profit. As a result, the private sector is far better at commercializing new technologies.

But a big argument against government intervention has to do with taxation. Let's look at that next.

RENT-SEEKING BEHAVIOR

The expenditure of money by businesses and individuals trying to influence the government.

CORRUPTION

Bribery and other illegal activities intended to influence government action.

LACK OF FLEXIBILITY AND INNOVATION

The lack of incentive in the public sector to put technological breakthroughs into widespread use.

INEFFICIENCY OF TAXATION

The reduction in production and sale which typically results from imposing a tax on a good or service.

The Inefficiency of Taxation

Any government, whether it's your local town or Washington, needs money to function, and that money usually comes from taxes: payments from individuals or businesses to the government. When the government imposes a tax on a market, the seller receives less than the buyer pays, so the tax pushes the market away from the competitive equilibrium. That is, it causes less to be produced and sold than would be the case otherwise. This is known as the **inefficiency of taxation.**

Let's see how this works. If there is a tax on hotel rooms, a tourist might pay $230 a night, but the hotel keeps only $200 and must give the other $30 to the local government. (San Francisco, for example, has a 14 percent hotel tax, which comes to $28 per night on a $200 per night room.) If there is a tax on income, the seller of labor (the worker) takes home less than the buyer of labor (the employer) pays. So if a person's yearly salary is $50,000, and she pays an income tax of $10,000, her take-home pay is $40,000.

SPOTLIGHT: CORRUPTION

Every year Transparency International, a Berlin-based organization, calculates the Corruptions Perception Index for most of the world's nations based on surveys and expert assessments. According to the organization, in 2010 the least corrupt countries were Denmark, New Zealand, and Singapore. The most corrupt were Somalia and Myanmar. The United States was the 22nd least corrupt country on the list of 180—just ahead of Uruguay.

Source: Transparency International, www.transparency.org.

Imposing a tax on a market typically hurts both buyers and sellers. Adding in the tax, buyers pay more than they would in competitive equilibrium. That causes them to reduce their quantity demanded (remember the law of demand from Chapter 2). After taxes, sellers receive less than they would in competitive equilibrium, so they reduce their quantity supplied (according to the law of supply in Chapter 2).

Let's look at the effect of a simple tax on the market for chairs in Figure 6.4. The market equilibrium without a tax occurs where the original supply and demand lines intersect (labeled *A*). Let's suppose the government imposes a tax—say $20—on the sale of every chair. After the tax is imposed, there is a gap between what sellers receive and buyers pay. Whatever the buyers pay, the sellers will receive $20 less, with the difference going to the government.

Where is the new equilibrium for this market after the tax is imposed? It still has to be true that quantity supplied and the quantity demanded are equal. But the new equilibrium quantity after the tax is imposed will be less than the old quantity. Buyers pay more (see the point labeled *B*), and sellers receive less (see the point labeled *C*) after transferring the tax money to the government.

It makes sense that a tax on something will reduce the quantity supplied and demanded. A tax on chairs makes them more expensive to buyers, which reduces the demand. The same tax, by reducing the price received by furniture manufacturers, causes them to cut back the production of new chairs.

The bigger the tax, the bigger the reduction in supply and demand in that market. At the extreme, the power to tax can be the power to destroy. Suppose every time you went to a movie theater you had to pay a $100 movie tax to the government. You would quickly stop going to the movies. If the government raises the tax on a good or service high enough, it can drive the quantity demanded down to zero.

Governments can impose taxes in many different ways (see Table 6.2). Each type of tax affects a different aspect of the economy. An excise tax, for example, is imposed on a specific good such as cigarettes or alcohol, and it reduces the consumption of that good. An income tax, as the name implies, lets the government take a percentage of pay. Because wages are the price of labor, an income tax reduces the amount of labor supplied

---

FIGURE 6.4 | How Taxes Affect a Market

This figure shows supply and demand in the market for chairs. With no tax, the market equilibrium is at point *A*. With a tax of $20 per chair, buyers pay more per chair (point *B*), and sellers receive less per chair (point *C*). The tax reduces the equilibrium quantity in the market.

TABLE 6.2   Some Common Taxes

This table shows some common taxes, the markets that are taxed, and the potential impact of each tax. The biggest tax in the United States today is the income tax.

Name of Tax	What's Taxed	Potential Impact
Income	Most sources of money coming into a household, including wages, interest, and business profits.	People put forth less effort to earn money.
Sales	The purchase price of most items; some states exempt certain purchases.	Consumers spend less, save more.
Excise	The sale of specific items such as cigarettes, liquor, or gasoline.	People consume fewer taxed items.
Payroll	Wages only; the main examples are Social Security and Medicare taxes.	Employers hire fewer workers.
Corporate profit	Profits made by a business.	Investors are less willing to put money into businesses.
Estate	Value of an inheritance; also known as the "death tax," the estate tax in 2007 exempted the first $2 million of assets.	Controversial; if people care about how much they will leave to their heirs, the estate. tax can lessen their desire to work
Property	Value of real estate.	People are less interested in buying real estate, reducing its value relative to other assets.
Capital gains	The increase in the value of an asset when sold.	Investors put less money into the stock market and other productive assets.
Wealth	Net worth of household (found in European countries such as France and Spain).	Controversial; possibly reduces the willingness of people to start new businesses because they are less likely to become wealthy.
Carbon tax	The carbon content of fuel.	People and businesses reduce their use of high-carbon fuels such as coal.

and demanded, though the precise size of this effect is subject to controversy among economists. And a carbon tax, as we will discuss in Chapter 19, gives utilities, businesses, and individuals an incentive to use fuels that put fewer greenhouse gases into the atmosphere.

But no matter which tax the government uses to raise revenue, the implication is the same: the larger the government, the more revenue it needs to raise, and the greater the impact on the economy. The inevitable result of "too much" government intervention in the economy is a slowing of growth and a lower standard of living. But how much is "too much"? That's the question economists disagree on.

THE RIGHT ROLE FOR GOVERNMENT ECONOMIC POLICY

In the previous section we saw that there are arguments for and against government intervention in the economy. So now we come to the critical question of economic policy: What is the right balance between the public and private sectors? We want to identify situations where markets fail to work as well as they might and where the pluses of government action outweigh the minuses.

Obviously, this is a question about which reasonable people might disagree. However, from an economic perspective, there are four main circumstances in which government economic intervention might be appropriate: *public good provision, market regulation, externalities,* and *income redistribution.*

Public Good Provision

In the United States and most other developed countries a long list of goods and services are provided to citizens primarily by the government.

PUBLIC GOODS
Goods and services that benefit many people in a city, region, or country to some degree.

These include national defense, police and fire protection, the road system, primary and secondary education, and public health efforts such as clean water. Individuals and businesses can add extra goods and services to these if they want—say, by hiring private security or by paying to go to private schools—but the major responsibility for national security, minimum education, and the other items on this list falls to the government.

These expenditures provide what economists call **public goods.** Public goods are goods and services that benefit many people in a city, region, or country—perhaps not equally, but to some degree. In contrast, the usual sorts of private purchases, such as a car or a house, benefit only the buyer and his or her family.

The classic public good is national defense because armed forces protect a whole country rather than any particular person. Fire departments generally protect all the buildings in an area because if one goes up in flames the others are in danger too. And most roads are available for anyone to drive on for free (only about 5,000 miles of U.S. highways have tolls on them, out of 4 million total miles of road across the country). After all, it wouldn't do you any good to be able to drive on the road in front of your house if you couldn't drive by your neighbor's as well.

Why does it make sense for the government to provide public goods? Think about the police patrolling your neighborhood and keeping your street safe. It would almost never be worthwhile for you to pay $60,000 a year to hire that officer. However, you might be willing to band together with 100 neighbors and pay $600 each. A public good needs to be paid for collectively because it benefits everyone.

But suppose you form a voluntary association to hire a police officer and one of your neighbors refuses to pay his share. After all, the cop on the corner will deter criminals whether or not your neighbor contributes anything. This is the **free-rider problem.** You can't stop people from benefiting from a public good even if they don't pay and thus get a free ride from everyone else's contributions. After a snowstorm, plowing the road benefits everyone who uses that road. National

---

SPOTLIGHT: DID THE GOVERNMENT CREATE THE INTERNET?

It's hard to remember a time when the Internet didn't exist. We take it for granted that we can turn on our computers and connect with other computers anywhere else in the world. Yet the communication protocols and standards enabling that miracle were encouraged and funded in good part by the federal government.

The key agency was the Advanced Research Projects Agency of the Defense Department, which first went by the acronym ARPA and then DARPA. Starting in the 1960s and continuing through the 1970s, DARPA funded the development of packet switching and the TCP/IP standards, which is the main way information is transmitted across the Internet. Then in the 1980s the National Science Foundation helped fund the first large-scale network, called NSFNET, and ensured that all computers followed the same communication protocol.

Today, of course, the physical elements of the Internet—the fiber optic cables, the network routes, the computers—are mostly privately owned and operated. Yet the standards that let all computers on the Internet communicate with each other are a public good that would have had a much tougher time coming into existence without government leadership.

Source: "A Brief History of the Internet," Internet Society, revised December 2003. www.isoc.org/internet/history/brief.shtml.

defense benefits everyone who lives in a country; it's not possible to selectively defend one person and not another.

The solution to the free-rider problem is government, which has the power to compel people to pay via taxes. Thus instead of private associations paying private security guards, the local government generally supplies police, supported by taxes. Fire departments, highway departments, and many other collective activities are also supported by taxes.

Another government activity that falls into the class of a public good is the collection of weather data and basic weather forecasting. Since it benefits everyone to know when a hurricane or blizzard is coming, it makes sense for the government to handle this activity. (See "Economic Milestone: The First Weather Satellite.")

Similarly, collecting basic economic data, such as the unemployment rate, benefits everyone. A private company would never be able to make enough profit to cover the costs of surveying 60,000 households every month to get this information. However, the benefits to society as a whole are high enough to make it worthwhile for us to allow the government to use tax revenues to provide this service.

One of the most important public goods the government provides is basic research. As we will see in Chapter 15, basic research—money spent on investigating fundamental questions such as those in physics, chemistry, biology, or mathematics—is essential for the progress of science. However, such basic research usually has no direct application in commercial products, so it's hard for private companies to invest in it. As a result, most spending on basic research comes from the government.

Once we get beyond a list of basic public goods, it becomes harder to find a political consensus about what the government should pay for. Here's one controversial example: education. Most people believe it's appropriate for the government to provide at least a high school education for everyone. However, there is intense dispute about whether the government needs to actually run the schools or whether it should just provide funding that families could use to pay for either a public or a private education for their children.

Or consider the public provision of wireless broadband service. Plenty of cities and towns have considered setting up their own free or low-cost broadband networks, but there have been nasty fights about whether it's appropriate for them to compete with the private sector telecom companies.

Probably the biggest issue, for now and the foreseeable future, is whether basic healthcare and retirement needs should be provided by the government or by the private sector. We will examine this question in Chapter 18.

Market Regulation

Markets don't govern themselves. They run by rules that determine which actions are legal and fair—and which count as unfair or against the public interest. For example, it's illegal for a supermarket to use scales that give the wrong weights. It's also illegal for pharmaceutical companies to sell drugs that have not passed government safety standards. And "lemon laws" let buyers return cars that have to be repeatedly repaired for the same problems.

In theory markets can enforce their own rules, up to a point. Trade associations can set rules that member companies have to follow. Consumers can choose not to patronize supermarkets that use unfair scales. Companies that make unsafe products

Economic Milestone

1960 THE FIRST WEATHER SATELLITE

One example of a public good is the collection of basic data about weather. The two cameras in the first weather satellite, TIROS-1, launched by the government on April 1, 1960, supplied the first continuous observations of global weather. Alas, TIROS-1 was not to have a long life, failing after only 77 days. Today the U.S. government has seven civilian weather satellites in orbit, and their pictures and data are freely available to anyone.

SPOTLIGHT: PRIVATE TOLL ROADS

We're used to thinking of highways as public goods, built and operated by state and local governments. Yet more and more states and municipalities, strapped for cash, are thinking about selling their toll roads to private companies that will collect the fees and handle maintenance. For example, New Jersey at one point considered selling either the New Jersey Turnpike or the Garden State Parkway—two of the most heavily traveled roads in the country. In 2011 the Texas legislature was debating whether to allow private investors to build new toll roads.

The allure of private ownership is not only financial but also political. These roads often need intensive maintenance, which must be paid for with tolls. But a politician who tried to raise tolls would become the immediate target of irate voters, most of whom drive. A private owner, the theory goes, would find it easier to take the unpopular step of raising tolls.

Why would investors buy or build toll roads? The reason is simple. Toll roads, especially in built-up areas, are practically a monopoly. Nobody is going to build an alternative to the New Jersey Turnpike—it would be far too costly. As a result, toll roads are a steady and low-risk source of revenues—something that makes them attractive for investors. Still, no one knows yet whether selling toll roads will turn out to be broadly politically acceptable.

acquire a bad reputation that consumers can research at the Better Business Bureau or on the Internet.

But in practice it's more workable for the government to provide and enforce **market regulation**: the basic rules companies and industries have to follow. For example, consider things as simple as commercial transactions between companies and sales to consumers. Almost every state government has adopted some variant of the Uniform Commercial

MARKET REGULATION
The role of the government in setting the basic rules for market competition.

Code (UCC), which lays out the basic rules for such transactions; these rules are enforced by the courts. The UCC includes important provisions such as the requirement that any goods sold be "fit for the ordinary purposes for which goods of that description are used." In other words, if someone sells you something, it has to do what was promised.

The government regulates, loosely or tightly, virtually every aspect of the economy. As we will see in Chapter 13, government regulators keep a close watch on the financial system, including banks, insurance companies, and investment banks. State and federal regulators try to monitor the safety of products ranging from toys to cars (at the federal level, that's the job of the National Highway Traffic Safety Administration). The marketing and development of new drugs and medical devices, the allocation of frequencies for different wireless devices, and the negotiation of trade treaties with other countries all fall under the jurisdiction of one or more regulators, as Table 6.3 shows.

Let's focus on two particular instances of regulation. The Federal Trade Commission (FTC) and the Department of Justice enforce **antitrust law.** Antitrust law is designed to ensure that companies don't unfairly try to get market power or reduce the amount of competition in a market or industry. These agencies have to approve large mergers and acquisitions that companies want to make so the government can ensure that the number of competitors in a market doesn't get too small. They watch for signs of collusion, a scheme in which competitors get together and try to push up prices. In other words, these government agencies are the defenders of competition.

For example, in 1997 the FTC blocked the proposed merger of Staples and Office Depot, two large office supply chains. The government's argument was that the merger would reduce competition and drive up prices. At the time the FTC said, "If the merger is allowed to proceed, consumers will pay millions more for their copy paper, envelopes, pens, and file folders." Since then sales at both Staples and Office Depot have

TABLE 6.3   Examples of Regulating Markets

The government regulates almost every market to a greater or lesser extent. The first column gives the type of regulation, the second column describes the goal of regulation, and the third column lists some government agencies involved in that type of regulation.

Type of Regulation	Goal of Regulation	Examples of Government Agencies
Supervising the financial and monetary system	Investors need to be treated fairly. Bank depositors need to be assured of the safety of their money.	Federal Reserve Board, Department of the Treasury, Securities and Exchange Commission, Comptroller of the Currency, Federal Deposit Insurance Corporation
Antitrust policy	Businesses have to compete fairly.	Federal Trade Commission, Department of Justice
Consumer protection	Consumers need to be able to trust the goods and services they buy.	Federal Trade Commission, Consumer Products Safety Commission, state agencies
Supervising commercial contracts	Businesses have to be able to make binding agreements.	Department of Justice, state agencies
Regulating key industries	Selected industries such as telecommunications, airplanes, and utilities need close supervision to balance industry and social needs.	Federal Communications Commission, Federal Aviation Administration, Federal Energy Regulatory Commission, state agencies
Regulating healthcare	Patients need to be able to depend on the drugs and medical devices they use.	Food and Drug Administration, Centers for Medicare and Medicaid Services
Negotiating trade policy	Rules for international trade have to be negotiated with other countries.	Office of the Trade Representative, Department of Commerce, Department of State

grown enormously, while the prices of stationery and office supplies have actually fallen.

While the government monitors the fairness of domestic markets, it is also responsible for keeping an eye on international markets. The central government of each country has the primary responsibility for negotiating its own rules for trade—which types of beef can be imported, which airlines can fly from London to New York, and whether foreign banks can buy up domestic banks.

The regulatory role of government is always changing with the economy. The recent housing bust brought new calls for regulation of home mortgages, and the development of new technologies requires new types of regulation as well. (See "How It Works: Regulating New Technology".) In every case, however, the need is to balance the benefit of regulation with the harm it might cause.

Externalities

The basic logic behind the success of a market economy is that when consumers and businesses strive to do the best for themselves, they benefit the entire economy. Thus a profit-maximizing company competes by cutting costs, introducing better products, and otherwise behaving in a way that improves the output of the economy.

That reasoning breaks down, however, if individual actions have side effects on others. For example, if you put a 20-foot-high flamingo statue in your front yard, it may please your

HOW IT WORKS: REGULATING NEW TECHNOLOGY

Is it legal to own a nuclear power plant in your basement? What rules govern private space travel? If you copy music onto your iPod, are you breaking the law? What are the rules for Internet pornography? Should humans be allowed to clone themselves?

One of the toughest tasks for government is regulating new technology. Economic progress is driven by technological change. But the dangers of new technology are usually unknown and potentially serious.

Everyone agrees that the government has the right to regulate technologies that could harm others—that nuclear power plant in your basement, for example, which could affect your neighbors. People also accept that the government needs to be able to control which new pharmaceuticals can be sold to patients. The Food and Drug Administration requires all drugs to pass safety tests and to be shown to actually work on people as promised.

Other technologies are more controversial. For example, the appropriate regulation of genetically modified food has been a subject of vigorous debate in both the United States and Europe. For now, Europeans are generally opting for tougher rules about the sale of such food than the United States.

Pollution is a negative externality.

artistic sensibilities. But it will negatively affect the views of your neighbors and perhaps reduce the values of their homes.

Economists call such secondary consequences of actions **externalities.** More precisely, an externality is the impact that the actions of an individual or business can have on others. Externalities can be either bad (negative) or good (positive). The classic example of a **negative externality** is pollution. A factory that emits noxious fumes is imposing a negative externality on nearby neighborhoods. As in the case of the Fukushima disaster in Japan, a nuclear power plant can affect the area around it if bad safety

EXTERNALITY
The impact that the actions of an individual or a business can have on others.

practices lead to an accident. On a more mundane level, if you insist on playing loud music late at night, you are imposing a negative externality on your neighbors. An airport imposes a negative externality on nearby residents in the form of noise from airplanes taking off and landing.

One of the most annoying externalities is an out-of-control car alarm. People buy alarms to deter thieves, which is an individual benefit. However, when a car alarm goes off in the middle of the night, it imposes negative externalities on everyone around—especially if it continues for a long time.

Positive externalities come about when your actions benefit other people. Suppose you have a sidewalk in front of your house that your neighbors also use. If you shovel your walk when it snows, that helps not just you but your neighbors, too. Similarly, if you paint your house, its added attractiveness helps increase the property values of your neighbors.

Here's another example of a positive externality. In the early days of the Internet, only a few people had e-mail accounts, and they could send e-mail only to each other. Now suppose you've just signed up with an Internet service provider for the first time. Suddenly your friends and business associates who already have accounts can e-mail you, so their connections have become more valuable to them.

In effect, your decision to pay for an Internet account has a positive impact on the people already on the Internet. This is what is known as a **network externality**: your decision to use a network affects the value of that network to other people.

There can be negative network externalities as well. If you decide to drive on a crowded highway during rush hour, the additional congestion you create may slow down other cars on the highway. This can be a big deal. If a road is close to capacity, then just a few additional cars can sharply slow down traffic and turn an orderly flow of cars into a traffic jam.

One important purpose of government is to convince people and businesses to do fewer of the things that create negative externalities and more of the things that create positive externalities. For example, environmental regulations limit the amount of pollution a factory or a car can produce. (We'll talk more about the environment in Chapter 19.) Zoning regulations prevent ugly industrial buildings from being constructed in residential neighborhoods. Building codes that reduce the risk your house will catch fire increase your safety, as well as the safety of your neighbors. Some highways impose higher tolls during rush hour as a way of persuading drivers to use the road at a less congested time. In effect, the higher tolls represent the extra costs each driver imposes on other vehicles.

Income Redistribution

A final important economic function of government is **income redistribution**—shifting money from rich to poor to close big income differences. Redistribution can take place through the tax system, through the distribution of benefits such as Medicare and food stamps, or through direct transfer of money such as unemployment insurance payments or income support for poor children.

This is one of the most controversial economy policy topics. Should the government help the poor? Some say, of course. Others say government's main responsibility is to provide opportunities for people who are willing to work hard, not to provide handouts. There are good arguments on both sides. In Chapter 17 we will look at income inequality and redistribution in much more detail.

CONCLUSION

As we've gone through this chapter, we've given the arguments, pro and con, for government intervention in individual markets. It's not a debate that can end in a clean knockout for either side. Each individual case, whether it's tighter regulation of the mortgage market or requiring more tests for new drugs, has advantages and disadvantages.

However, taking a broader perspective, there's one area where everyone can agree government has a key role: providing the economic statistics that enable policy makers, politicians, and businesses to know how the economy is doing. The next chapter begins our study of macroeconomics by looking at how we measure the size of the economy.

06

SUMMARY

1. Today the hand of the government is apparent in every corner of the economy. But before the Great Depression started in 1929, government had a much smaller role. During the Great Depression, President Franklin Roosevelt put into place a wide variety of new programs under the collective name of the New Deal. *(LO6-1)*

2. After the Depression and World War II ended, government spending and employment dropped but did not return to their pre-1929 share of the economy. In fact, government's role in the economy gradually expanded through the 1950s, 1960s, and 1970s. Starting in the mid-1970s, the public began to feel that government intervention in the economy had gone far enough. This was the beginning of the era of deregulation. *(LO6-1)*

3. The advantage of government intervention in the economy is that it directs economic activities to achieve desirable goals. This is often called the command-and-control approach to social and economic goals. *(LO6-2)*

4. The disadvantages include the incentive problem, rent-seeking behavior, and corruption. In addition, using taxes to raise revenues causes fewer goods and services to be produced and sold than would otherwise be the case. This is known as the inefficiency of taxation. *(LO6-3)*

5. The critical question of economic policy is finding the right balance between the public and private sectors. There are four circumstances when government intervention in the economy might be appropriate: public good provision, market regulation, externalities, and income redistribution. *(LO6-4)*

KEY TERMS AND CONCEPTS

private sector	incentive problem	market regulation
public sector	rent-seeking behavior	antitrust law
New Deal	corruption	externalities
oil price shock	lack of flexibility and innovation	negative externalities
deregulation	inefficiency of taxation	positive externalities
mixed economy	public goods	network externalities
command-and-control approach	free-rider problem	income redistribution

PROBLEMS

1. Which of the following measure the relative importance of government in the economy? *(LO6-1)*

    a) The number of cars per person.

    b) Government employment as a share of total employment.

    c) Energy use per person.

    d) Government spending as a share of GDP.

    e) Total taxes collected.

2. Which of these following programs were part of the New Deal? *(LO6-1)*

    a) National Public Radio.

    b) Medicare.

    c) Social Security.

    d) Federal minimum wage.

    e) Environmental Protection Administration.

3. Which of the following actions are examples of deregulation? Which are examples of increased regulation? *(LO6-1)*

    a) In 1996 Congress passed legislation—the Health Insurance Portability and Accountability Act (HIPAA)—requiring healthcare providers to protect the privacy of patient information.

b) In 2002 Congress passed legislation—the Sarbanes-Oxley Act—increasing financial reporting requirements for corporations.

c) In 1999 Congress passed legislation—the Financial Services Modernization Act—allowing banks, among other things, to sell insurance.

4. Which of the following is an example of a command-and-control approach? *(LO6-2)*

a) Requiring trucking companies to only buy new trucks that are low-pollution.

b) Charging a fee for use of a park.

c) Raising taxes to pay for a new bridge.

c) Offering low-interest loans to students.

5. The local government needs to replace all its traffic signals. Two companies are competing for this business. Company A spends $100,000 on buying a new, more efficient machine to make traffic signals. Company B spends $100,000 on campaign contributions for the city council. *(LO6-3)*

a) If Company B wins the contract, is this an example of perfect competition, market power, rent-seeking behavior, or monopoly?

b) Is Company B likely to charge a higher or a lower price for the traffic signals than Company A?

c) Would the taxpayers of the town prefer that Company A or Company B win the contract? Would the city council prefer that Company A or Company B win the contract?

6. Suppose the government taxes food according to its fat content. That is, the more fat a food contains, the higher the tax on it. *(LO6-3)*

a) Would this taxation raise or lower the prices consumers pay for fatty foods (including the tax)? Draw a graph to illustrate your answer.

b) Would this tax raise or lower the amounts of fatty foods consumers buy?

c) What effect would this tax have on the prices of nonfatty foods? (*Hint:* What happens to the demand schedule for nonfatty foods?)

7. Suppose the government decided to tax e-mail messages, text messages, and instant messages—say, at 5 cents per message. The money would be used to cut the income tax and sales tax on other goods and services. *(LO6-3)*

a) How many e-mail messages, text messages, and instant messages do you send each day? If you didn't change the number of messages you send, how much tax would you have to pay?

b) Would a tax of 5 cents per message reduce your use of messaging?

c) What effect do you think a tax on messages would have on the amount of spam sent on the Internet? Is this a desirable outcome?

8. Which of these government actions is justified by public goods, externalities, regulation, or redistribution? (More than one reason might apply in each case.) Explain your answers. *(LO6-4)*

a) New York City bans smoking in restaurants.

b) Congress renews the food stamp program, which gives poor people access to groceries at a discount.

c) Local governments open libraries that are available to anyone.

9. Communities sometimes take on large amounts of debt to build a new baseball or football stadium. The expectation is that a professional sports team can help create new jobs, give an area more visibility, and attract new businesses. *(LO6-4)*

   a) Is this example of government action—taking on debt to pay for a sports stadium—an example of a public good, an externality, regulation, or redistribution?

   b) Using the concepts in this chapter, explain why government funding of a new sports stadium might not produce the desired results.

10. In 2008 Mayor Michael Bloomberg proposed congestion pricing for New York City streets. Congestion pricing, in its simplest form, means that cars and trucks entering a specific highly congested area of Manhattan would have to pay an extra charge—perhaps as much as $8—during peak morning and evening rush hours. The proposal was approved by the New York City Council but turned down by the New York State Legislature. *(LO6-4)*

   a) Does this proposal rely on the idea of public goods, externalities, regulation, or redistribution?

   b) Show the effect of the congestion tax on a supply–demand diagram.

   c) Whom would it hurt, and whom would it help?

   d) Under what conditions is a congestion tax a good idea?

APPENDIX
DELVING DEEPER INTO MICROECONOMICS

LEARNING OBJECTIVES

After you read this appendix you should be able to:

LO6A-1 Explain the role of utility maximization in consumer choice and use the concept of price elasticity of demand.

LO6A-2 Explain the role of cost minimization in producer decisions and use the concept of price elasticity of supply.

LO6A-3 Explain the incidence of a tax.

Earlier in this textbook we laid out the basics of microeconomics: supply and demand, market equilibrium, profit maximization, and competition and market power. In this appendix we will explore several key topics in consumer choice and business decision making in more depth. These will help us understand some important issues and problems in today's economy.

First we will lay out the logic of utility maximization, which helps explain where the demand curve comes from and how consumers react to price changes. That will give us some insight into how consumers change their behavior in response to big changes in prices for items such as food and energy.

We'll also take a deeper look at demand elasticity.

In the second half of this appendix we'll examine the process of profit maximization, including how managers choose the best production techniques and where the cost function comes from. This will give us some insight into how companies make crucial production decisions, such as whether to move their operations to other countries.

We will finish the appendix by using the concepts of demand and supply elasticities to better understand who bears the burden of different taxes. In other words, when a tax is raised or lowered, who benefits and who loses? This is an important question as politicians debate future changes in the tax code.

CONSUMER CHOICE

We will start by developing a framework for understanding consumer choice. Recall that in Chapter 2 we described the demand schedule for buyers in a market. But now we are asking an additional question: where does a demand schedule come from? Getting the answer to this question is important for any company that makes or sells a consumer product such as shampoo, sports equipment, or motor vehicles.

More importantly, it also helps us better understand the economy we live in.

The Utility Function

To understand consumer decision making, economists generally start with the idea that each person has a **utility function.** You can think of a utility function as a little internal computer that accurately reflects a person's likes and dislikes. Given the actual goods and services the person is consuming, the utility function spits out a number that reflects the physical and emotional benefits the person gets—in other words, the **utility** of the person's consumption. A higher number is preferable, of course.

Each person's utility function is likely to be different. So, for example, if you like football games but don't care for opera, your utility function will give a strong positive weight to attendance at this weekend's football game and a negative weight to attendance at the opera.

The utility function also tells us how much benefit a person gets from purchasing and consuming more of the same thing—say, one car versus two cars, or one television versus two televisions. For example, we can write a utility function for a typical coffee drinker in Table 6A1.1. The first column of the table shows the number of cups of coffee the person drinks in a day. The second column shows the utility she derives from those cups of coffee.

One cup of coffee might give the person four units of utility (which economists sometimes call *utils*). Two cups a day give her seven total units of utility, and three cups give her nine units of utility.

We define **marginal utility** as the added amount of utility an individual gets from one more unit of consumption, holding everything else constant. For example, in Table 6A1.1 the marginal utility from the third cup of coffee is two, which is the difference between the utility for the third cup (nine) and the second cup (seven). Similarly, the marginal utility from the fourth cup of coffee is one.

Table 6A1.1 also illustrates the concept of **diminishing marginal utility**— the tendency for marginal utility to decline as consumption increases. That's typical for most goods and services: the more of a good you consume, the less added benefit from increasing your consumption.

The Budget Constraint

Your utility function is important to your spending decisions, but it's certainly not the only factor that determines what and how much you buy. Your **budget constraint** tells you what combinations of goods and services

MARGINAL UTILITY
The added utility from consuming one more unit of a good or service, holding everything else constant.

BUDGET CONSTRAINT
The combinations of goods and services you can buy, given the prices and the amount you have available to spend.

TABLE 6A1.1	The Utility Function of a Coffee Drinker

As someone drinks more cups during a day, the added utility of each additional cup falls.

Cups of Coffee in a Day	Utility (Measured in Utils)	Marginal Utility (Measured in Utils)
0	0	
1	4	4
2	7	3
3	9	2
4	10	1

you are able to buy, given the prices and the amount of money you have available to spend. The **rational individual** maximizes her utility, subject to her budget constraint.

For example, suppose your entertainment budget for the month is $60. You are going to spend that on some combination of going to the movies and eating out. The local movie theater charges $10 per ticket, whereas the local restaurant charges $20 for a dinner. Given the amount of money you have available, you want to make choices that give you the highest utility. For example, if you love movies, you might decide to go to one movie every week of the month ($10 × 4 = $40) and go out to eat once ($20), thus using your budget of $60. Someone else with the same budget constraint might decide to go to the movies twice ($10 × 2 = $20) and go out to eat twice ($20 × 2 = $40).

The budget constraint changes when the prices do. If the restaurant in Table 6A1.2 were to cut its price to $15 per meal, your set of affordable combinations would expand. If you didn't go to any movies, you could go out to eat four times a month rather than three. Or if you had been eating out twice and seeing two movies, now you could eat out twice and see three movies and still stay within your budget.

TABLE 6A1.2	An Example of a Budget Constraint

A person will choose how many movies and restaurant dinners to consume in a month subject to his budget constraint. In this case the total cost, which is the sum of the cost of the movies and the cost of the meals, cannot exceed $60.

Number of Meals Eaten Out in Month	Number of Movies Seen in Month	Price per Meal (Dollars)	Price per Movie (Dollars)	Cost of Meals (Price of Meal × Number of Meals)	Cost of Movies (Price of Movie × Number of Movies)	Total Spending (Cost of Meals + Cost of Movies)
3	0	$20	$10	$60	0	$60
2	2	$20	$10	$40	$20	$60
1	4	$20	$10	$20	$40	$60
0	6	$20	$10	0	$60	$60

The budget constraint also changes when the amount of money you can spend goes up or down. If you had $80 available for movies and eating out, that would give you a different set of choices.

Utility Maximization

A rational individual will choose goods and services to maximize utility, subject to his or her budget constraint. Because of diminishing marginal utility, you are likely to choose a combination of goods and services rather than blowing all your money on one item. To put it a different way: even if you enjoy riding roller coasters, and even if you say that riding roller coasters is your favorite thing to do, you are unlikely to want to ride roller coasters 12 hours a day, seven days a week. Diminishing marginal utility sets in quickly.

So the utility-maximizing decision is really about trade-offs, taking your budget constraint into account. Do you want to spend $5 on riding the roller coaster one more time, or would you rather use that money for two ice cream cones? Would you rather buy a used car or have enough money to take a trip? Would you rather spend money on a textbook or spend the same money on an extra cup of Starbucks coffee each week?

In each such case you are weighing the marginal utility of spending your last dollar on one good or service versus another. If you can raise your utility by switching to another combination of goods and services while sticking to your budget constraint, you will.

The utility-maximizing decision depends on the prices of the goods and services you are considering. If a price of a good or service changes, so will the budget constraint and the trade-offs that you have to make.

Price Elasticity of Demand

One of the key elements of economics is being able to quantify behavior. Among other things, we can measure the size and growth of the economy, the rate of change of prices, and the ups and downs of the stock market.

We can also quantify the reaction of consumers to big changes in prices. That's critical these days, when we have seen big swings in the price of essentials like food and gasoline. How much will the quantity demanded change when prices go up or down?

In Chapter 3 we examined the link between a price change and the reactions of buyers and sellers. We said that demand is *elastic* if a small price change produces a big change in quantity demanded. One example is restaurant meals, for which demand drops sharply as price increases. Demand is *inelastic* if a big price change produces only a small change in quantity demanded, as is true of gasoline. (We'll consider elasticity of supply later in this appendix).

Now we need to make these concepts more precise by assigning a number to elasticity. The

price elasticity of demand is the percentage change in quantity demanded that results from a 1 percent change in price. This will almost always be a negative number because an increase in price reduces the quantity demanded. But by convention economists usually just drop the negative sign and talk about price elasticity as a number.

For example, a price elasticity of 1 means that a 10 percent price increase leads to a 10 percent decrease in quantity demanded. An elasticity of 2 means that a 10 percent price increase leads to a 20 percent decrease in quantity demanded. An elasticity of 0.5 means that a 10 percent price increase leads to a 5 percent decrease in quantity demanded. In general, demand for a good or service is inelastic if its price elasticity is less than 1, and it's elastic if its price elasticity is greater than 1. (If it's exactly 1, we say that it has *unit elasticity*.)

Economists have estimated price elasticities for various goods and services. According to the Department of Agriculture, the price elasticity of food in the United States is close to 0.1, which makes it highly inelastic. That means if the price of food goes up by 10 percent, the quantity of food demanded decreases by less than 1 percent. As a result, changes in the price of food do not have very much impact on the overall consumption of food.

Most studies find that the price elasticity of gasoline is around 0.25. That is, if the price of gasoline goes up by 10 percent, the quantity demanded drops by about 2.5 percent. (That's over about a year or so. There's a bigger impact if we look further out because people switch to cars with lower fuel consumption.)

The price elasticity of demand can be applied to either an individual demand curve or a market demand

---

TABLE 6A1.3	**The Price Elasticity of Gasoline in Action**

Economic studies suggest that the price elasticity of gasoline in the short run is 0.25. That means a 10 percent increase in price will lead to a 2.5 percent decrease in the quantity demanded. In this example, the price increases by 10 percent from $3.00 to $3.30. The quantity demanded decreases by 2.5 percent from 800 gallons per year to 780 gallons.

Price (Dollars per Gallon)	Annual Quantity of Gasoline Demanded (Gallons per Year)
Before: $3.00	800
After: $3.30	780
Percentage change in price (3.30 − 3.00) / 3.00 = 10%	Percentage change (780 − 800) / 800 = −2.5%

PRICE ELASTICITY OF DEMAND

The percentage change in quantity demanded that results from a 1 percent change in price.

---

curve. Table 6A1.3 illustrates how a single individual's consumption of gasoline changes with price.

Starting from a particular combination of price and quantity, inelastic demand results in a more vertical demand curve than elastic demand. To see this, let's start with Figure 6A1.1, which shows the demand curve that corresponds to Table 6A1.3. Starting from the price of $3.00 per gallon and 800 gallons consumed, a 10 percent increase in the price results in

---

FIGURE 6A1.1	**Inelastic Demand for Gasoline**

This figure shows the demand curve corresponding to Table 6A1.3. With a price elasticity of demand of 0.25, a big percentage change in price produces a small change in quantity.

FIGURE 6A1.2 **A Hypothetical Elastic Demand for Gasoline**

Suppose that the price elasticity of gasoline suddenly jumps to 2. Then starting from the same combination of price and quantity, the demand curve is less vertical than it was in Figure 6A1.1.

Annual Quantity of Gasoline Bought (Gallons)

a 2.5 percent decrease in the quantity demanded. This represents a price elasticity of 0.25, which indicates inelastic demand.

Now let's assume that the price elasticity of gasoline suddenly jumps from 0.25 to 2—that is, from inelastic to elastic. Starting from the same combination of $3.00 per gallon and 800 gallons consumed, a 10 percent increase in price now results in a 20 percent decrease in the quantity demanded. Consumption of gasoline now drops from 800 gallons per year to 640 gallons per year, as shown in Figure 6A1.2, and the demand curve is less vertical.

PRODUCER DECISIONS

Now we shift our analysis from the demand side of the market to the supply side. In Chapter 4 we described the *cost function,* which reports how much it costs to produce each level of output. We used that information to analyze the process of profit maximization.

But where does the cost function come from? For any given level of output, managers have to figure out the least expensive production method. That process is known as **cost minimization.** In fact, often the biggest difference between a successful business and an unsuccessful business is which one does a better job of cost minimization.

Remember that a business usually has more than one way to produce the same output. For example, if you have a lawn-mowing business, you can use an army of workers equipped with hand mowers or one worker with a tractor. So your first step is to figure out which combination of inputs produces the desired output at the lowest cost. This cost-minimizing choice depends on the wages of the workers and the cost of the tractor and the gasoline needed to run it.

Or imagine you are the top executive of a small company creating and selling funny greeting cards. You have to ask the cost minimization questions first: is it cheaper to print the cards in the United States or overseas? Is it cheaper to have a staff of trained greeting card writers, or should you buy the copy inside the cards from freelancers? Obviously the answers to these questions depend on the prices of inputs such as labor, printing, and international shipping.

We will first consider how businesses achieve cost minimization. Then in the next section we will look at pricing and output decisions.

Choosing the Right Inputs

To see a simple example of cost minimization, let's think about a lawn-mowing service (also discussed back in Chapter 4). Suppose the business owner has agreed to cut 20 lawns a day in the neighborhood. Now he has a choice: he can hire five workers at the minimum wage (roughly $60 per day for each) with push mowers to do the task. Or he can hire one worker and rent a riding mower to cut the same 20 lawns. Which method should he choose?

The answer depends on the price of renting the riding mower. The option of hiring the five workers will cost $300 per day ($60 × 5). The option of renting the riding mower will be the daily rental cost of the mower plus the labor cost of one worker, which is $60. So renting the mower will be the preferred option as long as its rental cost is less than $240 per day ($300 − $60). But if the mower costs more than $240 per day, it's not worth it.

In general, a producer's choice of inputs depends on their relative prices. As an input becomes more expensive, all other things being equal, a business will want to use less of it. If you are running a factory and the cost of providing healthcare for your U.S. workers goes up, you're likely to reduce the number of U.S. workers by automating the assembly line or by moving the operation to China or Vietnam. If the cost of renting office space rises compared to other inputs, you'll put your workers in cubicles rather than offices, or you'll buy your workers laptops and have them work from home.

Substitutes and Complements in Production

We say that one input is a **substitute** for another if, when the price of one goes up, a cost-minimizing business uses more of the other (holding output constant). For example, factory workers in China are generally thought of as substitutes for factory workers in the United States. Voice mail systems are substitutes for secretaries. Teleconferencing is a substitute for air travel.

Sometimes, though, two inputs work together, so if you use less of one, you will use less of the other as well. We say that one input is a **complement** for another if when the price of one goes up, a cost-minimizing business will use less of the other (holding output constant). For example, freight transportation is a complement for foreign workers because if the price of shipping freight across the ocean goes up, there is less incentive to move production overseas. Cement is a complement for construction workers because as the price of cement goes up, less building occurs and therefore fewer workers are needed.

Sometimes it's not obvious whether two inputs are substitutes or complements. For example, are computers a substitute or a complement for educated workers? Prices of computers have plummeted over the past 20 years. If computers were a substitute for educated workers, they would have taken away jobs that educated workers would have done. But in fact the demand for educated

workers has soared over the past 10 years, and so have their wages. As a result, it seems almost certain that information technology is complementary to college-educated workers.

A Cost Minimization Example

Let's work through a simple example of cost minimization: if you are running a business, should you buy your own copy machine or send your documents out to a local copy shop? That's a decision many small businesses must make. If you buy a copy machine, you have to lay out anywhere from $200 to $1,200, depending on the speed and capacity of the machine you choose. And then there's the cost of the toner and paper, which could be 2–4 cents per copy. The alternative, of course, is to send the copying out, which could cost 10 cents or more per copy, depending on the quantity.

To make this decision, of course, we need to know the actual cost of the machine and the price per copy. Table 6A1.4 works through the cost minimization decision, assuming the cost of a copy machine is $300, the per-page cost if you own the machine is 2 cents per copy, and the per-page cost if you go to an outside shop is 10 cents per copy.

The calculations in the table show that for low volumes of copies, it's cheaper to use an outside copy shop. But once the volume gets high enough, buying a copy machine makes sense. The result is a *cost function*: for any level of output, we can tell what the cost will be. Producing 3,000 copies, for example, will cost $300. Producing 4,000 copies will cost $380.

In general, the best choice of inputs depends on the price of inputs and on a producer's expected scale of output. In the example just given, the decision of whether to buy a copy machine depends on how many copies you plan to make, holding input prices fixed. Similarly, in the case of the lawn-mowing company, the decision of whether to buy a tractor depends on how many lawns you need to mow, as well as on the relative prices of buying a tractor and renting it.

It's not unusual for the right mix of inputs for a small business to change as the business expands. A very small business may operate out of a spare bedroom, but a business with 10 employees needs its own office. A small business hires a

TABLE 6A1.4	The Copier Decision

Few small businesses can avoid the important copier decision: should they buy their own copy machines, with big up-front outlays and low per-page costs? Or should they use a local copy shop, with no start-up cost but a high per-page cost? The answer depends on the relative costs of the two options and the number of copies needed. The shaded regions represent the low-cost choices for selected copy volumes. For low volumes, the outside copy shop is preferable. For high volumes, buying a copier is better.

	Use Copy Shop	Buy Own Machine
Up-front cost	0	$300
Per-page cost	$ 0.10	$0.02

Number of copies	Total cost	
0	$ –	$ 300
1,000	$ 100	$ 320
2,000	$ 200	$ 340
3,000	$ 300	$ 360
4,000	$ 400	$ 380
5,000	$ 500	$ 400
6,000	$ 600	$ 420
7,000	$ 700	$ 440

part-time accountant; a bigger business has an in-house finance and legal department. These sorts of transitions make operating a business challenging.

Price Elasticity of Supply

In Chapter 3 we said that supply is *elastic* if a small price change leads to a large change in the quantity supplied. Similarly, supply is *inelastic* if a big price change leads to only a small change in the quantity supplied.

However, just as in the case of demand elasticity, we can be more precise. The **price elasticity of supply** is the percentage increase in the quantity supplied, given a 1 percent increase in the price. The price

PRICE ELASTICITY OF SUPPLY

The percentage change in quantity supplied that results from a 1 percent change in price.

FIGURE 6A1.3	Elastic Supply

When supply is elastic, a relatively small percentage change in prices produces a relatively large percentage change in supply.

elasticity of supply is generally a positive number because the supply curve is usually upward-sloping. For example, if the price elasticity of supply is 3, a 10 percent price increase will lead to a 30 percent increase in the quantity supplied. Supply is elastic if the price elasticity of supply is greater than 1, and it's inelastic if the price elasticity of supply is less than 1. Supply is perfectly inelastic if the elasticity is zero—that is, if the quantity supplied doesn't change, no matter how the price changes.

Figures 6A1.3, 6A1.4 and 6A1.5 show, respectively, elastic supply, inelastic supply, and perfectly inelastic supply. Each figure starts from the same combination of price P and quantity Q, and shows the reaction to the same price change P to P'. The change in quantity is biggest in Figure 6A1.3, smaller in Figure 6A1.4, and nonexistent in Figure 6A1.5. Starting from the same P and Q, the supply curve is more vertical when elasticity is smaller. In the case of perfectly inelastic supply, the supply curve is vertical.

TAX INCIDENCE AND ELASTICITY

Politicians are always talking about raising or cutting taxes. In fact, Congress seems to pass some kind of tax change every year, which affects the

FIGURE 6A1.4   Inelastic Supply

Starting from the same price *P* and quantity *Q*, the supply curve is more vertical when supply is inelastic than when it is elastic.

FIGURE 6A1.5   Perfectly Inelastic Supply

Perfectly inelastic supply corresponds to a vertical supply curve. No matter what the price is, the quantity supplied remains the same.

try to pass the tax on to consumers by raising the prices of shoes by $5. If they are successful, consumers will pay the shoe tax. The **incidence** of a tax identifies the people or businesses who ultimately have to pay a tax, whether or not they are the ones that actually write the checks to the government.

But here's the question that elasticity can help us answer: when can we pass a tax on to someone else? If you were the one being taxed, when could you get someone else to pay? The ultimate incidence of a tax depends on which side of the market—buyers or sellers—is more inelastic. For example, suppose the product is something buyers absolutely need, at least in the short run—say, gasoline to drive their cars to work. Now suppose the government increases the tax on gasoline (as of early 2011, the average tax on gasoline in the United States, a combination of federal and state taxes, was about 48 cents per gallon). Then in the short run, gas stations will be able to simply boost their prices by the amount of the tax because drivers won't have any choice but to pay the higher prices.

To put this a different way, if *demand* is inelastic, buyers have few alternatives, and they won't be able to object if sellers try to boost prices to pass along a tax. On the other hand, if *supply* is inelastic, sellers will be forced to absorb a tax themselves.

Figure 6A1.6 shows the effect of taxing a market in which demand is inelastic and supply is elastic, as is true for gasoline. In other words, purchasers don't have other choices, but sellers do. The tax shows up as the difference between what buyers pay and what sellers ultimately receive. But the impact is bigger on buyers than on sellers. In Figure 6A1.6 the after-tax price to buyers rises a lot, whereas the after-tax price paid to sellers barely drops.

amount that businesses and households have to pay the government.

But one of the big surprises of economics is that the ultimate *incidence* or burden of the tax may not fall on the person or company writing the check. Instead, it depends on the elasticity of supply and the elasticity of demand.

For example, suppose a local government levies a $5 tax per pair of shoes sold, to be collected from shoe stores. It might seem at first that shoe stores are being hurt by the tax. But the stores may

INCIDENCE
The people or businesses that ultimately have to pay a tax.

However, this may not be the final word on the incidence of the tax. There can be a difference between short-run and long-run elasticity in a market. Even if buyers don't have many options in the short run, in the long run they may be able to make big changes. Faced with higher gas taxes, for example, drivers will eventually buy more fuel-efficient cars, take public transportation, switch jobs to avoid long commutes, or move closer to their jobs. So in the short run a gasoline tax falls on drivers, but in the long run it may fall on the sellers of gasoline.

| FIGURE 6A1.6 | Taxation with Inelastic Demand |

Imposing a tax on a market with inelastic demand means that the after-tax price for buyers will increase by almost as much as the amount of the tax.

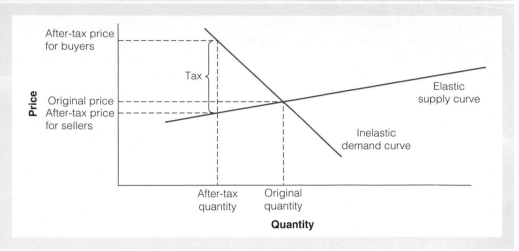

CONCLUSION

The fundamental lesson of this appendix is that as prices change, so does the behavior of consumers and businesses. The better we can understand these reactions, the better we can understand the economy around us. That's the virtue and importance of a deeper look at microeconomics.

06A   SUMMARY

1. A utility function reports a number that reflects the physical and emotional benefits a person gets from consuming different combinations of goods and services. Every person's utility function is different. Typically people get diminishing marginal utility from increasing consumption of the same good or service. *(LO6A-1)*

2. A budget constraint tells you what combinations of goods and services you can buy, given their prices and the amount of money you have available to spend. A rational person maximizes his or her utility subject to the budget constraint, which requires making trade-offs between different goods and services. *(LO6A-1)*

3. The price elasticity of demand measures the response of quantity demanded to price changes of a good or service. It is the percent-age change in quantity demanded that results from a 1 percent change in price. Demand is inelastic if the price elasticity is less than 1, and it's elastic if the price elasticity is greater than 1. *(LO6A-1)*

4. For any given level of output, the managers of a business have to figure out the least expensive production method. The cost-minimizing combination of inputs depends on the prices of the inputs. Two inputs are substitutes if raising the price of one increases the use of the other, holding output constant. Two inputs are complements if raising the price of one decreases the use of the other, holding output constant. *(LO6A-2)*

5. The price elasticity of supply is the percentage increase in the quantity supplied, given a 1 percent increase in the price. Supply is elastic if

the elasticity is greater than 1, and it's inelastic if the elasticity is less than 1. Supply is perfectly inelastic if the elasticity is zero—that is, if a change in price does not change the quantity supplied. *(LO6A-2)*

6. The incidence of a tax reflects who ultimately absorbs the burden of the tax. In general, the incidence of a tax depends on which side of the market—buyers or sellers—is more inelastic. *(LO6A-3)*

KEY TERMS AND CONCEPTS

utility function	budget constraint	substitute
utility	rational individual	complement
marginal utility	price elasticity of demand	price elasticity of supply
diminishing marginal utility	cost minimization	tax incidence

PROBLEMS

1. Diminishing marginal utility means that _____ *(LO6A-1)*

   a) marginal utility falls as consumption increases.

   b) marginal utility gets smaller over time.

   c) utility falls as consumption increases.

   d) utility gets smaller over time.

2. In the following table, the first column is the number of baseball games you attend in a month. The second column is the utility you get from these purchases. *(LO6A-1)*

Number of Baseball Games Attended in the Month	Total Utility	Marginal Utility
0	0	
1	10	?
2	20	?
3	30	?
4	35	?

   a) Fill in the third column with the marginal utility of each additional game.

   b) Is this a situation of diminishing marginal utility? Explain.

   c) Would you expect everyone to have the same utility function for baseball games? Why or why not?

3. You have $10 to spend on desserts for a week. You need to split it between cookies, which are $1 each, and ice cream cones, which are $2 each. *(LO6A-1)*

   a) What is the maximum number of ice cream cones you can buy in a week?

b) If you buy four cookies, how many ice cream cones can you buy?

c) Suppose the price of ice cream cones drops to $1. Write down all the combinations of cookies and cones that now meet your budget constraint.

4. Suppose the price elasticity of demand for sports cars is 2. When the price is $40,000 per car, a local dealer sells 100 cars over a year. *(LO6A-1)*

a) If the price per car rises to $44,000, what is the percentage change in the price?

b) What is the percentage change in sports car sales, given the elasticity?

c) What is the new sales level for sports cars?

d) What was the original revenue of the auto dealership from sports car sales? What is the new revenue? Did the price increase reduce or increase revenue?

5. The price of homes affects the number of new homes built—the higher the price rises, the more new homes are built. Economic literature suggests that a reasonable value for the price elasticity of supply for home construction is 3, so a 1 percent price increase generates a 3 percent increase in new home construction. *(LO6A-2)*

a) Suppose the average price of homes in a town is $300,000, and 100 new homes are constructed in the town each year. Now suppose the average price of homes goes up to $330,000. What is the new rate of home construction per year?

b) Instead of rising, suppose the average price of homes in the town falls from $300,000 to $270,000. What is the new rate of home construction per year?

6. A town decides to impose a new tax of 30 percent on food sold in its area. *(LO6A-3)*

a) Suppose the town is in the middle of the desert, so there are no other places nearby for people to buy food. Is the burden of the tax more likely to fall on food stores or food purchasers? Is this the result of inelastic demand, elastic supply, elastic demand, or inelastic supply? Explain your answer.

b) Now suppose the town is in the middle of a densely populated region of the country, so it's easy for food shoppers to go to stores in other towns. Is the burden of the tax more likely to fall on food stores or food purchasers? Is this the result of elastic demand, elastic supply, inelastic demand, or inelastic supply? Explain your answer.

7. Economists disagree about the magnitude of elasticity of labor supply. The labor market is a key part of the economy. Workers choose how many hours they will work, or even if they are going to take a job at all, depending on the wage they can get. The elasticity of labor supply tells us how much labor supply responds to changes in the wage. Some argue that it is quite low; others say that the elasticity of labor supply is much greater than 1.

This debate has important policy consequences. Suppose the government imposes a tax on wages, so there is a gap between the wage paid by employers and the wage received by workers. *(LO6A-3)*

a) Suppose the elasticity of labor supply is very low at the current level of employment. Does this tax have more effect on the wage received by workers, or on the quantity of labor supplied?

b) Now suppose the elasticity of labor supply is high at the current level of employment. Does this tax have more of an effect on the wage received by workers, or on the quantity of labor supplied?

c) Suppose you are a politician deciding whether to raise revenues by increasing taxes on high-income workers. Would you prefer that their supply of labor is elastic or inelastic? Explain.

07 THE FIRST STEP INTO MACROECONOMICS

LEARNING OBJECTIVES

After reading this chapter, you should be able to:

LO7-1 Define gross domestic product (GDP) and distinguish between final goods and services and intermediate inputs.

LO7-2 List and discuss the components of GDP.

LO7-3 Explain what GDP does not include.

LO7-4 Compare GDP and GDP per capita across countries.

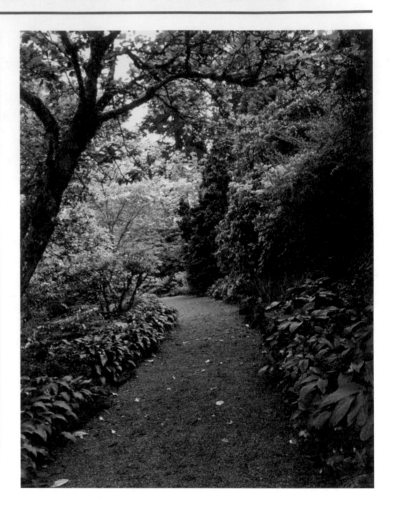

Up to this point we have focused our attention on the behavior of individual markets. We considered supply and demand in a single market, looked at profit-maximizing businesses, and discussed how government can affect a market.

Now we are going to take our first steps into **macroeconomics**—the study of the whole economy. This is the big picture that we read about online or see on television. What's happening to unemployment? Is the economy heating up or slowing down? Are we slumping into a recession or going into a boom? And what should Congress, the president, or the chair of the Federal Reserve do about it?

Macroeconomics addresses these questions and more. Over the next six chapters we will look at the core concepts of output, inflation, growth, and unemployment. We will discuss the Great Recession and how it hurt Americans. Then we will examine how government spending and taxation can influence the economy and the impact the Federal Reserve, the country's central bank, can have on interest rates and economic activity. In particular, we will look at the policy actions taken to fight the deep economic downturn.

Keep in mind, however, that there are quite a few macroeconomic topics about which economists don't agree. That's to be expected because macroeconomics explores the complicated interactions of many different parts of the economy. A decision by federal government to spend billions on new fighter planes can affect employment in the states where the planes are built. That increase in employment may affect the demand for new homes, which in turn may boost the demand for mortgage borrowing. Every part of the economy is interconnected.

The other reason for disagreement is the intensely political nature of many macro policy decisions. Republicans and Democrats in Washington differ on how much to spend, what kind of taxes to increase or cut, and how actively the government should intervene in the economy. As a result, disputes about macroeconomic policy quickly turn into political conflicts. During the presidency of George W. Bush, for example, Democrats repeatedly attacked the Bush administration for running a big budget deficit. Then after President Barack Obama took office, Republicans attacked the Obama administration for running a big budget deficit.

This chapter, however, will examine a relatively noncontroversial topic: the basic measure of the size of the economy, which is the gross domestic product or GDP for short. We mentioned GDP in Chapter 1, but we will look at it more closely now. GDP is the starting point for all macroeconomics—and for any discussion of the overall economy. We will discuss the different components of GDP and will finish by comparing the size of the U.S. economy with the economies of other countries.

MEASURING THE ECONOMY

When you visit a hospital or a doctor's office, a nurse generally takes your blood pressure, pulse, and temperature, weighs you, and perhaps draws blood samples. These measurements have three purposes. First, if anything has changed since your last visit, that could indicate a problem. Second, if you have a complaint, the measurements help pinpoint the cause. Finally, the information helps guide your treatment.

Measuring the economy has the same purposes: to identify economic problems, diagnose their causes, and figure out the right policy fixes. But taking the temperature of an economy as big as that of the United States is not an easy job. In fact, before the mid-1930s economists had no systematic way of measuring or tracking the economy as a whole. Government statisticians and industry trade associations could provide some information, such as the amount of freight being hauled by railroads or the amount of canned corn coming out of the nation's factories (a whopping 100 million cans in 1893, for those of you taking notes). But there was nothing anyone could point to and say, "*This* is how big the economy is."

When the Great Depression arrived in 1929, it suddenly became more important for us to know how the economy was doing. As we saw in the previous chapter, the economy was very sick during that time. There were loud calls for the government to do something about it, and economists were forced to come up with new tools and new ways of thinking. For the first time we needed an overall measure of the economy to see how bad economic conditions were and whether they were getting better. In the 1930s, economist Simon Kuznets, who later won the Nobel Prize in Economics, worked with a small staff to construct the first overall measure of the U.S. economy.

An ammunition plant during WWII. The government needed a measure of the economy to know how many wartime goods it could produce.

Kuznets's work represented a major break-through in economics. However, it was just the start. Over the next 10 years, the nation's economic statistics steadily improved. One major motivation for improving economic analysis was the international conflict with Germany and Japan in the early 1940s. Government military planners needed to know how big the economy was so they could figure out how many tanks, ships, and planes it could produce.

By the time World War II ended in 1945, the foundations for the current system of gathering economic statistics were in place. Today the Bureau of Economic Analysis (BEA), the Bureau of Labor Statistics (BLS), the Census Bureau, and the Federal Reserve are the main statistical agencies in Washington. They conduct surveys, collect information, and regularly publish reports on the key economic statistics, such as unemployment, inflation, productivity, and foreign trade.

GROSS DOMESTIC PRODUCT
The dollar value of the total output of the economy in a year.

The Basics of Gross Domestic Product

The BEA is charged with estimating output of the U.S. economy. The **gross domestic product** or **GDP** is the dollar value of the total output of the economy in a year. Collectively, all the statistics that feed into this process of estimating GDP are known as the **system of national accounts.** (The BEA also estimates quarterly GDP, which is economic output in each quarter of the year.)

Measuring the output of the largest economy in the world is a complicated task. GDP includes a wide range of goods and services—we'll explain next which ones belong and which ones don't. For now, think of that range as a long list going from automobiles (5.7 million sold in 2010) to baseball games (73 million fans attending in 2010), to college classes (an estimated 21 million students enrolled in higher education), to military strategy (919 generals and admirals in the United States armed forces), to haircuts (96,000 barbers and 770,000 hairdressers, hairstylists, and cosmetologists hard at work cutting hair), to paintball (an estimated 6.3 million people participated). No one really knows just how many different items this list contains, but it's certainly well into the millions for the United States, depending on how finely we cut it.

Such a list, even if we could compile it, would be interesting but not terribly useful. The different types of goods and services are all measured in different units. What have automobiles to do with admirals besides beginning with the same letter? Not much. And there's no easy way to add them all up.

But here's the key: if we can express each item on the output list as a dollar amount, the statisticians at the BEA can sum them into a figure for the total production of the economy. For example, in 2010 U.S. households spent $70 billion on new automobiles. We can add that to the billions spent for haircuts, the total amount spent on knee replacements, and the revenues collected by zoos and aquariums. After we have added our entire list of products and services, we have the output of the economy!

The Components of GDP

What goes into GDP? Here are its components:

- **Personal consumption:** goods and services for household use.

- **Nonresidential investment:** the long-lived buildings, equipment, and software that businesses purchase to use in production.

- **Residential investment:** the construction of new homes and the renovation of existing homes.

- **Change in private inventories:** goods produced by businesses that are not immediately purchased.

- **Government consumption and investment:** goods and services purchased by the government.

- **Net exports:** the difference between exports and imports.

Each of these amounts is measured in dollars, and gross domestic product consists of the sum of all of these:

GDP (in dollars) = Personal consumption + Nonresidential investment + Residential investment + Change in private inventories + Government consumption and investment + Net exports

Table 7.1 shows how the different components of GDP added up in 2010. For example, residential investment totaled $341 billion. Note that net exports were negative because the United States imported more than it exported (we'll discuss imports and exports later in the chapter).

No Double-Counting

We've listed the main components of GDP, but we seem to have left out some economic activity. For example, no category of GDP corresponds to, say, the spending by a business on janitorial services or electricity. In fact, all the intermediate inputs of businesses (described in Chapter 4) appear to be left out.

There's a reason for that. To eliminate double-counting, BEA statisticians count only the purchases of **final goods and services**—that is, goods and services that are bought by their ultimate users. Purchases of intermediate inputs are left out of GDP. **Intermediate inputs** include any goods and services bought by a business that are completely used up in production in less than a year.

Why do statisticians leave out intermediate inputs? Think about a restaurant that buys apples to make apple pie, which it then serves to customers. The apples are an intermediate input, and the apple pie is part of personal consumption expenditures. We don't want GDP to include both the apples and the apple pie because that would count the apples twice. Similarly, a printing company uses paper and ink to produce a book for sale to readers—say, this textbook. To avoid double-counting, only the purchase price of the book is counted as part of GDP.

FINAL GOODS AND SERVICES
Goods and services that are bought by the ultimate users.

TABLE 7.1	The Components of Gross Domestic Product, 2010

Below are the main components of GDP, along with their descriptions.

Category	Billions of Dollars in 2010	Explanation
Personal consumption	10,349	Vehicles, food, housing, medical care, education, consumer electronics, and everything else that households can consume.
Nonresidential investment	1,415	Computers, factory machinery, software, office buildings, airplanes, and all the other long-lived capital investments that businesses use for production.
Residential investment	341	Construction of new homes and renovation of existing homes.
Change in private inventories	72	Increase or decrease of inventories at manufacturers, wholesalers, and retailers.
Government consumption and investment	3,000	Salaries and benefits of government employees; purchases of supplies and equipment; and construction of buildings, highways, and other infrastructure.
Net exports of goods and services	−516	Exports of goods and services to other countries, minus imports of goods and services from other countries.
Gross domestic product	14,660	

Source: Bureau of Economic Analysis, www.bea.gov (as of April 2011). Numbers do not add exactly due to rounding.

However, a business can make some purchases that are included as part of GDP, like nonresidential investments in buildings, equipment, and software. What makes these different is that they are long-lived—that is, they don't get used up within a year. When the printing company buys a printing press—which may have a useful lifetime of 10 years—that's counted as a nonresidential investment. Similarly, the purchase of a commercial oven by the restaurant to bake the apple pies is a nonresidential investment and is included in GDP.

HOW IT WORKS: A TRILLION HERE, A TRILLION THERE...

The total GDP of the United States in 2010 was roughly $14.7 trillion. None of us sees a trillion of anything in our daily lives, so it's hard to get our arms around a number that big. Let's figure out how big it really is.

The thickness of a $1 bill is roughly .0043 inches. If we piled up 14.7 trillion dollar bills, they would make a pile a million miles high. That's four times the distance to the moon.

By contrast, if you make $50,000 per year, those dollars bills piled up would be 18 feet high—not nearly as impressive.

UNDERSTANDING GDP

Let's take a closer look at each component of GDP in more detail.

Personal Consumption

The biggest category of GDP is personal consumption, which accounted for $10.3 trillion in 2010. This enormous sum includes all sorts of goods that households spend money on, such as food, telephone services, personal computers, automobiles, and gasoline.

SPOTLIGHT: CONSPICUOUS SPENDING

When the BEA totals up spending on personal consumption or residential investment, it makes no judgment about an item's usefulness or social value. For example, in 2010 the residential investment component of GDP included construction costs for the enormous mansion being built in Tampa, Florida, by New York Yankee superstar Derek Jeter. With more than 30,000 square feet, 7 bedrooms, and 9 bathrooms, some Tampa residents call the mansion 'St. Jetersburg.'

Residential investment: Derek Jeter's mansion in Tampa, FL.

Meanwhile the personal consumption component of GDP includes spending on flashy jewelry, plastic surgery, expensive parties, all the champagne that professional athletes pour on each other when they win the championship. If you can spend it, the BEA can count it.

The category of personal consumption also includes the money consumers spent on pet food and on greeting cards. So when you buy holiday cards, you are contributing toward personal consumption and GDP. Religious intangibles—contributions to your local church, synagogue, or mosque—are counted as part of personal consumption. So are spending on education and contributions or bequests to universities. Gambling losses count as personal consumption, too, as does the latest video game.

One oddity of GDP statistics is that medical spending counts as part of personal consumption even if a health insurer or Medicare pays the bill. The reason is that the individual is the ultimate consumer of medical spending. If Medicare pays for your grandfather's heart surgery, that counts as personal consumption for him even though the money never touched his hands.

Nonresidential Investment

Another important GDP spending category is nonresidential investment. That's the total of outlays by businesses on the structures, equipment, and software they need to run their operations. Nonresidential investment includes computers on workers' desktops, office chairs, factory machinery, office buildings, power plants, wires to power plants, hospitals, medical equipment, and airplanes—anything that is used in production and that lasts for more than one year.

The pattern of nonresidential investment has changed over time. In the 1950s and the 1960s U.S. businesses put their money mostly into industrial and transportation equipment. Manufacturers were building and expanding factories, making everything from steel and cars to clothing and toys; as a result, they needed heavy machinery. At the same time, transportation companies were buying truck fleets to carry the raw materials to the factories and then shipping

Economic Milestone

1950 AUTO'S SHARE OF SPENDING HITS PEAK

Following World War II, factories switched from making tanks and planes to producing cars–lots of them. In 1950 spending on cars and parts exceeded 7 percent of personal consumption, an all-time record, as U.S. households moved out to the suburbs and adopted a car-oriented lifestyle. Today we are still driving, but we are devoting a much bigger share of our spending toward things like medical care and home computers. The car is no longer king.

the finished goods customers across the country.

The pattern of nonresidential investment has changed over time, reflecting the shift to a more global and information-based economy. Now many factories that feed U.S. stores are in China. As a result, U.S. companies have much less need to invest in industrial equipment at home.

Instead the biggest category of business investment spending today is software, which counts as investment even though it is usually not a physical product. The next biggest category is trucks, followed by communications equipment and computers. Altogether, information technology spending—computers, communications equipment, and software—now accounts for roughly 42 percent of nonresidential investment spending, up from just over 6 percent in 1950 (Figure 7.1).

Keep in mind a couple of important points. First, business investment counts toward U.S. GDP only if it happens in this country. So when a United States–based company like Intel spends billions to build a factory

A new factory counts as part of U.S. GDP only if it is built in the United States.

in Ireland, that does not count toward U.S. GDP. In contrast, when a foreign-based company such as Toyota lays out billions to build factories in Kentucky and Indiana, that *does* count toward nonresidential investment and GDP. Location—not ownership—matters for the calculation of GDP.

The other point is that most outlays by businesses are for intermediate inputs, so they don't count as part of nonresidential investment. When Walmart buys socks and sells them to consumers, the socks count as personal consumption. Only when Walmart builds a new supercenter are its construction expenses part of nonresidential investment. Similarly, purchases of food by restaurants are not counted in GDP, but the meals bought by diners count as personal consumption.

Residential Investment

Spending on the building of new homes and the renovation of existing ones is called *residential investment*. If you just rebuilt your kitchen for

---

FIGURE 7.1   Information Technology's Share of Nonresidential Investment

What are businesses spending on? Increasingly it's information technology equipment and software, which now account for 42 percent of nonresidential investment.

Source: Bureau of Economic Analysis (as of April 2011), www.bea.gov.

Construction expenses for new Walmart Supercenters are included in GDP.

$50,000, that's part of residential investment. The construction of that eyesore of a home down the street also counts as residential investment. However, if you buy an existing home for $500,000, that does *not* count as residential investment because no actual production or construction occurred—the house was already there. Remember, GDP calculates production of new goods and services.

Residential investment is highly volatile, which means it can quickly swing from high to low. Take a look at Figure 7.2, which measures residential investment as a share of GDP. Residential investment dropped to just over 3 percent of GDP in the recession of 1981–1982, when mortgage interest rates jumped so high that no one could afford to build or buy a home. Then in the housing boom year of 2005, residential investment topped 6 percent of GDP for the first time since the 1950s, when builders put up millions of homes for the generation of families formed after World War II. But the housing bust sent home construction plunging. In 2010 residential construction plummeted to only 2.3 percent of GDP, the lowest level in more than 50 years.

Government Consumption and Investment

Now we come to government. Clearly the federal, state, and local governments in the United States are an important part of the economy, spending a total of $5.6 trillion in 2010. And equally clearly, governments contribute to economic output. All those police, firefighters, and teachers aren't just saving lives and educating the next generation; they are contributing to GDP.

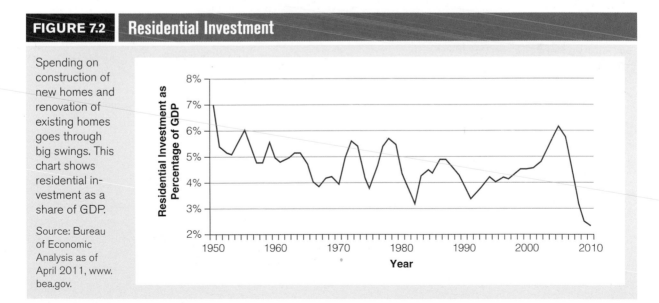

FIGURE 7.2   **Residential Investment**

Spending on construction of new homes and renovation of existing homes goes through big swings. This chart shows residential investment as a share of GDP.

Source: Bureau of Economic Analysis as of April 2011, www.bea.gov.

The government's direct contribution to GDP is called *government consumption and investment,* which includes all government purchases of goods and services, such as salaries paid to government employees. These goods and services are also called the **output of government.** (The government makes an indirect contribution to GDP as well, as we will see in a moment.)

Government *consumption* includes all the salaries paid to government workers, such as teachers, police, military personnel, U.S. senators, and the president. It also counts all purchases by the government for immediate use, including food for government cafeterias, pencils for government offices, and fuel for nuclear submarines.

Government *investment,* on the other hand, reports all purchases of long-lived assets such as tanks and planes, government buildings, and software. It also includes money the government spends on building and maintaining highways and airports. The purchase of a new fire truck is investment by your local government, but the salaries paid to firefighters are government consumption.

The output of government is thus equal to government consumption plus government in-

vestment. One major output of government is spending on national defense. Figure 7.3, shows how government's outlays for defense and nondefense goods and services have changed over time. Since the 1950s peak of the Korean War, defense spending has dropped as a share of GDP. Nondefense government spending on goods and services peaked in the mid-1970s. There was a slight reduction during the era of deregulation, as discussed in Chapter 6. Still, the pro- and anti-government political forces in the United States have mostly fought each other to a standstill over this period.

Figure 7.3 includes only government spending that is counted as part of GDP. However, as previously mentioned, there's a second way government indirectly contributes to GDP: money that is routed through the government for production actually done by the private sector. For example, Medicare and Medicaid are government programs that spend enormous sums, but most actual healthcare is performed by private hospitals and doctors. Because the government does not do the actual production, BEA statisticians don't count this type of government spending as government output.

FIGURE 7.3 | **Nondefense versus Defense Government Spending**

This chart shows government spending on nondefense goods and services versus defense goods and services. Both are measured as percentages of GDP, and include all levels of government.

Source: Bureau of Economic Analysis as of April 2011, www.bea.gov.

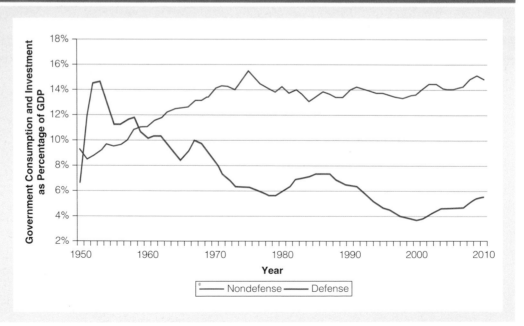

Similarly, government output does not include spending on Social Security, unemployment insurance, education grants, veteran benefits, food stamps, welfare payments, or housing subsidies.

Change in Private Inventories

The change in private inventories is a small but important component of GDP. This category represents the increase or decrease of inventories held by manufacturers, wholesalers, and retailers. Goods that are produced but are not immediately sold—like cars—go into inventories. When companies add to their inventories, this change contributes positively to GDP because the goods count as production even if no one has bought them yet. When companies draw down their inventories by selling goods, the change in this category is subtracted from GDP.

Inadequate inventory management used to play a significant role in making economic downturns worse. Before the information revolution, companies had a hard time tracking sales and inventories in real time. In fact, it was a ritual for many manufacturers and retailers to physically count their inventory once a year. The problem was that when the economy slowed, inventories would build up unrecognized. And when manufacturers finally realized their mistakes, they would need to work off these inventories by cutting back production and laying off factory workers.

But today information technology lets companies keep much better track of their inventories. In addition, many firms now manufacture cars, computers, or other products only when they actually have customer orders in hand and thus build up little or no unsold inventory. What's more, many goods consumed in the United States are now imported. As a result, when sales slow, inventories build up in foreign factories, where they do not count as part of U.S. GDP. As a result, inventory swings have become less important to the overall U.S. economy.

Net Exports

In this era of globalization, foreign trade is more important than ever. One measure of the contribution of the global economy to GDP is measured by *net exports,* which equal exports minus imports. **Exports** are goods and services produced in one country—in this case, the United States—and sold outside that country, so they count as part of gross domestic product. If a company builds a tractor in the United States for sale overseas, that's part of gross domestic product.

In contrast, **imports,** which are goods and services produced outside a country and consumed within that country, are considered in the GDP calculation with a negative sign. If you buy a toy from China that was imported into the United States for $5, that's $5 of personal consumption spending that wasn't for goods or services produced at home.

SPOTLIGHT: A DAY IN THE LIFE OF GDP

As you move through your day, almost everything you do is counted in GDP in one way or another. Consider the Bedell family in Catonsville, Maryland, a suburb of Baltimore. When we looked in on them in 2008, the family had three boys and two girls, ages 2 to 15. Most mornings the kids ate cereal for breakfast (that counts as personal consumption). Then two of the children were picked up by school buses (the buses, owned and operated by a private company, were counted as nonresidential investment when they were purchased). The salaries of their teachers, of course, counted as government consumption.

Both parents, John and Lisa, worked. Lisa was a nurse at a private nonprofit hospital in Baltimore. All the hospital equipment counted as nonresidential investment when it was purchased.

When the Bedell children came home, they often played video games (personal consumption) in the basement, which was just refinished in 2007 (the cost of the renovation counted as residential investment). And most components of the video game console were made overseas, so they counted as imports.

In 2010 the United States imported about $2.3 trillion of goods and services, and exported $1.8 trillion of goods and services. Because imports today exceed exports, net exports are negative (about $500 billion) Let's stop here for a moment. The fact that net exports are negative doesn't mean that global trade is bad for the United States. As we will see in Chapter 14, the United States benefits in many different ways from trade, including lower prices and faster innovation.

GROSS DOMESTIC PURCHASES

The amount spent by consumers, businesses, and government within the United States on final goods and services.

However, the fact that net exports are negative means that the United States is consuming more than it produces. **Gross domestic purchases** indicate the amount spent within the United States on final goods and services by consumers, businesses, and government. That is, it represents the *spending* activity of the whole country. In comparison, GDP is the amount of final goods and services *produced* in the United States. When gross domestic purchases are greater than gross domestic product, as is the case now, that means net exports are negative.

HOW IT WORKS: TRACKING THE GLOBAL CORPORATION

Large United States–based companies such as IBM, Intel, and GE have become increasingly global over the past 20 years. For example, GE, based in Fairfield, CT, is one of the most successful companies in the world. It collected $80 billion in sales outside the United States in 2010, finding ready customers for everything from turbines to jet engines to medical equipment to locomotives.

However, much of those overseas sales were the result of goods and services that were produced outside the United States. In 2010 GE's exports of American-made products totaled $17 billion, far less than total international sales.

In fact, GE, like many other large U.S. multinationals, has been expanding faster outside the United States. than within it, to take advantage of fast-growing regions such as Asia and the Middle East. At the same time, however, non-U.S. multinationals have been expanding within the United States. Ikea, the Swedish furniture company, contributed to U.S. GDP in 2008 when it opened a new factory in Danville, Virginia. Similarly, in 2010 the German company Siemens contributed to GDP in the United States when it built a new wind turbine factory in Hutchinson, Kansas.

WHAT GDP DOES NOT INCLUDE

GDP focuses primarily on the market economy—the part of the economy in which people get paid for the work they do. However, it does not cover the **nonmarket economy,** in which people may work just as hard but not get paid. For example, a stay-at-home parent is not given credit in the national income accounts for all the time and effort that go into raising children, cleaning house, and cooking food. That nonmarket labor disappears completely from GDP as if children magically raise themselves and homes stay clean without effort. All the hard work put in by volunteers at hospitals, schools, and religious organizations is not counted as part of GDP either.

The annual time use study by the Bureau of Labor Statistics shows that on average, U.S. adults spent 3.5 hours per day on unpaid work in 2009. That includes housework, child care, and volunteering. Surprisingly, they spent as much time, 3.5 hours per day, on paid work. (The reason that number seems low is that it includes weekends and the time of people who don't hold paid jobs, such as stay-at-home parents and the retired.)

If we counted those hours of unpaid work in GDP, how much would they be worth?

Let's suppose we compensated all the unpaid hours at the low figure of $7 per hour. Then unpaid work would be worth roughly $24 a day ($7.00 times 3.4 hours). With 365 days in a year, that means the unpaid work is worth about $9,000 per person, or about $2 trillion for the 240 million people in the United States who are 16 and older.

The omission of unpaid work from GDP creates some odd situations. For example, if a hospital moves an unpaid volunteer worker onto the payroll, GDP goes up even if the person is doing exactly the same amount of work as before. Similarly, if a mother who has been staying home to take care of her children takes a job outside the home and hires a nanny to watch the children, those child care activities move from the unpaid to the paid sector and now show up on the GDP ledger.

One final note: GDP also does not measure the **underground economy,** the portion of the economy that does not pay taxes or otherwise get reported to the government. That includes illegal activities such as drug dealing and off-the-book transactions such as the babysitter or the landscaper who gets paid in cash and does not report it to the Internal Revenue Service. Estimates vary widely, but the size of the underground economy in the United States could be as large as 10 percent of GDP.

INTERNATIONAL COMPARISONS OF GDP

So far we've been looking at the gross domestic product of the United States, which has the largest economy in the world. Other countries calculate their own GDP using roughly the same rules and principles. That allows us to see how the U.S. economy stacks up against the production of other countries.

An international comparison of GDP tells us which countries have the most production. It can also indicate which countries have the highest living standards. And of course we can still fulfill

> GDP does not include the nonmarket or underground economies.

one of the original purposes of gross domestic product, which is to calculate military capabilities (countries with higher GDP can generally produce more military ships, planes, and other equipment).

Today the largest economy in the world still belongs to the United States. China, which is number 2, has an economy half the size of that of the United States, followed by Japan and India.

GDP per Capita

GDP tells you how big an economy is—that is, how much it can produce. However, if we want to know which countries have higher living standards and which have lower, we need to look at population too. India, for example, has a bigger gross domestic product than does Sweden, but India also has many more people.

The key concept here is **GDP per capita,** or GDP per person. GDP per capita is the economic output of a country divided by the size of its population. In other words, GDP per capita measures the amount of output each person would get if the economic pie were sliced evenly.

Figure 7.4, shows the GDP per capita for selected countries. At the top are Norway, the United States, Switzerland, and Canada. Other European countries and Japan trail somewhat behind, followed by industrializing Asian countries such as South Korea. Then come middle-income countries such as Russia and Mexico. China has a GDP per capita roughly one-sixth that of the United States, while India's, even though it has been improving, is still well below the Chinese level. Bringing up the rear are poor countries such as Bangladesh and Ethiopia.

These numbers should be viewed a bit skeptically because it's hard to make economic comparisons across countries. What is true, though, is that looking at GDP per capita tells us that much of the world still has a long way to go before reaching the living standards of the United States and the big European countries.

| FIGURE 7.4 | An International Comparison of GDP per Capita |

This figure compares GDP per capita in 2010 for selected countries. Numbers are adjusted to reflect different price levels in different countries.

Source: International Monetary Fund, April 2011.

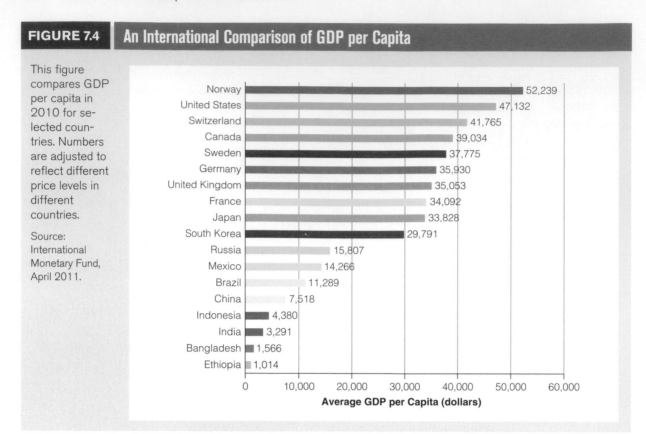

CONCLUSION

Measuring the size of the economy is the essential first step in macroeconomics. The key measure is gross domestic product (GDP), which enables us to put a dollar value on the output of the economy. We can also use GDP to compare different economies.

However, GDP is just a snapshot at a moment in time. In the next two chapters, we will go further and look at how the economy changes over time.

07 SUMMARY

1. The Great Depression and World War II forced economists to invent new tools for measuring an economy. They came up with gross domestic product (GDP), which is the dollar value of the output of an economy. Gross domestic product counts only purchases of final goods and services, not purchases of intermediate inputs. *(LO7-1)*

2. Gross domestic product includes personal consumption, nonresidential investment, residential investment, government consumption and investment, inventory investment, and net exports. *(LO7-2)*

3. GDP does not include the nonmarket economy, such as the work done by stay-at-home

parents and volunteers. It also does not include the underground economy of illegal and off-the-book activities. *(LO7-3)*

4. GDP and GDP per capita allow economists to compare living standards across countries. *(LO7-4)*

KEY TERMS AND CONCEPTS

macroeconomics

gross domestic product

system of national
  accounts

personal consumption

nonresidential investment

residential investment

change in private inventories

government consumption
  and investment

net exports

final goods and services

intermediate inputs

output of government

exports

imports

gross domestic purchases

nonmarket economy

underground economy

GDP per capita

PROBLEMS

1. Which of these is *not* a reason why we might want to measure the size of the economy? *(LO7-1)*

   a) To track the magnitude of recessions.

   b) To estimate the productive capacity of the country in case of war.

   c) To measure the happiness of people.

   d) To estimate tax collections.

   e) To compare living standards in different countries.

2. Suppose we have a small economy that produces only two goods: pineapples and commercial airplanes. *(LO7-1)*

   a) Here are the quantities produced and the prices for pineapples and commercial airplanes. What is the GDP of this country?

	Amount Produced	Prices
Pineapples	40,000,000 lbs	$1.00 per lb
Commercial aircraft	10 aircraft	$10 million per plane

   b) Suppose five additional planes were produced and sold overseas. Does that change GDP, and if so, how?

3. Indicate whether each of the following transactions is a part of final goods and services or an intermediate input. If it is part of final goods and services, indicate which GDP component it belongs to—personal consumption, nonresidential investment, residential investment, government purchases of goods and services, inventory investment, or net exports. *(LO7-1)*

   a) A restaurant purchases chopped meat to use in hamburgers.

   b) A restaurant buys new chairs for its dining room.

   c) A family on vacation in the United States rents a car.

   d) The local school district pays the salary of a first-grade teacher.

4. Consider a private detective agency, that does investigations for hire. In which category of GDP, if any, does each of the following spy expenditures belong, assuming that all purchases take place in the United States? *(LO7-2)*

   a) Purchases of miniature cameras for use in investigations.

   b) Purchases of Diet Coke for the agency cafeteria.

   c) The purchase of a new cell phone for the head of the agency.

   d) The purchase of a full set of James Bond movies for personal use by one of the agency's employees.

5. Indicate whether each of the following events causes GDP to increase, decrease, or stay the same, all other things remaining equal. *(LO7-2)*

   a) Consumers pay for fewer haircuts, and use the extra money to buy iPads that are made in China.

   b) Toyota builds a new car plant in the United States, and a same-size car plant run by Ford closes.

   c) Apple hires engineers and programmers in the United States to help design the next generation of iPads.

   d) Toyota builds a new car plant in the United States and reduces imports of its cars from Japan.

6. Which is the following is not included in GDP? *(LO7-3)*

   a) The value of the time of a stay-at-home parent.

   b) The purchase of a ticket to a Lady Gaga performance.

   c) The salary of a public school teacher.

   d) A new cell phone.

7. The rise of fast food restaurants such as McDonald's made it easier for families to go out to eat, rather than preparing their food at home. All other things being equal, the shift of food preparation from the home to the fast food restaurant had the effect of _____. *(LO7-3)*

   a) lowering GDP

   b) raising GDP

   c) leaving GDP unchanged

8. The following table gives the gross domestic product (in dollars) and the population for three countries. *(LO7-4)*

Country	Gross Domestic Product in 2010 (Billions of Dollars)	Population in 2010 (Millions of People)	GDP per Capita (Thousands of Dollars per Person)
Argentina	632	41	?
Turkey	957	71	?
Vietnam	276	88	?

Source: International Monetary Fund.

a) Calculate the GDP per capita for all three countries.

b) Which country has the highest GDP per capita?

c) Which country has the largest economy, based on GDP?

08 INFLATION

LEARNING OBJECTIVES

After reading this chapter, you should be able to:

LO8-1 Define inflation and calculate the inflation rate using the consumer price index (CPI).

LO8-2 Explain the difference between relative price shifts and the overall inflation rate.

LO8-3 Calculate and show how incomes and wages can be adjusted for inflation.

LO8-4 Discuss the impact of unexpected and expected inflation.

Everything has a price—that is, everything that is bought and sold in a market economy. In the United States there are billions of different prices. Some businesses, like airlines, change their prices every day, raising ticket prices on some routes and lowering them on others. Other businesses operate for years without changing their prices. Electronics stores always seem to be cutting their prices on computers, whereas colleges always seem to be raising tuition.

To get a clearer picture of what's happening to prices in the economy as a whole, we need to be able to average those billions of prices together. We want to know whether the *overall* level of prices is falling or rising, and how fast.

That rise in overall prices—also known as *inflation*—is a key measure of the health of an economy. If prices are rising too fast (rapid price declines do happen, though rarely), that's bad news for consumers and businesses. In fact, a main goal of economic policymakers around the world—particularly the people who run the central banks of each country—is to keep inflation under control.

In this chapter we take the next big step into macroeconomics by defining the idea of an average price level for a whole economy. We'll explain how we can use this average price level to calculate the inflation rate. We'll also compare a rise in the overall price level and a shift in relative prices, and show how inflation is adjusted for changes in quality. We'll look at the difference between expected and unexpected inflation and identify who gets helped or hurt by each. Finally, we'll end with a discussion of falling prices, which is known as *deflation*.

THE BASICS OF INFLATION

Suppose you were walking down the street, and every 10 feet a thief stole a nickel or a dime out of your pocket. The first few times it might be funny, but then you would start getting annoyed. After a while you'd realize that the steady theft of nickels and dimes was really making you poorer.

That, in a nutshell, is how inflation works. As prices rise, it's as if the money in your pocket were shrinking and becoming capable of buying less. Over the past 35 years, the overall price level in the United States has quadrupled. That means $25,000 in 1975 had the buying power of $100,000 today. It's as if each dollar today has become less valuable and is worth only a quarter of what it was worth 30 years ago. Or to put it a different way, if your parents earned $25,000 in 1975, and you are earning $100,000 today, you are not doing any better than they were.

The Average Price Level

At any moment in time, consumers will see the prices of some goods and services rising while other items are becoming cheaper. In February 2011, for instance, the prices of clothing, telephone services, and personal computers all fell. In the same month the prices of food, rent, new cars, tuition, and medical care, among other things, rose. In other words, that month was good for someone who was buying a new shirt and bad for someone who had to shell out bucks to fill a car with gas.

When we talk about inflation, though, we're concerned with what is happening to prices *across the entire economy,* not to any particular item or even category of items. The **average level of prices** in the economy measures how much it costs to buy a **market basket** of common goods and services. The U.S. Bureau of Labor Statistics (BLS) picks the contents of the market basket to represent the pattern of expenditures by a typical

AVERAGE LEVEL OF PRICES
A measure of how much it costs to purchase a market basket of goods and services.

CONSUMER PRICE INDEX (CPI)
A measure that tracks the average price level from a base year.

INFLATION RATE
The annual percentage change in the average price level.

U.S. household and gives each item a certain weight to represent its relative importance in the typical budget (see Table 8.1).

The single biggest part of the market basket is "owners' equivalent rent of primary residence," which is a measure of the cost of owning your home. (see "How It Works: Measuring the Price of Housing"). The second largest part of the market basket is food consumed at home, followed by medical care. Some items that get the most attention in the media, such as gasoline, account for only a small portion of the market basket.

Any particular person or household may have a pattern of expenditures different from the market basket. For example, if you are young, you will tend to spend more on education and less on healthcare than an elderly household. But the basket is reasonably representative of the typical expenditures of an average U.S household.

To make comparisons between years easier, the BLS has chosen 100 to represent the average 1982–1984 price level, and it now measures all other years relative to this base year. This measurement gives us the **consumer price index,** or **CPI,** which tracks the average price level in the United States.

For example, the CPI in 1992 was 140.3. That means the average price level in 1992 was 40.3 percent above the average price level in 1982–84. In Figure 8.1, we can see the consumer price index for the United States from 1950 to 2010.

For another example, we will look at three years. The CPI was 107.6 in 1985 and 218.6 in 2010 (both are marked in the figure). That means the average price level rose about 2 times between 1985 and 2010 because 218.1 divided by 107.6 is roughly about 2. This in turn means $2,000 today has roughly the buying power of $1,000 in 1985.

The Inflation Rate

We formally define **inflation** as a sustained upward movement in the average level of prices. The **inflation rate** is the annual percentage change

TABLE 8.1	Some Big Contributors to the Consumer Market Basket

This table shows the relative importance of different categories of goods in the market basket used to calculate the consumer price index. For a particular individual, of course, the percentages could be much different.

Category of Spending	Percentage of Market Basket, 2010	Includes
Owners' equivalent rent of primary residence	23.3	Owner-occupied homes
Food at home	7.8	Food bought for consumption at home
Medical care	6.6	Drugs, hospitals, physicians, insurance
Recreation	6.3	Consumer electronics, sporting equipment, pets, tickets to sporting events
Food away from home	5.9	Restaurants, fast food, school cafeterias
Rent of primary residence	5.9	Rented homes and apartments
Gasoline	4.9	Gasoline
Apparel	3.6	Clothing
New vehicles	3.5	Cars, SUVs, trucks
Communication	3.3	Postage, computers, telephone service, Internet service
Education	3.1	Tuition and books

Source: Bureau of Labor Statistics, www.bls.gov.

in the average price level, or a measure of how much the average price level changes over a year. Because the CPI tracks the average price level, the inflation rate is also the annual percentage change in the CPI. For example, the inflation rate for 2010 is the percentage change in the CPI from 2009 to 2010.

As Figure 8.2 shows, the annual inflation rate was low through most of the 1960s. In 1962, for example, the inflation rate was 1 percent, equivalent

HOW IT WORKS: MEASURING THE PRICE OF HOUSING

We all know what the price of a home means. Then why does the Bureau of Labor Statistics (BLS) measure the price of housing with the complicated phrase "owners' equivalent rent of primary residence"?

What the BLS is trying to measure is the price of a year's worth of housing services, rather than the price of owning the whole home forever. So rather than looking at the sale prices of homes, the BLS statisticians look at the price of renting similar homes for a year. They use that rental price as the "owners' equivalent rent of primary residence." The rent paid for a home is a pure measure of how much people are willing to pay, per month or year, for the privilege of living in that home for that period.

Usually the owners' equivalent rent is less volatile than home prices. For example, home prices soared by 80 percent between 2000 and 2006, but the owners' equivalent rent went up by only 20 percent. Then during the Great Recession, housing prices plunged by 30 percent between 2006 and 2010. However, the owners' equivalent rent actually rose by 8 percent because rents on comparable homes continued to rise.

Source: Bureau of Labor Statistics, www.bls.gov.

FIGURE 8.1   **The Consumer Price Index, 1950–2010**

The consumer price index (CPI) represents the average level of consumer prices based on a market basket of goods.

Source: Bureau of Labor Statistics, www.bls.gov.

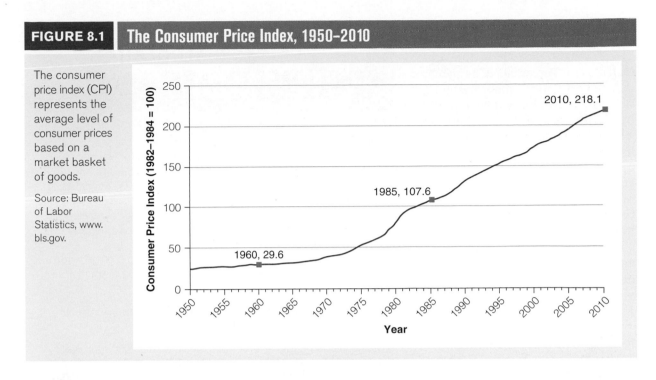

to the price of a $1.00 soft drink today going up by a penny in one year. On the other hand, the figure shows that inflation skyrocketed in the late 1970s and early 1980s, hitting 13.5 percent in 1980. In fact, inflation was generally identified as the biggest economic problem in those years. (Later in this chapter we'll explain why high inflation is so disturbing.)

Since 1990 the annual inflation rate has remained under 4 percent. In 2009 the annual

FIGURE 8.2   **Annual Consumer Inflation Rate, 1950–2010**

This figure shows the percentage increase of the average price level from one year to the next as measured by the consumer price index.

Source: Bureau of Labor Statistics, www.bls.gov.

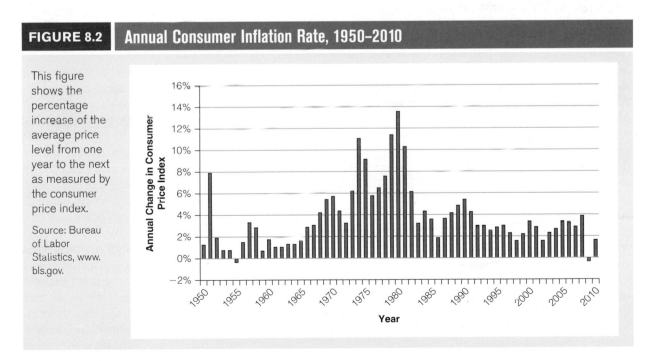

inflation rate was actually negative: the CPI fell from 215.3 in 2008 to 214.5 in 2009. (See "How It Works: Calculating Percentage Change.")

The CPI and the consumer inflation rate are published each month by the Bureau of Labor Statistics, which surveys 23,000 retail establishments and 50,000 households to update the prices in its market basket. The BLS then calculates how much the average price level changed that month. The BLS also calculates how much the average price level changed over the past year. For example, in February 2011 the CPI increased by 0.5 percent. In the previous 12 months prices had risen by 2.1 percent.

A related measure, also published by the BLS, is **core inflation.** That's the consumer inflation rate *without* taking food and energy into account. Why would we want to leave out food and energy? One reason is that those two categories happen to be volatile, sometimes spiking and then coming back down again. For example, if there's a frost in Florida, the prices of vegetables and fruit can jump and push up the overall inflation rate. But when the next growing season starts, those prices drop. Similarly, we've seen spikes in energy prices that have retreated when oil-producing countries put more oil on the market.

These big movements in food and energy prices can sometimes obscure what's happening to inflation in other goods and services. For example, from February 2010 to February 2011, the overall inflation rate was 2.1 percent, but the core rate was 1.1 percent.

Which number matters more? If we expect food and energy prices to come back down to "normal," then we should keep an eye on the core inflation rate. But if we expect food and energy prices to stay high, then the overall inflation rate is the one to watch.

HOW IT WORKS: CALCULATING PERCENTAGE CHANGE

Economics is concerned, in part, with how rapidly the economy changes over time. For example, the inflation rate indicates how fast the price level is rising. And in the next chapter we'll see that the growth rate indicates how fast the economy is expanding.

In both cases we measure the speed of change as an annual percentage change. A 1 percent inflation rate, for example, is a relatively small rise in the price level, whereas a 20 percent rise would be quite large.

Here's the formula for calculating percentage change when we know the original level of a measure, such as prices, and a new level measured later:

Percentage change = [(Original number − New number)/ Original number] × 100

Suppose, for instance, that the price of dinner for two at your favorite restaurant goes from $50 to $55. How big a percentage change is that? The percentage change from the original level of 50 to the new level of 55 is

[(55 − 50)/50] × 100 = [5/50] × 100 = 0.1 × 100 = 10%

Notice that multiplying by 100 in the last step simply converts the answer to a percentage.

RELATIVE PRICE SHIFTS

The inflation figures that get the most attention each month are the overall inflation rate and the core inflation rate. The Bureau of Labor Statistics also reports the inflation rate for subcategories of goods and services, narrowing the figures down to such individual fruits as apples, bananas, and oranges (including tangerines). Funeral expenses get their own price index, as do college textbooks, food from vending machines and mobile vendors, and "beer and other malt beverages away from home."

A **relative price shift** happens when the inflation rate of a good or service is significantly higher or lower than the overall inflation rate. If it's higher, then that good or service is getting more expensive over time relative to other possible purchases. If the inflation rate of

RELATIVE PRICE SHIFT

Where the inflation rate of a good or service is significantly higher or lower than the overall inflation rate.

TABLE 8.2	Shifts in Relative Prices, 2000–2010

This table shows some goods and services where prices have been rising much faster than the overall rate of inflation, and some for which prices have been rising much more slowly or even falling.

Selected Consumer Goods and Services	Average Annual Inflation Rate, 2000–2010 (%)
College tuition	6.8
Gasoline	6.4
Admission to sporting events	4.2
Medical care	4.1
Alcoholic beverages away from home	3.5
Owners' equivalent rent of primary residence	2.6
Haircuts and other personal services	2.6
All items	**2.4**
Airline fare	1.5
New vehicles	−0.3
Apparel	−0.8
Sports equipment	−0.9
Wireless phone service	−2.0
Toys	−5.6
Personal computers and peripherals	−16.4
Televisions	−16.7

Source: Bureau of Labor Statistics, www.bls.gov.

in items important to college students. The annual inflation rate for all items averaged 2.4 percent in the 10 years between 2000 and 2010. But the prices of goods such as apparel, toys, televisions, sports equipment, and automotive vehicles actually dropped over the same period. These goods have become relatively cheaper.

What other items have become relatively cheaper? The biggest declines have come in the technology area (not surprisingly), where consumer electronics, wireless telephone services, personal computers, and related items have dropped dramatically in price.

In contrast, the price of gasoline went way up due to a combination of the soaring demand for oil around the world and unrest in the Middle East. The relative prices of many services have risen as well; their inflation rates have been significantly higher than overall inflation. For example, looking at Table 8.2, we see that admissions to sporting events rose at a 4.2 percent annual rate between 2000 and 2010—far faster than the overall inflation rate, and probably due to the soaring pay of athletes. Other services with fast-rising prices included medical care and college tuition. (For an example of a recent relative price shift, see "Spotlight: The Price of Air Travel.")

Globalization and Inflation

One key reason why some goods have become relatively cheaper is globalization. The production of many goods has shifted from the United States and the developed countries of Europe to lower-cost developing countries such as China. That's certainly kept down prices for things like clothing and consumer electronics, which are mostly imported.

In contrast, it is much harder to shift the production of services overseas. When you get your hair cut, the person holding the scissors generally

a good or service is lower than the overall inflation rate, it's getting relatively cheaper.

If we look at the long-term inflation statistics in Table 8.2, we can see some large relative price shifts

Economic Milestone

1994 THE GREAT COFFEE CRUNCH

Coffee drinkers were hit by a very large relative price shift in 1994 because of a spate of natural disasters in coffee-growing countries that made coffee beans scarce: insects in Colombia, frost in Brazil, civil war in Rwanda. A pound of ground roast coffee rose from $2.50 in January of that year to $4.50 by August—a much bigger rise than the overall price level.

SPOTLIGHT: THE PRICE OF AIR TRAVEL

Air travel has become more popular in recent years. Planes are packed full, and delays are common because airports are so congested.

But have airplane tickets become cheaper or more expensive? According to the Bureau of Labor Statistics, the average price of plane tickets rose by 16 percent between 2000 and 2010. However, over the same period, the overall price index rose by 27 percent. In other words, air travel became a lot cheaper during that stretch compared to other goods and services. That helps explain why the number of air passengers increased over the period.

has to be at the same location as you. As a result, it is difficult to import haircuts. Medical care, too, has proven tough to outsource because much of it, from surgery to nursing to physical rehabilitation, has to be delivered in person.

But gradually companies are figuring out how to "offshore" parts of service industries. In theory, for example, you could do your homework assignments online and they could be graded by someone in India or the Philippines. Your X-rays can be read by technicians overseas, though that is still not common. As events like these become feasible, the trend for goods to become cheaper relative to services could slow down—or even reverse if the prices of services were to fall low enough.

Quality Improvements and Inflation

When is a price increase not really a price increase? The inflation rate is supposed to measure price changes of a fixed market basket of goods and services. But in the real world products are always changing. Companies introduce new products and improve their old ones.

Sometimes the price of a good or service rises because of an **improvement in quality,** which is a change in the nature of a good or service that increases its value for buyers. In that case, we don't count that price increase as part of the inflation rate. Suppose a car manufacturer decides to install antilock braking as a standard feature in all its cars and raises prices by $100 at the same time. According to BLS statisticians, that price increase should not enter into the calculation of inflation because it represents a quality improvement and not merely a price change.

When the quality or features of a product change slowly over time, it's relatively easy for the BLS to get a sense of how much of a price increase is related to changes in the product and how much represents a **pure price change.** A pure price change is simply a change in price without any change in the quality or nature of a product.

However, in areas of the economy where rapid technological change is taking place, an existing product or service can be replaced by one that's different and hard to compare to the original. For example, each generation of personal computers is faster than the one before. That makes the job of measuring inflation more difficult because even when the price seems to stay the same, the actual power of the computer is increasing, which makes computer power cheaper over time.

The same is true of consumer electronics. Consider, for example, the Sony Walkman, which was an enormous hit when it was introduced in 1979. It retailed for about $200 and held one audiocassette's worth of music, or roughly 15 songs. For the first time people could bring their music with them.

Compare that to the first iPod, which sold for $399 but held about 1,000 songs when Apple introduced it in 2001. If we are calculating the inflation rate for consumer electronics, should the difference between the Walkman and the iPod be counted as a price increase or a price decrease? The first iPod cost a lot more than the first Walkman; but the iPod had a much lower price per song (roughly 20 cents compared to about $1.30 for the Walkman).

The price comparison between the Walkman and the iPod is difficult enough, but at least they perform the same function: playing music on a portable device. Measuring inflation is even harder when technological change is disruptive—that is, when it enables us to do things that weren't realistically possible before, like having a GPS system in a car or taking a college course online.

The Walkman was an enormous hit in 1979.

ADJUSTING FOR INFLATION

In 1979 the typical U.S. household had an income of about $16,461. As of 2009 the typical household had an income of about $49,777 (where *typical* is defined as the median household, so half of U.S. households receive less than this household and half receive more). At first glance it looks as though incomes have tripled over this 30-year stretch.

But in fact almost all that apparent gain in income is canceled out by inflation. Over that same 30-year period the average price level has almost tripled as well. Some items have risen even more. College costs have skyrocketed: a year of tuition, room, and board at Yale University was $8,140 in the 1979–1980 school year. As of the 2009–2010 school year, it was $47,500, an increase of almost six times.

So if you merely compared household income over time without looking at changes in prices, you would run the risk of suffering from **money illusion.** Money illusion is the mistake that we make when we compare dollar amounts in different periods without adjusting for inflation.

Here's an example of money illusion. From 1955 to 1960, on a television show called *The Millionaire,* an eccentric old industrialist supposedly gave away a million dollars each week to a lucky person (it was staged, though). In 1999 a new television show called *Who Wants to Be a Millionaire* debuted, on which contestants answered Regis Philbin's questions with the ultimate goal of winning a million dollars. But when we look at the statistics published by the Bureau of Labor Statistics, we see that inflation has taken its toll on the prize: the average price level rose by more than six times between 1955 and 1999. So Regis would have to have given away more than $6 million to match the purchasing power of that anonymous (and fake) 1955 millionaire.

Avoiding Money Illusion

Suppose we have a quantity measured in dollars over time, such as our salary, the budget of our city or state, the price of our home, or the amount of money we have in the bank. To avoid money illusion, we must compare the change in these dollar figures with the inflation rate.

For example, suppose you are working and earning $50,000 per year. Your boss offers you a 3 percent raise of $1,500. Is that good news? It depends on the inflation rate. If inflation is running at 2 percent per year, then your 3 percent raise gives you an increase in purchasing power. But if the inflation rate is 4 percent, you are actually losing purchasing power because even with the increase, your income is going up more slowly than the average price level.

To avoid money illusion, the solution is to use the **real change,** which is the change in the money value after removing the effects of inflation (this is also sometimes called the **inflation-adjusted change**). A good rule of thumb for calculating the real change is to take the percentage change in dollars minus the inflation rate (there is a more precise formula for calculating the real change, which we show in the next section). We call the increase or decrease in a money value without adjusting for inflation

REAL OR INFLATION-ADJUSTED CHANGE
The change in a money value, after removing the effects of inflation.

the **nominal change.** So if your nominal percentage change in wages is 3 percent, and the inflation rate is 2 percent, then your real increase in wages is 3 percent minus 2 percent, or 1 percent.

We can apply the same principle to any other economic quantity measured in dollars. For example, it's important to adjust for inflation when we're looking at government budgets. Spending by a government agency may rise—but if it doesn't go up as fast as inflation, then the real value of the budget is falling and the agency is actually spending less, not more.

One example is federal spending on elementary and secondary education, which includes direct grants to the states, as well as things like the early education program Head Start, which assists children from low-income families. Federal spending on elementary and secondary education rose from $39.7 billion in 2006 to $40 billion in 2007; that was an 0.8 percent increase. But with inflation running at about 2.5 percent, real federal education spending actually declined by 1.7 percent (0.8% − 2.5%).

Real versus Nominal Dollars

The rule of thumb for calculating the real increase works well in most situations. But the most precise way to avoid money illusion is to transform the original dollar figures (also called *nominal* dollars) into *real* dollars (also called *inflation-adjusted* dollars).

How do we do this? We pick a base year—say 2005. We then use the consumer price index to adjust the nominal dollar figures for any other year to get real figures that eliminate the effects of inflation. The result is reported in "2005 dollars," or whatever the base year is.

Let's give a simple example first. Suppose that you earned $100,000 in 2005. Your boss decides to give you a raise of 3.2 percent in 2006, or $3,200 (that's 3.2 percent × $100,000). That seems like a fair amount of money.

But then you realize that the inflation rate in 2006 is 3.2 percent also, which cancels out your entire raise. In other words, your 2006 salary, expressed in 2005 dollars, is still $100,000. There's been no change in the your real salary at all!

SPOTLIGHT: WHICH MOVIE EARNED MORE MONEY?

Every year Hollywood proudly announces that a new blockbuster movie has broken all records. In 2007, for example, the top-grossing film was *Spiderman 3*, which had ticket sales of $337 million. By comparison, in 1989 the first Batman film earned a seemingly far less impressive $251 million.

But it turns out that when we adjust for inflation, Batman beat Spiderman with no problem. Batman took in $395 million in 1989, measured in 2005 dollars. But *Spiderman 3* had only $317 million in domestic ticket sales in 2007, also measured in 2005 dollars.

Source: www.boxofficemojo.com, Bureau of Labor Statistics.

Here is a formula for transforming a nominal amount into a real amount:

Real money amount = Nominal money amount × (Consumer price index for base year/ Consumer price index for current year)

For example, suppose we wanted to calculate real wages in 2005 dollars. According to the Bureau of Labor Statistics, in 2005 the average hourly wage for production and nonsupervisory workers—basically anyone who isn't a manager—was $16.13. By 2010, the average hourly wage had risen to $19.07. At first glance that seems like a pretty good increase.

But over the same stretch, the consumer price index rose from 195.3 in 2005 to 218.1 in 2010. So the real hourly wage in 2010, expressed in 2005 dollars, is:

Real hourly wage in 2010 = $19.07 × (195.3/ 218.1)

This calculation is outlined in Table 8.3. The third column reports the nominal wage for the two years. The fourth column reports the real wage, which is obtained by multiplying the second column—the inflation adjustment—by the nominal wage in the third column.

TABLE 8.3	Calculating Real Wages

This table shows how we can use the consumer price index to transform nominal hourly wages into real hourly wages.

	Consumer Price Index	Inflation Adjustment to "2005 Dollars"	Nominal Average Hourly Wage in Dollars	Real Average Hourly Wage in 2005 Dollars
2005	195.3	195.3/195.3=1	$16.13	$16.13
2010	218.1	195.3/218.1=0.9	$19.07	$17.08

Source: Bureau of Labor Statistics, www.bls.gov.

As shown in Table 8.3, the real hourly wage in 2010 was $17.08, measured in 2008 dollars. That's just a bit higher than the $16.13 average hourly wage in 2005. So shifting to real dollars has shown us that wages, adjusted for inflation, went up between 2005 and 2010, but far less than it appeared at first.

EXPECTATIONS AND INFLATION

So far we've been discussing how the average price level has changed over time. In effect, we've been looking backward and comparing different years. Now we will look forward into the future and introduce the intriguing idea of **expected inflation.** Expected inflation, as the name implies, is the inflation rate that consumers and businesses expect will happen over the next year or even further into the future.

Expected inflation forms the basis for pricing and wage decisions that businesses make. For example, if you are a company manager, and you expect a 3 percent inflation rate over the next year, you know your workers will need at least a 3 percent raise to stay even with inflation, and you will need to raise your prices at least 3 percent to cover your increased costs of doing business. Or if you are proposing a budget for a government agency and the expected rate of inflation is 5 per-

EXPECTED INFLATION
The inflation rate that consumers and businesses expect will happen over the next year or longer.

cent, you start with the assumption that the agency will need a budget increase of 5 percent if it is to deliver the same services next year.

Businesses and individuals form their inflation expectations based on their recent experience. So if inflation has been running at 2 percent a year, people generally expect that rate to continue. There's a certain amount of inertia in expectations. In fact, expectations are one reason why inflation, once it gets started, is so hard to drive out of an economy.

But the real question is what happens to expectations when there is a sudden jump in prices. For example, if the price of gasoline soars from, say, $1 a gallon to $3 a gallon, there's a risk that people will now expect that *higher* rate of inflation to continue.

A **wage–price spiral** occurs when businesses and workers boost prices and wages faster and faster to stay ahead of higher expected inflation. An economy stuck in a wage–price spiral is like a dog chasing its own tail. Expected inflation rises, so everyone boosts prices and wages more, which drives up expected inflation even faster.

Hyperinflation

In the worst possible case of wage–price spiraling we get **hyperinflation**—a very fast increase in the average price level. Rather than rising gradually, prices soar faster than the mind can follow. This

A 10 million boliviano note.

Brazilian cruzados replaced cruzieros to cope with hyperinflation.

danger seems to start when inflation gets into double digits like 15 percent or 20 percent a year. At that point, businesses and workers have no choice but to start building expected inflation into prices and wages, and inflation gets deeply embedded into the economy. If you were running a restaurant, you would no longer print menus. Instead you might put up a chalkboard with prices on it and raise the prices every day—or even twice a day.

Governments fervently want to avoid hyperinflation because it completely undercuts citizens' faith in the value of their money. In this situation, if workers are paid for their jobs in the morning, the value of the money has substantially fallen by the afternoon. People stop thinking about the future.

The most famous hyperinflation episode occurred in Germany in the 1920s. In 1919 one dollar was worth 8.9 German marks (a *mark* was the German currency at the time). By 1923 one dollar was worth *1 trillion* marks. In effect, German money was worth nothing, and barter became the order of the day. People's savings, pensions, and life insurance became valueless. Most economic

SPOTLIGHT: THE OIL TRIGGER

What starts a wage–price spiral? One cause, at least in the United States, is a sharp rise in oil prices. Because every industry needs energy, an oil price increase affects every part of the economy. That puts pressure on many companies to raise prices.

As mentioned in Chapter 6, the 1973 oil price shock happened in October after Egypt and Syria invaded Israel. While the war was still going on, the Arab oil-producing countries—led by Saudi Arabia, Kuwait, Iran, and Iraq—announced a sharp cut in oil production. In addition, these companies put an embargo on oil exports to the United States and some other Western European countries that were supporting Israel.

The oil embargo sent prices leaping—not just the prices of gasoline and heating fuel, but all sorts of other prices too. Businesses of all kinds had to pay higher energy costs to run their factories, heat and cool their offices, and transport their goods. As a result, they hiked the prices for their products. On top of that, companies had to invest a lot of money to buy more energy-efficiency equipment to try to use less energy.

The results were a big jump in the general price level (inflation) *and* a corresponding rise in expected inflation. What followed was a wage–price spiral that sent the inflation rate over 10 percent. Another oil price shock in 1979 followed the Iranian Revolution that deposed the Shah of Iran. Again energy prices soared, and both inflation and inflation expectations rose. As we will see in Chapter 12, the wage–price spiral did not end until the Federal Reserve took drastic action.

More recently, oil prices spiked in mid-2008 without causing a wage–price spiral. As this textbook is being revised in early 2011, oil prices are rising again, and gasoline prices are above $4 a gallon in many parts of the country. However, businesses and workers have not yet raised their inflation expectations for the future, perhaps because competition from overseas kept a lid on price and wage increases.

historians believe that the economic devastation from this hyperinflation was one factor that, by disrupting the German economy and undermining faith in the government, laid the groundwork for the Nazi takeover of Germany in the 1930s.

More recently, several South American countries have experienced hyperinflation, though not as bad as the German case. From 1989 to 1994 Brazil endured several years of inflation of over 1,000 percent, which means that prices rose by 10 times in a year. In 1985 Bolivia's inflation rate went over 11,000 percent. That means average prices went up by more than 100 times over the year. Or to put it a different way, a dollar would be worth a penny by the end of the year, and if a newspaper cost $1 at the beginning of the year, it would cost $100 by December.

To cope with hyperinflation, countries have to keep issuing currency in bigger and bigger denominations. For example, during its period of hyperinflation, Bolivia issued currency bills worth 10 million bolivianos each (the boliviano was the Bolivian currency then). Another alternative is to change the name of the currency and replace old bills with new ones. For example, in 1986 Brazil replaced its former currency, the cruzeiro, with the cruzado. The conversion formula was that each cruzado replaced 1,000 cruzeiros (in 1986 $1 was worth about 13 cruzados).

The Harm from Unexpected Inflation

What damage does inflation do? We'll examine two different cases. In this section we'll look at the impacts of *unexpected inflation,* when the actual inflation rate is much higher than expected. In the next section we'll consider more downsides of *expected inflation.*

Unexpected inflation happens when the rate of price increases suddenly accelerates well above what businesses and individuals were expecting. For anyone who is locked into a long-term contract of any sort, that makes a big difference. If you are supposed to *receive* money, unexpected inflation is bad for you. If you are supposed to *pay* money, unexpected inflation is good for you.

UNEXPECTED INFLATION
Sudden acceleration of the rate of price increases above what businesses, and individuals were expecting.

HOW IT WORKS: WHY UNEXPECTED INFLATION HURTS LENDERS

To understand how unexpected inflation hurts lenders, let's consider the simple example of a candy economy. Amanda has $10, which can buy a nice box of chocolates. But instead she lends Sam the $10 for a month, expecting to get back $10 plus $2 in interest (she figures the $2 will allow her to buy a soda to go along with the chocolate).

Unfortunately, over the month there is a sudden shortage of cocoa, and the price of a box of chocolate doubles to $20. So at the end of the month, when Sam gives Amanda $12 (the $10 plus interest), she can no longer afford the nice box of chocolates. Instead she has to settle for some M&Ms. As a lender, she has become the victim of an unexpected surge of candy inflation. If she had known this was coming, she would have asked for more interest or simply bought the chocolate before its price went up.

For example, consider the situation of lenders. A loan involves a transfer of money from lender to borrower, plus a promise from the borrower to pay back the money with interest sometime in the future. For example, the bank might lend you $100 with the requirement that you will pay back the money, plus $10 in interest, next year.

The problem for the lender is that if the price level unexpectedly jumps, that means borrowers get to pay back their loans with less valuable dollars. Suppose inflation unexpectedly turns out to be 10 percent for the year. When the bank receives repayment of its loan, the repayment is worth 10 percent less. In fact, if the inflation rate is high enough, the bank may actually lose money on the loan. Unexpected inflation helps borrowers, at least temporarily, because they are paying back their loans with inflated dollars. (See "How It Works: Why Unexpected Inflation Hurts Lenders.")

But the benefits to borrowers from unexpected inflation evaporate as soon as lenders realize that prices are rising. At that point they start raising their interest rates to compensate for the fact they are getting paid back in inflated dollars. That's what happened in the early part of the 1980s, when lenders kept interest rates high because they worried about a recurrence of the inflation of the 1970s.

The Harm from Expected Inflation

What happens if everyone expects the same rate of inflation that actually occurs? What is the harm from **expected inflation**? We've already mentioned hyperinflation. But what if inflation were only 7 percent or so? It might seem that expected inflation would be harmless if wages and salaries rise at the same rate as prices. If prices go up by 7 percent and wages go up by 7 percent, everyone is in the same relative situation they were in before, and nothing has really changed. In fact, one response to the high-inflation era of the 1970s was to put **cost-of-living adjustments** (COLAs) into many union contracts and government programs such as Social Security. A COLA automatically raises wages to compensate for inflation, so that if inflation is 7 percent, wages rise by 7 percent. Similarly, Social Security recipients have been protected from inflation since 1972: their payments rise along with consumer prices.

However, over time even expected inflation is a problem. First, if employers automatically bump up wages for inflation, they will have to raise prices to compensate for their increased costs. Thus cost-of-living adjustments build inflation into the economy and make a wage–price spiral more likely.

Second, economists have learned that higher levels of inflation are less predictable. If inflation is running at 2 percent this year, you can be pretty sure it will be close to 2 percent next year. But an inflation rate of 7 percent could be 12 percent or 3 percent next year. This makes it hard for businesses and households to make good decisions.

Finally, high levels of inflation increase the **cost of transactions**—the time and effort that go into managing your spending. If inflation is low, you can keep spending money in your checking account, where it is easy to get to, because you don't have to worry about it losing value. But if the average price level is rising quickly, you don't want to keep much money in cash or checking accounts because it quickly loses value. So you have to spend a lot of time making sure your money is in money market funds or someplace else where it will earn a high enough return to compensate for inflation.

The consensus among most economists is that policy makers should aim to keep inflation low—in the words of former Federal Reserve Chairman Alan Greenspan, "so low and stable over time that it does not materially enter into the decisions of households and firms." That level is generally accepted to be around 2 percent a year.

Deflation

If inflation is undesirable, why not strive for *deflation?* **Deflation** is an actual fall in the average price level. Don't confuse it with *disinflation,* which is a reduction in the inflation rate. If the inflation rate is 5 percent one year and 4 percent the next, that's disinflation. But if the inflation rate is −1 percent, that's deflation.

Deflation is not as bad as hyperinflation. Even though it may seem like a good thing for currency to become more valuable, economists usually agree that an economy should be kept away from deflation if possible for two reasons.

First, deflation usually means demand is so weak that businesses cannot raise their prices. The second problem with deflation has to do with loans. Remember that inflation hurts lenders because borrowers pay back loans in dollars that are worth less than expected. In the same way, deflation hurts borrowers because they are paying back loans with dollars that are worth more than expected. Indeed, if deflation hits wages as well as prices, your income may drop, but the size of that loan you took out stays the same. That's not a recipe for a happy life.

CONCLUSION

We've seen how inflation can change our picture of the economy. A high rate of inflation can eat away at the value of household income, wages, and any other monetary quantities.

But prices are not the only things that change over time. In the next chapter we will see how the economy's output changes over time as well.

08   SUMMARY

1. Inflation is a sustained upward movement in the average level of prices. The inflation rate is the annual percentage change in the average price level or its equivalent, the Consumer Price Index (CPI). The inflation rate in 2007, for example, was the percentage change in the CPI from 2006 to 2007. *(LO8-1)*

2. A relative price shift happens when the inflation rate of a good or service is significantly higher or lower than the overall inflation rate. Some goods or services have been getting relatively cheaper over time, whereas others have been getting relatively more expensive. *(LO8-2)*

3. Money illusion occurs when we compare dollar amounts in different periods without adjusting for inflation. To avoid money illusion, we need to adjust nominal changes in dollar amounts by the rate of inflation to get real changes. *(LO8-3)*

4. Expected inflation is the inflation rate that consumers and businesses expect will hold over the next year. Unexpected inflation happens when the rate of price increases suddenly accelerates above expected inflation. Unexpected inflation hurts lenders and anyone who is supposed to receive money under a long-term contract. Unexpected inflation helps anyone who is supposed to pay money under a long-term contract. A high level of expected inflation is harmful because it makes a wage–price spiral more likely, because it is unpredictable, and because it increases the cost of transactions. *(LO8-4)*

KEY TERMS AND CONCEPTS

average level of prices	improvement in quality	wage–price spiral
market basket	pure price change	hyperinflation
consumer price index	money illusion	unexpected inflation
inflation	real change	expected inflation
inflation rate	inflation-adjusted change	cost-of-living adjustments
core inflation	nominal change	cost of transactions
relative price shift	expected inflation	deflation

PROBLEMS

1. Which of the following statements is not true? *(LO8-1)*

   a) When the average price level rises, the price of all goods and services goes up.

   b) Owners' equivalent rent of primary residence is the biggest part of the market basket in the consumer price index.

   c) The market basket for the CPI represents the expenditures of a typical person.

   d) The CPI tracks the average price level.

2. The following table gives the the value of the consumer price index for 2003 through 2010. *(LO8-1)*

Year	Consumer Price Index
2003	184.0
2004	188.9
2005	195.3
2006	201.6
2007	207.3
2008	215.3
2009	214.5
2010	218.1

a) What was the inflation rate in 2003?

b) What was the inflation rate in 2007?

c) What was the percentage increase of the average price level from 2003 to 2010?

d) In what year was the inflation rate the highest? The lowest?

3. The following table that reports the average prices of gasoline and apples, as well as the consumer price index for three years. *(LO8-2)*

		Gasoline (Price per Gallon)	Red Delicious Apples (Price per Pound)	Consumer Price Index (1982–1984 = 100)
December	1987	$0.98	$0.55	115.4
December	1997	$1.24	$0.90	161.3
December	2007	$2.92	$0.98	208.9

a) What was the percentage increase in the price of gasoline from 1987 to 2007?

b) What was the percentage increase in the price of apples from 1997 to 2007?

c) Did the relative price of gasoline rise or fall from 1987 to 1997? That is, was the percentage increase in gasoline prices higher or lower than the percentage increase in the CPI?

d) Did the relative price of gasoline rise or fall from 1997 to 2007?

e) Did the relative price of apples rise or fall from 1987 to 1997?

4. Say whether each of the following represents a pure price change or an improvement in quality. *(LO8-2)*

a) The price of a home goes up.

b) The price of a home goes up after a complete renovation.

c) The latest model of a car is more expensive than the previous model, but it also has more features.

d) The price of a peach rises.

5. Suppose you are a Social Security recipient. In 2006 you receive $600 per month in Social Security benefits. In October of that year the Social Security Administration announces that the cost-of-living adjustment for 2007 will be 3.3 percent, roughly matching the overall inflation rate. *(LO8-3)*

a) How much will your 2007 monthly benefits be?

b) In real terms, do your benefits go up, go down, or stay the same?

6. One of the biggest decisions most of us have to make is which industry to look for work in. Compensation matters, but it also matters whether pay is rising or falling. The following table gives the annual average pay in five major industries for 2000 and 2009 (the figures include the pay of all workers, including top managers). *(LO8-3)*

a) Calculate the percentage increase in pay for each industry from 2000 to 2009.

b) What was the real percentage increase in pay for each industry from 2000 to 2009, using the rule of thumb that the real property tax increase is roughly the nominal percentage increase minus the inflation rate? (The CPI in 2000 was 172.2, and the CPI in 2009 was 214.5.)

c) Which industry had the biggest increase in real wages?

Average Annual Wages and Salaries (Dollars)*

Industry	2000	2009
Manufacturers	43,933	57,374
Retail trade	26,585	31,195
Finance and insurance	64,561	84,555
Computer systems design and programming	82,555	95,337
Hospitals	38,632	56,405

*Per full-time worker.
Source: Bureau of Economic Analysis.

7. The sports pages are always filled with news of the latest big contract an athlete has received. The following table shows the average price for major league baseball tickets for three years, the average player salary, and the consumer price index for those years. *(LO8-3)*

a) Calculate the real percentage increase in ticket prices from 1996 to 2001 and from 2001 to 2010.

b) Calculate the real percentage increase in player salaries from 1996 to 2001 and from 2001 to 2010.

c) Between 1996 and 2010 total attendance at major league baseball games grew from 60 million to 73 million, despite the increase in real ticket prices. Using your knowledge from Chapter 3, say whether this increase in attendance is more likely to represent a supply shift or a demand shift in the market for baseball tickets.

d) From the information provided below, do you think the rise in player salaries is the main cause of the rise in ticket prices? Explain.

	Average Ticket Price Major League Baseball (Dollars)	Consumer Price Index (1982–1984=100)	Average Player Salary (Dollars)
1996	11.32	156.9	$1,176,967
2001	17.64	177.1	$2,264,403
2010	26.74	218.1	$3,305,393

Source: Team Marketing Report, Associated Press.

8. Suppose the annual inflation rate has been 3 percent for several years. Then, without warning, it soars to 10 percent a year. Will each of the following individuals or businesses win or lose from such unexpected inflation? *(LO8-4)*

a) A tenant renting an apartment with a lease that fixes the rent for the next three years.

b) An automobile dealer who has leased a car to a buyer for three years with fixed payments.

c) A bank that has lent money to a family to buy a home with interest rates fixed for the next 30 years.

9. Which situation would most economists prefer? *(LO8-4)*

a) An unexpected drop in the inflation rate from 5% to 0%.

b) A steady 2% inflation rate.

c) An unexpected climb in the inflation rate from 3% to 6%.

d) An expected decline in the inflation rate from 3% to −2%.

09 GROWTH

LEARNING OBJECTIVES

After reading this chapter, you should be able to:

LO9-1 Explain the benefits of economic growth.

LO9-2 Calculate the economic growth rate.

LO9-3 Discuss the short-term and long-term change in living standards and calculate real GDP per capita.

LO9-4 List the forces driving economic growth.

LO9-5 Explain the role of government in economic growth.

LO9-6 Discuss the history of U.S. productivity growth.

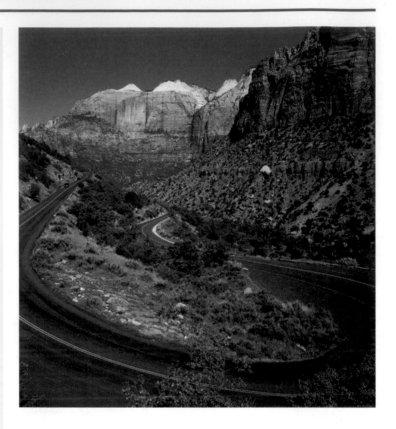

Here's the most important fact about modern economies: almost without exception, they grow over the long run. True, the U.S. was recently hit by a deep economic downturn that cut the production of goods and services for several years. But the general trend is still upward in most countries.

This record of success is encouraging and challenging at the same time. It's encouraging because when a country produces more goods and services, almost everyone is better off. An expanding economy almost always boosts living standards for the poor, frees up resources for the public sector, and lets the middle class enjoy more luxuries. But it's challenging because economic growth in a market economy often requires change and turmoil that make people uncomfortable.

In this chapter we will look at the benefits of economic growth. We will explore how growth is defined and measured. Finally, we will look at the key factors that help drive a country's economic growth over the long run.

THE SIGNIFICANCE OF GROWTH

What does it mean for an economy to grow from one year to the next? Simply put, an economy experiences **economic growth** if its production of goods and services increases. For example, suppose we have a simple economy that produces only one product: haircuts. This economy grows if its barbers and hairdressers begin providing more haircuts than in the past. (When an economy is growing, we also say it is "getting bigger.")

ECONOMIC GROWTH
When an economy's production of goods and services increases.

Improved Living Standards

Of course actual economies usually produce a much wider range of goods and services than just haircuts. In general, a growing economy usually produces more necessities, such as more food, better housing, and easier access to education and healthcare. A growing economy also generates more resources for leisure, recreation, and entertainment. In other words, economic growth makes most people better off in many different ways, both tangible and intangible.

What does this mean in concrete terms? Here's a simple comparison. Today, thanks to economic growth, virtually all homes in the United States have complete plumbing facilities (defined as hot and cold running water, a bathtub or shower, and a flushable toilet). But as recently as 1940, almost half of all U.S. homes lacked one or more of these essentials. That means a big change has occurred in the quality of daily life.

Or take something essential like the survival rate of newborns. In 1950 there were 29 infant deaths for every 1,000 live births in the United States. Over the next half century the U.S. economy grew enough to make it possible to devote more resources to better healthcare for pregnant women and newborns. As a result, the infant mortality rate plunged to only 6.4 infant deaths per 1,000 live births in 2009.

PRODUCTION POSSIBILITY FRONTIER
All the combinations of different goods and services the economy is capable of producing at a particular time, assuming full use of all resources.

That's still not as low as in some other industrialized countries, but it's far better than in the past.

On the lighter side, a bigger economy can also provide more variety in entertainment. In the 1960s a typical household had access to fewer than 10 broadcast television channels. Then cable television raised the number of available channels to 100 or more. Today the Internet opens a vast number of entertainment choices. And people are not just sitting in front of screens—they are going more places as well (see "Spotlight: Growth and Travel").

Production Possibility Frontier

One consequence of economic growth is that it gives us more choices. To see this, we will define the **production possibility frontier (PPF)** as all the combinations of different goods and services the economy is capable of producing at a particular time, assuming full use of all resources. To illustrate, let's look at a production possibility frontier for two outputs: healthcare and entertainment, shown in Figure 9.2. The PPF shows the different combinations of healthcare and entertainment the economy can achieve given our current state of knowledge and physical inputs. (Of course we could draw a PPF with any other two goods and services the economy can produce, like food and cars, or haircuts and homes.)

In this figure, the vertical axis measures the amount of entertainment the economy can produce, whereas the horizontal axis measures the amount of healthcare the economy can produce. The curved line shows all the different combinations of healthcare and entertainment that are possible. We can build hospitals, or movie studios, or some combination of them. Point *A* on the figure shows one possible combination of healthcare and entertainment that the economy can produce in a year.

SPOTLIGHT: GROWTH AND TRAVEL

Have you traveled abroad recently? In 2009 U.S. residents made 30 million plane trips overseas (that includes all countries except Mexico and Canada).

But it isn't just U.S. residents who are flying around the globe. Overseas travel is expensive, requiring enough money for a plane ticket, hotel rooms, and shopping. So a sure sign of economic growth in a country is when ordinary people have enough money and leisure time to travel overseas.

In the 1980s a wave of Japanese tourists hit the shores of the United States and other countries, reflecting increased prosperity in Japan. More recently there has been an explosion of tourists from Eastern Europe, China, and India as economic growth has boosted the number of people who can afford to travel. All across the country, from New York to San Francisco, tourist destinations are experiencing sky-high levels of foreign tourists.

Looking globally, international tourist trips increased by 37 percent between 2000 and 2010—much faster than the world population grew (see Figure 9.1). As long as the world economy continues to expand, this trend of rapid tourism should continue.

FIGURE 9.1
Percentage Change in International Tourist Trips, 2000–2010 The growth of international tourism has far exceeded the growth of the world population as many countries get richer.

Source: United States Office of Travel and Tourism Industries, United Nations World Tourism Organization.

FIGURE 9.2	The Production Possibility Frontier (PPF)

This example of a PPF shows all the combinations of entertainment and healthcare the economy can produce in a year. Point A shows one possible combination, as indicated by the dotted lines.

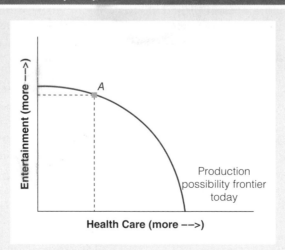

If the economy grows, the PPF moves outward, as shown in Figure 9.3. That is, the economy has a greater capability of producing more healthcare, or more entertainment, or both. Point B is one possible combination of healthcare and entertainment, but the economy is capable of producing any other combination on the PPF.

Growth versus the Zero-Sum Economy

If there is no growth, we have a **zero-sum economy.** This means if we want the economy to produce more of something—say healthcare—we have to accept

FIGURE 9.3   Growth and the PPF

As the economy grows, the production possibility frontier shifts outward. In this figure, growth means that it's possible to get more of both healthcare and entertainment. Point *B* corresponds to more healthcare and entertainment than point *A*, as the dotted lines show.

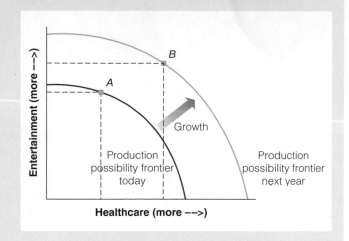

less of something else—perhaps entertainment. In Figure 9.4, if we are stuck on the same production possibility frontier (that is, no growth), then moving from point *A* to point *C* gives us more healthcare and less entertainment.

In contrast, a growing economy is **non-zero-sum.** So as the production possibility frontier moves outward, we could potentially get more of both healthcare and entertainment (point *B* in Figure 9.4).

This argument can be extended to income distribution. In an economy without growth, the only way for someone to get more goods and services is for someone else to get less—like kids squabbling over a piece of cake. More specifically, without growth, the only way to make low-income households better off is to take money away from middle-income or high-income households. (We'll examine income distribution in more detail in Chapter 17.)

On the other hand, it is possible for everyone to see their incomes rise if the economy gets bigger. In a growing economy, both rich and poor can enjoy a rising standard of living.

In fact, that is what has happened in the United States over the past 50 years. As the U.S.

ZERO-SUM ECONOMY

A situation where if we want to produce more of something, we necessarily have to produce less of something else.

economy expanded a World War II, the livi standard of poor peopl in the United States improved as well. Fewer people went hungry, the quality of housing rose, and virtually everyone acquired a television set. Now cell phones and access to the Internet are fast spreading into low-income households. As of early 2010, 66 percent of U.S. adults had a broadband connection at home.

In the poorest countries, economic growth can make a tremendous difference for the people at the bottom of the income ladder—even in something as basic as whether they have enough food to eat. As we will see later in this chapter, China has been able to maintain strong growth since the early 1980s, and India since the early 1990s. The result has been a sharp fall in the proportions of their populations that are undernourished.

What Growth Doesn't Buy

To finish this section, let us be clear: economic growth is not the only measure of a successful society. As we saw in Chapter 7, growth has not necessarily made us happier, at least judging by recent surveys. No one did such surveys back in 1900, but we cannot dismiss the possibility that people then were poorer than we are now but just as happy.

Moreover, there are other ways in which growth may have negative effects. Economic research suggests that the falling relative prices of food over time have increased food consumption. This may contribute to obesity—one of the key health issues facing the United States today. (We'll discuss the economics of healthcare in Chapter 18.)

FIGURE 9.4   **A Zero-Sum versus a Non-Zero-Sum Economy**

Suppose there is an economy that produces only healthcare and entertainment. In the absence of growth, getting more healthcare—moving from point *A* to point *C*—requires accepting less entertainment. However, if the economy grows, it's possible to get both more healthcare and more entertainment (point *B*).

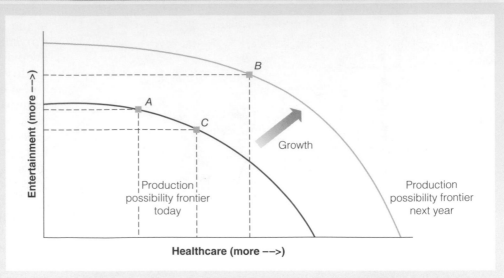

Finally, as we'll see in Chapter 19, published figures on economic growth leave out the issue of its impact on the environment, including global warming. Some of the impacts are quite serious, but we do not account for them when measuring growth.

Still, all other things being equal, economists generally believe that economic growth is a positive event. Few people cheer if government statisticians announce a low growth number.

MEASURING GROWTH

A typical economy produces a wide variety of goods and services, such as food, homes, cars, haircuts, and television shows. From Chapter 7 we already know we can combine these different goods and services into one number, *gross domestic product* (GDP), which measures the output of an economy in dollars. An increase in GDP over time can indicate economic growth.

However, we have to be careful here. There are two reasons why the dollar amount of output might rise, and only one of them counts as economic growth. First, an economy may actually be producing more

REAL GDP

Gross domestic product adjusted for inflation.

food, homes, cars, haircuts, and so forth. Or it may be producing the same amount of goods and services—or even less—but prices have gone up. That is, inflation may make it look as though the economy has grown more than it really has. How do we know the truth?

The solution is to adjust GDP growth for inflation. In practice that's a challenging task. Each quarter, statisticians at the Bureau of Economic Analysis (BEA) in Washington estimate the average price level for the whole economy, using hundreds of thousands of pieces of data. This is not the consumer price index with its basket of typical goods, but a broader measure that covers the prices of *all* items that go into GDP, including business investment, government consumption and investment, and foreign trade.

The BEA then adjusts GDP for inflation, using its estimate of the average price level for the whole economy. The result is called **real GDP,** which is gross domestic product adjusted for inflation. It is usually measured in 2005 dollars (as we defined in Chapter 8). When real GDP is increasing, that means that the output of the economy, adjusted for

FIGURE 9.5 | Economic Growth, 1950–2010

This figure shows the economic growth rate for each year. Note the negative growth for 2009.

Source: Bureau of Economic Analysis (as of April 2011), www.bea.gov.

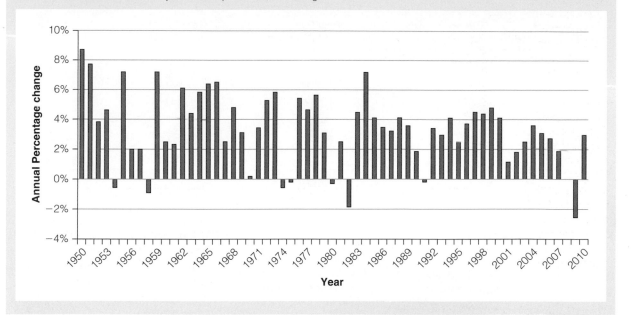

inflation, is increasing as well. As a result, economic growth is measured by the growth in real GDP over time.

When real GDP growth is positive, the economy's production of goods and services is increasing, and the economy is growing. For example, in 2004 the economic growth rate of the U.S. economy was 3.6 percent. That means the economy produced 3.6 percent more goods and services in 2004 than in 2003.

Looking at Figure 9.5, we can see clear signs of the Great Recession. Real GDP growth was zero in 2008, followed by negative growth in 2009. When growth is negative, that means the economy is shrinking.

GDP versus Real GDP

Let's make a clear distinction between GDP and real GDP. The growth rate of GDP includes both economic growth and the effects of inflation. In contrast, the growth rate of real GDP removes the effects of inflation. (See "How It Works: Calculating the Growth Rate.") Table 9.1 shows the relationship between GDP and real GDP in recent years.

HOW IT WORKS: CALCULATING THE GROWTH RATE

The Bureau of Economic Analysis regularly reports the growth rate of the U.S. economy, which represents the percentage increase in *real* gross domestic product. For example, in 2003 real GDP was $11,841 billion, measured in 2005 dollars. In 2004 real GDP was $12,264 billion, measured in 2005 dollars. The growth rate from 2003 to 2004 was 3.6 percent.

Billions of 2005 dollars

Real GDP in 2003	$11,841
Real GDP in 2004	$12,264

Growth rate $(12,264/11,841) - 1 = 0.036$
$= 3.6$ percent

TABLE 9.1	GDP versus Real GDP

Real GDP is measured in 2005 dollars, which removes the effects of inflation. The third column shows the growth rate of GDP, including inflation. The fourth column shows the growth rate of real GDP, which is adjusted for inflation.

	GDP (Billions of Dollars)	Real GDP (Billions of 2005 Dollars)	Growth Rate of GDP (%)	Growth Rate of Real GDP (%)
2005	12,638	12,638	6.5	3.1
2006	13,399	12,976	6.0	2.7
2007	14,062	13,229	4.9	1.9
2008	14,369	13,229	2.1	0.0
2009	14,119	12,881	−1.7	−2.6
2010	14,660	13,248	3.8	2.9

Source: Bureau of Economic Analysis (as of April 2011), www.bea.gov.

A Word of Warning

Keep in mind that a rise in real GDP for a whole economy doesn't mean the quantity of any particular good or service is also rising. It's possible for some parts of the economy to be shrinking while other parts are expanding. In 2007, for example, residential investment dropped sharply because fewer new homes were built. At the same time, though, households and businesses were spending more on computers and healthcare than ever before, helping real GDP rise overall.

THE INCREASE IN LIVING STANDARDS

So far in this chapter we've been talking about the growth rate of real GDP—that is, the rate at which the production of the whole economy is expanding. Now let's bring growth down to the level of the individual consumer. Remember that Chapter 7 defined GDP per capita as the gross domestic product divided by the population of the country—in other words, the amount of economic output each person would get if we split up the entire economy evenly and gave everyone a piece. As we saw, this is a rough measure of the average standard of living in the economy.

Now we can ask, "How fast is the average standard of living rising?" To answer this, we

REAL GDP PER CAPITA
Real GDP divided by the number of people in the country.

want to look at the change in GDP per capita. Of course we have to adjust for the effects of inflation. That means we're interested in the growth in **real GDP per capita.**

For example, in 2005 real GDP was $12,368 billion measured in 2005 dollars, as shown in Table 9.1 and reproduced in Table 9.2. The U.S. population was 296.2 million. Thus the real GDP per capita in 2005 was $42,688 (in 2005 dollars). If we divided real GDP equally among every man, woman, and child in the country, that's how much each person would get. In Table 9.2 we also do the same calculation for 2006 and come up with a real GDP per capita equal to $43,384 in year 2005 dollars. The growth rate of real GDP per capita equals the percentage change from 2005 to 2006, which in this case is 1.7 percent.

Short-Term versus Long-Term Growth

So far we have been looking at yearly growth, which falls into the category of **short-term growth.** But it's also useful to look at **long-term growth,** which is the average growth rate over 5 or 10 years or longer. In particular, we can look back and see how real GDP per capita has changed over history, which gives us some insight into how the standard of living has changed. The

TABLE 9.2	**Calculating Real GDP per Capita**

Dividing real GDP by the size of the population gives us real GDP per capita. From 2005 to 2006, real GDP per capita grew by 1.9 percent.

	Real GDP (Billions of 2005 Dollars)	Population (Millions of People)	Real GDP per Capita (Real GDP ÷ Population) (2005 Dollars)
2005	12,638	296.2	42,688
2006	12,976	299.1	43,384
Percentage Change from 2005 to 2006	2.7%	1.0%	1.7%

Source: Bureau of Economic Analysis, www.bea.gov.

chart of U.S. real GDP per capita in Figure 9.6 shows how much living standards have risen over more than two centuries.

With only a couple of major interruptions, real GDP per capita has been on a steady upward climb since the United States was founded. For example, let's look at 1905 on the chart. The president was Teddy Roosevelt, Russia was still ruled by a czar, and India was a British colony. Back then real GDP per capita in the United States in inflation-adjusted 2000 dollars was $5,465. Jump forward a century: in 2007 real GDP per capita was $38,291 in 2000 dollars. That's an eightfold increase in a century, or an average real growth rate of roughly 1.9 percent per year.

Here's another way to think about this. The much lower real GDP per capita in 1905, compared to 2007, reflects the lack of many goods and services that we take for granted today. In 1905 you couldn't take an airplane trip, listen to the radio, watch television, or use a computer because none of these technologies were in commercial use or even existed. Automobiles were rare, and antibiotics were not part of the medical toolkit. In effect, the productive capability of the economy was far lower—and so were living standards.

FIGURE 9.6	**Real GDP per Capita throughout U.S. History**

In most years since the country was founded, real GDP per capita has climbed.

Source: Louis D. Johnston and Samuel H. Williamson, "What Was the U.S. GDP Then?" MeasuringWorth. Com, 2010.

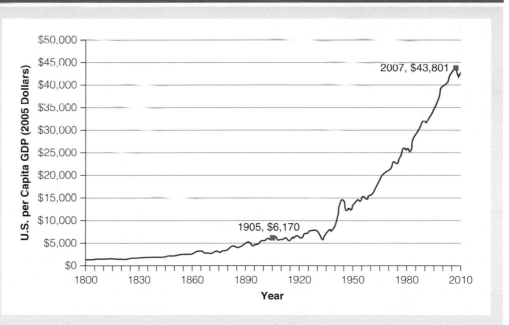

WHAT DRIVES GROWTH

What forces drive economic growth? What determines whether growth is fast or slow? In Chapter 4 you learned the production function of a business has five inputs: labor, capital, land, intermediate inputs, and business know-how. Given the levels of the different inputs, the production function tells us the output level of the business.

Similarly, the **aggregate production function** tells us the output, or GDP, of the economy, given its inputs. The list of inputs for the aggregrate production function includes the number of workers in the country (*labor*); the education and skill levels of these workers (what economists call *human capital*); equipment and structures (*physical capital*); raw materials such as oil and iron ore (which come from the *land*); and a final category we will call *knowledge* (which includes both technology and business know-how).

The economy grows when these inputs grow. That is, as the number of workers increases, the output of the economy tends to rise. Similarly, output rises as workers become more educated and skilled, as more physical capital is used, as

> **AGGREGATE PRODUCTION FUNCTION**
>
> The link between the inputs to an economy and its outputs.

more raw materials are mined and used, and as the economy accumulates more knowledge, as shown in Figure 9.7. In other words, the forces driving growth are the increases in the five different inputs to the aggregate production function.

Increase in Labor

As the number of workers increases, output increases too even if nothing else changes. That makes sense. A country like the United States experiences some growth simply because the number of workers generally increases over time.

In 1996, for example, the U.S. **labor force**—the number of people either working or actively looking for jobs—was 133.9 million. In 2006 the labor force was 151.4 million. On average the U.S. workforce has grown at roughly 1 percent annually in recent years.

The Census Bureau—which does population projections—expects the working-age population of the United States to keep growing, because there are many young people today and because of immigration. The latest forecasts from the Bureau of Labor Statistics project that

---

FIGURE 9.7   The Forces Driving Economic Growth

The economy grows when the inputs to the aggregrate production function increase, all other things being equal.

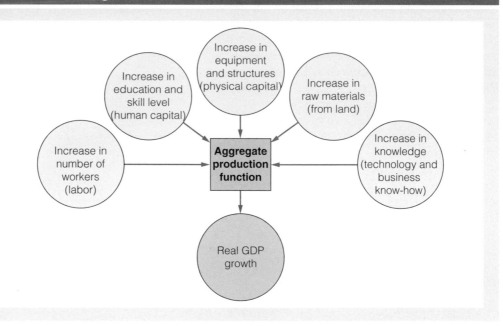

| FIGURE 9.8 | College Education and the Young |

The percentage of 25- to 29-year-olds who have completed college has risen over time, hitting a high of 30.8 percent in 2008. This rise in education has contributed to growth by making the workforce more skilled.

Source: Census Bureau, www.census.gov.

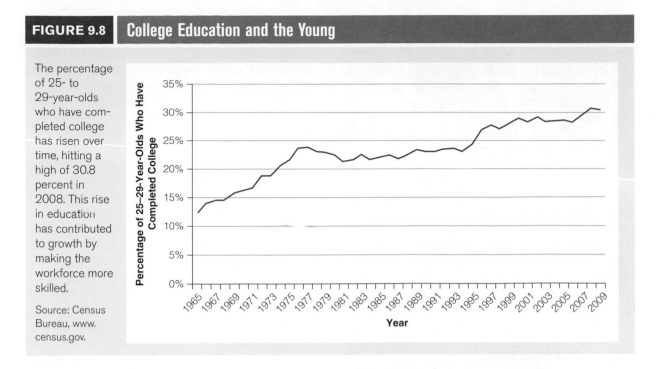

the workforce will expand by 8.2 percent between 2008 and 2018.

Increase in Education and Skills

Another way to boost aggregate production is to increase the skills or education levels of the workforce—that is, to increase **human capital.** In general, better-trained and educated workers can produce more. Education helps future workers develop critical skills. Equally important, educated workers seem to have an easier time adapting to new technology.

The education level of the U.S. workforce is much higher than it was in the past. Figure 9.8 shows that in 1965 only about 13 percent of U.S. adults between the ages of 25 and 29 had a college education. Back then it was more common for people to graduate from high school and go directly into a factory job. As of 2009, 30.6 percent of U.S. adults aged 25–29 had at least a bachelor's degree.

Equally important, it's become far more common to have at least some exposure to post–high school education. This change is related to the dramatic rise of two-year colleges, which today enroll more than 7 million students (see "Spotlight: Community Colleges and Economic Growth").

SPOTLIGHT: COMMUNITY COLLEGES AND ECONOMIC GROWTH

One essential force in the growth of human capital over the past several decades has been the community college system. Community colleges have been around for at least a century, but enrollments soared in the 1960s and 1970s. In 1963 enrollment in two-year colleges was 850,000. By 1973 this figure was 3 million, and by 1983 it had risen to 4.7 million. As of early 2011, more than 7 million students are enrolled in two-year colleges across the country.

The top fields for associate degrees in 2008–2009 were liberal arts, health, business, and security and protective services. As people graduate from community colleges and enter the workforce, their new education and skills contribute directly to the growth of GDP.

without factories to make microprocessors, memory chips, and video screens.

Generally, if we give a worker more and better equipment to use, we can assume that once the worker learns which buttons to press, he or she will be able to produce more output than with less useful equipment. A driver with a truck can deliver more packages than a messenger on a bicycle. A construction worker with a giant crane can lift more material faster than the same worker with a hand truck.

The positive impact of increased investment in physical capital is very strong in poor countries, where rural farmers and low-end workers have poor access to any machinery or equipment, and adding even a little can make a big difference. But investment in new equipment, software, and buildings is also an important driving force for growth in a developed country such as the United States. For example, if you order a shirt online, you are relying on the wires and fiber optic connections that link you to the retailer. You are also relying on the retailer's computers, which are housed in a building somewhere; on the designers and marketers of the shirt, who presumably work in an office building in the United States; and on fleets of ships and trucks that eventually bring the shirt from the factory, which may be located in another country. Without all this physical capital, none of this would happen. (See "Spotlight: Capital Investment in the Age of Google.")

Increase in Raw Materials

One essential input to growth is raw materials, which include everything from oil to iron ore to water. The importance of raw materials is obvious: you can't put up a building without iron ore, which is used to make the steel beams that hold up the building. Water is essential for drinking and for agriculture. The list goes on and on.

Historically, economies have consumed more raw materials as they have grown. For example, the United States used roughly 5.4 billion barrels of crude oil in 2010, up from 2 billion barrels in 1950. It's possible, however, that environmental considerations may slow this increase in raw material use in the future.

Increase in Knowledge

Increase in knowledge plays a crucial role in economic growth, especially in developed countries

An increase in physical capital can help an economy grow.

One new concern, however, is that the value of human capital seems to be rising more slowly in recent years. As Figure 9.8 shows, the percentage of young U.S. adults with a bachelor's degree appears to have flattened out in the late 1990s. If this trend continues, the United States will not be able to depend on better-educated workers as a source of economic growth.

Investment in Physical Capital

Economists have long focused on investment in physical capital—firms' purchases of equipment and buildings for production—as an essential ingredient for growth. Amost nothing can be done in today's economy without relying on or using physical capital in some way. You can't take goods or passengers across the ocean without a ship or a plane; you can't employ workers comfortably without putting a roof over their heads; and you can't build computers

SPOTLIGHT: CAPITAL INVESTMENT IN THE AGE OF GOOGLE

We usually think of Google as the producer of the ultimate in intangibles. After all, the search engine giant delivers nothing physical to its users.

But Google has to spend a lot of money on physical capital to deliver the Google experience. In particular, the company has built massive data centers around the world to execute nearly instantaneously all those searches its users request.

In 2006 *The New York Times* described a new data center Google was building in a rural section of Oregon:

> On the banks of the windswept Columbia River, Google is working on a secret weapon in its quest to dominate the next generation of Internet computing. But it is hard to keep a secret when it is a computing center as big as two football fields, with twin cooling plants protruding four stories into the sky.

From 2007 to 2010 the capital investment continued as Google spent almost $10 billion on property and equipment, much of it related to data centers and information technology infrastructure. Google's main competitors, Microsoft and Yahoo!, also poured large amounts into building their own data centers. In fact, these data centers are essential for competing in today's information economy—even if your product is as intangible as an Internet search.

Source: From *The New York Times*, 6/14/2006 © 2006 *The New York Times*. All Rights Reserved. Used by permission and protected by the copyright laws of the United States. The printing, copying, redistribution, or retransmission of the material without express written permission is prohibited.

such as the United States. Why? Because better **knowledge** means we have learned how to do something new, or learned how to produce something faster, better, or cheaper. In other words, we get smarter: we can produce more goods and services with the same amount of resources. For instance, food production has dramatically improved over the past 50 years because of enhancements in agricultural tools and techniques, seeds, fertilizers, and all sorts of related things.

Increases in knowledge include progress in science and technology, by which we learn more about the laws of nature and how to apply them. The results include better medicine, faster computers, and quieter airplanes that use less fuel.

Increases in knowledge also include improved business know-how: our greater understanding of how to arrange economic activities. For example, the invention of the credit card is important to our daily lives—but this has less to do with technology and more about realizing that people needed an easy way to make purchases on credit. As knowledge expands, more things become possible, and the economy grows.

GOVERNMENT AND GROWTH

As we saw in Chapter 6, the market economy does not function in a vacuum. The government plays an important role, setting laws and rules for everything from foreign trade to how mortgages are issued. (**Laws** are the actual legislation passed by Congress and state and local governments, whereas **rules** are the regulations issued by various government agencies.)

Some laws and rules encourage growth by making markets work better, whereas others, regardless of their original intentions, can discourage growth by making markets work less efficiently. For example, most economists would agree that a rule requiring everyone to hop on one foot before buying a car would probably be a bad idea. There might be some disagreement about whether a rule requiring that cars get tested for emissions each year is a good idea.

Most economists favor less government interference in the marketplace as the strategy most likely to produce steady growth. The idea behind this preference is that corporations and individuals are in a better position than the government to know what kinds of investments are most likely to pay off. After all, they reason, the government should not tell Intel what kind of microprocessor chips to make. Nor should it tell Donald Trump what hotels to put up.

Sometimes it's pretty clear that government is on the right track, exercising its power for the greater good. For instance, when a company is putting up a new structure such as an office building or a factory—an investment in physical capital—local governments often impose a long list of building code requirements, such as mandating a certain degree of resistance to fire, earthquakes, and storms. These requirements increase the cost of buildings and therefore slow down investment, but most people would agree that they are necessary.

Or consider the example of education. By law, everyone has to get an elementary and a high school education. That's the minimum amount of human capital that U.S. families are required to invest in. However, legislators could just as easily require everyone to pass at least two years of college—if they were willing to spend billions of dollars to build and staff new community colleges. For now, however, most people agree that completion of high school is an acceptable minimum.

In many cases, however, exactly where we want to draw the line on government interference is a subject of intense political dispute. Immigration is one example. At one extreme, the government could step completely out of the role of controlling the movement of labor across the border. Then immigration would be completely open. In the short run this might have a positive effect on growth because the population and the workforce would rise. But that's clearly unacceptable to a large proportion of citizens—and it would probably impose much bigger costs on local governments for education and healthcare.

We could keep offering examples because almost everything the government does—or doesn't do—can affect growth. But as we proceed through the following chapters, we will see other ways in which the government has an impact on growth. (For an example, see "Spotlight: The Chinese Government and Growth.")

SPOTLIGHT: THE CHINESE GOVERNMENT AND GROWTH

China illustrates how a shift in government policy can alter the long-term growth rate of a country. Until the late 1970s, the Chinese economy was tightly run by the Communist Party. Farms were managed collectively, which means farmers did not own their production; instead it was owned by the whole group. Most manufacturing was done in state-run factories with names like Beijing No. 7 Paper Mill. The combination of the largest population in the world and an inefficient economy made China one of the poorest countries in the world. In 1980 its GDP per capita was only about $400, which ranked China 144 out of around 150 countries.

All that changed under Deng Xiaoping, leader of the Chinese Communist Party from 1978 to the early 1990s. Deng instituted a series of economic reforms that included a move away from collective agriculture to more autonomy for individual households, such as deciding what to plant, choosing where to sell it, and getting much of the gains. Local officials and plant managers were given more freedom to run factories and businesses for profit instead of producing to meet government quotas.

The Chinese government still plays a very important role in that country's economy. Nevertheless, the increasing importance of markets in China is a good example of the kinds of changes in laws and regulations that make an economy work better. In addition, the Chinese have been investing in human capital at a high rate. For example, they geared up their higher education system to produce more than 6 million college graduates in 2010, up from about 1 million in 2001. That's an astounding jump that will pay off in faster economic growth in China's future. And China has been investing in knowledge: today it ranks below only the United States in spending on research and development.

As a result, the Chinese economy has grown at an average rate of 10 percent per year for the past 25 years. No one knows how long China will be able to maintain its rapid pace of growth. But at least for now, it's a role model for other developing countries.

PRODUCTIVITY

How can we summarize all these forces driving economic growth? Remember from Chapter 4 that we defined the *average product* for a business as output per worker. **Productivity** is the equivalent concept for the whole economy. That is, the productivity of an economy is its output for a given year divided by the total number of hours worked in that year, counting all workers. We use total hours, rather than number of workers, to adjust for the fact that not everyone puts in the same amount of time on the job. A sales clerk in a department store may work 20 hours in a week, whereas a highly motivated factory worker may put in overtime and work 60 hours a week; a corporate lawyer might work 90 hours.

> **PRODUCTIVITY**
> Economic output divided by the number of worker hours.

Productivity is a key concept for measuring the health and prosperity of an economy. The higher the productivity, the more output an economy can produce with the same number of workers. For example, China has more workers than the United States does, especially if we count farmworkers. But the United States has a much bigger economy because U.S. workers are more productive—they can produce more with the same or fewer inputs as Chinese workers can.

The **growth rate of productivity** is the percentage increase in productivity over a year, and it is among the economic statistics that economists watch most closely. If productivity growth is rapid, the same number of workers can produce more goods and services. That's good news: companies can afford to pay higher wages and still make a profit. Periods of solid productivity growth are usually also periods of rising living standards.

In contrast, low productivity growth, if it persists over a year or more, suggests the economy is stuck in a rut. Without much productivity gain, businesses have to either cut wages or boost prices to make profits.

The History of U.S. Productivity Growth

Since the end of World War II, the United States has experienced periods of both strong and weak productivity growth. Look at Figure 9.9, which shows the average rate of productivity growth for three different periods since 1947. One important note here: the productivity number reported by the Bureau of Labor Statistics focuses on the output of the "nonfarm business sector," which leaves out government, housing, agriculture, and nonprofits.

The first period, from the end of World War II to roughly 1973, was the **Golden Age** of U.S. growth. Productivity—output per hour—rose at an average of 2.8 percent per year. Not surprisingly, with that kind of productivity growth, everyone prospered. Real wage growth was strong, inflation was low, and living standards rose rapidly for most people.

This stretch of rapid productivity growth was also the period of government expansion described in Chapter 6. The construction of the interstate highway system, the massive program to put people on the moon, the creation of Medicare—it's no coincidence that these massive federal spending efforts came while productivity was growing quickly. With output per hour rising steadily, the economy was producing enough spare resources to expand government spending into new areas.

The era of rapid productivity growth ended around 1973. The immediate cause was the big jump in oil prices we described earlier, which made energy a lot more expensive and hurt the transportation and utility industries. But even after businesses learned to cope with more expensive energy, the earlier rate of productivity growth did not return.

Economists suggested a variety of possible explanations for the **productivity slowdown** of 1973 to 1995. One theory was that as the baby boom generation entered the workforce, these workers were young, inexperienced, and not highly productive. Another theory was that the environmental regulations passed in the late 1960s and early 1970s—such as the creation of the Environmental Protection Agency in 1970—were dragging down growth. Yet another theory proposed that U.S. workers were not saving and investing enough, which was holding back productivity. And still another theory suggested that there simply were not enough new products and

| FIGURE 9.9 | The Three Eras of Productivity Growth |

After World War II the United States experienced rapid productivity growth until the mid-1970s. Then productivity growth slowed for roughly two decades, followed by a speed-up as businesses learned how to use information technology and globalization.

Source: Bureau of Labor Statistics, www.bls.gov.

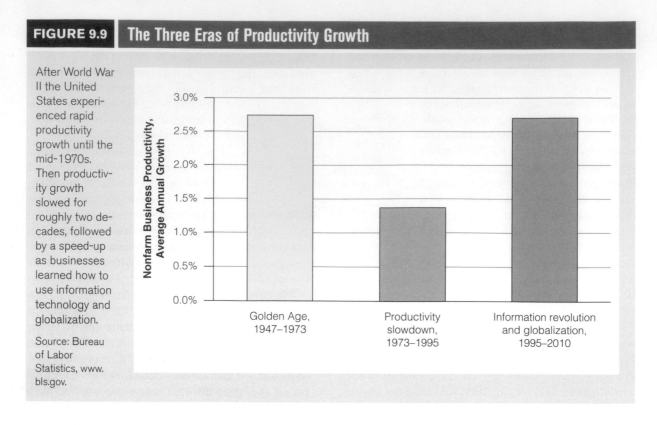

innovation. Businesses were churning out the same old cars and washing machines.

All of these factors probably contributed to the productivity slowdown. But no matter which reason was the most important, the total impact was clear: From 1973 to 1995 productivity growth slowed to only 1.4 percent per year, which was roughly half the previous rate. This meant that real wage gains for many workers were much smaller or even nonexistent. It also meant that U.S. consumers, strapped for money, were much less willing to pay high tax rates.

This productivity slowdown lasted until around 1995, when two things happened more or less simultaneously. First, the **information revolution** finally kicked in. Businesses learned how to use computers to produce more output with fewer workers, even as the rise of the Internet helped tie all those computers together. At the same time, there was a great expansion of **globalization** as businesses learned how to use foreign suppliers to cut their costs (we'll discuss globalization more in Chapter 14).

Together the combination of the information revolution and globalization has propelled a new productivity boom. Between 1995 and 2010, productivity growth rebounded to 2.7 percent, almost to where it was during the Golden Age.

CONCLUSION

Economic growth is one of the most important things we can know about an economy. If we can measure how fast real GDP is rising, then we can tell whether the typical standard of living in the country is increasing. Rapid economic growth cannot be taken for granted—it depends on increasing the inputs to the aggregate production function.

However, in any particular year, the economy may shrink rather than grow. That means economic growth is negative rather than positive, and it's bad news for consumers and for businesses. As we will see in the next chapter and afterward, trying to avoid periods of negative economic growth—a shrinking economy—is one of the main goals of economic policy makers.

09

SUMMARY

1. Economic growth leads to higher living standards. It also offers more choices. By pushing out the production possibility frontier, economic growth increases the productive capabilities of an economy. *(LO9-1)*

2. As we saw in Chapter 7, gross domestic product measures the output of an economy. Economic growth, or real GDP growth, is the increase in nominal GDP, adjusted for inflation. *(LO9-2)*

3. An increase in living standards can be measured by the increase in real GDP per capita, which is real GDP divided by the size of the population. In the United States, real GDP per capita has risen more or less steadily since the founding of the country. *(LO9-3)*

4. Economic growth is driven by several factors, including the number of workers, their education and skill, the amount of equipment and buildings, the availability of raw materials, and the amount of knowledge. Increases in any of these can help propel growth on a macro level. *(LO9-4)*

5. Government has an important role in promoting growth through laws and rules. However, there's much disagreement about where to draw the line between government and the private sector. *(LO9-5)*

6. Productivity is the average output per hour of work. Fast productivity growth is an indicator of the health and prosperity of an economy. *(LO9-6)*

KEY TERMS AND CONCEPTS

economic growth

production possibility frontier

zero-sum economy

non-zero-sum economy

real GDP

real GDP per capita

short-term growth

long-term growth

aggregate production function

labor force

human capital

knowledge

laws and rules

productivity

growth rate of productivity

Golden Age

productivity slowdown

information revolution

globalization

PROBLEMS

1. Which of the following statements is not true? *(LO9-1)*

    a) In a growing economy, the production possibility frontier moves inward.

    b) Two of the forces driving growth are increases in knowledge and increases in labor.

    c) The Golden Age of productivity growth ran from roughly the end of World War II to the mid-1970s.

    d) The arrival of the Internet helped spur an increase in productivity growth.

2. The following figure shows a production possibility frontier (PPF), today and next year, for an economy that makes food and cars. *(LO9-1)*

   a) Based on today's PPF, which point offers the higher production of cars?

   b) Which point on next yeat's PPF offers higher production of both cars and food compared to point *E*?

   c) Which point on next year's PPF offers lower production of cars compared to point *D*?

3. *Zero-sum* means that one person's gain is someone else's loss. *Non-zero-sum* means that it is possible for everyone to gain. Say whether each of the following represents a zero-sum or a non-zero-sum situation. *(LO9-1)*

   a) Three kids sharing a cookie.

   b) Two college students collaborating on a class project.

   c) Two baseball teams playing a game.

   d) A director and several actors making a movie.

   e) Two hotels competing for customers in a resort town where the total number of tourists stays the same.

4. The accompanying table shows real GDP from 2005 to 2010 for China, measured in billions of 2005 dollars. *(LO9-2)*

	Billions of 2005 Dollars
2005	5,364
2006	6,045
2007	6,903
2008	7,565
2009	8,523
2010	9,116

   a) In what year was Chinese economic growth the highest?

   b) By what percentage did the Chinese economy grow between 2005 and 2010?

5. Suppose we are looking at an economy that produces only toys. In 2009 the country's toy factories produced 5 million toys, which it sold on the international market for $10 per toy. In 2010 the country produced 6 million toys, which it sold for $12 per toy. *(LO9-2)*

   a) What was the percentage increase in the production of toys from 2009 to 2010?
   b) What was the gross domestic product of this economy in 2009? What was the gross domestic product in 2010? (Remember that GDP is the monetary value of the economy's output, valued at the market price.)
   c) What was the percentage increase in nominal GDP?
   d) What was the growth rate of the economy from 2009 to 2010? Explain.

6. The following table shows real GDP for both the United States and China, in billions of 2005 dollars. *(LO9-2)*

Real GDP, Measured in Billions of 2005 Dollars

	2008	2009
China	$ 7,565	$ 8,523
United States	$13,229	$12,881

   a) Which country's economy was larger in 2008?
   b) Which economy grew faster between 2008 and 2009?
   c) Which economy was larger in 2009?

7. The following table shows real GDP (in 2000 dollars) for Japan from 2005 to 2010, along with the population in each year. *(LO9-3)*

	Real GDP (Billions of 2005 Dollars)	Population (Millions of People)	Real GDP per Capita (Thousands of 2005 Dollars)
2005	3,873	127.8	___
2006	3,952	127.8	___
2007	4,045	127.8	___
2008	3,997	127.7	___
2009	3,788	127.6	___
2010	3,895	127.4	___

   a) Calculate real GDP per capita for each year.
   b) In what years did real GDP per capita fall?
   c) In what year did real GDP per capita rise by the biggest percentage?
   d) By what percentage did GDP per capita change from 2005 to 2010?

8. Say whether each of the following is likely to make real GDP for the United States rise or fall. *(LO9-4)*

   a) An increase in the number of college graduates.

   b) A war in the Middle East that cuts off the supply of oil to the rest of the world.

   c) A new technology that speeds up the construction of homes.

   d) A flu epidemic that forces people to stay home from work.

   e) The local fast food restaurant buys equipment to make more french fries at a time.

9. Identify which input (labor, human capital, physical capital, raw materials, or knowledge) is affected in the following scenarios. *(LO9-4)*

   a) An investment in new airports that cuts the number of flight delays.

   b) An earthquake that destroys a factory.

   c) Improved cash registers in stores.

   d) More immigrants entering the country.

   e) The discovery of natural gas under Pennsylvania.

10. For each of the following government laws and rules, identify whether it affects growth by influencing labor, human capital, physical capital, raw materials, or knowledge. *(LO9-5)*

    a) A new rule opening up more areas to oil drilling.

    b) A new law that provides more funds to support college scholarships.

    c) A new rule restricting how high an office building can be built.

    d) A new law that makes immigration into the United States more difficult.

11. Which of the following factors do not contribute to a slowdown in productivity? *(LO9-6)*

    a) Tighter environmental regulations.

    b) Low levels of savings and investments.

    c) Lower oil prices.

    d) Lack of innovation.

12. One country (call it A) can make 1,000 shirts with 50 hours of labor. A second country (call it C) can make 1,000 shirts with 75 hours of labor. *(LO9-6)*

    a) Calculate productivity for Countries A and C. Which one is higher?

    b) Suppose workers in Country A get paid $30 per hour and workers in Country C get paid $10 per hour. In which country is it more expensive to make a shirt (assuming that all other costs are the same between the two countries)?

10 BUSINESS CYCLES, UNEMPLOYMENT, AND INFLATION

Life would be much easier if everything were predictable. We could plan a trip to the beach and know it wouldn't rain. We could drive to work and pick the highway that didn't leave us stuck in traffic for an hour behind a jackknifed tractor-trailer. And best of all, in an ideal and stable world, we could be sure we'd never be unemployed.

But as we have all learned, market economies are subject to distressing turbulence. During the Great Recession that started in 2007, unemployment soared, millions of Americans lost their jobs and homes, banks were closed, and major companies such as General Motors were forced to declare bankruptcy. Some state and local governments had trouble paying their bills. The crisis was worldwide, hitting Europe and Japan as well as the United States. Countries such as Iceland, Ireland, Greece, and Portugal had to be bailed out.

Over the years economists have devoted enormous time and effort to understanding what causes economic fluctuations. In some ways modern economics began with the Great Depression of the 1930s (described in Chapter 6), when production and employment plunged in a very short time—not just in the United States but around the world. With one out of every four workers jobless and many factories closed down, the nation looked to economists to take a central role in setting government policy. They had to explain why the

Depression happened, how it could be ended, and how the United States could prevent something similar from happening in the future.

Since the 1930s there have been plenty of economic downturns or *recessions* in the United States and other industrialized countries. However, one of the great triumphs of modern economics is that no industrialized country has ever again suffered a depression of the same horrifying magnitude. Even the latest downturn, as bad as it was, was far less nasty than the Great Depression.

> **POTENTIAL GDP**
> The output of an economy, assuming no strains on production or unused resources.

In this chapter, we will look at the ups and downs of economies. We will show how an economy can deviate from a smooth upward path of potential gross domestic product (GDP). We will define *unemployment,* one of the key measures of an economy's health, and examine the balance between unemployment and inflation. And we will look at recessions: what they are, what kind of damage they can do, and what causes them. Then in the two chapters that follow, we will show how a government can use the tools of fiscal and monetary policy to help moderate the swings of an economy.

POTENTIAL VERSUS REAL GDP

Imagine you're driving along a smooth highway, moving at the same speed as the other cars on the road, so there's no pressure to speed up or slow down. You're listening to music, talking with your friends in the car, and enjoying the ride. Life is good.

Or you could be driving like a maniac—speeding up to 90 miles per hour to pass other cars, then suddenly jamming on the brakes just before you crash into the back of a truck or run into a pothole.

An economy is not a car, but it is useful to think about what it would mean for an economy to move along a smooth and sustainable path. If an economy is not jarred by outside shocks, if workers are fully employed but not overworked, if companies can sell everything they make without strain, and if there are no sudden stops and starts, then output will generally rise smoothly over time. **Potential GDP** is the output of an economy along this smooth path of growth, which assumes no strains on production or unused resources (a bit later in this chapter we'll explain more precisely what we mean by this). Potential GDP is measured in inflation-adjusted dollars like real GDP, and the rate at which it rises is the **potential growth rate.**

Potential Growth

The potential growth rate is driven by the factors we saw in the preceding chapter: growth of the labor force, availability of better-educated and more highly skilled workers, investments in physical capital, availability of raw materials, and increases in knowledge. We can also think of the potential growth rate over the long run as the combination of the long-term growth rate of the labor force and the long-term growth rate of productivity:

Potential growth rate = Long-term labor force growth rate + Long-term productivity growth rate

So if the labor force is growing at 1 percent per year, and productivity per worker is rising at 2 percent per year, then potential GDP (which is adjusted for inflation) is rising at 3 percent per year.

Estimating potential GDP is like drawing a line on a map to show where you are going. Economists project potential GDP into the future to forecast the sustainable growth path for an economy. If we plot potential GDP on a graph (see Figure 10.1), it generally looks like a smooth line.

The Output Gap

But the real GDP of an economy need not follow the same smooth path as potential GDP at all. At any moment, real GDP may be higher or lower than potential GDP, just as a car may be moving faster or slower than the flow of traffic on a road.

FIGURE 10.1	The Path of Potential GDP

As time goes on, potential GDP rises smoothly, reflecting the growth of productivity and the growth of the labor force.

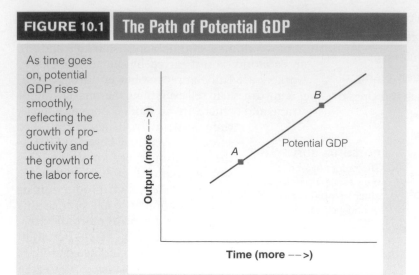

The **output gap** is the difference between real and potential GDP. The output gap is negative when real GDP is less than potential GDP, and it is positive when real GDP is greater than potential GDP (see Figure 10.2).

OUTPUT GAP

The difference between real and potential GDP.

Real GDP can be lower than potential GDP if there are unused resources in the economy, such as workers who don't have jobs, or workers who have jobs that don't use their education (like a PhD flipping hamburgers). Other unused resources include idle machines and empty office buildings.

During the Great Recession years of 2009 and 2010, the output gap was around 6 percent of GDP. This was a negative output gap—that is, real GDP was less than potential GDP.

But it's also possible for real output to exceed potential GDP. How? Imagine an economy consisting of five students. In theory they can study at an even pace all semester. That would be the path of potential GDP. However, in reality three of these students don't work very hard—they wake up late and spend more time at parties than they do studying. In this economy the actual output of work will fall short of potential, and the output gap will be negative.

Then comes the end of the semester. Suddenly the three slackers pump themselves full of caffeine and stay up around the clock to finish their assignments and study for exams. The output gap is positive during this period because their output exceeds their potential. As a result, their output is very high, but it's not sustainable. As we will see, there is a parallel between these students and the economy.

FIGURE 10.2	Potential versus Real GDP

The output gap measures the difference between potential and real GDP. When real GDP is greater than potential GDP, the output gap is positive. When real GDP is less than potential GDP, the output gap is negative.

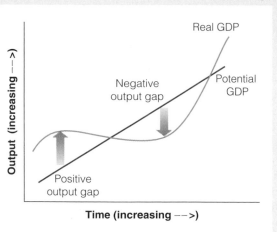

UNEMPLOYMENT

When real GDP drops below potential GDP, it means economic activity has slowed. Companies lay off workers or just don't hire. As a result, more workers become **unemployed**—that is, they don't have jobs but are actively looking for work.

Unemployment is a key measure of the ups and downs of an economy. The Bureau of Labor Statistics (BLS) estimates the number of unemployed workers each month

| **FIGURE 10.3** | **Unemployment Rate, 1960–2010** |

This chart shows the percentage of the labor force that did not have jobs but was actively looking for work.

Source: Bureau of Labor Statistics, www.bls.gov.

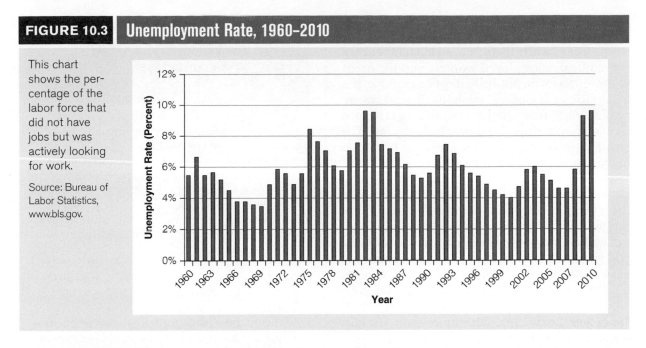

based on a nationwide survey of 60,000 people of various demographic characteristics. The BLS also estimates the number of employed workers each month. The **labor force** is the sum of the employed workers and the unemployed workers.

The **unemployment rate** is the percentage of the labor force that is unemployed. Note that the unemployment rate doesn't count people who are not looking for jobs because they have become discouraged and given up. Nor does it count people who are not working because they are going to school, taking care of children, or simply goofing off. Finally, the unemployment rate does not count the **underemployed**—people who are working part-time because they can't find a full-time job, or people who take jobs below their skill or education levels while they look for something better.

In March 2011 the unemployment rate was 8.8 percent, meaning that 8.8 percent of the labor force did not have jobs. Figure 10.3 shows how the unemployment rate has varied since 1960. Over that stretch, the annual average unemployment rate has gone as high as 9.7 percent in 1982 and as low as 3.5 percent in 1969. Despite the severity of the Great Recession, the annual unemployment rate hit only 9.3 percent in 2009 and 9.6 percent in 2010. (These are the annual averages; in particular months, the unemployment rate may have been higher or lower.)

Types of Unemployment

As we saw in Chapter 3, markets typically tend toward an equilibrium in which the quantity supplied equals the quantity demanded. If that were true in the labor market, everyone would have a job who wanted one. But the unemployment rate never falls to zero in this way—not in the United States or in any other country.

Economists have long puzzled over this fact and have come up with a variety of explanations. One reason unemployment is never zero is that the unemployment rate includes **frictional unemployment**—periods of temporary unemployment that correspond to short gaps between jobs. Frictional unemployment arises because there are usually at least a couple of weeks between the end of one job and the beginning of the next one, or between graduating from school and finding your first job. Even in the tightest labor market—or maybe *especially* in a tight labor market—people who are searching for work may actually turn some jobs down in hopes of getting a better one. This type of unemployment is also considered frictional unemployment.

> **UNEMPLOYMENT RATE**
>
> The percentage of the labor force that is unemployed.

Another reason why unemployment persists is **structural unemployment.** Structural unemployment occurs when there is a mismatch between the skills of unemployed workers and the needs of employers with unfilled jobs. For example, if a local factory is closing, the laid-off workers are probably not immediately qualified to take jobs as nurses even if the local hospital is hiring. The faster the economy changes, the more structural unemployment there will be.

But frictional and structural unemployment do not fully explain some of the big swings we see in the unemployment rate. Especially striking are the big jumps upward in some years, which we call **cyclical unemployment**—large jumps in unemployment tied directly to slowdowns in economic growth. In Figure 10.3 we see 19 years when the unemployment rate exceeded 6 percent on average for the whole year, including 1961, 1982, 1992, 2009, and 2010. With more than 150 million people in the U.S. labor force (as of March 2011), an 8.8 percent unemployment rate means more than 13 million people are out of a job. That's a lot of people.

The Unemployment Puzzle

In general, when the quantity supplied exceeds the quantity demanded in a market, the price falls. In the labor market, the price is the wage. So the unemployment puzzle is really a wage puzzle: when the unemployment rate is high, why doesn't the wage drop? One possible answer is that wages are **sticky.** That is, they don't change much in the short-term in response to economic conditions. For one thing, workers don't want to accept wage cuts in periods of high unemployment because they expect the labor market to quickly recover. In Figure 10.3 we see that the unemployment rate often goes up and then does in fact

HOW IT WORKS: LOCAL UNEMPLOYMENT

The unemployment number that's usually quoted is the unemployment rate for the entire country. But the Bureau of Labor Statistics also publishes the unemployment rates for many local areas. These give the percentages of the local labor force who are out of work and looking for a job.

Some areas have unemployment rates that are much lower than the national average. For example, in February 2011, the unemployment rate in Lincoln, Nebraska, was only 4.2 percent. Lincoln has a recession-resistant economy because it is the state capital and home to the University of Nebraska.

In contrast, El Centro, California, a small metropolitan area near the border with Mexico, had an unemployment rate of 26.9 percent in February 2011, the highest in the country. El Centro didn't lose that many jobs in the recession, but its labor force kept growing, sending unemployment higher.

To see the local unemployment rate for your area, go to the Bureau of Labor Statistics website (www.bls.gov/news.release/pdf/metro.pdf).

Source: Bureau of Labor Statistics.

come down within a couple of years. Another reason for sticky wages is that roughly 12 percent of the workforce belongs to **unions,** which are organized groups of workers that bargain collectively with employers. The contracts set the wages for the workers, making them harder to cut if things turn down. (We will further discuss labor markets in Chapter 16.)

Economic Milestone

2009 BIGGEST JOB CUTBACKS

Sometimes a milestone is negative; the biggest one-year loss in private sector jobs came in 2009. In that year private businesses reduced their employment by 1.9 million jobs. Roughly 1.6 million of those cuts came from manufacturing and another 1.1 million were in construction.

What's more, these were not temporary layoffs: many of those jobs were gone for good because companies permanently closed factories and moved production overseas. The result was an increase in structural unemployment.

THE TRADE-OFF BETWEEN UNEMPLOYMENT AND INFLATION

We just looked at the case in which actual GDP falls *below* potential GDP and more people end up without jobs. But what about the opposite case? As actual GDP rises *above* potential GDP, economic activity increases and unemployment falls. That's good. But the problem with increased economic activity is that inflation can rise; that is, prices and wages can start increasing at a faster rate.

> Inflation tends to rise if the unemployment rate is below the NAIRU. Inflation tends to fall if the unemployment rate is above the NAIRU.

Why should high GDP and low unemployment be linked to rising inflation? Here's one way to think about this: if the number of unemployed workers is low, it's harder for employers to find people to fill job openings. As a result, workers feel they have more power to ask for wage increases. Those wage increases drive up costs for companies and force them to raise prices. The higher prices eat away at the value of wages, and workers have to demand even bigger wage increases to keep up with inflation. The result is the sort of wage–price spiral described in Chapter 8.

In other words, if an economy runs too "hot"—that is, if GDP is too high relative to potential GDP—we get rising inflation. If an economy runs too "cold"—if GDP is too low relative to potential GDP—we get unemployment. As we will see in Chapters 11 and 12, one of the most important tasks for economic policy makers such as the Chairman of the Federal Reserve is to find the right balance between inflation and unemployment.

Inflation and Potential GDP

Earlier in this section we gave a basic description of potential GDP. Now that we have seen the link between inflation, GDP, and unemployment, here is a more precise definition:

Potential GDP = The maximum economic output an economy can sustain without increasing the inflation rate

When the economy is operating at potential, the rate of inflation is neither rising nor falling. This level of potential GDP is the point at which the forces of supply and demand are well balanced, given the existing labor force, technology, and stock of capital. That is why the potential growth rate is sometimes called the *speed limit* of the economy. If actual growth exceeds potential growth for too long, the economy overheats and inflation rises.

The Natural Rate of Unemployment

We can watch the unemployment rate to see whether economic output is approaching a level that causes inflation to accelerate. Milton Friedman, a University of Chicago economist who won the Nobel Prize in Economics in 1976, defined the **natural rate of unemployment** as the level at which inflation is more or less stable. When the unemployment rate is below the natural rate, inflation tends to increase, and when the unemployment rate is above the natural rate, inflation tends to fall. Another, rather long name for the natural rate of unemployment is the *nonaccelerating inflation rate of unemployment,* or **NAIRU** for short.

The NAIRU, or natural rate, is a key indicator of how hot an economy can run without pushing up inflation. As of early 2008 the NAIRU was 4.8 percent, as estimated by the Congressional Budget Office.

For example, in 1983, the NAIRU was about 6 percent and the actual unemployment rate was 9.6 percent. With so many people out of work and cutting back on their spending, demand was weak and businesses found it difficult to raise prices. In fact, the inflation rate fell sharply in 1983.

On the other hand, in 2000 the actual unemployment rate was 4 percent, lower than the NAIRU, which was about 5 percent. With lots of people employed and spending their wages, demand was strong and businesses were able to raise prices. As a result, the inflation rate rose in 2000.

When the unemployment rate is at or near the NAIRU, then it is likely that the economy is operating at potential. That's one reason why the unemployment rate is such a closely watched economic number.

RECESSIONS

Small deviations of real GDP from potential GDP or of the unemployment rate from the NAIRU don't matter much—just as you can drive slightly faster or slower than the flow of traffic on a highway without causing any big problems.

But large deviations from the potential growth path—especially deviations downward—are a problem. Think about what happens if your car stalls in the middle of a busy highway. Similarly, if GDP is running below its potential, everything in the economy suffers. It's harder to find a job, profits aren't as high, malls are empty, and tax revenues fall short of predictions. The world is a gloomier place.

If a downward deviation from potential growth becomes bad enough, an economy can actually shrink. A **recession** is defined as a significant decline in economic activity spread across an economy, lasting more than a few months. (Who identifies the official date when a recession starts? See "How it Works: Calling the Recession.")

The Business Cycle

Although all recessions are different, all display similar patterns. The **peak** is the date on which a recession starts—that's when the economy hits a high point and starts heading downward. The date on which the recession ends and the economy starts heading up again is called the **trough.** The **expansion** is the time from the trough, through recovery, and all the way to the next peak. This pattern of recession and expansion is known as the **business cycle;** see Figure 10.4 for a closer look at a typical cycle.

Despite its unusual severity, the Great Recession shows the same basic pattern as past downturns. The Great Recession officially started in December 2007, even though housing prices started dropping as early as 2006. The recession officially ended in June 2009, 18 months after it started, making it the longest, nastiest downturn since the Great Depression.

Figure 10.5 tracks real GDP through the recession, with the peak in the fourth quarter of 2007. The graph shows us that the initial stages of the

HOW IT WORKS: CALLING THE RECESSION

When is the U.S. economy in recession? That is, when is a decline in the nation's economic activity significant enough to qualify for this official designation? Oddly, government statisticians do not make this decision. Instead a private research group—the National Bureau of Economic Research (NBER)—decides the official dates on which a recession starts and ends.

The NBER is a Cambridge, Massachusetts–based organization that was founded in the 1920s to study the ups and downs of business cycles. Today, whenever there is an economic downturn, the Business Cycle Dating Committee of the NBER—made up of several prominent economists—meets to decide the official beginning and end dates of a recession, based on key figures like employment and retail sales.

RECESSION
A significant decline in economic activity spread across the economy, lasting more than a few months.

BUSINESS CYCLE
The recurring pattern of recession and expansion in an economy.

downturn were fairly mild. But after Lehman Brothers went bankrupt in mid-September 2008, the U.S. economy went into a steep plunge.

As we will see in the next two chapters, this was the period when the Federal Reserve, under Chairman Ben Bernanke, and the federal government, under President George W. Bush and President Barack Obama, took unprecedented monetary and fiscal policy measures to prop up the economy. During this stretch, there was widespread concern that even enormous government intervention was not going to be enough.

However, Figure 10.5 shows us that the government actions eventually seemed to be effective in stopping the plunge. The low point for real GDP came in the second quarter of 2009. We can see that real GDP, a measure of the output of the economy, had reached its previous peak by the end of 2010.

The Impact of Recession on Workers

Who suffers the most from a recession? Without question, unemployed workers and their

FIGURE 10.4 | A Typical Business Cycle

The peak marks the start of the recession, and the trough marks its end. A full business cycle runs from one peak to the next.

families suffer the most pain, especially those who do not have a savings cushion. From economic, political, and human points of view, a lengthy and deep recession can be a major disaster for individuals who lose their jobs.

The reason is simple: during a recession, if you lose your job, it's hard to find a new one. As the economy shrinks, factories close and companies stop hiring. And even after a recession is over it can take months or years for the labor market to revive. As a result, people who lose their jobs in recessions can find themselves unemployed for months or even years. That's long enough to outlast their savings, their healthcare benefits, and their ability to hold onto their homes. As this textbook is being revised in early 2011, private sector employment is still far below its earlier peak (see Figure 10-6).

The Impact of Recession on Businesses

Recessions hurt businesses as well as workers. As an economy slows, the demand schedules of most businesses shift to the left. For the same price, the quantity demanded falls, and therefore the quantity supplied also falls.

FIGURE 10.5 | The Great Recession: Real GDP

The figure shows the peak and trough of the latest business cycle. The line is real GDP in 2005 dollars.

Source: Bureau of Economic Analysis, www.bls.gov.

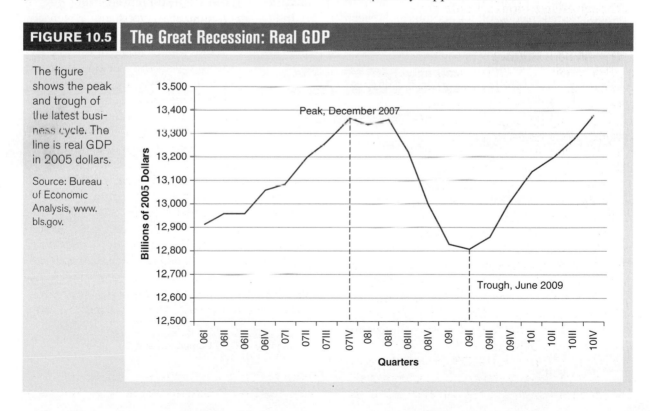

FIGURE 10.6 | The Great Recession: Private-Sector Jobs

The figure shows the path of private sector employment during the Great Recession. As of early 2011, private sector jobs were still well below their peak.

Source: Bureau of Labor Statistics, www.bls.gov.

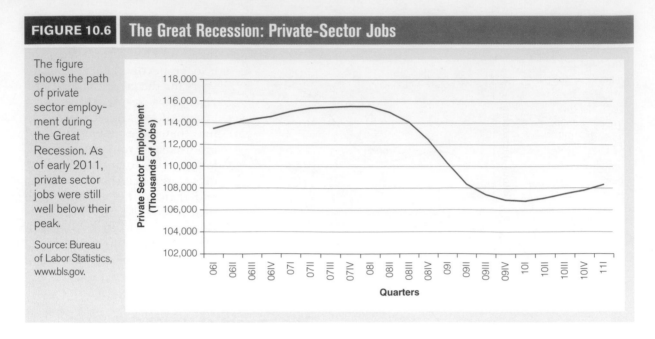

Figure 10.7 shows the supply and demand schedules for a typical market in an economy—say for cars. During a recession, consumers have less money to spend on new cars, and that causes the demand schedule to shift to the left. As a result, production of cars falls from *Q* to *Q*'. The auto companies are forced to offer discounts and special deals, so the price falls from *P* to *P*'. In fact, this is exactly what happened in the Great Recession. Motor vehicle sales collapsed to the point where General Motors and Chrysler were forced to declare bankruptcy and accept bailouts from the federal government.

But companies don't simply cut back on current production. In fact, all sorts of businesses— big banks, the mom-and-pop store at the corner—also cut back sharply on expansion and their plans for up-grades in recessions. Any spending they can post-pone, they will.

That's why recessions are usually accompanied by a rapid drop in purchases of capital equipment, such as machinery and computers, and an equally noticeable decline in the construction of commercial office buildings, factories, and other nonresidential structures.

In fact, an essential characteristic of a recession is that it is *broad-based*, so that the slowdown is

FIGURE 10.7 | The Effect of Recession on Car Companies

In a recession, demand for cars falls, and the demand curve shifts left. That reduces the quantity demanded and supplied for cars and typically causes car companies to offer customers better deals—that is, cheaper prices.

TABLE 10.1	What Typically Falls in Recessions

A recession is a broad decline in economic activity. In addition to the fall in real GDP, here are some other aspects of the economy that decline in most recessions.

Aspect of the Economy	What Happens in a Recession
Employment	Businesses lay off workers and cut back on hiring.
Retail sales	Many stores see falling sales, and some close.
Home construction	Fewer homes are built.
Housing prices	Home prices drop.
Household income, adjusted for inflation	Many households see their real incomes drop.
Business profits	Businesses make less money.
Business investment	Businesses spend less on physical capital, such as trucks, computers, and buildings.
Industrial production (the output of factories)	Factories produce less.
Tax revenues	Governments collect less tax.

spread across most of the economy. Table 10.1 lists some of the typical areas that are hit by recessions, including home construction and business profits. True, some industries tend to hold up better than others in recessions (see "Spotlight: Recession-Resistant Industries"). Nevertheless, these are the exception, not the rule.

WHY DO RECESSIONS HAPPEN?

If you see a car broken down by the side of the road, you don't know what happened. It could be that the driver was unlucky and hit a bad pothole. Or perhaps the driver neglected essential maintenance and the vehicle overheated. Or the car simply ran out of gas.

We face the same uncertainty when it comes to recessions. An economy may stall for a number of different reasons. The question of what causes recessions is one of the longest-running debates among economists, going back to the Great Depression. For our purposes here we just need to realize that recessions can have different triggers. Let's look at some of these: problems in financial markets, negative supply shifts, negative demand shifts, and inflation fighting.

Problems in Financial Markets

Recessions caused by a financial crisis are rare but challenging. Financial markets let individuals and businesses borrow money to finance everything from homes and cars to college educations. When financial markets stop working well, it becomes harder to borrow. When it becomes harder to borrow, the economy slows.

The Great Recession was caused, in large part, by problems in financial markets. As we'll see in Chapter 13, many consumers borrowed more than they should have, especially to buy homes. In particular, low-income homebuyers borrowed more than they could afford to pay back—the so-called subprime loans. And many banks lent more than they should have, helping fuel the housing boom.

But eventually the boom came to an end and was followed by a bust. Several big Wall Street firms either failed or were forced to sell themselves. Many homebuyers could not pay their mortgages.

After the bust, most banks tightened up their lending standards. As it became harder for consumers to borrow, there was less money available to buy homes and cars. It became harder for small businesses to raise the money they needed to operate and expand. The result was a sharp slowdown in the economy.

SPOTLIGHT: RECESSION-RESISTANT INDUSTRIES

In any recession, a few sectors usually avoid the general downturn and keep expanding. For example, entertainment spending is somewhat recession-resistant because people want to have fun to take their minds off their economic problems. Movie ticket sales held up well during the recession years of 2008 and 2009, spurred by the release of films such as *The Dark Knight*.

Another recession-resistant industry is healthcare. People keep getting sick whether the economy is up or down. Moreover, much of healthcare spending is funded by the federal government, which can keep spending even in a downturn by borrowing money.

As a result, healthcare employment typically keeps increasing even when other parts of the economy are shrinking. From December 2007 to December 2010, for example, hospitals, physicians' offices, and other healthcare businesses added roughly 800,000 jobs, while the rest of the private sector lost over 8 million jobs.

Negative Supply Shifts

Another significant cause of recessions is an unexpected negative supply shift, which moves the supply curve to the left for a broad array of markets. The classic example of such a negative shock is a sudden rise in the price of oil. For example, the 1973 oil price shock, described in Chapter 6, helped trigger the recession of 1973–1975. Similarly, Saddam Hussein's invasion of Kuwait in 1990, which pushed oil prices up, was one of the main reasons the U.S. economy slipped into recession that year. And the oil price increase of 2007 and 2008 helped slow the U.S. economy going into the early stages of the Great Recession.

An oil price increase is particularly harmful because it is a broad supply shift that affects most markets in an economy. By making energy and transportation more costly, the higher price of oil causes the supply schedule in many individual markets to shift left.

Consider, for example, the market for grocery items. These items are shipped to supermarkets from all over the country, so an increase in the cost of fuel translates directly into rising costs for supermarkets. As Figure 10.8 shows, a negative supply shift in a market tends to decrease the quantity demanded and increase the price.

If the higher price of oil affected only the grocery market, that would not cause a recession by itself. After all, grocery purchases, even though they account for billions of dollars of sales each year, are just a small part of the economy.

To cause a recession, a negative shift has to affect many markets simultaneously. In that case, it can decrease the output of the whole economy *and* push up inflation. That's exactly what happened after the oil price shock of 1973: the economy went into a combination of recession and inflation called *stagflation*. In every market where energy was an important cost, the supply curve shifted to the left—including the labor market because higher gasoline prices made commuting more expensive for most people.

Another example of a negative supply shift is a terrorist attack that forces businesses and governments to adopt tighter security measures. For example, suppose every box and container imported into the United States had to be checked for bombs. Such measures would make both shipping and transportation more expensive. The result would be a leftward shift in supply schedules over a broad range of markets, with the resulting fall in quantity and increase in prices that precipitate a recession. (To see an example of a narrow supply shift, take a look at "Spotlight: Do Hurricanes Cause Recessions?")

| **FIGURE 10.8** | **The Impact of a Negative Supply Shift** |

A rise in the price of oil can increase transportation costs for groceries and cause a shift in the supply curve to the left. That, in turn, reduces the quantity demanded and supplied. If this affects enough markets, it can cause overall economic output to decline.

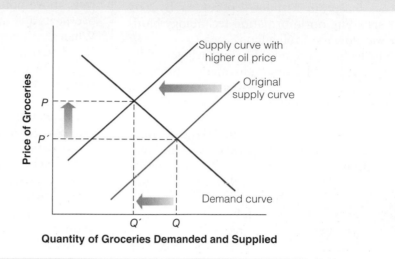

Negative Demand Shifts

A sudden and unexpected drop in demand can also cause a recession. Possibly the best example of a recession driven by a negative demand shift was the recession of 2001, which was caused primarily by a decline in business spending on computers, communications equipment, and other information technology gear. Until 2000 companies' spending on computers and information technology had been soaring for several different reasons. First, the dawning of the Internet age had created a surge of start-up dot-com companies, all of which had to spend heavily on computer equipment to get their operations up and running.

Second, businesses were scared of the "Y2K bug," which was the threat that older computer systems and programs would crash when the clock turned to January 1, 2000. As a result, many companies spent large sums of money replacing their old computers and programs. Third, telecom companies were spending billions laying down new fiber optic cable to handle all the future online traffic they expected.

But these sources of demand evaporated. Most dot-com companies failed. January 1, 2000, came and went (without a major hitch, as it turned out), and the need to fix the Y2K problem was over. And it turned out that the telecom companies had overspent because Internet traffic did not rise as fast as they expected.

SPOTLIGHT: DO HURRICANES CAUSE RECESSIONS?

Can a natural disaster such as a hurricane or an earthquake cause a recession? Perhaps, but history suggests that it is not likely in the United States. The worst recent natural disaster to hit the United States was Hurricane Katrina in 2005, which almost completely flooded New Orleans and much of the Mississippi coast. The storm caused at least $40 billion in losses and perhaps a lot more. At the same time, damage to the oil wells and refineries along the Gulf Coast drove gasoline prices up across the country.

But despite the devastation in New Orleans, GDP growth for the United States barely slowed in the third and fourth quarters of 2005. There are several reasons for the lack of overall economic impact. First, New Orleans, although a major city, contributed only a relatively small share to the whole U.S. economy. Second, many businesses with operations in New Orleans were able to move their production to other parts of the country. And third, the rebuilding effort, which included billions for repairing and upgrading dikes and levees, actually *added* to the level of economic activity in the United States.

So businesses, which spent $225 billon on computers and communications equipment in 2000, cut back sharply in 2001 and kept cutting. By 2003 their spending on information technology hardware was down to $160 billion.

This decline in demand helped trigger widespread layoffs. The unemployment rate in the San Jose, California, area—where major Silicon Valley tech companies such as Sun and Cisco are based—jumped from 2.5 percent in 2000 to 8.5 percent just two years later. Worldcom, a major telephone and Internet provider, went bankrupt in 2002, along with a host of smaller companies. All told, the "tech bust," as it was called, led to the 2001 recession. It was not a lengthy recession—only eight months—but it took a long time for jobs to recover.

We can imagine other scenarios for a recession driven by a decline in demand. For example, a deadly flu epidemic that kept people from shopping would reduce demand sharply, though it would probably also cut supply because many workplaces would close down as employees became ill.

Inflation Fighting

Let's come now to the final important cause of the recession: inflation fighting. If you run too fast and get overheated, you have to slow down for a while to catch your breath. Sometimes the economy gets into a similar situation: if output runs above potential for too long, the economy overheats and inflation rises, as discussed earlier. When that happens, economic policy makers at the Federal Reserve—the country's central bank—have to take inflation-fighting steps to slow growth. Sometimes they slow growth so much that the result is a recession.

For example, in 1980 and 1981 the inflation rate was running at 13.5 percent and 10.3 percent, respectively. That was way too high. So Paul Volcker, who was chairman of the Federal Reserve at that point, applied the brakes. To bring down inflation, he needed to get the unemployment rate *above* the NAIRU—which was about 6 percent at the time. That is, he had to intentionally force unemployment way up to reduce inflation.

That's exactly what Volcker did. He raised interest rates so high that businesses and consumers pulled back from borrowing. Purchases of homes and cars plunged, and the unemployment rate skyrocketed. He achieved his goal of reducing inflation—but the result was a deep recession that put millions of people out of work.

We have not had a recession caused by inflation fighting since 1981–82. But if prices start to increase at a rapid rate, the Federal Reserve could very well raise interest rates to slow the economy.

TABLE 10.2	**Recent Recessions and Their Causes**

This table lists some of the causes of recent recessions.

Recession Start Date	Type of Recession	Main Cause
November 1973	Negative supply shift	Sharp rise in oil prices
January 1980	Negative supply shift, inflation fighting	Sharp rise in oil prices combined with interest rate hikes by the Federal Reserve
July 1981	Inflation fighting	Interest rate hikes by the Federal Reserve
July 1990	Negative supply shift, inflation fighting	Oil price hike caused by Iraqi invasion of Kuwait, combined with interest rate hikes by the Federal Reserve
March 2001	Negative demand shift	Decline in tech spending by business
December 2007	Financial crisis	Excess borrowing

CONCLUSION

Market economies don't always grow at a steady rate. Sometimes they grow too fast for a period, creating the conditions in which inflation can get out of control. Other times, market economies shrink, turning into the unpleasant stretch that economists call a recession.

The ups and downs of economies described in this chapter will never go away. But they can be made less harmful by appropriate policy responses, as we will see in the next two chapters.

10 SUMMARY

1. Potential GDP is the output of an economy along a smooth path of growth, which assumes no strains on the economy or unused resources. Real GDP can be higher or lower than potential GDP. The difference between the two is known as the output gap. *(LO10-1)*

2. When real GDP drops below potential GDP, businesses cut back on hiring. The result is a rise in the unemployment rate—the percentage of the workforce that wants to work but cannot find jobs. Three types of unemployment are frictional, structural, and cyclical. *(LO10-2)*

3. If the unemployment rate rises above the natural rate of unemployment—also called the NAIRU—the inflation rate falls. If the unemployment rate drops below the NAIRU, the inflation rate rises. *(LO10-3)*

4. A recession is a significant decline in economic activity spread across an economy, lasting more than a few months. The beginning of a recession is called the peak, and the end of a recession is the trough. Recessions can hurt both workers and businesses. *(LO10-4)*

5. Recessions can have several different causes. These include problems in financial markets, negative supply shifts, negative demand shifts, and inflation fighting. *(LO10-5)*

KEY TERMS AND CONCEPTS

potential GDP

potential growth rate

output gap

unemployed

labor force

unemployment rate

underemployed

frictional unemployment

structural unemployment

cyclical unemployment

sticky wages

unions

natural rate of unemployment

NAIRU

recession

peak

trough

expansion

business cycle

PROBLEMS

1. Are the following situations more consistent with a positive output gap or a negative output gap? *(LO10-1)*

    a) Workers in a factory are putting in lots of overtime.

    b) The shopping mall seems empty on a Saturday afternoon.

    c) The roads are so crowded during rush hour that you have to leave early for work.

    d) You apply for a new job, and there are plenty of other applicants.

2. Do the following events increase or decrease potential GDP? *(LO10-1)*

    a) A decline in the number of new immigrants entering the country.

    b) A decrease in the purchases of new computers by businesses.

    c) The discovery of a new oil field in Texas.

    d) The discovery of a cheaper way of generating energy from sunlight.

3. The following table gives the potential GDP and real GDP for a very small economy, both measured in 2005 dollars. *(LO10-2)*

Year	Real GDP (2005 Dollars)	Potential GDP (2005 Dollars)	Output Gap
2001	100	100	—
2002	107	105	—
2003	110	110	—
2004	113	115	—

    a) Fill in the column for the output gap.

    b) Would you expect the unemployment rate to be higher in 2002 or 2004? Explain.

    c) In which year would you expect it to be easiest to find a job? (Assume that the NAIRU is the same each year.)

4. A man used to work for pay, but he is currently going to school and taking care of his family. We would count him in the category of _____ *(LO10-2)*

    a) unemployed.

    b) underemployed.

    c) employed.

    d) neither employed nor unemployed.

5. Say whether each of the following is more likely to be a case of frictional, structural, or cyclical unemployment. *(LO10-2)*

a) You graduate from college, and it takes you a month to find a job.

b) A furniture maker closes a factory in North Carolina and moves production to China. The laid-off factory workers have trouble finding new jobs because other furniture companies are doing the same thing.

c) A slowdown in sales causes the local department store to lay off workers.

d) There are plenty of "want" ads for nurses but few for factory workers.

6. Suppose the NAIRU is 5 percent, and the current unemployment rate is 4.5 percent. Are the following statements true or false? *(LO10-3)*

a) The inflation rate is likely to fall in future months.

b) Real GDP is likely higher than potential GDP.

c) We can find jobs for more people without increasing inflation.

7. Some recent inflation and unemployment figures for the United States are presented below. *(LO10-3)*

Year	Inflation Rate (%)	Unemployment Rate (%)
1996	3.0	5.4
1997	2.3	4.9
1998	1.6	4.5
1999	2.2	4.2
2000	3.4	4.0
2001	2.8	4.7

a) In what years does the inflation rate rise compared to the previous year?

b) What are the unemployment rates for the years when inflation rises?

c) Based on these data, was the NAIRU greater or less than 5 percent during this period? Explain.

8. The following table gives real GDP for a small economy going through a business cycle. *(LO10-4)*

Year	Real GDP (2005 Dollars)
2000	100
2001	104
2002	103
2003	106
2004	109
2005	112
2006	111
2007	110

a) Which years are peaks?

b) What are the starting and ending dates of the recession?

c) How many years does the expansion last?

9. Recessions affect many aspects of the economy. For each of the following economic quantities, say whether it rises or falls during a typical recession. *(LO10-4)*

   a) Construction of new hotels.

   b) Tax revenues.

   c) Airline workers.

   d) Workers who are overqualified for their current jobs.

10. Here are several economic events that could potentially help trigger a recession. Say which category each one falls into: negative supply shift, negative demand shift, inflation fighting, or problems in financial markets. *(LO10-5)*

    a) War in the Middle East destroys oil fields in Saudi Arabia.

    b) China suddenly cuts off imports to the United States.

    c) Inflation accelerates sharply to 10 percent a year.

    d) Mortgages become much harder to get because banks become less willing to lend.

11 FISCAL POLICY

LEARNING OBJECTIVES

After reading this chapter, you should be able to:

LO11-1 Identify key differences between the private sector and government.

LO11-2 Describe the short-term impacts of increased government spending and use the multiplier effect to calculate the effect of fiscal stimulus.

LO11-3 Summarize the limitations of using increased government spending to stimulate growth.

LO11-4 Discuss the ways that changes in tax rates affect the economy.

LO11-5 Explain how the budget deficit affects the economy in the short run and in the long run.

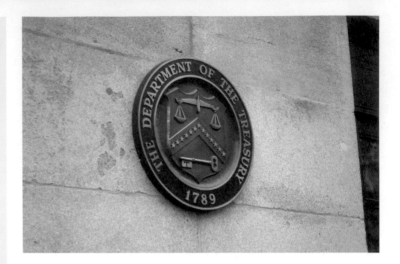

In 2008 and 2009 the federal government used its financial muscle to combat the Great Recession. President George W. Bush signed a bill to help prop up the failing banking system, and President Barack Obama followed with legislation that pumped $787 billion worth of federal spending and tax cuts into the faltering economy.

These increases in federal spending and cuts in taxes helped prevent the Great Recession from turning into something worse. But it also left the United States with a huge budget deficit as spending far exceeded tax revenues.

In this chapter we will analyze the economic effects of **fiscal policy**—that is, decisions about government spending, taxes, and debt in both the short run and the long run. In the short term, fiscal policy consists of the government's budget decisions that affect employment, output, and inflation over the next couple of years. That includes the spending increases and tax cuts that the government enacted to fight the Great Recession. In the long term, fiscal policy creates the link between government spending and taxation decisions and the country's economic growth.

Fiscal policy is probably the most politically charged area of economics. Each year lawmakers and government officials in Washington decide how to allocate trillions of dollars.

The result is a federal budget hundreds of pages long in which every sentence can make a big impact on someone's life or company. And of course, members of Congress get elected in part because of their ability to influence the budget in favor of individuals and companies that donated money to campaigns.

But leaving politics aside, reputable economists disagree about the right way to run fiscal policy. Some favor a larger role for the government, especially when the economy is in a slump. Others argue for shrinking government spending and taxation because they prefer less government interference and oversight. And a third group of economists focuses on reducing the size of the budget deficit, which is the difference between spending and revenue.

In this chapter we will lay out the basics of fiscal policy. We will discuss both the positive and negative impacts of government spending, taxes, and borrowing on the rest of the economy, presenting the different perspectives in an unbiased fashion. We will end this chapter by examining long-term fiscal policy.

THE GOVERNMENT AND THE ECONOMY

Imagine an armored car filled with a million dollars, making a pickup from a local bank. Now imagine a fleet of *3.5 million* armored cars, each with a million dollars in it. That's what you would need to carry the $3.5 trillion the federal government spent in fiscal year 2010.

If we add in the spending of state and local governments, the total would be even higher. In the fiscal year 2010, government at all levels—federal, state, and local—spent $5.5 trillion. Of that amount, $2.8 trillion paid for the salaries of government workers and for goods and services provided to the government. This is what we called "government output" in Chapter 7. The other $2.7 trillion went to **transfer payments**—government payments to individuals such as

HOW IT WORKS: LEVELS OF GOVERNMENT

In this chapter we talk about government as if it were one big entity. But there are three separate levels of government, each of which has different patterns of spending and taxation. The federal government, based in Washington, DC, spends mostly on national defense, Medicare, Medicaid, and Social Security.

In contrast, the 50 state governments and the more than 30,000 county and municipal governments have different sets of priorities. Their big expenses are education and local services such as police, fire protection, and waste collection. State governments also pay quite a bit toward Medicaid—the medical care for the poor.

Take the city of Springfield, Massachusetts, which has a population of 150,000 and is also home of the Basketball Hall of Fame (which, naturally, is shaped a bit like a basketball). In 2010 the city had a budget of $529 million. Out of that, 58 percent was spent on education, and 11 percent on public safety (police and fire). This is a very different spending pattern from that of the federal government's.

Social Security, Medicare, welfare, and other payments such as subsidies to businesses. In other words, one of government's most important roles is to act as a pipeline, shifting money from some people to others.

In many ways a dollar spent by the government contributes as much to economic output as a dollar spent in the private sector. Paying a schoolteacher's salary, fixing a bridge, or providing medical care for the elderly can be just as important—or perhaps even more important—to the economy than your neighbor's purchasing an expensive sports car.

However, there *is* a big difference between government and the private sector. In the private sector, businesses and individuals collect and spend money by means of market transactions. They exchange money either for goods and services, in the case of businesses and their customers, or for labor, in the case of workers and employers. All transactions are voluntary, so presumably all parties benefit.

What's more, as we saw in Chapter 5, private businesses are always under pressure to cut costs and find ways to become more efficient. If they don't do that, they are at risk of being put out of business by competitors.

Governments, in contrast, are under no such economic pressure to be efficient and innovative. Nobody is going to put the federal government out of business or take away its customers. Instead the level of government spending is set by the political system rather than the economic system, and that spending is funded through a combination of **taxation** and borrowing. Taxation, the main way the government raises money, is a legally required transfer of funds from individuals and businesses to the government. Governments also raise money by borrowing. Like private borrowers, governments have to pay interest on their debts. But unlike private borrowers, they can pay back their debts by raising taxes if necessary. For these reasons the government has a special role in the economy.

THE SHORT-TERM IMPACT OF GOVERNMENT SPENDING

Each year the federal budget is set through a complicated and exhausting process beginning in February, when the president proposes a budget for the next fiscal year (which starts on October 1 of each year). For the next nine months, various congressional committees and the executive branch wrangle over everything from the overall level of spending down to the smallest details, such as the funding for the Marine Mammal Commission (total 2010 budget: $3 million). Eventually Congress and the president agree on how much is to be spent and what the tax rules will be.

What's important here is that the level of spending is set through the political system. Congress and the president can decide to either increase or decrease government spending.

When Congress and the president decide to boost or cut federal spending, what happens to the rest of the economy? To make this more concrete, let's say they choose to boost spending by allocating an extra $10 million dollars for repairing a bridge that is about to collapse. We'll ignore for the moment the important question of where the added $10 million comes from (though we'll see later in the chapter that this makes a big difference to the economy).

The government spends some of the money on labor: architects and engineers to draw up the plans, truck drivers to move the supplies, construction workers to assemble the parts, police officers to supervise the site. It spends some money on equipment: cranes, drilling equipment, trucks. Other money goes for materials: steel, concrete, paint.

As you can see, repairing the bridge creates more demand for labor, materials, and equipment. In other words, the demand schedule for labor and the demand schedule for construction materials and equipment both shift to the right, as we see in Figures 11.1 and 11.2.

FIGURE 11.1	The Impact of Government Spending on the Labor Market

An increase in government spending pushes the demand curve for labor to the right, which boosts the quantity of labor supplied and demanded from L to L'.

Quantity of Labor Supplied and Demanded

FIGURE 11.2   The Impact of Government Spending on the Market for Construction Materials

When the government spends money to repair a bridge, that pushes the demand curve for construction materials to the right, which boosts the quantity of construction material supplied and demanded from Q to Q'.

The effect of the increase in government spending is to push up the quantity of labor from L to L' and to push up the quantity of construction materials from Q to Q'. In other words, unemployment falls because more workers are employed. And production increases because more construction materials are being demanded and supplied.

This brings us to the following general principle: in the short term, an increase in government spending lowers unemployment and increases GDP, all other things being equal. This principle is the essence of the **Keynesian approach** to macroeconomics, which uses increases in government spending and cuts in taxes (as we will see later in this chapter) to combat the effect of recessions. Such increases in government spending and cuts in taxes are called **fiscal stimulus** because they involve changes in fiscal policy. Economist John Maynard Keynes originally proposed the use of government spending to stimulate the economy in the 1930s during the Great Depression. He argued that the reason for the steep decline in GDP during the Depression was the lack of demand—a problem the government could correct by spending more.

Since then economists have had long and complex disputes about the validity of the Keynesian approach. Over time they have come to better understand many of its limitations, which we will discuss later in this chapter. However, facing a worsening recession in late 2008 and early 2009, most economists agreed that it was important for the government to support demand. The American Recovery and Reinvestment Act (ARRA) signed by President Obama in February 2009 was intended to stimulate growth and job creation by boosting demand (see Table 11.1).

The Multiplier Effect

Now let's continue our story of repairing the bridge. With more workers employed, the demand for consumer products goes up. Workers now have money to buy necessities like food, consumer durables like cars, and luxuries like occasional dinners out. That boosts spending, which increases sales across the whole range of businesses, including grocery stores, auto dealers, and restaurants.

Think about auto dealers, for example. Remember, the government itself doesn't buy any extra cars because it's repairing the bridge, but the newly hired construction workers do. If the government hires 1,000 construction workers, and 100

TABLE 11.1	Major Fiscal Stimulus Legislation, 2008–2010

Economic Stimulus Act
Date: February 2008, signed by President George W. Bush
Amount: $152 billion
Key aspects: Provided tax rebates for low and middle-income households and investment incentives for some businesses.

Troubled Asset Relief Program (TARP)
Date: October 2008, signed by President George W. Bush
Amount: $410 billion invested, $244 billion repaid (as of March 2011)
Key aspects: Gave the federal government authority to prop up the economy by investing up to $700 billion in troubled financial institutions and selected nonfinancial businesses.

American Recovery and Reinvestment Act (ARRA)
Date: February 2009, signed by President Barack Obama
Amount: $787 billion
Key aspects: Gave a wide range of tax reductions, including tax credits for college tuition, first-time home buyers, and home owners who invest in energy efficiency. Increased spending on healthcare and education, including aid to local school districts and Pell Grants. Invested in highway, bridge, rail, and air projects.

Tax Relief, Unemployment Insurance Reauthorization, and Job Creation Act
Data: December 2010, signed by President Barack Obama
Amount: $858 billion
Key aspects: Extended tax reductions that were going to expire as of December 2010. Extended unemployment benefits. Temporarily cut payroll tax.

of them buy new cars with their paychecks, that's 100 cars that weren't sold before.

The rise in sales across the board encourages private sector businesses to hire more workers as well: more car sales staff, more supermarket checkout clerks, more restaurant cooks. What's more, if sales go up enough, the auto dealers may be tempted to add another building to accommodate the new demand. And guess what? The construction company that builds the new auto dealership probably has to hire new workers too.

In other words, the initial government hiring effort creates enough additional purchasing power in the economy to induce another round of hiring in the private sector. And those extra workers, in turn, boost the economy with their purchases as well.

Taken together, this **multiplier effect** is the short-term boost in economic activity that flows from the government's spending increase (or tax cut, as we will see later in the chapter). A similar multiplier effect occurs for any

MULTIPLIER EFFECT
The short-term boost in economic activity from a government spending increase or tax cut.

type of government spending. For example, giving food stamps to poor households raises the demand for food, leading grocery stores to hire more cashiers. A purchase order for military submarines increases employment at the shipyards that keeps local stores humming, boosts construction of new homes for the shipyard workers, and perhaps even increases jobs at beach resorts as the workers can afford more family vacations.

We can state the multiplier as a **job multiplier,** which gives the total number of jobs created by one additional government-funded job. A job multiplier of 2 means that each new government job creates one new private sector job. A job multiplier of 1 means no additional private sector jobs are created.

Or we can state the multiplier as a **spending multiplier,** which gives the increase in GDP created by one additional dollar of government expenditures. Suppose the government spends an additional dollar on hiring workers or buying supplies. By itself that would boost GDP by $1 because government spending on goods and services is one component of GDP (as we saw in Chapter 7). But that dollar could have an additional effect as that new worker uses the new income to increase his purchases. A spending multiplier of 1.4 means that GDP goes up by $1.40 in response to the initial spending increase: $1 from the bigger government component and $0.40 extra in the private sector.

To put things in a wider perspective, suppose the government boosts spending by $100 billion. If the spending multiplier is 1.4, GDP will rise by $140 billion, including both the initial spending and its follow-up effects. That seems like a lot of money. However, with national GDP in early 2008 running at about $14 trillion per year, a $140 billion increase is equivalent to only about a 1 percent increase in GDP (1 percent = $140 billion/$14 trillion).

Economists use the multiplier to help estimate the impact of fiscal stimulus (see "Spotlight: The Impact of ARRA"). The multiplier can work at either the national or the local level. One of the best examples of the multiplier effect on the local level plays out in Washington, DC. The main employer in the District of Columbia is, of course, the federal government, which accounts for about 30 percent of all the area's workers. In fact, if it weren't for the federal government, most private sector businesses in Washington wouldn't be there, including many law firms and trade associations that lobby legislators and regulators. Without the government and the multiplier effect, Washington might be a small and sleepy village.

The Marginal Propensity to Consume

What determines the size of the multiplier? One factor is the **marginal propensity to consume (MPC),** which is the portion that households spend of each additional dollar they receive. Think about a construction worker being hired to build the bridge. When she gets the pay from her new job, she has the choice to spend the money or put it in the bank. If her marginal propensity to consume is .6,

MARGINAL PROPENSITY TO CONSUME
The portion that households spend of each additional dollar they receive.

SPOTLIGHT: THE IMPACT OF ARRA

From the beginning, President Obama and his team tried to track the impact of the American Recovery and Reinvestment Act (ARRA) on jobs. They required recipients to report on job creation and set up a website, www.recovery.gov, to offer the public this information.

Tracking the job creation, though, turned out to be more difficult than expected. Part of the problem was the sheer diversity of projects. ARRA-funded projects included everything from $23 million to help complete biking and walking trails near Philadelphia and Camden, NJ; to $73 million for the construction of "Warriors in Transition Barracks" for military personnel who were wounded in Iraq or Afghanistan; to $1.6 billion for cleaning up the Savannah River nuclear weapons site in South Carolina.

In the end, the best estimates of the job impact of ARRA came from the spending and job multipliers used by the Congressional Budget Office (CBO). In a February 2011 report, CBO estimated that spending on infrastructure had a spending multiplier of as little as 1, or as much as 2.5, spread over several quarters.

Based on this assumption, CBO estimated that the stimulus program raised GDP by $125 billion to $270 billion in 2009, and by $220 billion to $600 billion in 2010. Similarly, the CBO estimated that the stimulus raised employment by 500,000 to 900,000 jobs in 2009, and 1.3 million to 3.3 million jobs in 2010.

Source: The Congressional Budget Office, www.cbo.gov/ftpdocs/120xx/doc12074/02-23-ARRA.pdf and www.recovery.gov.

she'll spend 60 cents of that additional dollar and save the remaining 40 cents.

The higher the marginal propensity to consume, the bigger the multiplier will be, all other things being equal. If those newly hired construction workers run right out and buy cars, they'll give a big boost to the rest of the economy. More autoworkers will be hired, who in turn will go out and spend their wages on renovating their homes, say. That will lift the employment of carpenters, and so forth.

But if the newly hired construction workers sock all their money away in the bank, the short-term boost to the economy will be much smaller. Car sales won't go up, extra autoworkers won't be hired, and employment won't rise as much.

At one end of the scale, poor individuals typically have a marginal propensity to consume of close to 1. They are generally short of money for necessities. So given an extra dollar, they are forced to spend it all (a survey by the Federal Reserve suggests that only about one-third of low-income households do any saving).

In contrast, the richest individuals don't spend all their income, so if you give them an extra dollar, it's not likely to affect their spending habits much. Indeed, if you give Mark Zuckerberg of Facebook an extra $100, he's not likely to go on a buying spree. As a result, the rich have a very low marginal propensity to consume—perhaps close to zero.

The implication? The multiplier is higher if government spending goes, directly or indirectly, to people with a high marginal propensity to consume. A government project that hires unemployed workers into long-term jobs generally has a big multiplier effect because these workers are likely to spend a lot of their wages. But a program that hands out money to rich Americans is unlikely to have the same immediate impact on GDP.

Overseas Leakage

Another factor affecting the multiplier is the amount of money that's spent on goods and services produced in the United States versus the amount spent on imports. Government spending, if it is to boost output, needs to encourage production and employment in the United States. But in a world where so many products are made overseas, it becomes more likely that fiscal stimulus will lead to increased imports rather than to faster growth at home. This transfer of domestic economic stimulus to foreign markets is known as **overseas leakage.**

Leakage was less important in the past. In the 1960s, for example, imports of goods and services equaled only 4 percent of gross domestic purchases. Today imports of goods and services make up 16 percent of gross domestic purchases. For some types of goods, such as clothing and toys, imports supply more than half of all U.S. purchases.

As overseas leakage grows, the multiplier from fiscal stimulus shrinks. That's especially true when the government purchases directly from overseas suppliers, which completely skips any job creation in the United States (see "Spotlight: Fiscal Stimulus and the Buy American Provision").

SPOTLIGHT: FISCAL STIMULUS AND THE BUY AMERICAN PROVISION

ARRA, the 2009 stimulus legislation, was intended to create jobs for Americans. To that end, Congress wanted to discourage the stimulus funds from being used to buy imported goods. So the legislation contained a "Buy American" provision—public works projects funded by the legislation had to be built only using "iron, steel, and manufactured goods . . . produced in the United States."

Seems clear, right? Except that the legislation contained several large exceptions to the Buy American rule. The government is allowed to waive the rule if it costs too much to buy American, if American-made goods are not available in sufficient quantities, or if the agency overseeing a project says that requiring American-made products would be "inconsistent with the public interest."

For example, ARRA included funding for making high-speed broadband available to more people. But since most broadband equipment uses components from all over the world, the government had to issue a broad waiver of the Buy American requirement to achieve its goals. Another example: the Air Force wanted to construct housing for military families at an Alaskan base using ARRA funds. But the Air Force waived the Buy American requirements when it couldn't find domestic-made versions of a "Residential Style Polished Chrome Toilet Paper Holder" and other similar items.

In the end, it's hard to say how much impact the Buy American requirements had or how much of the fiscal stimulus leaked overseas. In a global economy, buying American is easier to say than to accomplish.

Source: Michael Mandel's blog, http://innovationandgrowth. wordpress.com/2011/04/18/air-force-certifies-the-weakness-of-domestic-manufacturing/

The Size of the Multiplier

With all the different factors affecting the impact of government spending on the economy, there is much disagreement among economists about the size of the job and spending multipliers. However, once you add together the direct and indirect effects of government spending, most estimates put both multipliers between 1 and 2.5. That means, for example, that one extra job in government can produce anywhere between 0 and 1 additional jobs in the private sector in the short run.

But as the next section shows, the exact size of the multiplier usually depends on where we are in the business cycle. What's more, the use of government spending to boost the economy comes with some troubling negative consequences, including inflation and debt. These, too, will be discussed in the next section and the rest of the chapter.

THE LIMITATIONS OF SPENDING STIMULUS

So far we've focused on one aspect of fiscal policy: how increased government spending can boost employment and GDP. In the short run this seems to imply that if the spending and job multipliers are greater than 1, a clear strategy exists for creating widespread prosperity: ramp up government budgets and watch the economy improve.

In fact, in the 1960s many economists and politicians believed that the government could get rid of unemployment and reduce poverty by stimulating the economy. In August 1964, for example, President Lyndon Johnson signed a bill that created the Job Corps, an agency that trained and found jobs for poor young people who might otherwise not be employed. The stated goal was to drive the unemployment rate down to 4 percent or less.

But economists gradually learned that there were plenty of downsides to stimulating the economy through fiscal policy. In fact, those downsides greatly limited the situations in which the government could use spending as an economic strategy.

The Perils of Inflation

Let's start with inflation. In the previous section we showed how the bridge repair effort by the government would increase the quantities demanded of labor, construction materials, and all sorts of other goods and services. But if we look again at Figures 11.1 and 11.2, we also see something else: an increase in wages and prices.

In other words, an attempt to use government spending to boost the economy also tends to create inflation. The extra government spending pushes up demand, and prices and wages rise faster than they would otherwise.

This makes sense. In the bridge example, the government would need to hire a lot of skilled construction workers. If they already had jobs in the private sector, the government would need to offer higher wages to lure them away. Similarly, the need for steel for the bridge is likely to raise the price of steel. As a result, in the short term, an increase in government spending raises wages and prices.

Which effect of government spending is likely to be stronger—the impact on output or the impact on inflation?

It depends on where we are in the business cycle. Remember from Chapter 10 that the business cycle consists of recession and expansion. During a recession, the unemployment rate rises above the natural rate. Real GDP drops and falls beneath potential GDP until the economy reaches a trough. Then the process reverses itself.

In the depths of a recession, when things seem miserable, there are plenty of underutilized resources—workers, factories, buildings, equipment. At that point, an increase in government spending can provide an effective boost to the economy. The job and spending multipliers will be relatively high, and the effect on inflation will be relatively low. For example, if there are many unemployed skilled construction workers, a new government bridge-building project can lower unemployment without depriving private companies of their workforce.

But what if the economy is already doing very well? Then most available resources and

> An increase in government spending tends to raise wages and prices in the short term.

workers are already being used by private industry. So if the government comes in and boosts spending, there will be a big effect on inflation, and relatively small job and spending multipliers. Returning to the bridge example, if most skilled construction workers are already employed in private jobs, the government's need for help with the new bridge will bid up the cost of workers rather than adding to employment.

In other words, an increase in government spending is more likely to have a positive impact on jobs and output when the economy is well into a recession, so that the unemployment rate is above the natural rate, and real GDP is below potential GDP. An increase in government spending is more likely to lead to higher inflation when the unemployment rate is below the natural rate and real GDP is above potential GDP.

Here's another way to think about it: in some respects, a recession is like a big pothole in a highway. It makes the ride bumpier, slower, and more dangerous. And just as a paving crew fills in the pothole with asphalt, the government can fill in the recession "pothole" by increasing spending. That gives business and individuals a smoother ride.

But what if the paving crew keeps pouring on asphalt after the pothole is filled? The cars don't move faster. Instead we just get a big bump in the road that may even cause more problems than the original pothole did. Similarly, if the government continues to boost spending after the recession is over, we get more inflation rather than faster growth.

Indeed, this explains why President Johnson's attempt to push the unemployment rate down below 4 percent in the 1960s didn't work over the long run. He could boost government spending, and he did, to create additional jobs at a time when the economy was already doing well. But that also led to an acceleration of inflation—not a good thing.

Lags in Policy

That brings us to the next problem: figuring out the right time for the government to spend. When an economy goes into recession, unemployment rises and real GDP falls below poten-

tial GDP. So according to the analysis we've just seen, boosting government spending in a recession should be **stimulative**—that is, it should have a good chance of pushing up output and reducing unemployment in the short run. But now here's a question: when an economic downturn hits, can Congress and the president increase government spending quickly enough to do any good?

This may seem like an odd issue, but it's tougher for them to do so than you might think. There are big **lags** in the government response. First, it takes time to recognize that the economy is in a recession. Moreover, any major project—like a new bridge—takes months or years to get going. The money has to be approved by Congress and signed by the president, which does not happen quickly. Then the construction contracts have to be given out, which is also not a quick process. Given that the recession of 1990–1991 and the recession of 2001 both lasted only eight months, the stimulative spending may not actually take effect until after the recession has ended.

If the spending comes when the economy is already out of recession, it is worse than simply being late: it adds to inflation. For that reason, in past downturns recession-fighting policy has focused on tax cuts (to be covered in the next section) and changes in monetary policy (to be covered in the next chapter).

Of course, the Great Recession lasted long enough for Washington to react with fiscal stimulus. The downturn started in December 2007, and ARRA was not passed until February 2009, 14 months later. However, the recession was still going on, and the stimulus was much welcomed.

TAXATION

Up to this point we've focused on the impact of government spending. But remember that the money the government spends has to come from somewhere. Either the government raises funds through taxes, or it borrows.

Let's first look at the economic effects of tax increases or tax cuts. Then in the next section we'll examine government borrowing.

TABLE 11.2	Major Types of U.S. Taxes

The biggest revenue source for the government is the federal income tax.

Name of Tax	What It Taxes
Income tax	All individual income including wages, gains from investments, tips, and lottery winnings
Property tax	The value of residential and commercial real estate
Payroll tax	Wage payments (paid by both employees and employers to fund Social Security and Medicare)
Corporate income tax	Corporate profits
Sales tax	Retail sales
Excise tax	Particular items such as gasoline, tobacco, and alcoholic beverages

The Basics

The main source of money for government spending is *taxation*. Taxes include a diverse collection of ways in which the government raises money: **income tax, property tax** on the value of homes and commercial buildings, **payroll tax** that funds Social Security and Medicare, **corporate income tax, sales tax** on retail purchases, and **excise tax** on gasoline, tobacco, and alcohol. In addition, there are all sorts of smaller taxes, such as taxes on hotel rooms, airline tickets, and sporting events (often called an *amusement tax*). Table 11.2 lists the major taxes in the United States.

We often complain about being overtaxed, and certainly the government collects a lot more tax than it used to. But compared to the size of the economy, tax collections have not changed much in the past 30 years or so.

In 1974 governments at all levels collected taxes and fees totaling roughly 28 percent of GDP. By comparison, taxes and fees were roughly 29 percent of GDP in 2007—just slightly bigger. The reason? Tax collections have risen enormously since 1974, but so has GDP.

Changes in the Tax System

The single biggest tax is the federal personal income tax. Figure 11.3 shows the income tax as a share of GDP, along with key changes in tax policy.

FIGURE 11.3	Federal Personal Income Tax as a Share of GDP, 1969–2009

After decades of political fights, the federal income tax as a share of GDP today is now at its lowest level in decades.

Source: Bureau of Economic Analysis, www.bea.gov.

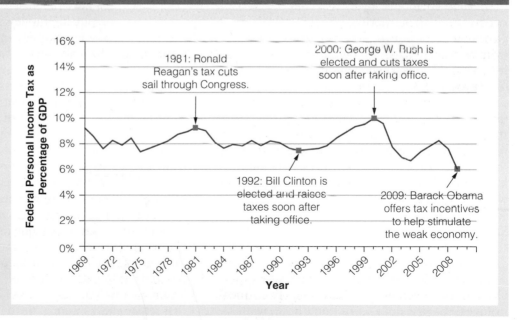

When the tax share rises, as it did in the late 1970s and the late 1990s, political pressure for tax cuts mounts. For example, the federal income tax as a share of GDP peaked at 9.3 percent in 1981, the year President Ronald Reagan proposed and got Congress to approve deep tax cuts. Similarly, the federal income tax share of GDP reached a peak of 10.0 percent in 2000, making it easy for President George W. Bush to make a case for cutting taxes.

But when the income tax share falls as it did in the early 1990s, it becomes easier for the legislature to pass tax increases. For example, the tax share reached a low of 7.5 percent in 1992, the year Bill Clinton was elected president. Once in office, Clinton proposed an income tax increase.

The big exception to this general pattern, however, is 2009. Despite the relatively low share of GDP going to the personal income tax, President Obama did not push to raise tax rates because of the weakness of the economy.

So far we have focused on the personal income tax. However, big shifts have occurred in other kinds of taxes. For example, the corporate income tax has shrunk as a share of the total tax pie. In part that's because corporations have good lobbyists, who help rewrite the tax code to favor them. But it's also the result of globalization, which means companies earn more of their money overseas. That makes it much harder for the U.S. government to tax company profits.

In comparison, a much bigger proportion of tax revenue now comes from payroll taxes—the taxes on wages that pay for Social Security, Medicare, unemployment insurance, and the like. Payroll taxes have been hiked several times as policymakers struggle to ensure that these programs are well funded. Currently employees pay 6.2 percent of their wages for Social Security, on income up to a maximum of $106,800 in 2010, and 1.45 percent of wages for Medicare, with no upper limit. Employers chip in the same amount. (We will discuss Social Security and Medicare further in Chapter 18.)

The Direct Impact of Taxes

Obviously if you pay a dollar to the government in taxes, that's a dollar you don't have available to spend. **Disposable income** is defined as the amount of income people have left after paying taxes.

Naturally tax cuts tend to boost disposable income, whereas tax increases tend to lower it (leaving out the effect of anything else the government might do). As a result, an increase in taxes will generally dampen spending, and a decrease in taxes will boost spending. In other words, tax cuts are stimulative, meaning that they lower unemployment and increase GDP in the short run, all other things being equal. By contrast, tax increases are **contractionary,** meaning they tend to reduce output and employment, all other things being equal.

Changes in taxes also have an impact on inflation. In particular, a decrease in taxes will boost wages and prices in the short term, all other things being equal. To see why, look at Figure 11.4, which shows the short-term impact of a reduction in income taxes on the market for cars. As taxes are cut, disposable incomes go up, which shifts the demand curve for cars (as well as for other goods and services) to the right. As a result, the new quantity demanded in the market is higher, and so is the price of cars.

> In the short run, tax cuts are stimulative and tax increases are contractionary, all other things being equal.

Using Tax Cuts to Fight Recession

If the economy goes into recession, the government can cut taxes as a way of putting money into the hands of people who may otherwise be struggling financially and unable to spend. In some ways this is similar to the argument in favor of boosting spending to fight recessions. As shown in Figure 11.4, a tax cut is stimulative.

What's more, as the effect of a tax cut spreads through the economy, economists can estimate the **tax multiplier,** which is the increase in GDP from a $1 cut in taxes. The tax multiplier depends on the marginal propensity to consume and overseas leakage, among other things.

However, for fighting recession, a tax cut has a big advantage over a spending increase: the tax cut can be put into effect more quickly. For example, in January 2008 President George W. Bush proposed a tax rebate—a type of one-time tax cut. The rebate was quickly passed by Congress. The first rebate checks were in the hands of Americans

FIGURE 11.4	The Stimulative Effect of a Tax Cut

A tax cut boosts the disposable income of consumers, which causes their demand curve for goods and services (such as cars) to shift to the right. This boosts the quantity supplied and demanded of cars while raising their prices.

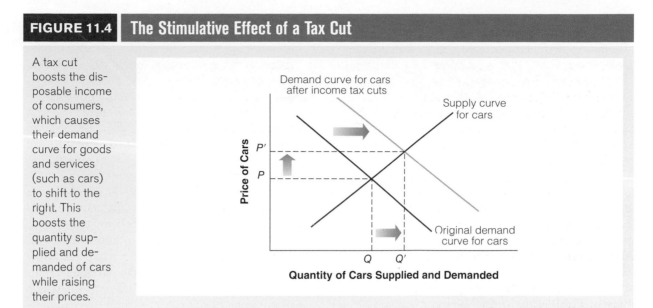

Incentives and Taxes

However, fighting recession is not the only reason why some economists and politicians favor lowering taxes. In the 1970s a group of economists began to focus on the negative **incentive effects** of taxes. That is, higher taxes discourage whatever activity is being taxed. So if labor income is heavily taxed, you are less likely to work hard. A high sales tax on clothing would make you less likely to buy clothing and more likely to buy something else. And a heavy tax on profits, which lessens the benefit of being successful in business, would make it less likely for you to start a new company.

This link between taxes and incentives is the essential insight of **supply-side economics.** Supply-side economics focuses on the **marginal tax rate:** the tax you pay on the last dollar of income you earn. For example, when the marginal tax rate is 30 percent, if you earn an extra dollar, the government gets 30 percent of it and you get 70 percent.

Different people may have different marginal tax rates, depending on their level of income and the tax code. The marginal tax rate is important because it determines your incentives for working a bit more. If your marginal tax rate were 95 percent, for example, it would not pay for you to increase your hours of work because the government would be taking 95 cents of every additional dollar you made. But if your marginal tax rate were 10 percent, the federal government's share would be close to zero.

Supply-side economics argues that cutting taxes gives people an incentive to work and invest more. Over the past 30 years many economists and politicians have accepted the proposition that cutting marginal tax rates can be beneficial. In the 1950s, as shown in Figure 11.5, the top marginal tax rate (the rate paid by those in the highest income brackets) was actually around 90 percent. To pick just one year—say 1955—the tax code called for a 91 percent tax rate on a married couple with a taxable income over $400,000 (adjusting for inflation, that $400,000 would be worth about $3 million today). That's an amazingly high tax rate.

But the top marginal rate was repeatedly lowered over time. In 2010 the top marginal rate for the federal income tax was down to 35 percent for married couples with taxable income over $349,700.

One extreme version of supply-side economics argues that cutting taxes can stimulate enough work and investment to actually *increase* tax revenues. That has been one argument given in favor

FIGURE 11.5 | **Top Marginal Tax Rates, 1913–2010**

The top marginal tax rate paid by Americans has fallen from 91 percent in the 1950s to 35 percent today.

Source: Tax Policy Center, www. taxpolicycenter. org.

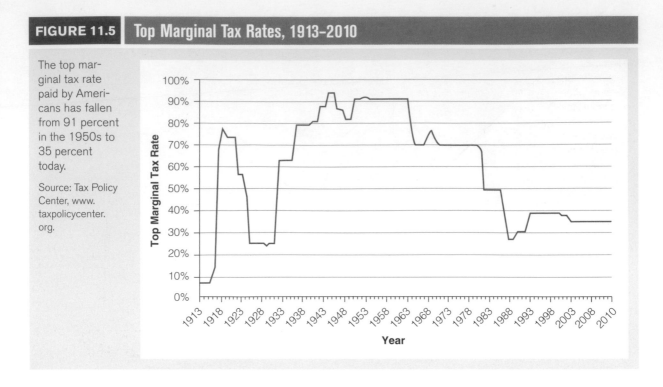

of tax cuts, starting with Ronald Reagan's 1981 cuts and continuing through to George W. Bush's tax cuts in 2001 and 2003. But most economists today accept that cutting marginal tax rates simply decreases tax revenues.

BORROWING

If there is a gap between spending and tax revenues—as there was in 2010—the government has to borrow money to make up the difference. On one level, borrowing by the federal, state, or local government is no different from an individual or company taking out a loan. But the government borrows on a scale that is unimaginable for an individual or a business—and this has an impact on the whole economy.

Budget Deficits and Surpluses

The excess of the federal government's spending over its revenues is the **budget deficit.** In fiscal year 2010 (which ended September 30, 2010)

BUDGET DEFICIT
The excess of the federal government's spending over its revenues.

the federal government spent $3.5 trillion and took in $2.2 trillion. The difference between the two ($2.2 trillion − $3.5 trillion) was the budget deficit, which totaled $1.3 trillion, coming to 8.9 percent of GDP.

To pay for a budget deficit, a government borrows money from investors. (In Chapter 13 we'll discuss government bonds, which are how the government borrows.) The total of all the government's borrowing is called the **public debt.** If the government runs a deficit, then the public debt increases. As of the end of 2010, the public debt was a bit less than $14 trillion.

We see in Figure 11.6 that from year to year, the budget deficit rises and falls, getting as deep as 10 percent of GDP in fiscal year 2009 (in the figure, negative numbers represent deficits, and positive numbers represent surpluses). There were several years, including 1999 through 2001, when the budget was in **surplus**—that is, revenues exceeded spending. Overall, the budget has mostly been in deficit in recent decades.

Why does the deficit swing so much? One reason is the state of the economy. Generally the deficit

FIGURE 11.6   Federal Budget Surplus or Deficit, 1961–2010

This chart shows the federal budget surplus or deficit as a share of GDP. Negative numbers are deficits, in which spending exceeds revenues. Positive numbers are surpluses.

Source: Office of Management and Budget, www.whitehouse.gov/omb.

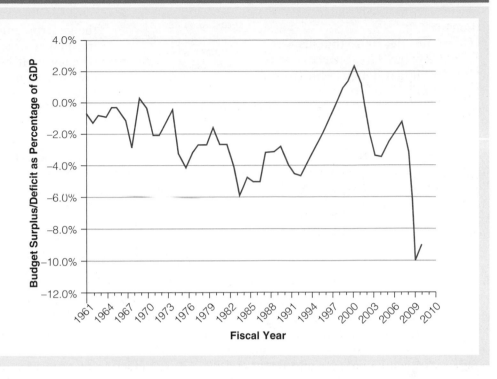

widens during recessions because workers and companies earn less income. As a result, less tax revenue comes in; and because unemployment is higher, the government also has to pay out more for unemployment insurance. During good times the deficit narrows because tax revenues rise along with the economy.

The deficit is also affected by changes in tax rates. The big tax cut put through by President Ronald Reagan in 1981 was one reason the deficit was so large in fiscal year 1983. Similarly, President George W. Bush's tax cuts helped flip the budget from a surplus in 2001 to deficits in subsequent years. Finally, deficits usually rise during wars because the United States, like other countries, is willing to borrow to finance national defense.

The Stimulative Effect of Bigger Deficits

In the short run, increasing the federal budget deficit has a stimulative effect on the economy. A bigger

> An increasing budget deficit stimulates the economy in the short run, all other things being equal.

deficit could occur if the government boosted spending without raising taxes by the same amount, or if it cut taxes without a matching cut in spending. In either case, more money would stay in the pockets of U.S. consumers and the government would have to borrow more.

For example, in 2001 President George W. Bush proposed a sharp tax cut, which Congress passed. Three things happened as a result. First, the federal budget went from $128 billion in surplus in 2001 to $158 billion in deficit in 2002. Second, the disposable income of U.S. consumers—that is, the income they had left after taxes were taken out—rose in 2002, even though employment was weak and the economy was sluggish. Third, consumer spending continued to rise as well.

These three facts are related. In general, an increase or decrease in the budget deficit serves as a rough-and-ready measure of the amount of fiscal stimulus applied to the economy. In this case the total fiscal stimulus was roughly equal to $286 billion dollars ($128 billion plus $158 billion, or the size of the swing from surplus to deficit).

Of course, the 2002 stimulus was dwarfed by the Great Recession, when the budget deficit went from $459 billion in 2008 to a staggering $1,413 billion in 2009. This was an enormous stimulus to the economy.

During a recession, the budget deficit generally increases because tax revenues weaken while expenditures rise. That increase in the deficit is known as an **automatic stabilizer** because the widening budget deficit pumps stimulus into the economy without the need for the government to change tax rates.

Crowding Out

However, government borrowing does have negative effects on the rest of the economy. When the budget deficit rises, the increased borrowing pushes the demand schedule for loans to the right, as we see in Figure 11.7. That in turn pushes the interest rate up from r to r'.

> An increasing budget deficit pushes up interest rates and crowds out private investment, all other things being equal.

The law of demand tells us that if something is more expensive, the market will buy less of it. So when the government's increased borrowing makes capital more expensive, business will be able to afford less investment in equipment and structures, and consumers can spend less on consumer durables such as homes and cars.

This phenomenon is known as **crowding out.** In effect, the government competes with the private sector for capital and elbows the private sector out of the way. Crowding out is bad in the short run because it lessens the stimulative effect of a bigger budget deficit. The fiscal stimulus may generate jobs and income, but it is accompanied by a reduction in private investment. Crowding out is also bad because with less capital investment, businesses are less productive. Over the long run, that means economic growth will be slower.

The damage done by crowding out is not as apparent as the pain of taxation. You can see how much the government is taking from you in taxes just by looking at your paycheck or tax returns. It's much harder to see how much government borrowing has raised the interest rate.

FIGURE 11.7 | **The Impact of Government Borrowing on Interest Rates**

As the government borrows more money, it pushes up demand for loans and raises the interest rate. That, in turn, discourages private borrowing.

Quantity of Money Borrowed and Lent

The Impact of Budget Deficits in the Long Run

No discussion of the budget deficit would be complete without a mention of its long run impact. In 2007 the U.S. federal budget deficit was 1.8 percent of GDP, roughly equal to its average over the past 20 years. By 2009 it was up to 10 percent of GDP, the result of the economic downturn plus the spending increases and tax cuts needed to fight the Great Recession. But even after the recession is over, the deficit may stay high as expenses rise for Medicare, Medicaid, and Social Security.

Most economists agree that a budget deficit equal to 10 percent of GDP or more would be an economic disaster. One problem is that the debt would grow faster than GDP, and so would the interest to be paid on the debt. The CBO report noted,

> The growth of debt would eventually accelerate as the government attempted to finance its interest payments by issuing more debt—leading to a vicious circle in which it issued ever-larger amounts of debt in order to pay ever-higher interest charges. In the end, the costs of servicing the debt would outstrip the economic resources available for covering those expenditures.

This is definitely not a desirable outcome. It is therefore necessary to get the long-term budget deficit under control, which means doing something about controlling the cost of Medicare, Medicaid, and Social Security. That's an issue we will cover in more detail in Chapter 18.

Putting It All Together

As we have seen, there are a lot of things going on simultaneously in fiscal policy. Congress and the president can raise or lower government spending. They can raise or lower taxes. Then the combination of these two decisions can lead to a bigger or smaller budget deficit, which changes the amount of borrowing.

All the fiscal policy actions put together can affect employment, output, inflation, and interest rates. It's useful to see all the impacts in one place. Table 11.3 summarizes the positive and negative impacts of the different actions the federal government can take. For example, lowering taxes can create jobs, boost GDP, and provide incentives for work and investment—but it can also widen the budget deficit and pump up interest rates.

The effects listed in the table work in the opposite direction as well. Suppose the government raised taxes. That would have a contractionary effect on employment and GDP while potentially reducing inflation and interest rates because the

TABLE 11.3   Summarizing the Impacts of Fiscal Policy

Fiscal Policy Action	How It Can Help	How It Can Hurt
Increase government spending.	Can create jobs and boost GDP, and perhaps do something useful with the spending—for example, building new bridges and highways.	Can boost inflation and widen the budget deficit, leading to higher interest rates and lower private investment.
Lower taxes.	Can create jobs and boost GDP, and provide incentives for work and investment.	Can boost inflation and widen the budget deficit, leading to higher interest rates and lower private investment.
Accept wider budget deficit.	Can create jobs and boost GDP. Other impacts depend on the particular combination of spending and tax changes.	Can lead to higher interest rates and lower private investment. Over the long run, can lower productivity and GDP growth.

government would be borrowing less, all other things being equal.

What Table 11.3 does *not* include is a summary of the relative sizes of the different effects. That's partly because they depend on where we are in the business cycle. It's also because economists disagree about which impacts are bigger. Is the incentive effect of a tax cut more or less important than its direct effect on jobs and GDP? You could poll 10 economists and get 10 different answers. That's what makes fiscal policy one of the most hotly disputed areas in economics.

CONCLUSION

We've seen in this chapter that fiscal policy can affect the economy. In the short run, the spending and taxation decisions of the government can influence output, employment, prices, and wages. That's especially important when the economy is going into a recession.

However, economists usually regard monetary policy—which is controlled by the Federal Reserve—as a more effective tool for adjusting the economy. That's what we will discuss in the next chapter.

11   SUMMARY

1. Fiscal policy is composed of decisions about government spending, taxes, and borrowing. The level of government spending is set by the political system, and that spending is funded through a combination of taxation and borrowing. *(LO11-1)*

2. In the short term, an increase in government spending lowers unemployment and increases GDP, all other things being equal. This is the essence of the Keynesian approach to macroeconomics, which uses increases in government spending and cuts in taxes to fight recessions. The multiplier effect is the overall boost in economic activity that flows from the spending increase. The size of the multiplier is determined, in part, by the marginal propensity to consume and the amount of overseas leakage. *(LO11-2)*

3. Stimulating the economy by government spending has a downside as well. In the short term, an increase in government spending can raise wages and prices and boost inflation. That's more likely if lags in policy make the fiscal stimulus show up after the recession is over. *(LO11-3)*

4. In the short term, a decrease in taxes lowers unemployment and increases GDP, all other things being equal. That same decrease in taxes tends to boost wages and prices, all other things being equal. Supply-side economics argues that changes in marginal tax rates affect incentives to work. In response to these arguments, marginal tax rates have come down substantially over time. *(LO11-4)*

5. Increasing the budget deficit can stimulate the economy, boosting employment and GDP. However, government borrowing can push up interest rates and crowd out private sector investment. *(LO11-5)*

KEY TERMS AND CONCEPTS

fiscal policy	fiscal stimulus	marginal propensity to consume
transfer payments	multiplier effect	overseas leakage
taxation	job multiplier	stimulative
Keynesian approach	spending multiplier	lag

income tax
property tax
payroll tax
corporate income tax
sales tax
excise tax

disposable income
contractionary
tax multiplier
incentive effect
supply-side economics
marginal tax rate

budget deficit
public debt
surplus
automatic stabilizer
crowding out

PROBLEMS

1. Identify whether each of the following government expenditures is a payment for goods and services or a transfer payment. *(LO11-1)*

   a) A local public school hires a new teacher.

   b) Medicare pays for a knee replacement for a 66-year-old.

   c) A poor family gets food stamps.

   d) The local Social Security office buys a new computer.

2. The federal government hires an extra worker but makes no other changes in taxation or spending. Identify whether each of the following is likely to rise or fall in the short run. *(LO11-2)*

   a) Federal government spending

   b) Unemployment

   c) Wages

   d) Real GDP

   e) The budget deficit

3. The accompanying diagram shows the supply and demand curves for desktop computers. Suppose the federal government decides to boost the economy by buying more computers. *(LO11-2)*

   a) Draw the new demand curve, and label the new equilibrium.

   b) Does the government purchase increase or decrease the price of computers?

   c) Does the government purchase increase or decrease the quantity of computers sold?

4. Suppose the job multiplier is 0.6. The government hires 1,000 workers. *(LO11-2)*

   a) How much does total employment rise or fall?

   b) How much does private sector employment rise or fall?

   c) Would you regard this as a successful?

5. Suppose you knew that the NAIRU (the nonaccelerating inflation rate of unemployment) was 5 percent. The current unemployment rate is 4.5 percent. *(LO11-3)*

   a) Is an increase in government spending more likely to increase output or to increase prices?

   b) Now the unemployment rate rises to 6 percent, but the NAIRU stays the same. Is an increase in government spending more likely to increase output or to increase prices?

6. Fiscal stimulus using increased government spending is best suited for _____ *(LO11-3)*

   a) fighting a short and shallow recession.

   b) fighting a long and deep recession.

   c) keeping an expansion from ending.

7. The federal government decides to impose a hefty tax on the sale of cars. *(LO11-4)*

   a) What is the effect on the number of cars sold?

   b) As the result of the tax, the government collects more revenue. What happens to the budget deficit?

   c) What is the effect of the tax on interest rates?

8. Over the last century, the top marginal tax rates in the United States have _____ *(LO11-4)*

   a) fallen to a low of 10% after supply side economics was introduced.

   b) remained stable at 35%.

   c) ranged from a low of 10% to a high of 90%.

   d) averaged out at about 45%.

9. Suppose that the economy is going into a recession. *(LO11-5)*

   a) Is a spending increase or a tax cut more likely to be an effective response to the recession? Explain.

   b) What effect will the tax cut have on the budget deficit?

10. The following table reports on GDP and government budget surplus or deficit for the United Kingdom (measured in dollars). *(LO11-5)*

   a) For each year, calculate the surplus or deficit as a percentage of GDP.

   b) In which year was the deficit the biggest as a percentage of GDP?

   c) In which year did the deficit as a percentage of GDP rise the most over the year before?

Fiscal Year	Surplus or Deficit (−) (Billions of Dollars)	GDP (Billions of Dollars)	Surplus or Deficit as Percentage of GDP
2000	1,516	48	−
2001	1,587	34	−
2002	1,647	−10	−
2003	1,730	−32	−
2004	1,837	−36	−
2005	1,932	−34	−
2006	2,050	−23	−
2007	2,168	−24	−
2008	2,214	−73	−
2009	2,127	−181	−
2010	2,173	−170	−

Data: International Monetary Fund, www.imf.org.

11. In January 2010 the Congressional Budget Office (CBO) estimated that it would cost $30 billion to send 30,000 additional American troops to fight in Afghanistan. Some of that money was spent on equipment and supplies produced in the United States. The rest was spent on paying local civilian employees and contractors in those countries, and on buying food and other local supplies. *(LO11-5)*

   a) Does the deployment of 30,000 additional U.S. troops to Afghanistan have a stimulative, a contractionary, or no effect on the U.S. economy? Assume that the extra expense is paid for by borrowing.

   b) Does the deployment of 30,000 additional U.S. troops to Afghanistan have a stimulative, a contractionary, or no effect on the Afghanistan economy? Assume that the extra expense is paid for by borrowing.

   c) Which creates more jobs in the United States? $30 billion for building and repairing highways in the United States, or $30 billion to send more troops to Afghanistan?

12 MONETARY POLICY

LEARNING OBJECTIVES

After reading this chapter, you should be able to:

LO12-1 List the three uses of money.

LO12-2 Describe the history and structure of the Federal Reserve System.

LO12-3 Identify the major goals of monetary policy, and list the policy tools used by the Federal Reserve.

LO12-4 Explain how changing the fed funds rate can affect the economy.

LO12-5 Discuss how the Federal Reserve can use direct lending to fight a financial crisis.

LO12-6 Compare and contrast monetary policy and fiscal policy.

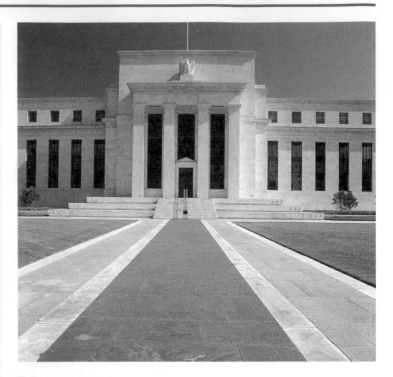

During the financial crisis of 2007–2009, the Federal Reserve, the nation's central bank, took unprecedented steps to keep the economy from collapsing. Led by Chairman Ben Bernanke, the Federal Reserve–also known as "the Fed"– lent more than a trillion dollars to banks and other financial institutions that were in danger of failing. At the same time the Fed cut its key interest rate, the fed funds rate, to nearly zero.

Combined with the fiscal policy measures described in Chapter 11, the Fed's actions helped prevent the Great Recession from turning into another Great Depression. In essence, the Fed did what it had been originally created to do: be the "lender of last resort" and preserve the stability of the financial system.

But the Fed has other responsibilities as well, including making sure that inflation does not get out of control.

In this chapter we will look at the history of the Fed and why it was created almost a hundred years ago. We'll explain the Fed's main goals and how it conducts **monetary policy,** using control over interest rates, direct lending to financial institutions, and other policy tools to influence the economy.

We'll look at the economic consequences of monetary policy, and we'll discuss some recent issues and problems faced by the Fed, including fighting the housing bust of 2007 and 2008.

THE USES OF MONEY

There are more ways to invest and make money today than ever before—and more ways to lose it too. We'll look at some of them in detail when we discuss the financial markets in the next chapter, but here we're concerned with the question, What is money?

On the simplest level **money** is made up of the bills and coins you have in your pocket, which have been printed or minted by the U.S. government (these are called **currency**). But money also includes the funds stored as electronic entries in your checking accounts and savings accounts.

Money serves three purposes. First, it is a **medium of exchange.** You can use money to buy goods and services and accept money in exchange for the goods and services you provide. A market economy would be impossible without money.

Second, money is a **store of value.** You can hold onto money to use later. So when you put your money into a bank, you expect that you will be able to take it out sometime in the future and that it will still be able to buy goods and services.

Third, money is a **standard of value.** It lets you make comparisons. If two houses sell for the same amount of money, then at that moment they are equally valuable. If you are willing to pay more for one car than another, then at that moment the first car is more valuable to you.

For all three uses of money, it doesn't matter whether you have cash in your pocket, write a check, or pull some money out of your savings account. All three are equivalent, which is why

MONETARY POLICY
The Federal Reserve's use of interest rates, direct lending to financial institutions, and other policy tools to influence the economy and support the financial system.

MONEY
A medium of exchange that also serves as a store of value and a standard of value.

we call them all *money.* (See "Spotlight: How Much Money Is There?")

However, money—whether it's a $10 bill or an entry in a bank database—always has an element of trust built in. When you work, you accept money for your labor, trusting that businesses you frequent will be willing to accept your tens and twenties in exchange for goods and services. And when you put your hard-earned cash in the bank, you trust that it will be worth something in the future when you take it out. If we lose trust, money can turn worthless in a moment. Those bills in your pocket would be nothing but pieces of green paper, and those electronic entries at the bank would have nothing to back them up.

Maintaining public trust in the value of a currency is paramount for a well-functioning economy. As a result, even the most free market–minded economists agree that a financial system needs a strong regulator with enormous powers. Therefore, in most countries printing money is strictly a government monopoly. In theory, anyone could print money. For example, Fred down the street could issue his own Fred money, and you'd have a choice about whether to accept it as legal tender.

Government-issued money has several advantages. First, everyone knows which bills are valid. There's no need to worry about whether that "Bank of Fred" currency will be accepted at the local store, or whether the Bank of Fred will go out of business next year, leaving you with worthless bills. There's also no need to try and figure out whether those twenties with a picture of Fred on them are worth more or less than the twenties issued by the "Bank of Sam."

Second, having a single source of money under government control makes it easier for policy makers to guide and control an economy. That is, the government can print money—and destroy it, if need be—to influence output, employment, inflation, and interest rates. Finally, having control over the money supply helps a government maintain trust in its money. The U.S. dollar is backed by the "full faith and credit" of

SPOTLIGHT: HOW MUCH MONEY IS THERE?

You might think it would be easy to figure out how much money there is. After all, the government knows the amount of currency—how many bills it prints and how many coins it mints. As of April 2011, there was about $950 billion in currency in circulation. But the definition of money is actually broader than that because people generally have only a small amount of cash in their pockets. Instead they keep their money in checking and savings accounts or earn interest in a certificate of deposit or a money market fund (we will describe these further in Chapter 13). Checking deposits are not much different from cash because they can be easily accessed by writing checks or using a debit card. It's a bit of a slower process to get at savings accounts, certificate of deposits, or money market funds, but the money is still accessible and spendable.

The Fed keeps track of two measures of the **money stock,** called M1 and M2. M1 includes currency and checking accounts, basically, whereas M2 adds in savings accounts, certificates of deposits, and money market funds As of April 2011, M1 was $1.9 trillion and M2 was $8.9 trillion. M1 and M2 used to be of great importance, but these days they are rarely mentioned by economists or by members of the Fed.

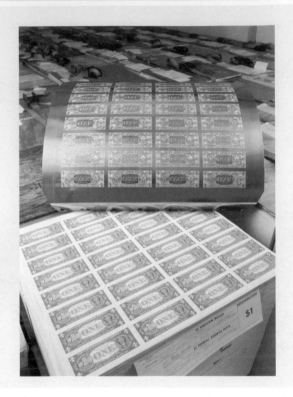

the United States government—and ultimately that is a very powerful thing.

THE HISTORY OF THE FEDERAL RESERVE

In the United States the prime guardian of the financial system is the **Federal Reserve System,** also known as the country's **central bank.** Congress founded the Federal Reserve System in 1913 in response to a financial panic in 1907. That panic—which few people except economists and historians remember today—wiped out several big banks and sent the stock market plummeting by nearly 50 percent. To avoid a repetition of this near disaster, it became clear that a strong central bank was needed to step in and help support the financial system when things went bad.

The creation of the Federal Reserve was a milestone in U.S. economic history. The Fed, as it is often called, had the power to issue currency, set key interest rates, and lend directly to banks—the first time a government agency was given such strong tools for directly influencing the economy.

The Structure of the Fed

The Federal Reserve was set up as a system of banks, not as a single bank. At the head is the Federal Reserve Board, based in Washington, consisting of a seven-person Board of Governors. The Federal Reserve Board is housed in an impressive building in Washington, DC, with very tight security. Congress also created 12 regional Federal Reserve Banks around the country, in part to gain the support of western and southern politicians. But creation of the regional banks also reflects the fact that the Fed was set up in 1913, when communication and travel were not as easy as they are today. As a result, having local branches, so to speak, was essential.

As the country's central bank, the Fed was designed to have quite a bit of independence. True, the U.S. president appoints the members of its Board of Governors, including the chairman. But the Fed funds its own operations, so it doesn't need budget allocations from Congress. And members of the Board of Governors serve 14-year terms, which end in different years, so a single president can't replace the whole board. The chairman of the board of governors, who holds most of the power, is appointed for a four-year renewable term. Alan Greenspan, for example, was first appointed chairman in 1987 and, through reappointments, served until 2006. Greenspan was followed as chairman by Ben Bernanke.

If the central bank were not independent, it could come under pressure to adopt monetary policies that benefit the political party in power but are not necessarily good for the country as a whole. For example, the central bank could cut interest rates just before an election to gain votes for the party in power.

THE GOALS AND TOOLS OF MONETARY POLICY

The Federal Reserve was created in response to a crash in the financial markets. Not surprisingly, its original purpose was to maintain financial system stability and people's trust in the currency. Although that aim is still important, over time the Fed has taken on a wider variety of objectives and concerns.

In 1978 Congress passed the Humphrey–Hawkins Act, which clearly specified a broad set of goals for the Fed:

> The Board of Governors of the Federal Reserve System and the Federal Open Market Committee shall maintain long-run growth of the monetary and credit aggregates commensurate with the economy's long-run potential to increase production, so as to promote effectively the goals of maximum employment, stable prices, and moderate long-term interest rates.

In other words, the Fed was supposed to strive for high job creation, low inflation, and low interest rates—something for everyone!

In reality, the Fed today does not follow the exact list of objectives in the 1978 legislation. Instead they have taken a slightly different form. Today the main **goals of monetary policy** are **controlling inflation, smoothing out the business cycle**, and **ensuring financial stability** (Table 12.1). We'll look at each of these in turn.

Controlling Inflation

Under most circumstances the top goal of monetary policy is to keep inflation under control. Central bankers have always worried about inflation because rising prices eat away at the value of money, as we saw in Chapter 8.

But that concern intensified after the experience of the 1970s, when the inflation rate spiked into the double digits. When Paul Volcker became chairman of the Fed in August 1979, the inflation rate was almost 12 percent—far too high to be acceptable—and Volcker's aim was to get it down in any way possible. As we will see later in this chapter, he succeeded—but at the price of a deep recession.

Economic Milestone

1998 CREATION OF THE EUROPEAN CENTRAL BANK

The Federal Reserve has been a role model for central banks in other parts of the world. The European Central Bank (ECB) was set up in 1998 to manage the euro, the European currency. Based in Frankfurt, Germany, the ECB is independent of political control, like the Fed. However, the ECB places more emphasis on controlling inflation than the Fed does.

TABLE 12.1	The Three Goals of Monetary Policy

Goal	Signs of Success
Controlling inflation	The inflation rate stays in the neighborhood of 2%.
Smoothing out the business cycle	Recessions are short and mild, and the unemployment rate stays relatively low.
Ensuring financial stability	Most borrowers are able to get access to loans relatively easily with little fear that financial institutions will go out of business.

Alan Greenspan, who followed Volcker as Fed chairman in 1987, repeatedly argued that a low, stable inflation rate was the best way to achieve strong economic growth. In 1988 he told Congress, for example, that the right goal for monetary policy was to guide the economy to

> a situation in which households and businesses in making their saving and investment decisions can safely ignore the possibility of sustained, generalized price increases or decreases.

In other words, the Fed should keep the rate of inflation contained so that no one really pays attention to it. How low a rate is that? Depending on whom you ask, it can be anywhere between zero and 2 percent per year.

One important point: you might think that if low inflation is good, then deflation—falling prices—must be better. But central bankers see deflation as a bad thing. As we saw in Chapter 8, falling prices hurt debtors because loans become harder to pay back.

Smoothing Out the Business Cycle

In the United States the Federal Reserve has the primary responsibility for fighting recessions. So when the economy slows and the unemployment rate starts to rise, the first thing that economists, businesspeople, and politicians want to know is this: what is the Fed going to do about it?

In response to rising unemployment, the main thing that the Federal Reserve can do is cut interest rates (we'll see how that works in the next section). Lower interest rates stimulate purchases of things like cars and homes, thus boosting the economy.

Ensuring Financial Stability

Under ordinary circumstances, people don't worry that their bank or other financial institution will go out of business overnight. However, in times of crisis, there's an understandable fear that your investments could suddenly vanish. When that happens, the role of the Fed is to calm things down by making sure banks and other financial institutions have the money they need to function.

In fact, the Fed is the **lender of last resort** during a financial crisis. Having a lender of last resort is essential for a well-functioning market economy because a meltdown in the financial markets would bring most transactions to a halt. In the worst case, businesses wouldn't be able to accept credit cards or pay their employees; individuals wouldn't be able to get access to their stock market accounts or other investments; home buyers wouldn't be able to get mortgages; and state and local governments might not be able to fund their daily operations.

Unfortunately this devastating scenario seemed possible in fall 2008 and early 2009. In one weekend in September 2008, the Wall Street firm Lehman Brothers went bankrupt because of risky investments and real estate loans. And the giant insurance company AIG had to be rescued with an $85 billion loan from the Federal Reserve. Frederic Mishkin, an economist who served on the Federal Reserve Board until just before the collapse, wrote in 2009,

> The collapse of AIG therefore revealed how risky the financial system had become and that any further systemic shocks to the financial system could result in a complete breakdown. . . .
>
> By March of 2009, the situation got downright terrifying. . . . The fear was not unjustified. If another Lehman Brothers had occurred at that time, the financial system would have imploded further, and it is likely that a depression would have ensued.

Figure 12.1 illustrates the impact of the financial crisis on stock prices and home prices.

| FIGURE 12.1 | The Financial Crisis: The Stock Market and the Housing Market |

The price of stocks and the price of homes both plunged in fall 2008 and early 2009, marking the acute phase of the financial crisis. Between early 2009 and early 2011 the stock market recovered, but housing prices stayed more or less flat.

Source: S&P 500; S&P/Case-Shiller Home Price Index.

Monetary Policy Tools

The Federal Reserve has three types of monetary policy tools available to help meet its goals (Table 12.2). For dealing with inflation and the normal ups and downs of the business cycle, the Fed can use its control over short-term interest rates. As we will see, this policy tool is effective for influencing the behavior of both consumers and businesses.

The second type of policy tool is direct lending to banks and other financial institutions. This is the big hammer in the Fed's toolbox, and Chairman Bernanke used it to the full extent during the financial crisis. Indeed, being able to draw on

| TABLE 12.2 | The Main Monetary Policy Tools |

- Control over short-term interest rates.
- Direct lending to banks and other financial institutions.
- Changes in the reserve requirement and other financial regulations.

funds from the Federal Reserve helped struggling financial institutions survive and kept the economy afloat. Later in this chapter we'll discuss the policy actions that the Federal Reserve took to preserve the stability of the financial system.

The third type of policy tool is changes in the reserve requirement and other financial regulations. The Fed has great regulatory power over many financial institutions, which it can use to influence the financial system. However, we will spend less time on this aspect of the Fed's powers.

CONTROL OVER SHORT-TERM INTEREST RATES

In this section we will look at how the Fed controls short-term interest rates and the impact of this control on the economy.

Open Market Operations

The Fed's most-used policy tool is its ability to control short-term interest rates. You already know that interest rates affect the cost of borrowing.

FIGURE 12.2 **How the Fed Cuts the Short-Term Interest Rates**

Making more money available to banks to lend shifts the supply curve for overnight loans to the right, which in turn reduces interest rates.

Short-term interest rates are relevant for loans with a relatively short length for repayment, like credit card balances and auto loans, and for adjustable-rate mortgages (these are home loans whose interest rates are allowed to rise at set times). Long-term interest rates, on the other hand, are relevant for loans such as 30-year fixed-rate mortgages and long-term corporate borrowing.

The Federal Reserve can influence short-term interest rates via **open market operations,** which increase or decrease the amount of money available to banks for lending out. (See "How It Works: Behind the Scenes at the Fed.")

Suppose the Fed wants to cut short-term interest rates. It executes an open market operation to make more money available for banks to lend. As a result, the supply curve for loans shifts right, as shown in Figure 12.2. The interest rate falls from r to r', and the quantity of loans made increases. This works the opposite way, too, of course. If the Fed reduces the amount of money available to banks to lend, the supply curve for loans shifts left. Interest rates rise, and the quantity of loans made falls.

Historically, the Fed has not tried to directly control interest rates on mortgages, credit cards, or auto loans (there's one recent exception that we will discuss in a moment). Instead the Fed targets a particular short-term interest rate called the

OPEN MARKET OPERATIONS

The process by which the Fed affects short-term interest rates.

fed funds rate. The fed funds rate is the rate banks charge each other for lending reserves overnight.

The fed funds rate is set by a vote of the **Federal Open Market Committee** (FOMC), which includes all seven members of the board of governors, and presidents of 5 out of the 12 Federal Reserve banks on a rotating basis. The FOMC meets eight times a year, or roughly every six weeks or so, to discuss the economy and decide on monetary policy; it typically issues a short statement after each meeting explaining its decision.

At each meeting of the Open Market Committee, the Fed tries to set the fed funds rate at a level that moves the economy in the right direction. Generally speaking, if the economy is running above potential GDP and inflation is too high, the Fed will raise the fed funds rate to slow the economy down. If the economy is running below potential and inflation is tame, the Fed will lower the fed funds rate to stimulate growth.

Which Interest Rates Can the Fed Affect?

You, as a consumer, will never pay the fed funds rate because it's an interest rate that banks charge each other. However, the Fed's control over the fed funds rate affects all other short-term interest

HOW IT WORKS: BEHIND THE SCENES AT THE FED

The Fed chairman doesn't have two desk buttons that say "lower" and "raise" to control interest rates. Instead, when the Fed wants to change monetary policy by lowering or raising short-term interest rates, it takes a more roundabout route.

The first thing to realize is that banks are required to keep a portion of their deposits either in cash in their vaults or on reserve with the Fed (hence the name *Federal Reserve*). The more reserves they have, the more they can lend.

So to lower interest rates, the Fed wants to make sure the banks have access to more reserves. That's what an *open market operation* does. In an open market operation, the Fed buys government bonds or other securities, usually from a big bank or other financial institution, and electronically credits the financial institution with more reserves. The previous owner of the securities now has money that didn't exist before, just as if the Fed had printed currency. The bank can now lend this extra money to borrowers, driving down short-term interest rates. Or it can lend the extra money to other banks, which then do more lending themselves.

Open market operations also work in reverse. If the Fed wants to raise rates, it sells some government securities it already owns. Then it reduces the money in the account of the purchaser. The net effect is that less money is available to be lent out and interest rates rise.

rates, including those of credit cards, auto loans, adjustable-rate mortgages, and rates on money market funds. True, they don't necessarily move in lockstep with the fed funds rate. General Motors and Ford might offer their customers a better interest rate on their cars even if the fed funds rate goes up. But in general, most short-term rates move more or less together.

For example, look at Figure 12.3, which reports two interest rates: the fed funds rate and the average interest rate on new car loans. You can see that in the early part of the 1990s, as the Fed was raising the fed funds rate (bottom line), rates on auto loans went up as well. Then from 2000 to 2003, when the Fed was cutting the fed funds rate, auto loan rates dropped too. Finally, they rose again when the Fed raised the fed funds rate from 2004 to 2006.

The same pattern is seen for the interest rates on credit cards

---

FIGURE 12.3 | **New Car Loans and the Fed Funds Rate**

Changes in the fed funds rate affect many other kinds of short-term interest rates. This figure shows how the interest rate on new car loans rises and falls with the fed funds rate.

Source: The Federal Reserve, www.federalreserve.com.

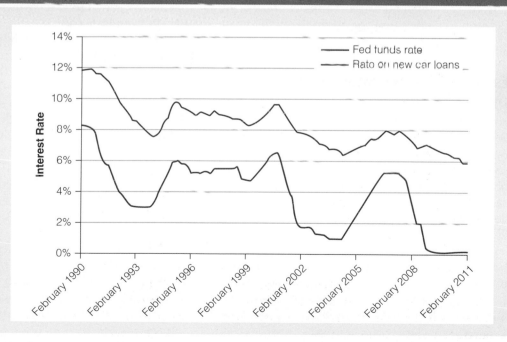

HOW IT WORKS: THE CONSUMER BENEFIT FROM RATE CUTS

When the Fed cuts the fed funds rate, other interest rates drop. And when other interest rates go down, you pay less if you need to borrow for a purchase.

Let's work through an example. Suppose you buy a $30,000 new car and take out a loan for the entire amount. In 2000 a bank would have charged you a 9.3 percent interest rate for a four-year (48-month) loan. But by 2004 the Federal Reserve had cut the fed funds rate 13 times, and the rates on auto loans had followed along. So in 2004 the comparable rate on the same auto loan was only 6.6 percent.

That rate decline would have reduced your monthly payment on the car from $751 to $713—roughly a 5 percent decline. To think about this another way, that decrease in payments is roughly equivalent to paying $28,500 for the car rather than $30,000. That's a big difference.

and many other types of short-term consumer and business loans. As the fed funds rate goes up and down, so do most other short-term interest rates.

Notice, however, that when the Fed cut the fed funds rate to nearly zero in 2008, the rate on new car loans did not drop very much. That was a sign of the financial crisis: banks charged high rates on loans because they didn't actually want to lend much.

Effect of Rate Changes on the Economy

As the Fed pushes short-term interest rates up or down, the effects of its actions are felt most directly by interest rate-sensitive sectors of the economy. These include motor vehicles sales, housing, and anything consumers buy with credit cards. These are the sectors of the economy dependent on short-term borrowing, so a rate change by the Fed affects the cost of their purchases.

In general, a decrease in the fed funds rate boosts spending and GDP, whereas an increase in the fed funds rate diminishes spending and GDP. Let's see how this operates; we'll start with motor vehicle sales. Most car buyers finance their

purchases either by borrowing money for their new vehicles or by taking out leases. The monthly payments vary according to the prices of the cars, the length of the loans or leases, and the interest rates. The higher the interest rate, the higher the monthly payment; the lower the interest rate, the lower the payment. (See "How It Works: The Consumer Benefit from Rate Cuts")

Figure 12.4 shows what happens in the car market when there is a decline in the interest rates on auto loans. Even if the prices of cars don't change, the quantity of cars demanded goes up when interest rates go down because the loan payments are lower. In the supply and demand diagram, that means the demand curve for cars shifts right when interest rates fall.

The result of these lower interest rates is that the quantity of cars demanded rises from Q to Q'. Similarly, if interest rates on auto loans rise, the demand schedule shifts left, and the quantity of cars sold drops.

Of course not only car sales are affected by changes in the Fed's interest rate policies. Let's think about credit cards, which consumers use to charge everything from groceries to tuition. Some people pay their charges off right away, but

FIGURE 12.4   **The Effect of Lower Rates on the Market for Cars**

As the interest rates on car loans fall, people buy more at a given price. The demand curve shifts to the right, and the equilibrium quantity in the market rises.

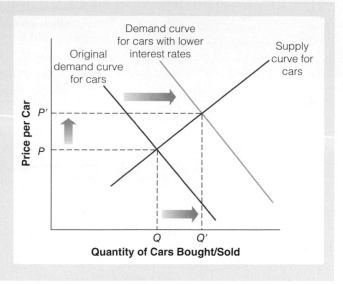

rises, so does the one-year mortgage rate. As a result, the Fed can directly affect the affordability of housing through monetary policy.

So taking it all together, the fed funds rate affects auto sales, retail credit card purchases, and the housing market. That explains why cutting the fed funds rate can boost GDP, at least in the short run. And it explains why raising the fed funds rate has the potential to significantly slow the economy. When it's more expensive to borrow, people make fewer purchases that require borrowing.

It's important to note here that monetary stimulus requires about 12 to 18 months for its full effect. These **monetary policy lags** have a big influence on how monetary policy is conducted. For example, if the economy is coming out of a recession, the Fed usually needs to start raising rates before the economy is back to full employment.

Finally, we mentioned a bit earlier that there's one exception to the rule that the Fed targets only the short-term fed funds rate. In the aftermath of the financial crisis, the Fed has also tried to influence long-term interest rates, including mortgage rates, through a policy known as "quantitative easing." However, it's not clear how effective this policy is or whether it will become a regular part of the Fed policy toolbox.

Effect of Rate Changes on Inflation

Take another look at Figure 12.4. When interest rates decrease, the demand schedule moves to the right. This pushes up the price of cars from P to P' while the quantity demanded rises from Q to Q'. That means a price increase is associated with a monetary stimulus.

In general, cuts in the fed funds rate put upward pressure on prices. Increases in the fed funds rate put downward pressure on prices. However, the exact link between monetary policy and inflation depends on the overall economic situation,

many others leave balances on their cards for a month or more. In fact, as of the end of 2010 U.S. consumers were carrying $800 billion in revolving (credit card) debt.

If you have credit card debt, you have to pay interest on it. As we will see in the next chapter, credit card companies vary the rates they charge according to the creditworthiness of borrowers. But on average, credit card rates move up and down when the fed funds rate increases or decreases. As a result, a decline in the fed funds rate is likely to reduce the cost of using your credit card, assuming you don't pay off all of your credit card bills right away. So we could draw a diagram like Figure 12.4 for all goods and services bought with credit cards. As interest rates fall, the demand schedule shifts to the right, boosting overall sales.

Finally we come to housing, one of the most important—and most complicated—markets in the economy. Most people buy their homes by borrowing through either a fixed-rate or an adjustable-rate mortgage. Interest rates on fixed-rate mortgages are tied to long-term interest rates, which are not directly affected by the Fed. But the interest rate on a one-year adjustable mortgage (in which the rate can change once every year) moves up and down with the fed funds rate. When the fed funds rate heads down, so does the one-year mortgage rate. And when the fed funds rate just as we saw in Chapter 11 for fiscal policy. Suppose actual GDP is below potential GDP and the unemployment rate is above the NAIRU (the nonaccelerating inflation rate of unemployment). In that case an interest rate cut will likely boost output without much fear of triggering inflation.

However, if actual GDP is above potential GDP or if the unemployment rate is below the NAIRU, an interest rate cut runs the risk of encouraging inflation. That's a great fear of central bankers.

> In general, a cut in the fed funds rate will put upward pressure on prices, while an increase in the fed funds rate will put downward pressure on prices.

Example: Volcker's Fight against Inflation

The modern era of monetary policy began when Paul Volcker became chairman of the Federal Reserve in 1979. Before that, the people who chaired the Fed did not fully understand that running an excessively loose monetary policy could lead to runaway inflation. Nor did they understand that the central bank had prime responsibility for bringing down high inflation.

In particular, Arthur Burns, who chaired the Fed from 1970 to 1978, believed that monetary policy was not an effective tool against inflation. In 1979, after leaving the Fed, he gave a speech called "The Anguish of Central Banking," in which he said,

> It is illusory to expect central banks to put an end to the inflation that now afflicts the industrial economies . . . their practical capacity for curbing an inflation that is driven by political forces is very limited.

As a result, when inflation accelerated in the mid-1970s after the oil price shock, Burns did not see it as the Fed's role to stamp it out. Instead he focused on cushioning the effects of the recession on unemployment—a seemingly compassionate maneuver that instead had the effect of letting inflation grow.

Volcker came into office with a different perspective: that the central bank has only not the power but the responsibility to reduce inflation. He quickly tightened monetary policy, sending interest rates skyrocketing and throwing the United States into the short recession of 1980 and the deep and nasty recession of 1981–1982 (see Figure 12.5).

FIGURE 12.5 | **Fed Funds Rate, 1970–2010**

This chart shows the fed funds rate over the past 40 years. It also shows how in 1981 the Fed jacked up interest rates to fight inflation. In 2003–2004 the Fed cut rates sharply to fight an economic slowdown and then cut rates to nearly zero in 2007 and 2008 to fight the financial crisis.

Source: The Federal Reserve, www. federalreserve.gov.

But this shock therapy worked. Inflation, which had been running sky-high, plummeted faster than almost anyone expected. Core inflation—leaving out food and energy—dropped from about 12 percent in 1980 to only 4 percent in 1983. The Fed's single-minded focus on inflation paid big dividends.

Example: Greenspan's Response to the 2001 Recession

Let's look at an example of how interest rates can be used to fight unemployment and boost growth. From 2000 through 2003 the United States experienced a sharp drop in business spending on information technology—the so-called "tech bust." Over the same stretch, the stock market plummeted because people realized that the value of some stocks had raced too high. The economy was also buffeted by the terrorist attacks of 2001, which destroyed the World Trade Center towers in New York.

In response, Greenspan cut the fed funds rate from 6.5 percent in 2000 to only 1 percent in 2003. Other short-term interest rates, such as auto loans, followed down as well. The point of such low rates was to encourage businesses and consumers to borrow and to keep the economy going when it was sluggish.

Greenspan succeeded in the sense that the recession ended in 2001. The economy grew in every year that followed. However, low rates did not help the job market much. The unemployment rate kept rising—from 5.3 percent in November 2001 to 6.3 percent by July 2003.

DIRECT LENDING AND OTHER TOOLS

When the two planes hit the World Trade Center on September 11, 2001, they destroyed the two towers and killed almost 3,000 people. The attack also shut down Wall Street, the biggest financial center in the world, and paralyzed the New York operations of many banks and other large financial institutions. The danger: "a domino chain of bankruptcies that would bring the financial system to a halt," in the words of a report from the St. Louis Federal Reserve Bank.

DISCOUNT WINDOW
A monetary policy tool that allows the Fed to lend money to financial institutions that are running short of funds.

To prevent this economic disaster from happening, the Federal Reserve immediately lent banks more than $45 billion to make sure they didn't run out of money. In fact, no banks failed in the aftermath of the terrorist attacks, and the economy kept functioning.

The response to the 9/11 attacks illustrates a crucial role of the central bank: to serve as the ultimate safeguard for the financial system when an unexpected crisis hits. To accomplish this role, the Fed can lend vulnerable financial institutions as much money as they need—money that's backed by the full faith and credit of the federal government. This usually ensures that banks and other financial institutions will have enough money to meet their financial obligations to depositors or to any other creditors.

To provide money to struggling financial institutions, the Fed has historically used a monetary policy tool called the **discount window.** (Although this isn't what actually happens, you can think of bank executives lined up at a teller's window.) In fact, a few hours after the September 11, 2001, terrorist attacks, the Fed announced, "The Federal Reserve System is open and operating. The discount window is available to meet liquidity needs."

The purpose of the discount window is to give financial institutions access to funds if they run short. To use the discount window, a bank would come to the Fed and ask to borrow money. It would then be charged the **discount rate.** The Fed usually sets the discount rate for banks 3/4 to 1 percentage point higher than the fed funds rate and adjusts them both at the same time. (The bank also has to put up collateral to prove that it can pay back the loan.) Under normal circumstances, the use of the discount window is usually viewed as a sign that a bank is mismanaged, so banks are reluctant to use it. But in a financial crisis it is an indispensable tool for getting money into the financial system quickly.

Example: The Fed's Response to the 2007–2009 Financial Crisis

In 2007 the housing boom turned to bust—in part because too many homes had been built and because too many loans had been made to borrowers with low incomes or bad credit histories—the so-called *subprime mortgages*. Home prices started to plunge, and many people with subprime mortgages couldn't afford to pay them back. The falling housing prices meant that residential construction dropped sharply. Homeowners also had to cut back on their spending because they could no longer easily borrow against the value of their homes.

The Fed addressed these problems by cutting the fed funds rate from 5.25 percent in summer 2007 to 2.0 percent by April 2008. That helped the economy by making borrowing cheaper.

But interest rate cuts weren't enough. As people started to have trouble paying back their loans, banks and other large financial institutions began reporting big losses. People feared that the troubles would spread and that a big bank might fail. There was an enormous amount of worry in the financial markets.

In response, Fed Chairman Ben Bernanke opened the discount window by encouraging financial institutions to borrow from the Fed as needed. But the discount window, in its usual form, was not enough to deal with the developing financial crisis either.

So the Fed came up with several new ways to lend to financial institutions, with complicated names like the term auction facility (TAF), the primary dealer credit facility (PDCF), the money market investor funding facility (MMIFF), and the term securities lending facility (TSLF). With one exception, these new ways of lending were all closed down by 2010 after the crisis subsided (so you don't have to the remember the names). But while they were in place, they enabled the Fed to get financially stressed banks and other financial institutions the funds they needed to stay afloat. Figure 12.6 shows the total of all the crisis-related lending by

---

FIGURE 12.6   **Fighting the Financial Crisis: The Fed Extends Credit to the United States and the World, 2007–2010**

To fight the financial crisis, the Fed lent dollars to a wide variety of financial institutions, both in the United States and abroad. In addition, the Fed provided other central banks with dollars to help stem the crisis in other countries. The amount outstanding peaked at about $1.6 trillion at the end of 2008. (The figure shows the four-week moving average of all credit extended by the Fed through the discount window, temporary direct lending programs, and lending to specific companies such as AIG.)

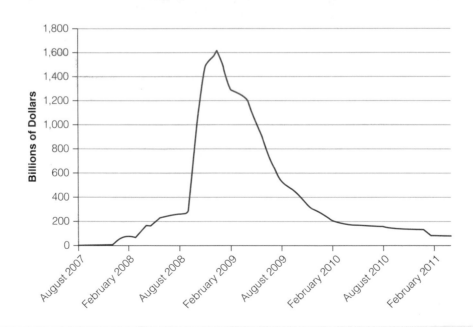

Source: The Federal Reserve, www.federalreserve.gov.

the Fed, which peaked at about $1.6 trillion at the end of 2008.

The Reserve Requirement and Other Regulations

Increasingly over time the Federal Reserve has taken the lead role in setting the regulations by which financial institutions can borrow and lend. By tweaking these, the Fed can exert control over the economy.

Three important regulations that the Fed controls are the reserve requirement, the interest on reserves, and the margin requirement. Remember from earlier in this chapter that banks have to keep a portion of their deposits either in cash in their vaults or on reserve with the Fed. For most banks this **reserve requirement** is 10 percent of deposits (it's less for smaller banks).

In theory, the Fed can exert influence over bank lending by controlling the reserve requirement. The more money they have to keep on reserve, the less money banks have available to lend. Less lending by banks means less spending by borrowers, which helps slow the economy. Alternatively, cutting the reserve requirement could give an extra boost to borrowing and lending.

The Fed also controls the **interest rate on reserves** that it pays banks. This is a new policy tool, so it's not clear how it will work in practice. However, cutting the rate on reserves should make banks more willing to use their funds for lending.

The **margin requirement** determines how much people can borrow when they buy stock. The higher the margin requirement (now at 50 percent for most stock purchases), the higher the percentage of cash down payment a purchaser must make when borrowing to buy securities. Raising the margin requirement makes it harder for investors to buy stock, and this has the effect of holding down the stock market.

However, changing either the reserve requirement or the margin requirement is a blunt tool for monetary policy that the Fed rarely uses. For example, the last time the Fed changed the reserve requirement was 1992. These instruments are always available, though, if the Fed needs them.

> Monetary policy is more flexible and less political than fiscal policy.

THE PRACTICE OF MONETARY POLICY

Some other important issues come up around monetary policy. These include how it compares to fiscal policy, the debate over rules versus discretion, and the question of what monetary policy can do over the long term.

Monetary versus Fiscal Policy

What are the similarities and differences between monetary and fiscal policy? Both can speed up or slow down the economy. The Fed can cut or raise rates, and Congress can boost or cut spending, or cut or raise taxes.

But several differences favor monetary policy as a tool when it comes to fighting inflation or smoothing out the business cycle. In particular, monetary policy is both more flexible and less political than fiscal policy. First, the Fed can act more quickly than Congress and the president because it doesn't have to go through the lengthy political process of passing legislation. In fact, if the need is great enough, the top decision makers at the Fed can raise or lower interest rates with just a telephone conference.

A second advantage is that the Fed, when it does act, can take action in baby steps. That means it can cut or raise rates a little bit at a time and see how the economy reacts before it goes further. Between June 2004 and June 2006, for example, the Fed raised interest rates 17 times, each time by a quarter of a percentage point. In contrast, Congress has to expend so much political energy to pass a big tax or spending bill that it can be done just once a year (or sometimes not at all). That makes monetary policy much more flexible than fiscal policy.

Finally, when the economy recovers from a downturn, the Fed can take back a monetary stimulus more easily than Congress can take back a tax cut or added spending. Think about it: when the Fed raises interest rates, making borrowing more expensive, people may complain. But the chairman of the Fed is not going to be fired because of that. In comparison, if a member of Congress votes to take back a tax cut, she can be sure her next election opponent will accuse her of having voted for a tax increase.

Discretion versus Rules

Economists now generally agree that central banks should focus on inflation. But there is still debate about whether the Fed should use a *rules-based* approach or an approach based on *discretionary intervention.* A rules-based approach does exactly what it says: it lays out a set of rules that clearly describe ahead of time what policies the Fed should follow, based on the state of the economy.

One example of a rules-based approach is **inflation targeting.** Inflation targeting says the Fed should publicly announce its inflation target—perhaps around 2 percent—and then commit itself to running monetary policy to hit that target. Fed Chairman Ben Bernanke is one of the main supporters of inflation targeting.

In contrast, the prime advocate of discretionary intervention was Alan Greenspan, who pre-

ceded Bernanke as Fed chairman. Greenspan believed that as the economy changed, monetary policy needed to adjust as well.

The clearest example of Greenspan's discretionary intervention came in 1996. That year the unemployment rate dropped below 5.5 percent, the level most economic forecasters had previously pegged as the NAIRU. Based on historical evidence, the right move for the Fed would have been to start raising rates to avoid an inflationary surge.

However, there was no sign of inflation accelerating, which puzzled the members of the FOMC. The minutes of their August 1996 meeting reported,

> Increases in prices had remained remarkably subdued for an extended period in relation to measures of resource utilization, notably the rate of unemployment. Such behavior differed markedly from the historical experience under similar circumstances.

SPOTLIGHT: THE FED'S BIGGEST MISTAKES

One problem with being the most powerful economic agency in the world is that when you make a mistake, it's a big one. The Fed's first mistake came during the Great Depression, the first major crisis the Fed faced. After the initial stock market crash in October 1929, the Fed loosened monetary policy, which was the right thing to do. By 1931, when the economy was just starting to recover, the Fed decided it would be a good idea to raise interest rates. The tightening continued on and off until 1933, helping contribute to an enormous number of bank failures and a widespread industrial collapse.

From this mistake the Fed learned its first important lesson: don't raise interest rates when the economy is collapsing. In the 1970s, however, the Fed made the opposite error. We saw in Chapter 10 how the oil price shock of 1973 helped create a deep recession. When that happened, the Fed cut rates, which was the right thing to do. However, it then made the mistake of keeping rates too low for too long after the recession was over. That fueled a tremendous surge in inflation. So the Fed's second lesson was this: don't cut interest rates when inflation is accelerating. Finally, many economists

argue that the Federal Reserve made a big mistake by keeping short-term interest rates too low for too long after the 2001 recession. This enabled a bubble to develop in the housing market, and set the stage for the financial crisis.

Fed mistakes contributed to bank failures in the Great Depression.

Meanwhile Chairman Alan Greenspan was giving speeches arguing that the economy was in the early stages of a productivity revival—the so-called "New Economy." This productivity revival would enable the economy to grow faster without igniting inflation. As a result, Greenspan advocated holding back on interest rate increases.

In fact, the Fed did not seriously start tightening monetary policy with rate increases until 2000, as we saw in Figure 12.5. This was one case in which the usual rules-based approach would have cut off the boom of the second half of the 1990s well before it was necessary.

Long-Term Effects of Monetary Policy

So far we've been discussing the short-term impacts of monetary policy. Can Fed actions have any long-term impact on unemployment and growth? Can the Fed lower the NAIRU or raise the long-term potential rate of growth?

Economists generally agree that monetary policy affects the long-term rate of inflation but has little direct effect, over the long term, on the rate of unemployment or the potential rate of growth. That is, if the Fed stimulates the economy in an attempt to keep unemployment below the NAIRU or actual GDP above potential GDP over the long term, the main result will be accelerating inflation. Workers will push up wages and businesses will push up prices, potentially leading to a wage–price spiral.

The best way to improve long-term growth has nothing to do with the Fed. Instead the country has to invest in physical and human capital and in the creation of knowledge, as we saw in Chapter 9.

These sorts of investments can help cut unemployment as well because firms that are growing and succeeding can hire plenty of workers and keep them employed.

However, there are two indirect pathways by which effective monetary policy can improve long-term outcomes. Low inflation makes the future more predictable, making it easier for businesses and individuals to plan and make good decisions. That tends to improve growth and employment in the long run. So if the Fed can hold inflation to around 2 percent or so, that's a plus for long-term growth.

In addition, if the Fed does a good job of smoothing out the business cycle, recessions will be few and mild. That makes it easier for businesses to take more risks in terms of investing in new technologies and opening up new business lines. In other words, the Fed's best long-term contribution to the economy is to manage it well by minimizing its ups and downs rather than stimulating it excessively.

CONCLUSION

The U.S. Federal Reserve was founded in 1913. Since that time, economists have become much more adept at using monetary policy to accomplish important goals, such as controlling inflation, smoothing out the business cycle, and ensuring financial stability. Most recently, to deal with the housing bust, the Fed had to find new ways of getting funds to vulnerable financial institutions.

But the economy is still evolving. In the next three chapters, we will explore the key driving forces for change in today's world: financial markets, international trade, and technological change.

12   SUMMARY

1. Money includes currency as well as the contents of checking and savings accounts. Money serves three purposes: a medium of exchange, a store of value, and a standard of value. *(LO12-1)*

2. The Federal Reserve was set up to support the financial system when things go bad. It was given the power to issue currency and set key interest rates—the first time a government agency was given such strong

tools for directly influencing the economy. *(LO12-2)*

3. The goals of monetary policy include controlling inflation, smoothing out the business cycle, and ensuring financial stability. To accomplish these goals, the Fed has several policy tools, including control over short-term interest rates, direct lending to financial institutions, and changes in reserve requirements and other financial regulations. *(LO12-3)*

4. The main interest rate that the Fed controls is the fed funds rate, using open market operations. Changes in the fed funds rate influence other short-term interest rates, such as the interest rates on auto loans, credit card debt, and adjustable-rate mortgages. *(LO12-4)*

5. The Fed uses its control over short-term interest rates to fight inflation and smooth out the business cycle. When the fed funds rate is cut, that encourages borrowing and spending in the economy and puts upward pressure on prices. An increase in the fed funds rate discourages borrowing and spending in the economy and puts downward pressure on prices. *(LO12-4)*

6. The Fed's prime weapon against a financial crisis is its ability to lend vulnerable financial institutions as much money as they need. To do this, it uses the discount window. During the financial crisis, the Fed created several new ways to lend money to hard-pressed banks and Wall Street firms. The Fed also has the power to change the reserve, the interest rate on reserves, and marginal requirements, but it has not used that power recently. *(LO12-5)*

7. The advantages of monetary policy over fiscal policy as a tool for influencing the economy are that monetary policy is more flexible and less political. The Fed can react more quickly, take action in small steps to see how the economy reacts, and change direction if needed. *(LO12-6)*

KEY TERMS AND CONCEPTS

monetary policy

money

currency

medium of exchange

store of value

standard of value

money stock

Federal Reserve System

central bank

goals of monetary policy

controlling inflation

smoothing out the business cycle

ensuring financial stability

lender of last resort

open market operations

fed funds rate

Federal Open Market Committee

monetary policy lags

discount window

discount rate

reserve requirement

interest rate on reserves

margin requirement

inflation targeting

PROBLEMS

1. Money has three roles: a medium of exchange, a store of value, and a standard of value. Which role is money playing in each of the following? *(LO12-1)*

   a) You go to the store and buy groceries.

   b) You put your money into a savings account.

   c) You write a check to make a purchase.

   d) You receive a paycheck from your employer.

   e) You have money taken out of your paycheck for your retirement account.

   f) You choose between two televisions, one costing $200 and the other costing $300.

2. You are playing a game of poker with some friends, using poker chips to bet, and to keep track of who is winning. At the end of the evening, the chips cashed in for money. Are these poker chips serving as a medium of exchange, a store of value, or a standard of value? *(LO12-1)*

3. The Federal Reserve was originally founded with the purpose of _____ *(LO12-2)*

   a) fighting inflation.

   b) fighting financial crises.

   c) printing money.

   d) controlling the economy.

4. One goal of the Federal Reserve is controlling inflation. Which of the following policy actions are likely to help the Fed meet that goal? *(LO12-3)*

   a) Cutting the fed funds rate to zero.

   b) Setting an inflation target of 2 percent.

   c) Raising the interest rate on reserves.

   d) Making a large loan to a big financial institution that is about to fail.

   e) Raising the discount rate.

5. Another goal of the Federal Reserve is ensuring financial stability. Which of the following policy actions are likely to help the Fed meet that goal? *(LO12-3)*

   a) Encouraging troubled banks to use the discount window.

   b) Reassuring investors that the Federal Reserve is standing behind the banking system.

   c) Raising the fed funds rate.

   d) Lowering the fed funds rate.

   e) Direct lending to troubled Wall Street firms.

6. Suppose the Fed raises the fed funds rate. For each of the following markets, explain what the effect will be on quantity and price. *(LO12-4)*

   a) Cars

   b) Homes

   c) Credit card purchases

7. The interest rates on many student loans, especially from private lenders, vary with the fed funds rate. Explain how monetary policy is likely to affect the demand for higher education. *(LO12-4)*

8. Suppose there is a sharp rise in oil prices that sends the price of gasoline to $6 per gallon. *(LO12-4)*

    a) If the output gap is large and positive, the Fed should _____ the fed funds rate.

    b) If the output gap is negative, the Fed should _____ the fed funds rate.

    c) If the inflation rate is already 6 percent per year, the Fed should _____ the fed funds rate.

9. The Fed's tool for helping financial institutions that are running short on money, even when the economy is not in crisis, is _____ *(LO12-5)*

    a) opening the discount window.

    b) lowering reserve requirements.

    c) lowering the fed funds rate.

    d) raising the Fed funds rate.

10. Monetary policy has little effect on which of the following economic outcomes? *(LO12-6)*

    a) Budget deficit

    b) Inflation

    c) Technological change

    d) Stability of the financial system

    e) Long-term productivity growth

11. Compared to fiscal policy, monetary policy is the preferred tool to fight inflation and smooth out business cycles because _____ *(LO12-6)*

    a) monetary policy is more sensitive to politics.

    b) monetary policy is more flexible.

    c) fiscal policy can be reversed faster.

    d) monetary policy is more discretionary.

APPENDIX
DELVING DEEPER INTO MACROECONOMICS

LEARNING OBJECTIVES

After reading this appendix, you should be able to:

LO12A-1 Define aggregate supply and aggregate demand.

LO12A-2 Describe the effect of an aggregrate supply or demand shift on prices and output.

In this appendix we will explore aggregrate supply and aggregate demand. This will give us a general framework for predicting the impact of various economic events—such as a sharp drop in home prices—on output and prices.

AGGREGATE DEMAND AND AGGREGATE SUPPLY

So far in this textbook we've used supply and demand diagrams to analyze individual markets. But economists also use supply and demand diagrams to think about the whole economy. In particular we talk about *aggregate demand* and *aggregate supply.*

Aggregate Demand

Aggregate demand is the sum of the quantities demanded from the different sectors of the economy: *personal consumption* (C), *nonresidential investment* (NR), *residential investment* (R), *government consumption and investment* (G), *change in private inventories* (I), and *net exports* (NX). These are the same sectors that make up gross domestic product, as we saw in Chapter 7, but now we have given them labels. The value of net exports, for example, is NX.

AGGREGATE DEMAND CURVE

The link between the average price level of the economy and the aggregate quantity demanded.

The equation for aggregate demand (AD) is therefore:

$$AD = C + NR + R + G + I + NX$$

The **aggregate demand curve** links the average price level of the whole economy with the aggregate quantity demanded. Obviously, as we've seen in earlier chapters, both the price level and output are almost always rising over time. Thus we can think of the aggregrate demand curve as a snapshot of the economy at a particular moment.

The aggregate demand curve is downward-sloping (see Figure 12A.1), which means that a higher overall price level means a lower quantity demanded by consumers, businesses, and government. This seems to make sense: we've seen over and over again in this textbook that in individual markets, higher prices mean lower quantities demanded.

FIGURE 12A.1   Aggregate Demand

The aggregate demand curve is downward-sloping. A higher price level *P* means a lower quantity demanded *Q*.

Real GDP

But the aggregate demand curve really doesn't work the same way as a market demand curve, even though it looks similar. The difference is that aggregate demand takes into account the price level for the entire economy. If that price level is higher, all prices are higher on average, including wages. Thus while the price of a restaurant meal may have gone up by 10 percent, your wages have gone up by 10 percent too—so that increase wouldn't stop you from buying a meal.

Economists have instead identified several other reasons why a higher price level means less aggregate quantity demanded. Two of these are the **wealth effect** and the **interest rate effect.** First is the *wealth effect*: if prices are higher, the cash in your pocket and your bank account is worth less. In other words, your real wealth (adjusted for prices) drops. If prices are lower, the cash in your pocket and your bank account is worth more. For example, if you have a $10 bill, and the price of a cup of coffee falls from $2 to $1 per cup, you can buy 10 cups with that money instead of only 5 cups. So higher wealth leads to more consumption.

AGGREGATE SUPPLY CURVE

The link between the average price level and the aggregate quantity of goods and services produced.

Second, rising prices also boost interest rates, and higher interest rates hold down business investment, residential construction, and consumer spending on things like automobiles, which are usually bought on credit. The link between prices and interest rates runs something like this: if prices are higher, you need to keep more cash on hand and in your checking account to pay your month-to-month bills. But that's money you can't deposit in your savings account, so it's not available for banks to lend out. With less money to lend out, the supply curve for loans moves to the left, and interest rates rise. This is the *interest rate effect.*

Aggregate Supply

Aggregate supply is the quantity of goods and services that the economy produces. Now let's look at the **aggregate supply curve,** which links the average price level of the economy with the aggregate quantity of goods and services produced. As in the case of the aggregate demand curve, we can think of the aggregate supply curve as a snapshot of the economy at a particular moment. In the long term, when prices rise, so do wages and all the other costs of production, such as rent and the costs of materials. From the perspective of a business, then, nothing much has changed—higher prices are balanced by higher costs. As a result, in the long run a rise in the overall price level does not change the quantity supplied, so the **long-term aggregate supply curve** is vertical—that is, suppliers produce the same amount no matter what the price level is.

Here's another way to think about the long-term aggregate supply curve. In the language of Chapter 10, long-term aggregate supply *Q* at any moment is the same as potential GDP at that moment. Potential GDP does not depend on the price level—rather, it reflects the economy's sustainable productive capacity.

However, the **short-term aggregate supply curve** is upward-sloping. If prices rise, it takes time for wages and other input prices to react. Here's one way to think about this: in most businesses, salaries and wages are adjusted only once a year (and if there's a union and a signed labor contract, it may

FIGURE 12A.2 | Long-Term and Short-Term Aggregate Supply

As the price level rises from *P* to *P'*, output increases from *Q* to *Q'* in the short term as output rises above potential. Over time, however, output falls back to *Q*, which can be interpreted as a return to the path of potential GDP.

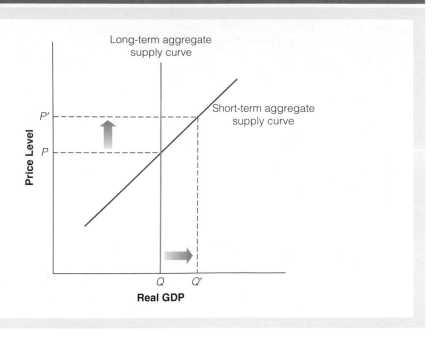

be several years before the contract expires). In other words, wages are **sticky,** meaning that they don't change right away.

So there's a period—after prices start to rise, and before wages respond—when labor gets relatively cheaper. During that period, a business can make more money by hiring additional workers and expanding. As a result, in the short run businesses will boost their production in response to an increase in the overall price level. You can interpret this as real GDP temporarily exceeding potential GDP.

But over time wages catch up with prices, and the economy returns to the long-run aggregate supply curve. Figure 12A.2 shows both the short-term and long-term aggregate supply curves.

Long-Term Aggregate Equilibrium

In Figure 12A.3, the long-term **aggregate equilibrium** occurs at the point where long-term aggregate quantity

supplied is equal to aggregate quantity demanded—that is, where the aggregate supply and demand curves cross. That gives us an equilibrium price level *P* for the economy and an equilibrium output *Q*.

In aggregate equilibrium, demand is just strong enough to get the maximum output from businesses

FIGURE 12A.3 | Aggregate Demand and Supply

The aggregate demand curve is downward-sloping, and the long-term aggregate supply curve is vertical. The equilibrium price *P* and output *Q* are shown at the point where the aggregate supply and demand curves intersect.

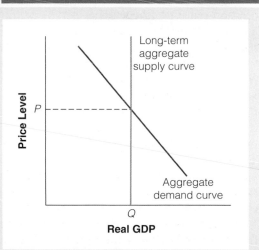

without creating upward pressure on prices. An economy at long-term aggregate equilibrium is therefore on the path of potential GDP, where there are no strains on production or unused resources.

REACTING TO EVENTS

The whole point of developing the aggregate supply—aggregate demand framework is to understand what happens when the economy is hit by a big event, like a sharp rise in oil prices, a fall in housing prices, or a terrorist attack. We can also use the aggregate supply-demand framework to assess the impact of different government policy actions.

Shifts in Aggregate Supply

Let's look first at events that cause a shift in aggregate supply—that is, a movement of the aggregate supply curve either left or right. The clearest example of a shift to the left is a terrorist attack that forces businesses and government to divert resources—money and people—to increased security. Every extra person working as a security guard, or guarding the border, is one less person available for productive work in a factory or an office. Every dollar put into security cameras is not available for new machinery and computers.

These resources are not available for production, which causes the long-term aggregate supply curve to shift to the left, as in Figure 12A.4. The result is that equilibrium output falls from Q to Q'. This decline can be interpreted as a reduction of potential output, which has the effect of slowing growth.

At the same time, all else being equal, the price level rises from P to P'. This can be interpreted as faster inflation, because the price level takes

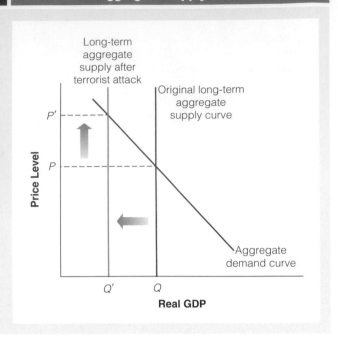

FIGURE 12A.4   A Decline in Aggregate Supply

An increase in antiterrorist security measures shifts aggregate supply to the left. That reduces potential output at any moment, which slows the economy's growth. It also drives up the price level, increasing inflation.

an extra bump up. In other words, anything that reduces the level of potential output pushes up inflation (by raising the general price level), which in turn holds down output and slows growth.

We would draw a similar diagram to illustrate the impact of rising oil prices, of the kind we saw in 2007 and 2008. The United States buys two-thirds of its oil consumption from overseas. So as the price of oil rises, the amount that the United States has to pay oil-exporting countries goes up. That leaves less money to invest in new equipment at home. What's more, some pieces of equipment that use a lot of energy may be unprofitable to use with fuel prices so high. That's why airlines cut back on their flights and took certain aircraft out of service.

As a result, rising oil prices cause the aggregate supply curve to shift to the left (similar to Figure 12A.4). That gives us what is known as **stagflation**—the combination of slow growth and inflation that we last saw in the 1970s. The bigger the rise in oil prices, the further that the aggregate supply curve shifts to the left. That means a bigger rise in overall prices and a deeper slowdown in growth.

FIGURE 12A.5 | An Increase in Aggregate Supply

The information revolution shifted long-term aggregate supply to the right. That increased potential output at any moment, boosting growth. It also pushed down the price level, reducing inflation.

On the other hand, we've seen events that have increased the level of potential output and shifted the aggregate supply curve to the right. The *information revolution*, described in Chapter 15, led to an increase in productivity as more and more businesses learned how to use computers. This is illustrated in Figure 12A.5 as the aggregate supply curve shifts to the right, equilibrium output increases from Q to Q', which can be interpreted as an upward boost to potential output, increasing the growth rate.

Figure 12A.5 also shows a drop in the price level from P to P'. This does not indicate actual deflation, but rather should be seen as a slowing of the inflation rate. This is what happened in the second half of the 1990s—rapid growth without inflation, or the opposite of stagflation.

There might be other reasons why the aggregate supply curve shifts to the right. Any significant technological change can increase aggregate supply. And many economists believe that cuts in marginal tax rates can increase the incentives to work and invest (as discussed in Chapter 11). That would increase output, and produce a diagram much like Figure 12A.5. However, there is great disagreement about how big an impact a marginal tax cut might have.

Shifts in Aggregate Demand

Many of the events that have hit the economy in recent years have affected the aggregate demand curve rather than the aggregate supply curve. Consider the financial crisis of 2007–2009. As home prices dropped, many households saw a large part of their personal wealth evaporate. What's more, it became harder for households to take out home equity loans, because their homes were worth less and banks were more reluctant to lend. And falling home prices meant a lot less construction of new homes by builders.

The result is lower personal consumption (C) and residential investment (R)—and since personal consumption and residential investment are both components of aggregate demand, that means the aggregate demand curve shifts to the left.

Take a look at Figure 12A.6. The first thing that happens when aggregate demand falls is that the equilibrium shifts from point A to point B along the short-term aggregate supply curve. Assuming nothing else changes, demand falls, the average price level decreases from P to P', and businesses drop their output from Q to Q' because they are less profitable. They hire fewer workers, the unemployment rate rises, and growth slows.

But over time, sticky wages and input prices fall along along with the overall price level. Business profitability goes up because firms are paying lower wages, so they hire more workers. The result is that output (and the unemployment rate) returns to the original level of Q. This can be interpreted as a return to the path of potential GDP. But the price level P'' is now much lower than the original price level P.

The implication is that the fall in housing prices leads to slow growth and to less inflation,

FIGURE 12A.6   A Decrease in Aggregate Demand

An event such as the housing bust shifts aggregate demand to the left. In the short run, the equilibrium moves from point *A* to point *B*, slowing growth. In the absence of any other negative shocks, the equilibrium would eventually move to *C*, on the long-term potential growth path but with lower levels of inflation.

with the economy eventually recovering, which means a return to the path of potential GDP. (This analysis assumes, of course, that nothing else changes. In the real world, oil prices rose at the same time that housing prices fell, which reduced aggregate supply and boosted prices even as aggregate demand was weakening.)

What about events that increase aggregate demand? The housing boom that ran until 2006 stimulated both personal consumption and residential investment. In the second half of the 1990s, the information revolution caused businesses to spend heavily on information technology, boosting nonresidential investment (NR) and lifting aggregate demand. And the combination of a depreciating dollar and growing foreign economies meant that consumers and businesses around the world could buy more U.S. goods and services. This helped fuel an increase in net exports (NX) in 2007 and 2008.

However, aggregate demand can also be increased by government intervention. Using fiscal and monetary policy, as described in Chapters 11 and 12, government policy makers can increase demand by cutting interest rates, cutting taxes, or boosting government spending.

For example, President Obama's fiscal stimulus package of 2009 created jobs and put money into the pockets of Americans, much of which they spent.

Let's see how we would represent a fiscal stimulus on an aggregate supply—aggregate demand diagram. Take a look at Figure 12A.7. The first thing that happens when aggregate demand rises is that the equilibrium shifts from point *A* to point *B*. Demand increases, the average price level increases from *P* to *P'*, and businesses boost their output from *Q* to *Q'* because it's profitable for them to do so. They hire more workers, and the unemployment rate falls.

But then wages rise, catching up to prices. Employers lay off some of their additional workers or cut back on hours. Output falls back from *Q'* to the original *Q*, returning back to potential GDP, and a higher price level, *P''*. That's a sign of potential inflation.

We can draw two conclusions from this analysis. First, attempts by the government to stimulate the economy and boost output above its long-term equilibrium level may succeed temporarily. In the long run, however, the main outcome of government stimulation is to increase prices

FIGURE 12A.7 | An Increase in Aggregate Demand

Fiscal or monetary policy stimulates the economy by shifting aggregate demand to the right. In the short run, the equilibrium moves from point A to point B, boosting growth. But eventually the equilibrium moves to C on the original long-term growth path but with higher inflation.

(and inflation). In other words, there is no sustainable way to drive unemployment down below its natural rate.

The second conclusion, though, is more optimistic. Suppose the economy suffered a negative demand shock, such as turmoil in the financial markets that made it hard for people to get mortgage loans. Then policies designed to stimulate demand, such as cutting interest rates, cutting taxes, or boosting government spending, could get the economy back to long-term equilibrium faster.

12A SUMMARY

1. Aggregate demand is the sum of the quantities demanded from the sectors of the economy. The aggregate demand curve links the average price level of the whole economy with the aggregate quantity demanded. (LO12A-1)

2. The aggregate supply curve links the average price level of the economy with the quantity of goods and services produced. The long-term aggregate supply curve is vertical, meaning that price changes have no effect on the quantity produced. The short-term aggregate supply curve is upward-sloping because price increases will induce businesses to produce more and hire more workers. (LO12A-1)

3. A shift of the long-term aggregate supply curve to the left will reduce output and boost the price level. This can be interpreted as a reduction in potential GDP and an increase in the inflation rate. A shift in the long-term aggregate supply curve to the right will increase output and hold down the price level. This can be interpreted as an increase in potential GDP and a decline in inflation. (LO12A-2)

4. In the short run, a rightward shift in aggregate demand—say because the government boosts spending—will increase output and prices. This can be interpreted as a boost to growth and inflation. In the long run, output will fall back to the long-term aggregate supply curve, but the average price level will remain higher. *(LO12A-2)*

KEY TERMS AND CONCEPTS

aggregate demand

aggregate demand curve

wealth effect

interest rate effect

aggregate supply

aggregate supply curve

long-term aggregate supply curve

short-term aggregate supply curve

sticky wages

aggregate equilibrium

stagflation

PROBLEMS

1. Which of the following statements is not true? *(LO12A-1)*

   a) Personal consumption is part of aggregate demand.

   b) If the price level rises, it becomes more attractive in the short run for businesses to hire workers.

   c) The wealth effect helps explain why the aggregate supply curve is upward sloping.

   d) The long-term aggregate supply curve is related to potential GDP.

2. Which of the following factors will affect the long-term aggregate supply curve? *(LO12A-1)*

   a) Productivity

   b) Unemployment rate

   c) Education of the workforce

   d) Government spending

3. In 2008 the price of oil briefly soared over $125 per barrel, a record at that time. *(LO12A-2)*

   a) Did the rise in the price of oil cause a shift in the aggregate supply curve or the aggregate demand curve?

   b) Draw an aggregate supply–aggregate demand diagram to illustrate the impact of the oil price increase. Label the original aggregate equilibrium and the new aggregate equilibrium. Does output *Q* rise or fall?

4. Suppose that the Federal Reserve cuts the fed funds rate. *(LO12A-2)*

   a) Does the cut in rates cause a shift in the aggregate supply curve or the aggregate demand curve?

   b) Draw an aggregate supply–aggregate demand diagram to illustrate the impact of the interest rate cut. Label the original aggregate equilibrium and the final aggregate equilibrium.

   c) Does output rise or fall in the short run? Does output rise or fall in the long run?

5. The aggregate supply–aggregate demand framework can be used to understand the impact of the financial crisis that hit the U.S. economy in 2007–2009. *(LO12A-2)*

   a) As part of the financial crisis, banks tightened lending standards for consumers, making it harder to borrow to buy a car or home. Did that cause the aggregate demand curve to shift to the left or right?

   b) Assuming everything else stays constant, does the shift in the aggregate demand curve cause the equilibrium output to rise or fall? Does it cause the equilibrium price level to rise or fall?

   c) Another effect of the financial crisis was that many businesses found it harder to borrow money to buy new equipment or pay for raw materials, so their production slowed. Did that cause the aggregate supply curve to shift to the left or right?

   d) Assuming everything else stays constant, does the shift in the aggregate supply curve cause the equilibrium output to rise or fall?

   e) Based on your answers to (a) through (d), did the financial crisis raise the equilibrium price level, lower the equilibrium price level, or have an ambiguous effect?

13 THE FINANCIAL MARKETS

LEARNING OBJECTIVES

After reading this chapter, you should be able to:

LO13-1 Discuss the demand and supply curves for loans and list some factors affecting interest rates.

LO13-2 Explain the role of a financial intermediary and discuss how banks work.

LO13-3 Describe the risk-return principle and explain how it applies to the stock market.

LO13-4 Review the benefits of the diversity of financial intermediaries.

LO13-5 Summarize the key causes of the financial crisis.

The first half of this textbook explored the basics of microeconomics and macroeconomics. Now we shift gears and focus on critical economic trends driving the news. This chapter and the next two will cover financial markets, technology, and globalization. The ups and downs of the stock market, the rapid growth of Google, and the shifting of jobs to China and India are topics that influence each of our lives.

In this chapter we will take a good look at financial markets. Over the past 25 years the financial markets and the businesses that participate in them—including banks such as JPMorgan Chase, investment banks such as Goldman Sachs, and stockbrokers such as Charles Schwab—have had an increasingly central role in our economy. More and more, the financial markets influence where we live, what we drive, and what our retirement will look like.

We've already encountered interest rates and how the Fed can control rates to influence the economy. Now we are going deeper into the financial markets, using the same microeconomics tools we've used already in this book. We will review some basics of borrowing and lending. Then we'll introduce the important ideas of financial intermediaries, the risk–return principle, and diversification. (Don't worry! We'll explain all these terms.) Along the way we'll describe some key institutions of the financial markets, such as the stock market and the bond market. We'll also explain how financial markets can go wrong, and what happened in the 2007–2009 financial crisis.

THE MARKET FOR LOANS

In earlier chapters we looked at simple lending and borrowing. Let's quickly review some terms and define some new ones. In any **loan,** a lender gives a borrower a sum of money called the **principal.** The price of the loan is its *interest rate,* which says how much the borrower has to pay the lender in exchange for the use of the money. For example, if the annual interest rate is 5 percent, the borrower has to pay the lender 5 percent of the principal in exchange for borrowing the money for a year. After some period of time, the borrower repays the principal to the lender, in addition to the interest already paid. The length of a loan is called its **term.**

Suppose a real estate developer wants to make money by building and selling some new houses in a previously rural area. Before she can sell the homes, the developer has to lay out a lot of money buying farmland, clearing the land with bulldozers, putting in the infrastructure (electricity, water, roads, sewer system), and actually building the homes. The process might take $3 million and a year or more.

Rather than taking this money out of her own pocket, the developer takes out a $3 million loan from a local bank, say at a 5 percent interest rate, to finance the construction. A year later she's built and sold the homes and has made enough money to repay the $3 million principal to the bank. In addition, she has to pay the bank 5 percent interest on the $3 million, which amounts to $150,000. So in total she pays the bank $3,150,000.

Because the borrower is actually a type of buyer who pays the lender—the seller—for the use of the principal for some length of time, we can think about this transaction in terms of the supply–demand framework we developed in Chapters 2 and 3. The interest rate is the price of using the money. The higher the interest rate, the higher the price.

Why Borrow?

Before we go further in our examination of the market for loans, let's ask a simple question: why borrow? Most typical households don't have enough cash on hand to afford the cars, the homes, the college educations, or the vacations they want. In theory they can save until they have enough money to pay cash, though that could take a while. Or they can borrow the money now and pay it back

SPOTLIGHT: ONE FAMILY'S LOANS

In 2008 we looked at Andrea Simmons and David Telep, a typical married couple living in the small town of East Hampton, CT, with a typical amount of debt. When they bought their house in 1991, it cost them $130,000, an amount that seems astonishingly low. Still, said David, who worked as a schoolteacher, the couple had to borrow $105,000 in order to afford the home. In 2008 they were paying a 4.75 percent interest rate on the mortgage, which they expected to have paid off in 2018.

Andrea and David had some other loans outstanding as well. For example, "we borrowed to buy a used sailboat in 2002," said David. That cost them about $8,000, but it enabled them to go sailing and vacationing with their three boys (aged 17, 15, and 11 in 2008). The next big question, of course: How much to borrow to pay for college? "We're working on that," said David.

TABLE 13.1	Some Common Types of Loans

Individual Loans	Explanation
Credit card	When a consumer charges a purchase on a credit card, the credit card company is effectively lending the consumer the money to make the purchase.
Education loan	Many students borrow to pay for their college education.
Home mortgage	The biggest single category of household borrowing is loans to buy homes.
Home equity	Home owners can borrow money for any purpose, based on the value of their home.

Business Loans	Explanation
Business expansion	Businesses use loans to buy the equipment and resources they need to expand.
Commercial mortgage	Businesses take out loans to buy industrial property and office buildings.
Inventory and accounts receivable loans	Sometimes companies borrow to finance the materials and services they need to make their products. They pay back the loans after they've sold the products and gotten paid.

over time, either by taking out loans or by charging the purchases on their credit cards (this is just like taking out a loan from the credit card company, only usually at a higher interest rate than you would pay at a bank). About three of every four U.S. families have some debt. The biggest single type of debt by far is mortgage debt, used to buy homes.

When businesses borrow, their typical goal is to finance their expansion—another building, more machines, more workers. An airline, for example, might borrow money to buy more planes or spare parts. A doctor's office might take out a loan to finance a new computer system. An electric utility might borrow to build a new power plant. These are all **future-oriented activities** intended to bring in profits over the long term, as opposed to buying supplies for immediate use. (See Table 13.1 for some common types of loans.)

The ability to borrow is important for healthy market economies. Without borrowing, there would be many fewer new businesses because potential entrepreneurs would have to save all the necessary money before their ideas could even get off the ground. Airlines could not buy new planes

unless they had millions of dollars in cash to pay for them (which they almost never do). JetBlue, the discount airline that started flying in 2000, borrowed hundreds of millions of dollars to buy planes. Trucking companies generally take out loans to pay for their fleets. And most office buildings, warehouses, and factories would not be constructed without borrowed money. In fact, the flow of borrowed funds nourishes productive capacity in every part of the economy.

The Demand Curve for Loans

Interest rates matter. The willingness of consumers and businesses to borrow rises as the interest rate falls—that is, the *law of demand* holds for loans. If the interest rate is low, both businesses and consumers are more likely to take on debt. But if the interest rate rises, the quantity of loans demanded will fall.

For example, the real estate developer in our previous example has to pay interest on the money she borrows to pay for the land and the construction. If a bank is willing to lend her the money to buy the land at only 1 percent interest per year,

TABLE 13.2	An Example of the Law of Demand in a Loan Market

This example shows why the quantity of loans demanded falls as the interest rate rises. A real estate developer is considering borrowing $3 million to buy land and build new homes. The process would take a year, after which she would sell the homes for $3.2 million. Here are her calculations under three different interest rate scenarios. As the interest rate goes up, it makes less sense to pursue the project.

	Low-Rate Scenario (Dollars)	Medium-Rate Scenario (Dollars)	High-Rate Scenario (Dollars)
Total Loan Needed to Purchase Land and Build Homes	3,000,000	3,000,000	3,000,000
Interest Rate on Loan	1%	5%	10%
Interest Cost	30,000	150,000	300,000
Total Amount to Be Repaid	3,030,000	3,150,000	3,300,000
Revenue from Selling the Homes	3,200,000	3,200,000	3,200,000
Profits	170,000	50,000	−100,000

she'll probably have the bulldozers roaring tomorrow. But if the interest rate is 10 percent per year, she'll be paying 10 times as much interest, and the loan to buy the land looks much less attractive.

Table 13.2 illustrates in more detail how higher interest rates can discourage borrowing. As before, it costs the developer $3 million to buy the land and construct the homes. As a result, she needs a $3 million loan. She hopes to sell the homes for $3.2 million, which will generate a $200,000 gain ($3.2 million minus her $3 million costs).

But wait! The developer also has to pay interest on the loan. If the interest rate is 1 percent, as shown in the first column of Table 13.2, her interest payment is $30,000 (1 percent of

In general, the willingness to borrow falls as the interest rate rises.

$3 million). That gives her a net profit of $170,000, so it makes sense to take out the loan.

Now take a look at the second column, where the interest rate is 5 percent. The interest payments are higher, and the net profit is lower. Still, the developer will go ahead.

But if the interest rate is 10 percent, as shown in the third column of the table, the interest payment is $300,000. Even after earning revenue of $3.2 million, her total costs have gone up to $3.3 million, and she actually makes a net loss of $100,000 on the deal. So being a smart entrepreneur, she doesn't take out the loan or build the homes. As others face the same situation, the higher interest rate ends up reducing the amount of borrowing.

Economic Milestone

2010 A LOW FOR THE MORTGAGE RATE

In October 2010 the interest rate on 30-year home mortgages dropped to only 4.2 percent, the lowest since the mid-1960s. Nevertheless, housing prices stayed low because of excess supply.

FIGURE 13.1 | The Basic Market for Loans

As the interest rate increases, the quantity of loans demanded goes down and the quantity of loans supplied goes up.

Households have the same response to high interest rates. If you are considering buying a new car, you're much more likely to go through with the purchase if you can get an auto loan at 1 percent per year rather than 10 percent. For example, if the car costs $30,000, a loan at 1 percent per year will cost roughly $300 in interest payments the first year. If the loan is at 10 percent, the first year's interest payments will come to $3,000. That's a big difference.

Because borrowing follows the law of demand, the demand curve for loans is downward-sloping, as we see in Figure 13.1 (we first saw the downward-sloping demand curve for loans in Chapter 3, but it's worth repeating). As interest rates rise, the quantity of loans demanded falls, all else being equal.

The Supply Curve for Loans

Why should anyone lend money? On one level the answer is obvious. Lenders have more money than they can use right away, so they lend it to someone else who is willing to pay for the privilege of using it.

But step back for a moment and imagine you have some spare money—that is, you are a potential lender. A friend or a relative wants to borrow the money and is even willing

As interest rates rise, lenders are willing to supply more loans, all other things being equal.

SPOTLIGHT: WHAT HAPPENS AFTER A BORROWER DEFAULTS?

When a borrower can't repay a loan, the lender will want to cut its losses. If the loan is a mortgage, the lender will foreclose on the home, which means it will take the property back from the owners, who will be forced to leave. The lender will then sell the home to get back whatever cash it can. If the loan is for a car, the lender will repossess the car and sell it. When Enron, the giant energy company, defaulted on its loans in 2001, its creditors sold off everything, including the tilted "E" logo in front of its headquarters.

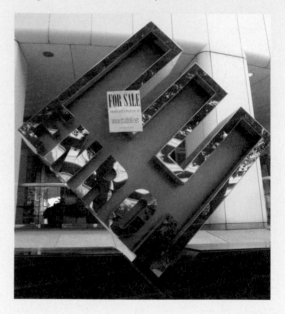

to pay interest. Why might you be reluctant to lend?

First, if you lend someone money, there's a risk the borrower may **default,** or fail to pay you back on time (or at all). The possibility of not getting paid back on a loan is known as the *risk of default.* (See "Spotlight: What Happens after a Borrower Defaults?")

Second, if you make a loan to someone, you don't have use of your money for the term of the loan. For example, if you lend your best friend or brother-in-law $10,000 to start a new business, that's $10,000 you don't have available for other purposes until he pays the money back. You may have unexpected medical costs, or you may want to buy a car, or you may want to put your money in a savings account where it could earn interest—but that money is not available to you.

The opportunity cost of not having your money available is known as the **time value of money.** Charging interest on the loan to your friend or brother-in-law is compensation for the fact that you don't have the money available for other uses.

For you to want to make a loan, the interest rate has to be high enough to compensate you both for sacrificing the time value of money and for bearing the risk of default. As a result, you are more likely to make a loan if you can charge a higher interest rate, all other things being equal. If rates get too low, it may be more worthwhile for you to put the money under a mattress or even spend it on yourself.

All lenders go through the same type of calculation. The result is an upward-sloping market supply schedule for lending, as shown in Figure 13.1. As the interest rate rises, lenders are willing to supply more loans, all other things being equal. This is the law of supply as applied to the loan market.

Some Factors Affecting Interest Rates

As we saw in Chapter 3, the price in any competitive market is set at the point where quantity supplied and quantity demanded are equal. The market for loans is no different. The interest rate in the loan market can be found at the point where the quantity supplied of loans is equal to the quantity demanded of loans. We look at the downward-sloping demand schedule for borrowing and the upward-sloping supply schedule for lending. The point where these two lines cross is the market equilibrium.

The equilibrium interest rate is determined by a host of factors. These include monetary and fiscal policy, which we looked at in Chapters 11 and 12. However, here we will pick out two other influences on rates: the strength of the economy and the borrowers' risk of default.

When the economy is stronger, businesses are more likely to invest because they expect they can make money. They anticipate rising demand for their output, so they borrow to build factories, open new offices, and buy more airplanes and trucks.

So a growing economy—or more precisely, an economy that is expected to keep growing—will cause the demand curve for loans to shift to the right. As we see in Figure 13.2, the equilibrium

FIGURE 13.2   **The Impact of a Stronger Economy on the Loan Market**

If businesses are seeing their revenues rise, that pushes the demand curve for loans to the right. The equilibrium quantity of loans increases from Q to Q', while the equilibrium interest rate rises from r to r'.

Supply curve for loans

New demand curve for loans

Original demand curve for loans

Interest Rate

Quantity Borrowed/Lent

FIGURE 13.3 | Why High-Risk Borrowers Pay a Higher Interest Rate

The supply curve for loans to high-risk borrowers lies to the left of the supply curve for low-risk borrowers. Thus the equilibrium interest rate r' charged to high-risk borrowers is higher than the rate r charged to low-risk borrowers.

SPOTLIGHT: CREDIT SCORES

How do lenders determine which borrowers are at high risk of default? Consumers receive a *credit score* based on payment history, amounts owed on other loans and credit cards, length of time those accounts have been open, and number of new accounts. Credit scores range from 300 to 850, with the highest numbers being the best. The safest households, with no history of late payments and not much debt, get offered the best rates. But even borrowers with spotty credit histories can usually get loans if they are willing to pay high enough rates. For example, in June 2008 the interest rate on a car loan could run from as low as 6 percent to roughly 15 percent, depending on your credit score, as Table 13.3 shows.

TABLE 13.3   How Credit Scores Affect Interest Rates

The higher your credit score, the lower the interest rate you have to pay.

Credit Score	Annual Interest Rate (National Average) for 36-Month Car Loan (%)
720–850	6.3
690–719	7.2
660–689	8.8
620–659	10.7
590–619	14.0
500–589	15.0

Source: Fair Isaac Corp. (as of June 15, 2008).

amount of loans increases from Q to Q', and the equilibrium interest rate increases from r to r'. In other words, interest rates are more likely to be higher in good times and lower in tough times, all other things being equal.

In tough times the process operates in reverse. If businesses are having trouble selling their products or services, they are less likely to borrow to expand. All other things being equal, the interest rate will fall.

Now let's look at a different factor influencing rates. Not every loan is paid back in full: some borrowers default, which means they cannot pay back the full amounts of their loans. Some borrowers have a higher risk of default than others. For example, someone who has a hard time holding a job is more likely to default than someone with a steady employment history. A well-established firm is less likely to default than one just starting up. Some industries, like restaurants, are notorious for their high number of failures, which leads to a high number of defaults on loans.

All other things equal, lenders are less willing to advance money to borrowers who are more likely to default. After all, lenders are in business to make money, not lose it when a borrower defaults. As a result, at the same interest rate, the quantity of loans made to high-risk borrowers is lower than the quantity of loans made to safer borrowers. This is equivalent to saying that the supply curve for borrowers at a high risk of default is left of the supply curve for loans to low-risk borrowers (as we see in Figure 13.3). As a result, the market equilibrium for high-risk borrowers has a higher interest rate (see "Spotlight: Credit Scores").

FINANCIAL INTERMEDIARIES

In the loan example we've been discussing so far, we did not ask one key question: Where does a lender get money to lend out? Or to put this in more specific terms, when a bank makes a $10 million loan to a real estate developer to build some new homes, where do those funds come from? After all, most of us don't have $10 million in our pockets.

Banks are financial intermediaries.

FINANCIAL INTERMEDIARY
Any financial institution, such as a bank, that collects money from suppliers of capital and funnels the funds to users of capital.

For the most part, the funds a bank lends come from its depositors. Individuals put their hard-earned cash into savings and checking accounts and certificates of deposit (certificates of deposit, also called CDs, are similar to savings accounts except that you agree to keep your money in the bank for a fixed time). The bank then lends those deposited funds to other consumers and to businesses. The bank pays interest to its depositors and receives interest payments from its borrowers. The loans are mostly mortgages, loans to established businesses, and consumer credit such as auto loans.

How do banks make profits? They generally charge higher interest rates on their loans than they pay on their deposits. For example, suppose a bank pays 3 percent annual interest on a $1,000 deposit, or

FIGURE 13.4 | Banks as Intermediaries

Banks take deposits from savers and then lend the money to borrowers.

$30 for a year (3 percent of $1,000). It then lends out that $1,000 and charges the borrower 5 percent interest, receiving $50 for a year (5 percent of $1,000). As a result, the bank makes $20 in profit. In addition, banks often charge sizable fees for various services; for example, if you try to write a check when you don't have enough money in your checking account, most banks will hit you with a fee of $25 or more.

Banks as Intermediaries

A bank, therefore, is both a buyer and a seller in the market for money. It collects money from depositors and funnels the funds to the individuals and businesses that borrow from the bank. (see Figure 13.4).

A bank is one example of what economists call a **financial intermediary** A financial intermediary is any institution that collects money from people or organizations, such as pension funds, with money to invest— what we will call the **suppliers of capital.** The financial intermediary then directs the funds to users of capital—people, businesses, or governments that are willing to pay for its use. In the case of the banks, the depositors are suppliers of capital and the businesses and individuals that borrow from the bank are **users of capital.**

In the following sections of this chapter we will talk about other financial intermediaries in the economy. But note here that banks have a special protected status. Banks are tightly

VENTURE CAPITAL FIRMS
Financial intermediaries that provide funds to risky start-ups.

regulated by the federal and state governments, and they are required to keep a certain amount of cash reserves. What's more, the Federal Deposit Insurance Corporation (FDIC), a government agency created during the Great Depression, insures bank deposits up to a certain size (currently $250,000). So even if your bank closed, the FDIC guarantees you would get your money back up to the insured limit. As a result, savings accounts and CDs have virtually no risk for the ordinary depositor.

Another Example: Venture Capital

Let's look now at a very different kind of financial intermediary, **venture capital firms.** Whereas banks lend money to established companies, venture capital firms provide funds to risky start-ups in their early years when no one else will give them money. The investment in these new companies is called, naturally, **venture capital.**

Well-known companies that received venture capital in their startup days include Intel, Apple, Google, Cisco, Federal Express, Yahoo!, and Amazon. More recently, the real estate site Zillow received venture capital funding, as did Facebook and YouTube. Such risky start-ups are the users of venture capital, and many would not exist if they had not received critical money at an early stage.

Venture capital firms are sometimes willing to fund ideas that look crazy at the time. Take

FIGURE 13.5	**Venture Capital Firms as Intermediaries**

Venture capital firms raise money from investors and invest it in small start-up companies.

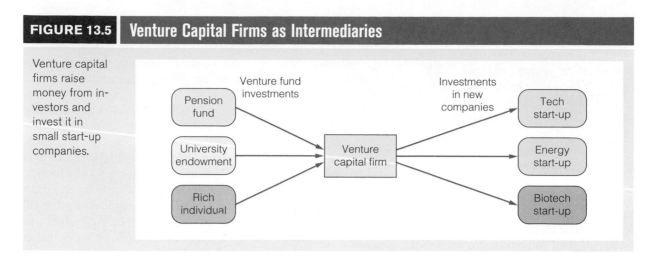

YouTube, for example. Most people know what YouTube is now, but when venture capital firm Sequoia Capital invested $11 million in the video site in 2005 and early 2006, nobody had any idea it was going to be such a hit.

Where does the money for venture capital come from? As shown in Figure 13.5, the suppliers of capital to the venture capital firms are pension funds, universities with big endowments, and other large institutions that can afford to take chances, as well as rich individual investors. They invest in venture capital firms such as Sequoia Capital and Kleiner Perkins, which are based in California and Boston respectively. These venture capital firms are the financial intermediaries—they take the money from their suppliers and decide which start-ups to invest it in.

Like banks, venture capital firms offer a path by which funds can move from suppliers of capital to users of capital (like a pipe for money). However, the goal of venture capital firms is to find new companies that are going to be big winners, like Google and YouTube. A rule of thumb is that only 1 out of 10 venture-funded start-ups will be a spectacular success. Only 3 out of 10 will even be profitable. The rest will fail or just barely continue to operate. Some venture-funded failures include Pets.com (which sold pet supplies online), Webvan (an online grocery store), and Global Crossing (a telecom company). (Pets.com was best known for its slogan, "Because Pets Can't Drive.") Unlike banks,

venture capital firms expect quite a few of their investments to fail. That's part of the cost of doing business.

RISK AND RETURN

The difference between banks and venture capital illustrates a key principle of financial markets: the link between risk and return. **Risk** is the possibility that something unexpected, either good or bad, will happen to your investment. **Return** is the gain on your investment in a year, measured as a percentage of the original investment. And **expected return** is the average return that you can expect over the long run.

For example, a savings account is a very low-risk investment, so you can sleep well without worrying about the safety of your funds. The return is the annual interest rate on the account (perhaps 0.5 percent as of April 2011). If you left $1,000 in a savings account for a year, it would earn just $5 in interest (0.5 percent = 0.005 = $5/$1,000). That's only enough for a few fancy cups of coffee.

By contrast, venture capital is a much riskier investment, but it has a much higher expected return or average return over the long run. In any particular year, there's a chance that start-ups will fail, leading to a very low return that year. But the average return on venture capital from 1990 to 2010 was about 25 percent per year. That means an investment of $1,000 would return $250 per year, on average, because the big winners, such as Google, more than compensate for the losses.

This is a specific illustration of a much more general rule: the **risk–return principle,** which says that the only way to get higher expected returns over the long run is to take more risks. The flip side is that safe investments will get lower expected returns, on average.

There are several different aspects to risk. First, an investment can be risky if there's a substantial possibility of big losses. For example, if a bank lends to businesses in a flood-prone area, it will not be a surprise if the businesses get flooded occasionally. And someone who invests in start-up companies shouldn't be surprised if a lot of them fail.

We can also think of risk as a measure of how much the value of your investment bounces around from week to week or month to month. If you buy the stock of a big company like Microsoft, there's almost no chance it will completely fail. But a month from now, the value of your investment could be 10 percent higher or 10 percent lower.

Finally, here's a third way of looking at risk. An investment or loan is riskier if it is likely to lose value at the same time your other investments or loans do. That is, a bank that makes most of its mortgage loans in one city is probably exposed to higher-than-usual risk if the real estate market in that city crashes because so many loans might default at the same time.

Risk also has different sources. **Default risk** is the possibility that a borrower won't pay back a loan on time, or at all. **Event risk** measures the odds that a major event, such as a terrorist attack, a big earthquake, or a hurricane, will affect the return on an investment. **Inflation risk** is the danger that inflation will suddenly accelerate, so you are being paid back in dollars that are worth less, as we saw in Chapter 8.

Still, no matter what kind of risk we are talking about, the basic principle is the same: It's tough to make big gains over the long run without taking risks. In economics, as we have mentioned before, there is no such thing as a free lunch. We'll return to this principle later in this chapter when we discuss the causes of the financial crisis.

THE RISK–RETURN PRINCIPLE
In a financial market, the only way to get higher expected returns over the long run is to take more risks.

The Stock Market and the Risk–Return Principle

To see the risk-return principle in action, we will turn our attention to the stock market. First we'll discuss the basics of the stock market, including how to calculate the total return on a stock. Then we'll show how the stock market offers both higher risks and higher expected returns than putting your money into a savings account or another safe investment.

A share of **stock** in a company is a piece of ownership in that business. **Public companies** are businesses that have sold shares of stock (also called **equity**) to the general public. Each share represents a very small piece of the company. Google, for example, now has roughly 300 million shares.

What does an investor get from buying a share of stock? Buying one share of Google, say, makes you a part owner of Google—of a very small part, certainly, but still an owner. Shareholders elect corporate boards of directors and vote on major actions such as mergers and acquisitions. If enough shareholders vote together, they can influence what a company does. Recent shareholder proposals at some companies have included limitations on the pay of top executives and requests for environmentally sound policies.

Share ownership also entitles you to a **dividend,** which is a portion of the company's profits that it pays out to shareholders each quarter. Some companies, like Google, make a lot of money but don't pay their shareholders any dividends. Other companies may continue paying dividends even if they report a big loss in a quarter or a year.

Perhaps most important, owning a share of stock gives you the right to sell it to someone else for a higher price than you paid for it—and that's where stock markets and stockbrokers come in. A **stock market,** as the name implies, is a market where shares of stocks are bought and sold. The main U.S. stock markets are the New York Stock Exchange (NYSE) and the NASDAQ, but there are stock markets in most major countries. (See "How It Works: Initial Public Offerings").

At any given moment the **market price** of a stock is the price at which it most recently traded. If there are many potential buyers of a stock, they have to be willing to pay a

SHARE OF STOCK
A piece of ownership in a company.

HOW IT WORKS: INITIAL PUBLIC OFFERINGS

What do companies get by selling shares of themselves? The short answer is that they get money for expansion or new equipment, or even for planned purchases of other companies. The first time a company sells shares to the public, it's called an **initial public offering** or **IPO.** When Google had its IPO in August 2004, it raised $1.2 billion from the sale of its shares, which it partly used to finance its acquisition of YouTube.

Sometimes companies have secondary public offerings in which they sell additional stock to raise money. In 2006 Netflix, which provides movies by mail and via online streaming, raised $105 million by selling stock to the public in a secondary public offering to expand its DVD library. It also needed funds to buy the equipment to provide movies online.

Investors don't typically buy their shares directly from the company that issued them. Instead they go through financial intermediaries such as **investment banks,** the stock market, and **stockbrokers,** which make it possible for companies to sell their shares and

for investors to buy and sell shares easily. Investment banks—big Wall Street firms such as Goldman Sachs, and Morgan Stanley—handle the initial public offerings and secondary offerings of companies. Stockbrokers such as Merrill Lynch, eTrade, and Charles Schwab handle the buying and selling of shares between investors.

Wall Street may go completely digital in the future.

higher price to get all the shares they want, and the market price rises. If there are many potential sellers of a stock, they have to be willing to accept a lower price to get rid of their shares, and the market price falls.

In general, the price of a share usually changes when the company is doing well or poorly. For example, Google initially sold shares to the public in 2004 for $85 each. But the company did so well that more people wanted an opportunity to own stock in it, and the price per share rose. Google's share price was over $500 in April 2011.

Share prices also react to changes in the future prospects of companies. If you think solar power is going to be the next big thing in the energy industry, you'll want to invest in companies that make solar cells because they'll be doing a lot of business in the future. If you believe oil prices will keep going up, you might invest in oil companies because they'll continue to be profitable. Rising share prices are therefore a guide—though an indirect and

TOTAL RETURN ON A SHARE OF STOCK
The change in the stock price, plus the dividend, divided by the original price. Usually reported as a percentage.

hardly a perfect one—to areas of the economy that investors expect to grow.

CALCULATING THE TOTAL RETURN It should be obvious that people buy stocks hoping to get back more than they put in. **Price appreciation** is the change that occurs in the price of a stock. The **total return** on a share of stock is the change in the stock price, plus the dividend, divided by the original price.

Table 13.4 shows how to calculate the total return on stock. For example, on the last trading day of 2004, the price of a share of Intel stock was $23.39. On the last trading day of 2005, a year later, the price had risen to $24.96 per share. In addition to that price appreciation of $1.57 per share, Intel had also paid out 32 cents in dividends per share during the year. As a result, the return on the stock in 2005 was $1.82 divided by the share price at the beginning of the period, $23.39. That gives a return of 8 percent.

TABLE 13.4	Calculating Total Return: Two Examples

The total return on a share of stock over a year is the change in the stock price, plus the dividend, divided by the original price. Here we calculate the total return in 2005 for two widely held stocks: General Motors and Intel.

Company	Stock Price on December 31, 2004	Stock Price on December 30, 2005	Price Appreciation in 2005 (Column 3– Column 2)	Dividend Payment in 2005	Price Appreciation +Dividend in 2005 (Column 4+ Column 5)	Total Return in 2005 (Column 6/Column 2)
(1)	(2)	(3)	(4)	(5)	(6)	(7)
General Motors	$40.06	$19.42	−$20.64	$2.00	−$18.64	−47%
Intel	$23.39	$24.96	$1.57	$0.32	$1.89	8%

Table 13.4 also shows that General Motors stock had a total return of −47 percent in 2005. That means you would have lost almost half your money if you had invested in GM stock at the end of 2004 and sold at the end of 2005. In 2006 the return on General Motor's stock, including the dividend, was more than 63 percent (not shown in the table). And the roller coaster continued: in 2008 GM's stock price plunged as auto sales were devastated by the financial crisis. In June 2009 the stock dropped to nearly zero when the company declared bankruptcy.

STOCKS AND RISK The share price of any single company can swing widely from day to day or month to month. This unpredictability makes an investment in the stock market much riskier than, say, depositing the same money in a savings account. But common sense and economic research suggests that holding a larger number of stocks, especially in a wide range of industries, may help smooth out the swings in the value of your overall investment because it's unlikely your stocks will all rise or fall at the same time. In fact, **diversification**—splitting your money across different investments—is a central principle of financial economics. Diversification can help you reduce risk without reducing expected return. We might also call this the "don't put all your eggs in one basket" rule.

DIVERSIFICATION
Splitting one's money across different investments can help reduce risk without reducing expected return.

Economists have spent many years exploring which investment mix offers the best trade-off between risk and expected return. One approach is to buy a wide basket of stocks, such as the 500 large companies which make up the S&P 500 Stock Index (see "How It Works: Tracking the Market.")

HOW IT WORKS: TRACKING THE MARKET

On any day some stocks are up while others are down. That's why we use a stock index to summarize the performance of the market. The two major stock indexes reported by the press and followed by financial professionals are the Dow Jones Industrial Average and the Standard & Poor's (S&P) 500 Index. The Dow, as it called, is based on the average share price of 30 stocks including Microsoft, McDonald's, and Home Depot. The S&P 500 Index, as the name suggests, includes 500 of the largest and best-known U.S. companies. The sets of companies in the two stock indexes are regularly readjusted to account for mergers, acquisitions, and growth (remember, a company has to be big to be in the S&P 500). Google, for example, was added to the S&P 500 in March 2006, replacing Burlington Resources, an oil and gas company.

FIGURE 13.6   The S&P 500 Stock Index, 1961–2011

This chart shows the monthly values of the S&P 500 Stock Index from January 1961 to January 2011.

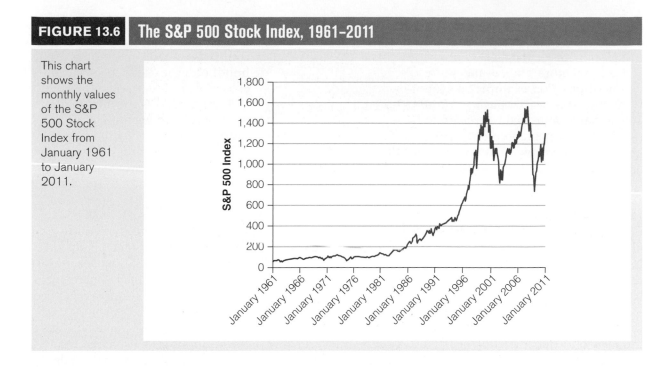

But the stock market is still risky even if you diversify. In good years, investments in the stock market can return 20 percent or more, as measured by the S&P 500. But in bad times the stock market can plunge quickly. Between February 2008 and February 2009, the market dropped by roughly 45 percent.

This unpredictability makes an investment in the stock market much riskier than, say, depositing the same money in a savings account. But as the risk–return principle says, along with the risk comes a higher expected return, based on the long-run history. For example, if you look at the S&P 500 Stock Index in Figure 13.6, you see that it zigs and zags, but the general trend over time has been upward. From January 1961 to January 2011, the S&P 500 Index rose an average of 6.3 percent per year. That's just price appreciation. If we include dividends, the return on S&P 500 stocks has averaged a bit below 10 percent per year.

One final point: As the financial markets become more thoroughly international, diversification increasingly means putting some money into foreign stock markets as well. While the New York Stock Exchange and the NASDAQ are still the largest stock exchanges in the world, they now account for only one-third of the market value of all the world's stocks. Other large stock exchanges are found in cities such as London, Tokyo, Hong Kong, Mumbai, and Shanghai.

THE DIVERSITY OF FINANCIAL INTERMEDIARIES

So far we've talked about three very different financial intermediaries: banks, venture capital firms, and the stock market. But the full list of financial intermediaries is much longer. For example, the **mortgage market** raises money for home loans and then funnels it to home buyers. This is the market that was hurt so badly by the housing crisis because so many mortgages went into default. Another crucial financial intermediary is the bond market, which is the main way that big companies and governments raise money. We'll discuss this market in the next section.

The fact that there are so many different ways to raise money is one of the strengths of the U.S. economy. It leads to more choice and more competition. For example, if you wanted to start a new business, you could charge your credit cards up to the limit, as some entrepreneurs do. Or you could borrow against your home through a home equity loan. Or if you were starting a technology business, you might be able to go to a venture capital firm for funds.

Multiple types of financial intermediaries lead to more competition and make it easier for businesses and individuals to raise money.

Visualize a large concert hall. If only one door is open, it will take a long time to get everyone in. Opening more doors speeds the process. In effect, having multiple ways to raise money removes bottlenecks from the financial system by opening up routes for individuals and firms to get funds.

These gains in the financial markets help other sectors of the economy that need to raise money—and that includes nearly everyone. A corporation has more options for raising money to erect a new factory that is expected to earn profits in the future, or to put up a new office building that will be filled with rent-paying tenants. Producers will find it easier to raise money from private investors to finance multimillion-dollar movies they hope will be big hits. Start-up companies will be more likely to get the money they need to develop new products. Airlines will be able to borrow money to buy new planes they expect to fly for years to come.

The Bond Market

Let's apply the principles of risk, return, and diversification to one of the main ways that corporations and government borrow: the **bond market.** It's essential to know at least a bit about the bond market if you want to understand how today's economy works.

Let's start with some terminology. A **bond** is a loan that entitles the lender—the **bondholder**—to get regular interest payments over time, and then to get back the principal at the end of the loan period. (The bond can be represented by an electronic notation or an actual piece of paper, but in either case the idea is the same.) We

BOND MARKET
The flow of funds from buyers of bonds to the corporations and governments that issue bonds.

call the borrower the *seller* of the bond; thus selling bonds is the same thing as borrowing money. The bondholder, or lender, is the purchaser of the bond.

Figure 13.7 shows how a bond works. At the beginning the borrower sells the bond and receives the loan (principal). The lender buys the bond and pays out the principal. Then over time the borrower pays interest and eventually repays the principal.

Most bond sellers promise to pay a fixed amount of interest per quarter or per year for the length of the loan. For that reason bonds are also known as **fixed-income securities.** Bond terms usually range from 1 to 30 years, though some companies like Walt Disney and Coca-Cola have issued 100-year bonds.

The suppliers of capital in the bond market are generally big institutions such as pension funds, life insurance companies, and mutual funds. In addition, U.S. bonds are often bought by foreign investors. The users of capital in the bond market are the borrowers, the bond sellers.

All other things being equal, borrowing by selling bonds is typically cheaper than taking a loan from a bank. One reason has to do with diversification. A bank that gives a big loan to a company has to consider the possibility, however minuscule, of a default. In the bond market, however, that big loan can be broken down into a lot of smaller bonds that are sold to many different investors. And each of those investors can hold bonds from different corporations. As a result, they are diversified, so any single default has only a small impact. That makes investors more willing to buy bonds of even riskier companies, so the supply curve is pushed to the right—keeping the interest rate lower than it would have been. Thus companies have been steadily relying more on the bond market than on borrowing from banks.

Government Borrowing

In Chapter 11 we talked about government borrowing and debt without discussing the precise way in which the federal government borrows. In

FIGURE 13.7 | How a Bond Works

In this diagram, the arrows represent the direction in which money moves. In the beginning the borrower sells the bond and receives money in return. The borrower has to pay interest and then pay back the principal.

fact, the federal government—or more specifically the Treasury Department—issues many securities each year to fund the budget deficit. It sells **Treasury bonds** with terms of 10 years and 30 years. The Treasury also issues securities with terms as short as one month; these are known as **Treasury bills.** When long-term interest rates are quoted in the press, they are usually the interest rates on 10-year Treasury bonds. The U.S. federal government is the biggest borrower in the world.

However, the federal government is also probably the safest borrower in the world. Its power to tax allows it to draw on the wealth of the entire U.S. economy to pay back any bonds it sells. As a result, the interest rates on Treasury bonds are lower than the rates corporations or individuals pay to borrow money for a comparable term. This is another application of the risk–return principle.

Bonds are also issued by state and local governments. Typically they borrow to fund long-term projects such as the construction and renovation of highways, airports, parking lots, sports stadiums, and schools.

In the forty years between 1970 and 2010, there were relatively few instances when state and local governments defaulted on bonds. This track record of safety enabled them to pay relatively low interest rates as well, though not as low

as the federal government. However, economists worry that the coming years will bring more examples of financially squeezed state and local governments simply not being able to make all the payments on their debt.

THE CAUSES OF THE FINANCIAL CRISIS

Now that we have developed an understanding of how financial markets work, we can ask some key questions: What caused the financial crisis? Why did the housing market, the stock market, and indeed the whole economy crash so suddenly? And can anything be done to avoid such crises in the future?

The first thing to realize is that financial markets are historically prone to **bubbles.** A bubble occurs when prices in a financial market rise for an extended period, and investors convince themselves that the increases aren't going to stop. At that point the bubble becomes self-feeding—believing that prices will go up, investors put more money into the market, which drives the prices well above a level that is sustainable over the long run.

For example, in the late 1990s there was a bubble in technology stocks. Many investors convinced themselves that the Internet was an unstoppable force that was going to keep driving up the stock price of both existing technology firms and start-ups. For example, the stock price of Corning—one of the world's biggest makers of fiber optic cable, used for high-capacity data transmission –went from $16 per share at the beginning of 1999, up to more than $100 per share in 2000, and then down to less than $2 a share in 2002. Fortunes can be made—and lost—with price movements like this.

The financial crisis of 2007–2009 was the result, in large part, of a bubble as well. This time the bubble occurred in the whole U.S. housing market, which represents a large part of the wealth of the country. From 1997 to 2006 the increase in housing prices far outstripped the rate of inflation. That increase, in turn, led to home buyers paying ridiculous prices for homes because they thought they would make a profit when they sold; home builders constructing more and more expensive new homes because they thought they would make a profit when they sold; and banks making questionable mortgages because even poor people could pay back their loans if they sold their homes in a rising market.

Weaknesses in financial regulation also helped contribute to the financial crisis. Regulatory agencies such as the Federal Reserve did not pay close enough attention to the rapidly evolving markets in complicated financial instruments known as derivatives. Using these derivatives, many large financial institutions were able to place big bets on the housing market, which would pay off as long as housing prices didn't fall. The financial institutions thought they had history on their side, because housing prices hadn't fallen nationwide since the Great Depression.

In the end, of course, the housing bubble burst, home prices went down, and everyone was left holding the bag. Some financial institutions, like Lehman, went bankrupt, while others came close. And the U.S. government had to borrow trillions of dollars to stimulate demand and keep the economy afloat.

Will this happen again? Generally after a big financial crisis, investors are wary for a while. But financial bubbles have happened before, and they will happen again.

CONCLUSION

The financial markets are extremely important to the economy. Without them, businesses would not be able to raise money for future-oriented activities, such as expansion. Governments would not be able to borrow to fund budget deficits and investment in infrastructure. Individuals would not be able to afford to buy as many big-ticket items such as homes and cars.

The next chapter will cover an equally critical feature of today's world: globalization. While financial markets are about transactions involving money, globalization is about movements of goods, services, and money across national borders. As we will see, such international trade brings up a whole new set of issues.

13   SUMMARY

1. The market for loans is essential for financing household consumption and business investment. The market for loans typically follows the laws of demand and supply. Higher interest rates reduce the quantity of borrowing, all other things being equal. Higher interest rates also increase the quantity of lending. *(LO13-1)*

2. Banks are examples of financial intermediaries. That means they collect money from suppliers of capital and funnel it to users of capital. Venture capital firms are other examples of financial intermediaries. They collect money from investors and funnel it to start-up companies. *(LO13-2)*

3. The risk–return principle says that in a well-functioning financial market the only way to get higher expected returns over the long run is to take more risks. The flip side is that safer investments will get lower expected returns, on

average. For example, an investment in the stock market, on average, has higher risks and higher expected returns than putting your money into a savings account. Diversification, which means splitting your money across different investments, can help you reduce risk without reducing expected return. *(LO13-3)*

4. The U.S. economy has many different kind of financial intermediaries. That's an advantage because it leads to more choice, more competition, and a lower cost of funds. One important financial intermediary is the bond market, which lets corporations and governments raise money by issuing bonds instead of borrowing from banks. *(LO13-4)*

5. The financial crisis of 2007–2009 was the result, in large part, of a bubble in the housing market. In addition, weaknesses in financial regulation enabled financial institutions to take too many risks. *(LO13-5)*

KEY TERMS AND CONCEPTS

loan	expected return	total return
principal	risk–return principle	investment banks
term	default risk	stockbrokers
future-oriented activities	event risk	stock trades
default	inflation risk	diversification
time value of money	stock	mortgage market
financial intermediary	public companies	bond market
suppliers of capital	equity	bond
users of capital	initial public offering	bondholder
venture capital firms	dividend	fixed-income securities
venture capital	stock market	Treasury bonds
risk	market price	Treasury bills
return	price appreciation	bubbles

PROBLEMS

1. Suppose a company borrows $10 million for a year at an interest rate of 6 percent annually, with all interest and principal to be paid at the end of the year. *(LO13-1)*

a) How much money will the company give the lender at the end of the year?

b) How much is the principal, and how much is the interest payment?

2. In each of the following scenarios, identify the borrower and the lender. *(LO13-1)*

   a) A corporation sells $1,000,000 in bonds to investors.

   b) A family takes out a mortgage from a bank for $250,000.

   c) A foreign investor buys $10 million in Treasury bonds.

   d) You buy a new coat with your credit card issued by your local bank.

3. Your brother-in-law wants to borrow $50,000 to start a new business selling T-shirts online. Will each of the following events make you more or less likely to lend him the money? Give the appropriate reason for each answer (time value of money or risk of default). *(LO13-1)*

   a) The interest rate on savings accounts goes up.

   b) Your teenager wins a full scholarship to college.

   c) You discover that your brother-in-law has started a business before and failed.

   d) Economists predict a recession for next year.

   e) Your neighbor comes to you with a hot stock tip.

4. For each of the following, identify the main suppliers of capital, the main users of capital, and the financial intermediary. *(LO13-2)*

   a) A bank credit card.

   b) An investment in a new mobile game company.

   c) A mortgage loan from a local bank.

5. Are the following statements true or false? *(LO13-2)*

   a) Venture capital goes to established companies such as General Motors and Procter & Gamble.

   b) Venture capital is a high-risk investment.

   c) The suppliers of capital in the venture capital are ordinary individuals.

   d) Venture capital firms expect that most of the companies they invest in will be big successes.

   e) The venture capital helps accelerate the adoption of new technology.

6. Two restaurants are on the same block. One has been open 10 years and is a thriving business. The other one has been open for only a year. They both want to expand. When the two owners go to the local bank looking for a loan, which one is likely to get a lower interest rate? Explain in terms of the risk-return principle. *(LO13-3)*

7. Following are the actual stock prices for Boeing on three dates, along with dividend payments. *(LO13-3)*

Date	Price of a Share of Boeing Stock
June 30, 2005	$66.00
June 30, 2006	$81.91
June 30, 2007	$96.16

	Dividend Paid on a Share of Boeing Stock
June 30, 2005–June 30, 2006	$1.10
June 30, 2006–June 30, 2007	$1.30

a) What was the price appreciation from June 30, 2005, to June 20, 2006, in dollars?

b) What was the price appreciation from June 30, 2006, to June 20, 2007, in dollars?

c) What was the total return from June 30, 2005, to June 20, 2006, as a percentage?

d) What was the total return from June 30, 2006, to June 20, 2007, as a percentage?

8. If you use a credit card, have you looked carefully at how much the credit card company can charge you for your unpaid balances? Probably not—but you might be surprised to find that the maximum interest rate on a typical card can go up to 25 percent or higher. True, virtually all states have usury (excess interest) laws that appear to limit interest rates. For example, in Michigan the usury limit is 7 percent. However, these laws are riddled with loopholes. They do not apply to national banks, including the ones that issue most credit cards. Nor do they apply to car financing companies or to late fees. In fact, the usury laws generally apply only to loans made between individuals or nonfinancial businesses, which of course are relatively rare. *(LO13-3)*

   a) What would happen if state governments tightened their usury laws so that nobody could charge more than 5 percent on any kind of debt? Would that restriction increase or decrease the quantity of loans demanded? Explain.

   b) Would tighter usury laws increase or decrease the quantity of loans supplied? Explain.

   c) Would tighter usury laws make it harder or easier to get a credit card? Explain.

9. A large company needs money to construct a new headquarters building. Which of these funding sources is the least likely source of financing for the construction? *(LO13-4)*

   a) Venture capital.

   b) The bond market.

   c) The mortgage market.

   d) The stock market.

10. When a company borrows money in the bond market, that means it _____ *(LO13-4)*

   a) buys bonds.

   b) sells bond.

   c) collects interest.

   d) sells stock.

11. If financial regulation had been stricter in the years leading up to the financial crisis, in all likelihood mortgage loans would have been harder to get. That would have meant that _____ *(LO13-5)*

   a) housing prices would have gone even higher.

   b) the housing bubble would have been less pronounced.

   c) the financial crisis would have been more severe.

14 INTERNATIONAL TRADE

LEARNING OBJECTIVES

After reading this chapter, you should be able to:

LO14-1 Explain why global trade has increased so much in recent years.

LO14-2 Summarize the main gains to trade.

LO14-3 Compare and contrast absolute advantage and comparative advantage.

LO14-4 Discuss the winners and losers from trade and analyze the arguments for protectionism.

LO14-5 Describe what it means for a currency to appreciate or depreciate.

LO14-6 List explanations for why the United States consistently runs a trade deficit.

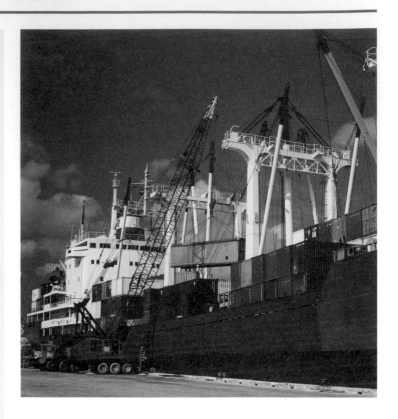

Over the past 20 years, foreign trade has soared, jamming the sea lanes with enormous cargo ships and filling ports around the world. The freight is coming by air too: air freight companies like FedEx have ordered special Boeing 747s with nose cones that flip open for big cargo. And undersea cables are sizzling with the flow of bits and bytes as U.S. companies hire programmers in Russia, designers in Taiwan, and customer service agents in India.

This is **globalization,** 21st-century style–the increasing exchange of goods, services, ideas, and people among countries. More and more local and national markets are going global as communication has become cheaper and easier and many trade barriers have been lowered.

Developing countries have embraced trade as the road to prosperity after seeing how exports helped China turn itself into a manufacturing powerhouse—and how India used service exports to jump-start its economy.

Today's trends confirm what economists have long argued: countries enjoy big gains from trade. These include lower product prices, faster growth, better use of resources, and generally higher living standards. However, trade and globalization can be disruptive. Workers and companies face increased competition and uncertainty, along with a frightening flow of jobs to overseas labor markets with nothing immediately apparent to replace them.

In this chapter we will examine some key issues and concepts connected with globalization, including the nature of international trade, the benefits from trade, the logic behind comparative advantage, and the winners and losers in globalization. We'll finish with a discussion of the trade deficit and exchange rates.

THE NATURE OF INTERNATIONAL TRADE

The current boom in international trade may be unprecedented in recent history. With almost no interruptions, exports rose from 19 percent of the global economy at the end of the 1980s to more than 32 percent in 2008, as Figure 14.1 shows.

Both **trade in goods** and **trade in services** have been soaring. Trade in goods happens when items are physically shipped from one country to another. These include commodities such as oil and copper; manufactured products such as clothing, furniture, and automobiles; and high-tech products such as computers and airplanes. When a product crosses the border, it becomes

---

FIGURE 14.1 **Global Exports (and Imports) as Percentage of Global GDP**

Over the past 20 years the volume of trade steadily climbed as a share of global output until the Great Recession.

Source: International Monetary Fund.

Chart: Global Exports (and Imports) as Percentage of Global GDP vs. Year (1989–2010). Line rises from about 18% in 1989 to a peak of about 32% in 2008, dips to about 28% in 2009, then rises to about 30% in 2010.

an *export* of the originating country and an *import* of the destination country.

Trade in services is becoming increasingly important to many countries. You might be wondering how we can trade a service. Service trade happens when a person or a company in one country provides a service to a resident of a different country. Let's start with service exports. When a foreign student comes to study at a college in the United States, the tuition payments count as payments for a U.S. service export (because the student, although physically in the United States, is still a resident of a different country). In other words, the United States is exporting education to the foreign country. Here's another example: When a television network in another country broadcasts a U.S. television show—say, *American Idol,* which is broadcast in more than 100 countries—it usually pays a fee to the U.S. owner of the show. That fee is reported as payment for service sector exports. The service category of exports of U.S. TV shows and movies was worth about $14 billion in 2009, compared to $2 billion in imports in the same category.

What about service imports? One example of service imports is spending on foreign travel: If a U.S. consumer travels to Shanghai, her hotel and meals there count as payment for a service import to the United States. When you call the help desk of a computer company and are connected to a customer service representative in India, that's a service export for India and a service import for the United States.

Companies in India now provide online tutoring for students in the United States at much lower prices than local tutoring enterprises—a differential Indian companies can afford to offer as long as the college graduates who work for them get paid much less than college grads in the United States. Healthcare is becoming globalized too, as more and more patients without medical insurance are trying to cut costs by having expensive procedures performed in other countries. A knee replacement operation, for example, might cost $25,000 in Singapore or $12,000 in India, including airfare and accommodations, compared to roughly $50,000 in the

United States. Such medical tourism could be the wave of the future.

Falling Natural Barriers to Trade

Why has trade risen so much in recent years? To answer, we first have to understand why trade *between* countries is different from trade *within* countries. Historically businesses that wanted to sell to buyers in another country faced both **natural barriers to trade** and **legal barriers to trade.** The natural barriers include such obstacles as distance, differences in culture and values, and the difficulty of delivering services remotely.

The legal barriers include tariffs, quotas, and other government actions that limit trade or make it more expensive.

But both natural and legal barriers to trade have become less important in recent years. That's due to technological advances, combined with a commitment among major countries to foster freer trade. In this new situation, global trade is feasible among a broader range of countries, involving more goods and services.

Let's start with the most important natural barrier to trade: distance. Distance obviously raises the cost of shipping. Distance also makes communication between buyers and sellers much more difficult. After all, if you have a problem with your purchase, would you rather be dealing with a seller in your town or 10,000 miles away?

As a result, countries have tended in the past to trade most with their close neighbors, which for the United States meant Canada and Mexico. These two countries are still important, as Figure 14.2a and Figure 14.2b show. However, as of 2010, China, on the other side of the globe, was the single biggest source of imports to the United States, passing Canada.

There are several reasons for the soaring U.S. trade with China. But one important factor is that the cost and time of shipping have become less onerous. The use of shipping containers—those 20-foot or 40-foot metal boxes that dominate ports—has dramatically reduced the amount of labor needed for ocean freight transportation (not to mention cutting the amount and cost of

> **NATURAL BARRIERS TO TRADE**
>
> Obstacles such as distance, differences in culture and values, and the difficulty of delivering services remotely.

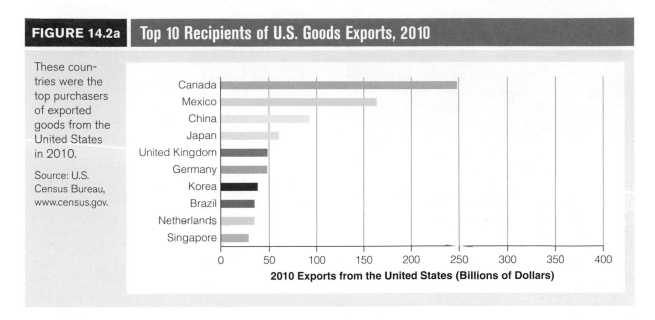

FIGURE 14.2a | **Top 10 Recipients of U.S. Goods Exports, 2010**

These countries were the top purchasers of exported goods from the United States in 2010.

Source: U.S. Census Bureau, www.census.gov.

Canada
Mexico
China
Japan
United Kingdom
Germany
Korea
Brazil
Netherlands
Singapore

2010 Exports from the United States (Billions of Dollars)

pilferage). The containers are packed at factories, trucked to ports, loaded onto ships, unloaded at their destinations, and trucked to stores or warehouses—all without needing to be unpacked again. Exporters and importers are also making much more active use of air freight to move high-value items such as semiconductors and perishable items such as seafood.

At the same time, the Internet and better technology have made communication over long distances much easier. When a factory in China is directly linked to the computer system of the U.S. retailer of its products, information about customer tastes and preferences can flow in real time, and coordination of production becomes almost as easy as if the factory were down the block.

The same ease of communication has reduced problems with different languages and different cultures, which have traditionally made selling overseas a tricky venture. In the past, U.S.

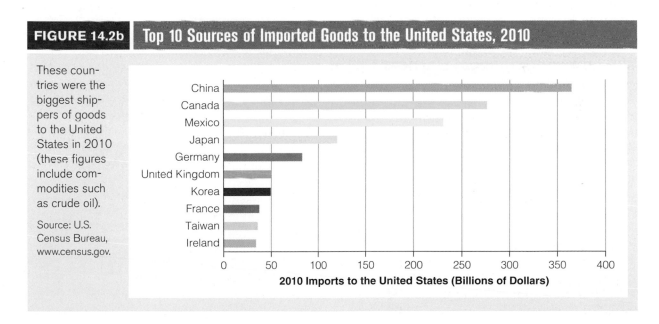

FIGURE 14.2b | **Top 10 Sources of Imported Goods to the United States, 2010**

These countries were the biggest shippers of goods to the United States in 2010 (these figures include commodities such as crude oil).

Source: U.S. Census Bureau, www.census.gov.

China
Canada
Mexico
Japan
Germany
United Kingdom
Korea
France
Taiwan
Ireland

2010 Imports to the United States (Billions of Dollars)

The use of shipping containers has facilitated long-distance trade.

companies often didn't understand the peculiarities of local cultures. For example, the Walt Disney Company stumbled badly when it built a theme park in France in the early 1990s. It didn't serve wine at its Paris theme park—an unpleasant surprise to French tourists who expected a glass of wine with lunch. Similarly, for years people made fun of the badly written instruction manuals that came with many imported electronics products.

But increasingly we live in a single global culture. You can tune in to CNN or MTV virtually anywhere in the world (see "Economic Milestone: MTV Goes Global"). And because more and more business executives travel internationally as part of their jobs, foreign countries are no longer as foreign. As a result, cultural barriers are less of a problem.

The Lowering of Legal Barriers

Another important reason for the increase in trade is the reduction of legal barriers. Historically countries have put tariffs and quotas on imported goods to raise money and protect their own industries.

SPOTLIGHT: WINDMILLS GO GLOBAL

To see another aspect of globalization, go to the little town of Fort Madison, Iowa, next to the Mississippi River. At a time when manufacturing jobs are disappearing all over America, Fort Madison has a factory that is actually expanding and hiring new workers. The surprise: the plant is owned and operated not by a U.S. company but by a large German company, Siemens AG.

The Siemens operation in Fort Madison makes the blades for "wind turbines"—that is the official name for the giant windmills that are increasingly generating electricity all around the country. The blades are an astounding 148 to 160 feet long, depending on the model, and drive wind turbines in California, Washington, Iowa, North Dakota, and Texas. When in place, the turbines themselves are higher than a 20-story building.

But there's one more part of globalization: the jobs at the Fort Madison factory depend on parts from overseas. Specifically, the part of the wind turbine that includes the rotors, the generators, and a lot of the control equipment is assembled in Brande, Denmark, and shipped to the United States. Such interconnectedness would not have been possible without the lowering of natural and legal barriers to trade.

Source: Author interviews.

Tariffs are extra charges or taxes levied on imports by a country, whereas **quotas** are numerical limits on the number of imported products coming into a country. For example, at one time it was not un-

Economic Milestone

1987 MTV GOES GLOBAL

The music video channel MTV was the first TV network to make the big jump across borders, starting with its first broadcast on a European channel in 1987. The company's music channels now include MTV China, MTV India, and MTV Nordic, which have helped create a shared global youth culture. Thus, besides being a service export itself, MTV also is one factor in lowering the cultural barriers to trade.

usual for countries to impose tariffs of 50 percent or more on imports, meaning that a company importing a shirt worth $100 would have to pay an additional $50 to the U.S. government.

Since the end of World War II, most countries—led by the United States—have made a concerted global effort to reduce tariffs, quotas, and other legal trade barriers. The first step came in 1947, when 23 countries signed the General Agreement on Tariffs and Trade (GATT). Successive rounds of negotiations reduced tariffs from an average of 50 percent to less than 5 percent among developed countries. In the following years more countries joined GATT as members.

In 1995 the members of GATT converted it into the World Trade Organization, with 150 members and a better procedure for resolving disputes. China joined the WTO in 2001—a big step. The WTO's rules governing world trade include

LEGAL BARRIERS TO TRADE
Tariffs, quotas, and other government actions that limit trade or make it more expensive.

about 550 pages of agreements, plus another 30,000 pages (!) that spell out in detail what each country has agreed to do to reduce tariffs and make trade cheaper and easier.

Why did the reduction of tariffs increase trade? The effect of a tariff is similar to the effect of a tax. The difference between what the consumer pays and what the importer receives is the tariff—so a 50 percent tariff, for example, adds 50 percent to the price of the import, and the consumer pays a higher price than the importer receives.

Another version of a tariff is a fixed dollar amount for each item imported. For example, a country could impose a $500 tariff on each imported car. That would add $500 to the price of the car, over and above the amount received by the importer.

Take a look at Figure 14.3. In the presence of such a fixed tariff, a consumer pays more than he or

FIGURE 14.3   Eliminating a Tariff Increases the Quantity of Imports

A tariff on imports creates a gap between what consumers pay (point A) and what the importer—the business actually importing the good—receives (point B). If the tariff is repealed, the market shifts to the equilibrium level (point C). The quantity of imports increases, the price paid by consumers decreases, and the price received by importers increases.

SPOTLIGHT: INTERNET GAMBLING AND TRADE

In the 1990s the little island nation of Antigua and Barbuda in the Caribbean hit on a great idea for economic growth: Internet gambling. The goal was to create jobs in Antigua while allowing customers—many of them from the United States—to gamble from the comfort of their homes. It was the ultimate service export.

Antigua's Internet gambling businesses thrived—until the United States put up new legal barriers to trade. To be more precise, in 1999 the U.S. government started a much-publicized crackdown on Internet gambling that, among other restrictions, made it harder to use credit cards online to gamble. That made it more difficult for U.S. residents to log onto gambling sites in Antigua. In 2006 the United States went further, actually banning Internet gambling (with a few exceptions) on the grounds that it was a danger to minors and a potential haven for organized crime.

Antigua complained to the World Trade Organization that the U.S. ban on Internet gambling was an unfair legal barrier to trade because it hurt Antigua's ability to export "gambling services." The WTO ruled that Antigua was right and denied the U.S. appeal.

Source: Lorraine Woellert, "A Web Gambling Fight Could Harm Free Trade," *BusinessWeek*, August 13, 2007.

straint agreement" limiting the number of cars they could ship to the United States. Even though it was "voluntary," this agreement was the equivalent of a quota because Japanese car makers abided by the limits. But because consumers were clamoring to buy Japanese-made cars, a waiting list grew for the hottest models. With Japanese cars in short supply in the United States, dealers could sell them for more—up to $1,000 more, by one estimate.

As tariffs and quotas have been reduced or eliminated, trade has become much easier. Countries can still put up plenty of legal trade barriers if they want (see "Spotlight: Internet Gambling and Trade"). But overall, the decline of tariffs and quotas has been a major factor driving the growth in imports and exports.

THE GAINS FROM TRADE

Now that we have seen the growing importance of trade, the next question is a simple one: Why do countries trade? Why go to all the trouble of hauling washing machines, cars, and all sorts of other goods halfway around the world?

Obviously a small country cannot produce everything it needs, so it must trade with others. But why should a large country like the United States—which can produce almost everything it needs within its own borders—import more than $2 trillion worth of goods and services each year? And why should countries from Austria to Zambia import $1.8 trillion worth of goods and services from the United States?

The answer is that there must be big enough **gains from trade** to justify the expenses and challenges of foreign trade. Let's look at what some of these gains from trade might be.

Lower Prices of Goods and Services

The main reason why we buy shirts or shoes made overseas is that they are less expensive than comparable domestic products. So a key gain from trade is lower prices.

she would otherwise, which reduces the quantity demanded (point *A* in the figure). Meanwhile, the importer receives less than it would have received without the tariff (point *B*).

When the tariff is removed, the price the consumer pays goes down. The revenue the importer gets to keep increases, and the quantity of imports supplied goes up (point C).

Trade negotiators have also worked hard to get rid of quotas, which are numerical limits on imports. In effect, quotas artificially restrict the quantity supplied to below the equilibrium level; that drives up the price. For example, in 1981 Japanese car makers accepted a "voluntary re-

For example, in 1996 the United States imported $7 billion worth of furniture from countries such as China, Canada, and Italy. By 2007 furniture imports had soared to $25 billion per year, with most of this increase coming from China. The reason? Chinese factories could deliver the same piece of furniture at a lower price than a U.S. furniture factory. Similarly, consumer items such as toys, clothing, and electronics are now mainly imported because they can be made much more cheaply outside the United States.

Look at Figure 14.4a. It shows the consumer price index for furniture, compared to the consumer price index for all goods and services. Between 1989 and 1996 the price of furniture rose at roughly the same rate as all consumer prices. But starting in 1996, something changed: the price of furniture began to fall while overall consumer prices kept heading up.

What changed in 1996? Figure 14.4b shows how imports of furniture into the United States skyrocketed after the mid-1990s. In particular, China became a much bigger source of everything from tables to bedroom sets. The imported furniture was considerably less expensive than its domestic-made counterparts—perhaps about two-thirds the price, according to people in the industry. As a result, consumers benefited.

In addition, the competition from imports forced domestic manufacturers to hold down their prices. Remember from Chapter 5 that a company with few competitors—a monopolist or an oligopolist—has market power and thus can keep prices higher than the competitive equilibrium. When an industry faces competition from imports, however, it's harder for businesses to exert market power.

Here's another example. At one time all the fresh flowers sold by florists, supermarkets, and gardening centers were grown in the United States. Today, however, about two-thirds or more of U.S. floral needs are imported, mostly from Colombia and Ecuador. The climate and long days in these countries, both of which are on the equator, let producers grow flowers such as roses and carnations all year long without expensive hothouses. In other words, these countries have relatively abundant resources of the type needed to grow flowers.

The United States could replace imports with domestic flowers—but that would require growers

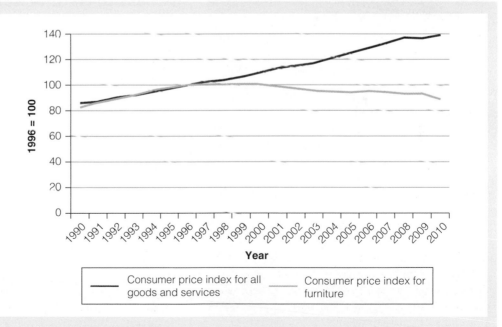

FIGURE 14.4a   Furniture Prices versus Overall Consumer Prices, 1990–2010

Between 1996 and 2007 the average price of furniture fell in the United States while the overall consumer price index kept moving up.

Source: Bureau of Labor Statistics, www.bls.gov.

_____ Consumer price index for all goods and services

_____ Consumer price index for furniture

FIGURE 14.4b | Furniture Imports to the United States, 1990–2010

Between 1996 and 2007 furniture imports into the United States more than tripled, with most of the increase coming from China. Those imports helped hold down prices.

Source: Bureau of Economic Analysis, www.bea.gov.

Furniture Imports to the United States, 1990–2010

Y-axis: Furniture imports (Billions of Dollars), from 0 to 30
X-axis: Year, from 1990 to 2010

Today about two-thirds or more of U.S. fresh flower purchases are imported.

to build expensive hothouses to yield a similar supply of blooms year-round. Domestic flowers would cost more, and the large investment of labor and capital required to build and maintain the hothouses would draw resources away from the rest of the economy.

Access to Natural Resources

Another gain from trade is access to natural resources that either are too expensive to be produced domestically or are not available in sufficient quantities. An obvious example is crude oil, which is essential for running a modern economy. The United States imports roughly two-thirds of its oil needs; cutting off that flow would send gasoline prices sky-high. Other industrialized countries, such as Japan and Germany, have no oil resources of their own and therefore have no choice but to import oil from other countries where petroleum is abundant, no matter what the price.

Meanwhile, there is a long list of important minerals that the United States does not produce at all. Niobium, for example, is a metal you may never have heard of. It's used to make superconductors and heat-resistant steel for items like jet engines and rockets. The United States has some low-grade niobium deposits in places like New Mexico, Idaho, and Alaska. But the last active U.S. niobium mine closed in 1959 because production was so expensive compared to other countries. So today the United States imports all its niobium, mainly from Brazil.

Access to Global Markets

Yet another gain from trade is that it gives companies access to global markets. Why is this important? The global market is bigger than any single national market, including that of the United States. So if you are running a company that has spent a lot of money developing a new product, you want to get the maximum benefit from your investment by selling it in the biggest market possible—that is, the global one.

A good example is the film industry. Big-budget movies with famous actors and lots of special effects are generally very expensive to produce; for instance, the third *Pirates of the Caribbean* movie, starring Johnny Depp, cost $300 million to make. But once a film is done, the cost of making copies and showing the film around the world is quite low. That's why movie companies try as hard as they can to export movies to other countries—especially action films, which attract a broad global audience. As a result, a typical successful Hollywood movie earns 60–70 percent of its box office revenues outside the United States, and its earnings from foreign distribution count as service exports.

Movies are an example of a business with high fixed costs and low marginal costs, as defined in Chapter 4. Such businesses make more profits by selling to a bigger market, so they are more profitable if they can sell globally.

Other industries also have large development costs for new products, making a global sales strategy essential. Consider the commercial airplane industry. There are only two major competitors right now: Boeing, a U.S.-based company, and Airbus, based in Europe. Developing a new airplane that's both safe and economical is an incredibly expensive proposition—it can cost as much as $15 billion. It would not be possible for either Boeing or Airbus to develop new planes if they restricted themselves to selling just to their home markets. As of March 2011 Boeing had unfilled orders for about 3,500 commercial airplanes, but only about one-quarter of these came from U.S. companies.

Access to New Ideas

A final gain from trade is access to new ideas from outside a country. Remember from Chapter 9 that knowledge is a critical factor driving growth. When countries trade, they not only exchange goods and services, but they also trade ideas, information, and new ways of doing things. That accelerates the development of new products.

Today many new U.S. products are either designed in countries other than the United States or are the result of cross-country collaboration. The first iPod, for example, was possible because Toshiba, a Japanese company, had developed a miniature hard drive. New pharmaceuticals are often developed and tested globally. The flat-panel LCD television became a commercial product because of work done in multiple countries (see "Spotlight: The Development of the Flat-Panel Television").

Some ideas that cross national borders are just fun. Remember Pokémon? That was the video game, card game, and television show that started in Japan and then crossed the Pacific to the United States in 1998. Built around the basic idea of capturing and training 151 "pocket monsters," the Pokémon craze seized the attention of kids across the United States. For a couple of years everyone with a small child knew about Pikachu, Charizard, and the rest of Pokémon.

Pikachu was arguably the most popular of the Pokémon imports.

SPOTLIGHT: THE DEVELOPMENT OF THE FLAT-PANEL TELEVISION

Walk into an electronics store and you'll see row after row of flat-panel LCD (liquid crystal display) televisions—all of them imported. The original idea for the flat-panel LCD screens was developed in the mid-1960s by a young U.S. researcher, George Heilmeier, who worked for RCA, the company that developed color TV.

Heilmeier thought then that a flat-panel TV that could hang on the wall was right around the corner. But the design problems were much more difficult to solve than he thought. It took 25 years—and concentrated research efforts by major companies in the United States, Europe, and Japan—before a flat-panel TV became a reality.

The process of producing a workable LCD TV would probably have been much slower if U.S. researchers had tried to do it alone. For one thing, television makers like RCA were reluctant to invest in LCDs, which were a threat to their existing business of producing glass picture tubes for televisions.

Moreover, the different countries had different strengths. One historian who looked at the history of the LCD screen wrote the following:

> America's strength was in its speed in creating new ideas and then demonstrating their feasibility. Europe's strength was in fundamental science and synthesizing basic materials. Japan's strength was in perfecting the implementation and moving it to mass production.

Today LCD screen manufacturers—mainly Japanese, Taiwanese, and Korean—are pouring billions of dollars into building mammoth TV factories in China and elsewhere. The result is that televisions keep getting cheaper, larger, and thinner.

Source: H. Kawamoto, "The History of Liquid-Crystal Displays," *Proceedings of the IEEE* 90, no. 4 (April 2002), pp. 460–500.

True, Pokémon showed up in ordinary imports of goods from Japan—games for the Nintendo Game Boy, stuffed Pokémon dolls, and the like. But on another level it was something different: the import of an idea.

ABSOLUTE ADVANTAGE VERSUS COMPARATIVE ADVANTAGE

Now that we understand the gains from international trade, let's examine who produces what. For example, why is so much furniture produced in China, while aircraft are produced in the United States?

Absolute Advantage

If it takes less labor, capital, and other inputs to produce the same good in one country than in another, the first country has an **absolute advantage** in that good. Saudi Arabia has an absolute advantage over the United States in oil production because the U.S. oil fields require much more complicated and expensive methods of pumping oil. Colombia has an absolute advantage over the United States in flower production: because of the equatorial sunlight, it takes less labor and capital to raise flowers there.

Let's look at another example. If one country has better and faster software programmers than another country does, the first country has an absolute advantage in software. The same software project will require fewer people; that is, the first country has higher *productivity* in software (remember that productivity was defined in Chapter 9 as output per hour of labor).

Sometimes absolute advantage is something that can be held for a long time, as in the case of Saudi oil. Sometimes it's fleeting. In the software example, it's possible for another country to train good programmers. If that happens, the absolute advantage disappears.

The Theory of Comparative Advantage

You might think that any country will produce and export the products in which it has an absolute advantage. Sometimes that's true. Saudi Arabia exports oil, for example, and Colombia exports flowers.

However, in general, what gets exported is determined by a more complicated set of factors than simply absolute advantage. Patterns of trade are determined by **comparative advantage.** That means a country will tend to specialize in the goods or services in which it has the biggest productivity advantage compared to other countries, or the smallest productivity disadvantage.

The easiest way to understand comparative advantage is with a simple example from daily life. Suppose that you are taking a car trip with a friend. You are slightly better at reading maps than your friend, but you are a lot better driver. In theory you could take on both tasks: drive, and then stop occasionally to read the map. But you will probably get to your destination faster if you take the role where you have the biggest advantage—driving—and let your friend take care of the navigating.

Now let's look at a similar sort of trade example. Imagine two countries. One country, *D*, has good dress designers and workers who are fast at sewing dresses. The other country, *P*, has poor dress designers and workers who are just a bit slower at sewing than their counterparts in country *D*. From this description, country *D* has an absolute advantage in both dress design and sewing.

> A country will tend to specialize in the goods or services for which it has the biggest productivity advantage or the smallest productivity disadvantage compared to other countries.

The theory of comparative advantage says that a trade between the two countries will make both countries better off. In particular, country *D* will probably specialize in dress design, where it has a big advantage. Country *P* will probably specialize in sewing the dresses, where it has only a small disadvantage. Country *D* can export dress designs to country *P* and get back inexpensive dresses in return.

Here's another way to think about comparative advantage. Suppose a country has a resource that is relatively abundant compared to other countries. It will want to specialize in an industry that uses that relatively abundant resource.

For example, China has a relative abundance of unskilled labor that has few better uses than working in manufacturing. How do we know this? In 2004 the average factory worker in China was paid 67 cents per hour, according to a study by the U.S. Bureau of Labor Statistics. (Figure 14.5 shows the hourly wage for manufacturing workers around the world.) If manufacturing

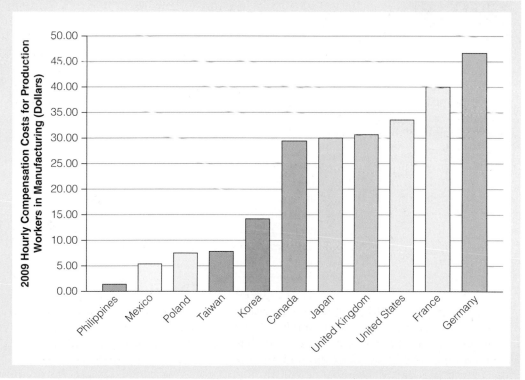

FIGURE 14.5 Labor Costs in Manufacturing, 2009

This figure shows hourly compensation costs in manufacturing around the world in 2009. The United States is lower than some of its major industrialized trading partners, but well above developing countries.

Source: Bureau of Labor Statistics, www.bls.gov.

SPOTLIGHT: OFFSHORING

Every economic era has its own new vocabulary. The current surge of globalization has brought us a new word: *offshoring*. Offshoring means the movement of jobs, especially in the service sector, to lower-wage countries.

Offshoring of service sector jobs was much more difficult before the age of rapid and cheap communications. The question now is, How far will it go? A 2005 study from the McKinsey Global Institute estimated that roughly 200,000 to 300,000 jobs would be lost each year to offshoring over the next 30 years. This is a significant but not overwhelming number. According to McKinsey's analysis only 11 percent of service jobs can be offshored. In healthcare only 8 percent of jobs can be performed remotely, but because healthcare employs so many people, that's a hefty chunk in absolute numbers.

The other issue is that developing countries, as they mature, may find better uses for their college graduates than answering phone calls from perplexed computer users in the United States. Already there are shortages of skilled, educated workers in India and elsewhere.

Source: D. Farrell and J. Rosenfeld, *U.S. Offshoring: Rethinking the Response,* McKinsey Global Institute, December 2005.

workers in China had a better alternative, their wage would be higher.

This low wage gives China a comparative advantage in many kinds of manufacturing. That's why it's cheaper for manufacturers in other countries to build and operate factories in China and to import goods from there.

A country's comparative advantage can change over time. Consider India, which got its start with customer call centers because it had a relative abundance of English-speaking college graduates who had no other good opportunities in the Indian economy. Therefore, these skilled workers were relatively inexpensive to hire. However, as India develops other industries that employ college graduates, such as consulting and programming, it may no longer have a relative abundance of college graduates. The wages of college graduates will go up, and India may lose its comparative advantage in call centers (see "Spotlight: Offshoring").

Note that you can't identify a country's comparative advantage just by looking at its own economy. You also have to know how it compares to its trading partners, and what they are producing. That's why it's called *comparative advantage*.

WINNERS AND LOSERS

One of the most politically contentious issues in the United States today is the impact of trade on individuals. The theory of comparative trade says that international trade will benefit an entire economy. However, nothing says that particular people or companies won't be hurt by trade. In this section we will look at the winners and losers from international trade.

Who Gets the Gains

As we discussed earlier, many benefits of trade show up as lower prices for all sorts of goods. So when you go to the store and buy an inexpensive shirt or a cheap piece of electronics, you are reaping the benefits of trade.

The implication is that the gains from trade are broadly distributed. Anyone who buys clothes, furniture, or electronics benefits from trade. That basically includes the entire population of the United States.

Trade has an even broader set of benefits. As a matter of history, countries that have been open to international trade seem to do better, in terms of growth, than ones that have been more closed off. China and India have done spectacularly well in recent years, largely because they are participating actively in the global economy. They followed different strategies: China has become a manufacturing powerhouse, shipping all sorts of toys, machinery, clothing, and other manufactured goods to the United States. India has concentrated on exporting business services, such as computer programming and customer service call centers. But the continued growth of each rests on trade with the rest of the world.

The Flow of Jobs

Now let's look at the losers from trade. On the face of it, imported goods and services displace domestically produced goods and services and cost a country jobs. And this actually happens—factories close, customer service call centers shift to India, and research facilities move out of the country.

FIGURE 14.6 | **Imports and Jobs**

The arrows on the right show how a purchase of imported furniture destroys manufacturing jobs in the United States. The arrows on the left show how that same purchase creates jobs in other industries.

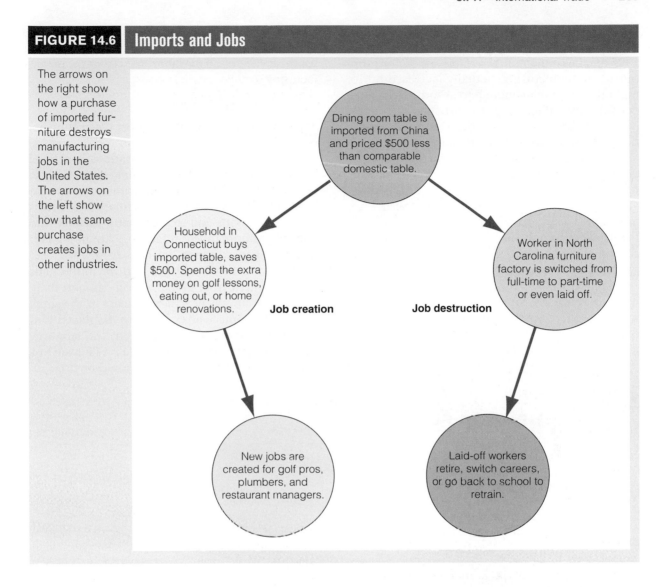

But this is the first step in a longer process that creates jobs as well as destroys them. Let's think about a consumer buying a new dining room table that was made in a Chinese factory, not one in North Carolina. The table costs a lot less—let's say $500 less—which is good news for the consumer and bad news for workers in furniture factories. Between 2000 and 2007, employment in the U.S. furniture industry dropped by roughly 150,000 jobs.

That's not the end of the story, though. A household that buys an imported dining room table now has an extra $500 to spend. Where does it go? Recreation, perhaps. Or eating out, college tuition, a massage, a visit to the doctor, or any one of a thousand different goods and services. No matter what the money is spent on, it generates new jobs—enough to at least replace the ones that were lost. Figure 14.6 traces the bad and the good sides of trade.

On a bigger and broader scale, this process of moving workers from manufacturing to other parts of the economy is exactly what has happened in recent years. The downside, though, was a loss of almost 6 million jobs in manufacturing between 1995 and 2010. What happened to the U.S. workers who were employed in the factories that are now shut? And what happened to all the young workers who would have been hired by those factories?

The short answer is that they found jobs in the rest of the economy—in construction, recreation, healthcare, consulting firms, restaurants, finance, and architectural and engineering firms. Between 1995 and 2010 the number of private sector jobs, outside manufacturing, actually increased by 15 million—more than enough to absorb all the jobs cut from manufacturing. In particular, the number of private sector jobs in the health and education industries increased by 6 million.

From the perspective of the factory workers displaced from their jobs, the import boom was terribly disruptive, forcing them out of work and requiring them to get added training or education to move into a new career. But from the perspective of the whole economy, the surge of imports lowered consumer prices and freed up millions of workers for gainful work in other parts of the economy.

To put this a different way, if the closed factories were to reopen tomorrow, millions of workers would have to be pulled from the rest of the economy to run them. Presumably they are working at new jobs and would be missed if they were gone.

The gain from international trade is that we not only get to consume the imported goods—we also get the benefit of all the labor freed from the manufacturing sector.

Losers from Trade

Now we come to one of the most distressing aspects of international trade. Both theory and experience strongly suggest that trade is beneficial for the economy as a whole. That is, on average, living standards should go up in an economy that is open to global markets. Consumers have access to cheaper goods and services, and workers who once might have toiled in factories are now available for other industries.

However, there's no rule that *all* individuals have to benefit from globalization. In fact, there will almost always be losers, at least in the short run—the people whose jobs are displaced and who have to move to other parts of the economy (see Spotlight: "The China Price"). This sort of

SPOTLIGHT: "THE CHINA PRICE"

U.S. manufacturers have been dealing with foreign competition for decades. But the influx of inexpensive Chinese imports has created many losers, as a 2004 article from *BusinessWeek* shows:

> From the rich walnut paneling and carved arches to the molded Italian Renaissance patterns on the ceiling, the circa 1925 council chamber room of Akron's municipal hall evokes a time when America's manufacturing heartland was at the peak of its power. But when the U.S.–China Economic & Security Review Commission, a congressionally appointed panel, convened there on Sept. 23, 2003, it was not to discuss power but decline. One after another, economists, union officials, and small manufacturers took the microphone to describe the devastation Chinese competitors are inflicting on U.S. industries, from kitchenware and car tires to electronic circuit boards.
>
> Despite buying the best computer-controlled gear, Douglas S. Bartlett reported that at his Cary (IL)-based Bartlett Manufacturing Company, a maker of high-end circuit boards for aerospace and automotive customers, sales are half the late-1990s level and the workforce is one-third smaller. He

> waved a board Bartlett makes for a U.S. Navy submarine detection device. His buyer says he can get the same board overseas for 40 percent less. "From experience I can only assume this is the Chinese price," Bartlett said. "We have faced competition in the past. What is dramatically different about China is that they are about half the price."
>
> "The China price." They are the three scariest words in U.S. industry. In general, it means 30 percent to 50 percent less than what you can possibly make something for in the United States. In the worst cases, it means below your cost of materials. Makers of apparel, footwear, electric appliances, and plastics products, which have been shutting U.S. factories for decades, know well the futility of trying to match the China price.

Since this story was written in 2004, the competitive pressure on U.S. manufacturers has only gotten more intense. Imports from China soared from $197 billion in 2004 to $365 billion in 2010.

Source: P. Engardio and D. Roberts, "The China Price," *BusinessWeek,* April 12, 2004.

HOW IT WORKS: HELPING THE LOSERS

The overall economy benefits from trade, but some individuals and companies are almost inevitably going to be hurt. As a result, there's a logical role for some form of trade adjustment assistance to compensate the losers.

Trade adjustment assistance can include support for retraining; income support during a transition from one career to another; relocation assistance; temporary government payments for health insurance; and incentives to businesses to help create new jobs.

Since at least the 1970s the United States has tried various forms of trade adjustment assistance. However, there's little evidence that the programs have been successful. Depending on which economist you talk to, the reason is either that the programs were underfunded or that it's hard for the government to intervene in labor markets (or both).

displacement and movement is not just a side effect of trade, however—it's part of the key mechanism by which trade raises overall living standards.

In the short run, the transition costs of adjusting to trade can be large in both time and money. When a factory closes, some workers retire early; the rest have to retrain themselves for new jobs and move to other parts of the country if necessary. Many displaced workers have to return to school to qualify for new jobs, which can be an expensive and time-consuming proposition, even if the new jobs pay more. That's why the government might have a role assisting people in making the transition (see "How It Works: Helping the Losers")

What about over the long run? The rule of thumb is simple: all other things being equal, globalization benefits people whose skills are relatively scarce in world markets. It hurts people whose skills are relatively common. In general, better-educated workers should do better in a globalized economy because most countries have a smaller proportion of college graduates among their citizens than the United States does.

Arguments for Protectionism

Economists believe, and the evidence shows them to be correct, that international trade is beneficial to any economy. Yet globalization is regularly attacked by politicians who believe it harms too many workers. There are often demands for a return to **protectionism**—the use of tariffs, quotas, or other trade barriers to protect domestic jobs and businesses.

Are there good arguments for protectionism? Some economists point out that trade can sometimes be **disruptive,** which means that it can impose big economic and social adjustment costs. In developed countries, small towns are often organized around local factories. So when that factory moves to Mexico or China, it affects everyone in the town, not just the workers in the factory.

The problem of disruptive trade is bigger in developing countries that have a large agricultural subsistence sector composed of poor farming households who survive by selling small amounts of crops locally. The danger here is that foreign competition in agriculture could leave whole villages and regions like these without a livelihood. For that reason, trade treaties typically allow poor countries to protect at least some of their agricultural industries.

Another reason given for protectionism, the **infant industry** argument, is simple: An infant industry is a new or a small industry in a country, which is vulnerable to being crushed by better-funded and more mature foreign competitors. Given a chance to grow while protected, however, the new industry could be a viable global competitor. (See "Spotlight: How Canadians Nurture Their Music.")

In theory this argument makes sense. But in practice it rarely seems to work because it reduces competition. In the 1980s Brazil wanted to develop its own computer industry. So the government imposed restrictions on the use of imported computers and software, and set up regulations that forced domestic computer makers to use domestically made parts.

The result was to cut Brazil off from the rapid technological progress being made in the

SPOTLIGHT: HOW CANADIANS NURTURE THEIR MUSIC

The Canadian government has mounted a determined effort to protect and foster Canadian culture, which it regards as vulnerable to being overwhelmed by its giant U.S. neighbor. This effort includes setting rules for the kind of music radio stations can play to ensure that Canadian musicians get enough exposure to do well.

The regulations require that broadcasters devote at least 35 percent of their popular music selections to Canadian songs. And what makes a song Canadian? Well, it's not enough that the performer is Canadian—either the music or the lyrics have to be written by a Canadian as well, or the song has to be recorded in a Canadian studio. (There are other possibilities, but that's the basic idea.)

The biggest winners from the Canadian content rule are young bands who get more airtime than they would otherwise. Well-known bands that benefited from this exposure in their earlier days include Nickelback and Barenaked Ladies.

Source: "Canadian Content Requirements for Music on Canadian Radio," Canadian Radio-Television and Telecommunications Commission, www.crtc.gc.ca/eng/cancon/r_cdn.htm.

global computer industry. As a result, Brazil's computers lagged several years behind those in the rest of the world and were more expensive too. What's worse is that the rest of the Brazilian economy suffered because of the country's inability to use the fastest, cheapest computers available.

Another justification for protectionism is **unfair competition.** This usually refers to cases in which a foreign country subsidizes its exporting industries by lowering their taxes, offering them low-cost loans, or just giving them money. Armed with such a subsidy, the foreign industry can afford to price its products more cheaply. The result is that subsidized industries can get a bigger share of the global marketplace.

For example, Airbus, the European airplane manufacturer, has access to low-cost loans from European governments. In effect this is a subsidy because Airbus can borrow money at a lower interest than it could as a "normal" company. Boeing, its U.S. competitor, has complained that these loans give Airbus an unfair advantage.

On the face of it, unfair competition looks a bit like cheating. However, if one country subsidizes its exports, that may benefit consumers in other countries. Suppose the government of Fiji decides to subsidize its tourist industry by giving anyone who comes to the island a free room and meals. Obviously this will attract travelers who might have gone elsewhere. For example, some tourists who might have spent time in Hawaii will go to Fiji instead, hurting the Hawaiian tourist industry.

But the tourists themselves will be better off: Free room and meals in Fiji—what could be better? In fact, the gains to consumers will exceed the losses to domestic industries, as in any other form of trade. However, losing jobs to unfair competition seems, well, unfair, because it comes about as the result of government decisions rather than pure economic competition.

Probably the most compelling reason to maintain some trade barriers is concern about protecting important defense-related industries. During peaceful times it doesn't matter whether factories are in the same country as their goods' ultimate consumers. It's in the interest of the exporting countries to keep shipping their goods. After all, what else are the factories for?

But a major war changes these calculations. Once shooting starts, you don't want to find out that all your bullets are made in the country you're fighting. Or that all the special steel in your missiles and all the electronics in your fighter planes are made in a neutral country that can't provide any more supplies because the shipping lanes are closed by war. Or even that the supply of computer and communications equipment, so essential for running a modern economy, starts drying up because so much of it is produced abroad.

National security requires balancing the economic benefits of trade against the potential vulnerabilities of a global supply chain during war. In ordinary times, outsourcing cuts costs and enables the defense dollar to go further. But it may take too much time to rebuild factory capacity during war.

For that reason, it's generally accepted that countries can protect some portion of defense-related production. The U.S. Department of Defense, for example, has to get much of its specialty steel in weapons systems and military aircraft from domestic steel mills. Critical electronics must be made domestically as well. However, the United States has still not figured out the right balance between low cost and national security.

EXCHANGE RATES

Let's turn our attention to exchange rates, which is an aspect of trade we have not yet considered.

Almost every country has a national currency. The best known are the dollar (United States), the euro (France, Germany, Belgium, Greece, Spain, Ireland, Italy, Luxembourg, the Netherlands, Austria, Portugal, and Finland), the yen (Japan), the pound (Great Britain), and the yuan (China). But there are currencies for small countries that receive almost no attention, including the Albanian lek, the Bangladesh taka, and the Paraguay guarani.

For two countries to trade, they need to be able to convert one currency to another. Suppose Honda makes a motor scooter in Japan and ships it for sale in Los Angeles. The workers in Japan are paid in yen, but the U.S. consumers who buy the motorcycles pay dollars for them. At some point, if Honda wants to keep operating its factories and paying its workers, it has to turn those dollars into yen.

The **exchange rate** is the rate at which one currency can be converted into another. For example, on April 25, 2011, one dollar was worth 82 yen. That same dollar could also be turned into 0.68 euros or 45 Indian rupees. You can think of the exchange rate as the price of buying one currency.

EXCHANGE RATE
The rate at which one currency can be converted into another.

In most cases exchange rates between currencies are **floating,** which means they are set in the foreign exchange markets. Currency traders buy and sell dollars for yen, or yen for euros, or euros for the Thai baht or the Indonesian ringit. The exchange rate is determined by the outcome of market transactions, and it can swing dramatically.

Some currencies do not float; instead their exchange rate is **pegged,** which means the government of the country manages the exchange rate to keep it fixed relative to another currency. For example, some Caribbean countries, including Aruba and the Bahamas, peg their currencies to the dollar (one Bahamian dollar equals one U.S. dollar, for example). Some African countries, such as Chad and Senegal, peg their currencies to the euro.

For many years China pegged its currency, the yuan, to the U.S. dollar at a rate of 8.3 yuan to the dollar. As of July 2005 the Chinese government began allowing the exchange rate to change slowly (Figure 14.7). As of April 2011 a dollar was worth only 6.5 yuan.

When an exchange rate changes so that one currency can buy more of another, we say the first currency is **appreciating** and the second currency is **depreciating.** For example, based on Figure 14.7, we can say that the yuan appreciated against the dollar between July 2005 and April 2011 and the dollar depreciated against the yuan. Similarly, in July 2002 one dollar could be traded for about one euro. Since then the dollar has depreciated while the euro has appreciated. When this textbook was revised in April 2011, one dollar could buy only 0.68 euros; in other words, the dollar has gotten cheaper relative to the euro.

Effects of Appreciation and Depreciation

What happens when one currency depreciates relative to another? To make this concrete, let's suppose the dollar depreciates relative to the euro: one dollar buys fewer euros, and one euro buys more dollars. This affects the price of imports and exports.

Consider what happens when a U.S. maker of construction equipment ships a massive crane to

---

FIGURE 14.7 | **The Exchange Rate of the Yuan versus the Dollar**

The chart shows the number of yuan a dollar can buy. As the number has fallen over time, the dollar has depreciated against the yuan.

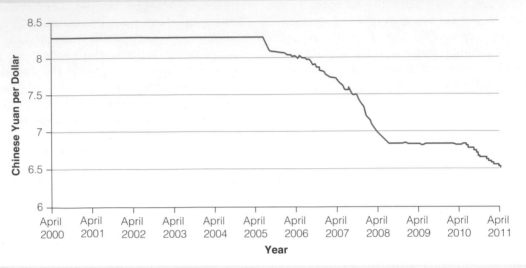

Source: The Federal Reserve, www.federalreserve.gov.

Europe that is priced (in dollars) at $100,000. If the exchange rate is one dollar for each euro, that crane sells for 100,000 euros, as line A in Table 14.1 shows. But if the dollar depreciates to $1.30 for each euro, the crane sells for roughly 77,000 euros (€) to European buyers. The crane is the same price in dollars, but it becomes cheaper for European buyers, as line B shows.

Here's another example, also from Table 14.1. Consider a German car priced at 40,000 euros. If it is shipped to the United States at a time when the exchange rate is one dollar for one euro, its price would be $40,000, as shown in line C. Now suppose the dollar depreciates, so one euro is worth $1.30. That same 40,000-euro car would cost roughly $52,000 in the United States, as shown in line D.

TABLE 14.1 | **How Depreciation Works**

A depreciating dollar raises the price of imports to domestic buyers and cuts the price of exports to foreign buyers.

A crane is exported from the United States to Europe. After the dollar depreciates, the price of the crane in euros falls.

	Original Price in Dollars	Dollars per Euro	Price in Euros
A	100,000	1.00	100,000
B	100,000	1.30	76,923

A car is imported from Europe to the United States. After the dollar depreciates, the price of the car in dollars goes up.

	Price in Dollars	Dollars per Euro	Original Price in Euros
C	40,000	1.00	40,000
D	52,000	1.30	40,000

The bottom line is that imports become more expensive when a currency depreciates. Similarly, exports become cheaper when a currency depreciates. If imports become more expensive, the law of demand suggests that purchases of imports will fall. And when exports become cheaper, purchases of exports should rise. As a result, when a currency depreciates, its trade deficit should eventually shrink over time, all other things being equal.

The other thing that happens when a currency depreciates is that assets in that country—real estate, stocks, and so forth—become cheaper for foreign investors to buy. Think about this. Suppose you have a U.S. home selling for $300,000. If the dollar–euro exchange rate is one for one, then a European buyer would have to pay 300,000 euros (€). But if the dollar depreciates to $1.30 for each euro, the price of that home in euros falls to only 230,000. Suddenly, U.S. real estate looks much cheaper to European investors, even if nothing has changed about their price in dollars.

THE TRADE BALANCE

Let's finish this chapter by looking at the **trade balance,** the difference between exports and imports of goods and services. If a country's trade balance is negative—that is, if imports exceed exports—we say that the country is running a **trade deficit.** As we will see in this section, the amount that the United States borrows is closely related to the size of its trade deficit.

The U.S. trade deficit has grown rapidly in recent years, as Figure 14.8 shows. How did the U.S. trade deficit get so large? On one level, the answer is straightforward. Exports have grown at

---

FIGURE 14.8   **Goods and Services Trade Balance as Percentage of GDP, 1975–2010**

In this chart, when the trade balance is negative, the United States is running a trade deficit. In 2010, for example, imports exceeded exports by $516 billion, or 3.5 percent of GDP. Because the trade balance is negative, the bars stretche downward.

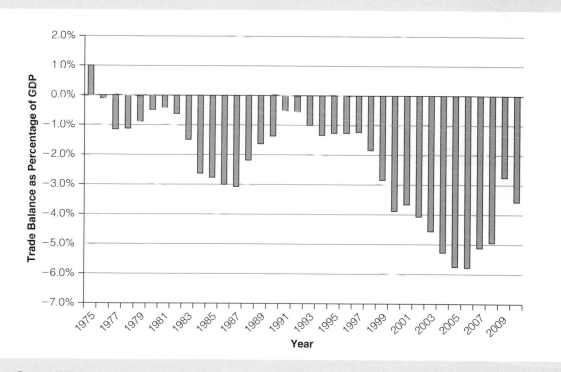

Source: Bureau of Economic Analysis, www.bea.gov.

TABLE 14.2	Explanations for the U.S. Trade Deficit

"It's Our Fault"

U.S. consumers borrow too much.

The U.S. government borrows too much.

U.S. manufacturers can't compete.

"It's Their Fault"

Other countries restrict imports from the United States.

Other countries unfairly subsidize their exports.

"It's No One's Fault"

The United States is a successful rich economy, able to afford imports.

The United States is a successful rich economy, making it a magnet for lending from other countries.

roughly the same rate as the economy as a whole, but imports have grown much faster. In particular, imported goods from China have soared from $15 billion in 1990 to $321 billion in 2007 to $365 billion in 2010.

But economists disagree about how to interpret the growing trade deficit. There are many explanations for the trade deficit, which fall into three general categories: "It's our fault"; "It's their fault"; and "It's no one's fault" (see Table 14.2).

Some Explanations for the Trade Deficit

Let's start with "It's our fault." Because the big trade deficits started in the 1980s, some economists have put the blame solidly on the actions of U.S. manufacturers, consumers, and governments. The deficit was caused, some say, because U.S. manufacturers are incompetent and unable to compete with overseas rivals, which is why U.S. consumers have been buying imports. Others blame the trade deficit on overspending by U.S. consumers. If consumers would cut back on their purchases instead of borrowing heavily to buy imported goods such as cars, toys, and electronics, the trade deficit would shrink or even vanish. Along the same line, many economists argue that the big trade deficit is the result of overspending by the federal government. In other words, big budget deficits cause big trade deficits.

What about "It's their fault"? Some economists, politicians, and business leaders blame the trade deficit, at least in part, on decisions made by foreign countries. For example, during the 1980s the United States ran big trade deficits with Japan, which seemed to be using non-tariff barriers to keep out U.S. exports. More recently, as we will see later in this chapter, China has been following an exchange rate policy that keeps Chinese imports to the United States cheaper than they should be.

Finally, some economists believe the United States trade deficit may simply reflect the strength of the U.S. economy, rather than its weakness. People in the United States have high enough incomes to be able to afford high levels of consumption, including imports. Moreover, the United States, the largest and most stable economy in the world, is a magnet for lending from other countries. Ask yourself this: If you were a Chinese billionaire, would you like to keep all of your wealth in China, or would you prefer

Economic Milestone

1975 THE LAST TRADE SURPLUS

In 1975 the United States ran a small excess of exports of goods and services over imports, as a weak economy cut consumer demand. That was the last U.S. trade surplus. Since then the United States has registered 35 straight years of trade deficits.

to move half of it to the comparative safety of the United States?

The truth is, all these explanations have an element of truth. The trade deficit does reflect U.S. overspending in part, decisions by other countries in part, and the wealth and health of the U.S. economy in part.

Paying for Trade

But no matter what explanation for the trade deficit you accept, this is true: If you buy an imported toy, bottle of wine, or car, you have to pay for it, one way or another. As economists say, there is no such thing as a free lunch. A country must pay for its imports somehow. There are four ways to do this (see Table 14.3).

One way to pay for our imports is to send back exports of our own goods and services. The United Arab Emirates sends us oil, and we send commercial aircraft, military aircraft, and drilling equipment. Australia sends us wine, uranium, and beef, and we send excavating machinery, agricultural machinery, drugs, and medical equipment.

But what if we are running a trade deficit with a country? When China ships us a container ship full of toys, what do we send China in return? One possibility is that China and other countries can give us the goods and services on credit, like a bar that lets its patrons run tabs. As of the end of 2010, the United States owed more than $8 trillion to the rest of the world. The biggest chunk of that was roughly $4.4 trillion in borrowing by the federal government.

TABLE 14.3	**Four Ways to Pay for Imports**

- Sell exports to foreign purchasers.
- Borrow money from foreign investors.
- Sell assets such as stock or real estate to foreign investors.
- Allow foreign companies to build factories or other facilities in the United States.

Is that a lot of money or a little? On one level it's a lot of money because it's roughly $27,000 per person, and paying back that much debt may decrease the amount of money available for our future consumption. On the other hand, if our economy is growing fast enough, even a high level of obligations may not be a problem. A fast-growing country will likely have enough future income to pay back accumulated debt—much as a family with a rising income can pay back the mortgage it used to buy a house.

Alternatively, we can pay for imports by selling other countries valuable U.S. assets. These can be stock shares in U.S. companies, for example; as of the end of 2010, foreigners owned $4.4 trillion in U.S. stocks. Or we can sell some of our real estate to foreigners to help pay for our imports. In the late 1980s, for example, when the United States was running a large trade deficit with Japan, Japanese companies bought a chunk of Rockefeller Center in New York City and Pebble Beach Golf Club in California, among other purchases.

A fourth way of paying for imports is to encourage foreign companies to invest directly in the United States by building factories and office buildings here. Such foreign investment includes Toyota's construction of billion-dollar factories in Georgetown, Kentucky, and San Antonio, Texas.

CONCLUSION

In the past, you might not have given a moment's thought to China, India, or any other faraway country. Today, however, globalization is one of the key driving forces of the economy, and there's no way to understand your future without some knowledge of international trade.

Still, globalization would not be possible without breakthroughs in communication and transportation. That's what has enabled national economies to be tied closer together. It's these sorts of technological improvements that we will discuss in the next chapter.

14 SUMMARY

1. The current boom in international trade may be unprecedented in recent history. Both trade in goods and trade in services have expanded. The increases are due to falling natural barriers to trade such as distance, and falling legal barriers to trade such as tariffs. *(LO14-1)*

2. The gains of trade include lower prices of goods and services, access to natural resources, access to global markets, and access to new ideas. For example, international trade allows consumers and businesses to buy lower-priced imports. *(LO14-2)*

3. If it takes fewer resources to produce the same good in one country than in another, the first country has an absolute advantage in that good. However, patterns of trade are determined by comparative advantage rather than absolute advantage. Comparative advantage means that countries specialize in the products or services for which they have the biggest productivity advantage—or the smallest productivity disadvantage. *(LO14-3)*

4. The theory of comparative advantage says that there always is a trade between two countries that makes both better off. You cannot identify a country's comparative advantage by just looking at its own economy. You also have to know how it compares to its trading partners. *(LO14-3)*

5. Economists believe that the gains from trade are broadly distributed. However, particular people and companies may be hurt by trade. In the short run, the transition costs of adjusting to trade can be large. Arguments for protectionism include the disruptive effects of trade, the desire to protect infant industries, concerns about unfair competition, and the need to protect important defense-related industries. *(LO14-4)*

6. The exchange rate is the rate at which one currency can be converted into another. If the exchange rate changes so that one currency can buy more of another, we say that the first currency is appreciating and the second is depreciating. A depreciating currency makes imports more expensive to domestic buyers and exports cheaper to foreign buyers. *(LO14-5)*

7. There are several explanations for why the United States has been running big trade deficits. These include overconsumption by the United States, policies by foreign countries that keep out U.S. exports, and the strength of the U.S. economy. *(LO14-6)*

KEY TERMS AND CONCEPTS

globalization	gains from trade	exchange rate
trade in goods	absolute advantage	floating exchange rate
trade in services	comparative advantage	pegged exchange rate
natural barriers to trade	protectionism	currency appreciation
legal barriers to trade	disruptive trade	currency depreciation
tariffs	infant industry	trade balance
quotas	unfair competition	trade deficit

PROBLEMS

1. Identify each of the following transactions as an import, an export, or neither, from the perspective of the United States. *(LO14-1)*

   a) You purchase a BMW made in Germany.

   b) You purchase a Toyota Camry made in Toyota's Kentucky plant.

   c) Air France, an airline based in Paris, purchases a new 777 airplane from Boeing, a company based in Seattle.

   d) You call customer service for your computer and are connected to a service representative in India.

   e) You study in another country for a year.

2. Suppose the quality of U.S.-made bulldozers declined. How would this change impact the following? *(LO14-1)*

   a) The supply curve for imported bulldozers to shift to the left, shift to the right, or stay the same?

   b) The demand curve for imported bulldozers to shift to the left, shift to the right, or stay the same?

   c) The quantity of imports to rise, fall, or stay the same?

3. The U.S. imposes a new tariff of $5.00 on every pound of imported cheese. *(LO14-1)*

   a) Does imposing the tariff raise or lower the prices U.S. consumers pay?

   b) Does it raise or lower the prices foreign cheese producers receive for the cheese they sell in the United States?

   c) Does imposing the tariff increase or decrease the quantity of imported cheese?

   d) What impact does the tariff have on the supply and demand curves for domestic cheese?

   e) What happens to the prices and quantities of domestic cheese sold?

4. This chapter identifies four different gains from trade: lower prices of goods and services, access to natural resources, access to global markets, and access to new ideas. For each of the following situations, say which gain from trade is the most important and explain why. *(LO14-2)*

   a) In 2010 Microsoft received $26 billion in revenue from customers outside the United States.

   b) The United States imports 94 percent of the platinum that it uses.

   c) The Wii video game machine, designed in Japan by Nintendo, was a big hit in the United States.

   d) The price of furniture in the United States has dropped as more has been imported from China.

5. One important gain to trade is access to global markets. That's likely to be important if _____ *(LO14-2)*

   a) U.S. wages are rising.

b) the U.S. is growing faster than other countries.

c) other countries are growing faster than the U.S.

d) wages in other countries are falling.

6. Suppose that because of climate or some other reason, Country A's wheat farmers have higher productivity than Country B's wheat farmers. That is, on the same size farm, Country A can grow twice as much wheat as Country B with the same amount of labor. *(LO14-3)*

a) Is this an example of absolute advantage or comparative advantage? Explain.

b) Does this mean Country A will necessarily export wheat to Country B? Explain.

7. Suppose that a massive oil field was discovered in Michigan. If it was large enough, we would expect that _____ *(LO14-3)*

a) oil imports would increase.

b) the U.S. would become a net exporter of oil.

c) oil consumption would fall.

d) the U.S. would lose its comparative advantage in oil drilling.

8. Suppose that Chinese manufacturers develop the ability to build a good car that costs only $5,000. They start shipping it to the United States. For each of the following groups, say whether they are likely to win, lose, or not be affected much by the Chinese imported cars. *(LO14-4)*

a) Low-income American families.

b) High-income American families.

c) U.S. autoworkers.

d) U.S. auto companies.

9. At the end of 1993 the exchange rate between Mexico and the United States was 3.1 pesos to the dollar. By the end of 1994 the exchange rate was 5 pesos to the dollar, and at the end of 1995, it was 7.7 pesos to the dollar. *(LO14-5)*

a) Over this period, did the dollar appreciate or depreciate against the peso?

b) A $1,000 piece of construction equipment made in the United States would have cost _____ pesos in 1993. It would have cost _____ pesos in 1995.

c) Would you expect exports from the United States to Mexico to rise or fall over this period?

d) Suppose it cost 1,000 pesos to make a television set in Mexico in the early 1990s. That was equivalent to _____ dollars in 1993 and _____ dollars in 1995.

e) Would you expect imports from Mexico to the United States to rise or fall over this period?

10. The currency of Iceland is called the krona. In July 2007, the exchange rate was roughly 60 krona to a dollar. In July 2011, the exchange rate was roughly 120 krona to a dollar. *(LO14-5)*

a) Over this period, would you expect exports from the United States to Iceland to get cheaper or more expensive in Iceland?

b) Would you expect living standards in Iceland to rise or fall?

c) Is the krona appreciating or depreciating against the dollar?

11. In June 2007 a U.S. toy company was forced to recall 1.5 million "Thomas the Tank Engine" toys because they contained lead paint. The toys had been made in China. Several other recalls of Chinese-made toys with excess lead followed. *(LO14-6)*

a) What effect, if any, would you expect these recalls to have on the demand curve for Chinese-made toys?

b) What effect, if any, would it have on the supply curve of Chinese-made toys?

c) If the result were tighter regulation, what would be the impact on prices and the volume of imports?

d) Would tighter regulation of Chinese-made toys increase or decrease the U.S. trade deficit?

15 TECHNOLOGICAL CHANGE

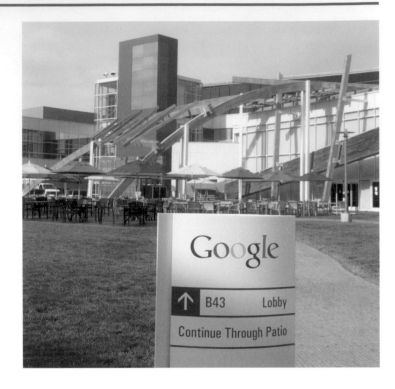

The growth of the modern market economy is in many ways the story of technological change. Basic science—the urge to understand nature—has been harnessed to the profit motive, and the combination has been exceptionally potent.

Finding the next big thing is a good way to make money. James Watt invented the steam engine in the 1700s to pump water out of mines and became rich in the process. Henry Ford invented the assembly line and the Model T automobile and created one of the greatest fortunes in U.S. history. Larry Page and Sergey Brin invented a better search engine, and the result—Google—made them both billionaires.

It's a virtuous circle. Economic incentives encourage people and businesses to create and commercialize new technology, and then technological change and innovation drive economic growth. In fact, one of the greatest advantages of the U.S. economy, compared to its rivals in Europe and Japan, has been its ability to take new ideas and commercialize them quickly.

In this chapter we will use our tools of supply and demand to understand the economics of technological change.

We'll describe the different kinds of innovation and look at the factors affecting the supply of and demand for innovation.

THE NATURE OF TECHNOLOGICAL CHANGE

As we saw in Chapter 1, **technological change** is an improvement in knowledge that increases the range of goods and services that the economy can deliver. By definition, technological change expands the limits of what we can produce, given today's natural resources and workforce. Technological change leads to **innovations,** which are new products and processes.

Without technological change, it's impossible to get sustained increases in living standards. Imagine, if you would, today's world with the technology from a century ago. No antibiotics or television—they didn't exist in 1910. You could buy your own small airplane because by 1910 the Wright brothers were offering the Wright Model B for sale. However, there would be no commercial air travel for years. The best car available in 1910 was the Ford Model T, which Henry Ford started selling in 1908. There was no long-distance

> Technological change expands the limits of what we can produce, given today's natural resources and workforce.

telephone service and certainly no Internet. Your life expectancy was only 51 years, and air conditioning had not been invented.

Remember, however, that technological progress has not been steady over the past 100 years. Instead it has proceeded in waves. One wave came in the first half of the 20th century, with amazing breakthroughs like antibiotics, radio, air travel, television, widespread use of electricity, cars, plastics, and other new materials that had never existed before. For example, nylon, the first synthetic fiber, was invented in 1935.

The next stretch—from roughly 1950 to 1975—had fewer big breakthroughs. Instead it was a productive period of building on earlier innovations. Companies refined and improved their new products, in some cases in major ways. For example, the shift from black-and-white to color television happened in the 1960s and 1970s (in 1966 NBC became the first network to broadcast its shows in color). Airlines introduced widespread use of jets, which replaced propeller-driven planes and improved speed and passenger comfort.

However, in the 1970s it became clear that two highly touted breakthrough technologies were failing to deliver much in the way of economic benefits. The first was space travel. Putting a person on the moon in 1969 and making five additional landings over the next three years was a great public relations achievement. But despite all the hoopla, the manned space program, including today's space shuttle launches, has generated relatively few economic returns so far. Our major economic uses of space today, including the launching of weather and communications satellites, mainly predate the beginning of the manned space program.

The second big failure from an economic perspective was nuclear energy, which was supposed to be a limitless source of cheap power. When the first nuclear power plants were built after World War II, utility companies expected the cost would fall, just as other new technologies had become cheaper over time.

Innovation took flight starting with the Wright brothers.

Instead nuclear power plants became more expensive to operate and build, and safety considerations loomed larger—especially after the 1979 accident at Three Mile Island in Pennsylvania and the 1986 Chernobyl disaster in Russia. U.S. utility companies, which stopped ordering nuclear power plants after Three Mile Island, have been planning to build more, but that will be slowed down by the 2011 Fukushima incident in Japan.

The Information Revolution

Of course while space travel and nuclear power were falling short of expectations, there was one enormous technological breakthrough: computers. In 1971 Intel created the first microprocessor—a computer on a chip—for use in a Japanese calculator. In 1977 Apple, led by Steve Jobs and Steve Wozniak, introduced the Apple II, the first real mass-market personal computer. IBM produced the IBM PC in 1981, using an operating system from Microsoft, then a small, unknown company.

These events created enormous excitement and press attention at the time. The new companies and their inventions also produced a generation of

MOORE'S LAW
The historical pattern that microprocessors double their performance every 18–24 months.

billionaires and multibillionaires, led by Bill Gates, the founder of Microsoft. Yet economists were justifiably skeptical about personal computers' impact on the economy. At the time there was no sign they were really changing how business was done or helping the United States compete better in global markets. They seemed more like toys.

But electronic devices grew smaller, faster, cheaper, and more powerful each year, following **Moore's law.** Named for Geoffrey Moore, one of the founders of Intel, Moore's law says that microprocessors double their performance every 18–24 months. That is, with the same resources, over time we can do a lot more computing. In rough terms, as Figure 15.1 shows, today's personal computers are 10,000 times more powerful than the ones available in 1980.

Sometime in the early 1990s, computers became powerful enough to make a real difference in the economy. This advance ignited the **information revolution,** which means the application of the additional processing capacity of the new generation of computers to a wide variety of new uses. These included sophisticated financial models for banks and Wall Street firms, corporate databases for retailers and manufacturers, and computer games of all sorts.

FIGURE 15.1   How Fast Can We Compute?

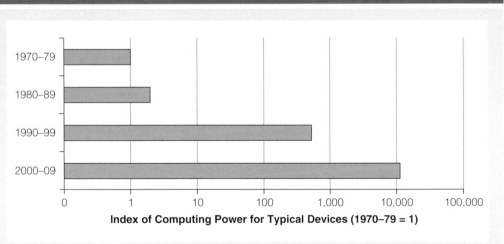

The modern era of computing started in the 1970s, with the invention of the microprocessor and the introduction of the Apple II, the first mass-market personal computer. By one measure, today's computers are 10,000 times more powerful than those early devices.

Source: W. Nordhaus, "Two Centuries of Productivity Growth in Computing," *Journal of Economic History,* March 2007.

HOW IT WORKS: E-COMMERCE

One of the most important uses of the Internet is for e-commerce: buying and selling over the Web. More and more retail sales are conducted via the Internet, and virtually every business of any size has a website. Even when actual sales are made in person, shoppers use the Internet to collect information beforehand.

Still, e-commerce is relatively small. According to the Census Bureau, e-commerce sales in the fourth quarter of 2010 came to only 4.3 percent of total retail sales. That makes sense: There are so many things, such as gasoline, that simply can't be bought online.

However, e-commerce is growing quickly. Between the fourth quarter of 2007 and the fourth quarter of 2010, e-commerce sales grew by 22 percent. Meanwhile, the rest of retail sales fell by 1 percent. If this pattern persists, e-commerce will take a larger and larger share of the retail sales total.

Perhaps most important, as computers became faster, they revolutionized communications. The Internet is based on the idea that information of any sort—a Web page, an e-mail message, a picture—can be broken into little packets of information and routed to the right destination. This sort of networking would not be possible without very fast computers.

Similarly, fast and cheap computing was the essential factor behind the development of the iPhone, which would not have been possible in 1985 or even 1995. Nor would YouTube, which depends on fast communications to let users upload and view online videos. And most important, globalization could not have come about without the fast, cheap communications that let customer service representatives in India answer calls from customers in Idaho.

THREE TYPES OF INNOVATION

Our society and our economy have been shaped by technological change and innovation. Yet not all innovations have the same degree of impact. In fact, we can identify three different channels by which technological change and innovations can affect businesses and consumers—and thus the economy.

Productivity Enhancements

Suppose Toyota figures out how to produce cars with fewer parts or with fewer steps on the assembly line. Then it can produce and sell the same number of cars as before at a lower cost. This is an example of a **productivity-enhancing innovation.**

> **PRODUCTIVITY-ENHANCING INNOVATION**
> Technological change that shifts the supply curve to the right.

In general, a productivity-enhancing innovation in an industry gives you more of the same product, holding fixed the resources used. That has the effect of shifting the supply curve to the right. The reason is that businesses can afford to produce more output for the same cost, typically reducing the market price and increasing the quantity sold in the market.

Productivity-enhancing innovations can be small and gradual—or large and disruptive. The small ones are common because companies are forever tinkering with their operations to cut

Economic Milestone

1935 FIRST SYNTHETIC FIBER

Chemists at DuPont learned how to turn coal into a silk-like fiber they called *nylon*. Within a few years nylon and other synthetic fibers were being used in parachutes and women's stockings. In toothbrushes they replaced boar's hair bristles. Soon the production and use of synthetic fibers had become a multibillion-dollar industry.

costs or boost output. Such small innovations don't change the nature of the final product or service, though sometimes they reduce its cost a bit. There hasn't been a huge change in cars in 40 years despite many cumulative innovations in design and engineering: They still perform the same functions as they did before power steering and automatic transmissions, for instance, and they still get you there in roughly the same time.

However, some productivity-enhancing innovations can have a major impact across the entire economy. Computers and electricity are general-purpose technologies that we can apply in almost every industry to boost output and lower costs. Electricity enables energy to be generated in one place and distributed, quietly and safely, to light homes and offices, to run labor-saving motors and machinery, and to power refrigerators. Computers and the miniaturization of data storage devices have changed almost every aspect of our public and private lives, from communication to banking to entertainment.

New Goods and Services

A second kind of technological change yields the **creation of new goods and services,** enabling people to do things that weren't possible before. These are not mere improvements but spectacular jumps forward that change daily life. Television, for example—the beaming of live pictures into the home—had no analogue in the past. Now it eats up an average of over two hours per day for adults (three hours per day on weekends!).

Or consider the cell phone. On one level it's just another way to make a phone call, something that has been possible since 1876. But on another level the portability of the cell phone lets us be permanently connected to the communications grid no matter where we are. That's a major change in how we live our lives, as evidenced by the number of people who walk through the streets with their phones pressed to their ears. Additionally, smartphones, such as the iPhone, are powerful enough to substitute for computers in many applications.

And what about the combination of the Internet and a powerful search engine such as Google? Together the two enable you to do incredibly fast searches, at no cost, across an enormous set of information. In theory if you had enough money or time, you could have done something similar in the past by poring through library stacks and reading endless rolls of microfilm. But the truth is that the Google–Internet combination is a truly new service that was not available before.

Some innovations fit more than one category: They both enhance productivity *and* provide new goods and services. In the early part of the 20th century, as electricity became more common, it replaced other forms of power in factories. This was productivity-enhancing because electricity cut costs without changing what the factories produced. But electricity also created the opportunity for firms to produce new goods and services, such as elevators and escalators, that did not exist before.

Quality of Life

A **qualify-of-life innovation** does exactly what it says: enhance the quality of life for you and those around you. The clearest example is an improvement in healthcare technology that lets you or your loved ones live

CREATION OF NEW GOODS AND SERVICES
Technological change that lets people do things they could not do before.

QUALITY-OF-LIFE INNOVATION
Technological change that enhances the quality-of-life for you *and* for those around you.

Economic Milestone

1941 FIRST TV COMMERCIAL

The Bulova Watch Company ran a short ad before the television broadcast of a Brooklyn Dodgers–Philadelphia Phillies baseball game. Bulova paid less than $10 for the 20-second spot, which was the first TV commercial. By providing television stations with a source of revenue, commercials turned the innovation of television into a rapidly expanding business.

SPOTLIGHT: THE BIOTECH REVOLUTION

The next big wave of innovation may come from *biotechnology,* which is the use of new techniques to modify living cells and biological molecules. Scientists have labored hard in recent years, and there have have been enormous advances in this area. These include the decoding of the human genome; a much deeper understanding of how the human body works; and the ability to manipulate the internal workings of cells. Stem cell research (an intensely controversial topic) is generally considered part of biotechnology as well.

Biotech has the potential to allow enormous breakthroughs in medical care, agriculture, and even energy. In theory, once we know the underlying workings of the human body, it should be possible for us to create drugs or treatments targeted directly at any medical or genetic problems. We could even create new plants that are more efficient at turning sunlight into usable fuel, or converting garbage into power.

However, so far biotech has promised a lot more than it has delivered. The first biotech drug arrived on the market in 1982, and since then there have been a fair number of success stories but no big blockbusters. There has been no biotech equivalent of Google.

Should we be pessimistic about this progress? Not necessarily. Remember that the microprocessor was invented in 1971, and for the next 20 years economists regularly complained that it wasn't having much of an impact on the economy. Indeed, Nobel Prize–winning economist Robert Solow wrote in 1987, "You can see the computer age everywhere but in the productivity statistics."

It wasn't until the mid-1990s—25 years after the first microprocessor was made—that the information revolution took off. The lesson is that new technologies mature slowly. Biotech, despite all its grandiose promises and failures, may only now be getting to the point where it will make a big difference.

longer or better. For example, Alzheimer's disease—a debilitating form of dementia involving loss of memory and alterations to thinking—currently afflicts 4 million U.S. adults, mostly the elderly, and that number is likely to rise quickly as the population ages. Right now there is no cure. But if medical science could produce a way of even reducing the severity of Alzheimer's, that would be a tremendous quality-of-life innovation (for a source of possible innovations in healthcare, see "Spotlight: The Biotech Revolution").

Technological advances that reduce pollution also fall into the category of quality-of-life innovations. Less pollution does not necessarily show up in any of the usual measures of economic output (as we will see in Chapter 19). Nevertheless, most people prefer a cleaner environment for its health benefits, for the beauty of nature and the safety of wildlife it

enhances, and for its beneficial impact on our planet's ecology.

What's the difference between a quality-of-life innovation you enjoy and an ordinary innovation that gives you pleasure—say a new generation of iPads? In the language of Chapter 6, a quality-of-life innovation generates *positive externalities* or reduces *negative externalities.* Diminishing pollution affects many people simultaneously. Similarly, an improvement in the health of a parent will improve our quality of life as well.

INNOVATIVE ACTIVITIES
Economic activities directed primarily at creating and developing new products, processes, ideas, knowledge, and technology.

INNOVATIVE ACTIVITIES

Where do innovations come from? They don't simply fall out of the sky. Instead innovation and technological change are the direct result of **innovative activities.** Those

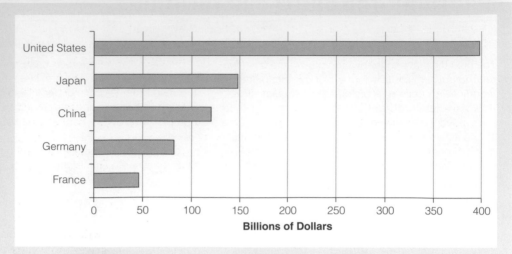

FIGURE 15.2 | **The United States Leads in R&D Spending, 2008**

If research and development were a sport, the United States would be a gold medal winner. This chart shows the top five countries in the world, ranked by spending on R&D. In fact, the United States spends more than the other four countries combined.

Source: The Organisation for Economic Cooperation and Development (OECD), www.oecd.org.

are any economic activities directed primarily at creating and developing new products, processes, ideas, knowledge, and technology. One example of an innovative activity would be a scientist studying the biochemistry underlying cancer. Another example would be an automobile company devoting resources to developing a fully electric car. Still another example would be an entrepreneur starting a new company to develop a new type of microprocessor, or a company employing programmers and artists to create a new video game.

The amount of money available for **research and development (R&D)** is the most important measure of the amount of innovative activities going on in an economy. R&D represents money and resources—particularly human resources—that economies or businesses devote to science and technology. It can be undertaken by corporations, by the government, or by scholars in academic settings. Corporate funding for the development of a new drug, for example, comes under the heading of R&D. So does a government research grant to a physics professor for the study of superconductors. In sum, R&D is anything that moves the frontier of science and technology forward.

Figure 15.2 shows that in 2008 the United States spent $398 billion on R&D. Measured by total dollars, the United States is by far the largest spender on R&D in the world, accounting for roughly one-third of all R&D money. The next largest is Japan, followed by China, though there is debate about whether such Chinese spending is being correctly measured. Most countries spend little on R&D.

In 2008 the United States spent $69 billion on **basic research,** which is devoted to scientific investigations that have no immediately obvious commercial applications. In the past, big companies like AT&T and IBM did basic research in their labs. For example, two researchers at AT&T's Bell Labs, Arno A. Penzias and Robert W. Wilson, won the 1978 Nobel Prize in physics for their discovery of faint background radiation remaining from the "big bang" explosion that is believed to have given birth to the universe.

Today, however, basic research is performed mostly in universities and nonprofit institutions and is funded primarily by the federal government. Corporations, under much more intense competitive pressure, have focused their attention on applied research and development. **Applied research** is scientific research focused on solving real-world problems, while **development** is aimed at creating commercial products. For example, if a pharmaceutical company spends heavily to test different approaches for fighting cancer, that is applied research. But testing a particular drug counts as development.

The Market for Innovative Activities

Traditionally economists have treated technological change as a kind of black box, driven by nonmarket factors such as government funding for R&D. To some extent that's still true. In particular, spending on basic R&D, which has no immediate economic payoff, is money that must come mainly from the government or from universities.

But in many other cases we can think about innovative activity as a service that can be bought and sold in a market, just like any other service (Figure 15.3). First, innovative activities have a price. The price of research, for example, might be the salary for a scientist for the year and the price of renting or buying the equipment. Or imagine that rather than trying to create new products by itself, a frozen-food business pays a scientific research laboratory to do its development (such firms exist—for example, SRI International, with about $500 million in revenues per year). In that case, the price of innovative activities is the amount the frozen-food company pays per month to the scientific research firm.

The **supply curve for innovative activities** tells us the quantity of innovative activities that are supplied, given their price. For example, given the wages paid to scientists, the supply curve tells us how many people will be available for science and engineering jobs, as opposed to law or other occupations.

Similarly, the **demand curve for innovative activities** tells us the quantity of innovative activities businesses will want to fund, given the price. For example, given the wages paid to engineers and scientists, the demand curve tells us how many resources a business is willing to devote to creating a new product. The willingness to spend on knowledge creation, of course, depends on how much profit the business can expect to make from the new product, and whether it's easy for competitors to copy.

Consider, for example, the market for research into cancer-fighting drugs. The price of research is the amount of money a business pays for, say, one year's worth of research by a scientist. The greater the price, the more scientists will move into anticancer research, so the supply curve slopes up. Meanwhile, the higher the price of such research, the less of it drug companies will want to buy. Hence the demand curve for innovative activities slopes down. For another example of the market for innovative activities, see "Spotlight: Private Space Tourism."

How does this market-based view of innovation help us? It tells us that if we want more innovation, we should look at factors that shift the supply and demand curves. That's what we will look at in the next two sections.

FIGURE 15.3 The Supply and Demand of Innovative Activities

This figure shows supply and demand curves for innovative activities. The price might be the salary for a scientist, and the quantity might be the number of scientists employed.

Supply curve for innovative activities

Demand curve for innovative activities

Price of Innovative Activities

Quantity of Innovative Activities Supplied and Demanded

SPOTLIGHT: PRIVATE SPACE TOURISM

For an example of the market for innovative activities in action, consider private space travel. Since the first manned space flights in 1961, space travel had been solely the responsibility of government agencies, mainly in the United States and Russia. These agencies did not operate by markets. Instead they were willing to spend tens of billions of dollars to put people into space for both prestige and research.

Private businesses could not afford that kind of money. For private space travel to become a reality, it had to become a lot cheaper than government-funded space travel—and just as safe. For years that didn't seem possible.

But recently, two sets of market forces converged to make private space travel possible. First, there is suddenly greater demand for private space travel by a long line of rich individuals willing to pay big bucks to go into space. That made it more attractive to research relatively inexpensive space travel. Second, new materials made it possible to build a safe spacecraft more cheaply.

In other words, both the demand and supply curves for the development of relatively inexpensive space travel shifted to the right. The result was far more research into private space travel. In 2004 a spacecraft called *SpaceShipOne* became the first privately funded, manned spacecraft to arrive in space at an altitude of more than 70 miles. (In the process, it won a $10 million prize.)

This showed that private space travel was possible. Now Virgin Galactic—a company started by Virgin Atlantic owner Richard Branson—has a long waiting list of people willing to pay $200,000 for a six-minute trip into space. Test flights have started, and a "spaceport" is being built in New Mexico.

See Virgin Galatic, www.virgingalactic.com, for more information.

INNOVATION: THE SUPPLY SIDE

In this section we will look more closely at factors that can move the supply curve for innovative activities. These include the availability of scientists and engineers, availability of venture capital, and

location in an innovation cluster. In the next section we'll also examine the factors that can cause the demand curve for innovative activities to shift.

Availability of Scientists and Engineers

A key factor affecting the supply curve for innovative activities is the availability of scientists and engineers—the people who perform actual research and development. That's consistently a problem in the United States because the number of people getting PhDs in science and engineering has not kept up with demand.

Part of the problem is simply that wages for scientists and engineers have not risen as fast as the wages for other occupations a highly educated person can enter. According to one survey, the median salary 10–14 years after getting a doctorate is $80,000 for a biologist, $75,000 for an earth scientist, and $93,000 for a chemist. That's quite low considering that these people

FIGURE 15.4 | How Immigration Affects the Market for Engineers and Scientists

An increase in immigrant engineers and scientists pushes the supply curve for engineers and scientists to the right and lowers their wage.

Supply curve for native-born scientists and engineers

Supply curve for scientists and engineers including immigrants

Demand curve for scientists and engineers

Wage for Scientists and Engineers

W
W'

E E'

Employed Scientists and Engineers

typically had to study for five or more years to get a PhD. In comparison, a smart student can get a law degree or an MBA and earn much more with fewer years of education.

As a result, many members of the scientific and engineering workforce in the United States are originally from other countries. Some enter the United States as graduate students and remain here to work; others come because they are offered jobs.

There's a heated debate about whether the immigration of skilled scientists and engineers is a good thing for the United States. On the one hand, it pushes the supply schedule of the market for scientists and engineers to the right, lowering the pay of U.S. scientists and engineers, as shown in Figure 15.4. On the other hand, it raises the number of engineers and scientists, which pushes the supply schedule for innovation to the right and increases the amount of innovation, as shown in Figure 15.5. The net result, as is true for most types of foreign trade, is that the influx of foreign-born scientists and engineers is probably a good thing for the country as a whole, but is problematic for a subgroup of the population.

Availability of Venture Capital

It doesn't do any good to have a bright idea if you can't support yourself and a small staff to develop it. And banks typically won't lend money to brand new businesses without a track record of profits.

One solution to this problem is *venture capital*, which we discussed in Chapter 13. Venture capital funds collect money from insurance companies, pension funds, college endowments, and wealthy individuals, and they invest those funds in high-risk technology start-up companies. Venture capitalists closely monitor the start-up companies they invest in, help them with key strategic decisions, and even replace the company founders if it looks like they are not up to the task.

FIGURE 15.5 | How Immigration Affects Innovation

Immigration increases the supply of engineers and scientists, which pushes the supply curve for innovative activities to the right. The result is more and cheaper innovation.

Supply curve for innovative activities

Supply curve for innovative activities, including immigrant scientists and engineers

Demand curve for innovative activities

Price of Innovative Activities

P
P'

I I'

Quantity of Innovative Activities

Venture capitalists expect that most of their investments will not create successful companies. In fact, they accept a failure rate that would make a banker's hair turn gray. Most companies funded by venture capitalists never become profitable, and eventually close.

However, the big successes—starting with Intel and running through Yahoo! and Google—are truly impressive and make up for many failures. Venture capitalists who invested in Google, for example, made quite a bit of money. Over the past 20 years, the average return on venture capital investments has been around 16 percent per year, compared to about 10 percent for the stock market.

The availability of venture capital has the effect of shifting the supply schedule for innovation to the right. What's interesting is that venture capital itself is actually a relative innovation in the financial markets. The first modern venture capital fund was started in 1946. Other countries have some venture capital, but far less than in the United States.

Location in an Innovation Cluster

If you list some of the great tech companies of the world, a healthy share of them started in the area south of San Francisco now known as Silicon Valley. Two engineers named Gordon Moore and Bob Noyce founded Intel in 1968 in Santa Clara, California, then a sleepy little town about 20 minutes south of Stanford University. Google has its headquarters in Mountain View, the next town north of Santa Clara, and Facebook is based in Palo Alto, just a bit closer to San Francisco.

It's not simply coincidence. The chances of innovations occurring seem to improve when innovative companies are clustered together because they can share ideas and workers. A pool of skilled and experienced labor moves from company to company. There are good resources, like lawyers who understand technology and start-ups. And there are sources of financial support, like nearby venture capital firms.

In addition, innovation is easier when there is a major university nearby. Google and Yahoo!

INNOVATION CLUSTER

A region where the resources for innovation are plentiful so that the supply curve for innovative activities is shifted to the right.

were both started by Stanford students. Other technology hot spots include Cambridge, Massachusetts, which has become the world center for biotech, and Bangalore, which has become the center for software in India.

In other words, an **innovation cluster** is a region where the resources for innovation are plentiful so that the supply curve for innovative activities is shifted to the right. As a result, innovation is easier for a business located in an innovation cluster like Silicon Valley.

Once innovation clusters get started, they tend to persist. Silicon Valley, for example, has retained its magic. Some of the hottest new companies, like YouTube, have started there in recent years (see Table 15.1). The power of clustering continues.

TABLE 15.1

Some Top Silicon Valley Companies

Below is a partial list of major tech companies headquartered in the Silicon Valley/San Francisco region of California. The list spans Hewlett-Packard, founded in 1939, to YouTube, founded in 2005. Facebook was originally started in Cambridge, Massachusetts, but currently has its headquarters in Palo Alto, California.

Company	Date Founded
Apple	1976
Cisco	1984
eBay	1995
Electronic Arts	1982
Facebook	2004
Google	1998
Hewlett-Packard	1939
Intel	1968
Intuit	1983
Linden Lab (Second Life)	1999
Oracle	1977
Yahoo!	1994
YouTube*	2005

*Bought by Google in 2006.

INNOVATION: THE DEMAND SIDE

The demand for innovative activities is a tricky thing to measure. Everybody likes the newest or best technology—unless your job is being eliminated by automation, or your home is threatened by pollution from a new factory down the street, or your scenic view is blocked by energy-generating windmills. The truth is that it's not unusual for new technologies to face opposition—from existing companies, from workers who feel their jobs are threatened, or simply from ordinary people who don't like change.

That's why technological change needs to be propelled by a strong force—which usually is the profit motive. What sustains innovation is the fact that businesses can make money from it. Although in theory the government can fund and encourage innovative activities, in practice no society has been able to sustain a commitment to innovation over a long period without the profit motive.

So let's look at the factors that can determine the demand curve for innovative activities.

Return and Risk from Innovative Activities

The demand for innovative activities is closely tied to their ability to create profits for companies and benefits to society. Economic studies repeatedly show that the **return from innovative activities**—that is, the long-term payback to businesses from spending on research, development, and all sorts of other activities that have the potential of producing innovations—is very high. For example, a dollar spent on R&D can yield an average return of 25–50 percent per year. That's excellent. By comparison, the average annual return from investing in the stock market is about 10 percent.

However, most corporate executives view R&D spending with trepidation because the chances of failure are so high. Although the return on R&D spending is high, all sorts of things can go wrong when you try something new. In other words, the **risk from innovative activities**—the possibility that spending on R&D and other innovative activities will not pay off—is high.

The pharmaceutical industry understands the risk of innovative activity well. Drug companies

start with literally thousands of compounds they have reason to think might be good candidates to treat illness. Then each compound goes through a multistep, multiyear process including laboratory evaluation, animal testing, testing on humans, and then clinical trials to see whether the new drug safely does what it's supposed to do and is measurably more effective than existing treatments. At any step along the way, a proposed compound can fail expensively, and many do. In the end, very few successful new drugs are introduced each year.

Corporate executives have another reason for being reluctant to put money into R&D and other innovative activities. In many cases the company that pays for research may not get all or even most of the benefits. The private return from innovative activities is the gain to the original company sponsoring the research, while the social return from innovation is the benefit to the whole economy. In general, the social return will be much greater than the private return because it's difficult to keep good ideas fenced in.

Xerox is a classic example of a company that came up with great ideas but reaped little benefit from them. In the 1970s the Rochester, New York–based company had a research facility in Palo Alto, California, that helped develop many great innovations for the personal computer, including the mouse and the graphical user interface. But Xerox, mainly focused on copiers at the time, was slow to take advantage of these innovations. Instead Apple and Microsoft developed the graphical user interface and made big money from it. The social return to innovation was very high in this case, and the private return to the original inventor was low or practically zero.

Patents and Other Intellectual Property Protection

Companies are more likely to invest in creating innovative new products and services if they can make money with them. And making money is more likely if they can protect their innovation from being copied, at least for a while. For this reason, the United States and other developed countries have several different means of **intellectual property protection**—that is, laws that make it difficult to copy innovations.

The most important means of protection against copying is a **patent,** granted by the U.S. Patent and Trademark Office (USPTO) to a person who "who invents or discovers any new and useful process, machine, manufacture, or composition of matter, or any new and useful improvement thereof." Such a patent is a grant from the government that allows an inventor to control the use of his or her innovation for a set period, currently 20 years. In particular, the inventor has the "the right to exclude others from making, using, offering for sale, or selling the invention throughout the United States."

Inventions protected by patents run the gamut from very important to totally weird. In the 1800s Thomas Edison patented the electric lightbulb, the microphone used in telephones, the phonograph, and the motion picture camera. AT&T patented the transistor, which was invented in AT&T's Bell Labs in 1948. More recently a researcher patented embryonic stem cells. More oddly, patent #6960975 was granted to "a space vehicle propelled by the pressure of inflationary vacuum state"—in other words, an anti-gravity device.

Patents have two purposes. First, they allow an inventor to benefit from innovation by making it harder for others to duplicate it. If you have a patent on an invention, no one can use your invention without your permission until the patent runs out.

The second purpose of a patent is to encourage inventors to share ideas with the rest of society. You can license your invention to others, allowing them to use it, and collect royalties from them (a share in their profits). Without patents, you might be tempted to conceal your idea to protect it from imitators.

The transistor patent is an interesting case. The three scientists credited with inventing the transistor won a Nobel Prize for their achievement, but their employer, AT&T, never got any economic benefits. At the time the company was fighting an antitrust suit, and it was sensitive about its public image. AT&T was therefore willing to license the patent rights to the transistor for a relatively low fee. Then as part of the 1956 settlement of the antitrust suit, it let anyone use the transistor patent without charge.

Thomas Edison at work.

Intensity of Competition

Remember from Chapter 5 that in a competitive market, companies with a lower cost curve drive out ones with a higher cost curve over the long run. If you have an innovation that allows you to offer the same or better product at a lower cost, you'll be more successful in the marketplace.

Innovation is one of the key ways to get a competitive advantage. Boeing gets more orders by creating more fuel-efficient airplanes than the ones sold by Airbus. One computer manufacturer gets an advantage by designing a computer that is faster and cheaper than those of its rivals.

Thus a key factor driving demand for innovative activities is **intensity of competition**. One of the most important benefits of economic competition is that it spurs faster creation and adoption of new technology by both existing firms and new firms. Let's be blunt: most companies would avoid the risk of innovation activity if they did not face the threat of competition.

A note of caution here: if a market is close to pure competition, profits may be low. If so, no companies may have enough extra money to spend on long-run research. What's more, rivals may immediately copy any new ideas that one company comes up with. As a result, economists sometimes worry that too much competition may slow down technological change.

The Diffusion of New Technologies

If you buy a sandwich and eat it, nobody else can eat it. In contrast, if you spend money developing a new technology, the knowledge you create can be used by someone else as long as it is not restricted by a patent.

Technological diffusion is the process by which new ideas spread from one person or business to other parts of the economy. It sometimes seems as if any successful idea is immediately picked up and imitated by competitors. The initial success of *American Idol* in 2002, for example, quickly brought forth all sorts of competitors, like *America's Next Top Model* (started in 2003), *The Apprentice* (started in 2004), and so forth.

However, in most areas of the economy, technological diffusion takes longer than in entertainment. In medicine, for example, it takes a long time for doctors to adopt new and better

HOW IT WORKS: INNOVATION AND YOUTH

It often seems as if young people adopt new technologies faster than middle-aged or older workers. In part that's because the young have more malleable minds. But there are also economic reasons why young workers get more benefits from spending time learning something new.

Think about it this way. A 25-year-old worker can expect to be in the labor force for another 40 years. A 55-year-old worker can expect to be employed for another 10 or so years. That means the young worker will get many more years of benefits from learning how to use, say, instant messaging. That's a big economic incentive.

In addition, the 55-year-old worker is typically paid more. That means the opportunity cost of his or her time is higher than for the 25-year-old. So the older worker gets lower benefits and higher costs from spending time learning a new technology. That helps explain why many older workers seem to lag in adopting current innovations.

treatments, even for common problems such as strokes and heart attacks.

The same thing is true in corporations. Economic studies show wide differences between the productivity levels of different factories making the same products. Some people and companies are more willing to take the risk of adopting a new technology, whereas others wait until that new technology is mature (see "How It Works: Innovation and Youth"). It can take 10, 20, even 30 years before an innovation spreads through the whole economy. The process of technological diffusion is slow and gradual.

CONCLUSION

It's impossible to imagine what today's economy would be like without technological change, globalization, and financial markets, the topics of this chapter and the previous two. The most vivid example is the Internet, which was tiny 15 years ago and now pervades our entire lives. At the same time, our ties to other countries have transformed the whole economy, while the ups and downs of the financial markets have had a pervasive impact.

In particular, change affects all of us in our working lives—what type of work we do, how we are paid, who hires us, how we spend our days. In the next chapter we will examine the labor market, which is one of the most important markets in the economy. That will help us better understand why some people are gaining from financial markets, globalization, and technological change, while others seem to be worse off.

15 SUMMARY

1. Technological change is the introduction to the market of new goods and services, or new processes of production, that did not exist before. Without technological change, it's impossible to get big increases in living standards. The most recent wave of technological change was the information revolution. Following Moore's law, electronic devices get smaller, cheaper, faster, and more powerful every year. *(LO15-1)*

2. Three types of innovation are productivity enhancements, the creation of new goods and services, and quality-of-life improvements. *(LO15-2)*

3. Traditionally economists have treated technological change as a kind of black box, driven by nonmarket factors. But it has become clear in recent years that the creation of new knowledge is an economic activity or service that can be bought and sold just like any other service. Innovative activities are any economic activities directed primarily at creating and developing new ideas, new knowledge, and new technology. *(LO15-3)*

4. Innovative activities can be bought and sold in the market. The supply curve for innovative activities tells us the quantity of innovative activities that are supplied, given their price. The supply curve for innovative activities can be affected by the availability of scientists and engineers, access to venture capital, and location. *(LO15-4)*

5. Similarly, the demand curve for innovative activities tells us the quantity of innovative activities that businesses will want to fund, given the price. The demand curve for innovative activities can be affected by the return from innovative activities, by patents and other forms of intellectual property protection, and by the intensity of competition. Unlike ordinary goods and services—which can be consumed by only one buyer—new technologies and ideas can spread from one person or business to the rest of the economy. *(LO15-5)*

KEY TERMS AND CONCEPTS

technological change

innovations

Moore's law

information revolution

productivity-enhancing innovation

creation of new goods and services

quality-of-life innovation

innovative activities

research and development (R&D)

basic research

applied research

development

supply curve for innovative activities

demand curve for innovative activities

innovation cluster

return from innovative activities

risk from innovative activities

intellectual property protection

patent

intensity of competition

technological diffusion

PROBLEMS

1. Which of the following is not a benefit of technological change? *(LO15-1)*

   a) Improved living standards.

   b) Faster growth.

   c) Longer work hours.

   d) Longer lives.

2. Suppose that Moore's law no longer was true, so that microprocessor performance stopped improving. For each of the following statements, say whether the end of Moore's law would make it more or less likely. *(LO15-1)*

   a) Cell phones getting smaller.

   b) The cost of Internet service rising.

   c) The creation of new companies like Facebook.

   d) Supermarkets charging a fee for using a credit card.

3. Say whether each of the following is mainly a productivity-enhancing innovation, a creation of new goods and services, or a quality-of-life innovation. Explain. *(LO15-2)*

   a) A car that emits less pollution.

   b) A car that uses less gasoline.

   c) A drug that cures lung cancer.

   d) A teleportation device that can move you instantaneously from one spot to another.

4. Which of the following represents an increase in innovative activity? Explain. *(LO15-3)*

   a) A drug company hires more scientists to work on a new cancer drug.

   b) A department store hires more sales clerks.

   c) A university buys faster computers for its research labs.

   d) An automobile manufacturer tells its engineers to figure out how to reduce the cost of car production.

5. U.S. companies are opening research facilities in China and India, where the lower cost of labor lets them hire more scientists and engineers. Consider a company trying to develop the next generation of cell phones. *(LO15-3)*

    a) Draw the supply and demand curves for innovative activities directed toward the development of new cell phones.

    b) Suppose the company moves some of the development of new cell phones to China and India. Does this affect the supply curve or the demand curve for innovative activities? Show the change on your supply–demand diagram.

    c) What happens to the quantity of innovative activity when new research centers open abroad? Do we get more or fewer new models of cell phones?

6. There's a very heavy concentration of biotechnology firms in the Boston area, closely attached to the Massachusetts Institute of Technology. This concentration of biotech is usually considered one of the premier innovation clusters in the United States. If you were starting a new biotech company, which of the following would be an advantage of locating in the Boston area? *(LO15-4)*

    a) A large pool of well-trained scientists.

    b) Warm climate.

    c) Lack of competition from other companies in the same industry.

    d) Easy access to special technical equipment.

7. Suppose that a drug company spends $1 billion developing a new treatment that potentially cures cancer. *(LO15-4)*

    a) Is the private return from this innovative activity is best measured by increased life expectancy for patients, or by higher profits for the drug company?

    b) Is the social return from this innovative activity is best measured by increased life expectancy for patients, or by higher profits for the drug company?

8. Imagine that a company has a monopoly on video game sales in a country. That is, it is the only company allowed to develop and sell new video games. The company has a choice: it can spend $100,000 to slightly update its best-selling game, or $100 million to write a completely new game, which might or might not be a success. *(LO15-5)*

    a) As a monopolist, explain which choice the company might make.

    b) Now suppose the video game company faces new competition in the form of a hot new game imported from another country. Explain which choice the company might make.

9. Suppose workers are going to retire at a higher age and stay in the workforce longer. *(LO15-5)*

    a) Does the higher retirement age increase or decrease the willingness of workers to learn new technology?

    b) Does postponed retirement affect the supply curve or the demand curve for innovative activities? What happens to the quantity of innovative activities?

10. In February 2008, Speedo, the swimsuit manufacturer, launched a new model called the LZR Racer. The company boasted that it took three years of research and

development to design the swimsuit, which was intended to help swimmers go through the water faster. Within the first five months, competitive swimmers wearing the LZR had set 44 world records. As the result of all the good publicity, Speedo was able to sell the swimsuit to ordinary buyers for $550—much more than it could charge for its other swimsuits. *(LO15-5)*

a) What is the return to Speedo for all its spending?

b) Identify two risks for Speedo.

16 ECONOMICS OF THE LABOR MARKET

LEARNING OBJECTIVES

After reading this chapter, you should be able to:

LO16-1 Define the labor supply and demand curves.

LO16-2 Identify factors affecting labor market equilibrium.

LO16-3 Explain why different workers may receive different wages.

LO16-4 Describe effects of government regulation on the labor market.

LO16-5 Identify the forces driving long-term labor supply.

Technology and globalization are inexorably transforming the nature of work. Your bank no doubt has automatic tellers; your local supermarket may have self-service checkout counters; and most calls you make to businesses are probably answered by recorded voice mail rather than by real people. Manufacturing operations are increasingly moving to China, Eastern Europe, Mexico, and other low-wage countries. And more and more companies are taking their customer service operations to any country that can lay down a fiber optic communications cable and train English-speaking workers.

As this textbook is being revised in early 2011, Americans are struggling with high unemployment. Nevertheless, the Bureau of Labor Statistics reports that 59 percent of the U.S. adult population in 2010 still had jobs—about the same as the 57 percent who were employed 40 years ago.

The *labor market*—the buying and selling of the time and effort of different kinds of workers—is still the most indispensable market in the economy. There is no productive activity that does not require some input of labor. True, the nature of work changes: people become fashion designers rather than secretaries, network technicians rather than factory workers. But in the end, human input is essential for all productive activities.

Understanding the labor market, and how it evolves, is crucial for understanding the world we live in. In many respects the labor market functions the same way as the basic markets we described in Chapters 2 and 3. *Wages*—the price of labor—are set by the interaction between supply and demand, just like prices in the market for fruit or for homes.

But there is, of course, a big difference between fruit and people: people have rights, and unlike fruit they complain bitterly when they feel they've been unfairly treated. As a result, the labor market has some special characteristics, including rules regulating how many hours people can be required to work and the minimum wage they must be paid. In this chapter we will explore the nature of the labor market in the United States and the global economy. In addition, we will explain the similarities and differences between the labor market and the other markets we've studied so far.

THE BASICS OF THE LABOR MARKET

When you're looking for a job, it may feel as if the odds are against you. There are so few open positions, and so many applicants who want to be hired. A company advertising a desirable, high-paying job may receive hundreds or even thousands of résumés, especially when the economy is weak.

But turn the situation around, and imagine that you are a manager trying to fill an open position. You have a mental picture of the skills, experience, and personality the perfect job candidate will have. Yet that perfect person may be impossible to find, especially if you can't pay a high enough wage to get the sort of person you want. As a result, some positions may stay open for months or even years. In February 2011 U.S. businesses reported 3.1 million open positions, even though more than 13 million people were unemployed and searching for jobs.

SPOTLIGHT: THE RISE OF THE ONLINE JOB SEARCH

Employers with a job opening used to have limited options for filling it: they could put a help-wanted ad in the local newspaper, or they could ask friends and acquaintances whether they knew anyone who was qualified. Both avenues were chancy. Friends might not know anyone right for the job. And the best candidate might not read the newspaper that week—or worse, might live in a different city.

In 1994 a Boston area advertising executive named Jeff Taylor created an alternative: the Monster Board, an online site for matching job seekers with employers. At the beginning it listed about 200 job openings, but over time it grew. In 1999 the site was renamed Monster.com.

Monster.com and sites like it improve the job search process in two ways. First, they ensure that people looking for jobs and employers looking for workers are no longer geographically limited. If you live in South Dakota, you can look for jobs in San Francisco. Second, they make it much easier to search for the particular characteristics of the job or the job candidate you desire. In the end, this should result in faster, better job matches and a better-functioning labor market.

In some ways the labor market is a giant matching game in which job seekers hop from interview to interview, and managers roll prospective employees in and out of the office, with everyone looking for the right fit. The pain of matching is eased by such innovations as online job sites that make it easier to quickly scan many potential jobs and candidates. (See "Spotlight: The Rise of the Online Job Search.")

Economic Milestone

1969 THE SHORTEST STRETCH OF UNEMPLOYMENT

In 1969 workers without jobs were unemployed for less than eight weeks, on average. That's the shortest time on record. By contrast, in mid-2008 an unemployed person was out of work for an average of 17 weeks.

The Labor Supply Curve

What happens before the job search? Let's focus on the worker's side of the labor market first. The worker's first and most important decision is a simple one—should I look for a job or do something else? In other words, what is the opportunity cost of working? (In Chapter 2 we defined *opportunity cost* as the value or benefit of the next-best alternative use of time or money.) Remember that people have alternatives to working a steady job. For example, they can go to college or graduate school. They can stay home with their kids or grandkids. They can be supported by their parents or other relatives, or they can receive Social Security checks from the government. Or, especially if they are young or retired, they can travel or simply be at loose ends.

The **labor force** is the part of the adult population that is either working or actively looking for a job. An individual chooses whether to be in the labor force or not. The **labor force participation rate** is the share of the adult population that is in the labor force. In the United States as of March 2011, 70 percent of men and 58 percent of women 16 years old or over were in the labor force. These numbers reflect the reality that even today it is still socially more acceptable for women than for men to take off time from paid work, especially when raising children.

The **labor supply curve** tells us, given the wage, how many people are in the labor force—that is, working or looking for work (see Figure 16.1). Alternatively, it can tell us the total quantity of labor hours supplied (remember from Chapter 4 that labor can be measured by either people or hours). Generally speaking, the labor force participation rate of men between 25 and 54 is not very responsive to changes in pay. However, young people, women, and senior citizens are more likely to make decisions about whether to look for work based on the available pay. For example, the high-paying tech jobs of the 1990s caused many young people

| **FIGURE 16.1** | **Labor Market Supply and Demand** |

The intersection of the labor demand schedule and the labor supply schedule determines the equilibrium wage *W* and the equilibrium quantity of labor *L*.

Quantity of Labor (Number of Workers Demanded and Supplied)

LABOR SUPPLY CURVE
The line on a graph that reports, for each level of wages, how many people are in the labor force, or the total quantity of labor hours supplied.

to forgo graduate school and go directly to work for a tech firm. Then when the economy went into recession in 2001 and information technology companies experienced a sharp drop in demand, young people started applying to graduate schools instead. Similarly, the Great Recession increased the number of people who wanted to go to business schools.

The labor force participation rate of adults over 65—a growing part of the workforce—is sensitive to the wages they might receive. That makes sense: they are already receiving Social Security benefits and have a bit more flexibility about whether they work.

In some jobs, such as retailing, it's also possible to choose whether you work full-time or part-time. In these types of jobs, it is natural to write the labor supply curve in terms of the total quantity of working hours that people are willing to supply.

So if three people are willing to work half-time—20 hours per week—at the going wage, that would be 60 hours per week of labor supplied.

The next decision is usually about what kind of job to look for. This is the **job market decision.** If you have an accounting degree, for example, you could look for a job as an accountant. Or you could try to get work as a cashier, or a computer programmer, or a journalist, or an actor. Each of these jobs is in a different labor market.

Each labor market has its own labor supply curve. In its simplest form, the labor supply curve for a given job reports how many people are looking for that kind of job at a particular wage. (Or if we think of labor supply as measured in hours, the labor supply curve reports the total quantity of hours of labor people are willing to supply for that job at a particular wage.) The general rule is straightforward: if the wage for a job increases, more workers (or more hours) will be available for that job. This is the law of supply applied to the labor market.

Where do the additional workers come from? Some are lured into the labor market from other activities, such as schooling. Some switch from other lines of work. Schoolteachers sometimes become construction workers when the pay for construction climbs high enough. Economics and finance professors move into high-paying Wall Street jobs; journalists go into public relations. Government officials are hired at much higher pay by firms that lobby their former agencies.

The Labor Demand Curve

Recall from Chapter 4 that businesses choose how many workers to hire because they have identified the number of employees that will help maximize their profit. This may seem obvious, but plenty of employers, like governments and nonprofits, such as most hospitals, have goals other than profit when they hire workers.

Let's look inside the mind of a manager at a profit-making business deciding whether to hire an additional worker. On the plus side is the increased production or output that an extra worker generates. This is called the **marginal product of labor.** For example, the marginal product of an added worker in a hair salon is the additional haircuts the salon can provide because of that worker. The marginal product of an extra stockbroker is the additional trades he or she brings into the brokerage house.

The **marginal revenue** of an additional worker is the extra revenue his or her efforts add to the business. In the simplest case, the marginal revenue is equal to the price of the output times the marginal

LABOR DEMAND CURVE

A line on a graph that reports, for each level of wages, how many workers businesses will want to hire, or the quantity of labor hours demanded.

product. For example, if the marginal product of an additional hairdresser is six haircuts per day, and the price of a haircut is $20, then the marginal revenue from hiring that added hairdresser is $120 per day.

To make the hiring decision, a manager must compare the added revenue generated by an additional worker to the added cost of hiring that worker. The **marginal cost of labor** is the wage the company must pay the additional worker. (We will think of the wage as including the cost of **benefits,** such as employer-provided healthcare insurance, and other supplements to the basic paycheck.)

In the short run, economic logic calls for the manager to keep hiring workers as long as their marginal revenue exceeds the wages paid to the workers (including benefits). As long as that's true, the additional workers will add to the profit of the business.

For jobs where workers are hired by the hour, such as retail sales clerks or waiters, the marginal revenue of labor is the extra revenue from one more hour of labor, while the marginal cost of labor is the hourly wage. The same rule applies: managers will increase the quantity of hours demanded as long as marginal revenue exceeds marginal cost.

The **labor demand curve,** also shown in Figure 16.1, reports, for each level of wages, how many workers businesses will want to hire, or the quantity of labor hours demanded. Generally, as the wage rises, businesses will want to hire fewer workers or pay for fewer labor hours.

An Example of Labor Demand

Let's work through an example of labor demand, using the case of a hair salon, as mentioned back in Chapter 2. The first two columns of Table 16.1 give the salon's production function. The first column shows the number of hairdressers employed by the salon, while the second column, labeled output, gives the number of clients the salon can serve in a day (and assuming one haircut per client). The first hairdresser can take care of six customers in a day, and so can the second. A third hairdresser is a bit less productive because he keeps bumping into the other two and has to wait to use some of the equipment. These problems get a little

TABLE 16.1	The Labor Demand Decision

Here's how the owner of a hair salon might decide how many workers to hire, given the price of each haircut and the amount each worker gets paid. The rule is to keep hiring more workers as long as marginal revenue is greater than marginal cost

			If the Price Is $20 per Haircut		If Each Worker Gets Paid $90 per Day		
Labor (Number of Workers)	Output (Total Number of Haircuts per Day)	Marginal Product (Number of Haircuts per Additional Worker)	Total Revenue (Dollars)	Marginal Revenue (Dollars per Additional Worker)	Total Labor Cost (Dollars)	Marginal Labor Cost (Dollars per Additional Worker)	Profit (Dollars)
1	6	6	120	120	90	90	30
2	12	6	240	120	180	90	60
3	17	5	340	100	270	90	70
4	21	4	420	80	360	90	60
5	24	3	480	60	450	90	30

more severe with each added hairdresser. As a result, the marginal product per hairdresser falls as more hairdressers are hired.

Suppose the market price for haircuts is $20 per cut; that's cheap for many areas of the country. The fourth column shows the total revenue of the salon, assuming each client pays $20 per cut. The fifth column shows the marginal revenue from adding each additional worker. We can see that marginal revenue declines as more workers are hired. The marginal revenue of the first worker hired is $120, whereas the marginal revenue of the fifth worker is only $60.

That's the revenue side; what about the cost side? The Bureau of Labor Statistics reports that the average national wage for hairdressers and cosmetologists is $13 per hour. So let's suppose the market wage for hairdressers is roughly $90 for a seven-hour day ($13 × 7 = $91). The **market wage** is the prevailing normal wage for a particular type of job. Then the marginal cost of each additional worker is $90 per day.

The salon owner will want to hire additional hairdressers as long as they increase his or her profit. In other words, the marginal revenue has to exceed the marginal cost. Looking down the table columns, we see that marginal revenue ($120) exceeds marginal cost ($90) for the first worker. The same is true for the second and third workers. For the fourth worker, marginal revenue is less than marginal cost. So the profit-maximizing owner hires the first three hairdressers and politely says no to the fourth.

We can check this conclusion by a different route. If we subtract total cost from total revenue, what's left is profit. That's the far right column of the table. We can see that the salon reaches its maximum profit with three workers—precisely the same conclusion as before.

So now we know that if the wage is $90 per day, the firm will hire three workers. A similar calculation shows us that if the wage is $70 per day, the firm will hire four workers (because the marginal revenue of the fourth worker is $80, which is greater than the wage, but the marginal revenue of the fifth would be only $60). And if the wage is $110 per day, the firm's labor demand will be two workers (because the third worker has a marginal revenue of only $100). Higher wages lead to less hiring, and lower wages lead to more.

LABOR MARKET EQUILIBRIUM AND WAGES

We've seen that in the labor market managers are busy making hiring decisions, based on the going wage for a job. But where does that wage come from? In the world of economics, the answer is simple: the wage is set by the interaction of supply and demand in the labor market, just like any other market.

The basic mechanism is that the wage rises (or falls) to the point where the number of workers available for a particular type of job is just equal to the number of workers that businesses are willing to hire. That is the **labor market equilibrium** as shown in Figure 16.1. (We'll leave aside for the moment the fact that there are always some workers who are between jobs or unemployed.) Alternatively, for jobs that are hired by the hour, the labor market equilibrium is the wage at which the quantity of labor hours supplied is equal to the quantity of labor hours demanded.

The equilibrium wage W is affected by anything that affects the supply and demand curves, just as we described in Chapter 3. Consider, for example, the market for accountants in a city. The demand for accountants comes from accounting firms, companies that need accountants to do their books, ordinary people who need help with their taxes, and government agencies that need accountants to keep track of where the people's tax money is going. The supply of accountants includes people currently working as

> **LABOR MARKET EQUILIBRIUM**
> The wage at which the number of workers available is equal to the number of workers businesses are willing to hire. Alternatively, the wage at which the quantity of labor hours supplied is equal to the quantity of labor hours demanded.

accountants, new graduates with accounting degrees, and people working in other lines of work who have accounting training.

Let's suppose that the government passes legislation requiring companies to document all their financial decisions more closely. In fact, in 2002 Congress passed the Sarbanes–Oxley Act (known as Sarbox for short), which requires public corporations to meet much more rigorous financial accounting standards. To implement Sarbox, companies had to hire more accountants, which shifted the demand curve for accountants to the right (see Figure 16.2). The result of such a shift? The equilibrium wage rises from W to W', and the quantity of accountants rises from L to L'. In reality that's exactly what happened after the law was passed. Despite an overall weak labor market, the demand for accountants grew, pushing up salaries.

The Impact of Technological Change

Technological change can have a profound impact on both the labor supply schedule and the labor demand schedule. Think about the automobile, which came into widespread use in the early 1900s. Whole new job classifications were created that didn't exist before, including petroleum geologist, oil field worker, and gas station attendant. The demand for skilled mechanics increased dramatically because workers were needed who could repair the new "horseless carriages," which were prone to regular breakdowns. At the same time, the increasing use of automobiles *decreased* demand for some types of jobs, such as making saddles and harnesses for horses.

More generally, technology can be either a substitute or a complement for labor. Technology is a substitute for labor if businesses hire fewer workers at the same wage. Technology is a complement for labor if businesses hire more workers at the market wage. For example, a bulldozer is a substitute for unskilled labor because at any wage it dramatically reduces the demand for workers with shovels.

Or consider some more recent examples. The widespread use of automated telephone answering

FIGURE 16.2 | The Changing Labor Market for Accountants

The demand curve for accountants shifts to the right after the government increases requirements for financial reporting.

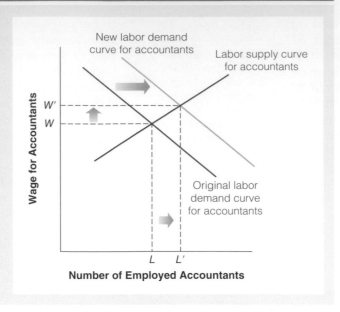

New labor demand curve for accountants

Labor supply curve for accountants

Wage for Accountants

W'
W

Original labor demand curve for accountants

L   L'

Number of Employed Accountants

systems—voice mail—dramatically reduces the need for secretaries and phone operators because a caller can leave a message without talking to a person. (See "Economic Milestone: The First Voice Mail System.") However, new technology can also *increase* the demand for certain kinds of workers. In the 1990s there was a great need for network specialists—the people who set up computer networks and keep them running.

The availability of online shopping is another example. It shifts the demand for labor in two ways. First, when you can buy clothes while sitting at your home computer, that reduces the quantity demanded of retail sales clerks—a substitution effect. On the other hand, it increases the demand for people who can program store

The speed of technological change has benefited educated workers.

Web sites, as well as for truck drivers to deliver the goods to your home.

Most recent technological innovations have acted as substitutes for low-skilled labor and complements for high-skilled labor. That is, the voice mail system eliminated the job of the secretary, but not the job of the manager. Factory automation reduced the number of assembly-line workers, but not the number of people needed to design and create new products. Web sites for buying airline tickets mean fewer reservation clerks are needed, but pilots are still in high demand.

The speed of technological change benefits educated workers. In eras of rapid change, businesses want workers who can learn new technologies quickly. That generally boosts the demand for educated workers, who find it easier to adapt.

But here's a question: Will future technological change continue to favor educated workers? Not necessarily. For decades, science fiction writers and technological prophets have speculated about artificial intelligence software that could take over the functions of human managers and professionals. So far the capabilities of artificial intelligence have fallen far short of such hopes. But as computers grow more powerful, there may come a generation of artificial intelligence programs smart enough to substitute for human judgment.

Economic Milestone

1975 THE FIRST VOICE MAIL SYSTEM

There was nearly a century between the invention of the telephone and the introduction of the first voice mail system. Maybe that was too little time: in a 1997 survey, U.S. adults called voice mail the number one technology that should never have been invented. Nevertheless, voice mail is one of the clearest examples of technology substituting for labor. It has transformed the staffing of many offices by reducing the need for assistants.

| FIGURE 16.3 | The Labor Pool Effect of Globalization |

Because a growing number of jobs can now be done overseas, U.S. companies face a supply curve for labor that has shifted to the right. Assuming no change in demand, that drives the equilibrium wage down from *W* to *W'*.

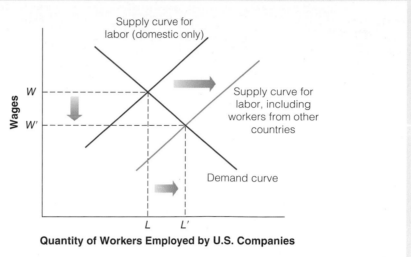

The Impact of Globalization

Historically most labor markets were local. After all, whether you were a manager, a factory worker, or a secretary, your employer expected you to physically show up at the place of business every day. But today globalization and advances in communication technology make it possible for multinational companies to hire and communicate with workers across the country or on the other side of the world. And these are not just low-level production jobs. More and more U.S. companies are having their research and development work done in Korea, Taiwan, China, or India.

As a result, when U.S. companies look to hire, they face a labor supply curve that has shifted to the right because a larger pool of workers is available globally for any job. We will call this the **labor pool effect** of globalization (see Figure 16.3). Assuming no change in demand, the labor pool effect causes wages in the United States to drop because U.S. companies can now employ low-wage workers in China, India, and other developing countries.

But globalization can also have a positive impact on labor demand because U.S. companies can produce not just for the U.S. market but for the German, Chinese, and Indian markets as well. As we saw in Chapter 14, most large U.S. companies, and many small ones, have tapped into overseas demand as a good way to increase sales.

We will call this the **market expansion effect** of globalization. Globalization means more potential customers, more potential sales—and potentially more labor demanded by U.S. companies. This translates into a rightward shift of the labor demand curve for U.S. companies, as shown in Figure 16.4. Assuming no change in labor supply, this can drive up the wage the companies pay.

The overall impact of globalization on wages depends on whether the market expansion effect is stronger than the labor pool effect. For U.S. manufacturing workers, the labor pool effect has been greater than the market expansion

Boeing planes are sold around the world.

FIGURE 16.4 | The Market Expansion Effect of Globalization

Because companies have better access to growing overseas markets, the demand schedule for labor has shifted to the right. Assuming no change in labor supply, that boosts the equilibrium wage from *W* to *W'*.

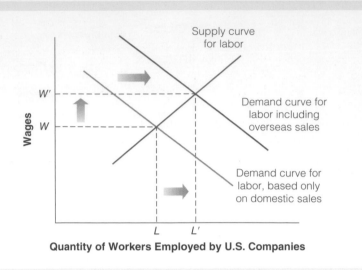

effect. U.S. manufacturers are selling a lot of goods overseas, but they are using overseas factories to produce those goods. So while total revenue for these firms is going up, the demand for U.S. factory labor is going down.

But plenty of workers in the United States have benefited from access to the global economy. For example, big Wall Street brokerages and investment banks, such as Goldman Sachs, have been very successful at operating abroad, and the resulting profits have created new jobs and higher wages at home. (See "Spotlight: The Global Movie Star" for another example of a winner from globalization.)

SPOTLIGHT: THE GLOBAL MOVIE STAR

At least so far, some of the biggest winners from the market expansion effect have been U.S. movie stars. Consider Johnny Depp, star of the *Pirates of the Caribbean* movies. The three movies took in impressive box office revenues of $1 billion in the United States. But overseas box office revenues were an astonishing $1.6 billion, according to *Box Office Mojo,* an online movie publication. No wonder Depp now ranks as one of the best-paid U.S. actors.

So far U.S. movie stars haven't suffered much from the labor pool effect. Stars like Depp don't fear competition from Indian film stars such as Shah Rukh Khan, who has won India's equivalent of the best actor prize six times (though some immigrant actors have done well in the United States, such as Welsh-born Catherine Zeta-Jones and Arnold Schwarzenegger, originally from Austria).

It's not impossible to imagine that Bollywood—India's equivalent of the Hollywood movie machine—or some other filmmaking region could start producing viable global stars. But it hasn't happened yet.

WHY NOT ALL WORKERS ARE THE SAME

Suppose there is a sudden increase in the demand for experienced accountants. That will likely boost the wages for accountants, but it will probably not affect the pay for nurses. Similarly, an increase in the demand for nurses is unlikely to boost the pay for accountants.

Accountants and nurses are not competing for the same jobs. Each occupation requires different skills, qualifications, and experience. That's not to say an accountant can't retrain to be a nurse, or vice versa. But it's a slow process, and most people won't do it.

The labor markets for accountants and for nurses are **noncompeting labor markets.** Two labor markets are noncompeting if the workers in one market do not compete for jobs in the other.

In fact, the overall U.S. labor market is really a collection of many smaller labor markets. Surgeons don't compete for the same jobs as fast-food cooks. Airline pilots don't compete for the same jobs as major league baseball players.

This lack of competition helps explain the big differences in what different workers are paid. Surgeons get paid an average of $220,000 per year, whereas fast-food cooks make an average of $18,000—but a cook can't apply for a job as a surgeon. Similarly, airline pilots and flight engineers earn, on average, $117,000 per year, whereas the average pay for major league baseball players at the start of the 2010 season was over $3 million—but no one would suggest that highly skilled pilots would make good second basemen.

Education

But why should there be separate labor markets? To put this another way, what's to stop any worker from competing for a highly paid job? Some labor markets, like those for professional athletes or opera singers, are walled off by the need to have particular skills that are rare and cannot be easily acquired.

More generally, in today's labor market, education has become the key qualification that workers

NONCOMPETING LABOR MARKETS
When workers in one market do not compete for jobs in the other.

EDUCATION PREMIUM
The added pay for getting a college degree.

need. Employers for many good jobs increasingly want to see a bachelor's or associate degree, depending on the position. There were once a sizable number of well-paid U.S. factory jobs that required at most a high school diploma, but those jobs have mostly melted away, and there is a much tighter link between education and income than before.

Obtaining an education, especially a college or graduate degree, can be an expensive proposition, but it can also yield high returns in terms of better pay and benefits and lower unemployment. For example, according to the U.S. Census Bureau, the average full-time worker with a bachelor's degree earned $68,812 in 2009. A similar worker with only a high school diploma earned $39,937. The added pay for getting a college degree is the **education premium.** Over a 40-year work career, the average college graduate, whether male or female, earns far more than the average high school diploma holder.

To be sure, Figure 16.5 shows that the education premium has not widened since 2000. However, higher wages are not the only benefit of earning a college degree. Data from the Bureau of Labor Statistics show that better-educated workers also have a lower unemployment rate, as Table 16.2 reveals.

Why should college-educated workers get paid so much more? One possible reason is that college teaches skills and knowledge that make future workers more productive. That shifts the demand curve for college-educated workers to the right, driving up their wage *and* making them less likely to be unemployed.

But that's not the only possible explanation. Perhaps college doesn't teach much but instead provides a way of identifying smart people who are able to follow directions. That is, a college degree signals to future employers that you are smart enough and dedicated enough to pass four years' worth of classes. In essence, college is one long test.

But no matter what the explanation, the question remains: if going to college has such a big payoff, why doesn't everyone get a college degree? One reason, of course, is that going to school is an expensive proposition. The cost of tuition, textbooks, and other supplies can be sizable. (Room

FIGURE 16.5   Inflation-Adjusted Earnings by Education Level

Holders of bachelor's and advanced degrees saw their earnings rise in the 1990s, adjusted for inflation. But since 2000 inflation-adjusted pay has been flat or down for all education levels.

Source: Census Bureau, www.census.gov.

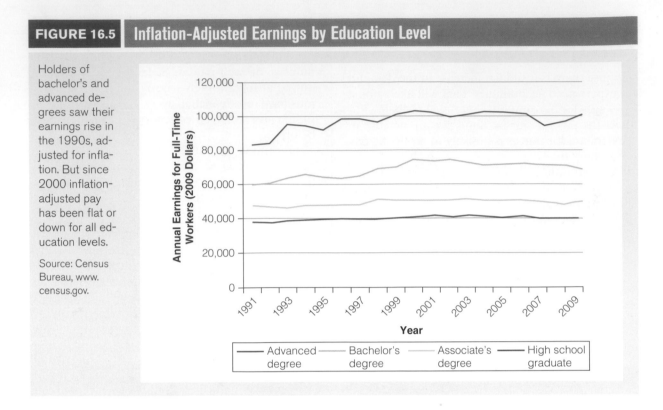

and board—the cost of housing and eating—would have to be paid whether or not the student is in school.)

The biggest cost, though, is the value of the earnings you've lost because you are in school rather than working. This is the opportunity cost of education. If it takes 25 hours a week to complete a full-time program, you have 25 fewer hours a week to work for pay. So the true economic cost of college is tuition and all its other costs *plus* forgone earnings.

Incidentally, the opportunity cost of education helps explain why it's easier to go to school when you're young. Your wage is lower when you're young, so you lose less money by going to school in your teens and twenties than you would if you went later. In other words, you might be giving up a $15,000-a-year job at McDonald's to go to college now rather than a $60,000-a-year job as a stockbroker.

Age and Experience

Does experience make a difference? Older workers do earn more than younger workers—up to a point. Data from the Census Bureau show that wages generally hit their peak when workers are between 45 and 54 (see Figure 16.6). Pay levels off or falls a bit in people's late 50s and early 60s, before retirement. For example, in 2009 workers with a college education and a full-time job who

TABLE 16.2   Education and Unemployment

Better-educated workers are less likely to be unemployed. In 2010 the unemployment rate for college graduates was only 4.7 percent, compared to 10.3 percent for high school graduates with no college education.

	Unemployment Rate, 2010 (%)
Less than a high school diploma	14.9
High school graduate, no college	10.3
Some college, no degree	9.2
Associate degree	7.0
Bachelor's degree and higher	4.7

Source: Bureau of Labor Statistics, www.bls.gov.

FIGURE 16.6 | **Earnings of College-Educated Workers by Age: 2009**

For full-time workers with a bachelor's degree, average pay rises with age, peaking when workers are 45–54 years old.

Source: Census Bureau, www.census.gov.

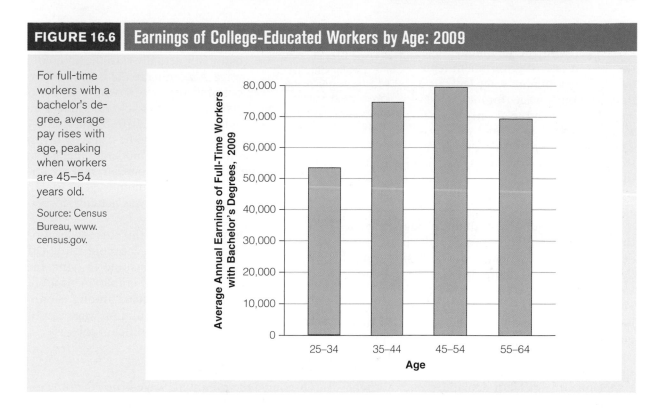

were between 45 and 54 years old earned an average of about $79,535 per year. Comparably educated workers between 55 and 64 earned only $69,410 a year.

There are plenty of reasons why pay should rise with age. Experience clearly improves performance, up to a point. Many jobs require a learning curve, often years long, before you achieve full proficiency. One suggestive fact is that it takes roughly 10 years to achieve expert competence in a game where strategy and analysis are important, such as chess. Moreover, the longer you work at a particular company, the more you build up firm-specific experience—knowledge of how to get things done within that company. Most firms value this knowledge in their employees.

Finally, research has shown that verbal and interpersonal skills stay at high levels as people age. In the 1984 presidential debates, Ronald Reagan, then 73 years old, quipped, "I will not make age an issue of this campaign. I am not going to exploit, for political purposes, my opponent's youth and inexperience." At the time his opponent, Walter Mondale, was 56 years old.

But as workers age, other types of physical and cognitive capabilities decline. Reasoning abilities, mental speed, and the ability to remember events drop off significantly before 50 years of age. Painters, musicians, and writers seem to achieve their peak creative output in their 30s and 40s. Moreover, in a fast-changing economy, knowledge and experience depreciate quickly. As we saw in Chapter 15, young people have more incentive than do older workers to invest in learning new technologies because they have more time left in the workforce to use their new knowledge.

REGULATION OF THE LABOR MARKET

The labor market is one of the most intensely regulated parts of the economy. There are rules governing everything from work hours to child labor to the minimum wage to employment discrimination to retirement benefits. In Chapter 6 we discussed the role of government in the economy; here we'll explore some rules and laws that specifically govern labor markets.

The Minimum Wage

Let's start with the **minimum wage,** the clearest case of government regulation. The minimum wage law sets a floor for hourly wages for most workers. When introduced in October 1938, the federal minimum wage was 25 cents per hour! But that wasn't as low as it sounds—the average wage in manufacturing at that time was 62 cents per hour. As of March 2011, the federal minimum wage was $7.25 per hour.

What effect does the minimum wage have on the labor market? This is one of the most hotly debated topics in economics. The basic supply–demand analysis is straightforward: a minimum wage lifts the wages of the lowest-paid workers above their market wage. As a result, employers have to cut back on their hiring because the marginal revenue of some workers is below their wage.

A minimum wage creates a situation of excess supply in the labor market. The higher wage lowers the quantity of labor demanded and raises the quantity supplied. In other words, some people who want jobs can't get them.

The usual example is a fast-food restaurant, which employs a lot of low-paid young workers to stay open long hours. If the minimum wage were increased, it might not be profitable for the restaurant to stay open quite so late. The result would be fewer work hours, and perhaps fewer workers hired.

Figure 16.7 shows graphically the impact of instituting a minimum wage. L is the equilibrium employment without the minimum wage law, and W is the equilibrium wage. When a minimum wage law is imposed that raises the wage to W', that lowers the quantity of labor demanded from L to L'.

However, we don't know whether the drop from L to L' is big or small. A series of studies done in the 1990s suggested that raising the federal minimum wage by a moderate amount would have only a small negative effect

> **MINIMUM WAGE**
> A wage floor set by the government that lifts the wages of the lowest-paid workers above their market wage.

on employment, if any. There are a few reasons. First, not many workers nationally actually earn the minimum wage. According to the Bureau of Labor Statistics, only 6 percent of workers were paid at or below the minimum federal wage in 2010. Second, many employers seem to be relatively insensitive to small or moderate changes in the minimum wage when it comes to making hiring decisions. Third, the minimum wage in March 2011, adjusted for inflation, was actually 15 percent below its level in 1979.

In the end, it seems that the current level of minimum wage gives an acceptable trade-off between improving pay for some low-income workers while pushing down employment a bit. However, there is no consensus among economists about how high the minimum wage can be boosted without causing significant job loss.

The Working Day

Of course the minimum wage is not the only example of government regulating labor markets. Consider the length of the working day. Today the 8-hour day and the 40-hour workweek are ingrained into our culture. But those conditions are the result of hard-fought and sometimes violent disputes between unions and employers. In

FIGURE 16.7   Labor Supply and Demand with a Minimum Wage

The original equilibrium wage is W. The minimum wage raises the wage to W' while lowering the quantity of labor demanded from L to L'. With the minimum wage the quantity of labor supplied L'' is higher than L'.

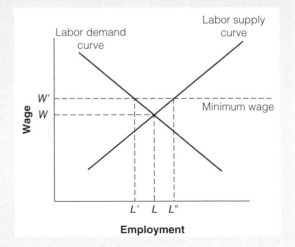

SPOTLIGHT: LICENSES FOR MANICURISTS

To see how occupational licensing requirements work, let's take a look at manicurists, also known as "nail technicians." Most states prohibit someone from working as a manicurist unless they have passed certain hurdles. In Arkansas, for example, budding manicurists must take 600 hours of course instruction at an approved school of cosmetology. In addition, they have to pass both a written and a practical exam. A sample question on the written exam might ask how manicuring instruments should be treated after each use (answer: cleaned and disinfected). The practical exam asks the candidate to do tasks such as doing a manicure, applying a nail tip, and so on.

The licensing requirements are not trivial. A required manicurist course might cost $4,000 and consume the equivalent of 75 full working days, or more than three months. Studying for the written and practical exams requires time and materials as well.

What are the arguments for and against licensing? On the plus side, the licensing requirements force manicurists to learn at least the basics of health and safety. That's a good thing at a time when people are more worried than ever about being infected with something that is not easily treatable. Licensing also enforces some minimum of skill at doing nail care.

On the minus side, the licensing requirement reduces the supply of manicurists because it rules out people who don't have enough money or time to pay for the course. This, in turn, has the effect of driving up the wages paid to manicurists, which in turn raises the price of a manicure.

week into effect at the beginning of 2000. Many companies struggled with the law, and by 2005 the government relaxed the standard, saying that it was making businesses less competitive.

Licensing

Government often intervenes in labor markets by setting **licensing requirements** for certain professions. That is, you need to receive permission from the government before doing certain jobs (see "Spotlight: Licenses for Manicurists").

It makes sense to license certain occupations, such as doctors and pharmacists. You want to know that the doctor who treats you has at least a minimum amount of training and experience. The same is true for the pharmacist who fills your drug prescriptions. It can also be argued that restricting who can practice law makes sense.

But sometimes the oddest professions require licenses. In the state of California, for example, you need to be licensed to be a boxing matchmaker, a brake lamp adjuster, or an aesthetician (someone who works in a beauty salon). You need a license to run a cemetery or an aelectronics repair business, sell mattresses or bedding, process anchovies, cut and wrap butter for sale, or manufacture margarine. It's not hard to imagine that the true purpose of some licensing requirements is to restrict competition by making it more difficult for people to qualify for certain occupations.

Unions

A **union** is a group of workers that bargains collectively with employers for wages (including benefits) and working conditions. At one point unions were extremely important in

1886, nationwide demonstrations to shorten the workweek—which then averaged 60 hours—turned into riots around the country. And it wasn't until 1938 that the federal government passed effective rules to set a 40-hour workweek, with a requirement for overtime pay for many workers.

What effect does regulating the workweek have on the labor market? Suppose a new law reduces the legal workweek to 35 hours. Then the employer would have two choices. She could pay overtime wages to encourage everyone to work 5 more hours, which would obviously be more expensive. Or she could hire and train extra workers to make up for everyone else's reduced hours. Training is expensive; so is paying benefits such as healthcare to more workers. As a result, limitations on work hours impose extra expenses on businesses.

This is exactly what happened in France, which put a 35-hour work-

UNION
A group of workers that bargains collectively with employers for wages (including benefits) and working conditions.

FIGURE 16.8   The Impact of Union Membership on Wages

In some cases unions can push up wages. However, the resulting employment level will be less than the competitive market equilibrium.

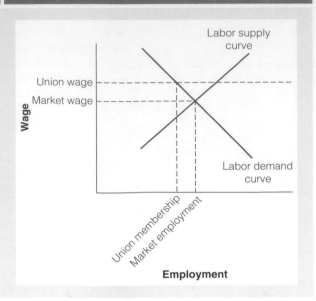

the economy. In the 1950s, for example, roughly one-third of workers belonged to unions, compared to 12 percent today. Only 7 percent of private sector workers now belong to unions, compared to 36 percent in the public sector. Indeed, the largest union is the National Education Association, which has 3 million members, mainly teachers.

Wage setting with collective bargaining is very different from wage setting in a competitive market like the ones we've discussed in this chapter so far. In collective bargaining, the employer talks with the representatives of the union to come up with an acceptable deal. The employer's ultimate resort is to fire the workers, and the ultimate threat of the union is to walk off the job or go on strike and deprive the employer of skilled and experienced labor.

Bargaining takes place against a backdrop of laws and regulations that determine what is acceptable: When is it legal for an employer to hire replacement workers? When is it legal for a union to picket a workplace? All this is governed in the United States by the National Labor Relations Act of 1935 and the Taft-Hartley Act of 1946. Compliance is monitored by the National Labor Relations Board, whose members are appointed by the president. In addition, individual states are allowed to pass "right-to-work" laws, which mean that employees cannot be compelled to join a union.

When they're effective, unions can raise pay and improve working conditions for current workers. By definition, that means pushing wages above the equilibrium market level, as Figure 16.8 shows.

Under what conditions can unions be effective at raising wages? First, it has to be difficult for a company to hire replacement workers. In the airline industry, the pilots' union is generally more effective at raising wages than is the flight attendants' union. Planes can fly with substitute flight attendants, but it's much harder to replace trained pilots at short notice. That gives the pilots more leverage in bargaining for wage increases.

Second, unions are more effective when it is difficult for nonunion competitors to enter an industry. The public sector is heavily unionized, in part because there is little or no competition for most government functions. Private companies can do some government jobs, like waste collection, but it is much less usual to have a private company handle police or fire protection, or even public school education. The scarcity of other options for getting the work done is another way in which unions gain bargaining leverage.

Why has private sector unionization fallen sharply in recent years? Globalization is one key reason. When whole factories can move to other countries, the possibility of a union strike becomes much less threatening to employers. That helps explain why strikes have become far less common in recent years. Figure 16.9 shows that work stoppages due to strikes have become both less common and shorter in the last 50 years. The only recent exception was 2000, when actors working in radio and television commercials went on strike for half the year.

FIGURE 16.9 | Days of Work Lost to Work Stoppages, 1965–2010

As unionization has become less important in the American economy, work stoppages due to strikes have become less common and shorter.

Source: Bureau of Labor Statistics, www.bls.gov.

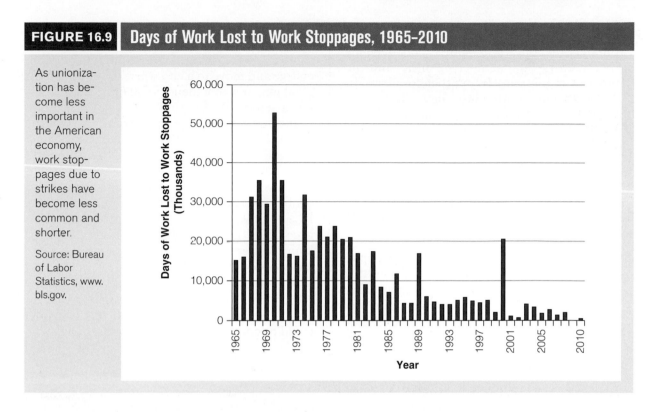

Despite this strike, however, there is no evidence that fewer commercials were made or shown in that year.

LONG-TERM LABOR SUPPLY

To end this chapter, we will look at the **long-term labor supply:** the predicted size of the labor force in a country or a region at some point in the future. Economists and businesses worry about the long-term labor supply because it affects the growth rate of the economy, future tax revenues, and the ability of businesses to find workers.

Working-Age Population

As we saw earlier in this chapter, the labor force depends on the size of the population and the labor force participation rate. However, for long-term forecasts of the labor supply, economists usually focus on changes in the size of working-age population (ages 20–64).

In 1980, when the baby boom generation was hitting working age in large numbers, the labor force was growing at 1.8 percent per year. The second peak came around 2005, when the children of the baby boom generation were entering the workforce.

Going forward, however, the rate of growth of the working-age population drops sharply. Between 2008 and 2018, the working-age population is expected to grow at 0.7 percent. Then between 2018 and 2028, the growth rate is expected to drop to only 0.2 percent per year. That's astoundingly slow.

There are two implications of this slowdown in the growth rate of the working-age population. First, it may become difficult for businesses to find enough skilled and educated workers in the United States, especially as older workers retire. This will put more pressure on workers to get an education.

Second, as we will see in Chapter 18, this slowdown will make it harder to pay for Social Security and Medicare because these programs are funded by payroll taxes paid by workers. Fewer workers will mean less payroll tax available to help support retirees.

The Impact of Immigration

Ultimately the long-term labor supply depends on two factors—the number of births and the number of immigrants from other countries. In recent years immigration into the United States has been quite high. Pulled by economic opportunity in the United States and a lack of good jobs in their own countries, the foreign-born labor force increased by 2.3 million workers between 2005 and 2010. That's about the same size as the increase in the native-born labor force. In other words, without immigration, the growth rate of the labor force would have been much slower.

Immigration is a highly controversial topic. Immigration clearly shifts the labor supply curve to the right—in a big way. All other things being equal, this decreases wages while increasing the level of employment in the United States. Economic research has not nailed down the size of this wage effect from immigration, though it's certainly real.

This concern about immigration driving down wages fuels much of the political debate over immigration policy. People are worried that the influx of foreign-born workers makes it harder for U.S.-born workers to get paid well.

But that's not where the story stops. Immigration also shifts the demand curve for labor to the right, which helps push up wages. Why? Immigrants are consumers as well as workers. They buy homes: 57 percent of foreign-born families in the United States own their homes. They buy food and furniture, use telephones and banks, and shop for cars and toys. As a result, immigrants not only increase the supply of labor; they also increase the demand for goods and services, and therefore the demand for labor. This may be especially true in cities such as New York and Los Angeles, which have vibrant immigrant communities.

These two opposing effects of immigration help explain why there is much disagreement among economists about the actual impact of immigration on wages. Reputable estimates range from a big negative impact to almost no impact at all.

Location

Another aspect of the long-term labor supply is location. People move around. They change jobs and relocate from one area of the country to another—from Texas to California or from Cleveland to New York City. They graduate from college and move to a city where they've landed a good job, or where their spouse or friend has gotten a good job. Or they take a big leap and change countries—moving from Mexico to the United States, or from the United States to China or some other country where the opportunities seem better.

As people move, the supply of labor in a region or country changes over months or years. If a region is attractive to enough people—because of climate, job opportunities, cost of living, or presence of cultural institutions—the local labor supply will grow. The development and widespread use of air-conditioning in the 1930s made warm-weather states like Florida and Georgia more attractive because people could be comfortable during the hot summers.

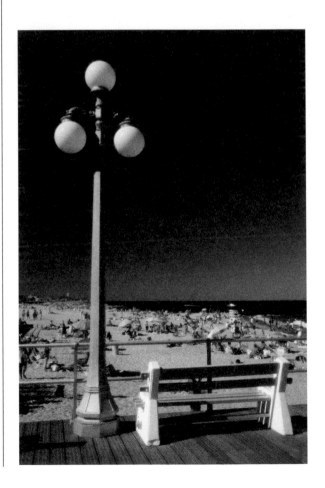

Meanwhile, certain areas of the country are losing working-age population because of their lack of jobs, combined with colder climates. That's especially true in the manufacturing areas of the U.S. Midwest. The population of Cleveland fell by 17 percent between 2000 and 2010, according to the Census Bureau. The populations of Pittsburgh and Buffalo were down by 9 percent and 11 percent, respectively. These are places where young people are moving out, shrinking the labor force.

Where do they go? Young college graduates like to live where there are lots of other young college-educated people (if you are single, you certainly understand). Similarly, educated workers go where they can find cultural opportunities, which creates enough demand to attract even more cultural opportunities.

CONCLUSION

Every worker, from the president of the United States to the housekeepers in the local hotel, participates as a seller in the labor market. Similarly, almost every business, from the largest down to almost the smallest, is a buyer in the labor markets. Indeed, labor markets are pervasive in today's economy.

But something else is pervasive as well: the sense that someone else is being paid more than you. In the United States economy, there's a very wide gap between the highest and lowest paid workers. That fact distresses many people, and may be a social problem—and that's why the next chapter will take up the tough problem of the distribution of income and inequality.

16 SUMMARY

1. The labor force is the part of the population that is either working or actively looking for a job. The labor force participation rate is the share of the population in the labor force. The labor supply curve tell us, given the wage, how many people are in the labor force or the total number of labor hours supplied. The labor demand curve reports how many workers businesses want to hire, given the wage. Businesses want to expand their employment as long as the marginal revenue from an additional worker exceeds the wage paid to the worker (including benefits). *(LO16-1)*

2. Labor market equilibrium is affected by various factors, including government legislation, technological change, and globalization. For example, the market expansion effect of globalization causes the labor demand curve to shift to the right, boosting equilibrium employment and wages. *(LO16-2)*

3. Workers differ by education, age, and experience. Higher-educated workers get paid more, but the education premium has not widened since 2000. *(LO16-3)*

4. The labor market is heavily regulated. The minimum wage law sets a floor for hourly wages for most workers. This has the effect of raising wages for a small number of workers and somewhat reducing employment. Another regulation limits the workweek for many workers and requires the payment of overtime rates for anything above that. A union is a group of workers that bargains collectively with employers for wages (including benefits) and working conditions. An effective union can raise pay above the equilibrium level, which reduces employment. *(LO16-4)*

5. The long-term labor supply is expected to grow more slowly in coming years. That will affect the ability of businesses to find enough skilled and educated workers. One critical factor determining future labor supply is the number of immigrants. *(LO16-5)*

KEY TERMS AND CONCEPTS

labor force

labor force participation rate

labor supply curve

job market decision

marginal product of labor

marginal revenue

marginal cost of labor

benefits

labor demand curve

market wage

labor market equilibrium

labor pool effect

market expansion effect

noncompeting labor markets

education premium

minimum wage

licensing requirements

union

long-term labor supply

PROBLEMS

Mc Graw Hill **connect**™
ECONOMICS

1. Identify which of the following statements is false. *(LO16-1)*

   a) The Internet makes it easier for employers to find potential job candidates.
   b) High unemployment means there are no job openings.
   c) The labor demand curve slopes down.
   d) The labor market is in some ways different than other markets.

2. The following table shows the production function for a bicycle manufacturer. *(LO16-1)*

Number of workers	Number of bicycles produced per week
1	3
2	7
3	10
4	12
5	13

   a) Suppose that the weekly wage is $850. What is the marginal labor cost of the second worker per week?
   b) Suppose that the price of a bicycle is $450. What is the marginal revenue of the third worker, per week?
   c) How many workers does the bicycle manufacturer employ if the price per bicycle is $450 and the weekly wage is $850?
   d) If the price per bicycle drops to $300, what happens to the number of employed workers?

3. Consider the labor demand curve for a city. For each of the following events, say whether the labor demand curve shifts to the left, shifts to the right, or stays in place. Explain. *(LO16-2)*

   a) The local factory installs a robot assembly line.

   b) The local wage increases.

   c) The local factory is able to sell more products overseas.

   d) A new department store opens in town to compete with existing retailers.

4. A restaurant installs an automated conveyor belt system for getting food from the kitchen to customers' tables faster, with fewer dropped plates. Is this technology a substitute or a complement for the following jobs? *(LO16-2)*

   a) Waitress.

   b) Conveyor belt mechanic.

   c) Cook.

   d) Cashier.

5. Identify whether each of the following situations is an example of the market expansion effect or the labor pool effect of globalization. *(LO16-2)*

   a) A furniture maker shifts production from the United States to China.

   b) Merck, the big U.S. pharmaceutical company, hires more scientists in the United States so it can develop drugs to sell in overseas markets.

   c) A U.S. newspaper hires reporters in India to write about the U.S. stock market.

   d) A U.S. magazine hires reporters in the United States to write about the Indian stock market.

6. Indicate whether each of these factors will increase or decrease the odds that a young person in the United States will choose to get a college education. *(LO16-3)*

   a) An increase in the global number of unskilled workers.

   b) Increased industry investment in technology.

   c) Increased college tuition.

   d) Increased pay for high school graduates.

   e) Rising wages in India for college-educated workers.

7. Suppose a law is passed forcing everyone to work until age 69. *(LO16-3)*

   a) In March 2011 the labor force participation rate of people aged 65–69 was 33 percent. After the law is passed, will the labor force participation rate of this group go up or down?

   b) What will be the impact of the new law on the labor supply curve? Will it shift left, shift right, or stay in place?

   c) Will the new law raise wages, cut wages, or leave them the same?

8. Suppose labor laws in China were changed to require a higher minimum wage for Chinese workers. *(LO16-4)*

   a) What would happen to the price of Chinese-made products?

   b) How would that affect the labor demand curve for U.S. factory workers?

   c) What would happen to U.S. factory wages?

9. A town changes its zoning regulations to close down all its dance clubs because too many workers are staying out late and aren't able to come to work the next day. *(LO16-4)*

   a) In the short run, does the labor supply curve shift to the left, shift to the right, or stay the same? What happens to production in the town?

   b) The town develops a reputation as a boring place, so young people no longer want to live there. In the long run, does the labor supply curve shift to the left or the right?

   c) In the long run, would you expect wages and employment to go up or down? Explain your reasoning.

10. Consider the long-term labor supply curve for a city. For each of the following events, say whether the labor supply curve shifts to the left, shifts to the right, or stays in place. Explain. *(LO16-5)*

    a) The tuition of the local community college is raised.

    b) The local wage increases.

    c) The minimum wage in a neighboring city is increased.

    d) The city receives a sudden influx of immigrants from another country.

11. This chapter focused on individuals who work for an employer. But in March 2011 almost 9 million Americans reported that they were self-employed—that is, they worked for themselves. This raises an interesting question: Should more young people be willing to try starting their own businesses? Bill Gates was 20 years old when he started Microsoft. Sergei Brin and Larry Page were 25 when they founded Google. Inexperience and youth didn't seem to stop them from becoming billionaires well before the age of 30. On the other hand, most new businesses either fail or don't produce a profit for several years. *(LO16-5)*

    a) What are the advantages of starting a new business when you are young? (*Hint:* Consider opportunity cost.)

    b) What are the disadvantages of starting a new business when you are young? (*Hint:* Think about the different skills you might need.)

17 THE DISTRIBUTION OF INCOME

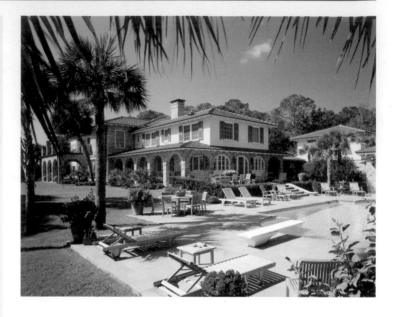

In 2009 Mark Hurd, then chief executive officer of tech giant Hewlett-Packard, received approximately $30 million in salary, bonus, and other compensation. In the same recession year roughly one-quarter of all U.S. households had incomes of $25,000 or less.

That gap—between $30 million and $25,000—demonstrates the wide spread of incomes in the U.S. economy. In recent years the economy has produced a growing number of very high-income winners: corporate executives, athletes and entertainers, hedge-fund and private equity managers, and technology entrepreneurs. Mark Zuckerberg, founder of Facebook, went from college student to billionaire in just three years. That's the good news.

Unfortunately there seems to be a growing gap between the people with very high incomes and everyone else. In particular, the country's overall prosperity seems to have missed a large number of low-income households. The percentage of U.S. citizens living in poverty—that is, with incomes below the official poverty line—is actually higher today than it was for most of the 1970s.

This income gap is one of the most important topics in economics, yet it is also one of the most controversial. Does having such a wide spread between top and bottom provide an incentive to try harder, or does it discourage effort and create political resentment? Is it unfair that some people make millions of dollars and others earn very little, or is it unfair to take money away from people who have earned it to give it to others who have less?

In this chapter we'll lay out the basic facts about the distribution of income in the United States. We'll discuss some reasons why the income gap may have widened in recent years, and we'll examine the justifications for income redistribution. Then we'll finish with a look at racial and gender discrimination in pay.

INCOME DISTRIBUTION

A description of the share of households at different income levels.

THE BASICS OF INCOME DISTRIBUTION

The starting point for any discussion of U.S. incomes is the data produced each year by the statisticians at the Census Bureau. Each March the department asks a sample of about 76,000 households about their **income**—that is, how much money they received in the previous year from various sources such as their jobs, the interest on their savings accounts, the dividends on their stocks, their Social Security payments, and their profits if they own businesses. This sample is large enough to let the statisticians draw conclusions about the whole population. Then the Census Bureau reports its findings, together with information about the characteristics of the households (a *household* is a group of people living together in one housing unit).

Figure 17.1 shows some basic information about the **income distribution**—that is, a description of the share of households at different income levels. For each level of income in 2009, Figure 17.1 reports two numbers: the share of households in that income category, and their share of the country's total income. For example, 50 percent of households received between $0 and $50,000 in 2009. These households, taken together, received 19 percent of U.S. total income.

At the upper end of the distribution, roughly 2 percent of households in the United States had income over $250,000 in 2009. But that relatively small number of people also received 13 percent of the country's total income, much bigger than their share of the number of households.

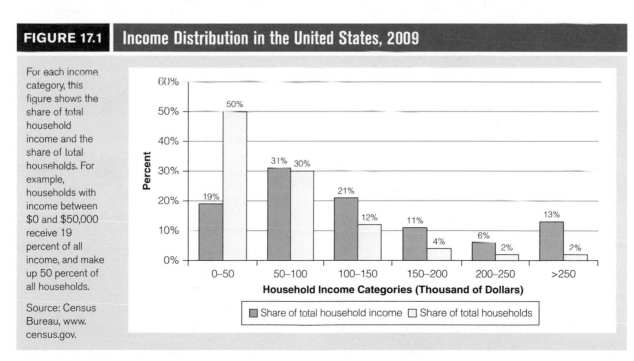

FIGURE 17.1 **Income Distribution in the United States, 2009**

For each income category, this figure shows the share of total household income and the share of total households. For example, households with income between $0 and $50,000 receive 19 percent of all income, and make up 50 percent of all households.

Source: Census Bureau, www.census.gov.

Household Income Categories (Thousand of Dollars)

■ Share of total household income   □ Share of total households

TABLE 17.1	The Quintiles of Household Income, 2009

Each row shows the minimum income that a household needs to get into each group. For example, to be in the top 5 percent of households requires an annnual income of at least $180,000.

Income Quintiles, 2009

Top 5%	$180,000
Top quintile	$100,000
Fourth quintile	$61,800
Third quintile	$38,530
Second quintile	$20,450
Bottom quintile	$0

Source: Census Bureau, www.census.gov.

Quintiles

Figure 17.1 looked at the distribution of income in terms of monetary ranges. But economists also like to think about income distribution in terms of **quintiles.** A quintile represents 20 percent of households. For example, the bottom quintile is the 20 percent of families with the lowest incomes. The top quintile is the 20 percent of families with the highest annual incomes (the top quintile is usually also subdivided into the top 5 percent and the top 1 percent).

Table 17.1 shows the minimum income needed to get into each quintile in 2009. If you worked full-time and earned the national minimum wage ($7.25 an hour at the end of 2009), your total earnings for the year would be $14,500, which is in the first quintile. A household income of $20,450 is needed to get you into the second quintile.

On the other hand, 5 percent of U.S. households earn incomes of $180,000 or higher. This category includes highly educated households. Many lawyers, successful small business owners, and doctors fall in the top 5 percent (the average salary of an obstetrician–gynecologist was in excess of $200,000 in 2009, according to the Bureau of Labor Statistics). Many highly paid corporate managers are in the top 5 percent as well. (See "Spotlight: CEO Pay.")

SPOTLIGHT: CEO PAY

Among the best-paid workers in the United States are the chief executive officers (CEOs) of big companies. They typically get salary and bonuses, often running into the millions of dollars. In addition, they usually are granted stock in their companies, or the option to buy stock at a fixed price. This stock-related pay can be very valuable.

In 2010 the typical CEO at a large company was paid $9.6 million, up 12 percent from the year before, according to calculations by *The New York Times.* By contrast, average hourly earnings of all private sector workers rose less than 2 percent. One of the biggest changes in the economy over the past 20 years has been the rapid increase in pay for top corporate executives. What are large companies like Hewlett-Packard paying for? First, running a large multinational corporation successfully is a tough job. Corporate boards (who hire CEOs) perceive that few people have the experience and leadership ability to do this work. In other words, the labor supply is relatively skimpy. So it's worth paying a lot to hire and retain a good CEO.

A second possible reason for high CEO pay could be called the *tournament effect.* By making the CEO job so lucrative and therefore desirable, high salaries in effect set up a tournament in which many middle-level managers compete hard to make it up the ladder. Thus well-paid jobs at the top stimulate work effort throughout an entire organization

Another justification for huge pay packages—especially for pay in the form of stock and stock options—is the need to give corporate managers incentives to make decisions in the best interest of shareholders. A CEO who owns stock options or stock in his or her company will be more motivated to manage the firm so as to boost the company's share price, which is what shareholders want.

The final reason for high pay is simple. In many corporations, the CEO controls who gets to sit on the board of directors. And guess who votes on CEO pay? The board of directors. This sort of arrangement helps explain why CEO pay keeps going up.

Source: "The Drought Is Over," *The New York Times,* April 10, 2011.

The top 5 percent also includes virtually all major league athletes. For example, the minimum salary for major league baseball players in 2009 was $400,000. That number would put a player and his family into the top 5 percent of households.

80/20 RATIO
One measure of the spread between high-income and low-income households.

Finally, the top 5 percent of households also includes quite a few two-earner families, in which both members of a couple work at good jobs. That is, if both people earn $90,000 a year, that would push a household into the top 5 percent.

One Way to Measure Inequality

Income inequality, generally speaking, is the disparity between high-income and low-income households or individuals. There are several different ways to measure the degree of income inequality, but here's one of the most widely used. Remember that a quintile represents one-fifth or 20 percent of households. The income level that marks the dividing line between the bottom quintile and the second quintile is called the 20th percentile because 20 percent, or one-fifth, of households fall below that level (see Figure 17.2). The income level that marks the dividing line between the top quintile and everyone else is called the 80th percentile because 80 percent of households have incomes below that level. In 2009 the income level for the 20th percentile was $20,450, and the income level for the 80th percentile was $100,000.

We can think of the households in the top quintile as "high-income" and the households in the bottom quintile as "low-income." From that perspective, we can calculate the **80/20 ratio**—that is, the 80th percentile of income divided by the 20th percentile of income. For Figure 17.2, the 80/20 ratio is $100,000/$20,450, which is roughly 5 (or more precisely 4.89, but we will round up to 5). In other words, high-income households have an income that is at least 5 times that of low-income households.

An 80/20 ratio of 5 means that high-income households earn a lot more than low-income ones. By contrast, if the 80/20 ratio is close to 1, high-income and low-income households have relatively similar incomes, and the degree of inequality is low.

CHANGING INCOME INEQUALITY

Most economists believe the distribution of income has widened over the past 25 years. In other words, income inequality has increased. However, there is no consensus about whether the increase in inequality has been large or small. It depends on which data source you look at and which measure of inequality you use.

The 80/20 Ratio

Let's start by looking at the 80/20 ratio, which the Census Bureau calculates each year based on its survey of income. Figure 17.3 shows that the 80/20 ratio has been rising over time, which means the spread between high-income and low-income households has been widening. In 1975 high-income households had incomes at least 4 times those of low-income households. By 2006 that difference had widened appreciably.

However, judging by Figure 17.3, the increase in inequality has been slow and gradual rather than dramatic. High-income households have seen their incomes rise faster than their

| FIGURE 17.2 | One Way to Measure Inequality |

The spread between the 20th percentile and the 80th percentile of income indicates the degree of income inequality.

Source: U.S. Census Bureau, www.census.gov.

| FIGURE 17.3 | The Rising 80/20 Ratio, 1975–2009 |

The ratio of the 80th percentile to the 20th percentile has gradually increased over time, suggesting an increase in inequality.

Source: Census Bureau, www.census.gov.

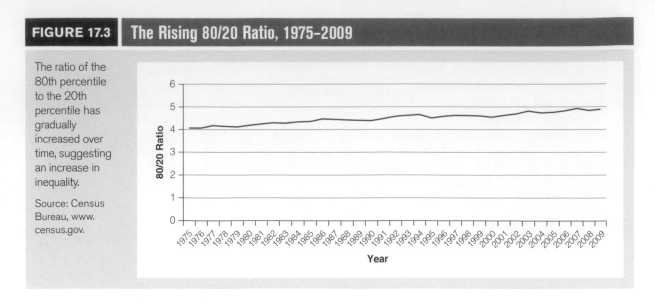

low-income counterparts over the past 30 years, but the difference is not that great.

An Alternative View

Some economists have disputed this relatively benign view of slow-rising inequality. In particular, researchers Thomas Piketty and Emmanuel Saez looked at tax return data from the Internal Revenue Service, under the reasonable assumption that people are more likely to be truthful to tax collectors about their incomes than to surveyors from the government.

In particular, Piketty and Saez examined the top 1 percent of individual tax returns, ranked by total reported income. They calculated the total income of this group and compared it to the total income reported on all tax returns.

It turns out that the share of reported income going to the top 1 percent has risen sharply over the past 30 years. In 1975 the top 1 percent of taxpayers got about 9 percent of total income, as shown in Figure 17.4. By 2008 the top 1 percent of taxpayers were getting 21 percent of all income; that's a stunning increase.

Not surprisingly, this view has itself been disputed by other economists, who argue that tax return data have all sorts of problems. In particular, they do not include Social Security payments, which are a large part of income for many elderly taxpayers. And tax return numbers may be distorted by tax evasion. Nevertheless, whether you trust the 80/20 ratio or the tax

return data, it seems likely that income inequality has increased.

Reasons for Rising Inequality

Economists are still not sure what has caused the increase in income inequality since the 1980s. However, they have suggested several different reasons, each of which may explain part of the increase (see Table 17.2).

First, the introduction of computers into the workplace in the 1980s and the 1990s seems to have favored skilled and educated workers. Remember that before the early 1980s, virtually no one had a personal computer at work. By the end of the decade, personal computers were everywhere. The new technology eliminated or reduced the need for certain low-skilled jobs, and it put a premium on the ability to understand and use sophisticated equipment. The result was an increase in the *education premium* in the 1980s, as we saw in the previous chapter in Figure 16.5. As the pay gap between the college-educated and those with less education widened, it led to more income inequality.

Another cause for widening inequality, especially in recent years, is foreign trade. This explanation used to be controversial among economists, but it has become much more widely accepted. Prior to the 1980s, workers with a high school education could find well-paying jobs in manufacturing. Many of those jobs have now vanished because low-cost imports from China and elsewhere

FIGURE 17.4   Share of Reported Income Going to Top 1 Percent of Taxpayers, 1975–2008

Data from U.S. tax returns show an increasing concentration of reported income at the very top. The top 1 percent of taxpayers garnered 21 percent of total income in 2008.

Source: E. Saez, "Striking It Richer: The Evolution of Top Incomes in the United States," July 2010.

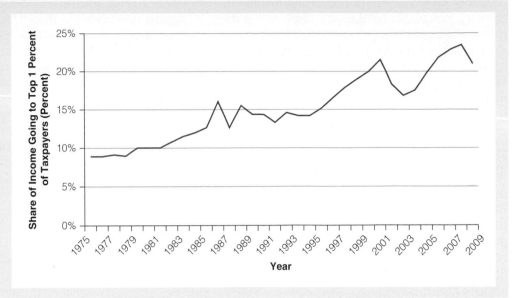

have reduced the size of the U.S. manufacturing sector. In other words, the *labor pool effect* of globalization has caused wages for low-skilled workers to fall (as described in Chapter 16). At the same time, highly skilled workers have benefited from the *market expansion effect* of globalization, at least until now.

Another cause of widening income inequality is what we might call the **superstar economy**. In many fields—sports, entertainment, consulting, academics, law—there is a widening gap in compensation between the top people and the merely competent ones. As the economy evolves from local to national and even global markets, companies are reaching out to the best talent they can find. The reason is simple: If you are accused of a crime, you want the best criminal defense attorney if you can afford him or her, rather than the 10th best or a competent but average one. If you are a big company looking for help with a tough problem, you'd rather go to one of the top consulting firms rather than get a second stringer.

TABLE 17.2   **Possible Reasons for Increasing Inequality**

Economists have come up with several different explanations for why the U.S. income distribution gap is widening.

Reason	Explanation
Rapid technological change	The increased use of information technology favors educated workers.
Growth of foreign trade	Competition from low-wage countries has hurt less skilled workers.
Shift to "superstar" markets	To a greater degree, the top people in a field do much better financially than everyone else.
Changes in government policy	The minimum wage has not risen as fast as inflation, while taxes have been cut for high-income households.

This means that the top people in any field end up doing very well.

Finally, government action—or inaction—has probably played a role in increasing income inequality, though it's hard to say just how big this role is. For example, some economists believe that the minimum wage helps reduce income inequality by boosting the pay of low-income workers. However, as discussed in the previous chapter, the minimum wage has not kept up with inflation over the past 30 years.

Poverty

Another way to assess the distribution of income is to look at the **poverty rate,** which is the percentage of people living in households that earn incomes below the poverty line. The **poverty line** is an income level that is supposed to indicate the lowest acceptable living standard in the economy. It is adjusted for inflation each year and depends on the number of people in the household. In 2009 the poverty line for a family of four was $21,954.

POVERTY RATE

The percentage of people living in households with incomes below the poverty line.

Figure 17.5 shows that over the past 40 years the poverty rate been as low as 11.1 percent in 1973 and as high as 15.2 percent in 1983. But it doesn't look like there's been much progress against poverty since the 1970s. In fact, the data show that the poverty rate has risen in recent years. This reflects a combination of the financial crisis, high unemployment and lack of real wage growth for many Americans.

However, the official poverty rate does not tell the full story of how the people at the bottom of the income distribution are doing. One reason is that the government's calculations of the poverty rate exclude noncash benefits such as food stamps and healthcare programs such as Medicaid (a *noncash benefit* is any income support that the government provides other than a direct check to the recipient).

It's also important to remember that a household classified as poor in the United States may have a higher standard of living than the typical person in another country. Over time, some countries have closed the income gap with the United States, but it's a slow process. (See "How It Works: Global Catch-Up.")

FIGURE 17.5 | **The Poverty Rate, 1966–2009**

The percentage of the U.S. population living below the poverty line has not fallen much in 30 years.

Source: Census Bureau, www.census.gov.

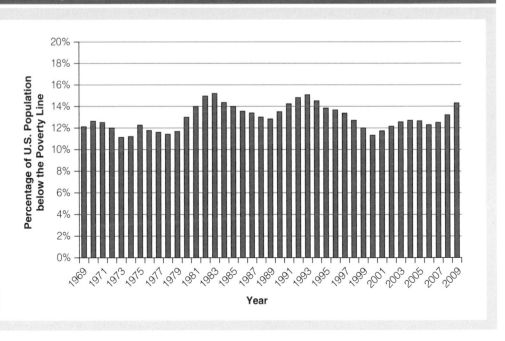

HOW IT WORKS: GLOBAL CATCH-UP

Are emerging countries catching up to the industrialized countries? Figure 17.6 shows GDP per capita for six important emerging economies compared to the United States. For example, in 2005 Brazil was at 20 on the graph, meaning that Brazil's per capita GDP in 2005 was 20 percent of that of the United States. So if the line on the chart is rising, that means the country is catching up with the United States. If it's falling, it's losing ground.

What's striking is that out of the six countries on this chart, three have lost ground compared to the United States since 1980 (Brazil, Nigeria, Mexico); two have gained some ground (India, Egypt); and only one (China) has significantly closed the gap with the U.S.

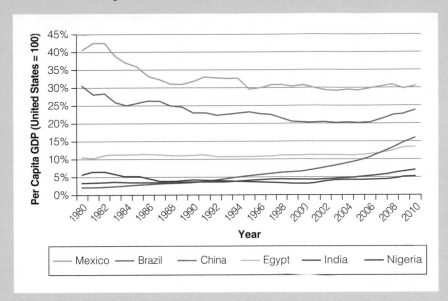

FIGURE 17.6
GDP per Capita: Six Important Emerging Economies. This figure shows the GDP per capita of six emerging countries as compared to the United States from 1980–2010.

THE DEBATE OVER INEQUALITY

When we consider rising income inequality in the United States and what economists, politicians, and the public want to do about it, we find enormous and passionate differences of opinion. Virtually everyone would agree that a rich country like ours cannot allow its citizens to starve, no matter how poor they may be. Yet people argue about whether the government should act to reduce inequality and, if so, by how much. We summarize these ideas in Table 17.3 and discuss them next.

Two Competing Notions of Fairness

Supporters of government intervention argue that an economy with wide gaps between rich and poor is inherently unfair and immoral. It's not right, they say, for one person to live in a shack and go hungry while someone else lives in a mansion. The gaps between vast wealth and poverty in the same economy, or even the same city, are morally problematic for many people.

Those in favor of government action use this argument to support many different kinds of intervention, including using the tax system to even out incomes; offering subsidies for necessities

TABLE 17.3	The Pros and Cons of Government Intervention to Reduce Inequality

For every argument in favor of government taking an active role to reduce inequality, there's an argument against government action.

	Arguments in Favor of Government Intervention to Reduce Inequality	Arguments against Government Intervention to Reduce Inequality
Fairness	A wide gap between rich and poor is unfair and immoral.	Taking money away from individuals who have earned it is unfair and immoral.
Growth	More equal societies experience stronger growth.	Allowing big rewards to go to the most successful performers helps motivate creativity, innovation, and hard work.
Politics	Big income differences cause political strife and eventually undermine support for a market economy.	A policy devoted to reducing inequality eventually leads to political control of the economy and an increase in rent-seeking behavior.
Data	Income distribution statistics understate inequality because they undercount high-income households.	Income distribution statistics overstate inequality because they do not include noncash benefits and fail to take economic mobility into account.

like housing, food, education, and medical care; providing income support for families and children; and retraining workers for better jobs. These programs all exist today, though not funded to the level that their supporters want.

However, an appeal to fairness can also underpin an argument *against* government intervention. Income support programs cost money, which has to come from somewhere—mainly taxes. Many people believe it is not fair to take money away from those who have earned it: "I worked many hours to earn my money—why should the government take it away and give it to someone else?" Whether or not you agree with this argument, it has proven to be politically potent enough over the past 20 years to win support for tax cuts at both national and local levels.

Inequality, Growth, and Politics

Some supporters of government intervention use a pragmatic rather than a moral argument. They point out that big income gaps cause social stresses and political strife that impede the functioning of the economy. For example, if people in the bottom half of the income distribution are doing poorly, they are more likely to press for restrictions on foreign trade. That's bad for economic growth.

Moreover, in a global economy in which education is increasingly important, a national economy with many poor and unskilled workers is increasingly at a disadvantage. That's one reason why many corporate executives are concerned about poverty and education.

On the other hand, opponents of government intervention argue that inequality could actually be good for growth. How so? In a market economy, you motivate effort and creativity by giving bigger rewards to the most successful performers. The economy functions better if people have an incentive to try as hard as they can, so a bigger gap between winners and losers means a bigger incentive to succeed.

This is one of the guiding principles of *supply-side economics,* discussed in Chapter 11. Starting with President Ronald Reagan, a significant number of politicians and economists have argued that taxing the rich too heavily lessens their incentive to work hard because they don't get to keep what they earn. From the same perspective, some people believe the fear of unemployment and poverty is important for motivating the poor to work rather than stay at home on welfare.

There's another reason why government intervention might be a drag on growth. Remember that in Chapter 6 we discussed *rent-seeking behavior,* which includes activities, such as lobbying, undertaken for the sole purpose of influencing government decisions. The more the government intervenes in the economy for good purposes such as helping the poor, the more tempting it is for lobbyists and special interest groups to try and get a share of the government pie for themselves. This can be an enormous burden on the economy; it diverts resources and leads to bad decisions.

Misleading Statistics

As we saw earlier in this chapter, economists do not agree about how much income inequality has risen. Supporters of government intervention argue that the official figures put out by the Census Bureau understate inequality. In fact, an analysis of income distribution based on tax returns—which are arguably more complete than the census survey—seems to show greater increases in income inequality (as shown in Figure 17.4).

On the other hand, the figures may overstate inequality because they don't include noncash benefits such as Medicare and food stamps. The figures also don't take into account **income mobility,** which describes the changes in your income level over your lifetime. There may be years when you have very low income—when you are young, for instance—and times when your income is much higher. For example, imagine an economy in which all young workers earned $20,000 per year, and all middle-aged workers earned $100,000 per year. If we looked only at the figures for one year, we'd see a big gap between the poor and well-off households. But if we tracked people's income through their lifetimes, we'd see that this was a highly equal society in which everyone's income rose equally as they matured.

TAXES AND REDISTRIBUTION

We are going to focus here on the most common form of government intervention: the use of the tax system for **redistribution.** Redistribution is government action that transfers money from high-income to low-income households. Some amount of redistribution is essential for fixing the inequities produced by a market economy and for ensuring that poor people have enough money to live.

In theory, a tax system could be an effective mechanism for redistributing income. Suppose,

REDISTRIBUTION
Government action that transfers money from high-income to low-income households.

for example, we imposed a high tax rate—say 90 percent—on anyone earning over $100,000. Then the **after-tax income distribution**—that is, what's left after the tax is taken out—would be much more equal than the **pretax income distribution.**

We call the share of total income a household pays in taxes the **effective tax rate** (by contrast, the marginal tax rate is the share of the last dollar going for taxes). An income tax is **progressive** if high-income households pay a higher share of their income in taxes than do low-income households; that is, high-income households have a higher effective tax rate. For example, the federal income tax is progressive because the tax rate rises as household income rises. A progressive tax tends to make the after-tax income distribution more equal than the pretax income distribution.

For example, Table 17.4 shows how a progressive income tax can reduce inequality. Suppose the government collects a 10 percent tax on incomes up to $50,000, and then a 30 percent tax on everything a household earns above that (obviously this is a simplified version of the actual tax system). Then a household with a $20,000 income will pay $2,000 in taxes (10 percent of $20,000). A household with a $200,000 income will pay $47,000 in taxes (10 percent of the first $50,000 plus 30 percent of the remaining $150,000).

In this example, the high-income household pays about 24 percent of its income in taxes, and the low-income household pays 10 percent. This difference in tax rates tends to narrow income inequality. Before taxes, the high-income household has an income 10 times that of the low-income household as shown in the right column of Table 17.4. After taxes, the ratio falls to 8.5—still a lot, but not as much as before.

In contrast, a tax is **regressive** if it makes low-income households pay a bigger share of their incomes than high-income taxpayers. Consider a sales tax, for example. A sales tax is typically equal to some percentage of the money spent on purchases. That is, households pay the tax on the portions of their incomes that they spend but not on the portions saved.

As a result, the sales tax is regressive. Most low-income households don't do much saving, so they pay sales tax on almost their entire incomes. However, high-income households don't spend

---

TABLE 17.4 **An Example of a Progressive Income Tax**

In this example, households pay a 10 percent tax on income up to $50,000, and 30 percent on everything over that. As a result, households with higher incomes pay a higher effective tax rate.

	Low-Income Household	High-Income Household	Ratio of High Income to Low Income
Before-tax income	$20,000	$200,000	10 to 1
10% tax up to $50,000	$ 2,000	$ 2,000	
30% tax on everything over $50,000	$ 0	$ 45,000	
Total tax	$ 2,000	$ 47,000	
Effective tax rate (as a percentage of before-tax income)	$ 10%	$ 24%	
After-tax income	$18,000	$153,000	8.5 to 1

---

all their incomes, so they pay a lower share of their incomes in tax. That is, if you earned $1 million per year but spent only $10,000, you could pay the same sales tax as a family earning $10,000 and speading $10,000.

Table 17.5 shows a more realistic example of a regressive sales tax in action. The tax rate is 6 percent on all purchases, so the low-income household—which spends everything—ends up paying a sales tax of $1,200 (6 percent of $20,000). But the high-income household, because it spends only half its income, pays $6,000 in taxes (6 percent of $100,000). That means the after-tax ratio of high income to low income actually *increases* from 10 percent to 10.3 percent because of the sales tax.

Adding It All Up

Figuring out whether the whole U.S. tax system is progressive or regressive is not easy because U.S. citizens pay a lot of different taxes, including income tax, sales tax, property tax, and payroll tax (for Social Security and Medicare). Some of these, like the income tax and property tax, are progressive. Others, like the sales tax and the payroll tax, are regressive.

What's more, there have been multiple recent changes to the tax code, including big tax cuts in 1981, 2001, and 2003, and big tax increases in 1990 and 1993. In fact, Washington has changed the tax law almost every year.

Surprisingly, after all these changes, the federal tax system is about as progressive now as it

---

TABLE 17.5 **How a Regressive Sales Tax Works**

In this example, households pay a 6 percent sales tax on all spending.

	Low-Income Household	High-Income Household	Ratio of High Income to Low Income
Before-tax income	$20,000	$200,000	10 to 1
Amount spent	$20,000	$100,000	
Amount paid on sales tax of 6%	$ 1,200	$ 6,000	
Percentage of before-tax income paid in sales tax	$ 6.0%	$ 3.0%	
After-tax income	$18,800	$194,000	10.3 to 1

FIGURE 17.7   **The Effective Federal Tax Rate for the Top 1 Percent of Taxpayers, 1979–2007**

The effective federal tax rate for the top 1 percent is about the same as it was in 1981.

Source: Congressional Budget Office, June 2010.

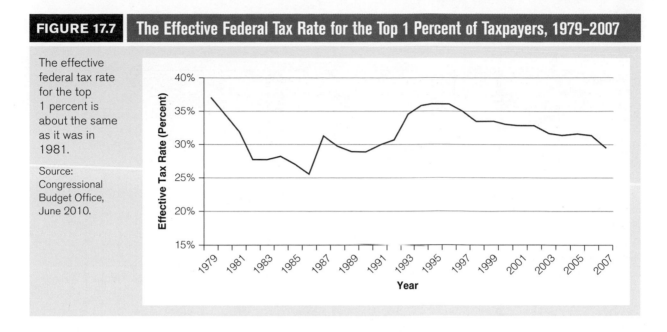

was in 1981, when President Ronald Reagan took office. For example, those in the top 1 percent income bracket paid 31.8 percent of their income in federal taxes in 1981 (including income taxes, payroll taxes, gasoline and other excise taxes, and their share of corporate income taxes). That's according to the nonpartisan Congressional Budget Office. After President Reagan cut taxes for high-earning households, the effective tax rate for the highest-earning 1 percent dropped as low as 25.5 percent. Then tax increases by President Bill Clinton in 1993 pushed the effective rate at the top as high as 36 percent, which his successor, President George W. Bush, lowered again. Thus the effective tax rate on top-income individuals in 2007, the last year for which data are available, was 29.5 percent (see Figure 17.7).

However, it is true that the poor now pay a smaller share of their income in federal taxes today than they did in 1981. The reason is that both Republicans and Democrats have been willing to ease the tax burden on the poor, so more and more low-income households pay little or no federal income tax. According to the 2007 tax code, a married couple with two young dependent children could make as much as $40,000 without paying any federal income tax.

The question of redistribution will continue to be important in the future. It's unlikely, though, that we will see government intervention making a dramatic change in the distribution of income.

EARNINGS AND LABOR MARKET DISCRIMINATION

Now we turn to another aspect of income inequality: the question of discrimination in labor markets. **Labor market discrimination** occurs when one person is paid less or treated worse on the job than an equally qualified person because of his or her race, gender, or some other characteristics. One government responsibility is to enforce workplace antidiscrimination laws. These may differ by city, by state, and by occupation. On the national level, for example, the Equal Employment Opportunity Commission (EEOC) enforces laws forbidding employment discrimination based on age, race, color, religion, gender, national origin, or disabled status.

Despite such laws, a reality of today's labor market is that some groups—notably women, blacks, and Hispanics—consistently earn less on average than others. Women earn less on average than men, while blacks and Hispanics earn less on average than whites. Figure 17.8 provides some comparative figures for 2010, based on Bureau of Labor Statistics data. For example, the median weekly earnings of adult male workers were $824 per week, compared to $669 for adult female workers (*median* means the midpoint— half the members of a given group earn more than the median, and half earn less).

FIGURE 17.8   Weekly Earnings by Gender and Race, 2010

This chart shows the median weekly earnings for full-time workers in several gender, race, and ethnicity subgroups. For example, typical white male workers earned $850 per week, compared to only $684 for black male workers.

Source: Bureau of Labor Statistics, www.bls.gov.

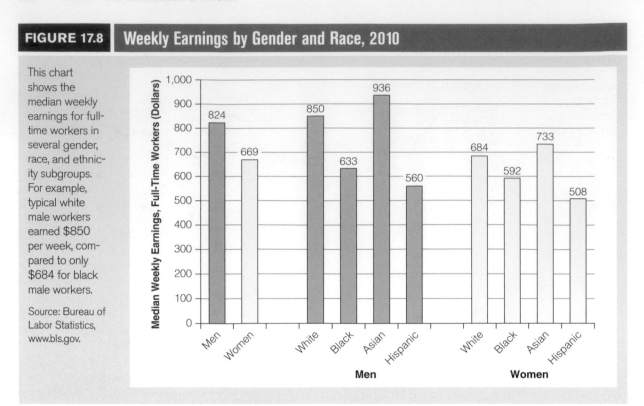

How much of these disparities comes from illegal discrimination, and how much from other sources? In addition to discrimination, there are three main reasons earnings could differ by gender and race: differences in education, differences in experience, and differences in occupational choices.

Let's start with education. As we saw earlier in the chapter, better-educated workers generally earn higher pay. Today women have pretty much the same education levels as men, so education differences can't explain much of the gender pay gap. As of 2009, 29.1 percent of women 25 years and over were college graduates, compared to 30.1 percent of men; that's hardly a difference at all. And if we look at men and women aged 25 to 29, the difference actually reverses. In that age group, 34.8 percent of women were college graduates, compared to 26.6 percent of men.

However, education differences can explain part of the pay gap for blacks and Hispanics because it is still true today that non-Hispanic whites have a higher average level of formal education than do comparable blacks and Hispanics. Among 25- to 29-year-olds, only 19.0 percent of blacks

and 12.2 percent of Hispanics had four years or more of college. In comparison, 37.2 percent of non-Hispanic whites in that age group were college-educated.

If we stopped here, it would look as though differences in education go a long way toward explaining why non-Hispanic whites earn higher wages than do blacks or Hispanics. But the situation is a bit more complicated. Some people argue that blacks and Hispanics face unfair obstacles in attending and graduating from college because they tend to come from poorer families who have a harder time paying for education and because they face discrimination getting into and attending college. To the extent that these two factors are true, differences in educational attainment themselves reflect economic inequality and discrimination.

Similar complications come up when we look at differences in pay between men and women working full-time. This pay gap has narrowed substantially over time, but it is still there. As Figure 17.9 shows, in 2009 the median weekly earnings of full-time female workers were only about 80 percent of earnings of comparable male workers.

FIGURE 17.9 **Women's Median Weekly Earnings as a Percentage of Men's**

Women's wages have been catching up with men's, but there is still a gap.

Source: Bureau of Labor Statistics, www.bls.gov.

A big part of this pay gap reflects the tendency of many occupations to be filled mainly by one gender or the other. Occupations that are heavily female tend to be paid less. For example, most lawyers still are men, whereas 86 percent of paralegals are female (as of 2010). Over 70 percent of dentists are male, while 95 percent of dental hygienists are female.

To what extent does the gender segregation of occupations reflect discrimination, and to what extent does it reflect choice? Why should most dentists be male and virtually all dental hygienists female? Some economists assert that women choose lower-paid occupations with more flexible hours, such as teaching, rather than better-paid but more time-consuming occupations, such as being corporate executives. Other economists find this reasoning flimsy and argue that there is still widespread discrim-ination against women in traditional male occupations, which drives women away from better-paying jobs.

CONCLUSION

Just by the numbers, there is clearly income inequality in the United States. Equally clearly, it has been increasing in recent years, with an increase in the share of income going to the top earners.

However, there is little agreement among economists about why inequality is rising and what can be done about it. Some argue that there is little that government can and should do. Others believe that taking action to reduce inequality is one of the most important responsibilities of government. This question is likely to be one of the more controversial ones in economics for many years to come.

17 SUMMARY

1. The Census Bureau tracks the nation's income distribution each year, based on a survey. A quintile represents 20 percent of all households. The 20th percentile is the income level that marks the dividing line between the bottom quintile and the second quintile, whereas the income level that marks the dividing line between the top quintile and everyone else is called the 80th percentile. One way to measure income inequality is the 80/20 ratio, which is the 80th

percentile of income divided by the 20th percentile of income. A high 80/20 ratio means that high-income households earn a lot more than low-income households. *(LO17-1)*

2. Income inequality in the United States has been increasing over time. However, the size of the increase depends on what measure you use. The reasons for rising inequality include rapid technological change, the growth of foreign trade, a shift to superstar markets, and changes in government policy. Another way to assess inequality is to look at the poverty rate, which measures the percentage of the population living in households with incomes below the poverty line. *(LO17-2)*

3. Economists disagree about whether more government intervention is needed to reduce income inequality. These disagreements involve issues of fairness, growth, politics, and data problems. *(LO17-3)*

4. The tax system can be used to redistribute income from high-income households to low-income households, thus reducing inequality. A progressive tax like the income tax reduces inequality, whereas regressive taxes like sales or payroll taxes increase inequality. *(LO17-4)*

5. Another aspect of income inequality is discrimination in labor markets. That means one person is paid less or treated worse on the job because of his or her race, gender, or some other characteristic. *(LO17-5)*

KEY TERMS AND CONCEPTS

income
income distribution
quintiles
income inequality
80/20 ratio
superstar economy

poverty rate
poverty line
income mobility
redistribution
after-tax income distribution
pretax income distribution

effective tax rate
progressive taxes
regressive taxes
labor market
  discrimination

PROBLEMS

connect
ECONOMICS

1. Look at Figure 17.1, on page 337, which gives some basic information about the income distribution in 2009. *(LO17-1)*

   a) What percentage of households received between $100,000 and $150,000 in income in 2009?

   b) What percentage of total income did this group get?

   c) What percentage of households received between $0 and $100,000 in income in 2009? (*Hint:* You can add the percentages of different categories.)

   d) Look at the households with incomes over $250,000. What percentage of total income did this group get?

2. The following table gives 10 occupations and their average annual wages in 2009, as determined by the Bureau of Labor Statistics (these are nationwide averages across all experience levels). *(LO17-1)*

Occupation	Average Annual Wage (Dollars)	Quintile
Compensation and benefits managers	95,230	–
Elementary schoolteachers	53,150	–
Fashion designers	74,410	–
Network administrators	70,930	–
Paralegals and legal assistants	50,080	–
Registered nurses	66,530	–
Security guards	26,430	–
Shampooers (in hair-cutting establishments)	18,890	–

a) Using Table 17.1, on page 338, identify which quintile an average worker in each occupation would be in, assuming a one-earner household.

b) Suppose a fashion designer married a security guard, and they both kept working. Which quintile would their household be in?

c) Suppose a network administrator married a registered nurse. Which quintile would their household be in (assuming both keep working)?

3. The table below gives the 80th and 20th percentiles of household income for 1989 and 2009, measured in inflation-adjusted 2009 dollars. *(LO17-1)*

	1989	2009
	Household Income in Inflation-Adjusted 2009 Dollars	
80th percentile	89,707	100,000
20th percentile	20,203	20,453
80/20 ratio	?	?

a) Calculate the 80/20 ratio for each year.

b) Did inequality increase between 1989 and 2009? Explain.

c) Based on this table, do you think that poor families were worse or better off in 2009 compared to 1989? Explain.

4. Which of the following is not a reason for rising inequality? *(LO17-2)*

a) Widespread use of computers.

b) Rising enrollments at community colleges.

c) Increased global competition from China and other low-wage countries.

d) The widening education premium.

5. Suppose that we have a country with a population of 30 million, where 3 million are below the poverty line. What would the poverty rate be? *(LO17-2)*

   a) 10%
   b) 30%
   c) 3%
   d) 15%

6. Many CEOs of large corporations have enormous pay packages in the tens of millions of dollars per year. Such high pay helps contribute to income inequality because the vast majority of people earn much less. Suppose Congress passed a law that saying that the annual pay for any job could not exceed $500,000 per year. What effect would this law have on the market for corporate executives? *(LO17-3)*

7. It's sometimes said, half in jest, that the best anti-poverty policy is to simply give the poor more money. Which of the following would be a disadvantage of such a policy? *(LO17-3)*

   a) More equal societies tend to experience greater growth.
   b) People would have less incentive to work hard.
   c) Big income differences cause political strife.
   d) A wide gap in income is immoral.

8. Suppose our tax system imposed a 30 percent tax rate on income up to $50,000 and a 10 percent tax rate on income over $50,000. *(LO17-4)*

   a) Would this tax system be progressive or regressive?
   b) The Social Security tax is 6.2 percent of wages, up to a maximum of $106,800 in 2011. For incomes above that maximum, no additional taxes are paid. Is the Social Security tax progressive or regressive?

9. Which of the following situations most clearly represents labor market discrimination against women? *(LO17-5)*

   a) A man earns $50,000 per year, and a woman in a different occupation and the same education and experience earns $40,000.
   b) A woman earns $75,000 and a man with less experience earns $70,000.
   c) A man earns $50,000 per year, and a woman in the same occupation with the same education and experience earns $45,000.
   d) A woman earns $100,000 and a man with less experience and more education earns $110,000.

18 ECONOMICS OF RETIREMENT AND HEALTHCARE

LEARNING OBJECTIVES

After you have read this chapter, you should be able to:

LO18-1 Apply the life cycle theory of retirement and identify the main sources of retirement funds.

LO18-2 Explain the difference between defined benefit and defined contribution retirement plans.

LO18-3 Summarize the demographic challenge facing Social Security and describe the possible solutions.

LO18-4 Describe the healthcare life cycle, its problems, and the role of health insurance.

LO18-5 Discuss reasons why healthcare spending is rising so quickly.

There are few certainties in life, but here are two scenarios that are probable. First, at some point you will likely get sick and need the services of a doctor and perhaps a hospital. And second, you will eventually grow old and be ready to (or be forced to) retire.

Because these scenarios are likely for most people, the questions of how society is going to pay for healthcare and retirement are two of today's most important economic issues.

Both require us to take care of people who may not be in a position to care for themselves. As a result, the normal market solution of letting individuals make their own decisions doesn't always work. It is not socially acceptable to allow old people to live in squalor because they cannot work anymore. And it is not socially acceptable to let old or poor people suffer or die because they cannot afford medical care.

That's why the United States has adopted a mixed private–public system to provide for both retirement and healthcare. Retirement income comes from personal savings, employer retirement plans, and government programs (mainly Social Security). Healthcare comes through personal spending, employer-provided insurance, and government programs (mainly Medicare for the elderly and Medicaid for the poor).

The problem, though, is that this mixed public–private system is expensive, and it is getting more so as the population ages. What's more, many people believe the U.S. healthcare system does not work well and leaves too many people unprotected. That led President Barack Obama to sign healthcare reform legislation in March 2010. This complicated bill, which we will discuss later in this chapter, transforms the healthcare sector. Yet while this textbook is being revised, opponents are trying to roll back portions of the legislation.

In this chapter we will look at the economics of retirement and healthcare. We will lay out the basic life cycle theory, which explains how retirement would work in the absence of Social Security and pensions. We will describe how the current retirement and healthcare systems are financed, and why they will run into financial problems in the future. Finally, we will discuss President Obama's healthcare reform effort.

CH 18 Economics of Retirement and Healthcare **355**

THE BASICS OF RETIREMENT

Before we examine the current system of retirement, we should understand how individuals might finance their spending in old age by themselves, without any assistance from the government or from employer retirement plans. Remember, retirement means you no longer have income from work.

The Life Cycle Theory of Retirement

The **life cycle theory of retirement** describes what could happen if there were no government or business-supported programs for the elderly. It says people spend when they are young, save during the latter part of their working lives, and then spend while they are retired. According to this hypothesis, in your early years your income is low, and you need to spend money on education and buying a home. In your middle and later working years, your income rises, and you have the opportunity to pay off your debts, save money, and build your wealth. Then, when you retire, you spend your nest egg.

This life cycle theory is illustrated in Figure 18.1. The graph shows how your **net worth**—your total assets minus your debt—starts out negative as you borrow for a home and education. Your net worth turns positive as your income rises, followed by a decline after you leave the workforce. Whether your net worth actually drops to zero depends on how long you live after retirement and on how much you spend—and whether you want (or are able) to leave an inheritance to your heirs.

Problems with the Life Cycle Theory

In some ways, the life cycle theory seems reasonable as a prescription for action. It suggests a strategy for everyone to provide for their own retirement without the need for any government intervention. All that's required is the willingness to save for the future.

FIGURE 18.1   The Life Cycle Theory of Retirement

According to the life cycle theory of retirement, the young borrow for education and to buy homes. The middle-aged pay off their mortgages and build savings. Then in old age, people use their savings to pay for medical and living costs.

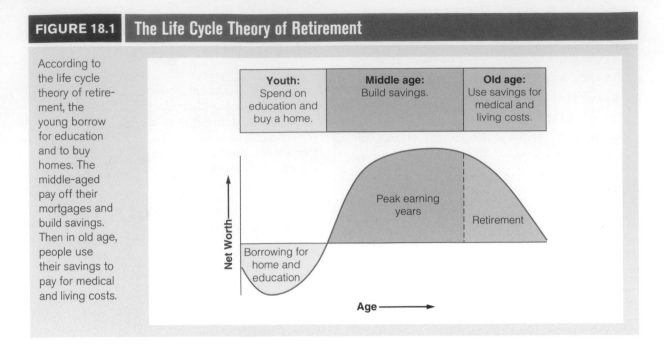

But at least two things can go wrong with this simple vision. First, poor people are often not in a position to save much for retirement. Because their incomes are low, all their earnings go for necessities such as food and housing. No savings accumulated when working means no savings available for old age. According to the Federal Reserve's Survey of Consumer Finances, only 42 percent of families save regularly. Call this the **retirement poverty problem.**

Second, it's difficult to know how much money to put away in savings to cover all the eventualities. For example, the amount of savings you need for retirement depends on how long you will live after retirement. Today if you are 35 years old, you can expect to live until 80—but there's a 25 percent chance you will live until at least 90, and a 10 percent chance you will reach 95! Should you save enough to cover 15 years of retirement, 25 years, or even more? No one knows. Call this the **retirement uncertainty problem.**

RETIREMENT POVERTY PROBLEM

Poor people often don't have enough income to save for retirement.

RETIREMENT UNCERTAINTY PROBLEM

Individuals don't know how long they will live after they retire.

The length of your life is not the only unknown making it difficult to plan the right amount of money to save for retirement. Depending on your assumptions, the amount of money you need can vary enormously. Will you or your spouse be stricken by an illness that requires expensive treatment and leaves you poor? Will the investments into which you put your savings do well or poorly? Will inflation be high enough to eat away at the value of your savings?

Because running out of money can leave you poor in old age, you need to save extra. The need to save extra money for retirement should lower your consumption and living standards during your working life.

Sources of Retirement Income

The combination of the retirement poverty problem and the retirement uncertainty problem means that individual savings by themselves are not enough to provide for retirement.

Today economists talk about the **four-legged** stool of retirement income: part-time work, **employer retirement plans, Social Security,** and individual savings. Employer retirement plans, which we will discuss in the next section, are provisions for retirement that your employer contributes to on your behalf. And Social Security—which we will discuss at length later in this chapter—is income the government provides to older citizens.

Table 18.1 lays out the sources of income in 2009 for U.S. adults aged 65 and over. Their single largest source of support was Social Security, which accounted for 41 percent of their income. The next biggest source was earnings from current work, showing that many older people are still working part-time. Amazingly, income from assets—that is, the result of individual savings—accounted for only 11 percent of income for adults 65 and over. That's because most people reach old age without much savings.

In fact, if you did want to fund your retirement completely out of individual savings, you would require a truckload of money. The exact amount would depend on what assumptions you made about your return on investments and

TABLE 18.1	**Where U.S. Adults Aged 65 and Over Get Their Money, 2009**

This table shows that Social Security is the single biggest source of funds for people aged 65 and over.

	Percentage of Average Income for People Aged 65 and Over
Earnings from Work	26
Social Security	41
Public and Private Defined Benefit Pensions	18
Defined Contribution Plans and Individual Retirement Accounts	1
Income from Assets	11
All Other	3

Source: Employee Benefit Research Institute, www.ebri.org.

how long you would live. (See "How It Works: How Much Do You Need to Save for Your Own Retirement?")

HOW IT WORKS: HOW MUCH DO YOU NEED TO SAVE FOR YOUR OWN RETIREMENT?

Suppose you had to fund your retirement entirely out of your own savings—that is, with no Social Security checks or payments from employers. How much would you need in savings when you retire?

The answer to this question is not simple: It depends on how much income you want, how long you will live, and what kind of risks you want to take with your investments. Obviously, the longer you live, the more savings you need. And if you want to put your money into safe investments, you will have to compensate for their low average rate of return by saving more.

For example, suppose your target income for retirement is $50,000 per year, adjusted for inflation. If you expect to live 25 years after retirement—until age 90—and you want to put your money in risk-free certificates of deposit, you'll need to save at least $1.1 million by age 65. If you're willing to put your money into conservative stocks, you'll need only $700,000—but then you take the risk that the value of the market might fall and take some of your money with it. There are no guarantees.

EMPLOYER RETIREMENT PLANS

In some ways the existence of employer retirement plans is a bit of a surprise. After all, why should employers care about what happens to their workers after they stop providing productive labor?

But in fact, in the late 19th century, employers discovered that setting up a retirement plan was a good way of attracting and keeping high-quality workers. Today there are two types of employer retirement plans, *defined benefit* and *defined contribution*. In this section we will discuss the differences between the two, and the limitations of employer retirement plans in general.

Defined Benefit versus Defined Contribution

A **defined benefit plan** gives you a predetermined amount of money monthly when you retire. The exact amount depends on how much you earned during your work life, how long you were employed with that company, and the age at which you retired. The amount received may or may not be adjusted for inflation. This is the classic employer-provided pension.

Defined benefit plans are funded primarily by the employer. In the case of private employers, the money comes from pretax profits (that is, the amounts a company contributes to a pension plan for its employees are not subject to the corporate income tax). The company invests the money in the stock market and in bonds. If the stock market goes up, the employer might be able to provide the pension without putting in any money of its own. But even if the investments fall short, the employer is responsible for making the promised future payments.

Defined benefit plans used to be common. In 1980, 84 percent of full-time employees in large and midsized private firms were participating in defined benefit plans. In particular, big companies such as General Motors and IBM almost always had generous defined benefit plans. Many

> **DEFINED BENEFIT PLAN**
> A retirement plan that pays retirees a predetermined amount of money monthly.
>
> **DEFINED CONTRIBUTION PLAN**
> A retirement plan where the payments depend on the return on investments.

government employees today still have good defined benefit plans.

In recent years, however, more and more private employers have been moving to **defined contribution plans.** Such plans require employees—and usually employers as well—to put money each month into an account, which the employer then invests. The actual monthly payment to the retired worker, however, depends on how the investment does over time. As a result, the retirement benefits are not guaranteed.

The most important form of defined contribution plan today is the **401(k) plan,** named for the corresponding section of the tax law. Generally in a 401(k) plan a participant will decide how much of his or her pretax income should be put into the retirement account (within government-set limits). The employer then matches the contribution, either partly or in full. For example, a worker earning $100,000 per year might put 5 percent of her pretax salary, or $5,000, into her 401(k) account. At the same time, her employer might match 3 percent of her pretax salary, or $3,000. The total contributions would be 8 percent of her salary, or $5,000 from the worker and $3,000 from her employer, per year.

Participants in 401(k) plans can generally choose whether to invest their funds in the stock market (in the United States or abroad), put them into interest-paying money market accounts, or put them into other kinds of investments. No taxes are imposed on those funds as long as they stay in the 401(k) account. They are taxed only when withdrawn to pay for retirement expenses.

The Limitations of Employer Retirement Plans

Employer retirement plans can be useful in raising individuals' retirement income. However, they do not solve the retirement poverty problem. Full-time workers are more likely to be in a retirement plan than those who work part-time. Better-paid workers are more likely to have retirement benefits than those who are paid less.

HOW IT WORKS: CHOOSING NOT TO PARTICIPATE

Many people have access to defined contribution plans at work but choose not to participate. For example, according to the Bureau of Labor Statistics, 48 percent of private sector low-wage workers have access to a defined contribution plan but only 29 percent participate in them. There are a variety of reasons. Some people don't have any spare cash to save; some don't think about the future; some don't realize the company contributes to boost their savings; some simply forget to file the right forms.

To address this problem of nonparticipation, in 2006 economists pushed for a change in the laws governing retirement plans to make it easier for employers to automatically enroll workers in 401(k) plans. Workers can still opt *not* to contribute, but they have to make an active choice in that case. The expectation is that this will raise participation rates over time.

What about the retirement uncertainty problem? If you participate in a defined benefit plan, in theory it will pay you the same amount monthly as long as you live. That provides a certain measure of security. However, defined benefit plans have a big downside: they assume the company will be able to provide enough money to fund all future benefits. If a company goes bankrupt or fails, the money to fund the pension plan may not be there.

To avoid the heavy burden of defined benefit plans, many companies have been switching to defined contribution plans, which transfer the risk to individual workers. With a defined contribution plan, you still have to worry about how your investments will do and whether you will live long enough to exhaust your savings.

SOCIAL SECURITY

Social Security was introduced as part of the New Deal in 1932 to help address the retirement poverty problem. It takes a different approach to retirement income than either individual savings or employer retirement plans. Both of those sources of income are based on the idea of saving now and building assets for the future.

In contrast, Social Security levies a tax on current workers to pay for the retirement of yesterday's workers. In other words, income is transferred from current workers to current retirees. At the same time there is an implicit commitment that the next generation will do the same when current workers retire. Figure 18.2 shows how Social Security modifies the life cycle model we described earlier in the chapter.

In principle, Social Security can solve both the retirement poverty problem and the retirement uncertainty problem. Because Social Security is funded by current taxes, it can offer a decent retirement income to low-income workers without requiring them to contribute that much during their careers. Indeed, Social Security has made a major contribution to lowering the poverty rate of older retirees.

FIGURE 18.2	**The Life Cycle with Social Security**

The retirement life cycle changes once Social Security is introduced. Each generation is supported in retirement by the ones that come after.

Young: Pay taxes to support the old.	**Middle age:** Pay taxes to support the old.	**Old:** Use transfers from young and middle-aged for living costs.

Moreover, because Social Security draws on current taxes, it can offer people retirement benefits as long as they live. That means workers don't have to save up huge nest eggs to account for the possibility of living to age 80, 90, or more.

How Social Security Works Today

As we saw earlier in the chapter, Social Security provides 41 percent of the income of people aged 65 and over. Because of its importance to the economy, it's good to know how the program works today. First, the Social Security Administration, which runs the program, has a formula for determining your monthly benefits. That formula depends on the average of how much you earned during your lifetime, adjusted for the rise in average wages over time. The formula is **progressive** so that low-income workers get back higher percentages of their lifetime average incomes than do better-paid workers. The benefits are also indexed to inflation—so as prices rise, the benefits rise to keep pace with them.

Second, there's a formula for determining how much payroll tax you and your employer pay each year to fund Social Security. As of 2010 you pay 6.2 percent of your wages up to a $106,800 wage cap, and your employer pays an equal amount. The cap is raised each year to account for inflation. These taxes are paid into the Social Security trust fund (officially called the Old-Age and Survivors Insurance and Disability Insurance Trust Fund), invested in Treasury bonds, and then paid out in benefits to current retirees.

Third, and most important, there's no real link between the taxes you pay and the benefits you receive later in life. Congress can raise and lower the benefit formula as it likes—and it has done this many times. It can also raise and lower the tax rates as it likes—as it has done many times. There's no direct connection between the two, and there never has been. Early recipients received far more than they put in, whereas many current high-income workers are likely to get only a small return on their payroll taxes.

OLD-AGE DEPENDENCY RATIO
The ratio of the size of the older population to the size of the working-age population.

The Demographic Challenge Facing Social Security

The concept of Social Security works well when the population is expanding. In this scenario, a large working population has to support a smaller number of elderly people. Paying off the previous generation is cheaper than saving for yourself.

It also helps if real wages are rising over time, as has been true over the past 75 years. Then the younger generation is better off than the older generation, making it easier for them to pay Social Security taxes.

But funding Social Security becomes more difficult when population growth slows. The clearest sign of the funding problem comes from the **old-age dependency ratio,** which is the ratio of the size of the older population (65 years and older) to the size of the working-age population (ages 20 through 64). For example, a ratio of 0.2 means there are five working-age people for every older person to support. The lower the old-age dependency ratio, the less tax burden each worker has to support the older population.

Figure 18.3 shows the history of the old-age dependency ratio, along with the projections of the Social Security Administration through 2075. The ratio goes from 0.2 to 0.4, which means instead of 5 workers supporting every retiree in 2075, there will be only 2.5 workers. The burden on each worker will double.

Will Social Security Run Out of Money?

You've probably heard this over and over again: "Social Security is going to run out of money." That's partly true, but it's also misleading. Right now Social Security is running a small surplus: the amount generated by the Social Security payroll tax exceeds the amount being paid out in benefits to current retirees. As of the end of 2009, there was roughly $2.5 trillion in this fund, held in federal government bonds (these bonds are promises from the government to pay recipients in the future). In effect, the Social Security trust fund has lent the rest of the government its surplus.

FIGURE 18.3	**The Demographic Challenge of Social Security**

The old-age dependency ratio will double over the next 50 years.

Source: Social Security Administration, www.ssa.gov.

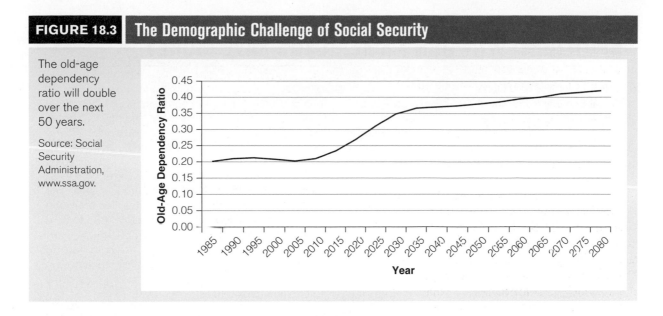

Fixing the Retirement Shortfall

What will happen in the future? The Social Security Administration offers multiple projections, depending on its assumptions about growth, demographics, and other variables. However, based on its intermediate projection in 2010, the cost of Social Security benefits due will exceed the income from payroll taxes starting around 2015 or so.

From that point on, there will be a **financing gap** between taxes and spending that the Social Security Administration will fill with the assets in the trust fund, which are Treasury bonds. To come up with the cash to pay Social Security recipients, the Social Security Administration will have to redeem the bonds, which are obligations of the U.S. government. And to pay these bonds off, Congress and the president will have to agree either to raise income taxes or to cut other types of spending.

In other words, once the cost of Social Security exceeds the proceeds from its payroll tax, the government will have to come up with the money, one way or another.

Fixing the Retirement Shortfall

There are four possible responses to the Social Security financing gap: cut benefits, raise payroll taxes, fund the gap from general revenues, or privatize Social Security. Let's look at the pluses and minuses of each of these, and whether and how they might be combined.

CUTTING BENEFITS The most likely response to the financing gap is probably a reduction in Social Security benefits. A 30 percent reduction of benefits from their expected levels would bring the cost of Social Security back in line with costs.

However, the cut in benefits need not be a reduction in payments across the board. It could come in the form of a higher retirement age, for instance. That makes sense, given that people are living longer. However, a higher retirement age might be hard on workers who do physical labor like loading trucks or construction, which is tougher when you are in your 60s.

Economic Milestone

1940 THE FIRST SOCIAL SECURITY RECIPIENT

Ida May Fuller, a legal secretary in Ludlow, Vermont, received the first monthly Social Security retirement check in January 1940, three years after the program started collecting taxes. During that time Fuller paid a total of $24.75 in payroll taxes. She lived until 1975, and she collected $22,889 in Social Security benefits.

SPOTLIGHT: WHY DON'T AMERICANS SAVE MORE?

Social Security is not about to disappear, but its benefits are likely to be trimmed in the future. That means Americans should be saving more for retirement. The **personal savings rate** is equal to personal savings as a percentage of disposable personal income, which is income after taxes. The personal savings rate dropped from over 10 percent in the early 1980s to a low of 1.4 percent in 2005. Since then it has bounced back up to around 6 percent as households reacted to the recession by spending less.

Still, most economists agree that a 6 percent personal savings rate is not nearly enough. Why don't Americans save more? One reason is that historically U.S. consumers have had access to a lot more credit than consumers in other countries; this let them keep buying instead of saving. Second, the housing boom in the 2000s increased the value of homes around the country and made U.S. home owners feel wealthier, encouraging them to consume beyond their incomes and driving down savings. Finally, some countries, such as China, do not have an organized system, like Social Security in the United States, for providing support for the elderly. Therefore people have to save to provide for their own old age.

Sooner or later, Americans are going to have to boost their personal savings. That may mean buying smaller cars and homes, or cutting back on personal entertainment expenses.

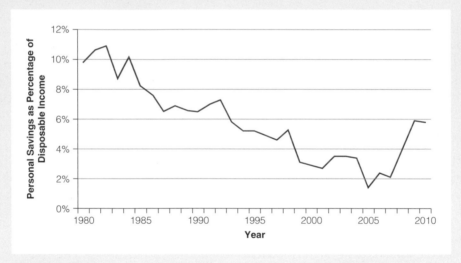

FIGURE 18.4

The Personal Savings Rate, 1980–2010 Personal savings as a percentage of disposable income hit a low in 2005 as Americans borrowed against their homes. But since then households have been tightening their belts.

Source: Bureau of Economic Analysis, www.bea.gov.

Another possibility is a reduction in benefits for high-income workers. That would be less harmful because these people are expected to have good savings and alternative sources of income. But such a targeted reduction in benefits would be likely to erode the political support for Social Security because high-income voters would get less from the program, making them less likely to support it.

RAISING THE PAYROLL TAX Another possible response—either by itself or combined with a benefits reduction—is an increase in the amount that Social Security receives from payroll taxes.

One way to achieve this is to raise the Social Security payroll tax rate, which is currently 6.2 percent of wages from both workers and employers.

Another way to raise payroll taxes is to lift the Social Security cap—that is, the maximum amount of income that can be taxed. For example, in 2010 the Social Security cap was $106,800. If a worker made $200,000 that year, he or she paid Social Security tax on only the first $106,800 earned. Raising or eliminating the cap on Social Security taxes would increase tax revenues.

FUNDING WITH GENERAL REVENUES It is inevitable that at least a portion of the Social Security gap will be funded out of general revenues, which include personal and corporate income taxes. When the Treasury bonds in the Social Security trust fund are cashed in, that money will come out of the overall federal budget—in the form of higher taxes, lower spending, or both. When the trust fund has been completely depleted, Congress and the president will have the option to use the same flow of funds from general revenues—personal and corporate income taxes, primarily—to directly support Social Security benefits.

But will there be the political desire and will to do this? It probably depends on how well the economy is doing. If growth has been strong and real incomes have risen, workers may feel able to pay a bit more in taxes to support older citizens. But if growth has been weak, the natural tendency will be to force everyone to cut back—which includes cutting Social Security benefits.

PRIVATIZATION The first three responses to the Social Security shortfall keep the basic structure of today's retirement system. **Privatization,** in contrast, refers to an overhaul of the Social Security system that takes the radical step of moving more of the decisions and responsibility of retirement saving into the private sector while preserving a basic safety net for the poor and unlucky.

Many versions of privatization have been proposed. The most basic version is a defined contribution plan: the money from each individual's

payroll taxes would go into a personal account rather than a national trust fund. Each individual would then be responsible for investing the money to have enough from retirement.

In this scenario the government role would be to set rules for how much workers would have to contribute and how they would be allowed to invest. In addition, the government would "top up" the accounts of low-income workers—that is, the government would contribute enough money to make sure everyone had a minimum amount in his or her account.

The benefit of privatization is that if the economy and the stock market were to do well, people might retire with more money than they would have gotten through Social Security. And because it would be mandatory for people to build up their personal accounts, there would be more savings in the economy and likely more growth.

The downside of privatization is the retirement uncertainty problem: workers would once again have to worry about whether they will have enough money to support themselves through old age. If the economy does poorly, the returns on personal accounts will be lower—and instead of having guaranteed payments as they do now, retired workers will share the pain with current workers. Moreover, there's a large transition problem because workers who are now close to retirement age don't have an opportunity to build up personal accounts to replace the Social Security payments they have counted on. This is not an easy problem to solve.

In the end, it's likely that the Social Security shortfall will be solved through a combination of all four approaches—some reductions in benefits, increased payroll taxes, some reliance on general revenues, and perhaps personal accounts added to the current system. The exact mix, however, will depend on the next generation of politicians and economists.

THE BASICS OF HEALTHCARE SPENDING

We now turn from retirement and Social Security—which is a large but manageable problem—to healthcare, which is a large but thus

FIGURE 18.5 | National Health Expenditures as a Percentage of GDP

Spending on healthcare has taken a growing share of the economy over the past half century.

Source: Centers for Medicare and Medicaid Services, www.cms.gov.

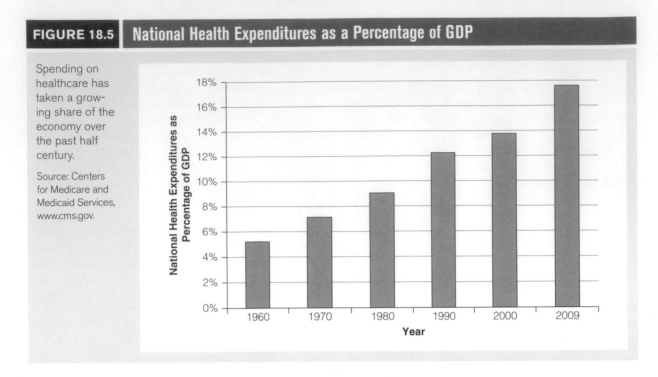

far unmanageable challenge. Healthcare today is the largest sector of the economy. In 2009 Americans spent $2.5 trillion on healthcare, including drugs, hospital care, and nursing homes. That's roughly 17.6 percent of the economy, bigger than food or housing.

More important, healthcare's share of the economic pie has been growing, as Figure 18.5 shows. Similarly, healthcare has accounted for a big share of job growth in recent years (see "Spotlight: Healthcare and the Job Market"). Compared to other countries, the United States spends far more on healthcare per person. (See Figure 18.6).

If these trends continue, healthcare could equal 30 percent of the economy by 2075. Imagine a world where every third building is a hospital, nursing home, or doctor's office! As a result, the question of how to slow the growth of healthcare spending, while still maintaining or even improving care for everyone, is one of the biggest issues facing policy makers.

The Healthcare Life Cycle

To understand why healthcare spending is such an issue, let's start by looking at the basic eco-

nomics of healthcare. In most markets, decisions to purchase and consume are voluntary. You choose when and how to buy a new car or a new home. By contrast, in the healthcare market consumption decisions are usually forced by an external event such as getting sick. There are

SPOTLIGHT: HEALTHCARE AND THE JOB MARKET

Along with rising healthcare spending come healthcare jobs—lots of them. A growing share of the workforce is employed as nurses, doctors, medical technicians, home health aides, and all the other occupations that provide healthcare. In 2010, health services—including hospitals and doctors' offices—accounted for almost 13 percent of all private sector jobs. What's more, healthcare makes up a critical part of job growth. From 2000 to 2010, healthcare services added 2.9 million jobs. Meanwhile the rest of the private sector lost 6.6 million jobs.

Source: Bureau of Labor Statistics, www.bls.gov.

FIGURE 18.6 | Per Capita Healthcare Spending across the World, 2008

The United States spends far more on healthcare, per person, than do other industrialized countries.

Source: The Organisation for Economic Cooperation and Development (OECD), www. oecd.org.

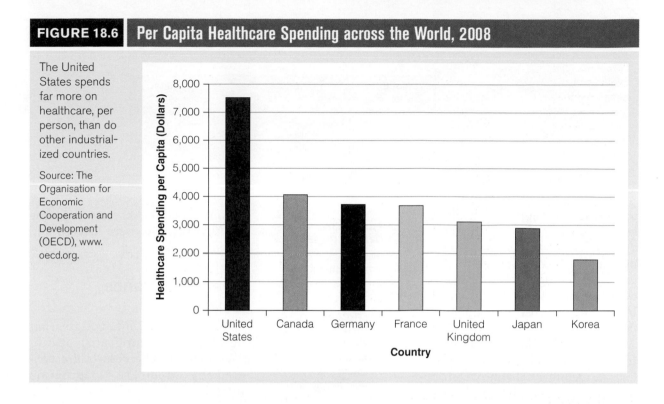

three types of health events. First, there's the flow of ordinary healthcare expenses when you are young and middle-aged: dental and vision costs, occasional visits to the doctor for the flu or sports-related injuries. Second, there's the catastrophic health event, which becomes more likely in middle age: getting cancer, for example. Finally, there's the inevitability of a steady stream of old age–related health expenses as you age: heart attacks, strokes, cancer, and expensive end-of-life care.

In the absence of government- or business-supported health insurance, these three stages make up the **healthcare life cycle.** Let's consider what the healthcare system would look like if it were completely paid for by individuals as they used it. The young and middle-aged would probably pay for their ordinary healthcare expenses out of their own pockets. Both young and middle-aged people would buy **catastrophic health insurance,** which would cover the high expenses incurred for a catastrophic health event but not ordinary healthcare expenses (for example, it would pay for the hospital and physician services for a serious accident, but not for an

ordinary visit to the dentist). Middle-aged people would pay more for catastrophic insurance, of course, because the odds of something going seriously wrong are higher in middle age than in youth.

However, it would be very expensive to buy insurance to cover old age–related healthcare expenses. The reason is straightforward: because old age–related healthcare expenses are nearly inevitable, the insurance company would have to charge high premiums to pay all the expected claims. At some point it would not be financially worthwhile for an older person to buy medical insurance.

Thus in a healthcare life cycle, middle-aged individuals would expect to pay their old age healthcare expenses out of their own pockets. That means they would have to sock away an enormous amount during middle age to cover most of their medical costs (see Figure 18.7).

Problems with the Healthcare Life Cycle

The life cycle approach to healthcare has the advantage of treating medical care like any other

FIGURE 18.7 | The Healthcare Life Cycle

How individuals might pay for healthcare by themselves.

Youth:	Middle age:	Old age:
Pay for basic health expenses.	Pay for basic health expenses. Buy insurance against catastrophic health events. Save for old age health expenses.	Use savings for medical costs.

good or service. People buy healthcare according to their income and desires; doctors, hospitals, and drug companies supply healthcare services and goods according to their cost functions; and the price of healthcare is set by the interplay between supply and demand.

However, the life cycle approach to healthcare has the same two problems as the life cycle approach to retirement, plus another problem of its own. First, it leaves the poor exposed to medical disasters because they cannot afford to pay for insurance; that's the **healthcare poverty problem.** Second, it puts people in the position of projecting how much money they will need to pay for healthcare when they are old—a difficult task because medical expenses are so high and so unpredictable. That's the **healthcare uncertainty problem.**

Finally, the life cycle approach to healthcare also suffers from the **adverse selection** problem. Adverse selection is the tendency for insurance to be purchased by those who are more likely to make claims. In particular, health insurance is more likely to be purchased by people who are sick and less likely to be purchased by people who need it less—the ones who are healthy. Thus any health insurance plan—including the catastrophic insurance plan needed by the young and middle-aged—will tend to have the sickest people (an "adverse selection" of the population) in it. This drives up insurance rates because the plan must pay a lot more in claims (compared to how much it receives in premiums)

HEALTHCARE POVERTY PROBLEM
Poor people often do not have enough income to pay for health insurance.

HEALTHCARE UNCERTAINTY PROBLEM
People don't know how much money they will need to pay for healthcare in old age.

ADVERSE SELECTION PROBLEM
The tendency of insurance to be purchased by those who are more likely to make claims.

than it would if everyone, including healthier people, were insured and paying premiums.

Health Insurance Coverage

Over time the United States has developed a complicated healthcare system. The elderly are covered by **Medicare,** a program introduced by President Lyndon Johnson in 1965. Low-income children, their parents, and individuals with disabilities are covered, not always completely, by **Medicaid,** which was also introduced by President Johnson. Many workers were covered through **employer health insurance plans.**

This healthcare system helped solve the healthcare uncertainty problem because the elderly knew they would be covered by Medicare no matter how long they lived. Workers, especially at larger companies, typically had access to

TABLE 18.2	Who Doesn't Have Health Insurance: 2009

	Percentage without Health Insurance Coverage, 2009
Household income	
Greater than $75,000	9.1%
Less than $75,000	21.4%
Age	
Under 18	10.0%
18–34 years	29.7%
35–64 years	18.0%
Size of employer	
100 or more employees	13.3%
Fewer than 100 employees	29.6%

Source: Census Bureau, www.census.gov.

good healthcare services through their employers' plans, including doctor visits, hospital care for major accidents or illness, and some types of prescription drugs.

However, the previous system had many gaps and did not fully solve either the healthcare poverty problem or the adverse selection problem. Poor families—especially those employed at low-wage or part-time jobs at small companies—were often without healthcare coverage. Similarly, if you lost your job, it was often hard to obtain new health insurance at a reasonable cost. Meanwhile, many young Americans were not covered because health insurance seemed too expensive to be worthwhile (see Table 18.2).

The Obama health insurance reform bill, signed March 2010, was designed to close most of the gaps in the health insurance system. The key features of the bill addressed both the healthcare poverty problem and the adverse selection problem. On the one hand, the legislation included extensive tax credits and subsidies to help low-income households buy health insurance. On the other hand, the Obama health reform package also included an "individual mandate": a requirement that almost everyone has to enroll in a health insurance plan or pay a fine.

As this textbook is being revised in early 2011, opponents of President Obama's health-

HOW IT WORKS: IS HEALTH INSURANCE REALLY INSURANCE?

By definition, "insurance" is the payment of regular small premiums in exchange for coverage in the case of an expensive but rare event. The classic case is fire insurance: only one of 300 living units has a fire every year, but if you do have a fire, it can destroy your whole house. As a result, most people pay a regular premium to receive compensation if their house should burn partially or fully.

On the other hand, you would never buy "food insurance." There would be no point because you have to buy food every week. Moreover, you would be continually filing claim forms with your "food insurer," who would question whether you really needed that extra bag of popcorn.

Health insurance combines both these kinds of events. It covers rare catastrophic and expensive events, as well as the flow of ordinary healthcare expenses.

care reform are attempting to modify or repeal the legislation. It is unclear how successful they will be.

THE RISING COST OF HEALTHCARE

A crucial fact about today's economy is that healthcare spending per person has consistently risen faster than income per person. In other words, the richer we get, the more we spend on doctor's visits, medical tests, mental healthcare, cosmetic surgery, and almost every other form of necessary or elective care.

For a few years in the 1990s, healthcare spending seemed under control. But in recent years costs have jumped again. One measure of this increase is the consumer price index for medical care, which includes both healthcare services (doctors and hospitals) and healthcare products (drugs and equipment). Between 1995 and 2010

TABLE 18.3	Six Reasons Why Healthcare Costs Are Rising Quickly

Reason	Explanation
Demographic change	An aging population needs more healthcare.
Rising incomes	A richer population is willing to pay for more healthcare.
Third-party payments	Spending decisions are made by doctors and patients, but most of the payments come from insurance companies and the government.
Tax deductions for employer healthcare	Workers are not taxed on company-funded healthcare spending.
Rapid technological progress	New healthcare technologies are expensive.
Bad medicine	Some healthcare practices don't work.

the price to consumers of medical care rose at an average annual rate of 3.8 percent. Meanwhile the price of everything else rose at an annual average rate of only 2.3 percent.

Why the big disparity? Economists have explored several reasons why healthcare costs are so difficult to control. These reasons are summarized in Table 18.3; let's look at them more closely.

Demographic Change

Obviously older people use more healthcare than younger people do. For example, Table 18.4 shows that the cost of providing healthcare to the typical older person in 2004 was $14,797, compared to only $2,650 for the typical young person (the latest data available as this textbook

TABLE 18.4	Healthcare Spending in the United States by Age

Age	Personal Healthcare Spending per Person, 2004	Average Annual Growth, 1987–2004 (%)
Total	$ 5,726	6.5
0–18	$ 2,650	6.8
19–64	$ 4,511	6.6
65+	$14,797	6.2

Source: Centers for Medicare and Medicaid Services, www.cms.gov.

is being revised). So as the percentage of the population who are 65 and older rises, healthcare spending should inevitably rise.

However, **demographic change**—the changing distribution of age groups—is only a partial explanation for rising healthcare costs. Table 18.4 also shows that in each age group, healthcare spending is increasing at roughly the same rate. That means healthcare costs would be rising even if the population today consisted of only, say, 19- to 64-year-olds.

Rising Incomes

Many people believe healthcare is a *luxury good,* as defined in Chapter 3: one whose consumption goes up sharply when incomes rise. The argument runs something like this: we have all the physical goods we need—food, housing, transportation, and entertainment. So as we get richer, we don't spend the extra money on a fourth car or a fifth television set. Instead we spend it on healthcare.

This probably explains part of the rise in healthcare costs. In fact, U.S. adults seem willing to spend a bit extra to be able to quickly see a doctor rather than waiting months for an appointment. And they are willing to pay for additional tests just to have some peace of mind.

Third-Party Payments

Imagine that the store manager at your local supermarket was allowed to choose the foods you buy. He or she would make up the list, fill your shopping cart, and then bill your insurance company. You'd likely end up eating some tasty but expensive items that you otherwise would not have bought.

Similarly, when it comes to healthcare, the person making decisions is often not the patient but the doctor. Roughly 85 percent of healthcare spending is paid for by a **third party**—a health insurance plan, Medicare, or Medicaid. That means the normal constraints on purchases are not present. In theory, a doctor can order expensive tests and treatments without worrying about whether they are actually worth the money, and the patient can agree without worrying about whether she will have to pay for them. In fact, if the doctor is worried about being sued for malpractice by an unsatisfied patient, ordering extra tests for self-protection becomes a rational decision.

This is different from the usual sort of market we discussed in earlier chapters. Typically, when we talk about buyers in a market, we assume the buyer is also the ultimate consumer of the good or service being purchased. So when you buy a car, you'll pay for extra options like special shiny trim only if you think they're worth their cost.

In practice, both private health insurers and Medicare closely scrutinize doctors' decisions and refuse to pay for care they think is excessive. However, many economists believe that if patients had to pay their own healthcare costs, they would spend more frugally.

> Healthcare is a luxury good because people spend a lot more on it as their incomes rise.

Tax Deductions for Employer Healthcare

By law, employer contributions to healthcare plans do not count as taxable income. In other words, if a worker receives a dollar in wages, he or she has to pay federal, state, and local taxes on that money. But if the employer spends that same dollar on improving the company healthcare plan—say, by paying for a broader array of benefits for workers—then no one pays any taxes on it.

It's a general principle that if something is untaxed, you receive more of it. In this case, there's an incentive for workers to receive their compensation as health insurance, which is untaxed, rather than as wages, which are taxed. That helps explain why healthcare spending is so high.

Rapid Technological Change

In recent years the United States has poured hundreds of billions of dollars into medical research. The result has been all sorts of new medical technologies, pharmaceuticals, and procedures intended to improve health and save lives. One example is better cardiac care. From 1994 to 2004 the number of people dying from coronary heart disease declined 18 percent, even as the number of older people rose.

But this technological progress has come with a big price tag. New drugs to fight cancer are often spectacularly expensive. Genentech, one of the leading biotech firms, charged $4,400 a month for its cancer-fighting drug Avastin when it was first introduced in 2004. Advanced equipment like an MRI machine is also expensive.

Even some advances that look like they should save money actually don't. Using drugs to treat depression and other mental illness is cheaper, on a per-person basis, than sending the same person to a well-paid psychologist or psychiatrist. Yet because the use of the drugs allow more people to be treated, the total cost to the United States of treating mental health problems has risen. From 1995 to 2005 (the latest data available as this textbook was being revised) spending on mental health drugs grew at a 17.5 percent annual rate, compared to only a 4.2 percent annual gain for all other types of mental health spending. That's according to a report by the Substance Abuse and Mental Health Services Administration. This is similar to what happened in the computer industry in the 1990s. As computers became less expensive and more powerful, they became more useful, so households and companies ended up spending more money on information technology in total.

Bad Medicine

Could it be that we are simply wasting money on unnecessary medical procedures? Doctors and

SPOTLIGHT: HOW WELL DOES HEALTHCARE WORK?

We spend an enormous amount on healthcare, but here's a key question we rarely ask: Does all that money improve our health? With most purchases in a market economy, you know whether you received value for the money you paid. For example, when you buy a car, you know whether or not it runs well.

The simplest way to assess the quality of our healthcare system is to look at the change in our **life expectancy,** or expected years of remaining life, based on today's healthcare system. (Obviously there is no way to predict future medical breakthroughs, so we must ignore them in this analysis.) Life expectancy for newborns—the usual number cited—has risen a lot because of better care for pregnant mothers and young children. In 1900 life expectancy at birth was only 47.3 years. In 2009, the latest year available, life expectancy at birth had risen to 78.2 years. That's a big gain.

However, we can also look at life expectancy at age 50, and that picture is not so rosy. As Figure 18.8 shows, at the beginning of the 20th century, a 50-year-old U.S. adult could expect to live to 71.3 years. Today that's increased only up to 81.1 years.

Considering how many billions of dollars have been poured into cancer and heart disease research in recent years, it's a bit of surprise that the life expectancy of the middle-aged hasn't increased more.

One hypothesis is that we have been taking worse care of ourselves—getting less exercise and eating too much—even as medical science has gotten better. Alternatively, inefficiencies in the healthcare system may prevent the delivery of good medical care to many adults. Or surprisingly, medical science may still not have advanced far enough to be translated into enough new drugs and treatments to make a difference.

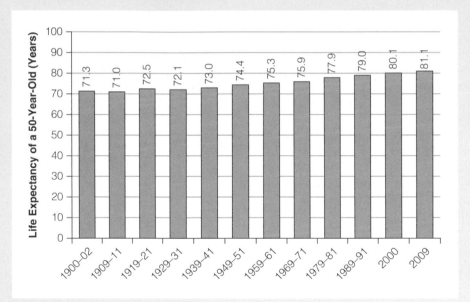

FIGURE 18.8
Life Expectancy of a 50-Year-Old

Source: National Center for Health Statistics, www.cdc.gov/nchs.

hospitals don't always know what works and what doesn't. For example, there's some dispute about whether commonly prescribed medications such as Lipitor (for reducing cholesterol) have the impact on heart disease that doctors expected. This will continue to be an important topic in years to come. (See "Spotlight: How Well Does Healthcare Work?")

Policy Responses

In several places in this textbook, we have discussed the controversy over the role of government in the economy. As we have seen, government economic intervention is a plausible and sometimes necessary remedy when private markets fall short. That's especially true when we focus on social issues, such as the lack of medical care for poor people.

On the other hand, we also saw in Chapter 6 that government action is accompanied by several downsides. These include the *incentive problem* because government managers don't have to worry about making a profit; *rent-seeking behavior,* which leads companies to divert resources to lobbying public officials rather than improving productivity; and *the lack of flexibility and innovation* that can occur because government officials may be too cautious about making big changes.

This debate about the role of government in the economy is always going on, but it is especially intense in healthcare. Everyone agrees that something needs to be done because of the combination of rising costs and dissatisfaction with the current system. Yet economists and policy makers are divided about whether to increase the role of the government or reduce it.

CONCLUSION

The economic problems of funding retirement and healthcare are closely linked, but they are not the same. The Social Security financing gap is large but relatively straightforward to fix. By contrast, no one yet has a handle on the right way to deal with fast-rising healthcare costs.

The next and final chapter will focus on another issue likely to be debated for years: how to handle energy, pollution, and global warming. We will lay out the dimensions of the economic problem, and discuss potential policy alternatives.

18 SUMMARY

1. The life cycle theory of retirement says people spend when they are young, save during the latter part of their working lives, and spend while they are retired. Two things can go wrong in the life cycle model. First, poor people often cannot save much for retirement. Second, it's difficult to know how much money to put away in savings to cover all eventualities. The four components of retirement income are part-time work, individual savings, employer retirement plans, and Social Security. *(LO18-1)*

2. Employer retirement plans can be useful in raising individuals' retirement incomes. The two types of employer retirement plans are defined benefit plans and defined contribution plans. However, they do not solve the poverty problem. Meanwhile defined contribution plans, although increasingly common, do not solve the uncertainty problem. *(LO18-2)*

3. Social Security levies a tax on current workers today to pay for the retirement of yesterday's workers. Currently Social Security is the single largest source of support for U.S. adults aged 65 and over. The concept of Social Security works well when the population is expanding, but funding Social Security becomes more difficult when population growth slows. That means we will likely need some combination of benefit cuts, tax increases, funding with general revenues, and privatization. *(LO18-3)*

4. Funding healthcare poses a bigger challenge than Social Security. The healthcare life cycle raises three problems that must be solved: the healthcare poverty problem, the healthcare uncertainty problem, and the adverse selection problem. *(LO18-4)*

5. Healthcare expenditures have been rising steadily as a share of GDP. The reasons include demographic change, rising incomes, third-party payments, tax deductions for employer healthcare, rapid technological progress, and bad medicine. *(LO18-5)*

KEY TERMS AND CONCEPTS

life cycle theory of retirement	401(k) plan	healthcare uncertainty problem
net worth	progressive	adverse selection problem
retirement poverty problem	old-age dependency ratio	Medicare
retirement uncertainty problem	financing gap	Medicaid
four-legged stool	privatization	employer health insurance plans
employer retirement plans	personal savings rate	demographic change
Social Security	healthcare life cycle	third party
defined benefit plan	catastrophic health insurance	life expectancy
defined contribution plan	healthcare poverty problem	single-payer system

PROBLEMS

1. Consider the life cycle theory of retirement. *(LO18-1)*

   a) In which stage do workers accumulate savings for retirement?

   b) An individual who comes from a long-lived family needs to pay special attention to which retirement life cycle problem?

   c) Social Security payments are adjusted for inflation. That helps solve which retirement life cycle problem?

2. Suppose that you reach 65 years old, and had $100,000 in an investment that pays a return of 5% per year. *(LO18-1)*

   a) If you withdraw $10,000 at the end of each year for living expenses, how many years will it take before your investment is gone? (*Hint:* Go year by year and calculate the return on the investment and then the amount remaining after the withdrawal).

   b) If you withdraw $5,000 at the end of each year for living expenses, how many years will it take before your investment is gone?

3. Employer retirement plans are an important element of retirement income. *(LO18-2)*

   a) Suppose that in addition to your salary, your employer invests a sum of money in the stock market each year in your name. Then, when you retire, you get the current value of the invested money. Is this a defined benefit or a defined contribution plan?

   b) Suppose the plan is set up so that it is invested only in the stock of the company you work for. Which life cycle retirement problem does this *not* solve?

4. The labor force participation rate of an age group is the percentage of people of that age who are either working or actively looking for jobs. Would you expect the existence of Social Security to increase or decrease the labor force participation rate for people aged 65 and over? Explain your answer. *(LO18-3)*

5. Most economists agree that immigration helps improve the finances of the Social Security system. *(LO18-3)*

   a) To benefit Social Security funding, would we prefer immigrants to be old or young? Explain.

   b) Would the finances of Social Security benefit more from low-wage immigrants or high-wage, highly skilled immigrants?

   c) Assume that about half of illegal immigrants actually pay Social Security taxes, but they are unlikely to collect benefits. Based on that assumption, do illegal immigrants help improve the finances of the Social Security system? Explain.

6. The following table gives the population at different ages for the city of Elizabeth, New Jersey, in the 2000 census. *(LO18-3)*

Age	Number of People
Under 5 years old	9,266
5–17 years old	22,414
18–19 years old	3,432
Ages 20–64	73,415
Ages 65 and over	12,041

   a) What is the old-age dependency ratio in Elizabeth?

   b) Table 18.4 showed the annual cost of healthcare per person, by age. Suppose the annual cost of educating the average 10-year-old is $10,000. According to the data in Table 18.4, is the cost of education plus healthcare for a 10-year-old greater or less than the healthcare cost for an adult older than 65?

7. In this chapter we identify several kinds of events that can affect your health. *(LO18-4)*

   a) Name them and explain their differences.

   b) Which ones are covered by employer healthcare plans?

8. In this chapter we identify several reasons that might explain why healthcare costs have risen so rapidly. Fill in the blanks in the following statements. *(LO18-5)*

   a) In a state with a young population, healthcare costs would be rising _____ than the rest of the country.

   b) If workers were forced to pay income taxes on the value of their employer-provided healthcare benefits, then the growth rate of healthcare costs would _____.

   c) If we could identify the healthcare practices that don't work, then the cost of healthcare would _____.

   d) If patients were forced to pay more of their medical bills, that would worsen the _____ problem.

9. Lung cancer is the leading cause of cancer-related deaths among both men and women, with an estimated 160,000 deaths in 2007. Suppose a drug was approved that immediately cured lung cancer. *(LO18-5)*

a) In the short run, is that drug likely to increase or decrease healthcare spending? Explain.

b) In the long run, is that drug likely to increase or decrease healthcare spending? Explain.

19 ECONOMICS OF ENERGY, THE ENVIRONMENT, AND GLOBAL CLIMATE CHANGE

Two key topics for us are the economics of energy and the economics of the environment. They are closely related to each other because much of the pollution emitted today is related to the production and use of energy.

In this chapter we examine three key aspects of the economics of energy and the environment. First, we will look at the balance between supply and demand for energy in the short run. This is a topic of enormous importance, especially since we have seen big swings in the price of gasoline and oil in recent years.

Second, we will consider the sustainability of our energy supplies in the long run. As countries such as China and India increase their output and improve their standards of living, they also increase their consumption of energy. How will the world economy meet those energy needs? Will the price of oil and other energy sources increase sharply? Is there a role for government intervention to either encourage the development of new sources of energy or to encourage energy conservation?

Third, we will examine the economic impact of pollution, including the economic consequences of global climate change. We look at this from an economic perspective, asking how we can cost-effectively reduce pollution's effects on the environment. We examine the pros and cons of different approaches, including using the market as a tool for reducing pollution.

THE BASICS OF ENERGY CONSUMPTION AND SUPPLY

Let's start by looking at the basics of energy consumption and supply. Energy is one of the most important markets in the economy. Every family, every business, and every organization uses energy, so any changes in the price of energy affect everyone simultaneously.

Energy Consumption

Economic history has been the story of rising energy consumption—energy to power factories, move vehicles, heat and cool homes, and so forth. At each step of the way, energy use per person in industrialized countries has risen. Figure 19.1 shows energy usage in the United States over the past 150 years, measured as millions of British thermal units per person per year. (A British thermal unit, or BTU, is a measure of energy; 1 gallon of gasoline is equivalent to 124,000 BTUs.)

Over this century and a half, energy usage per person has more than tripled. However, the oil price shock of 1973 (mentioned several times

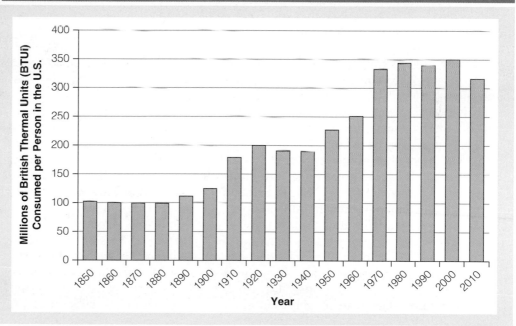

FIGURE 19.1   U.S. Energy Consumption per Person, 1850–2010

Per capita consumption of energy rose dramatically for more than a century but has been basically stable since the mid-1970s.

Source: Energy Information Administration and author calculations.

FIGURE 19.2 | **Global Energy Consumption per Person, 2008**

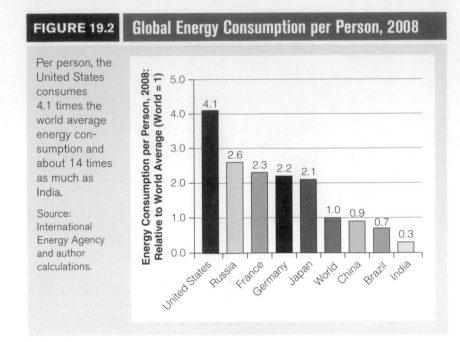

Per person, the United States consumes 4.1 times the world average energy consumption and about 14 times as much as India.

Source: International Energy Agency and author calculations.

earlier in this textbook) seems to have marked the end of unbridled energy use. Since the mid-1970s, energy use per person in the United States has remained more or less the same from year to year, with a slight drop after the financial crisis.

Still, the United States today uses more energy per person than most other countries. Data from the International Energy Agency show that the United States uses about 4.1 times the world average (see Figure 19.2). In contrast, Japan, with the second-largest industrialized economy in the world, uses 2.1 times the world average energy per person, or roughly half what the United States uses.

Why is Japan's energy consumption per person so much lower than that of the United States? One reason is that, compared to Americans, Japanese tend to live in smaller homes that cost less to heat and cool. Japanese homes also are more likely to have energy-efficient appliances. Perhaps most important, Japan is a much more compact country than the United States, so less travel—which consumes gasoline or jet fuel—is required to get from one point to another. The distance between Japan's two largest cities, Tokyo and Osaka, is only 250 miles. The two largest U.S. cities, New York and Los Angeles, are roughly 2,500 miles apart in contrast.

Developing countries such as China and India, although sprawling geographically, use much less energy per person than the United States. That's because they have less industry and are poorer. Over the long run, however, as these countries become richer and more heavily industrialized, they will almost inevitably use more energy.

Energy Supply: Fossil Fuels

Where does our energy come from? From an economic perspective, this is an important question because different fuels have different supply and demand characteristics. The most widely used energy source is **fossil fuels,** which include coal, crude oil, and natural gas. These are all found underground and have been produced over millions of years by the transformation of dead animals and plants. Fossil fuels are **nonrenewable:** there is a limited quantity of them (though as we will see, no one knows how much).

To use fossil fuels, we must first locate them underground, which may be quite difficult. For example, in recent years it's been necessary to hunt in nearly inaccessible areas—such as far offshore—to find new oil fields. Then fossil fuels have to be extracted from the ground by digging mines (for coal) and by drilling wells (for oil and natural gas). This effort requires vast sums—in 2010 Exxon-Mobil, the world's largest oil company, spent $32 billion on exploration and capital investment.

Once the wells and mines are in place, the **marginal cost of extraction** is the amount of money it takes to get one more ton of coal, one more barrel of oil, or one more cubic foot of natural gas out of the ground. This can vary greatly. In some cases the coal or oil lies close to the surface, so the marginal cost of extraction is low. For more inaccessible fields, the marginal cost of extraction may be high.

From our discussion of profit maximization earlier in the textbook, we might think that companies will mine coal or pump oil and gas as long as the marginal cost of extraction is less than the market price. After all, they make a profit on anything they can sell for less than the marginal cost.

However, when it comes to a nonrenewable resource, that's not quite true. The businesses will take into account the fact that the price of the coal, oil, or natural gas may rise in the future because there is only a limited amount in the ground. This implies that the energy companies may not produce as much as they possibly could. They may rationally want to leave some supply in the ground—even if it was profitable to extract today—because they expect the future price to rise. Suppose, for example, the marginal cost of extraction is $50 per barrel of oil, and the price of oil today is $55 per barrel. That sounds profitable, but if the company expects the price to rise to $100 per barrel next year, it makes sense to not pump everything today.

When they pump oil or mine coal, the companies will probably first want to take it from the oil fields or coal mines where the marginal cost of extraction is the lowest. So we extract natural resources from the cheapest places. As those are exhausted, we get our energy from more expensive locations. Eventually, as the marginal cost of extraction rises, we shift to other energy sources.

Solar power is one source of renewable energy.

Energy Supply: Renewable and Nuclear

Now we turn our attention to the two other main sources of energy: renewable energy and nuclear power. **Renewable energy** includes solar power, wind power, hydroelectric power, and the energy products made from newly grown plants and trees. This last category includes ethanol, a gasoline replacement, which can be made either from corn (corn ethanol) or from agricultural wastes and nonfood plants (cellulosic ethanol).

Renewable energy sources such as solar power have relatively low variable costs—after all, the sun is free, and so are wind and rushing water. However, they are not yet able to provide power for transportation applications, such as cars, so they cannot replace gasoline and other uses of petroleum. Moreover, solar panels have high fixed costs. Installing a solar power system that supplies most of the electricity for an average-sized house might cost $20,000 in an area with lots of sun. This means that solar power is not yet economically competitive with fossil fuels, though it is likely to be in the future.

The final category of energy source is **nuclear power,** which uses the contained nuclear reaction of uranium or some other radioactive element to power an electric generator. Nuclear power, like solar power, is likely to be a growing source of energy in the future, in part because nuclear power does not emit carbon and does not contribute to global climate change. However, the Fukushima nuclear disaster in Japan will make countries much more safety-conscious. (See "Spotlight: Energy-Related Disasters.") As a result, the cost of building and operating nuclear power plants, already high, is likely to rise.

SPOTLIGHT: ENERGY-RELATED DISASTERS

Unfortunately, 2010 and 2011 were big years for energy-related disasters. On April 20, 2010, the British Petroleum (BP) Deepwater Horizon oil rig exploded in the Gulf of Mexico and triggered the biggest accidental oil spill in history, a sea-floor oil gusher that flowed for three months until it could be successfully plugged. The spill damaged marine and wildlife habitats, hurting the Gulf's fishing and tourism industries.

On the other side of the globe, and nearly a year later (March 11, 2011), the Fukushima Daiichi nuclear power complex in Japan was wrecked by a mammoth tsunami from one of the largest earthquakes on record. As this textbook is being revised, the result has so far been a partial meltdown of fuel, venting of radioactive gases and water, and an evacuation of the surrounding area. The combination of tsunami-related damage and high radioactivity means the utility that owns the facility has still not been able to get the situation under full control.

However, neither disaster is likely to derail the global need for more energy. After the oil spill, the Obama administration ordered a six-month moratorium on drilling, and BP faces fines and penalties of as much as $21 billion. Now, a year later, Congress is debating whether to accelerate the approval process for new rigs.

Similarly, countries such as China and India are still planning to go ahead with their large-scale programs for building nuclear power plants, even though the ultimate scope of the Fukushima disaster is not yet clear. In addition to the direct costs of dismantling the damaged plants—which could require more than $10 billion—the people evacuated from the nearby regions will need to be compensated. Moreover, nuclear plants will need to meet ever-higher and more expensive safety regulations. Still, it is difficult to see a way of meeting the energy needs of fast-growing economies without nuclear power, especially since nuclear power does not contribute to global warming.

Distribution of Supply

Since the 1970s the sources of the world's energy supply have shifted, as Table 19.1 shows. Crude oil has become less important as an energy source while, nuclear energy has become more important.

However, in other ways the distribution of energy production has been surprisingly stable. In 1973, before the oil price shock, fossil fuels made up 87 percent of world energy production. Today that's fallen only a tad, to 81 percent. Renewable energy rose from 12 percent of production in 1973 only to 13 percent in 2008. In particular, solar, geothermal, and wind power as a share of global energy supply barely increased over this period.

Economic Milestone

1885 THE FIRST INTERNAL COMBUSTION-POWERED VEHICLE

The internal combustion engines that now dominate the landscape are just over a century old. They were invented by Nicholas Otto of Germany in 1876. But it wasn't until 1885 that George Daimler, also of Germany, was the first person to use a gasoline-powered internal combustion engine to drive a vehicle. Daimler went on to found the auto company that now bears his name, Daimler, the maker of Mercedes-Benz vehicles.

TABLE 19.1	**Where the World's Energy Comes From, 1973 and 2008**

The world's sources of energy have remained relatively stable since the mid-1970s.

	Percentage of World's Energy Supply	
Energy Source	1973	2008
Coal	24.4	27.0
Crude oil	46.2	33.1
Gas	16.0	21.1
Nuclear	0.9	5.8
Hydro	1.8	2.2
Combustible renewables and waste*	10.6	10.0
Solar, geothermal, wind, and other	0.1	0.7

Source: International Energy Agency, www.iea.org.

*Wood and similar products.

The Price of Energy

What do we know about the price of energy? The easiest energy commodity to track is gasoline, which touches all of us. If the price of gasoline, adjusted for inflation, goes up, that means, as we saw in Chapter 8, that gasoline prices are rising faster than the overall price level. If the inflation-adjusted price of gasoline is falling, that means gasoline prices are rising more slowly than the overall price level.

Figure 19.3 shows that between 1961 and 2002 inflation-adjusted gasoline prices actually fell. True, there were several spikes in prices, most notably an enormous one in the late 1970s and early 1980s. But even that spike faded away relatively quickly. Until fairly recently there was no sign that gasoline (or other fossil fuels) was getting more expensive relative to other goods and services.

This was the era when Americans bought lots of fuel-guzzling cars and sport utility vehicles. Remember that consumers react to prices. With fossil fuel prices stable and relatively low, it makes perfect sense that consumption of fossil

FIGURE 19.3	**The Real Price of Gasoline**

Until the last few years, the price of gasoline, adjusted for inflation, was lower than it was in the 1960s.

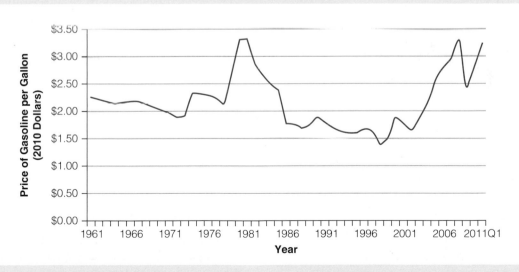

Source: Energy Information Administration and author calculations.

fuels remained high, and there was little impetus to switch to other forms of energy.

But starting in 2002, the real price of gasoline has been climbing. As a result, energy consumption and production patterns started to shift. However, despite the rise in energy prices, it was still not clear whether the spike was temporary or permanent. The long-term economics of energy is the subject of the next section.

ENERGY SUSTAINABILITY

The rapid growth of China and India suggests that we can expect rising energy demands worldwide for the foreseeable future. Will our supplies of energy be up to the task? The main danger is not that we will run out of energy. Instead the potential problem is a sharp and sudden increase in the *price* of energy sometime in the future, which will significantly constrain economic growth.

ENERGY CONSERVATION
A shift in economic activities to reduce the use of energy.

The Long-Term Future of Oil

We will focus here on the long-term future of oil for several reasons. First, as we've seen in Table 19.1, oil is still the single most important source of

SPOTLIGHT: THE MARCELLUS SHALE

Sometimes new energy supplies come from surprising places. In recent years geologists and energy companies have located a major new source of natural gas under parts of Ohio, West Virginia, Pennysylvania, and New York. The natural gas is embedded in a rock formation known as the Marcellus Shale, a mile or more beneath the ground, and extracted by a new drilling technique known as "hydraulic fracturing." The good news is that the drilling and extraction of the natural gas will create jobs and income in economically struggling regions. The bad news is that hydraulic fracturing, or 'fracking,' has the potential to do damage to the environment if not done carefully. As we will see in this chapter, new supplies of energies often come with environmental side effects.

energy globally. Second, if developing countries such as China and India follow the path of the industrialized countries, their use of oil will soar as they buy more cars. Third, oil is the energy commodity that is closest to exhaustion.

Let's begin by looking at a bit of history. People have worried about "running out" of petroleum since the oil price shock of the 1970s. But as we saw in Figure 19.3, gasoline prices came back down and stayed down for many years. One reason is that oil companies kept finding new oil fields. The second reason for the stability of oil prices was the very low marginal cost of extraction in the Middle East oil fields, where most of the world's reserves are located. That low marginal cost put a ceiling on all energy prices because oil can be used for producing electricity and heating, as well as transportation.

However, some oil experts fear that global production of oil may be nearing its highest point. This is called the **peak oil theory.** It doesn't mean we are about to run out of oil completely. Rather, according to the peak oil theory, the big oil fields in the Middle East are going to be less productive than expected, reducing the amount of oil available each year to the world economy at any given price.

If we think about a supply–demand diagram for crude oil, the peak oil theory predicts that the supply curve for crude oil will shift to the left. Such a shift would force a significant increase in the price of oil and a reduction in the quantity of oil demanded.

The Economics of Conservation

So far we've been considering the supply side of the energy market. Now let's look at the demand side of the market. In particular, let's consider **energy conservation,** which is a shift in economic activities to reduce the use of energy.

There are three types of energy conservation. First, there is conservation that arises out of the normal working of the market: when the price of something goes up, you use less of it. If the price of gasoline rises, you drive less or buy a more fuel-efficient car. More broadly, consumers and businesses respond to rising energy prices by reducing their consumption of gasoline, electricity, and other forms of energy.

FIGURE 19.4	Energy Conservation in Response to a Supply Shift

If the supply curve for gasoline shifts to the left, the market equilibrium moves from point *A* to point *B*. The market quantity of gasoline falls from *Q* to *Q'*, and the market price rises from *P* to *P'*.

Figure 19.4 illustrates this form of conservation in the gasoline market. Suppose something happens to shift the gasoline supply curve and drive up prices—perhaps the Middle East oil fields are becoming depleted faster than expected, so the marginal cost of extraction rises. This causes the market equilibrium to shift from point *A* to point *B*. As the figure shows, this represents a *movement along the demand curve* for gasoline (remember that the concept of a movement along a demand curve was defined in Chapter 3). The price of gasoline rises, and the quantity of gasoline supplied and bought falls.

The second type of energy conservation is the result of direct government intervention to control economic activity to achieve a desirable goal—the **command-and-control approach**, as we defined it in Chapter 6. One important example of command-and-control conservation is the fuel efficiency standard for cars (also known as the CAFÉ standards). Since 1974 automakers have had to meet an average "miles per gallon" target for all the cars they sell. The goal is to ensure that U.S. motorists are driving more fuel-efficient cars.

COMMAND-AND-CONTROL APPROACH

Direct government control over economic activity to achieve a desirable goal.

MARKET-BASED APPROACH

Changing the price signals faced by consumers and producers in order to move their behavior in the desired direction.

In addition to fuel efficiency standards, the government has tried a variety of different methods over the years to encourage conservation. One of the biggest moves was the passage of the National Maximum Speed Law in 1974, which forced states to reduce the maximum speed limit to 55 miles per hour. Economists disagree about how much fuel that restriction saved, but in any case the law was repealed in 1995.

Figure 19.5 shows how such speed limits affect the market for gasoline. The law shifted the demand curve to the left (unlike Figure 19.4, which was a movement along the demand curve). The equilibrium shifted from point *A* to point *B*, and the quantity of gasoline supplied and bought fell.

The third type of conservation is also the result of government intervention, but using a **market-based approach**. A market-based approach changes the price signals that consumers and producers face in order to move their behavior in the desired direction. However, rather than directly telling people what to do, a market-based approach gives them more options.

One example of a market-based approach is raising the tax on gasoline. This discourages the

| **FIGURE 19.5** | **The Effect of a Speed Limit on the Gasoline Market** |

One example of a command-and-control conservation measure was the 55 miles-per-hour speed limit, repealed in 1995. It had the effect of shifting the demand curve for gasoline to the left. In this diagram, the market equilibrium shifts from point *A* to point *B*, and both the market quantity and the market price fall.

A market-based approach to energy conservation can also use carrots rather than sticks. That is, instead of taxing energy consumption, the government can offer tax credits for such actions as putting up energy-efficient buildings or improving the energy efficiency of existing

use of gasoline by most drivers, but it allows people who really need to drive to get the fuel they need. Figure 19.6 illustrates the impact of a gasoline tax. Remember from Chapter 6 that a tax on a good or service generally lowers the quantity demanded and supplied in a market.

| **FIGURE 19.6** | **Energy Conservation with a Gas Tax** |

A tax on gasoline can reduce the quantity supplied and bought.

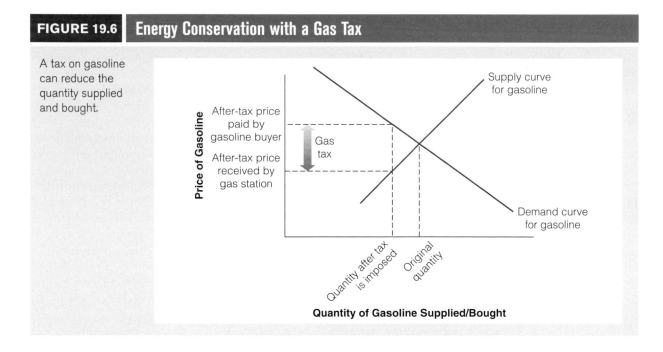

homes. In 2008, for example, the New Jersey state government offered $20 rebates to people who bought energy-efficient air conditioners.

Let's finish up this section by asking simple question: Why does the government need to *do anything* about encouraging conservation? Why not just let higher prices and the normal workings of the market do the work of bringing down energy consumption?

There are several reasons why the government might want to intervene in energy usage. First, individuals sometimes put too little weight on the future. So the price of oil or other forms of energy today may take insufficient account of the fact that there is a limited supply of oil in the ground. In that case, government intervention corrects for short-sightedness.

Second, government-led conservation measures can help accelerate the development of new energy technologies. For example, a tax on gasoline encourages car companies and other businesses to research alternatives to gasoline-powered internal combustion engines. By making existing energy sources more expensive, the government is sending a signal that it's worthwhile to take the risk of pursuing innovative activities in the energy area.

Third, energy usage of fossil fuels typically generates pollution, greenhouse gases, and other negative *externalities* (which were defined in Chapter 6). The measures used to encourage conservation also have the side benefit of reducing negative externalities, as we will see a bit later in this chapter.

Alternatives to Fossil Fuels

If prices of oil and petroleum products such as gasoline were to continue to rise, would there be any good alternative fuel sources? The short answer is "not yet." As Table 19.2 shows, each alternative source of energy available today has some key disadvantages, which explains why oil is still the most significant source of energy for the global economy.

However, when we look at the list of alternatives in Table 19.2, we also need to consider the role of *technological change,* which we discussed at length in Chapter 15. History tells us

SPOTLIGHT: SHOULD THE UNITED STATES HAVE A HIGHER GASOLINE TAX?

Compared to other industrialized countries, the United States imposes very low taxes on gasoline. The combination of state, federal, and local gas taxes came to an average of 48 cents per gallon in January 2011. Many European and Asian countries impose a much higher tax, on the order of $3–$5 per gallon.

Many economists believe the United States should boost its gas tax to at least $1.00 per gallon. That would encourage energy conservation, as well as reducing the pollutants and greenhouse gases created by gasoline combustion. However, the political opposition to an increase in the gas tax is enormous, especially in large states whose residents drive long distances. What's more, a gas tax would be regressive because gasoline is a bigger portion of the budget of low-income families.

that technological change is both important and unpredictable. Over the long run, the solution to rising energy prices is likely to include technological breakthroughs that make one or more of the alternatives in Table 19.2 more compelling—or perhaps make it possible to commercialize an energy source that is not even in the table. In 1900 a list of serious competitors to trains would not have included airplanes.

For example, scientists have known for decades how to produce ethanol from wood and agricultural waste products. This is known as cellulosic ethanol (as distinct from corn ethanol, which comes from a food plant). However, the process is still too expensive and not economically viable. Many businesses are doing research in this area, and a breakthrough could make cellulosic ethanol a much more attractive substitute for gasoline.

TABLE 19.2	**Alternatives to Fossil Fuels**

Each alternative to oil has both advantages and disadvantages.

Alternative Source	What It Is	Economic Advantages	Economic Disadvantages
Solar	The use of energy from the sun to either generate electricity or heat water.	Very low operating costs.	Very high initial cost compared to fossil fuels; more usable in some locations than others.
Nuclear	The use of nuclear reactions to generate electricity.	Low fuel costs.	High capital costs; high operating expenses for safety reasons; possibility of major disasters.
Ethanol and other biofuels	Fuels derived from plants or other biological products.	Can substitute directly for gasoline.	Corn ethanol competes with food crops for agricultural land. Cellulosic ethanol, made from agricultural wastes and nonfood plants, is still not economically viable.
Hydro	The use of running water to generate electricity.	Very low operating. costs	Limited amount available; river dams endanger salmon and other fish populations.
Wind	The use of wind to generate electricity.	Very low operating costs.	Not always available; generators are large and highly visible in the landscape.
Fuel cells	The use of hydrogen to generate electricity.	Theoretically low operating costs.	Very high initial costs, and no infrastructure yet in place to generate and deliver hydrogen.

ECONOMICS OF THE ENVIRONMENT

Now let's turn our attention from the economics of energy to economics of the environment. In this section we consider the negative impact of **pollution,** an unwanted side effect of economic activity.

Sources of Pollution Externalities

The key concept in environmental economics is *externalities.* A negative externality is a negative side effect from an exchange that affects someone other than the buyer and seller. For example, a loud car causes noise externalities for the people who live in the neighborhood of the driver. A sewage treatment plant causes odor externalities for people nearby.

One important source of pollution externalities is the production and use of energy. For example, a plant burning coal to generate electricity produces externalities in the form of various air pollutants such as sulfur dioxide and nitrogen dioxide. These pollutants help produce urban smog and acid rain, which damages forests. Vehicles burning gasoline also produce those pollutants, plus carbon monoxide and a variety of other problematic compounds. And virtually any process using fossil fuels produces greenhouse gases, such as carbon dioxide, which contribute to global climate change.

However, there are other sources of pollution beyond energy-related ones. For example, manufacturing residues and chemicals create water pollution when they are dumped into rivers or onto the ground, from which they seep into nearby streams and aquifers. Old industrial sites sometimes leave behind contaminated land.

SPOTLIGHT: WINDMILL POLLUTION

Windmills would seem to be the perfect energy source for the 21st century. Apparently nonpolluting and with no by-products, they use a completely renewable resource—the wind—that no one else wants.

Yet many people find that windmills cause a kind of externality: visual pollution. Across the country

people and communities have opposed the construction of windmills for power. The reason is simple. Today's power-generating windmills are typically over 400 feet high, or as tall as a 30-story building. Put 10, 20, or 50 of them on top of a hill to catch the winds, and they can be seen for miles. In other words, they harm environmental amenities.

The best-known fight against windmills occurred in Massachusetts, where one developer proposed in 2001 to put 130 windmills into Nantucket Sound outside Cape Cod. The local and summer residents of Martha's Vineyard and Nantucket—including some well-known people like Walter Cronkite—fought these windmills for years. As of early 2011, the proposal has received all of its permits and is about to start construction.

Source: A. Aston, "The War over Offshore Wind Is Almost Over," Businessweek.com, June 26, 2008.

The Impact of Pollution Externalities

Economists have identified many negative impacts from pollution. First, **health impacts** include loss of life and reduction of health caused by externalities. For example, air pollution increases asthma and bronchitis—killing people and causing them to miss work and be admitted to hospitals.

A second negative impact from pollution is **material and crop damage,** which represents the harm to buildings and to agriculture from pollution. If you see grime and soot covering a city building, that's material damage.

Next is the **harm to environmental amenities,** which includes negative effects of pollution on natural resources that people enjoy. Examples include untreated sewage ruining an unspoiled beach and noise disturbing a quiet residential neighborhood. (See "Spotlight: Windmill Pollution.")

Finally, pollution can cause **ecological damage,** which is damage done to the functioning of an ecosystem, including harm to plants and animals. An obvious example of ecological damage is an oil spill that kills thousands of fish and birds. But any kind of pollution can hurt an ecosystem.

Measuring the Damage Done by Pollution Externalities

We'd like to be able to translate the costs of pollution externalities into monetary terms. That would make it easier to figure out which aspects of pollution do the most damage, helping us choose environmental policies with the biggest benefits.

Let's start with the health impacts of pollution. To put a monetary value on these negative externalities, regulators and economists use what they call the **value of a statistical life.** This odd phrase describes a monetary value we treat as the cost of an additional death from pollution. It is *not* what a person would pay to avoid dying. Rather, it represents the value that we as a society put on having one person not die from pollution.

To estimate this number, the two main techniques that economists use are known as *revealed preference* and *stated preference*. **Revealed preference** is an approach that analyzes the choices people make in their daily lives to change their risk of death or injury. For example, if we look at patterns of job choice, how much of a lower salary are they willing to accept to take a job with a somewhat smaller chance of death or injury? How much are consumers willing to pay for a new automobile safety feature that slightly reduces the chance of dying in an accident? By analyzing consumption and labor market behavior, economists can calculate how much value people put on avoiding death or injury.

The other technique is **stated preference,** which involves surveying individuals and asking how much they would pay to reduce their risk of death. One way is to simply ask them how much they would pay to reduce their chances of dying by 1 percent over the next five years.

But economists have found it's hard for people to answer that question directly. Instead, stated preferences surveys usually set up a comparison between two situations and ask people to choose between them. For example, a question might go something like this:

> Suppose you have a choice between two jobs at companies A and B. The jobs are identical except for one fact: At company A you will be exposed to a chemical that has a 1 in 100 chance of causing a fatal illness over the next five years. The job at company A pays $100,000 a year, and the job at company B pays $50,000 a year. Which one do you choose?

This is not an easy question to answer—but it gives some insight to your trade-off between money and the odds of dying.

The combination of revealed preference and stated preference gives a range of numbers for the value of a statistical life, but as of 2010 the Environmental Protection Agency (EPA) uses about $7.9 million for this figure.

We can use similar techniques of revealed and stated preferences to judge the value of environmental amenities. For example, suppose that the breathtaking scenic views from the top of a mountain are being reduced by pollution, and we want to know the monetary value of the damages. One possibility is that we can look at records of home sales to see how much extra people are willing to pay for a home on that mountaintop versus one in a valley. This revealed preference helps estimate the value of a mountaintop view. Alternatively, we can survey people, asking how much they would pay to preserve the views.

The ecological damage done by pollution is usually addressed through stated preference methods because no one really has a direct monetary stake in ecology. For example, the Hawaiian hoary bat—found only in Hawaii—is on the endangered species list (www.fws.gov/Endangered/species). Suppose someone asked you how much you would be willing to pay to preserve its habitat. You might say 5 cents; but if we multiply that 5 cents by the 300 million people in the United States, the total amount people would be willing to pay to help the hoary bat is $15 million ($0.05 × 300 million).

Finally, the monetary value of material and crop damage from pollution can usually be calculated directly. The loss of crops, for example, is simply what those crops would have brought on the open market. The damage to buildings is valued at what it would cost to repair them.

Taking these factors together, we can add the various costs of the externalities generated by a particular type of pollution to get a total cost figure. This figure may have a wide range, but as we will see in the next section, it is helpful in thinking about economic policy.

Costs in a Market with Externalities

In a typical market, a cost function sums up all the expenses of production borne by the seller. The marginal cost curve tells us the additional costs of producing one more unit. So the marginal cost of a cell phone, say, is the additional cost to the phone maker of producing that phone.

However, the cost function for a business omits the externalities of production—that is, the costs imposed on people other than the seller. In particular, it does not include the negative externalities produced by the business, such as air, water, or noise pollution.

FIGURE 19.7 | Effect of a Noise Externality

If airlines had to pay for the noise externalities generated by their flights to a town, then they would provide less service to that town. The number of passenger seats available, assuming that the price of a ticket stayed the same and all planes flew at capacity, would drop from Q to Q'.

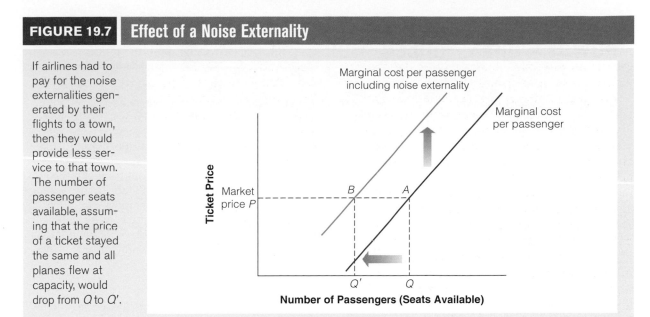

The fact that the cost function is missing the externalities makes a big difference. Let's think about the airlines that use an airport in a town. Each airline has a cost function, which depends on labor (pilots, flight attendants, mechanics), capital (airplanes, primarily), and jet fuel. The more flights into the town, the higher the costs. If the air travel market into this town is competitive, then each airline adds capacity until the price of a ticket is equal to the marginal cost of an extra passenger. This is the principle for profit maximization in a competitive market, as described in Chapter 5.

But notice what is *not* in the cost function: the extra noise pollution that hits the residents of the town because of the additional flights. One more daily 11 p.m. arrival, for example, can cause sleepless nights for thousands of people—but the airlines don't have that in their cost function.

Let's assume, using revealed and stated preference, that we've done all the calculations and surveys necessary to calculate the monetary value of the noise externality. For the sake of argument, let's say the noise externality caused by an extra flight is valued at $500. If we assume that the typical plane has 50 passengers and it flies completely full, then the *extra* marginal cost per passenger is $10.

If the airline was actually forced to pay the negative externality—that is, pay an extra $10 for each passenger—that would affect its decision about how many planes to fly into the town. It might be more reluctant to add capacity, and the price of the tickets would have to be higher.

Let's show this graphically in Figure 19.7. In a competitive market, the airlines will add seats up to the point where the price of a ticket equals the marginal cost of another passenger (leaving out the noise externality). That's point A on the diagram.

Now let's suppose the price stayed the same, but the airline had to pay the $10 noise externality as well. Then the marginal cost curve would shift upward because the cost would be $10 higher for each passenger. The result would be that the airline would want to fly fewer planes to the town. That's point B on the diagram.

This example is an oversimplifcation, of course. If the supply of flights into a town falls, that's likely to lead to higher ticket prices and a lower number of people who want to fly.

But despite the oversimplification, the basic intution of this example is straightforward: in general, if sellers have to take into account the negative externalities produced by their good or service, then they probably will choose a lower level of output.

HOW IT WORKS: "GREEN" GDP

One of the goals of economic policy makers is to increase economic growth, which is the increase in real gross domestic product (GDP). But there's a problem—the official government calculation of GDP includes the output of factories, power plants, and refineries, but it does not subtract the environmental damage done by the pollution they produce. That means policy decisions may be distorted.

To get a more accurate accounting of the costs and benefits of growth, some economists have tried to calculate what is called *green GDP*. Green GDP counts the production of the country as a positive but subtracts damages to the environment. Such negatives include depletion of natural resources and harm to forests, water resources, and other parts of the environment.

Measuring green GDP turns out to be a difficult task because economists can't agree on what should be counted on the environmental side. However, it seems likely that the Bureau of Economic Analysis will eventually provide supplementary numbers showing the environmental impact of the economy.

CONTROLLING POLLUTION

How do we get polluters to change their behavior to take account of the negative externalities that they generate? In the airline example we made the assumption that the airlines had to pay for the negative noise externalities that they generated. But in the real world, it's not as easy as that.

Imagine, for example, a small town of people who live around a lake. They dump their wastewater in the lake, which ends up being severely polluted. The members of the town council vote and decide that these discharges into the lake need to be substantially reduced. How should they accomplish this change?

The most straightforward way is to issue regulations restricting how much waste each family or business can discharge into the lake and establishing fines or jail sentences for the violators. That's how most pollution control is done today. However, as we will see in this section, economists have come up with alternative ways of controlling pollution that may produce better results.

Command-and-Control Approaches

As we saw in the section about energy conservation earlier in this chapter, the government can use a command-and-control approach to reduce pollution. That means the government tells business and consumers what to do and what not to do. Here are a couple of examples. In 1972 the Environmental Protection Agency banned the pesticide DDT because of concern about the harm it caused to the environment and both human and animal health. Similarly, in 1973 the EPA issued regulations forcing refineries to sharply reduce the amount of lead they put in gasoline to make car engines run better. Studies had shown that the lead from gasoline ended up in the air and on outdoor and indoor surfaces, and this lead was especially poisonous to children.

Overall, command-and-control regulations have helped reduce pollution in the United States and other developed countries. Figure 19.8, for example, shows the emissions of carbon monoxide, a toxic gas produced by internal combustion engines. The Clean Air Act, passed in 1970 by Congress, required that emissions of carbon monoxide be sharply curtailed. In response, the EPA issued strict regulations detailing how much carbon monoxide cars could produce. The result: automakers installed catalytic converters in cars, which turn carbon monoxide into carbon dioxide. The amount of emitted carbon monoxide fell by half from 1970 to 2006, despite a large increase in the number of vehicles.

The benefit of the command-and-control is that you know what you're going to get as a

FIGURE 19.8

The Decline in Carbon Monoxide Emissions, 1970–2008

Regulation helped drive the decline in airborne pollutants, such as carbon monoxide.

Source: Environmental Protection Agency, www.epa.gov.

result—in this case less pollution. You can simply ban the offensive actions or substances or require the use of a particular antipollution technology. Command and control can be appropriate for pollutants that have large and immediate negative health effects because stopping their use is clearly the best strategy for safeguarding the public.

However, command-and-control approaches have a big disadvantage: they're inflexible and usually force all pollution emitters to meet the same standards or install the same equipment. That can be expensive and perhaps counter-productive, especially if the regulations take effect very quickly.

For example, let's go back to the problem of noise pollution at airports. Suppose that the federal government made a rule that all airlines could no longer use older, noisier planes, in order to address noise complaints from people living near airports. What would happen then? Suddenly United States airlines would have to ground most of their fleet (since they tend to have aircraft that average over 10 years old). The result: bankrupt airlines and sharply higher ticket prices for passengers. That's not a good idea at all.

Market-Based Approaches

As we saw for energy conservation, market-based approaches to controlling pollution work by changing the price signals that people and businesses face in the market. Such price signals give people and businesses incentives to produce less pollution while giving them more options than the command-and-control approach.

One example of using a market approach to reduce the amount of pollution is to tax the product or process causing the externality. The government can use that tax to make sure buyers and sellers take into account the externalities of their actions affecting third parties.

Let's see how this might work, using your computer as an example. Computers and monitors contain sizable amounts of toxic metals, such as lead, cadmium, and mercury. A typical computer monitor, for instance, can contain several pounds of lead, which can seriously damage children's brains if inhaled or ingested. When it's time to dispose of the computer, if it is simply thrown in a landfill, these toxic metals are released—harming human health and the environment.

Now suppose a tax is put on the computer according to the amount of toxic metals it contains. The more lead, cadmium, and other toxins in the computer, the higher the tax is. Faced with these incentives, computer manufacturers will look for ways to reduce the amounts of toxic metals. In other words, the tax forces the computer manufacturers to bear part of the externality.

In the air travel example, a similar solution for reducing the externality from noise would be to make the airlines pay a tax for each landing and takeoff. The exact amount of the tax would depend on the noisiness of the aircraft. Extremely noisy planes would pay a steep tax, while quiet planes would pay no tax at all. The result would be an extra encouragement for airlines to upgrade their fleets to quieter models.

Another market-based approach for reducing pollution is the use of **tradable pollution permits.** A pollution permit gives a business the right to emit a particular amount of pollution. For example, since 1995 electric utilities in the United States have needed pollution permits (also called *allowances*) to emit sulfur dioxide, the pollutant that causes acid rain.

The idea of issuing permits to pollute may seem like a funny concept. But they can be highly effective in reducing pollution. First, only a certain number of permits are issued, which provides a cap on the amount of pollution (that's why such programs are often called **cap-and-trade systems**). The cap can be reduced over time.

More important, these permits can be bought or sold. If a business has a permit to emit some amount of pollution, it has three choices. It can use the permit itself. It can decrease its own pollution and sell the permit to another business that needs it more. Or it can buy more permits if reducing its own pollution is too expensive.

The ability to sell permits for a profit gives firms an incentive to cut their own emissions more than required. In other words, there is a reward for virtue. And the permits are sold to companies that have the hardest time cutting their pollutants.

GLOBAL CLIMATE CHANGE

Now we will focus on one particular environmental problem: greenhouse gases such as carbon dioxide. Greenhouse gases arise primarily from the combustion of carbon-based fossil fuels, such as coal, oil, and natural gas. The current scientific consensus is that the buildup of greenhouse gases will significantly warm the earth over the next several decades.

This is an economics textbook, so we will not address here the science of climate change. There is still enormous disagreement about the exact timing and degree of global climate change, and these facts will be debated for years to come. However, assuming global climate change is happening, we can look at potential policies to adapt to global climate change and to mitigate its effects.

The Potential Costs of Global Climate Change

Let's start by quickly reviewing some of the potential economic costs of global climate change. The effects of global climate change on agriculture could be far-reaching. Higher temperatures, of course, would change where certain crops could be grown. Crucially important would be the change in rainfall patterns. Certain food-growing regions could be turned into dust bowls, while other areas might become more productive.

Higher temperatures could increase the severity of hurricanes, leading to the possibility of economically devastating natural disasters. And rising sea levels could threaten many of the world's largest cities, including New York and London.

Still, one of the greatest uncertainties connected with global climate change is identifying which parts of the world would be hurt the worst and which parts might possibly be better off. This uncertainty makes it much harder to get countries to work together: it's harder to help the people who are going to be hurt if we don't know who they are ahead of time.

Policy Response: Adaptation

What can we do about global climate change? The responses fall into two broad categories: *adaptation* and *mitigation*. **Adaptation** is the alteration of consumer and business behavior to reduce the damage from global climate change. **Mitigation** includes policies to significantly reduce emissions of greenhouse gases. We'll look at adaption in this section and mitigation in the next section.

In some ways adaptation is similar to the usual demand response to a price change. Remember from the law of demand that as the price increases, the quantity demanded goes down. For example, if there is a drought in the coffee-growing regions of Colombia and the price of a cup of coffee goes up, you adapt by consuming less.

On a much larger scale, adaptation to global climate change represents the same sort of response. Suppose the rise in temperatures shifts the main wheat-growing region of the United States northward. Gradually farmers will change the crops that they plant to take account of the new temperature and rainfall patterns. Similarly, a rise in the sea level will cause people to adapt, either by moving further back from the coast or by building in a way that resists the water.

Adaptation is a useful strategy for a rich country like the United States, which can afford to rebuild homes and farms to take account of changing climate. But it is much more difficult for poorer countries, which do not have the resources to adapt.

Moreover, even within the United States, the costs of adaptation fall very unevenly. Suppose you own a small home right along the New Jersey coast line. Then if the sea levels rise, you will basically be wiped out because you will have no way to sell.

The question, then, is whether the government should help the adaptation process in this case, perhaps by buying out homes. More generally, is there a role for government in speeding adaptation to global climate change by helping resettle people? In the extreme, could we imagine moving large numbers of people from tropical countries—which may become unbearable—to the now-comfortable temperatures of northern Canada and northern Russia? A difficult question, for sure—but one that could conceivably make economic sense.

Policy Response: Mitigation

If adaptation by itself is not enough, the question becomes how best to mitigate the harm caused by climate change. Can any of the policies we've suggested to control pollution work to slow the activities that contribute to global climate change? The command-and-control approach is too ponderous a solution for a goal as broad as controlling the emission of greenhouse gases. The government would have to regulate every use of fossil fuel. The resulting degree of control might harm the economy and would likely stifle much innovation.

Instead the preferred approach for mitigating global climate change is the effective use of price signals. The priority is to effectively slow the emission of greenhouse gases while doing the minimum possible damage to the economy. That means giving people and businesses maximum incentives to research and adopt new technologies. Let's compare two widely discussed solutions: a **carbon tax** and tradable permits.

One proposed means for reducing the incentive to burn fossil fuels is a *carbon tax,* which would vary for different fuels according to their carbon content. Fossil fuels such as coal would bear the heaviest taxes because such fuels have a high carbon content, which means they emit the most greenhouse gases when they burn. Fuels with a lower carbon content, such as natural gas, would be taxed at a lower rate.

Over the long run a carbon tax would encourage less use of high-carbon fuels and more use of low-carbon fuels. It would also make fossil fuels more expensive across the board, thus reducing their consumption.

As a result consumers and businesses would find it worthwhile to invest in energy efficiency. For example, it would become much more cost-efficient to improve the insulation in a house to retain heat rather than to use more fuel. The carbon tax would also encourage the development and use of alternative technologies, such as solar power, by boosting demand for them as the cost of fossil fuels rose.

There are problems related to the carbon tax, however. The first is that it's a tax, and no one likes taxes. Worse, it would be a *regressive* tax because poor families devote a larger share of their income to energy than do high-income families. That's why some economists propose using the proceeds from a carbon tax to reduce other taxes, especially for the poor.

The other proposed alternative is to use a system of tradable pollution permits discussed earlier in the chapter. In the context of greenhouse gases, this is usually called a *cap-and-trade system.* Already in effect in Europe, a cap-and-trade system has the government issue a limited number of tradable permits for greenhouse gas emissions. The number of permits sets the total cap on emissions.

Then each company has a choice in what it does with its permits. It can use its permits. It can buy more permits from other companies if it exceeds its carbon emission allowance. Or it can sell its permits if it's managed to reduce its emissions.

The buying and selling of permits allows companies to make extra money by reducing greenhouse gas emission further than required. In effect, it offers an incentive to be environmentally sound.

In theory, either a carbon tax or a tradable permit system should work to reduce greenhouse gas emissions. But it's not clear yet which one will be more politically acceptable or workable in the United States. Nor is it clear yet whether fast-growing developing countries such as China and India will be willing to restrict their greenhouse gas emissions.

CONCLUSION

This chapter has discussed some of today's most important economic issues: energy, environment, and global climate change. With these topics likely to be at the top of the news for the next several years, economics is going to play a crucial role in the energy and environment debate.

We've come to the end of the textbook, but not the end of economic topics. New problems and questions are going to arise, and you now have the tools to understand them.

19 SUMMARY

1. Energy consumption per person has been flat in the United States since the mid-1970s. Nevertheless, on a per-person basis the United States still uses more than four times the world average. About 81 percent of the world's energy comes from fossil fuels, which are nonrenewable. Crude oil is still the single largest energy source. The quantities supplied of crude oil and other nonrenewable energy sources depend on the market price, the marginal cost of extraction, and the amount thought to remain in the ground. Other energy sources include nuclear power, hydropower, and solar power. *(LO19-1)*

2. There are three types of energy conservation. First, the normal response is to reduce the quantity demanded of energy when its price goes up. This is a move along the demand curve. The second type is command-and-control, which represents direct government intervention to reduce the use of energy. The third type is a market-based approach, which uses price signals to change the incentives of consumers and businesses. *(LO19-2)*

3. Pollution produces negative externalities, which affect someone other than the buyer or the seller in a market. Pollution externalities can lead to health impacts, material and crop damage, harm to environmental amenities, and ecological damage. The monetary value of the damages done by pollution externalities can be estimated using revealed or stated preferences. *(LO19-3)*

4. Pollution can be reduced by either the command-and-control approach or the market-based approach. One example of a market-based approach is a tax on pollution. Another example is the use of tradable pollution permits. *(LO19-4)*

5. Global climate change, because of the buildup of greenhouse gases, is a critical environmental and economic issue. Possible policy responses include adaptation and mitigation. *(LO19-5)*

KEY TERMS AND CONCEPTS

fossil fuels

nonrenewable energy

marginal cost of extraction

renewable energy

nuclear power

peak oil theory

energy conservation

command-and-control approach

market-based approach

pollution

health impacts

material and crop damage

harm to environmental amenities

ecological damage

value of a statistical life

revealed preference

stated preference

tradable pollution permits

cap-and-trade system

adaptation

mitigation

carbon tax

PROBLEMS

1. In 2008 the price of jet fuel soared because of the sharp increase in the price of crude oil. *(LO19-1)*

   a) What effect did that price increase have on the supply curve for airplane travel?

   b) Show on a supply–demand diagram what changed.

   c) What happened to the price of air travel tickets?

   d) What happened to the quantity of air travel?

2. The Department of Energy (DOE) projects that the price of electricity, adjusted for inflation, will remain roughly flat for the next 25 years. Meanwhile the price of gasoline, adjusted for inflation, is expected to rise by about 50 percent. *(LO19-2)*

   a) If the DOE is right, is that likely to increase or decrease the demand for electric cars?

   b) The DOE projection assumes that the amount of electricity generated from renewable resources such as solar power will rise about 75 percent over the next 25 years. Suppose that the price of oil soars, so that utilities close their oil-powered generators and decide to invest even more in renewable energy. Is that likely to raise or lower the price of electricity?

3. It is common to use the tax system to help support new energy technologies. The federal government, for example, offers a tax credit for some hybrid vehicles (gas–electric combinations that use less gasoline than conventional internal combustion engines). *(LO19-2)*

   a) What effect does the tax credit have on the number of hybrid vehicles sold?

   b) Does the tax credit raise or lower the price charged by sellers of hybrid vehicles?

4. A potential negative impact of energy generated by windmills is _____ *(LO19-3)*

   a) visual pollution.

   b) negative health effects.

   c) ecological damage.

   d) crop damage.

5. The patrons at a local bar get rowdy on Friday and Saturday nights and wake up the 10 residents of the adjacent apartment building. The town economist surveyed the residents, and found that each of the residents would be willing to pay $15 per night, on average, to not be woken. *(LO19-3)*

   a) Calculate the size of the negative externality per night.

   b) Calculate the size of the negative externality over the course of the year (assuming 50 weeks).

6. Suppose a town has lots of noisy restaurants that disturb their neighbors. The citizens would like to reduce the noise level without driving all of the restaurants away. *(LO19-4)*

   a) Suppose the town issues fines for exceeding noise limits. This is an example of the _____ approach to pollution control.

b) Alternatively, the town decides to issue tradable "noise permits" that allow restaurants to make a certain amount of noise each night. This is an example of the _____ approach to pollution control.

c) Suppose there are six restaurants making the same amount of noise each night, but the town would like to get the number down to three. Is the fine-based or the tradable permit approach likely to work better?

d) If the town succeeds in reducing the number of noisy restaurants, is the price of a meal likely to rise or fall?

7. Every household produces garbage, some more than others. In town A the local sanitation department will collect all the garbage that households put out. In town B the residents have to pay per bag to have their garbage collected. In all other respects the towns are identical. *(LO19-4)*

a) In which town would the residents produce less garbage? Explain.

b) Suppose town A finds itself with soaring garbage costs because too many households put out 5 or 10 bags of garbage per week. To solve this problem the town imposes a new rule saying that households can put out only three bags of garbage. What type of households would be hurt by this rule?

c) Would you prefer to live in town A (with the maximum number bag rule) or town B? Explain.

8. Economists regularly suggest that the United States needs to raise the gasoline tax. *(LO19-4)*

a) The following table lays out the share of expenditures spent on gasoline and motor oil by households with different levels of income. Using the table, explain why a higher gasoline tax would be regressive or progressive.

b) The data for the table come from 2009. Between 2009 and 2011, the price of gasoline has risen sharply. What would you expect has happened to spending on gasoline as a share of total spending?

Income Level	Spending on Gasoline as Percentage of Total Expenditures, 2009*
Less than $70,000	4.7%
$70,000–$80,000	4.3%
$80,000–$100,000	4.1%
$100,000 and more	3.2%

Source: Bureau of Labor Statistics.
*Includes motor oil as well.

9. Consider the following actions for dealing with global climate change. Identify whether each represents adaptation or mitigation. *(LO19-5)*

a) Building up tall levees to stop the rising ocean from flooding a town.

b) Raising the tax on gasoline.

c) Giving a subsidy for people to buy hybrid cars.

d) Giving a subsidy for people to buy air conditioners for their homes.

GLOSSARY

A

401(k) plan A common type of retirement plan that allows employees to save pretax income, often matched in part by the employer.

80/20 ratio A measure of income inequality obtained by dividing the 80th percentile of income earners by the 20th percentile.

absolute advantage A situation in which one country can produce a particular good or service with less labor, capital, and other inputs than another country.

adaptation The response of consumer and business behavior to a change in conditions—for example, the alteration of behavior to reduce the negative impact of global climate change.

advance purchase discount A reduced price given for buying in advance, so that prices differ according to when purchases are made.

adverse selection The tendency of insurance—health insurance in particular—to be purchased by those who are more likely to make claims.

advertising Paid communication with potential customers through a public medium such as television, print, or a website.

after-tax income distribution The spread of incomes after taxes have been taken out.

aggregate demand The sum of the quantities demanded from all sectors of the economy.

aggregate demand curve The link between the average price level of the whole economy and the aggregate quantity demanded.

aggregate equilibrium The price where aggregrate quantity demanded equals aggregate quantity supplied.

aggregate production function The link between the inputs to an economy and its outputs.

aggregate supply The quantity of goods and services that the economy produces.

aggregate supply curve The link between the average price level of the whole economy and the aggregate quantity of goods and services produced.

antitrust law Government regulation intended to maintain competitive markets and discourage unfair accumulation of market power.

applied research Scientific research focused on solving real-world problems.

automatic stabilizer The tendency of the budget deficit to increase during recessions because tax revenues slow and certain types of spending, such as unemployment insurance, increase. The result is a fiscal stimulus for the economy.

average level of prices A measure of how much it costs to purchase a market basket of goods and services.

average product The total output of a business divided by the number of labor hours or by the number of workers. Also *output per hour* or *output per worker*.

B

barrier to entry Anything that makes it difficult for a new competitor to enter a market.

basic research Scientific investigations that have no immediately obvious commercial applications.

benefits The part of worker compensation that includes employer-provided healthcare insurance and other supplements to the basic paycheck.

bond A loan that entitles the lender to get regular interest payments over time, and then to get back the principal at the end of the loan period. Also called a *fixed-income security.*

bond market One of the main ways corporations and governments borrow.

bondholder The purchaser of a bond.

borrowing Accepting money from a lender with the obligation to pay it back later.

bubble A situation where the price of an asset, such as housing, rises far above sustainable levels.

budget constraint The combinations of goods and services an individual is able to buy, given prices and the amount of money available to spend.

budget deficit The excess of the federal government's spending over its revenues.

business cycle The recurring pattern of recession and expansion.

business know-how The knowledge and technology necessary for the production process.

business savings The part of corporate profits that is not distributed in the form of stock dividends or some other payment to owners.

buyers In a market, the consumers or businesses that exchange their money for goods and services from others.

C

cap-and-trade system See *tradable pollution permits*.

capital The long-lived physical equipment, software, and structures a business uses in its production process.

carbon tax A tax on fuels that depends on the amount of carbon in the fuel.

catastrophic health insurance Insurance that covers the very high expenses incurred by a serious illness or accident but does not cover ordinary health expenses.

central bank The official institution that controls monetary policy in a country.

centrally planned economy An economy in which most economic activities are controlled by the government.

ceteris paribus A Latin phrase meaning "all other things equal."

change in private inventories Increase or decrease of inventories at manufacturers, wholesalers, and retailers.

collusion An illegal practice in which two or more oligopolists work together to keep the prices of their products artificially high.

command-and-control approach An approach to regulation that directly specifies certain market outcomes and activities to achieve desirable goals.

comparative advantage The tendency of countries to specialize in the goods or services in which they have the biggest productivity advantage or the smallest productivity disadvantage.

competitive market A market that is characterized by *perfect competition*.

complements Two inputs that are used together, such that when the price of one goes up, a cost-minimizing business uses less of the other.

consumer price index (CPI) A measure that tracks the average price level, starting from a base year.

contractionary A description of a government policy action, such as a tax increase, that reduces output and pushes up unemployment in the short run.

controlling inflation One key goal of the Federal Reserve, which tries to keep inflation below a certain level.

core inflation A measure of consumer inflation that omits the changes in food and energy prices.

corporate income tax A tax collected on corporate profits.

corruption Bribery or other illegal activities intended to influence government actions.

costs The money a business pays for its inputs.

cost function Reports the total cost of producing each level of output.

cost minimization The process of choosing the lowest-cost way of producing a given level of output.

cost of accumulating business know-how Outlays that increase a company's knowledge and capabilities.

cost of capital and land Outlays for buying or renting equipment, structures, and land.

cost of intermediate inputs Outlays for goods and services purchased from other companies.

cost of labor Monetary outlays for labor, including benefits.

cost of transactions The time and effort that go into managing spending.

cost-of-living adjustments (COLAs) An automatic rise in wages to compensate for inflation.

creation of new goods and services Technological change that allows people to do things they could not do before.

crowding out A decline in private investment that results from an increase in government borrowing that pushes up interest rates.

currency Bills and coins used as money.

currency appreciation A change in an exchange rate allowing one currency to buy more of another.

currency depreciation A change in an exchange rate allowing one currency to buy less of another.

cyclical unemployment Large jumps in the unemployment rate that are tied directly to business cycles.

D

default Failure of a borrower to pay back a loan to the lender on time, or at all.

default risk The possibility that a borrower won't pay back a loan on time, or at all.

defined benefit plan A retirement plan that pays retirees a predetermined amount of money monthly.

defined contribution plan A retirement plan that pays retirees an amount of money that depends on the return on investments.

deflation An actual fall in the average price level.

demand curve A line on a graph showing the link between price and quantity demanded.

demand curve for innovative activities Reports the quantity of innovative activities businesses will want to fund, given the price of those innovative activities.

demand schedule The link between a buyer's quantity demanded and the price.

demand shift A change in the amount buyers want to purchase at a given price.

demographic change A changing distribution of groups in a population.

deregulation The process of reducing government control over markets.

development Innovative activities that are aimed toward creating a commercial product.

diminishing marginal product A situation where marginal product declines as a business adds workers without changing other inputs.

diminishing marginal utility The tendency for marginal utility to decline as the consumption of a good or service increases.

discount rate The interest rate at which the Fed lends money to financial institutions through the discount window.

discount window A monetary policy tool that allows the Fed to lend money to financial institutions that are running short of funds.

disposable income The amount of income people have left after paying taxes.

disruptive trade Trade that imposes big economic and social adjustment costs.

diversification The process of splitting one's money across different investments to help reduce risk without reducing expected return.

dividend A portion of a company's profits that it pays out to shareholders each quarter.

downward-sloping demand curve A demand curve that is consistent with the law of demand, so that an increase in price leads to a decline in quantity demanded. As a result, the line slopes down when read from left to right.

E

ecological damage Negative effects of pollution on the functioning of an ecosystem, including harm to plants and animals.

economic competition The effort by people and businesses to achieve a desirable outcome, given what everyone else is doing.

economic growth The increase in an economy's production of goods and services. Usually measured by the growth in gross domestic product adjusted for inflation.

economics The study of how individuals, businesses, and governments make decisions and trade-offs in the face of scarce resources.

education premium The added lifetime pay for getting a college degree.

effective tax rate The share of income a household pays in taxes.

elastic demand Intuitively, a situation in which a small change in price has a big impact on quantity demanded. More precisely, a situation in which the price elasticity of demand is greater than 1.

elastic supply Intuitively, a situation in which a small change in price has a big impact on quantity supplied. More precisely, a situation in which the price elasticity of supply is greater than 1.

employer health insurance plan A health insurance plan set up by and partly paid for by an employer. Employees are usually required to pay a fraction of the cost in monthly premiums.

employer retirement plan Provisions for retirement that an employer contributes to on behalf of an employee.

energy conservation A shift in economic activities to reduce the use of energy.

ensuring financial stability One key goal of the Federal Reserve, which tries to keep the financial system functioning well.

equilibrium price The price at which the quantity supplied in a market equals the quantity demanded.

equilibrium quantity The quantity corresponding to the equilibrium price. At that price, there's a match between what buyers want and what sellers are willing to supply.

equity Shares of stock.

event risk The odds that a major event will affect the return on an investment.

excess demand A situation in which quantity demanded exceeds quantity supplied at the current market price.

excess supply A situation in which quantity supplied exceeds quantity demanded at the current market price.

exchange rate The rate at which one currency can be converted into another.

excise tax A tax collected on particular items such as gasoline, tobacco, and alcoholic beverages.

expansion The period of time from a recession trough all the way to the next peak.

expected inflation The inflation rate that consumers and businesses expect will happen over the next year or longer.

expected return The average return that you can expect on an investment over the long run.

exports The goods and services produced in a country and sold outside that country.

externality The impact that the actions of an individual or business can have on others.

F

fed funds rate The short-term interest rate controlled by the Federal Reserve. Also, the rate banks charge each other for lending reserves overnight.

Federal Open Market Committee (FOMC) The 12-member group at the Federal Reserve that votes on monetary policy.

Federal Reserve System The central bank of the United States.

final goods and services The goods and services that are bought by ultimate users.

financial intermediary Any institution, such as a bank, that collects money from suppliers of capital and funnels the funds to users of capital.

financial markets The parts of the economy connected with borrowing, investing, or transferring money. Also called the *financial system*.

financial system See *financial markets*.

financing gap A mismatch between the amount of money coming in and the amount of money that needs to be paid out. In this book the term *financing gap* refers to a long-term problem facing the Social Security system.

fiscal policy Decisions about government spending, taxes, and borrowing in the short and long run.

fiscal stimulus Increases in government spending and cuts in taxes designed to boost the economy.

fixed costs Costs that are difficult to change in the short run.

fixed-income securities Bonds that entitle the lender to receive regular interest payments over time.

floating exchange rate An exchange rate between two currencies that is set in the financial markets.

fossil fuels Nonrenewable energy sources such as oil and natural gas that have been produced over millions of years by the transformation of dead animals and plants.

four-legged stool A metaphor for the four main components of retirement income: part-time work, individual savings, employer retirement plans, and Social Security.

free-rider problem Occurs when individuals benefit from a public good that they have not helped to pay for.

frictional unemployment Periods of temporary unemployment that correspond to short gaps between jobs.

future-oriented activities Activities intended to bring in profits over the long term.

G

gains from trade The benefits from participating in trade relationships with other countries.

GDP per capita The economic output of a country, divided by the size of its population.

global market A market where buyers and sellers can be located anywhere in the world.

global market economy A collection of all the different participating markets in the world interacting simultaneously.

globalization The increasing exchange of goods, services, ideas, and people among countries.

goals of monetary policy The main goals of monetary policy are controlling inflation, smoothing out the business cycle, and ensuring financial stability.

Golden Age The period from the end of World War II to roughly 1973 characterized by rapid increases in productivity and a rising standard of living.

government consumption and investment The goods and services purchased by the government.

government intervention Actions taken by the government to affect the economy.

government savings The excess of government revenues, mainly taxes, over government spending.

Great Recession The deep economic downturn that started in December 2007.

gross domestic product (GDP) The dollar value of the total output of an economy. Based on final goods and services produced in a year.

gross domestic purchases The amount spent within the United States on final goods and services.

growth rate of productivity The percentage increase in productivity over a year.

H

harm to environmental amenities Negative effects of pollution on natural resources that humans enjoy, such as lakes, beaches, and clear skies.

healthcare life cycle The pattern of spending on healthcare over the span of an individual's life, in the absence of government or business-supported health insurance.

healthcare poverty problem The problem that poor people often do not have enough income to pay for health insurance.

healthcare uncertainty problem The problem that people don't know how much money they will need to pay for their healthcare in old age.

health impacts (of pollution) The loss of life and reduction of health caused by pollution.

human capital The education and skill level of a workforce.

hyperinflation A very rapid increase in the average price level.

I

implicit collusion Occurs when oligopolists let one company—the market leader—set prices in the market without direct communication.

imports Goods and services that are produced outside a country and consumed within that country.

improvement in quality A change in the nature of a good or service that increases its value for buyers.

incentive effect When a tax discourages the economic activity being taxed.

incentive problem The potential lack of pressure on public sector managers because governments don't need to make a profit.

incidence The individual or business that bears the actual burden of a tax, regardless of who actually writes the check to the government.

income The amount of money an individual receives in a year from various sources.

income distribution Share of households at different income levels.

income inequality The disparity between high-income and low-income households or individuals.

income mobility The change in an individual's income over his or her lifetime.

income redistribution A policy of transferring income from high-income households to low-income households.

income tax A tax collected on individual income.

index fund An investment whose value tracks the performance of a broad stock market index, such as the S&P 500.

inefficiency of taxation The reduction of production and sales which typically results from imposing a tax on a good or service.

inelastic demand A situation where the quantity demanded does not change much even if the price changes significantly. More precisely, a situation where the price elasticity of demand is less than 1.

inelastic supply A sitution where the quantity supplied of a good does not change much even if the price changes significantly. More precisely, a situation where the price elasticity of supply is less than 1.

infant industry A new or a small industry that is vulnerable to being crushed by better-funded and more mature foreign competitors.

inferior good A good for which the quantity demanded falls as income increases.

inflation A sustained upward movement in the average level of prices.

inflation rate The annual percentage change in the average price level.

inflation risk The danger that inflation will suddenly accelerate.

inflation targeting The idea that the Federal Reserve should publicly announce its inflation target and then commit itself to running monetary policy to hit that target.

inflation-adjusted change The change in a money value after removing the effects of inflation.

information revolution The application of additional processing capacity of new generations of computers to a wide variety of new uses. Enabled businesses to produce more output with fewer workers.

initial public offering (IPO) The first time a company sells shares to the public.

innovation New products and processes.

innovation cluster A geographic region in which the resources for innovation are plentiful and the supply curve for innovative activities is shifted to the right.

innovative activities Any economic activities primarily directed at creating and developing new products, processes, ideas, knowledge, and technology.

inputs The goods and services a business or an economy uses to produce outputs.

intellectual property protection Laws that make it more difficult to copy innovations.

intensity of competition The pressure on businesses to innovate to get a competitive advantage.

interest rate The amount a borrower has to pay a lender each year in exchange for the use of the lender's money; given as a percentage of the loan.

interest rate effect One reason why aggregate quantity demanded falls as the average price level rises.

interest rate on reserves The interest rate that the Federal Reserve pays on reserves held by banks.

intermediate inputs Any goods or services purchased from other businesses and used up in production.

investment banks The financial intermediaries that handle the initial public offerings and secondary offerings of companies.

invisible hand A term to describe a situation in which individual actions of buyers and sellers tend to result in a positive social outcome.

J

job market decision An individual's decision regarding what kind of job to look for.

job multiplier The total number of jobs created by one additional government-funded job.

K

Keynesian approach An approach to macroeconomics that uses increases in government spending and cuts in taxes to combat recessions.

knowledge A category of input in the aggregate production function that includes both technology and business know-how.

L

labor The inputs supplied by various types of workers. Measured by the hours of work or the number of workers.

labor demand curve Reports how many workers businesses will want to hire, or how many hours of labor they will want to pay for, given the market wage.

labor force The part of the adult population that is either working or actively looking for a job.

labor force participation rate The percentage of the adult population in the labor force.

labor market The market where workers sell time on the job in exchange for money.

labor market discrimination When an individual is paid less or treated worse on the job than an equally qualified person because of his or her race, gender, or some other characteristic.

labor market equilibrium The wage at which the quantity of labor supplied is equal to the quantity of labor demanded. Alternatively, the wage at which the number of workers available is equal to the number of workers businesses are willing to hire.

labor pool effect A situation where the labor supply curve in a given market shifts to the right because there is a larger pool of workers available globally.

labor supply curve Reports, for each level of wages, how many people are in the labor force, or the quantity of labor hours supplied.

lack of flexibility and innovation The lack of incentive in the public sector to put technological breakthroughs into widespread commercial use.

lag The length of time between recognizing that the economy is in recession and getting fiscal stimulus or monetary stimulus into effect.

laissez-faire economy An economy with few government regulations or laws.

land The actual ground used by a business. Distinct from the buildings on the land.

law of demand The tendency of quantity demanded to rise if the price falls, all other things being equal.

law of supply The tendency of quantity supplied to rise if the price rises, all other things being equal.

laws Acts of legislation.

legal barriers to trade Tariffs, quotas, and other government actions that limit trade or make it more expensive.

lender of last resort The Fed's role of lending to financial institutions to keep them in business and to keep the financial markets functioning in a time of crisis.

lending from the rest of the world Flows of money into the United States from outside the country, in the form of loans or other investments.

licensing requirements Course and examination requirements that an individual must pass to be licensed to practice an occupation.

life cycle theory of retirement The pattern of spending and saving for retirement over an individual's lifetime in the absence of government and business-supported assistance for the elderly. Posits that people spend when they are young, save during the latter part of their working lives, and spend when they are retired.

life expectancy The number of years an individual is expected to live, given his or her current age and available medical knowledge.

loan A sum of money that a lender gives a borrower, which is expected to be repaid with interest.

local market A market where buyers and sellers are geographically close to each other.

long-term aggregate supply curve The long-term link between the average price level of the economy and the quantity of goods and services produced.

long-term cost function The link between the output of a business and the cost of producing that output, allowing for all inputs to be changed.

long-term costs See *fixed costs*.

long-term growth The average economic growth over longer periods such as 5 or 10 years.

long-term labor supply The predicted size of the labor force in a country or a region in the future.

long-term profit maximization Profit maximization by businesses, assuming that all inputs can be changed and that there is the option to shut down.

luxury good A good whose demand rises sharply as income increases.

M

macroeconomic policy Government intervention to improve the performance of the economy. In particular, the use of monetary and fiscal policy to smooth out business cycles.

macroeconomics The study of the overall economy.

margin requirement The regulation that determines how much money a person can borrow when buying stock.

marginal cost The added expense of producing one more unit of output.

marginal cost of extraction The amount of money that it takes to get one more ton of coal, one more barrel of oil, or one more cubic foot of natural gas out of the ground.

marginal cost of labor The wage a firm must pay for an additional worker or for an additional hour of labor.

marginal product of labor The extra amount of output a firm can generate by adding one more worker or one more hour of labor.

marginal propensity to consume The portion that households spend of each additional dollar they receive.

marginal revenue The additional money a business gets from producing and selling one more unit of output; or the additional money that a business gets from adding one more worker or one more hour of labor.

marginal tax rate The tax a person pays on the last dollar of income earned.

marginal utility The added amount of utility an individual gets from one more unit of consumption of a good or service, holding everything else constant.

market basket The typical household pattern of expenditures on goods and services that is used to calculate the average price level.

market demand schedule A sum of the demand schedules for all the individual buyers in a market.

market economy A collection of all the different markets in a given area.

market equilibrium A situation in which the quantity supplied and the quantity demanded in a specified market are equal. See *equilibrium price* and *equilibrium quantity*.

market expansion effect An increase in labor demand when businesses can sell to overseas customers.

market mechanism The process by which a market reaches equilibrium without a central planner. See *invisible hand*.

market power The ability to raise prices above the level that perfect competition would produce by restricting the quantity supplied.

market price The typical price at which a good or service sells in a market. Also, the current price at which a share of stock can be bought or sold.

market regulation The role of government in setting basic rules for market competition that businesses have to follow.

market shift A shift of the demand or supply curve to the left or right, often as the result of events external to the particular market; a change in the quantity demanded or quantity supplied at a given price.

market structure Market classification according to the number of buyers and sellers and the intensity of competition.

market supply schedule The sum of the supply schedules for all the individual suppliers in a market.

market transactions The activity of exchanging goods and services that other people are willing to pay for.

market wage The prevailing normal wage for a particular type of job.

market-based approach Government action to change the price signals faced by consumers and producers in order to move their behavior in the desired direction, such as polluting less or emitting fewer greenhouse gases.

markets A way for buyers and sellers to voluntarily exchange goods and services for money.

material and crop damage Negative effects of pollution on human structures and agriculture.

Medicaid A government-funded health plan that helps cover healthcare costs of low-income children, parents, and others.

Medicare A government-funded health plan that helps cover healthcare costs of older individuals.

medium of exchange The property of money that it can be used to buy goods and services.

minimum wage A wage floor set by the government that lifts the wages of the lowest-paid workers above their market wage.

mitigation The implementation of policies and programs designed to significantly reduce emissions of greenhouse gases.

mixed economy An economy that is mainly market-based but also includes a significant role for government.

monetary policy The Federal Reserve's use of interest rates, direct lending to financial institutions, and other policy tools to influence the economy and support the financial system.

monetary policy lags The amount of time a monetary stimulus requires before it will have an effect on the economy.

money A medium of exchange that also serves as a store of value and a standard of value.

money illusion The mistake of comparing dollar amounts in different time periods without adjusting for inflation.

money stock A measure of the amount of money in an economy.

monopolistic competition A situation where a market has many sellers with similar but not standardized products.

monopoly A situation where a market has only one seller, and buyers have no good alternatives.

Moore's law The historical pattern that microprocessors double their performance every 18–24 months.

mortgage market The market for home loans.

movement along a demand curve The effect of a price change on the quantity demanded.

movement along a supply curve The effect of a price change on the quantity supplied.

multinational A business that operates in multiple countries.

multiplier effect The short-term boost in economic activity that flows from the government's spending increase (or tax cut).

mutual funds A financial intermediary that, for a fee, invests the money of customers in a group of stocks.

N

Non-accelerating inflation rate of unemployment (NAIRU) Also called the *natural rate of unemployment.*

national market A market where buyers and sellers can be in different parts of a country.

national savings The sum of personal savings, government savings, and business savings.

natural barriers to trade Obstacles to trade that include distance and differences in cultures.

natural monopoly An industry in which it may make economic sense to have only one supplier.

natural rate of unemployment The level of unemployment in the economy at which inflation is more or less stable. Also called *NAIRU.*

negative externalities An undesirable impact that an economic activity can have on others.

negotiated price A price that is determined on a case-by-case basis as a result of negotiation between individual buyers and sellers.

net exports The difference between exports and imports.

net worth Total household assets minus liabilities.

network externality How the decision of a person to use a network affects the value of that network to other people.

New Deal A collection of public programs that President Franklin Roosevelt instituted to alleviate economic suffering during the Great Depression.

New Economy The period between 1995 and 2007 when productivity growth rebounded almost to what it was during the Golden Age.

new entrants New businesses competing in an existing market, or existing businesses that are expanding into a new market.

new markets Markets with new products and services, or markets that include mostly new buyers and sellers.

nominal change The increase or decrease in a monetary value over time without adjusting for inflation.

noncompeting labor markets Occurs when the workers in one labor market do not seek jobs in another.

nonmarket economy The part of the economy where people perform productive work without getting paid. Includes child-rearing and volunteer work.

nonrenewable energy Sources of energy like fossil fuels that have only a limited supply.

nonresidential investment The buildings, equipment, and software that businesses purchase to use in production.

non-zero-sum economy Occurs when an economy can produce more of one good or service without having to curtail production of another.

normal good A good whose demand rises more or less in step with income.

nuclear power An energy source using contained nuclear reactions to generate electricity.

O

oil price shock The events occurring in 1973 when the Organization of Petroleum Exporting Countries (OPEC) put an embargo on oil shipments to the United States and several European countries. Skyrocketing oil prices followed, which helped trigger an era of high inflation.

old-age dependency ratio The ratio of the size of the older population (65 years and over) to the size of the working-age population (ages 20 through 64).

oligopoly A situation where a market has only a small number of sellers producing similar products.

open market operations The process by which the Federal Reserve affects short-term interest rates.

opportunity cost The value or benefit of the next-best alternative use of money or time.

output gap The difference between real and potential GDP.

output of government The government's purchases of goods and services. Also called *government consumption and investment*.

outputs The goods and services a business sells to customers.

outsourcing Shift of labor to third parties to handle tasks once done by a firm's own employees.

overseas leakage A situation where fiscal stimulus leads to increased imports rather than to faster growth at home.

P

patent A protection against copying granted by the U.S. Patent and Trademark Office to inventors for their discoveries.

payroll tax A tax collected on wage payments, paid by both employees and employers to fund Social Security and Medicare.

peak The date a recession starts—the high point of an economy before its decline.

peak oil The theory that global production of oil may be nearing its highest point.

pegged exchange rate Occurs when the government of one country manages its exchange rate to be fixed in relation to another currency.

perfect competition A situation in which all buyers and sellers in a market are price takers.

personal consumption The goods and services bought by households.

personal savings What remains from household income after taxes and consumption spending are taken out.

personal savings rate Savings by households as a share of disposable income.

pollution One important negative externality from economic activity.

positive externality A desirable impact that an economic activity can have on others.

potential GDP The output of the economy along a smooth path of growth, assuming no strains on production or unused resources.

potential growth rate The rate at which potential GDP increases; also the combination of the long-term growth rate of the labor force plus the long-term growth rate of productivity.

poverty line An income level that is supposed to indicate the lowest acceptable living standard in an economy; it depends on the number of people in the household and is adjusted for inflation each year.

poverty rate The percentage of people living in households that earn incomes below the poverty line.

pretax income distribution The spread of incomes before taxes have been taken out.

price The rate at which buyers and sellers exchange money for a good or service.

price appreciation An increase in the price of a stock.

price elasticity of demand The percentage change in quantity demanded that results from a 1 percent change in price.

price elasticity of supply The percentage change in quantity supplied, given a 1 percent change in price.

price takers Buyers and sellers who take the market price as given and make their buying and production decisions accordingly.

principal The sum of money in any loan that the lender gives the borrower.

private return from innovative activities The gain to an original company that devotes resources to innovative activities.

private sector The economy outside of government, including privately owned businesses.

privatization The shifting of certain aspects of government programs, such as Social Security, to the private sector.

product A good or service.

production The process of turning inputs into outputs.

production function The link between the inputs of a business and its outputs.

production possibility frontier (PPF) All the combinations of different goods and services the economy is capable of producing at a particular time, assuming full use of all resources.

productivity Economic output divided by the number of labor hours worked.

productivity slowdown The period from 1973 to 1995 in which productivity grew at a much slower pace than in the Golden Age.

productivity-enhancing innovation Technological change that provides more of the same product while holding inputs constant. It has the effect of shifting the supply curve to the right.

profit The difference between revenues and costs.

profit maximization The main objective of a business in a market economy: finding a way to achieve the largest difference between revenue and costs.

profit-maximizing rule A profit-maximizing business will increase production as long as marginal revenue exceeds marginal cost.

progressive tax A tax that requires high-income households to pay a higher tax rate than low-income households.

property tax A tax collected on the value of residential and commercial real estate.

protectionism The use of tariffs, quotas, or other barriers to trade to protect domestic jobs and businesses.

public companies Businesses that have sold shares of stock (also called *equity*) to the general public.

public debt The total of government borrowing.

public goods Goods and services that benefit many people in a city, region, or country.

public sector The portion of the economy that includes the federal, state, and local levels of government.

pure price change An increase in the price of a good with no change in its quality or characteristics.

Q

quality-of-life innovation Technological change that enhances the quality of life for you and those around you.

quantity demanded The amount of a good or service that a buyer is willing to purchase at a given price.

quantity supplied The amount of a good or service that a seller is willing to supply at a given price.

quintiles 20 percent of a group. Used when considering income distribution.

quotas Government-imposed disincentives to trade that include numerical limits on the number of imported products coming into a country.

R

rational individual A person who maximizes his or her utility, subject to a budget constraint.

real change The change in a quantity adjusted for inflation. See *inflation-adjusted change.*

real GDP Gross domestic product, adjusted for inflation.

real GDP growth The growth in gross domestic product adjusted for inflation. Also known as economic growth.

real GDP per capita Real GDP divided by the number of people in a country. Serves as a measure of the standard of living.

recession A significant decline in economic activity spread across the economy, lasting more than a few months.

redistribution The transfer of money from high-income to low-income households.

regressive tax A tax that requires high-income households to pay a lower tax rate than low-income households.

relative price shift A situation where the inflation rate of a good or service is significantly higher or lower than the overall inflation rate.

renewable energy Energy sources such as wind and solar power.

rent-seeking behavior Occurs when businesses spend money trying to influence the government.

research and development (R&D) Money and resources—particularly human resources—that economies or businesses devote to science and technology.

reserve requirement The requirement that banks keep a portion of their deposits either in cash in their vaults or on reserve with the Federal Reserve.

residential investment The construction of new homes and the renovation of existing homes.

retirement poverty problem The problem that poor people often don't have enough income to save for retirement.

retirement uncertainty problem The problem that individuals don't know how long they will live after retirement.

return The gain on your investment in a year, measured as a percentage of original investment.

return from innovative activities The payback to spending on innovative activities such as R&D.

revealed preference One way of putting a monetary value on the health impacts of pollution, based on analyzing the choices that people make in their daily lives to change their risk of death or injury.

Also used to assess the monetary value of harm to environmental amenities.

revenue The amount of money companies get from selling their products or services.

risk The possibility that something unexpected, either good or bad, will happen to an investment.

risk from innovative activities The possibility that spending on innovative activities such as R&D will not pay off.

risk of default The possibility of not getting paid back on a loan.

risk-return principle The concept that the only way to get higher expected returns over the long run is to take more risks.

rules Regulations issued by various government agencies.

S

safety net Government programs that provide a measure of economic security for the poor, the sick, and the vulnerable.

sale price A price intentionally set below the market price to stimulate purchases.

sales tax A tax collected on retail sales.

satiation The point at which the value of additional consumption of a good or service goes to zero.

sellers Businesses or individuals who receive money in exchange for supplying goods and services.

shift in tastes A shift in the demand curve for a good or service based on a change in consumer preferences.

short-term aggregate supply curve A curve that shows the short-term link between the average price level and the quantity of goods and services produced.

short-term cost function The link between the output of a business and the cost of producing that output, assuming that fixed costs cannot be changed.

short-term costs See *variable costs*.

short-term growth Economic growth over a single year.

short-term profit maximization The process of running a business to achieve the greatest excess of revenues over costs, assuming that fixed costs cannot be changed.

shutdown decision A business decision to keep operating or not, based on the level of profits.

single-payer system A proposed health plan in which healthcare spending for everyone is paid for through the government.

smoothing out the business cycle One key goal of the Federal Reserve, which tries to keep the economy from dropping into a steep recession.

Social Security The government program that provides income support to older citizens who have contributed during their working years.

spending multiplier The increase in GDP created by one additional dollar of government expenditures.

stagflation A combination of slow economic growth and rapid inflation.

standard of value The use of monetary values to make comparisons between different items.

standardized products Outputs that differ from each other in only a small number of easily identifiable features.

stated preference One way of determining the monetary value of the damage done by pollution, based on surveys of individuals or other direct queries.

sticky wages Wages that don't change much in the short term in response to economic conditions.

stimulative A government policy action, such as a tax cut, that pushes up output and reduces unemployment in the short run.

stock A piece of ownership in a company. Also called *equity.*

stockbrokers The financial intermediaries that handle the buying and selling of shares between investors.

stock market A market in which shares of stocks are bought and sold.

stock trade The purchase or sale of a share of stock by an investor.

store of value The property of money that it can be used for purchases in the future.

structural unemployment A situation in which there is a mismatch between the skills of unemployed workers and the needs of employers with unfilled jobs.

substitute Two inputs are substitutes if a business will use more of one when the price of the other rises.

superstar economy Situations in which there is a widening gap in compensation between the top people and the merely competent.

suppliers of capital The investors who provide the funds. In the banking system, for example, the suppliers of capital are the depositors in the bank.

supply curve A line on a graph showing the link between price and quantity supplied.

supply curve for innovative activities Reports the quantity of innovative activities that are supplied, given their price.

supply schedule The link between a seller's quantity supplied and the market price.

supply shift A change in the amount sellers produce at a given price.

supply-side economics A school of economic thought that emphasizes the importance of low marginal tax rates.

surplus A situation where government revenues exceed government spending.

system of national accounts All the statistics that feed into the process for estimating the quarterly and annual output of the U.S. economy.

T

tariffs Extra charges or taxes levied on imports by a country.

tax incidence The people or businesses who ultimately have to pay a tax.

tax multiplier The increase in GDP from a $1 cut in taxes.

taxation The main way the government raises revenue from individuals and businesses.

technological change An improvement in knowledge that increases the quantity and range of goods and services an economy can deliver.

technological diffusion The process by which new ideas spread from one person or business to other parts of the economy.

term The length of a loan; the period of time during which a borrower repays principal back to a lender.

third party In healthcare, an external organization that pays for healthcare services for an individual.

time value of money The opportunity cost of not having one's money available for use for some period.

total cost The sum of costs for each of the inputs used in production.

total return The total return on a share of stock is the change in the stock price, plus the dividend, divided by the original price.

tradable pollution permits A government-endorsed "allowance" that gives a business the right to emit a particular amount of pollution. These permits can be traded or sold among private businesses.

trade balance The difference between exports and imports of goods and services.

trade deficit Occurs when a trade balance is negative so that imports exceed exports.

trade in goods Exchanges that occur when sellers physically ship items to another country.

trade in services Exchanges that occur when a person or a company in one country provides a service to a resident of a different country.

transfer payments Payments from government to individuals, including unemployment benefits and Social Security benefits.

Treasury bills Securities the federal government issues with terms as short as one month.

Treasury bonds Securities the federal government issues each year to fund the budget deficit with terms as long as 10 years and 30 years.

trough The date on which a recession ends and the economy starts heading up again.

U

underemployed Individuals who take jobs below their skill or education levels or who are working part-time involuntarily.

underground economy The portion of the economy that does not pay taxes or otherwise get reported by government.

unemployed A description of individuals who do not have jobs but are actively looking for work.

unemployment rate The percentage of the labor force that is unemployed.

unexpected inflation The sudden acceleration of the rate of price increases above expected inflation.

unfair competition In global trade, cases in which a foreign country favors its own exporting industries by lowering their taxes or giving them some other subsidy.

union A group of workers who bargain collectively with employers for wages, benefits, and working conditions.

upward-sloping supply curve A supply curve that is consistent with the law of supply, so that an increase in price leads to an increase in quantity supplied. As a result, the line slopes up when read from left to right.

users of capital The eventual recipients, such as borrowers, of funds from a bank or other financial intermediary.

utility A measure of the physical and emotional benefits a person gets from consumption.

utility function The link between the goods and services a person consumes and his or her utility.

V

value of a statistical life A monetary value economists treat as the cost to society of an additional death—in this book, from pollution.

variable costs Costs that managers can quickly raise or lower by decisions they make today.

venture capital The funds provided to risky start-ups by venture capital firms.

venture capital firm Financial intermediaries that provide funds to risky start-ups.

volume discount A price set below the market price to reward buyers who purchase a large quantity of items.

W

wage–price spiral A situation that occurs when businesses and workers boost prices and wages to try to stay ahead of rising expected inflation.

wealth effect One reason why aggregate quantity demanded falls as the average price level rises. Also, the phenomenon in which higher wealth leads to more consumption.

Z

zero price Occurs when an additional unit of a good or service is offered at no cost to buyers.

zero-sum economy When the only way an economy can produce more of something is to produce less of something else.

PHOTO CREDITS

INDEX